CONFRONTING SEXISM AND VIOLENCE AGAINST WOMEN

A Challenge for Social Work

An imprint of Addison Wesley Longman, Inc.

New York • Reading, Massachusetts • Menlo Park, California • Harlow, England
Don Mills, Ontario • Sydney • Mexico City • Madrid • Amsterdam

Editor-in-Chief:	*Priscilla McGeehon*
Acquisitions Editor:	*Janice E. Wiggins*
Senior Marketing Manager:	*Wendy Albert*
Project Coordination and Text Design:	*York Production Services*
Cover Designer:	*Kay Petronio*
Full Service Production Manager:	*Valerie Zaborski*
Manufacturing Manager:	*Hilda Koparanian*
Electronic Page Makeup:	*York Production Services*
Printer and Binder:	*R.R. Donnelley & Sons, Co.*
Cover Printer:	*The Lehigh Press, Inc.*

For permission to use copyrighted material, grateful acknowledgment is made to the copyright holders on pp. 329–330, which are hereby made part of this copyright page.

Library of Congress Cataloging-in-Publication Data

Stout, Karen D.
   Confronting sexism and violence against women: a challenge for social work/Karen D. Stout, Beverly McPhail.
      p.   cm.
   Includes bibliographical references and index.
   ISBN 0-8013-1757-6
   1. Social work with women—United States.   2. Women—Crimes against—United States.
   3. Sex discrimination against women—United States.   4. Sexual harassment of women—United States.
   I. McPhail, Beverly A.   II. Title.
   HV1445.S76   1998
   362.82'92'0973—dc21
                                                                    97–35328
                                                                    CIP

Please visit our website at http://longman.awl.com

ISBN 0-8013-1757-6

   345678910—DOC—01009998

CHAPTER-BY-CHAPTER OVERVIEW

Chapter 1
PRESENTING THE CONTINUUM: A BRIEF OVERVIEW

Sexism and violence perpetrated against women is a serious and pervasive problem affecting all women in one form or another, and social workers must be prepared to address these vital issues at both the personal and the political levels. This chapter outlines a continuum model for understanding such assaults.

Chapter 2
WOMEN'S INSTITUTIONAL STATUS

Sexism and violence against women is embedded in the very fabric of our society—encoded in our laws and entrenched in our attitudes. This chapter outlines how the major institutions in our society—politics, the economy, religion, and family systems—support, maintain, and condone the subordination of women. In this chapter, as in all the subsequent chapters, both policy and practice implications are formulated.

Chapter 3
PSYCHOLOGICAL WOUNDS

Many of the assaults against women leave physical bruises and scars, but some also leave less visible wounds, which affect women's psyches. This chapter describes the hazards of being raised female in a misogynistic society by focusing on gender socialization, internalized oppression, and the effects of secondary victimization inflicted by traditional mental-health systems. In this chapter, and throughout the text, the unique implications for women of color, lesbian women, disabled women, and other stigmatized populations of women are discussed.

Chapter 4
GENDERED COMMUNICATION

Sexism so imbues our everyday actions that it influences the words we speak and the way we touch. This chapter examines exclusionary and hateful language, differential-status indicators, and the use of space and touch to demonstrate dominance and power.

Chapter 5
ECONOMIC ASSAULT ON WOMEN

Unequal power results in unequal economic opportunities and outcomes. This chapter details women's secondary economic status, including such topics as the wage gap, unpaid labor, glass and Lucite ceilings, and the impoverishment of women.

Chapter 6
CONTROLLING WOMEN'S BODIES: HEALTH AND REPRODUCTIVE FREEDOM

In a patriarchy, women's bodies are not their own. This chapter details how women's bodies are controlled in the area of reproductive freedom and women's health by such tactics as fetal-protection policies and *medicalization* of women's health.

Chapter 7
PORNOGRAPHY AND PROSTITUTION

Prostitution and pornography are two vital topics demanding social workers' attention and analysis. This chapter examines the commercialized use of women for men's sexual pleasure, as represented in violence against women in the sex industry.

Chapter 8
SEXUAL HARASSMENT: ASSAULTS ON WOMEN AT WORK AND AT SCHOOL

Daily, women run a gauntlet when obtaining an education, working outside the home, or even walking down the street. This chapter looks at the definitions, causes, and consequences of sexual harassment and the role that social workers can play in addressing and ending this assault.

Chapter 9
WOMEN WHO ARE BATTERED

Sometimes, lovers break more than hearts. This chapter addresses the physical, sexual, and emotional abuse inflicted on some women by their intimate partners.

Chapter 10
SEXUAL ASSAULT

Power and control can be expressed through sexual aggression. This chapter focuses on rape: the causes and consequences of stranger rape, acquaintance rape, and marital rape, as well as the implications for practice and policy.

Chapter 11
BATTERED WOMEN WHO KILL AND FEMICIDE: THE FINAL ACTS OF VIOLENCE AGAINST WOMEN

The last point on the continuum involves death, both of women who are killed and of women who kill their batterers. The final act of violence is presented both as a distinct issue and as a culmination of the sexism and violence that preceded this final point on the continuum.

Chapter 12
PERSONAL AND PROFESSIONAL IMPLICATIONS: A CONVERSATION WITH SOCIAL WORKERS

The last chapter summarizes themes developed throughout the book and includes discussion of vicarious victimization, connecting the "isms," and a message to male social workers. Social workers who are actively engaged in the struggle to address the issues presented in the continuum and detailed in the previous chapters discuss both the joys and the pain of doing such work. They examine these feelings from both professional and personal perspectives.

CONTENTS

Chapter 6

CONTROLLING WOMEN'S BODIES: HEALTH AND REPRODUCTIVE FREEDOM   134

Chapter 7

PORNOGRAPHY AND PROSTITUTION   159

Chapter 8

SEXUAL HARASSMENT: ASSAULTS ON WOMEN AT WORK AND AT SCHOOL

Chapter **9**

WOMEN WHO ARE BATTERED   211

Chapter **10**

SEXUAL ASSAULT   251

Chapter *11*

BATTERED WOMEN WHO KILL AND FEMICIDE: THE FINAL ACTS OF VIOLENCE AGAINST WOMEN

Chapter *12*

PERSONAL AND PROFESSIONAL IMPLICATIONS: A CONVERSATION WITH SOCIAL WORKERS

PREFACE

$\mathcal{T}$he purpose of this book is to describe the vast array of issues related to sexism and to violence against women. Because of the prevalence and severity of sexism and violence affecting women, and because issues related to sexism and violence are often compartmentalized or separated, a continuum conceptualization is offered. A *continuum model* informs by demonstrating how one form of sexism and violence cannot readily be distinguished from another; each element in the continuum shades into the other elements. A critical focus is on the connections among various forms of violence, rather than on a distinct set of discrete problems that women address. Similarly, the need to confront sexism and violence against women at multiple levels is introduced, and multilevel practice and policy strategies are proposed. For example, in practice courses on planning and administration, students are often offered information about sexual harassment. However, there is a fine line between sexual harassment and the general status of women within organizations, gender-related pay inequities, and differential treatment of women and men, which is often reflected by gendered communication patterns. Further, the content of sexual-harassment discussions often focuses on the quid pro quo forms of harassment (e.g., "have sex with me or lose your job"), slighting the physical and sexual assault that may be part of the harassment. This example illustrates the complexity within a single issue confronting women. The same women who have been confronting sexual harassment in the workplace may also have been experiencing battering, sexual assault, economic discrimination, or other physical or psychological assaults in their life experiences outside the workplace. Too often, social work materials, the media, and lay publications present unidimensional explanations about women's experiences when, in fact, women's lives and problems are multidimensional, complex, and interrelated. Similarly, many social work practice courses offer individual-level change strategies (e.g., individual, couples, or group counseling) while neglecting the importance of effecting social change as an intervention or a prevention-change strategy.

We offer the approach to examining issues related to sexism and violence against women used in this book from an unapologetic feminist perspective. Both of us have a feminist world-view, which informs our practice and our ideological perspectives. Feminism has been defined as everything from "believing in equal rights for women" to a slogan often seen on T-shirts by Cheris Kramarae and Paula Treichler proclaiming that "feminism is the radical notion that women are people," to a quote attributed to Rebecca West around 1913, noting, "I'm not sure exactly what a feminist is, I just know I get called one anytime my actions differentiate me from a doormat." As the variety of these slogans suggests, feminism and feminists are not a unidimensional phenomenon. Bricker-Jenkins and Hooyman (1986) have noted both that feminism is distinguished by its ideology and that ideology is at the core of feminist practice. Further, those authors suggest that feminism is tentative and is always becoming. However, there are ideological themes that have emerged from feminist thought: ending patriarchy, empowerment, process, the personal is political, unity–diversity, validation of the nonrational, and consciousness raising as praxis (Bricker-Jenkins & Hooyman, 1986). In just the time it has taken us to work on this book, we found validation from the notion of feminism as always becoming. Each day, new information, new insights, and new contradictions arose, which made our work more challenging, more interesting, and—at times—more frustrating, as there is no one feminist position or way of practice. We hope that the readers of this text will use the ideas set forth as a way to begin a dialogue, certainly not as an end product or as *the* answer from *the* experts. We share our thoughts, informed by feminist ideas and practice, to create a dialogue among our readers, to generate interest in ending sexism and violence against women, and to keep challenging ourselves to learn more, to do better, and to engage in more dialogue with other social work practitioners.

As social work educators, we understand the pressures of conforming to curricular standards and to university and school mission statements. We are proud to be part of a profession that mandates the inclusion of content on women, persons of color, and gay and lesbian persons. However, too often, that content on women, persons of color, and gay and lesbian persons is presented in a single class session with a single focus: women who are battered, women and depression, lesbian women, women living with AIDS, and so on. Yet each of these problems has a context, in and of itself, and in relationship to the other problems. It is difficult to understand the complexity of a woman who is experiencing depression without a thorough understanding of all of the forces that collude to maintain a structure where women are the most frequent victims of depression. Further, in part because of the structure of social work education, policy classes are often remiss in discussing both the practice and the practical implications of agency, state, and national policy. Practice courses often beautifully address issues related to women's experiences with violence yet do not address the policy implications that might support the practice content. Because of the separateness too often apparent in structures of social work education content areas, it is important that materials be offered, which bring to students' attention both the issues and the change strategies, both practice and policy. In that vein, this book was developed because we believe that women's lives are too important, too dynamic to be addressed as a peripheral, though mandated, discussion topic.

ORGANIZATION OF THE TEXTBOOK

Each chapter in this book addresses forms of sexism and violence against women. *Chapter 1* introduces the need for scholarship on sexism and violence against women for social work practice and introduces the continuum model. *Chapters 2–11* focus on particular elements of the continuum: women's institutional status, psychological wounds, gendered communication, economic assaults, control of women's bodies, pornography and prostitution, sexual harassment, women who have been battered, sexual assault, battered women who kill, and femicide. These chapters take the reader through many forms of societal and individual acts of violence against women. **Strategies for Change** sections, which offer practice and policy implications, are included in Chapters 2–11. The last chapter encourages the reader to examine how these forms of sexism and violence may affect them personally or vicariously. That chapter concludes with personal notes from each of us. As women and as social workers, we have been or are personally affected by many issues addressed in the text, and we chose to share some of our experiences with our readers.

This book could be used in a variety of courses both within and outside of the social work curriculum. The most obvious courses would focus on women's issues. Both of us have taught women's issues and feminist practice courses and we found that in order to cover the multitude of issues and practice strategies that could be offered, many books were needed on single content areas: battered women, sexual-assault survivors, group practice, community practice, and so forth. With *Confronting Sexism and Violence Against Women,* we have brought together all of these content areas into one text so that several books may not be necessary. This book is also appropriate for family-violence classes, and also designed to be useful for courses on diversity, as well as practice and policy courses.

A THOROUGH INTEGRATION

As noted, each chapter introduces information on the issues associated with various forms of sexism and violence against women. We set forth information and analysis related to each of these topics, with the purpose of providing a knowledge base on these issues. The next major section of chapters 2–10 focuses on strategies for change for students to consider—from social work practice with individuals, staging of demonstrations, group work, and conscious-

ness raising to changing agency, professional, and national policies.

When discussing issues of importance to women, it is critical to include the experiences of all women. The realities of all women must be directly named and included. Pharr (1988) makes this point by writing,

> A very small but powerfully effective first step we can take is to say the word lesbian. We must say it in positive ways in our everyday conversations as we affirm different sexual identities, and we must say the word lesbian *when we talk about our work with women. It is not enough to say that our organization is for* all women *because women from groups that have never been considered the norm are still rendered invisible under the term all women. (p. 46, emphasis in original)*

Throughout this book, we address concerns related specifically to women of color, low-income women, lesbian women, women who are physically disabled, and older women. Each chapter includes information on one or more of these populations. Within the "circle of women" (Bricker-Jenkins, December 1996, personal communication), each group's special experiences are illuminated. For example, the chapter on battering focuses on practice issues with Latina, African-American, Asian-American, and lesbian women. The problem section of the chapter on sexual assault presents the special issues that emerge for African-American, Latina, and disabled women. However, the chapter on economic discrimination focuses a great deal on low-income women. Perhaps we can simply note that each chapter is inclusive *and* diverse.

Woven into the chapters are issues related to the specific continuum element being discussed and to concerns of special populations of women, as well as strategies for change. While each chapter pays careful attention to a particular element, each chapter is also intricately related to every other chapter. For example, one cannot divorce the economic status of women from the issues related to women used in the sex industry, and gendered communication easily merges with sexual-harassment issues. Just as the problem areas shade into each other, so do the strategies for change. Although we discuss the use of media as a change strategy only in Chapter 2, in that chapter's discussion of the institutional status of women, we recognize that the development of media skills is just as important in confronting the issues of sexual harassment, sexual assault, pornography and prostitution, and femicide. In some ways, dividing this book into chapters could lead into the old trap of seeing each form of sexism or violence as distinct. However, the intent is to awaken the reader to the overwhelming tasks ahead, which are necessary to confront, and even better to end, violence against women. Just as a single consumer visiting a social worker's office is a person who is both influencing and being shaped by her or his environment, so each chapter in this book is both influencing and being shaped by content that comes before and after it.

Having taught women's issues and feminist practice courses for a number of years, we found that many times, students needed information that could be used *today!* While neither of us feels that graduate or undergraduate students should be spoon-fed material, both of us have a commitment to providing materials that would easily translate into practice. As a result of our experiences, we have included some how-to information, which we hope will help social workers and other helping professionals to prepare for action.

Finally, at times, one or both of us have chosen to relate personal experiences or to speak directly to the reader through the text. As social workers and as women, it is not possible for us to completely divorce ourselves from the content of the text, and we believe that we have some experiences that might initiate discussion or validate readers' experiences. Therefore, we occasionally shift from third person to first person throughout the book.

ACKNOWLEDGMENTS

This book has been shaped by vision, accidents, cooperation, and conflict—all of which we are grateful for. The persons and institutions who helped us shape this work are many, and we thank you all, from the students in the first course we ever taught to the former and current staff at Longman, especially George Hoffman and Janice Wiggins who provided the means to translate our ideas into book form. Janice has been a constant source of warm support and friendly competence. We also appreciate the efforts of her able assistant Katya McElfresh. (Welcome to social work!)

Both of us are grateful to Pat Palmer, Kate Carlson, and Claude LaBrosse for the practice-strategy pieces they contributed to the book. Juliet Austin supported this work greatly with a library search after the first draft to obtain articles suggested by the first round of reviewers. Further, Pat, Juliet, Wendy Nes, Marty Collier, and Ellen Stevens joined us for a potluck dinner one evening to brainstorm about what might become a part of this text and shared in our joys and struggles throughout the process. Gary Norman helped with switching computer formats and did some reference work for us. Both of us have been supported by the faculty, staff, and students of the University of Houston Graduate School of Social Work (GSSW). We especially acknowledge GSSW Deans Karen S. Haynes (now President of University of Houston—Victoria) and Karen A. Holmes for their leadership, vision, and support of our goals—including this book. Howard Karger and Bob Fisher were great book-writing role models, friends, and listeners throughout this process, and we thank them for supporting our work in so many ways. Former students Dawn Nelson, Mary Jo Galle, and Cindi Hunter gave us insight into their student perspective on the first draft of the text, which for us was a tremendous complement to the academic reviewers. We appreciate the time they took to inform us of what was good and what was missing from the draft they read. Finally, all the students who took women's issues and feminist practice courses with us informed us greatly, challenged us, and gave us energy and excitement for this text. We thank you all so very much.

The reviewers of this text took it from its roughest draft through the final revisions, and the book is better because of their many suggestions, mandates, and supportive comments. We thank each of you:

Daniel Saunders, *University of Michigan*

Jill Rosenbaum, *Cal State Fullerton*

Joan M. Jones, *University of Wisconsin—Milwaukee*

Rosalie Ambrosino, *University of Texas—Austin*

K. Jean Peterson, *University of Kansas*

Migdalis Reyes, *San Jose State*

Marion Wagner, *University of Indiana at Indianapolis*

Jacqueline Nielson, *Southeast Missouri State University*

K. Jean Peterson, *University of Kansas*

Mary Bricker-Jenkins, *Temple University*

Finally, we are grateful to Kirsten Kauffman and the staff at York Production Services who provided editing services, patience, and much polishing of the manuscript. Their talents are much appreciated.

Beverly McPhail

Writing acknowledgments is a little like accepting an Oscar: You have just a few moments (or in this case, a few lines) to thank all the many people who have made this moment and this book possible. I echo all the previous acknowledgments and add a few personal ones of my own.

My first thanks and great appreciation go to my co-author, Karen Stout, for allowing me the opportunity to work on this exciting project with her. It has been a challenge and a delight. Our relationship has developed over the pages of this book, and I am most grateful for this opportunity, as well.

I must also thank a number of people who have played an important role in my development, both personally and professionally. Their roles in my life have been varied, ranging from teachers to mentors, supervisors, therapists, friends, and colleagues. Their knowledge and influence has greatly contributed to who I am as a woman, a feminist, and a social worker. I truly am standing on the shoulders of these wise

women: Karen Holmes, Karen Haynes, Barbara Winston, Diana Storms, Barbara Ellman, and Pat Palmer. I would also like to recognize a profeminist ally who has been influential: Jeff Basen-Engquist. I would also like to thank Nancy Johnson-Gallagher, Pat Palmer, and Sandra Lopez for their careful reading of and comments on different portions of the manuscript. My special thanks go to Kim Kulish for the wonderful photographs that enhance the text, as well as Joan and Kyle Kulish for their encouragement and support throughout the years.

Finally, I would like to thank my parents, Virginia and Angus McPhail, for their unwavering support, as well as my three special sisters, Meredith, Kimberly, and Christine. Kevin Kulish, my husband, is also my partner, friend, and coparent, who makes all my work possible with his love, support, respect, and unfailing good humor.

Then, I come to my sons, who were simultaneously my biggest inspiration for writing the book and my greatest distraction from ever completing the book. For Justin and Josh, who daily challenge my notions of what it means to be a feminist mother of sons and who enrich my life in countless ways, all my love.

Karen Stout

There is a feminist folk song by Holly Near which speaks to the importance of women in women's lives. I need to acknowledge the women in my life who have made this work possible: to the hundreds of battered women and their children who trusted me enough to tell me of their hurt and pain as they left their homes in search of safety and support; to shelter workers, across this country, who work for low wages and too little professional respect in exchange for the comfort in knowing they can make a difference in women's lives, now and in the future; to women social work students, searching for recognition of their experiences in academia, in their personal lives, and in the profession—especially to Mary Jo Galle, Dawn Nelson, and Cindi Hunter, who critiqued an early version of this text; to the talented women faculty at the University of Houston GSSW, who have been sources of inspiration and support, especially Karen Haynes, Karen Holmes, Ellen Stevens, Jean Latting, and Susan Robbins; to my dearest friends Jean Frank and Laura Stephenson for helping me sort through personal and professional conflicts that arose during the course of this writing journey; to Juliet Clarke for taking in my girls on many occasions and for her humor and support, and to my co-author, Beverly McPhail, for her great thinking, writing, organizational abilities, creative style, patience, and friendship, and for helping this vision come to fruition—I am truly indebted and grateful.

During the final stages of writing this book, the deaths of both of my grandmothers caused me to reflect and renew my gratitude to the women who came before me, who shaped my life, nurtured me, and changed the world in their lifetime. Women such as one of my grandmothers, who was called before the Dean of Students for wearing pants in the 1910s, gave birth to ideas that have just kept multiplying. My mother, Ann Edwards, is the absolutely best person I know, and I thank her for all the joy, sense of purpose, and opportunities she has given to me. Making the circle of women complete would be acknowledgment of the girls in my life: my sisters, Megan and Sarah Stout, and my daughters, Brenna and Delaney Catlettstout. To Brenna who thought I was writing a book on pumping breast milk and who, when angry with me, would tell me to go work on that "darn book" and to Delaney who squirmed in the womb for her first 9 months and then squirmed in her swing her next 6 months while I tried to write: You are truly loved and cherished. Keep your strong voices and caring spirits. Mommy loves you now and forever and wrote this "darn book" out of her vision for a world that would lovingly embrace and shelter all the girls and women of the world.

Finally, I acknowledge all of the precious women and men in my life—family members, friends, current and former students, Longman and York Production Services staff, and colleagues who have embraced and held me up since by breast cancer diagnosis in the fall of 1997. I particularly thank my husband, Don Catlett, for his love and caring through this challenging time in our lives. I acknowledge and thank my oncologist, Dr. Root: (1) for being the first medical professional since my diagnosis to ask me "who I am" besides "a left breast, intraductal carcinoma with positive nodes", and (2) because I want to get on his good side as I fully expect him to work with me to end breast cancer in both of our lifetimes!! I couldn't have finished the work on this book without my family of origin and choice and I'm grateful. Thank you, Mom, Dad, Cathy, Betty, George, Bud, Dan, Joe, Christin, Ron, Cathy, Beverly, Pat, Kathy, Jean, Susan, Laura, Marty, Wendy, Bob, Juliet C., Paul, Nadine, Diana, Karen, Ellen, Lacey, Barbara, Juergen, Juliet A., Susan, Gary, Howard, Marsha, Toby, Denny, Suzy, Jim, Terri, Lin, Jeff, Mitzi, Beth and Toni. My life is full and rich because of each of you. Your commitment to me and your commitment to ending sexism and violence against women truly is making this world a better place to be.

REFERENCES

Bricker-Jenkins, M., & Hooyman, N. (Eds.) (1986). *Not for women only: Social work practice for a feminist future.* Silver Spring, MD: National Association of Social Workers (NASW Press).

Pharr, S. (1988). *Homophobia: A weapon of sexism.* Little Rock, AR: The Women's Project.

Chapter 1

PRESENTING THE CONTINUUM: A BRIEF OVERVIEW

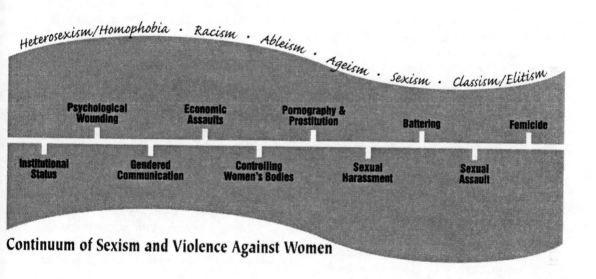

Heterosexism/Homophobia · Racism · Ableism · Ageism · Sexism · Classism/Elitism

| Psychological Wounding | Economic Assaults | Pornography & Prostitution | Battering | Femicide |

| Institutional Status | Gendered Communication | Controlling Women's Bodies | Sexual Harassment | Sexual Assault |

Continuum of Sexism and Violence Against Women

> As perceived psychological, social and economic harm is validly considered as injury, and as the assailant does not have to use his fists, boots, knife, gun, baseball bat, or lead pipe to be considered assaultive, the victim does not have to demonstrate fractures, technicolor bruises, 45 stitches, or semen in her vagina or anus in order to be aggressed against. Thus, sexual coercion, sexual harassment, "brow beating," restriction of educational and employment opportunities, or economic threats can validly be considered aggressive behavior.
>
> *Stark-Adamec and Adamec, 1982, p. 2*

*C*age. *Consider a bird cage. If you look very closely at just one wire in the cage, you cannot see the other wires. If your conception of what is before you is determined by this myopic focus, you could look at that one wire, up and down the length of it, and be unable to see why a bird would not just fly around the wire anytime it wanted to go somewhere. Furthermore, even if, one day at a time, you myopically inspected each wire, you still could not see why a bird would have trouble going past the wires to get anywhere. There is no physical property of any one wire, nothing that the closest scrutiny could discover, that will reveal how a bird could be inhibited or harmed by it except in the most accidental way. It is only when you step back, stop looking at the wires one by one, microscopically, and take a macroscopic view of the whole cage, that you can see why*

1

the bird does not go anywhere; and then you will see it in a moment. It will require no great subtlety of mental powers. It is perfectly obvious that the bird is surrounded by a network of systematically related barriers, no one of which could be the least hindrance to its flight, but which, by their relations to each other, are as confining as the solid walls of a dungeon.

It is now possible to grasp one of the reasons why oppression can be hard to see and recognize: One can study the elements of an oppressive structure with great care and some good will without seeing the structure as a whole, and hence without seeing or being able to understand that one is looking at a cage and that there are people there who are caged, whose motion and mobility are restricted, whose lives are shaped and reduced. (Frye, 1983, pp. 4–5)

In 1983, Marilyn Frye made this wire-cage analogy to focus attention on the systematic oppression of women. The many elements of sexism and violence against women, which are the focus of this book, can be conceptualized as the oppressive wires that create the structure of the analogous birdcage. When looking individually at a single aspect of sexism or violence (e.g., exclusionary language, media depictions of women, fetal-protection policies, or pornographic depictions of women in the workplace), it may appear that the problems facing women are perhaps a troublesome barrier, but not oppression, and certainly not a cage or a dungeon. When these aspects are taken together and viewed with other problems confronting women (e.g., sexual harassment, battering, rape, and femicide), one can begin to visualize a structure taking a more restrictive and foreboding form. Making the connections among various irritating, restrictive, life-threatening, and life-ending experiences of women is an important task for the social work profession to undertake. Van Soest (1996) wrote, "To practice in this increasingly diverse and inequitable society, social work students must understand the patterns, dynamics, and consequences of

societal oppression and translate that understanding into actions designed to facilitate change" (p. 191).

Turner, Singleton, and Musick (1984) defined oppression as, "a situation in which one, or more, identifiable segments of the population in a social system systematically and successfully act over a prolonged period of time to prevent another identifiable segment, or segments, of the population from attaining access to the scarce and valued resources of the system" (pp. 1–2). According to Turner, Singleton, and Musick's definition of oppression, sexism and violence have systematically and successfully worked over a long period of time to deny resources to women. Doesn't the fear of rape, which immobilizes some women and restricts many women, limit women's access to resources of the system? Doesn't the 59 cents Latina women earn, as compared to each $1.00 earned by white men, prevent Latina women from attaining valued resources?

In another examination of the meaning of the word *oppression,* Frye (1983) paid attention to the root of the word: *press.* She noted, "Something pressed is something caught between or among forces and barriers which are so related to each other that jointly they restrain, restrict or prevent the thing's motion or mobility" (p. 2). To be restrained or restricted or to have one's mobility threatened is very much oppression, and as such, it presents a challenge to social workers to work toward ending the individual, institutional, and cultural oppression of women.

Examining the effects of oppression on individual women, Findlen (1995) suggests, "Almost every woman has experienced the feeling of being mistreated, trivialized, kept out, put down, ignored, assaulted, laughed at or discriminated against because of her gender" (p. xii). Similarly, Patricia Ireland (1996), a leader of the National Organization of Women (NOW), describes some of her experiences with sexism and violence:

The year I got married, reproductive freedom was still not recognized as a constitutional right.

Birth control was illegal, even for married couples, in some states, and illegal abortion was the leading cause of maternal death in this country.

The year I started law school, child care was still seen as a commie plot. In vetoing a child-care bill, Richard Nixon, in a message written by Pat Buchanan, called it "the Sovietization of American children."

When I was well into my legal career, head and master laws, which made husbands absolute rulers over their wives and families, were still in force in many states.

For those too young to remember, it may sound like I'm describing the Middle Ages. But these conditions were enshrined in law in this country until very recently—in some cases, less than twenty years ago. (p. 4)

The rationale for the need to focus on sexism and violence against women rests on two premises: (1) The social work profession needs to highlight and present more in-depth materials on the very real and everyday forms of violence women experience; and (2) those experiences should be presented in the context of the misuse of power and control, instead of as individual deficits or problems warranting individualized treatment. Further, a feminist perspective has often been missing from discussions on sexism and violence. Boneparth and Stoper (1988) suggest,

Feminism is the most powerful revolutionary force in the world today. And feminism is urgently needed in a world that is not working, [is] dangerously out of control, and is losing a sense of what it means to be human. In getting at the heart of sex bias, feminism is challenging the social fabric of society, its political orientation, and the decisions of its political authority. And, it is challenging all political and social systems. (p. xiii; emphasis in original)

The identification, description, and feminist analysis of issues presented in this text is only possible due to the women leaders who came before us. The second wave of feminism has roots in the civil rights, New Left, peace,

and gay and lesbian liberation movements. The movement for providing battered women's shelters has roots in the antirape movement, which was firmly grounded in the women's liberation movement. Within social work, the National Committee on Women's Issues of the National Association of Social Workers (NASW) sponsored the first National Conference on Social Work Practice in Sexist Society in 1980, where more than 800 women gathered to share their visions (Bricker-Jenkins & Hooyman, 1986a). In addition, The National Committee on Women's Issues created the Feminist Practice Project to address the development and dissemination of descriptive information on feminist practice in social work. In 1980, the Association for Women in Social Work and *Affilia—The Journal of Social Work with Women* were founded, and the Council on Social Work Education formed its Commission on the Status of Women (Bricker-Jenkins & Lockett, 1995). Further contributing to the emergence of feminist practice in social work are numerous books and articles "which shared a conviction that a simultaneous focus on the personal and the political was necessary and methodologically possible; thus, feminist practice held the promise of achieving the profession's espoused purpose of integrating 'cause and function' in a unitary method of practice" (Bricker-Jenkins & Lockett, 1995, p. 2531).

While it is beyond the scope of this chapter and even of this book to provide further historical analysis of feminist efforts within and outside of social work, it is not beyond our scope to recognize the importance of naming and recognizing feminist accomplishments. Susan Schechter, author of *Women and Male Violence: The Visions and Struggles of the Battered Women's Movement* (1982, pp. 2–3), provides an important example regarding the necessity of recognizing feminist accomplishments:

In the Foreword to Sheltering Battered Women, *a national survey of battered women's refuges in*

1981, Nancy Humphreys, the president of the National Association of Social Workers, fails to mention the grassroots and feminist efforts that led to the creation of services for abused women. Instead, she attributes the national recognition of battered women's plight to "society."

> *"The battered woman is not a new problem. Rather, it is society's awareness of this problem that is new. Society's recent interest in, and sensitivity to, the issue of violence ... has made it possible for the many victims to come forward and seek help."*

The president of the National Association of Social Workers is wrong. "Society" did not recognize battered women; feminists and grassroots organizers did. Nowhere in her introduction is this fact acknowledged, so unwittingly, her statement rewrites the history of the battered women's movement.

Feminist contributions to changing the world and changing social work have been phenomenal, the battered women's movement being just one example. This book focuses on the work that feminists have done, and that still needs to be done, to address sexism and violence against women. Sexism and violence against women manifests itself in a multitude of forms, is prevalent and often severe, and can leave survivors with physical or psychological scars, separately or in combination. In response, women have organized; resisted; created communities, social service agencies, and alternative service organizations; developed theory; and implemented practice and policy strategies to challenge and end the violence (Bricker-Jenkins, Jan. 1997, personal communication). The remainder of this chapter explores the need for a focus on sexism and violence against women, and it introduces the need for both a contextualized approach and a distinctive framework for understanding and addressing issues related to sexism and violence against women. Specifically, a continuum model is explained as the framework that organizes this book.

Author's Perspective

A year does not go by in any school of social work where I (Karen Stout) have taught that a student does not have a crisis related to battering—whether it be herself being battered or stalked, concern about a friend, a client who deeply touches the student, or memories of a mother or other family member being battered. One such student, who experienced a crisis, was Jennifer (pseudynm). Jennifer was a quiet, older student who was bright and endearing, due to her eagerness to learn, her sense of humor, and her insights about content. I was always pleased, when I walked into a new class, to find that Jennifer was enrolled. I also knew that Jennifer was a formerly battered woman and hoped that she felt some safety in my classes. One night, Jennifer came to me. She had been brutally beaten and began to tell her story. While her story of terror, rape, and beatings is not repeated here, to ensure Jennifer's anonymity and safety, critical factors emerged that are informative about why we social work professionals must begin to take sexism and violence against women seriously and why we must include it in our developing knowledge base. Apparently, some of Jennifer's classmates knew of the battering and had encouraged her to "confront him and leave him!" Jennifer had been appreciative of the assertiveness techniques taught in some of her first-year practice courses and decided to take the advice of her classmates to behave assertively toward her partner. She asserted her rights to him. He then beat the hell out of her. She came to me in fear for her life.

So-called conventional wisdom failed for this social work student. In fact, "Assertiveness 101" could have gotten her killed. Nearly 20 years of work on violence against women can help us as social workers to refocus our messages and energies so that we can avoid the pitfalls inherent in such imprudent advice. This book pulls together research and practice experiences that can help social workers take enlightened steps forward in order to begin transforming their practice with survivors of sexism and violence.

Crises such as Jennifer's are very much the reason why this textbook was written, and they clearly show a rationale for why social workers must do more to understand the oppression of women in its many forms. Wetzel (1986), in the premiere issue of *Affilia,* noted, "Social workers continue to relegate women to the periphery of the profession, viewing them as a marginal special interest group" (p. 5). As a result of marginalization, a focus on women is often seen as unnecessary or as "just" a special interest. Wetzel further noted that justice for women (locally, nationally, and internationally) will not occur as long as people keep the issues of women on the periphery. Smith (1986) suggested that the notion that women's issues are peripheral or narrow is a myth. She challenged this myth with the following comments:

> This myth once again characterizes women's oppression as not particularly serious and by no means a matter of life and death. I have often wished I could spread the word that a movement committed to fighting sexual, racial, economic, and heterosexist oppression, not to mention one which opposes imperialism, anti-Semitism, the oppressions visited upon the physically disabled, the old and the young, at the same time that it challenges militarism and imminent nuclear destruction, is the very opposite of narrow. (p. 50)

Clearly, a multitude of issues and systems have been challenged by feminism in order to end the oppression of women. In addition to these feminist concerns are the simple facts that most social work constituents are women, most social workers are women, and the majority of people in this world are women. The issues and the populations addressed in this book are not peripheral or narrow at all. Certainly, this single textbook does not begin to capture what could, should, or might be known about women. With its focus on sexism and violence, it does not capture all the joys of womanhood; nor does it try to provide the definitive word on practice and policy strategies. Finally, in this book, we do not attempt to develop a theory to explain or predict the manifestation of violence against women. Instead, we identify important issues that have profound consequences for women's lives, and we suggest that when viewing a single issue, that single wire on the bird cage, social workers must also reflect on other issues that exacerbate the situation or experience.

BACKGROUND:
THE PERSON-IN-ENVIRONMENT CONTEXT

Feminist scholars recommend a contextualized approach to understanding and presenting issues related to sexism and violence against women. Bart, Miller, Moran, and Stanko (1989) introduced a special issue of *Gender and Society,* targeting violence against women, by stating, "All forms of violence against women and girls are interrelated. Wherever one starts one's analysis, with rape, incest, sexual harassment, battery or pornography, the systemic nature of these injuries emerges. . . . Yet the media treat each issue separately, and usually one at a time, so that people do not learn about their systematic interrelation" (p. 433). Further, Bart, Miller, Moran, and Stanko advocate that within all societal systems, the feminist message should clearly be that male violence is institutionalized and systemic. Collins (1990) suggests that African-American feminist thought emphasizes three levels as areas where domination exists and as potential areas of resistance: (1)

personal biography; (2) group or community cultural context created by race, class, and gender; and (3) social institutions.

The language of contextualization is familiar to social workers. Contemporary social work professes to be rooted in drawing connections between private and public issues and between micro and macro practice. Haynes and Holmes (1994) clearly note, "Social workers see people as they interact with, and are affected by, their environment. We acknowledge explicitly that no one lives in a social vacuum. This is referred to as the *person-in-environment perspective*" (p. 236; emphasis in original). Similarly, Fisher and Karger (1997) draw attention to the need for contextualization. They suggest, "Contextualization differentiates the social work approach to individual problems from a purely psychological approach. Moreover, contextualization is essential to affecting both individual and social change. Anchoring study and practice—whether macro or micro— to a structural analysis of social conditions and the goal of social change is what makes social work *social*" (p. xi; emphasis in original). Because of the interrelatedness of issues, feminist practice is often generalist in nature—addressing "private troubles to public issues" (Bricker-Jenkins & Hooyman, 1986b, p. 29). Both the profession of social work and individual social workers can become leaders in the struggle to end violence against women, once they accept the challenge to address sexism and violence with a person-in-environment, contextualized perspective.

CONCEPTUALIZING SEXISM AND VIOLENCE AGAINST WOMEN—A CONTINUUM MODEL

During the mid-1970s, a grassroots organization, the Movement for a New Society, offered a continuum model (see diagram on each chapter opening) as a tool for analyzing violence against women (Bricker-Jenkins, Jan. 1997, personal communication). I (Karen Stout) used this analysis tool when I was employed at a shelter for battered women from the late 1970s to the early 1980s. Since that time, I and others have used and continually adapted this continuum model as a framework to help people understand the dynamics of battering. The model has also been a useful tool to facilitate understanding that battering is not an anomaly in a society that demeans, dismisses, and victimizes women.

The continuum of sexism and violence against women presented in this text focuses on the following elements: institutional status of women, psychological wounding, gendered communication, economic assaults, control of women's bodies, pornography and prostitution, sexual harassment, women who are battered, sexual assault, and femicide. *Institutional status* refers to the status of women within major systems: political, economic, religious, and family systems. In addition, institutional status has been broadened to include an examination of how research affects women and how the media portray women. *Psychological wounding* describes the hazards of being raised female in a misogynistic society. One student reported that after reading a draft of this chapter for a women's issues class, she cried, and as she spoke of her pain in relation to this chapter, she cried again. She noted, "There are so many losses that I have suffered. I had hoped to protect my daughter from the same loss of self-esteem, from restricted choices, but each day I see how much she has been harmed—just because she is a girl." Some of the symptoms women present to clinicians—such as low self-esteem, depression, and concerns over body image—are clearly associated with being female. The chapter on psychological wounds is premised on the types of wounding that often occur even if a woman has not been harassed, battered, or sexually assaulted; yet it recognizes that such wounds often become intensified and more raw with each additional assault the woman faces in schools, on the streets, or in relationships. *Gendered communication* speaks to the differential treatment that so often emerges through our language (exclusionary, negative, and hateful speech), through differential-status indicators, and through the use of space and touch to illustrate dominance and power. *Economic assaults* refer to the economic inequities that women face. The chapter also describes how women's unpaid work is devalued, how women often pay more than men do for the same products, and how the glass and Lucite ceilings keep women from advancing in the paid work spheres. *Control of women's bodies* directs attention to women's lack of control over reproductive decisions and to how health-care systems have assaulted women through inadequate research, the pathologizing of normal healthy functions, and fetal-protection policies. *Pornography and prostitution* addresses the commercialized use of women for men's sexual pleasure. This topic, framed as violence against women used in the sex industry, is often absent from discussions on violence against women, and its inclusion represents the need for social workers to expand their knowledge and practice base to include stigmatized women. The chapter on *sexual harassment* takes a view of women's reality inside academic and paid work environments. Too often, women face hostile and even dangerous conditions that threaten their economic livelihood. The inquiry about *women who are battered* confronts the reality that those who profess to love us sometimes do tremendous physical and emotional harm to us. Also addressed are issues of power and control within relationships, as well as the many forms of violence that women who are battered experience. The investigation of *sexual assault* presents the way in which sexual means are used to assume power and control over women. Many women are sexually assaulted each day, and many more live in fear and take measures to prevent sexual assault each day. Finally, the continuum ends in *femicide,* the killing of women (p. 1). In addition, issues associated with racism, heterosexism, ageism, ableism, and classism/elitism interact with and

compound the complexities of each individual element and of the continuum as a whole.

A *continuum* is defined as "a continuous extent, succession, or whole, no part of which can be distinguished from neighboring parts, except by arbitrary divisions" (*American Heritage Electronic Dictionary,* 1992, Houghton Mifflin Co.). The elements of the continuum, labeled in the figure that opens each chapter (see page 1) and described previously, represent arbitrary divisions. The continuum framework offered in this book suggests that all elements of the continuum graduate into each other and are interrelated, connected, and often indistinguishable. Kelly (1988) wrote, "The concept of a continuum can enable women to make sense of their own experiences by showing how 'typical' and 'aberrant' male behaviour shade into one another" (p. 75). For example, when addressing issues related to battered women, the elements of psychological wounding, gendered communication, economic assaults, sexual assault, and femicide are all likely aspects of the presenting problem of battering. The role of pornography and prostitution may also emerge as issues in the context of the battering and secondary assaults by the health-care industry can possibly occur, linking battery to the control of women's bodies. Similarly, the sexual harassment of a woman often occurs within the context of women's institutional status, gendered communication, economic assaults, battering, sexual assault, and femicide.

Viewers of the continuum tend first to notice that sexism and violence against women moves from subtle and covert to obvious and overt forms of violence, or as Stanko (1985) observed, from "typical" to "aberrant" behavior. Many people tend to place value judgments on the severity of different acts of violence. For example, they may suggest that pornography is worse than sexist advertisements, or that an employer who sexually harasses an employee is worse than a producer of pornographic pictures. In turn, the harassing employer may appear mild, compared with the man who rapes his date or the man who batters his wife. Most people will quickly admit to abhorring the behavior of the man who rapes, yet even the rapist may not be viewed as being as bad as the man who kills a woman. Given that orientation, as social workers isolate events, other issues tend to be ignored or excused as less life-threatening forms of violence against women (Stout, 1991). The assertion made throughout this text is that all forms of sexism and violence against women warrant the attention of social workers, as all such forms are harmful to individuals and to women as a class. All elements of the continuum are impacted by racism, homophobia, heterosexism, classism/elitism, ableism and ageism. Again, visualize the bird cage and how each wire fits together with all of the rest to create an oppressive structure.

We hope that the visual representation of violence against women shown in the continuum encourages social workers to think about the prevalence, severity, subtleties, and insidious nature of sexism and violence against women. A clear implication is that acts of violence against women are not isolated and that social work professionals must examine the context and culture in which violence prevails when working with victims, survivors, and perpetrators.

LIMITATIONS OF A VISUAL REPRESENTATION OF A CONTINUUM AND ALTERNATIVE MODELS

The continuum framework presented in this book is a linear presentation going from typical to aberrant forms of sexism and violence against women. Within this framework, various decisions on ordering the continuum's elements have emerged over the years, based on perceptions of participants regarding whether the problem seems to be more of a nonviolent control mechanism versus a means of encouraging and actualizing physical violence against women. However, a linear presentation may be misleading in asserting that one act causes another or that one

crime is worse than another. Determinations regarding severity and placement on the continuum become difficult in the areas of economic assaults, pornography, sexual harassment, battering, sexual assault, and femicide. Many sexual harassment victims are beaten and raped. Rape victims are often beaten. Battered women are often raped. Women are starving around the world and in this country as a result of a blatantly discriminatory economic system. Any one of these crimes can result in femicide. Add to this continuum the factors related to multiple oppressions, and the ordering and severity may change.

Feminists have offered many different models and images to analyze violence against women. We present a linear continuum as a way of introducing and organizing the topics of this book. Frye (1983) provides the birdcage analogy, which is an inviting image. Bricker-Jenkins (1996, personal communication) uses a web, which shows the interrelationships of elements in the material. Kelly (1988) uses a continuum, yet orders it by prevalence, not severity. Elisabeth Moen (Jan. 1997, personal communication), a doctoral student in social work at the University of Umea in Sweden, portrays similar content with a spiral. Others have suggested visualizing a tree, the roots of which are deeply embedded in a patriarchal culture, with branches heavy under the weight of oppression. With all of these representations, the idea is that the interrelationships are present and need to be understood conceptually in order to develop meaningful social work theory, practice, or policy. Each reader's own learning style, ideology, theoretical orientation, and even imagination will affect the manner in which she or he chooses to integrate and visualize the material.

Reactions to the Continuum

It is sometimes difficult and painful to make connections and to analyze the interrelationships among forms of sexism and violence. When this material has been used in presentations, many listeners have reacted very strongly to the issues, the content, and the connecting framework. On the topic of language alone, students have had very mixed reactions. One student reported, "Language, a sensible place to start, brought to my attention things I never knew, never saw, of which I was unaware. I shall relentlessly be sensitive to nonsexist language in the spoken and written word" whereas another student suggested, "I feel being concerned with the language we speak is carrying it too far."

A common initial reaction to the content addressed in the continuum model is anger. The content on violence against women does not tend to elicit gender-neutral feelings. Some men have reported feeling scapegoated, picked on, or portrayed solely as a violent class of individuals. Other women and men have regarded women's reactions to the content as "shrill" or "irrational." One person who attended a weekend workshop on this content noted that it was a "crusade," not a class. The intent of this text is certainly not to portray women as angels and men as devils. Throughout this text, we emphasize how much social workers need to learn to better serve victims and survivors of violence. While we do not single out men as the only ones who need to learn this content, we do hope that men, alongside women, will benefit from the content. The anger that emerges as a result of opening one's eyes to the continuum is legitimate. Social workers need to be able to hear the anger of oppressed populations. How can social workers help to confront oppression if they are uncomfortable with the anger of oppressed people? Female survivors will often be angry. Social work professionals, female and male, need to hear people's anger and to develop the empathy that comes from truly listening to and hearing another person's reality (Stout, 1991).

Another common reaction to the content is fear. Women students have expressed fear of walking to their cars on campus and of repeat-edly checking the locks on their doors at home after their exposure to the content included in this text. Other women have commented that suddenly they see violence everywhere: on the television, in the grocery store, with clients, and in every possible private and public arena. Unfortunately, violence against women is pervasive. The task becomes to confirm reality and to take action to ensure that these issues do not become minimized or negated. Feelings of fear, the reality for many women, can be transformed to empowerment. Tifft (1993) suggests, "Empowerment can be fostered by *contact* to counter feelings of isolation, *awareness* to contravene feelings of isolation, and *action* to negate domination and oppression" (p. 145; emphasis in original). For example, one year, almost half of the second-year graduate class at the University of Houston Graduate School of Social Work (GSSW) took the women's issues class, where sexism and violence against women is covered in depth. Many of the students had felt they were among just a minority of feminist students; they had felt *isolated* until they came in *contact* with other women and men who had similar concerns. On finding each other, many found the support and strength needed to take *action* on classroom and policy issues that concerned both them and the women and men with whom and for whom they would be working.

Finally, students exposed to this content have confirmed its relevance to social work practice. One student commented, "Sexism and racism are such a part of our culture that we often don't recognize them unless we train ourselves to be alert to their appearance, for they come in so many forms."

It is our hope that similar dialogues will occur about the material in this text. Obviously, we hope that both the content and the process of your dialogues will have a positive impact on you, personally and professionally. Our favorite student comments about this material are those indicating that people are reconceptualizing and actively processing (whether in agreement or disagreement) the information. For example, a student wrote, "My personal reaction to the course content has several dimensions. I felt defensive at times, surprised, offended, frightened, angry, and eventually felt empowered by the information that was presented." Finally, another student poignantly described the continuum presentation by stating, "I thank you for the experience; even though I've lost an innocence, for this I mildly grieve, I've gained a power—the power of enlightenment, and that is far more useful."

A CALL TO ACTION

Patricia Ireland, in her 1996 book entitled *What Women Want*, addressed the pain that accompanied her realization of the wrongs she had experienced in her life. She noted, "I was also afraid to lift the lid off my feelings of resentment at the ways I was treated as a woman. In some sense, I was right to be afraid. Once I opened my eyes, I could not really, wholly, close them again" (p. 5). Later in the book, she described the power of change:

> *All of us can improve our own lives and the lives of other women by influencing the people around us every day. We can keep a straight face when someone tells a racist, sexist, or homophobic "joke" and suggest that the person explain it, because we just don't see the humor. We can tell the truth about our lives and be proud of overcoming violence, incest, or rape. We can refuse to be intimidated by harassment or lesbian-baiting and refuse to be forced into denying our sexuality. All of these things can help move public opinion and ultimately public policy. (p. 303)*

Finally, Ireland concludes, "Just as we began this century by winning the right to vote, I

African-American women attend a town hall meeting in South-Central Los Angeles. Photo © 1996 Kim Kulish.

want us to end this century by taking real political and personal power" (p. 307). That seems an appropriate challenge as the year 2000 approaches. There is so much that every person can do to confront injustice every day of every week of every year.

Often, when we address students on the responsibility to work toward social justice, several students will sigh and suggest that it will be all that they can do to go to their paid work from 8 to 5 and then go home to their second shift of unpaid labor. Yet if social workers are truly centered on understanding the concepts of the person-in-environment or the "personal is political" in their professional outlook, they will see that their work for social justice encompasses both their paid work and their home work. As Ireland (1996) suggested, each of us

can stop laughing at injustice and start speaking the truth. One person, informed on issues related to sexism and violence against women, can help the woman who is being battered to help the woman who is being harassed, who can help the woman who is being denied equal pay. The work that must be done can be shared with those who come to social workers for assistance, with allies, and with those who are closest to us. The work to be done is not centered on individual solutions. It is work to be done in concert with others. It is organizing, marching, creating, visualizing, doing magic, enacting, sharing, and changing ourselves and others (Bricker-Jenkins, Jan. 1997, personal communication). If the work that must be done is shared, if it is movement work, transformational change will finally emerge.

REFERENCES

Bart, P., Miller, P., Moran, E., & Stanko, E. (1989). Guest editors' introduction. *Gender & Society, 3,* 431–435.

Boneparth, E., & Stoper, E. (Eds.). (1988). *Women, power and policy.* New York: Pergamon Press.

Bricker-Jenkins, M., & Hooyman, N. (Eds.). (1986a). *Not for women only.* Silver Spring, MD: NASW Press.

Bricker-Jenkins, M. & Hooyman, N. (Eds.). (1986b). Grounding the definitions of feminist practice. In M. Bricker-Jenkins & N. Hooyman (Eds.), *Not for women only* (pp. 25–33). Silver Spring, MD: NASW Press.

Bricker-Jenkins, M., & Lockett, P. W. (1995). Women: Direct practice. In *Encyclopedia of Social Work* (pp. 2529–2538) Silver Spring, MD: NASW Press.

Collins, P. (1990). *Black feminist thought.* New York: Routledge.

Findlen, B. (Ed.). (1995). *Listen up: Voices from the next feminist generation.* Seattle: Seal Press.

Fisher, R., & Karger, H. (1997). *Social work and community in a private world.* White Plains, NY: Longman.

Frye, M. (1983). *The politics of reality: Essays in feminist theory.* Trumansburg, NY: Crossing Press.

Haynes, K. S., & Holmes, K. A. (1994). *Invitation to social work.* White Plains, NY: Longman.

Ireland, P. (1996). *What women want.* New York: Dutton.

Kelly, L. (1988). *Surviving sexual violence.* Oxford, England: Polity Press.

Schechter, S. (1982). *Women and male violence.* Boston: South End Press.

Smith, B. (1986). Some home truths on the contemporary Black feminist movement. In N. Van Den Bergh & L. Cooper (Eds.), *Feminist visions for social work.* Silver Spring, MD: NASW Press.

Stanko, E. (1985). *Intimate intrusions: Women's experience of male violence.* London: Routledge & Kegan Paul.

Stark-Adamec, C., & Adamec, R.C. (1982). Aggression by men against women: Adaptation or aberration? *International Journal of Women's Studies, 5,* 1–21.

Stout, K. D. (1991). A continuum of male controls and violence against women: A teaching model. *Journal of Social Work Education, 27,* 305–319.

Tifft, L. (1993). *Battering of women: The failure of intervention and the case for prevention.* Boulder, CO: Westview Press.

Turner, J., Singleton, R., & Musick, D. (1984). *Oppression: A socio-history of Black–White relations in America.* Chicago: Nelson-Hall.

Van Soest, D. (1996). Impact of social work education on student attitudes and behavior concerning oppression. *Journal of Social Work Education, 32,* 191–202.

Wetzel, J. (1986). Global issues and perspectives on working with women. *Affilia, 1,* 5–19.

Chapter

2 WOMEN'S INSTITUTIONAL STATUS

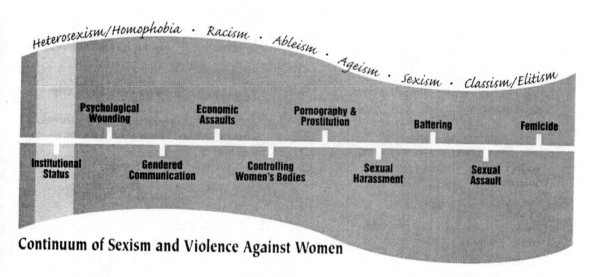

Continuum of Sexism and Violence Against Women

Heterosexism/Homophobia · Racism · Ableism · Ageism · Sexism · Classism/Elitism

Psychological Wounding · Economic Assaults · Pornography & Prostitution · Battering · Femicide

Institutional Status · Gendered Communication · Controlling Women's Bodies · Sexual Harassment · Sexual Assault

"Math Class Is Tough"

Mattel's Talking Barbie Doll
(pulled from distribution after protests by many smart women)

*I*n Chapter 1, while introducing the continuum concept, the importance of contextualization was stressed. Part of the context when examining sexism and violence against women includes the roles women have and have not played within major societal institutions. The set of institutional roles for women is being termed "women's institutional status," as an element of the continuum of sexism and violence against women. This chapter examines the role of research for its part in excluding women and in maintaining the status quo. In addition, the purpose of this chapter is to describe women's institutional status in key socialization systems: political, economic, media, religious, educational, and family systems. Women have often been excluded from the knowledge base, and, as this chapter also highlights, women have too often been excluded from decision making in major societal institutions. When women are not part of the knowledge base and the decision-making process, their voices and their needs are not fully addressed.

Those absences, those unheard voices, and those unfilled voids have underpinned a culture of sexism and violence against women.

Inspire Me

Everybody needs someone to show them
what is possible
Everybody needs someone to go as far as
she can go
I need to stand upon the shoulders of giants
I need a woman a woman who's as big as me.

When I was a little bitty baby sitting on my
mama's knee
I looked around to see just what the future
had in store for me
I needed to see women who were living
without limits
I needed to see women making history.

So I said,
Give me a woman who can climb the
tallest mountain
Give me a woman who can swim across the
widest sea
Women need women who lead lives of bold-
est daring
Tell me their stories they inspire me.

Give me Amelia who went soaring cross
the ocean
Winnie Mandela who is going to set her
people free
Judy Chicago who breaks all artistic silences
These women leave a precious legacy.

When I was a young teenager reading my
Seventeen
I looked around to see just what the future
had in store for me
Women in the fashion mags were too small
for my dream
I needed to see women just as big as me.

So I said, give me a woman. . . .

I know of women all across the nation
Leading lives of courage in the face of fear
and poverty
One leaves an abusive home, one raises her
five children
Women, we need a new mythology.

Now that I'm a grown up woman living in society
I still look around to see just what the future
holds for me
I still need women who are shooting like
the comets
So I can leave my own starlight in this galaxy.

And I say, give me a woman. . . .

Won't you please tell me their stories, they
inspire me.
I'd like to tell you their stories, they inspire me.
Won't you please tell me your story, you inspire me.

Words and music by Libby Roderick

The issues related to women's institutional status tend to be regarded as the status quo. Many have come to accept that men are the nation's leaders in the economy, religion, media, education, and even within the family. These institutional systems cannot be ignored as consideration is given to issues related to sexual harassment, battering, sexual assault, gendered communication, women's health, and the psychological wounding of women. It is within the context of the systems highlighted in this chapter that sexism and violence against women exists and is allowed to persist. Many call this set of systems underpinning a culture of sexism and violence against women "the patriarchy" literally by the father.

Bhasin (1993, 1994) described patriarchy as power relationships in which men dominate women and as a system in which women are subordinate in numerous ways. Schaef (1981) broadened the definition of patriarchy by including the domination of men of color. She named the current institutional systems the "White Male System." She described this system as one in which the power is vested in white men (many would add that heterosexual white men enjoy the greatest power). This system too often becomes defined as reality, and those who suggest an alternative reality are carefully scrutinized and often ridiculed or ostracized. She likened the acceptance of this system to pollution: "When you are in the middle of pollution, you are usually unaware of it (unless it is especially bad). You eat in it, sleep in it, work in it, and sooner or later start believing that that is just the way the air is" (p. 4). Living, learning, and being socialized in a system where women are subordinate or invisible indoctrinates people into that perspective.

A 1995 Gallup poll, conducted in 22 countries, found some interesting international perceptions about the status of women and men (Gallup, 1996). For example, the majority of people in nearly two-thirds of the countries polled felt that their society was biased (favorably) toward men. In most of the countries, men were seen as having more courage than women and to be more aggressive and ambitious, while women were viewed as patient, emotional, and talkative. The U.S. respondents had one of the highest preference ratings for the "traditional family"—male as breadwinner and woman as homemaker. In all but 2 countries, women were more likely than men to indicate that if they were reborn, they would prefer to be reborn as the opposite sex. Further, in all but 2 countries, more respondents expressed a preference for working for a man. However, despite these somewhat stereotypical responses internationally, respondents in all but 1 country believed their government would be better if more women were in politics (Gallup, 1996).

The purpose of this chapter is to highlight the white-male-dominated systems that are so pervasive and that have an everyday impact on women and men in this society. Improving the status of women must become an important is-

sue for social workers. Although the media and political pollsters have in recent years declared "The Year of the Woman," women are still seeking equity and fair representation in most of our societal systems. This chapter first reviews how research has often neglected women's concerns and then reviews women's status in several key systems—economic, media, educational, political, religious, social work, and family systems. Finally, change strategies are proposed to place women's needs in the forefront of national and professional agendas.

INTRODUCTION TO THE ISSUES

The Problem of Research

Weick (1994) called social workers' attention to how those who have suffered discrimination have been injured by social messages and practices. Because of these harms, she directs attention to the need to become aware of our own and other people's experiences with oppression. This book addresses many forms of oppression, from the status of women through the murder of women. A subtle but powerful form of oppression, a force to be reckoned with, concerns the manner in which research has ignored, dismissed, or pathologized women. Becoming aware of messages and practices stemming from erroneous or incomplete knowledge about sexism and violence against women is an important step toward reaching the goal of social change and social justice.

Mincing no words, Spender (1982) wrote, "While the subject of male control has for centuries been a problem for women, it has not presented a serious problem for men, with the result that they have not addressed the topic and have often dismissed the whole area as unimportant and insignificant—and they have been in the position to have their assessment accepted by women as well as by men" (p. 15). Women's experiences with heart disease have been a serious problem, yet even as recently as

1988, women were not included in a major study of that disease; as a result, that study did not provide information for women on whether "an aspirin a day would keep our heart troubles away." Breast cancer has been a serious problem for women, yet in a study on how obesity affected breast and uterine cancer—only men were used in the sample (Laurence & Weinhouse, 1994). For lesbians, who may have a two to three times higher risk for breast cancer, as compared with heterosexual women, this lack of appropriate research is a serious problem (Laurence & Weinhouse, 1994). Yet, as Spender (1982) suggests, it has not been a problem for the patriarchy, so the problem has not been adequately addressed. In addition, it takes only a cursory reading (though a careful reading is suggested) of Shilts's (1987) extraordinary book *And the Band Played On* to know that gay men and men of color have also been systematically excluded from or harmed by the status quo. Not until 20,849 people had died from AIDS-related illnesses did former President Ronald Reagan even mention the word AIDS; moreover, when he finally did say the word "AIDS," he did not mention the words "gay men." His policies tremendously influenced funding for research that could have saved lives (Shilts, 1987). Instead, people died and continue to die.

Consider the topic of sexual harassment for a moment. Women have participated in the paid labor force for many years. The phenomenon of women working outside of the home was not invented during the second wave of feminism or by feminism at any time. People know that women worked outside of the home because many of their mothers, grandmothers, and great-grandmothers participated in the labor force—especially women from working-class backgrounds. There had been hundreds of studies on organizational behavior prior to the mid-1970s. Why then was it not until the mid-1970s that sexual harassment was addressed in profes-

sional literature? Because researchers failed to study sexual harassment, it continued to contribute to harsh working environments for women, and policies were not developed to address the problem.

The same questions can be asked about alcoholism. It is no secret that women have been substance abusers for many years, yet it was not until the 1970s that the first U.S. congressional hearings on women and alcohol were held. Around that time, research and services began to address women's problems with alcohol. Many undesirable outcomes have resulted from these exclusions. Lives have been lost; serious health problems, such as alcoholism, have continued unidentified and untreated.

Eichler (1991) named the problems related to exclusion *androcentricity*. She defines *androcentricity* as "essentially a view of the world from a male perspective" (p. 5). She explained,

> From an androcentric perspective, women are seen as passive objects rather than subjects in history, as acted upon rather than actors; androcentricity prevents us from understanding that both males and females are always acted upon as well as acting, although often in very different ways. Two extreme forms of androcentricity are gynopia (female invisibility) and misogyny (hatred of women). (p. 5)

Issues related to power and politics have a great deal to do with issues of invisibility and with how misogyny creeps into the knowledge base, as researchers have the power to define reality. They have the power to pose research questions that are inclusive or exclusive, racist or nonracist, sexist or nonsexist; that maintain the status quo or promote social change; or even that foster discrimination or enhance understanding. Research texts often suggest that research-based knowledge is incremental. Spender (1982) suggested that incrementalism works only for groups of people who have been included. She noted, "While men take it for granted that they can build on what has gone before, selecting, refining, adapting the knowledge they have inherited to meet their needs, women are constantly required to begin with a blank sheet" (p. 17).

How researchers will fill in those blank sheets will be affected by politics. DiNitto and Dye (1987) suggested that *politics* can be defined as *who* gets *what, when,* and *why*. Politics is a part of who becomes reviewers for editorial boards, who then decide which articles will be published in social work journals. Politics is a part of determining what problems are deemed worthy of grant funding. All of these factors help to shape which research questions are studied and subsequently published, and which then influence public policy and practice knowledge.

Politics, especially in relationship to research practice, is often seen as separate from the scientific method. Haynes (1996) stated that all social work is political and "that we [social workers] become explicitly and purposely so" (p. 275). Unfortunately, it is often oppressed and marginalized groups of people who are accused of being political. Carniol (1990) addressed this issue:

Curiously, professionals who are accepting of the status quo and its downward flow of power are not seen as political. Yet when social workers support an upward flow of power they are accused, at least by some, of being "political," that is, of doing things viewed as "unprofessional." (p. 134)

Being cognizant of power and politics is crucial to understanding the dynamics of sexism and violence against women. Cummerton (1986) called to our attention the political nature of feminist research, stating, "Research in a feminist perspective is clearly political in that its ultimate goal is to improve the quality of life for women and for other oppressed populations. Research *for* women rather than research *on* women remains a major theme in this perspective" (p. 87). An implication of this perspective is that the researcher becomes a change agent

and that "many feminist research projects focus on substantive areas that are of little interest to the dominant white male heterosexual power structure" (Cummerton, 1986, p. 96).

The importance of the feminist perspective for oppressed groups was clearly articulated by Wood (1994) in a discussion of standpoint theory:

To survive, subjugated persons have to understand both their own perspective and the viewpoints of persons who have more power. To survive, subjugated persons have to understand people with power, but the reverse is not true. From this it follows that marginalized groups have unique insights into the nature and working of a society. Women, minorities, gays and lesbians, people of lower socioeconomic class, and others who are outside of the cultural center may see the society from a perspective that is less distorted, less biased, and more layered than those who occupy more central standpoints. Marginalized perspectives can inform all of us about how our society operates. (p. 52)

This theoretical perspective would suggest that the knowledge base must become more inclusive if social workers and others are to understand the nature of power and the reality of the day-to-day lives of the people whom social workers serve. Swigonski (1994) pointed out the congruence between standpoint theory and feminist research and concluded, "The research base of social work needs both passion and objectivity. Standpoint theory provides an avenue for achieving a profoundly relevant and impassioned objectivity that honors and celebrates cultural diversity with a scholarly rigor" (p. 392). Feminist research may be a model that can help social workers move toward greater inclusion and contextualization in research practice, which in turn can enhance the knowledge base related to issues of sexism and violence against women.

Knowledge about women and other oppressed groups has been largely minimized in the professional literature—despite the overwhelmingly female composition of both the social work profession and the population it serves. In addition, in spite of the structural forces that serve to maintain inequality in this society, much of the research focus has been on intrapsychic and interpersonal factors. For example, McMahon and Allen-Meares (1992) reviewed all of the articles published in *Child Welfare, Social Casework, Social Work,* and *Social Service Review* during the 1980s, and found that of 1,965 articles published in these journals, only 5.95% (*n* = 117) proposed some type of intervention with ethnic minorities. Of these 117 articles, only 22.2% recommended an institutional intervention. The authors concluded, "In general, the majority of articles surveyed attempted to understand minorities acontextually, that is, without reference to the real social processes, such as racism and poverty that shape people's lives" (p. 537). This individualistic and adjustment-oriented research focus has prompted feminist and Afrocentric critiques of the adequacy of social work research and even its fit with the profession's mission of social justice.

Brieland (1990) pointedly questioned whether the profession today would even recognize Jane Addams as a social worker. Brieland noted that research was a piece of the work done by our social work forebears, for the purpose of social change, as opposed to individual change or adjustment. "Residents [of Hull House] became technical experts on their neighborhood, and survey data were used with the city council and the state legislature to back up demands for change" (p. 136). Brieland asked that social workers reflect on the following question: "Has social work abandoned social reform and substituted modest efforts at advocacy—mostly for the needs of one client at a time?" (p. 138). The McMahon and Allen-Meares (1992) findings suggest that addressing the needs of one client at a time continues to be the tradition in social work research. If practice is to be grounded in research, it is time for change.

Authors' Perspective

Despite the aforementioned criticisms of research practices and the continuing need for knowledge building on issues affecting women's lives, the past 20 years have given social workers, other professionals, and the public an enormous body of literature on which to draw to learn about sexism and violence against women. Fifteen years ago, if a student had come to our offices to borrow materials on battering, we would have given her or him a fairly large box filled with articles and books. Now when students come to our office for materials on battering, they are quizzed for 30 minutes or so to determine *which* box of books and articles will be most helpful for their particular focus on the issue (e.g., effects on children, psychological characteristics of men who batter, expert witnesses, historical explanations). The variety of perspectives on this issue is the impetus for writing this textbook. Because there is so much information on intrapersonal, interpersonal, family, group, and community practice and on policy issues related to sexism and to violence against women for *each* topic, social workers often fail to notice the larger context, fail to observe important interrelationships, and fail to make fundamental connections.

The following sections present connections and interrelationships by illustrating how major societal institutions have worked to institutionalize discrimination and stereotypical images of women.

Institutional Status

Volumes have been written on how key societal institutions socialize, indoctrinate, support, or even negate the will and the capacity of humans to develop and flourish. Issues that concern women, as noted in Chapter 1, are neither few nor narrow. Hence, it is important to highlight key systems to note how women have been influenced by and have influenced those systems.

Women's Economic Status

All of Chapter 5 is devoted to the important issue of women's economic status. In brief, according to Women's Action Coalition (WAC) statistics (1993):

- Of all children in female-headed households, 57% live in poverty.
- In the United States, $24 billion is owed mothers for unpaid child support.
- Minority women comprise only 3.3% of women corporate officers.
- Female lawyers are partners in only 6% of law firms.
- In 1987, disabled women earned 38% less than did nondisabled women.
- In 1990, 46% of working women were employed in service and administrative support jobs, such as secretaries, waiters, and health aides.

Julian and Kornblum (1983) suggested a baseball metaphor for looking at the economic status of women. They asserted, "If you are a female, that's one strike against you; if you are either a poor female or a nonwhite female, that's two strikes against you; if you are a poor, nonwhite female, you have struck out" (p. 337). Jesse Jackson, in his powerful address to the 1988 Democratic Convention, noted that women cannot buy milk or meat more cheaply than can men, so women deserve equal pay for the work that they do. Chapter 5 addresses the issues of women in poverty, pay equity, and the glass ceiling, as well as the related strategies for social change. It is important to note here that economic inequities continue to be a major systemic issue that must be addressed by helping professionals.

Woman living in a downtown Los Angeles homeless camp. Photo © 1996 Kim Kulish.

The Political Dimension

It was not until 1920 that women, after a long struggle, won the right to vote in this country. During that struggle, many women who supported women's right to vote faced "rejection, ridicule, and outright mockery. They were accused of being socialists, of trying to destroy the home, of threatening states' rights and of distracting the nation from its war effort" (Scott, 1995, p. 1G). Only a few generations of women have voted in the U.S. electoral system. Just a few years ago, in 1991, through the confirmation hearings for Justice Clarence Thomas the nation apparently awakened to the issue of sexual harassment and also to the realization that the members of the judicial committee of the U.S. Senate were all white and all male. The image of that all white male panel was imprinted on the minds of many Americans, and many became committed or recommitted to ensuring that more women are elected to government office. The history of women's involvement with the political system has been fraught with difficulties and limitations, yet it also has given us a lot of our early women leaders (Sojourner Truth, Elizabeth Cady Stanton, Tye Leung Schulze, Francis Willard, Patsy Mink).

As social workers, we can take pride that the first woman elected to congress was also the first social worker in Congress: Jeannette Rankin in 1917. Today, another one of our own, Barbara Mikulski, M.S.W., is a member of the U.S. Senate. The 105th Congress will have nine women serving in the U.S. Senate: Senators Mikulski, Bailey-Hutchison, Murray, Feinstein, Boxer, Snowe, Collins, Landrieu, and Moseley-Braun. Six of these women were elected in the first national election after the Justice Thomas confirmation hearing. Despite these gains, however, the U.S. Senate is still only 9% women, and just 6% of the membership of the House of Representatives is female. In 1994, women governed only three states (Kansas, New Jersey, and Oregon) and held only 18% of the seats in state legislatures. Of the 100 largest cities, only 19 had women as mayors (Haynes, 1994). These numbers reflect both progress and the need for continued efforts to secure more representation by women at all levels. Social workers can take pride that along with Senator Barbara Mikulski, four members of the House of Representatives are social workers: Debbie Stepanow, Ron Dellum, Edolphus Towns, and Ciro Rodriquez.

Frase-Blunt (1991, p. 18) found that Latina women "are woefully underrepresented in politics, especially at the national level. According to figures from the National Association of Latino Elected and Appointed Officials, only 17 of the 926 Hispanic women elected officials serve at state level or higher." Yet, Hardy-Fanta (1992) noted that the stereotypical perception of Latinas as submissive or passive is contrary to the role Latinas play in mobilizing Latino communities. She found that politically active Latinas placed more emphasis on connectedness and on grassroots politics than on electoral politics.

U.S. Senator Barbara Mikulski, Democrat from Maryland, holds an M.S.W. and is one of nine women in the U.S. Senate.

Some people may wonder whether having more women representatives in the electoral political process would really make a difference in the lives of women and men. Carroll (1992) has noted the tendency to point to Margaret Thatcher or Indira Gandhi to conclude that the election of women will not help women's status. Contrary to this perception, Carroll found, "Most women state legislators do work on legislation aimed at helping women, and proportionately more women than men legislators place top priority on legislation dealing with women's issues, health care issues, and children's welfare issues" (p. 38). The March, 1996, *National NOW Times* headlined a viewpoint article, "'Insider' Women Are Still Making a Difference," citing a record amount of health-care funding for women's health, passage of the Family Leave and Medical Leave Act, and the forced resignation of Senator Bob

Packwood, who was alleged to have committed numerous acts of sexual harassment during his tenure as a United States Senator—all of which occurred through the leadership of women in Congress.

Looking to the international realm, many other countries have had women as their presidents or prime ministers, and some countries also have much greater representation of women in their legislative body. Table 2.1 presents data on women's political status in some selected countries. Data from an international perspective show that the United States is not a leader in electing women to political office. Also, U.S. voters have not elected a woman to their highest elected office—the presidency. As of early 1997, approximately 5 of 190 nations had women leaders: Norway, Nicaragua, Sri Lanka, Bangladesh, and Ecuador (Petty, 1996). On the other hand, Native American women can boast of both Wilma Mankiller, a social worker, as a recent (until 1995) Chief of the Cherokee Nation, and Ada Deer, who was elected Chief of the Monominee Tribe in 1973. Historically, Lakota women were central in Sioux government.

> Many women were filling the sacred and traditional role of chiefs, council of mothers or grandmothers, beloved women whose word was final for the people. . . . However, the Anglo-European male insistence on only men being in power changed Native societies forever from matriarchal to patriarchal. . . . It was to lead to the total disappearance of Native women as policy and political leaders in tribes. It was to lead to the total invisibility of Native women in the Native world and the white world. It was to lead to Native women being stereotyped as squaw or beast of burden. (Whitehorse Cochran, 1991, p. 197)

Jackson (1992) suggested that if the United States maintains the same rate of progress toward electing women to political office, it will be the year 2056 before women comprise half of the members of state legislatures; it is worth noting here that women have been elected to

Table 2.1
Women's Political Status Internationally

Country	% Women in major national legislative body
United States	6.4
Canada	13.2
China	21.3
Denmark	33.0
Finland	38.5
India	7.1
Iran	1.5
Japan	2.3
Mexico	12.4
Nicaragua	16.3
Norway	35.8
Sweden	38.1
United Arab Emirates	0.0
United Kingdom	6.3
Vietnam	17.7
Zimbabwe	12.0

Data from Franck, I., & Brownstone, D. (1993). The Women's Desk Reference. New York: Viking Press.

state legislatures much more quickly than to the national legislative level. Raising money continues to be a problem for women candidates. Fortunately, groups such as EMILY's (Early Money Is Like Yeast) List have emerged to raise money for women candidates.

Although professional social workers are rare on the national political level, social workers have many skills, such as their ability to work with people at multiple levels; such an ability could well serve social workers interested in electoral politics. Edolphus Towns (D, NY) is a social worker in the U.S. Congress, and he appreciates the skills a professional social worker can bring to government service. He has noted, "I cannot think of any educational underpinning better suited to a career in government and politics than social work" (Towns, 1991, p. 33).

Media Misrepresentations

Wood (1994) wrote of the distorted view of the world the media presents. If people relied on media images alone, the following images would be accepted:

> White males make up two-thirds of the population. The women are less in number; perhaps because fewer than 10% live beyond [age] 35. Those who do, like their younger and male counterparts, are nearly all white and heterosexual. In addition to being young, the majority of women are beautiful, very thin, passive and primarily concerned with relationships and getting rings out of collars and commodes. There are a few bad, bitchy women, and they are not so pretty, not so subordinate, and not so caring as the good women. Most of the bad ones work outside of the home, which is probably why they are hardened and undesirable. The more powerful, ambitious men occupy themselves with important business deals, exciting adventures, and rescuing dependent females, whom they often then assault sexually. (p. 232)

Jackson (1992) noted that 97% of print ads show women either in an image that puts the woman down (such as a sex object or a victim) or in a stereotypical role—mother, wife, or secretary—and that 1 of every 15 films has a rape scene. Wood (1994) described basic themes evident in the media: (1) under representation of women, (2) stereotypical portrayals of women and men, and (3) stereotypical images of relationships between women and men. The implications of media themes include the fostering of unrealistic and limited gender ideals, the pathologizing of the female body, and the normalizing of violence against women (Wood, 1994).

Wolf (1991) strongly voiced her concern about the pathologizing of women's bodies. She wrote, "The larger world never gives girls the message that their bodies are valuable simply because they are inside them. Until our culture tells young girls that they are welcome in any shape—that women are valuable to it with or without the excuse of 'beauty'—girls will continue to starve" (p. 205). Girls and women need

to be affirmed not only for their shape but also for their skin color. Yang and Ragaza (1997) cited a study by Thomas Schwartz, which found that the number of women of color in full-page ads in *Vogue, Cosmopolitan,* and *Mademoiselle* was 0% in the late 1960s, a mere 5% in the late 1970s, and dropped to 1.6% in the late 1980s.

The display of violence against women in the media is not a new phenomenon. In 1978, London drew attention to advertising images of violence against women: "In record-album photos, in fashion and men's magazines layouts, in department store windows, on billboards and other advertisements women are increasingly shown bound, gagged, beaten, whipped, chained, or as victims of murder, sexual assault, gang rape" (p. 510). Chapman (1978) gave a startling example of an advertisement depicting violence against women: "A boutique in Cambridge, Massachusetts has shown a mannequin as a dead woman, blood coming from her mouth, placed in a trash can. Men's shoes are placed at her head and neck, with the caption, 'We'd kill for these'" (p. 259).

Although Chapman's example is extreme (though not unusual), more subtle images are flashed numerous times every day in advertisements: a shadowy figure looming over a woman, women shown in vulnerable positions, dogs attacking women, and images of startled women. In *Ms.* magazine, each issue highlights sexist ads, and many of those portray violence against women. Chapman (1978) suggested, "Picturing the victimization of women has long been found effective and profitable. It has now become a principle technique in advertising campaigns, even those geared to a predominantly female market" (p. 259).

Motion pictures also depict sexism and violence against women as an acceptable male–female dynamic. Even Paul Newman, a favorite actor of many women and men, has hit women in many of his movies. In both *The Verdict* and *Absence of Malice,* he struck a woman as a means of settling a conflict. Sonkin, Martin, and Walker (1985) wrote about the movie *The Verdict*, noting, "We have our hero, a hard-working attorney who is working with a woman on a case. The long and short of it is that the woman is also working for the other side in the case and betrays our hero. What does he do when he finds out? He punches her in the face, at which time the audience applauds" (p. 181). In 1994, Wood concluded, "Thus, the research that demonstrates connections between sex-stereotypical media and acceptance of sexual violence is consistent with that showing relationships between more extreme, pornographic media and acceptance of and use of violence" (p. 256).

Disney movies have been heavily criticized for their role in teaching girls to look for salvation in the form of relationships with men while often shunning other women as competitors, rather than allies. In Disney's *Little Mermaid*, the young mermaid was willing to give up her voice in pursuit of a man she had glimpsed only once. In the movie *The Beauty and the Beast*, the messages were even more sinister, encouraging young girls to overlook the so-called hero's abusive behavior, in the hope that the heroine's love could change him. In another Disney movie, the true story of Pocahontas's courage and daring in bridging two cultures was distorted to provide a fictional love story. Over and over again, girls learn that the love of a man can be their only salvation.

Parenti (1993) suggested that even news broadcasts are likely to misrepresent oppressed groups:

> Those who have position and wealth are less likely to be slighted in news reports than [are] their critics, and they are more likely to be accorded adequate space to respond on the infrequent occasions they are attacked. The media are less energetic in their search for a competing viewpoint if it must be elicited from labor leaders, environmentalists, feminists, peace and disarmament advocates, communists, civil rights supporters, Black or Latino protesters, Third World insur-

> gents, American supporters of Third World insurgents, the poor, and the oppressed. (pp. 198–199)

Wood (1994) concurred that news programming has been biased. She described how the morning news shows focused on women's hormonal changes when Pat Schroeder ran for U.S. president and Geraldine Ferraro for vice president. Yet when it was disclosed that former President Bush was taking Halcion (a psychoactive drug), little attention was paid to possible effects on his judgment. Similarly, during the Gulf War, when a woman soldier became a prisoner of war, attention was focused on the woman as a sexual object. Male prisoners of war were shown in uniform, but the woman's photo was a glamour shot from her school yearbook (Wood, 1994).

Focusing on the print news media, Martindale (1997) analyzed how The *New York Times* portrayed the largest U.S. minority groups (African Americans, Latinos, Asian Americans, and Native Americans). She found that these media focused disproportionately on crime for Latinos, African Americans, and Asian Americans; and on the problems of Native Americans and Asian Americans. She concluded, "This kind of coverage reinforces the claim that the media present minorities as people outside the mainstream of U.S. society by portraying them as problem people" (p. 94).

> If you had relied on the white press of that day, you would have assumed that blacks were not born, because the white press didn't deal with our births.
>
> You would have assumed that we didn't finish school, because the white press didn't deal with our educational achievements.
>
> You would have assumed that we didn't get married, because the white press didn't print our wedding announcements or pictures of black brides and grooms cutting cakes.
>
> You would have assumed that we didn't die, because it didn't deal with our funerals. . . .
>
> So says John J. Johnson, publisher of Ebony magazine, describing the year 1945 in his national bestseller, Succeeding Against the Odds.
>
> Fast-forward to 1995. African Americans, along with Latinos, Asians, and Native Americans, are still essentially an "invisible people"

when it comes to editorial coverage and advertisements. You can also assume that they don't read, write or edit because the white press doesn't hire them. (Brown, 1997, p. 155)

In 1995, the rap music of African-American artists became a campaign issue, due to the words of violence used in some musicians' lyrics. Importantly, hooks (1994a) has cautioned us not to make young African-American men scapegoats for violence in the media. She noted,

Without a doubt black males, young and old, must be held politically accountable for their sexism. Yet this critique must always be contextualized or we risk making it appear that the problems of misogyny, sexism, and all the behaviors this thinking supports and condones, including rape, male violence against women, is a black male thing. And this is what is happening. Young black males are forced to take the heat for encouraging via their music the hatred of and violence against women that is a central core of patriarchy. (p. 116)

Further, hooks has encouraged us to examine the Academy Award–winning movie *The Piano* and compare the images this highly acclaimed movie portrayed to the messages of some rap artists. According to hooks, "Violence against land, natives, and women in this film, unlike that of gangsta rap, is portrayed uncritically, as though it is 'natural'—the inevitable climax of conflicting passion. . . . While I do not think young black male rappers have been rushing in droves to see *The Piano*, there is a bond between those folks involved with high culture who celebrate and condone the ideas and values upheld in this film and those who celebrate and condone gangsta rap" (pp. 120–121).

Social workers must challenge media images of women. Cultural images that dismiss and demean women create an environment that allows sexism and violence against women to become culturally rooted through our advertisements, news programs, movies, television programs, and music.

Taking Action

When you see a sexist ad on television, call and let that network *know* you object to ads showing women in a negative, offensive light. Call the main headquarters for the network (ABC: [212]456-7777; CBS: [212]975-4321; NBC: [212]664-4444; and FOX [310] 277-2211) and ask for the Office of Broadcast Standards and Practices. Tell them the name of the product being advertised, and voice your objection to the ad. Networks have been known to pull commercials if they suspect [that] continuing to run the ad will lose them loyal viewers.

From: Jackson, D. (1992). How to make the world a better place for women in five minutes a day (p. 124). New York: Hyperion.

Educational Inequities

A Native American Woman's Experience

It is almost impossible to explain to a sympathetic white person what a typical Indian boarding school was like; how it affected the Indian child suddenly dumped into it like a small creature from another world, helpless, defenseless, bewildered, trying desperately and instinctively to survive and sometimes not surviving at all. . . .

Even now, in a good school, there is impersonality instead of close human contact; a sterile cold atmosphere, an unfamiliar routine, language problems, and above all the mazaskan-skan, that damn clock—white man's [sic] time as opposed to Indian time, which is natural time. Like eating when you are hungry and sleeping when you are tired, not when that damn clock says you must.

From: Crow Dog & Erdoes, 1990, pp. 28–29.

An African-American Woman's Experience

When we entered racist, segregated, white schools we left a world where teachers believed that to educate black children rightly would require a political commitment. Now, we were mainly taught by white teachers whose lessons reinforced racist stereotypes. For black children, education was no longer about the practice of freedom. Realizing this, I lost my love of school. The classroom was no longer a place of pleasure or ecstasy. School was still a political place, since we were always having to counter white racist assumptions that we were genetically inferior, never as capable as white peers, even unable to learn. Yet, the politics were no longer counterhegemonic. We were always and only responding and reacting to white folks.

From: hooks, 1994b, pp. 3–4.

Two different women from two different cultural backgrounds faced hostile educational systems. Unfortunately, these women's individual, unique experiences are not uncommon. The American Association of University Women (AAUW) (1991/1994) found that in adolescence girls' self-esteem scores plummet from their healthy self-esteem scores in elementary school. African-American girls maintain a sense of esteem in family and community interactions but "experience a significant drop in positive feelings about their teachers and schoolwork" (p. 9). This study also found that Latina girls began their educational experience with higher self-esteem than white girls, then "between elementary school and high school, their personal self-esteem drops 38 points, more than the drop for any other group of girls" (p. 9). Sadker and Sadker (1994, p. 13) poignantly wrote,

> Like a thief in school, sexist lessons subvert education, twisting it into a system of socialization that robs potential. Consider this record of silent, devastating losses.
>
> • In early grades girls are ahead of or equal to boys on almost every standardized measure of achievement or well-being. By the time they graduate from high school or college, they have fallen back. . . .
>
> • Boys are much more likely to be awarded state and national college scholarships.

> • The gap does not narrow in college. Women score lower on all sections of the Graduate Records Exam, which is necessary to enter many graduate programs. . . .

Sadker and Sadker continued with a long list of ways in which girls fall behind in academic achievement, then these authors addressed other difficulties girl face, such as sexual harassment, teenage pregnancy, and economic discrimination. They concluded, "If the cure for cancer is forming in the mind of one of our daughters, it is less likely to become a reality than if it is forming in the mind of one of our sons. Until this changes, everyone loses" (p. 14).

Through data from Sadker and Sadker and from AAUW-commissioned studies, the nation became aware that girls are shortchanged early in the educational process and often never catch up—in educational achievement (particularly math and science) and in self-esteem. Higher educational systems also pose barriers for women. Academic women face challenges in seeking to be included and valued. Simone (1987) found that women faculty members are more likely to hold part-time positions, to be off the tenure track, and to have lower salaries and lower academic ranks. Women are also more often regarded as teachers, rather than given the more prestigious designation of scholar or researcher. The absence of family leave and other family-friendly policies makes it difficult for some faculty women to integrate career with family. Finally, male perspectives are often seen as more valuable than female ones, and research on and for women is often devalued.

Lesbians and gay men must often struggle to meet basic safety needs in an educational environment. Griffin (1992) researched issues related to gay and lesbian educators and found that "all decisions to take a risk were accompanied by fear" (p. 175). Griffin further found that all of her research participants sought to protect their reputations from the negative effects of being identified as a gay man or a lesbian. Strategies to protect their reputations were these: "All participants sought to establish themselves as 'super teach-ers': totally competent, above reproach, and conscientious about their professional respon-sibilities" (p. 173). Their students face similar challenges. Uribe and Harbeck (1992) exam-ined adolescent homosexuality and bisexuality and found that youths devise concealment strategies that often leave them emotionally and socially impaired.

Only 1.3% of college presidencies are women of color (Wilson, 1989), and they "will have to struggle against long ingrained male prejudices to get faculty appointments and to re-ceive objective evaluation of their work, particu-larly if they choose to do research in ethnic stud-ies" (p. 95). Coleman-Burns (1989) suggested that African-American women must play a cen-tral role in intellectual leadership. She spelled out four reasons for the necessity of having African-American women intellectual leaders:

(a) they comprise a large segment of the nation's university and college population; (b) they, like all women, are the carriers of culture in the so-ciety, and are seeking an equal role in determin-ing the direction of our society and creating that culture; (c) they offer a new and different body of scholarly knowledge as a result of their his-toric position as intellectual and political critics of American society and its culture; and (d) they provide a link between the emerging radical thinking of African American men and Euro-pean American women.

Despite many women's ability and willing-ness to learn and to serve as intellectual leaders, it appears that for many oppressed peoples, the entire educational process, as students or as teachers, has been a system that has historically been for and about preserving the status quo and the patriarchy. Haynes (1994) reminded social workers (a) that it was not until 1979 that the Council of Social Work Education (CSWE) mandated that course content include topics related to women and to ethnic minori-ties and (b) that this content tends to be an ex-tra—isolated as a single topic within a course or separated as an isolated elective course.

Given this context, Paulo Freire's (1970/1993/1994) analysis of the educational process is one for social work students and ed-ucators to seriously ponder. He noted,

The truth is, however, that the oppressed are not 'marginals,' are not people living outside of soci-ety. They have always been 'inside'—inside the structure which made them 'beings for others.' The solution is not to 'integrate' them into the structure of oppression, but to transform the struc-ture so that they can become 'beings for them-selves.' Such transformation, of course, would un-dermine the oppressors' purposes; hence their utilization of the banking concept of education to avoid the threat of student conscienizacão. (p. 55)

An African-American feminist writer and edu-cator, bell hooks is a passionate supporter of the ideals of Paulo Freire and often writes about the need for transformational change in institutions of higher education. She wrote, "If we examine critically the traditional role of the university in the pursuit of truth and the shar-ing of knowledge and information, it is painfully clear that biases that uphold and maintain white supremacy, imperialism, sex-ism, and racism have distorted education so that it is no longer the practice of freedom" (1994a, p. 29).

The transformation of educational systems is an important issue facing society as a whole and helping professionals in particular. From preschool through doctoral education, some members of oppressed groups and their allies are asking for inclusion and for an expanded knowledge base. By listening to those voices, employing new educational pedagogies, and forming coalitions, we may work toward bring-ing about the transformations so vital to living, working, and prospering in an increasingly global society.

Religious Systems

Bhasin explained (1994, p. 10),

All major religions have been created, inter-preted and controlled by upper class and upper

caste men; they have defined morality, ethics, behavior and even law; they have laid down the duties and rights of men and women, the relationship between them. They have influenced state policy and continue to be a major force in most societies; in South Asia their power and presence are enormous. In India, for instance, in spite of the fact that it is a secular country, a person's legal identity with regard to marriage, divorce and inheritance is determined by his or her religion.

Sanford and Donovan (1984) wrote that Protestantism, Catholicism, and Judaism are the most popular religions in the United States. They suggested that religion fulfills many different needs of people, for example, "the need for community, the need for rules, limits and a sense of order, the need for a sense of connection to something larger than oneself, the need for acknowledgment and expression of the spiritual aspects of being, the need for the mysteries of the universe and human existence to be acknowledged and explained, the need to come to terms in some way with the fact of mortality, and the need for a sense of purity and goodness" (p. 162).

Along with the fulfillment of these types of needs, religion can also cause harm. Sanford and Donovan (1984) noted that these three Judeo-Christian religions all have a long patriarchal history in doctrine and in practice. Progress toward more gender-sensitive doctrine and practices includes more inclusive language and challenges to the orthodox Jewish tradition in which men begin each day by thanking God that they are not women. Nonetheless, patriarchal forms of religion continue to cause harm. God is primarily described as being a white man; women are described as bringing evil into the world, and suffering is presented as the path to salvation (Sanford & Donovan, 1984). Ruether (1983/1993) suggested that repugnance against the idea of women in the ministry is often conveyed with the question, "Can you imagine a pregnant woman at the altar?" (p. 195).

Comstock (1993) has addressed the patriarchal nature of the Bible and the patriarchal sexual ethics it prescribes. He summarized the patriarchal sexual-ethics messages as follows:

> *Worthwhile women produce sons for men; when the Bible heralds the passing of generations, it does so by naming fathers and sons; when the Bible needs a metaphor for sin, it uses a woman's sexual rebellion against her master; when the Bible needs a scapegoat for wickedness, it uses those whose sexual practices are neither heterosexual nor procreative. Quite obviously the Bible is stacked in favor of heterosexual males ruling household, tribe, and nation; and a central factor in maintaining position is their control of sexual behavior. ... Within such a patriarchal framework, therefore, lesbians and gay men should not be surprised to find passages that malign us. (p. 38)*

Spong (1991) is optimistic about the emerging role and influence of women. He predicted, "It is only a matter of time before all vestiges of the ecclesiastical oppression of women will come to an end. A woman bishop of Rome, sitting on the throne of Saint Peter as pope, is inevitable" (p. 6). Despite trends toward inclusion of all women and gay men in many denominations, religious institutions, like the culture surrounding these institutions, have been slow in changing. Ruether (1983/ 1993) suggested that women often are still relegated to secondary roles within the ministry, as assistants in charge of children and older adults.

One part of the work done by persons involved in the battered women's shelter movement has been to transform religious doctrine and practice. Philibert-Ortega (1996) wrote about the House of Ruth's work with churches:

> *During one of our presentations, a priest disclosed his prior experiences working with battered women. He used to tell women to pray harder and submit. He has now changed his responses to victims, and his awareness has resulted in his counseling battered women differently and providing them with appropriate religious and secular options. (p. 30)*

Gnanadason (1996) reported that in 1994, the Ecumenical Association of Third World Theologians had a "Women Against Violence Dialogue," in which women theologians from 24 countries issued a statement. Gnanadason reported the following statement: "We must deconstruct the theo-ethical language and practice that produces, sustains and legitimates violence against women and we must reconstruct liberating discourses of resistance and well being. We dare not, however, allow ourselves to be only reactive, but we must allow the work of women against violence to generate new theological categories and visions" (p. 24).

Fortune and Wood (1988) discussed the difficulty of not only transforming religious institutions but also ensuring that spirituality is addressed in work with survivors of sexual and physical violence. They noted,

> Often regarded with suspicion by other feminists, particularly within the movement to end violence against women, the Center [The Center for the Prevention of Sexual and Domestic Violence] persists in affirming spirituality as a necessary dimension of this work. Spirituality is the last "closet" of the women's movement. Because traditional institutions and faith practices have done so much harm to so many women, some feminist organizations reject any semblance of religious or spiritual activity. Many women, however, have retained those aspects of their faith that have nurtured and supported them, and some are now willing to speak openly about such things. (p. 120)

South Asian women have expressed similar concerns. For example, the group Sakhi for South Asian Women (1996) wrote an article describing the role of religion in South Asian communities. One woman, while working with an art therapist, designed a temple that included the Lord Ganesha, a Hindu god considered the "Remover of All Obstacles." The woman explained her design by noting, "Whenever I am in trouble, I pray to my God Ganesha. I know that he will help me" (p. 8). Sakhi for South Asian Women staffers wrote, "It is important to remember that most women

from South Asia have grown up in environments that respect religious beliefs. For a woman who seeks homage and spirituality in religion, the support of her religious community, when she decides to leave a relationship, can therefore be crucial" (p. 8).

As noted in the beginning of this section, religious practices have been barriers, as well as sources of strength, to many women and men. Sermabeikian (1994) suggested that social workers need to respect clients' spiritual values and, in doing so, "may discover that therapeutic benefits can be accomplished through them" (p. 182). Work must be continued on all fronts to ensure that women's needs are known, respected, and acted on within this critical system.

Social Work Systems

Social work, as an institution, has not been free of male bias and discrimination. Karen Haynes, social worker and president of the University of Houston—Victoria campus, noted in a 1994 keynote address: "The rhetoric is that we are a woman's profession when the reality is that women are neither in leadership positions in proportion to their numbers, women are not setting our professional agenda, nor are women necessarily well served by our profession" (p. 10). Haynes (1994) supported these statements by noting that from 1960 to 1980, only 20% of the nationally elected National Association of Social Workers (NASW) presidents were women, and none of the national executive directors were women. Since 1980, only one woman has served as executive director (and for only 1 year). Further, women hold only 20% of leadership positions in social work agencies.

Addressing social work education, Petchers (1996) expressed surprise "that women compete and are at all successful in an academic structure that was designed for men a century ago" (p. 29). Within social work education, women do outnumber men at the lowest levels—instructors and assistant professors. Yet less than 10% of women are full professors in social work education (Haynes, 1994); and women are greatly overrepresented in the often lowest-paying positions as field liaisons and practicum administrators (Sowers-Hoag & Harrison, 1991). Sowers-Hoag and Harrison expressed concern for the future of women in social work education, writing, "In the face of reversing affirmative action policies in the United States, however, prospects for major or swift improvement are guarded, and extra efforts are needed to maintain the initial successes of women in academia" (p. 327).

Family Systems

While Pat Buchanan, Republican presidential candidate in 1992 and 1996, was traveling around the country loudly proclaiming his "cultural revolution" platform, many women have feared that a part of that revolution would result in turning back the clock on the many gains made toward gender equity within families. It should not be a surprise, however, that so-called family values would remain a hotly debated topic in this country. Families, in all of their forms, are powerful socialization forces and have profound effects on the lives of women and men. Feminists have frequently been accused of being antifamily. In part, this antifamily criticism comes from (a) the efforts of many feminists to expose the politics of family life, such as violence, power inequities, and gender socialization in the family, and (b) feminist efforts to promote a broader, more inclusive view of healthy families (e.g., lesbian families of choice, male- or female-headed single-parent families, parenting without marriage or male partnership, and dual-wage-earner families). Anderson (1991) credited feminism for providing the "intellectual context for understanding the transformation of gender relations in families" (p. 236). This section of this chapter provides a brief overview of gender socialization and violence within families, to highlight the manner in which families, as a system, have served to support the patriarchy and

have contributed to the psychological wounding of women (and men).

Socialization of Females For as long as we can remember, the behavior of men and women has been shaped by adherence to sex roles. *Sex roles* are "the pattern of behaviors, attitudes, and mental and emotional characteristics that a society associates with females or males" (Franck & Brownstone, 1993, p. 636). Historically, sex roles were presented as being biologically determined or ordained by God. Sex roles have often been seen as irrefutable and immutable. There have often been harsh penalties for women and men who stepped outside of prescribed roles. Penalties have ranged from ridicule and ostracism to confinement in jails or asylums. The ultimate punishment was death, such as by stoning women who had intercourse outside of marriage or by burning independent and women-loving women as witches.

Today the emphasis on predetermined, biologically based differences has been replaced with a growing emphasis on the role of culture, with the family as a critical aspect of the culture, a teacher of gender roles. Gender roles vary in different societies in different times in history, often to suit the political and economic needs of the culture. A prime example is the account of women's dramatic role changes during World War II. Prior to the Second World War, women were taught that they were weaker and less able and capable than men. Middle-class women's assigned place was to be at home, assuming the presumed proper role of wife and mother. With the simultaneous male civilian labor force drain and increased production demands of the war, women were actively recruited to the labor force, often in difficult and demanding jobs. "Rosie the Riveter" was featured on a poster commissioned by the War Production Committee (Greene, 1990). The depiction of a strong woman, flexing her muscles and stating "We can do it!" promoted women's strength, capability, and patriotism. Yet when the war was over and men wanted to reclaim their jobs, the myth of women's weakness and natural place in the home was again advanced. Women were forced out of their jobs, and the child-care facilities that had been opened and operated by corporations and the federal government were closed. Television programs of this era, such as *Leave It to Beaver* and *Father Knows Best* promoted and idealized the role of women as subordinate homemakers.

Gender stereotypes endure today. With the second wave of the women's movement in the 1960s, there was a brief movement to raise children in nongendered, nonsexist ways. Although children's names and clothes became more androgynous, this movement affected only a small counterculture that never became mainstream. Although some may protest that things have changed, we would argue this point. The practice of placing newborn infants in either pink or blue blankets continues today, and this sex-role-stereotypic practice is only the beginning. Just try giving a male infant a pink sleeper, and see the furor such a gift can create! If you are still disbelieving, walk down the distinctly boy and girl aisles in any toy store, or ask a young child about the differences between boys and girls. Even at early ages, children quickly absorb society's messages about gender. Also, play the game suggested by Vinton and Nelson-Gardell (1993), called, "If there is equality between the sexes, then how come_____exists?" and make your own list of answers to the question.

Many aspects of women's and men's lives are determined by rigid sex-role stereotypes that are often strictly enforced, both formally and informally. These rigid roles are detrimental to both sexes. They restrict and hamper human growth and development. Rigid roles prevent girls and boys from really learning who they truly are, as they are taught instead, who they must be. Boys are encouraged to roam, experiment, and take risks. Girls are taught to be good and nice. Girls are taught that their primary role is to nurture and care for others, while boys are encouraged to be active agents on their own behalf. Girls are taught not only to be good, but also to look good. Girls internalize society's standards of beauty and perfection, which are often introduced in their homes.

This socialization process is based on a patriarchal model that values boys and the characteristics associated with masculinity. Girls are deemed inferior and deficient by contrast. For instance, the worst names you can call a boy are "girl" and "sissy." The extreme end of the continuum of valuing boys over girls is demonstrated by both the number of female infanticides in China, as a result of the one-child-per-couple population-control policies, and the number of abortions of female fetuses in India after amniocentesis is conducted for the specific purpose of sex selection.

In the United States, a study cited by DeBold, Wilson, and Malave (1993) offers an interesting demonstration of how quickly boys and girls learn the increased value and benefit of being male:

Girls and boys both seem to understand that life for boys and girls, men and women is very different. The Michigan Board of Education recently published a statewide study of students'

This Nancy *cartoon illustrates the absurdity of stereotypical images of women and girls.*

perceptions of what it is to be male or female in this society. When asked how their lives might be different if they were the opposite sex, nearly 50 percent of the girls spoke of the advantages to being a boy, while only 7 percent of the boys saw advantages to being a girl. While the girls found it interesting or exciting to think of life as a boy, nearly 20 percent of the boys have extremely hostile, derogatory responses. A surprising number of boys said that they would commit suicide if they were girls. One boy wrote, "I would kill myself right away by starting myself on fire so no one knew." (p. 9, emphasis in original)

Stereotypes, often introduced and valued within families, are also supported by many of society's other institutions, as well. For instance, many religious doctrines teach women to be dutiful, self-sacrificing, and subservient to men. The media often limit the depiction of women to that of sexual objects, while advertisements portray women as empty-headed consumers of cleaning supplies. Families often buy into this notion by having daughters assume the cleaning roles, while sons mow lawns and haul trash.

An active way of teaching daughters and sons gender roles is through parental role modeling. Hochschild (1989) studied dual wage earners with young children. One of her findings was that women worked about 15 hours a week more than men did—most of this during the so-called second shift (after they arrived home from work). In a year's time, women worked the equivalent of a full month of 24-hour days more than their male partners did. As a result of her qualitative analysis, she suggested,

One reason women take a deeper interest than men in the problem of juggling work with family life is that even when husbands happily shared the hours of work, their wives felt more responsible for home and children. More women kept track of doctors' appointments and arranged for playmates to come over. More mothers than fathers worried about the tail on a child's Halloween costume or a birthday present for a school friend. They were more likely to think about their children while at work and to check in by phone with the babysitter....

Another reason women may feel more strained than men is that women more often do two things at once—for example, write checks and return phone calls, vacuum and keep an eye on a three-year-old, fold laundry and think out the shopping list. Men more often cook dinner or take a child to the park. Indeed women often juggle three spheres—job, children, and housework—while most men juggle two—job and children. For women, two activities compete with their time with children, not just one. (pp. 7–9, emphasis in original)

Sons and daughters watch mothers work this extra 15 hours a week and observe the types of things for which she is responsible in the family; their observations serve as role models. Mom takes care of thank-you notes; Dad takes children to sporting events. Dad fixes bikes; Mom fixes lunch. Such behavior becomes a critical part of how girls and boys learn how men and women are supposed to be. DeBold, Wilson, and Malave (1993) summarized a dilemma facing adolescent girls as they try to transform themselves to fit within a patriarchal culture. They suggested that girls come up against a wall; this wall is a culture that devalues women and portrays women in sexual terms. In order to get through this wall, girls have to give up a part of themselves. Once they have broken through and are accepted, suddenly this transformed self becomes reality. The result is that girls have to give up their desires, knowledge, and needs in order to fit into the culture. Adolescent girls often have an acute sense of what is just, what is right. As they watch the gender-role patterns operating in their homes, they often realize the inequities and power differentials at work. Yet, at some point, they find themselves adapting and changing themselves to become what they once despised—a stereotypical woman.

Violence in Families Family, whether biological, adoptive, reconstituted, or created from community, has been projected, and sometimes experienced, as a place of nurturance, safety, encouragement, and challenge. Peplau (1979)

and Huston and Ashmore (1986) bring to our attention some of the components of close relationships, which may not often be in the forefront of our minds when we are considering intimate relationships. Peplau (1979) stated,

Americans are sentimental about love. In thinking about romance, we emphasize intimacy and caring; we like to view our lover and the relationship as unique. We deemphasize the part that cultural values and social roles play in determining whom we love and how we conduct ourselves with them. In particular, we neglect a crucial aspect of love relationships—power. (p. 106)

Huston and Ashmore (1986) like Peplau (1979) noted that intimate relationships involve more than the senses of belonging and of closeness people seek in such relationships. Conflict and anger are also inherent in close relationships. They suggested that vulnerability and hostility are more likely to be experienced in intimate relationships than in casual relationships. Unfortunately, violence has been a means through which many intimate partners have chosen to exercise power and to channel their frustrations and anger. Levinson (1981) presented data suggesting that, worldwide, women are the preferred victims of family violence. In this country, females are disproportionately represented as victims of incestuous assault, sexual harassment, rape, and battering. Lincoln and Straus (1985), focusing on the idealized view of the family relationship, noted that crime in the family has not been given serious study: "One reason may be that it is something most people do not want to think about because it forces one to come to grips with the fact that the family is less than the perfect institution which most people want it to be" (p. 5).

The sexual abuse of female children is one type of crime in the family that many people have not wanted to recognize as part of family dynamics. While incidence rates vary in the liter- ature, it appears that from 19 to 45% of girls have been sexually abused (Russell, 1983; Wyatt, 1985). Sexual abuse has been associated with eating disorders (Steiger & Zanko, 1990), and literature reviews have shown that childhood sexual abuse is associated with depression, substance abuse, prostitution, suicidal ideation, and multiple personality disorders in adulthood (Mennen, 1990; Ratican, 1992). Judith Herman, a pioneer in exposing the issue of the sexual abuse of girls, recalled the advice she received from supervisors when working with adult survivors of sexual abuse in the early 1970s.

"I would say, 'This is what she told me,'" Herman recalls. "And my supervisors would say either, 'Poor naïve resident, don't you know that women fantasize about this sort of thing?' or, 'Don't touch this, the patient can't handle it.' Now of course the patients were bringing it up because they wanted to talk about it. So to the extent that I followed the advice of my supervisors, I was not successful with my patients." (Hawkins, 1991, p. 44)

Denial by professionals often matches the denial used by survivors (Barrett & Trepper, 1992), by survivors' family members, and by society at large. Denial, however, does not address the trauma girls face as victims of sexual abuse. Finkelhor (1988) outlined four *traumagenic* (trauma engendering) dynamics that help explain the impact of sexual abuse: traumatic sexualization, betrayal, stigmatization, and powerlessness. Finkelhor defined a *traumagenic dynamic* as "an experience that alters a child's cognitive or emotional orientation to the world and causes trauma by distorting the child's self-concept, worldview, or affective capacities" (p. 354).

Sexual abuse, including sexual abuse in families, is a betrayal to the victim, to all other members of that family system, and to the concept of family. As mentioned earlier in this section, people occasionally suggest that feminists are antifamily. Yet to us, it seems antifamily *not* to address the socialization process and the violence occurring in families, which *undermine* family stability and can physically and emotionally harm important members of families—women and girls. We would like to see strong, vibrant families of all forms in our society and believe that by valuing all the members in a family and by working to end sexism and violence against women, we can begin the process of creating and promoting healthy families and a much healthier society.

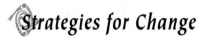

Strategies for Change

PRACTICE FOR CHANGE

This practice section focuses on using the media and legislative processes to create social change. Too often, *practice* is inferred to mean working only with individuals, families, or small groups. When addressing institutional abuses, the practice and policy implications must also be at that level. Too often, individuals have been taught to adapt or to cope with abuse, and victims have been blamed for the abuse, when the institutions need to be changed. Further, community is often seen as an abstract entity, and the victim feels helpless to do anything to effect change. We hope that all social workers have a desire to effect social change and will acquire intervention skills for use at multiple ecological levels—including effecting change at the community and national level.

In this strategies section, we discuss working with the media and challenging any media misinformation, activating computer networks, and working within electoral political systems. It is important to note that using the media and legislative processes to create change is a critical change strategy for every issue presented in this text, not just for changing minds and attitudes about women's status. Therefore, while we present these key practice strategies in this chapter, we hope you will use this information in your advocacy work to create economic jus-

tice, to advocate for women who have been battered, and to promote change in the many, many other issues that confront women.

USING THE MEDIA TO CREATE CHANGE

Three primary media strategies are introduced here: (1) forming truth squads to challenge misinformation presented in the media, (2) writing op-ed pieces for newspapers, and (3) presenting effective radio or television interviews.

Truth Squads

Amidei (1982) introduced truth squads as a way of countering misinformation presented in the media. A *truth squad* consists of people mobilized to correct misinformation disseminated by the media. Too often, the poor, women, ethnic minorities, and other oppressed groups are portrayed inaccurately or stereotypically in the media. Leaving these images unchallenged allows the images to settle in as part of the nation's consciousness. Amidei encourages social workers to form truth squads to counter these images and misconceptions.

For example, perhaps a group of social work students have a strong interest in improving the lives of parents receiving Temporary Aid to Needy Families (TANF). That group might form a truth squad around that issue. They would need to familiarize themselves with the media outlets in their area and determine who has access to which media outlet. Perhaps the person who drives to work at 7:30 A.M. would monitor the local radio talk show at that time. Someone who diligently reads one local paper would monitor that paper, the avid television news watcher would be in charge of that outlet, and several in the group who are connected to different news groups on the Internet would be assigned that medium. Each member of the group would be responsible for correcting misinformation in the member's assigned source.

Strategies could include the following: (1) immediately calling in to correct the information, (2) writing to the producer with corrected information, or (3) contacting the reporter directly to educate her or him on the issue. Again, this simple strategy involves diligently monitoring issues of concern and challenging misinformation at every possible outlet. The goal is for the public to receive information that accurately conveys the realities of AFDC/TANF policy (in this example), as well as the impact of AFDC/TANF policy on individuals.

Op-ed Newspaper Articles

Opinion-editorial (op-ed) Op-ed articles are an effective way for social workers to communicate with the public (Stoesz, 1993). Stoesz outlined the advantages of op-ed pieces for addressing social problems:

> First, it provides almost immediate response to a community problem, because the time between submission and publication is typically one week. Second, coverage is as extensive as the circulation of the newspaper. Third, because the Op-Ed section of the newspaper provides elected officials with an opportunity to check the pulse of the community on local issues, an Op-Ed offers access to important decision makers. Fourth, photocopies of op-ed pieces are useful addenda for grant applications, an indication that the personnel of an agency are concerned about community problems. Finally, newspapers usually pay about $100 per Op-Ed, a modest source of revenue. (p. 367)

An op-ed piece is generally three to four pages in length and "should be written in a provocative, 'punchy' style without footnotes" (Stoesz, 1993, p. 367). A major focus of an op-ed piece is to frame or to enter community discussions on social or agency issues. Haynes and Mickelson (1997) noted, "Editorials, like coverage of media events, are more likely to get included or covered if they are tied in with an is-

sue which is current and of public interest" (p. 116). MacEachern (1994) lists seven characteristics of a newsworthy story: (1) It's new, (2) it's timely, (3) it's colorful, (4) it involves substantial numbers of people, (5) it revolves around a crisis, (6) it involves controversy, and (7) it includes celebrities who are participating (pp. 190–191). Stoesz called attention to the idea that as more of the responsibility for human problems is shifted to the local level, social workers will increasingly need to be attentive to public opinion in their area, and an op-ed piece is a way to influence the public.

Using Television and Radio to Effect Change

Television

Haynes and Mickelson (1997) stated that television is the most powerful medium and that the evening news is an effective arena for influencing public opinion and for changing public policy. Further, they noted that with television, the sound bite becomes an essential format for communication. Generally, a person will have 10 seconds of air time. The message, then, must be brief, well-stated, and delivered with passion. Preparation is the key to an effective presentation. Prior to being interviewed, it is important to pull relevant statistics and to plan the main point—that is, the sound bite. Further, whenever possible, it helps to speak with the reporter before she or he arrives on site, both to get the facts of the case and to get a feel for what angle the reporter is using to cover the story.

Kahn (1991) talked about the value of reframing interviewers' questions during a live interview:

> Sometimes, particularly, if you're on a live interview on radio or television, you can answer a question that isn't quite what you want to talk about by quietly changing the subject. Only the most aggressive reporters are going to stop you and say, "That isn't what I asked about." Most of them will let you talk as long as it's interest-

ing. You might practice in the practice sessions how to change the subject during the course of an interview. This is a useful way of getting information across the way we want it presented. (p. 221)

Preparation is the number-one requirement for effective television interviews. Other relevant concerns have to do with how to make the best appearance. For example, look at the interviewer (not at the camera) when being interviewed, unless you are making a plea to the audience. If you will be bothered by having shiny spots on your face when you're watching the show, then we encourage you (female or male) to put a bit of powder on your face or to rub your face with a damp paper towel before the interview. If you have a habit of smiling when nervous and you're talking about a serious issue during the interview, then make a conscious effort to demonstrate the appropriate affect.

Regarding appearance, a student once told us that he wore a monogrammed sweater during an interview. He recalled that none of his friends talked about the important comments he made during his television debut, instead, they just teased him about the "RAH" on his shirt. Rah, Rah, Bob! As a result of this experience, he encouraged his classmates not to trivialize the matter of what to wear and to give consideration to the overall media presentation of content, tone, and appearance. Finally, anything said to a reporter should be considered on the record and available to be reported.

Practice helps a great deal toward making an effective television statement. Perhaps for part of a class session, social work students could have a professor from their college's journalism school either give a lecture on the do's and don'ts of television interviews or hold a practice lab session, with journalism students interviewing members of the class. Individuals from the class may also wish to meet with a newscaster, friend, or colleague whose media presence is respected, to get tips on performance enhancement.

Authors' Perspective

We encourage the reader to *not* feel obligated to be interviewed. Often, as professionals, we feel compelled to respond, and as normal human beings, we sometimes feel flattered to be asked. However, there are some stories that you may not want to associate with, and there are some media in which you may not excel. Beverly McPhail prefers the written medium of newspapers. Karen Stout prefers radio and television, but is not an effective participant on television panel shows; therefore, she always inquires about the format of the show and the specific topic under discussion. We all have our strengths, as well as our preferences. We know that social workers in rural areas are asked to be experts on everything! We encourage you to use the media well—which suggests speaking on those issues, and only those issues, where you can make an informed contribution.

Radio

Radio eliminates the need to think about appearance. Instead, you can focus on content and delivery. Again, preparation is critical, but with radio, it's often possible to have a page of notes for refreshing your memory on key points, phrases, and statistics. We encourage you to have only a single page of notes because (a) you're probably not going to have time to rummage through your notes, and (b) paper crackling will not enhance your delivery style.

Haynes and Mickelson (1997) noted,

The best example of how effective talk radio can be is illustrated by how right wing conservatives have used radio to get their message to millions.

Talk radio is great for public service announcements (PSAs), which can be helpful in educating the community about concerns or actions that need to be taken. This medium has not been utilized to its fullest by social workers. (p. 116)

As with television, clarification about the format and audience prior to the interview can aid with preparation. Is the audience considered progressive, young, Christian? What is the current event behind the interview? Does the show include a call-in component? Doing homework on these types of considerations can ensure that you can direct your preparation to aim at the audience who will be listening. If the show includes a call-in component, it's often helpful to review the myths and stereotypes on the topic under review, and to have the appropriate facts to counter the myths readily at hand (or in your head). By thinking ahead about common questions or concerns about an issue, you are less likely to feel stuck if the material gets reframed in a negative manner, and you increase the likelihood that you will disseminate the correct information to your listening audience.

CREATING PHONE TREES AND COMPUTER NETWORKS

Diane MacEachern, in her 1994 book *Enough Is Enough: The Hellraiser's Guide to Community Activism,* suggested organizing phone trees and computer networks to mobilize people— quickly. She suggested that small groups can simply distribute a membership list to each member and call people in the order on the list. Should someone not be available, that person's name is skipped. Large groups often require more elaborate procedures. She suggested having a *coordinator* who maintains a list of all names, addresses, and phone numbers on a card or a computer file. Members have assignments as activators and phoners. The coordinator gets the process going by phoning the ac-

tivators and giving them all the relevant member and action information. *Activators* then phone the *phoners,* each of whom contact 5–10 members to encourage them to act on the issue at hand.

Computer bulletin boards allow a message to be posted—one time. Members can then send and receive messages through their computers. This medium requires that members have access to a computer, a modem, and telephone line. MacEachern (1994) noted that "American Online, CompuServe, Prodigy, and Internet are networks popular among general users; EcoNet, HandsNet, PeaceNet, and the WELL are networks specially designed for nonprofits and social interest organizations" (p. 53). Computer bulletin board service groups can also send out requests to other related groups to inform and to encourage action.

EFFECTING LEGISLATIVE CHANGE STRATEGIES

Social workers have the opportunity to participate in every realm of political practice. Social workers serve as elected officials, campaign chairpersons, lobbyists, candidates, and voter-registration officials, and they often present testimony to legislative bodies. This practice section focuses on writing letters and on presenting testimony to legislative bodies.

Letters

Haynes and Mickelson (1997) pointed out that legislators *do* read letters from constituents. In fact, they read mail from constituents carefully. A letter indicates a great deal of concern—that is, you took the time to write. Effective letter-writing tips from Haynes and Mickelson include the following:

Letters to legislators should be short, to the point, and credible. Write one or two pages at most. Confine yourself to one subject area or bill. . . .

Legislators are quite busy and long letters are time-consuming. However, do not sacrifice clarity and completeness for brevity. Describe your position exactly and, if necessary, provide documentation. State your purpose in the first paragraph and then elaborate in the text. The use of facts combined with personal experiences, whether yours or your client's, is most effective. State the action you want the legislator to take. Whether you want him or her to vote yes or vote no on a bill, cosponsor legislation: be specific. (p. 98)

Postcards, telegrams, and form letters are not good substitutes for a personal letter—yet are probably better than no communication at all.

Legislators respond best to positive communication. Haynes and Mickelson (1997) also suggest thank-you notes to legislators when you agree with their positions and their votes. (See Table 2.2 for addresses and salutations for national officials.)

Testimony

Haynes and Mickelson (1997) remind us:

Testimony by both the practitioner and the client is an extremely dynamic lobbying tool and is most dramatically done by the practitioners and

Table 2.2
Addresses and Salutations for Selected Elected and Appointed Officials

Address	Salutation/Closing
President	
The President	Dear Mr./Ms. President
The White House	Very Respectfully Yours
1600 Pennsylvania Avenue, NW	
Washington, DC 20500	
E-mail: president@whitehouse.gov	
Vice President	
Vice President	Dear Vice President (insert last name)
Old Executive Office Building	Sincerely Yours
Washington, DC 20500	
E-mail: vicepresident@whitehouse.gov	
U.S. Senators	
The Honorable (insert full name)	Dear Senator (insert last name)
United States Senate	Sincerely Yours
Washington, DC 20510	
U.S. Representatives	
The Honorable (insert full name)	Dear Representative (insert last name)
U.S. House of Representatives	Sincerely Yours
Washington, DC 20515	
Cabinet Members	
The Honorable (insert full name)	Dear Secretary (insert last name)
Secretary of (insert department)	Sincerely Yours
Washington, DC (insert zip)	

Information compiled from Haynes, K., & Mickelson, J. (1997). Affecting change: Social workers in the political arena. *New York: Longman.*

clients directly affected. It may be more persuasive than the most expensive lobbyist who, after all, must rely on secondary sources, such as aggregate data or "secondhand" stories. Thus, the client or social worker who can present facts, personal vignettes, and scenarios, and who also is a constituent, can play a significant role for clients and in major policy settings—a role that no other individual or group can fill. (p. 74)

Legislative committees have a tremendous amount of work to accomplish during the legislative session. Committees will often use testimony to gather a great deal of information on the bill under review in a limited amount of time. Testifying before legislative committees is an opportunity for social workers to give input to a particular committee.

You should thoroughly prepare your testimony to be brief (5 to 10 minutes in most cases). Distribute written copies of the testimony to committee members, their aides, and the media members present (Haynes & Mickelson, 1997). While you should be prepared with written copies of your testimony in hand, you should not read it to the committee. Make the testimony conversational (but not chatty), and maintain eye contact with committee members. If committee members ask questions, and you don't know the answer, do not bluff. Instead, tell the committee that you do not have the information requested at this time, but as soon as it can be secured, you will forward it to them (if, in fact, this can be done in a timely manner). Follow-through then becomes critical, as credibility—personal and professional—is at stake. Personalizing the testimony can help legislators relate the issue to how it affects their constituents (Haynes and Mickelson, 1997).

Affirmative Action program supporter protesting in Sacramento, California. Photo © 1996 Kim Kulish.

POLICY FOR CHANGE: AFFIRMATIVE ACTION

The policy issues related to equality and justice are, of course, numerous and are all important. Just a few of the important policy changes for social workers to advocate for include securing an Equal Rights Amendment, pay equity legislation, and the Employment Non Discrimination Act (ENDA), which would prevent lesbians and gay men from being fired because of their sexual orientation. This policy-change section, however, focuses on the issue of affirmative action as an important policy for social workers to learn more about and to work toward, thereby ensuring support for and valuing of programs attempting to include more men of color and more women.

Affirmative-action principles are a source of disagreement within the social work profession, as they are in the larger society. In essence, many white males feel that they are victims of reverse discrimination and suggest, or strongly assert, that all persons of color and all white women are given unfair advantages under affirmative-action policies (Stout and Buffum, 1993). Similarly, some persons of color and some white women are concerned that others might believe that they did not earn their positions if affirmative-action policies are in place. In contrast, proponents of affirmative action suggest that white men have an inherent and unfair advantage and, therefore, affirmative-action policies are critical to ensuring fairness and promoting equity. In other words, proponents hold that without affirmative-action protections, white men will continue to have the unfair advantages that historically have placed them in the top positions in most societal systems.

Many definitions of affirmative action have been offered. Jones (1981) stated that the purpose of affirmative action "is to achieve distribution throughout occupational and professional categories, or other life chances, that is appropriately representative of the diversity of population generally" (p. 467). Jesse Jackson (1987) wrote that affirmative action is creative justice and asserted that affirmative action is necessary if we are to achieve educational and economic parity. Lovell (1978) stressed that affirmative action is more than a passive statement of nondiscrimination; instead, it requires active programs for influencing systems of hiring.

In 1993, author Karen Stout and her colleague Bill Buffum wrote,

> *Traditional social work values are coming into heated conflict around the issue of affirmative action. The idea of affirmative action assumes that there is injustice which exists and which should be redressed, even at the possible expense of some individuals. Social workers battle for social justice for their clients, but the waters are muddied when social workers themselves are affected. (p. 126)*

NASW has well-developed policies and procedures for meeting affirmative action goals. All states must meet specific goals and must follow specific procedures for the hiring of office staff and directors, the election of state board members, and the appointments to state committees. NASW policy requires that elections and appointments be conducted in a manner ensuring that the leadership reflects the gender and the racial and ethnic makeup of the chapter membership. Elections are designed to ensure that the elected leadership will have proportionate representation of persons from the gender and the racial and ethnic groups composing the membership. The most common strategy for achieving these goals is to *double-slate* the candidates. This means that persons from racial and ethnic minority groups run against persons from racial and ethnic minority groups; women run against women, and white men run against white men. Some social workers believe that such a policy is unfair to white males. Others applaud the professional organization for ensuring diversity in leadership positions.

Again, affirmative action programs are being dismantled across the country. Social workers are not immune from public debates of issues, nor should they be. As controversy builds on this critical issue, serious debate and strong policies are needed within the profession. Stout and Buffum's (1993) research found that social workers in Texas felt more favorably toward affirmative-action policies if they knew someone (including themselves) who had benefited from such policies. Similarly, social workers held a less favorable opinion if they felt that they or others they knew had been harmed by such policies. Therefore, it would be advantageous for social workers to listen to persons inside and outside of the profession, to learn how affirmative action has helped to diversify work environments and how individuals perceive affirmative-action policies as being supportive of their career goals.

SUMMARY

In many ways, such as through research practices and religious doctrines and practices, women have been marginalized, kept from full and informed participation. The losses resulting from such marginalization can be counted in terms of the loss of women's lives, the limited numbers of inspiring role models for women, and the absence or minimization of women's input into systems that so directly affect their lives. Viewed separately, each system is seen as neglectful or remiss. Taken together, the network of systems truly does seem stacked against women, despite the major gains made during the twentieth century. To tackle the enormous challenges ahead in order to fully include women in major systems and to fairly represent women in those systems, social workers can develop skills and can implement policies to effect change. In fact, to paraphrase Ed Towns (1991; D [Democrat], NY [New York]), we know of no other profession so distinctly qualified to undertake such a challenge. The social work profession, through its members, is in a position to positively effect change regarding the status of women, given its emphasis on person-in-environment considerations and the CSWE mandate to teach social workers about policy and research, in addition to human behavior theory, practice, and field education.

To end this chapter on a challenging note, we present a poem by Marge Piercy (1987). Her urging to act in concert with others is not only inspirational, but also absolutely necessary if women are going to take their rightful place in all societal institutions.

The Low Road

What can they do
to you? Whatever, they want.
They can set you up, they can

bust you, they can break
your fingers, they can
burn your brain with electricity,
blur you with drugs till you
can't walk, can't remember, they can
take your child, wall up
your lover. They can do anything
you can't stop them
    from doing. How can you stop
them? Alone, you can fight,
you can refuse, you can
take what revenge you can
but they roll over you.

But two people fighting
back to back can cut through
a mob, a snake-dancing file
can break a cordon, an army
can meet an army.

Two people can keep each other
sane, can give support, conviction,
love, massage, hope, sex.
Three people are a delegation,
a committee, a wedge. With four
you can play bridge and start
an organization. With six
you can rent a whole house,
eat pie for dinner with no
seconds, and hold a fund raising party.
A dozen make a demonstration.
A hundred fill a hall.
A thousand have solidarity and your own
newsletter.
ten thousand, power and your own paper;
a hundred thousand, your own media;
ten million, your own country.

It goes on one at a time,
it starts when you care
to act, it starts when you do
    it again after they said no,
It starts when you say *we*
and know who you mean, and each
day you mean one more.

Marge Piercy

REFERENCES

Anderson, M. (1991). Feminism and the American family ideal. *Journal of Comparative Family Studies, 22,* 235–245.

Amidei, N. (1982). How to be an advocate in bad times. *Public Welfare, 40,* 37–42.

AAUW (1991/1994). *Shortchanging girls, shortchanging America.* Washington, DC: American Association of University Women (AAUW).

Barrett, M. J., & Trepper, T. S. (1992, May/June). Unmasking the incestuous family. *Networker,* pp. 39–46.

Bhasin, K. (1993, 1994). *What is patriarchy?* New Delhi: Kaj Press.

Brieland, D. (1990). The Hull-House tradition and the contemporary social worker: Was Jane Addams really a social worker? *Social Work, 35,* 134–140.

Brown, C. (1997). Changing the face of the magazine industry: *Black Enterprise, Essence,* and *Ebony.* In S. Biagi & M. Kern-Foxworth (Eds.), *Facing difference: Race, gender, and mass media* (pp. 154–159). Thousand Oaks, CA: Pine Forge Press.

Carniol, B. (1990). Social work and the labor movement. In B. Wharf (Ed.). *Social work and social change* (pp. 114–143). Toronto: McClelland and Stewart.

Carroll, S. J. (1992). Women state legislators, women's organizations, and the representation of women's culture in the United States. In J. Bystydzienski (Ed.), *Women transforming politics* (pp. 24–40). Bloomington, IN: Indiana University Press.

Chapman, J. R. (1978). The economics of women's victimization. In J. R. Chapman & M. Gates (Eds.), *The victimization of women* (pp. 251–269). Beverly Hills: Sage Publications.

Coleman-Burns, P. (1989). African American women— Education for what? *Sex Roles, 21,* 145–160.

Comstock, G. (1993). *Gay theology without apology.* Cleveland, OH: Pilgram Press.

Crow Dog, M., & Erdoes, R. (1990). *Lakota woman.* New York: HarperPerennial.

Cummerton, J. (1986). A feminist perspective on research: What does it help us to see? In N. Van Den Bersh & L. Cooper (Eds). *Feminist visions for social*

work (pp. 80–100). Silver Spring, MD: NAJW Press.

DeBold, E., Wilson, M., & Malave, I. (1993). *Mother daughter revolution: From betrayal to power.* Reading, MA: Addison-Wesley.

DiNitto, D., & Dye, T. (1987). *Social welfare politics and public policy* (2nd ed.). Englewood Cliffs, NJ: Prentice-Hall.

Eichler, M. (1991). *Nonsexist research methods.* New York: Routledge.

Finkelhor, D. (1988). The trauma of child sexual abuse. *Journal of Interpersonal Violence, 2,* 348–366.

Fortune, M., & Wood, F. (1988). The Center for the Prevention of Sexual and Domestic Violence: A study in applied feminist theology and ethics. *Journal of Feminist Studies in Religion, 4,* 115–122.

Franck, I., & Brownstone, D. (1993). *The women's desk reference.* New York: Viking.

Frase-Blunt, M. (1991, October). Soldaderas: Hispanic women face the '90s. *Hispanic,* pp. 12–18.

Freire, P. (1970/1993/1994). *Pedagogy of the oppressed.* New York: Continuum.

Gallup Organization (1996). *Gender and society: Status and stereotypes.* (Report available from 47 Hulfish Street, Princeton, NJ 08542.)

Gnanadason, A. (1996, Fall). Violence against women: Women against violence. *NCADV Voice,* pp. 22–24.

Greene, C. E. (1990). Rosie the riveter. In A. H. Zophy & F. M. Kavenik (Eds.), *Handbook of women's history* (p. 523). New York: Garland.

Griffin, P. (1992). From hiding out to coming out: Empowering lesbian and gay educators. In K. Harbeck (Ed.), *Coming out of the classroom closet* (pp. 167–196). Binghamton, NY: Harrington Park Press.

Hardy-Fanta, C. (1992). Latina women and politics in Boston: Somos la vida, la fuerza, la mujer. *Latino Studies Journal, 3,* 38–54.

Hawkins, J. (1991, March/April). Rowers on the river styx. *Harvard Magazine,* pp. 43–52.

Haynes, K. S. (1994, October 7). *Women in the profession: Rhetoric, realism, risk.* Paper presented at the Indiana Social Work Educators' Conference, Indianapolis, IN.

Haynes, K.S. (1996). The future of political social work. In P. R. Raffoul & C. A. McNeece (Eds.), *Future issues for social work practice* (pp. 266–276). Boston, Allyn & Bacon.

Haynes, K., & Mickelson, J. (1997). *Affecting change: Social workers in the political arena* (3rd ed.). New York: Longman.

Hochschild, A., with Machung, A. (1989). *The second shift*. New York: Avon Books.

hooks, b. (1994a). *Outlaw culture*. New York: Routledge.

hooks, b. (1994b). *Teaching to transgress*. New York: Routledge.

Hoyt, C. (1984). Pornography and women's civil rights. *Response to the Victimization of Women and Children, 7*, 5–7.

Huston, T., & Ashmore, R. (1986). Women and men in personal relationships. In R. Ashmore & F. Del Boca (Eds.), *The social psychology of female and male relations*. New York: Academic Press.

Jackson, D. (1992). *How to make the world a better place for women in five minutes a day*. New York: Hyperion.

Jackson, J. (1987). *Straight from the heart*. Philadelphia: Fortress Press.

Jones, J. E. (1981). "Reverse discrimination" in employment: Judicial treatment of affirmative action programmes in the United States. *International Labour Review, 120*, 453–472.

Julian, J., & Kornblum, W. (1983). *Social problems*. Englewood Cliffs, NJ: Prentice-Hall.

Kahn, S. (1991). *Organizing: A guide for grassroots leaders*. Silver Springs, MD: NASW Press.

Laurence, L., & Weinhouse, B. (1994). Outrageous practices. New York: Fawcett Columbine.

Levinson, D. (1981). Physical punishment of children and wifebeating in cross-cultural perspective. *Child Abuse and Neglect, 5*, 193–196.

Lincoln, A. J., & Straus, M. A. (1985). *Crime and the family*. Springfield, IL: Charles C. Thomas.

London, J. (1978). Images of violence against women. *Victimology, 2*, 510–524.

Lovell, C. (1978). Three key issues in affirmative action. In S. Slavin (Ed.), *Social administration: The*

management of social services (pp. 447–450). New York: Haworth Press and CSWE.

MacEachern, D. (1994). *Enough is enough: The hellraiser's guide to community activism*. New York: Avon Books.

Martindale, C. (1997). Only in glimpses: Portrayal of America's largest minority groups by the *New York Times, 1934–1994*. In S. Biagi & M. Kern-Foxworth (Eds.), *Facing difference: Race, gender, and mass media* (pp. 89–94). Thousand Oaks, CA: Pine Forge Press.

McCullough, M. (1996, March 11). Lesbian mom loses case again. *Houston Chronicle*, p. 19A.

McMahon, A., & Allen-Meares, P. (1992). Is social work racist? A content analysis of recent literature. *Social Work, 37*, 533–540.

Mennen, F. (1990). Dilemmas and demands: Working with adult survivors of sexual abuse. *Affilia, 5*, 72–86.

Parenti, M. (1993). *Inventing reality: The politics of news media*. New York: St. Martin's Press.

Peplau, L. A. (1979). Power in dating relationships. In J. Freeman (Ed.), *Women: A feminist perspective* (pp. 106–121). Palo Alto, CA: Mayfield.

Petchers, M. (1996) Debunking the myth of progress for women social work educators. *Affilia, 11*, 11–38.

Petty, J. (1996). Only 5 of 190 world leaders are women. How are they doing? *Ms., 6*(5), 20–23.

Philibert-Ortega, G. (1996, Fall). Church and shelter collaboration. *NCADV Voice*, 29–30.

Piercy, M. (1987). *The moon is always female*. New York: Alfred A. Knopf.

Ratican, K. (1992). Sexual abuse survivors: Identifying symptoms and special treatment considerations. *Journal of Counseling and Development, 71*, 33–38.

Ruether, R. R. (1983/1993). *Sexism and God-talk*. Boston: Beacon Press.

Russell, D. 1984. *Sexual exploitation: Rape, child sexual abuse, and workplace harassment*. Beverly Hills, CA: Sage.

Sadker, M., & Sadker, D. (1994). *Failing at fairness*. New York: Simon & Schuster.

Sakhi for South Asian Women (Fall, 1996). Role of religion in South Asian community. *NCADV Voice*, pp. 7–9.

Sanford, L., & Donovan, M. (1984). *Women and self-esteem*. New York: Penguin Books.

Schaef, A. W. (1981). *Women's reality*. San Francisco: Harper & Row.

Scott, J. (1995, August 20). Women won the vote. *Houston Chronicle*, p. 1G.

Sermabeikian, P. (1994). Our clients, ourselves: The spiritual perspective and social work practice. *Social Work, 39*, 178–183.

Shilts, R. (1987). *And the band played on*. New York: St. Martin's Press.

Simeone, A. (1987). *Academic women*. South Hadley, MA: Bergin & Garvey Publishers.

Sonkin, D. J., Martin, D., & Walker, L. E. (1985). *The male batterer: A treatment approach*. New York: Springer.

Sowers-Hoag, K., & Harrison, D. (1991). Women in social work education: Progress or promise? *Journal of Social Work Education, 27*, 320–328.

Spender, D. (1982). *Invisible women*. London: The Women's Press.

Spong, J. (1991). *Rescuing the Bible from fundamentalism*. New York: HarperCollins.

Steiger, H., & Zanko, M. (1990). Sexual traumata among eating disordered, psychiatric, and normal female groups. *Journal of Interpersonal Violence, 5*, 74–86.

Stoesz, D. (1993). Communicating with the public. *Social Work, 38*, 367–368.

Stout, K., & Buffum, W. (1993). The commitment of social workers to affirmative action. *Journal of Sociology & Social Welfare, 20*, 123–135.

Swigonski, M. (1994). The logic of feminist standpoint theory for social work theory. *Social Work, 39*, 387–395.

Towns, E. (1991). Closing Keynote address, May 1, 1991 Sixth Annual Futures Conference, Houston, TX.

Uribe, V., & Harbeck, K. (1992). Addressing the needs of lesbian, gay, and bisexual youth: The origins of PROJECT 10 and school-based intervention. In K. Harbeck (Ed.), *Coming out of the classroom closet* (pp. 9–28). Binghamton, NY: Harrington Park Press.

Vinton, L., & Nelson-Gardell, D. (1993). Consciousness-raising through teaching about the global oppression of women. *Affilia, 8*, 91–102.

WAC (Women's Action Coalition). (1993). *WAC stats: The facts about women*. New York: The New Press.

Weick, A. (1994). Overturning oppression: An analysis of emancipatory change. In L. Davis (Ed.). *Building on women's strengths* (pp. 211–228). Binghamton, NY: The Haworth Press.

Whitehorse Cochran, J. (1991). Steadily, one-by-one pulling ourselves out. In J. Whitehorse Cochran, D. Langston, & C. Woodward (Eds.), *Changing our power: An introduction to women's studies* (pp. 194–201). Dubuque, IA: Kendall/Hunt Publishing.

Wilson, R. (1989). Women of color in academic administration: Trends, progress, and barriers. *Sex Roles, 21*, 85–97.

Wolf, N. (1991). *The beauty myth*. New York: Anchor Books.

Wood, J. (1994). *Gendered lives*. Belmont, CA: Wadsworth.

Wyatt, G. (1985). The sexual abuse of Afro-American and white American women in childhood. *Child Abuse and Neglect, 9*, 507–519.

Yang, J., & Ragaza, A. (1997). The beauty machine. In S. Biagi & M. Kern-Foxworth (Eds.), *Facing difference: Race, gender, and mass media* (pp. 11–14). Thousand Oaks, CA: Pine Forge Press.

PSYCHOLOGICAL WOUNDS

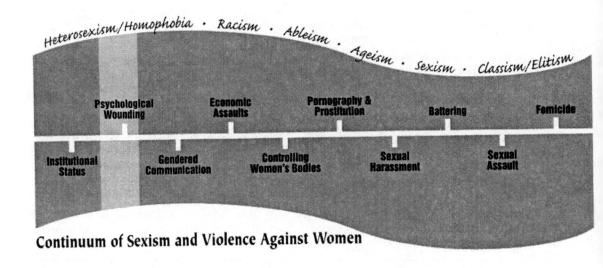

Heterosexism/Homophobia · Racism · Ableism · Ageism · Sexism · Classism/Elitism

Psychological Wounding — Economic Assaults — Pornography & Prostitution — Battering — Femicide

Institutional Status — Gendered Communication — Controlling Women's Bodies — Sexual Harassment — Sexual Assault

Continuum of Sexism and Violence Against Women

> *What are little girls made of?*
> *Sugar and spice and everything nice,*
> *that's what little girls are made of.*
>
> *What are little boys made of?*
> *Frogs and snails and puppy dogs' tails,*
> *That's what little boys are made of.*
>
> *Anonymous Nursery Rhyme*

*T*his simple, innocuous-sounding nursery rhyme, recited to babies for countless centuries, begins the rigid gender-role indoctrination process that has been handed down from generation to generation. Although, in the past, we thought that gender roles were natural, immutable facts of life, assigned by both deity and biology, we now know that gender is a cultural construct that serves the societal needs of the time. This chapter focuses on how our patriarchal society has profound psychological impact on girls and women.

The chapters that follow this one discuss violent assaults perpetrated on women. Such assaults often leave tangible evidence, although in some cases, these assaults are minimized and even denied. In the aftermath of sexual assault, we can see the victim's fear; with battering, we can often see bruises such as black eyes; and with femicide, we sadly observe the sheet-covered body. Less tangible, however, are the psychological wounds inflicted on women by the process of growing up in a patriarchal society. Like the air we breath, such assaults are often invisible and unacknowledged. The process is subtle, insidious, and ever-present. Women virtually breathe in multitudes of hurtful and restricting messages each time they inhale. Girls and women are deeply affected by this trauma, but because the process is so subtle and pervasive, such trauma is deemed natural and normal.

Many of the physical assaults perpetrated on women leave psychic scars as well. Following rape and battering, many women report depression, anxiety, and low self-esteem. These sequelae of violence are discussed in subsequent chapters. In addition, however, women who have not been harassed, raped, or battered often report similar negative feelings. This psychological wounding is the result of growing up in a society that dehumanizes and devalues women. The risk factors for receiving such wounds are not only rape and battering, but also merely being female in a society that values only males. Women are oppressed in this society, and this oppression has psychological, as well as physical, economic, and social ramifications.

This chapter outlines some of the psychological effects of growing up female in a society that devalues the feminine. Included is a discussion on how some of these wounds are inflicted, such as the gender socialization process, internalized oppression, the wholesale adoption of male models of mental health, and the subsequent secondary victimization women receive when they turn to mental health professionals for assistance.

Violence perpetrated on women affects varying numbers of women, as the following chapters describe, yet society's psychological assaults affect all women. While no woman is immune, some girls are more affected than others, and girls have varying amounts of support in resisting the socialization process. We would like to caution our readers that not all of women's mental health problems can be laid at the feet of the socialization process or of internalized oppression. Each young girl is influenced by her own personality, childhood experiences, and biological factors, as well as by external traumatic events. Additionally, each girl has unique experiences with sexism, racism, classism, and homophobia, as well as other forms of oppression, such as ableism and oppression based on appearance. This chapter merely presents another piece of the complex picture of the female experience.

INTRODUCTION TO THE ISSUES

The Socialization of Girls

The socialization of girls in this culture was briefly discussed in Chapter 2, on the institutional status of women. To review, whether a newborn possesses a vagina or a penis has profound implications for how the child will be socialized in this culture. Rigid gender roles are enforced and reinforced by other social institutions, such as educational, economic, and political systems; the media; and family and friends. Although the roles are changing and broadening to some extent, in general, gender roles remain rigid, and stereotypes abound.

Mary Pipher's best-selling book details the results of such rigid gender socialization on adolescent girls. In *Reviving Ophelia* (1994), Pipher describes how patriarchal culture causes girls to abandon their true selves and take up false selves in order to bow to peer pressure and other social pressures to take up the female role. She spoke bluntly when saying,

> *America today is a girl-destroying place. Everywhere girls are encouraged to sacrifice their true*

selves. Their parents may fight to protect them, but their parents have limited power. Many girls lose contact with their true selves, and when they do, they become extraordinarily vulnerable to a culture that is all too happy to use them for its purposes. (p. 44)

Both men and women face difficulties because both sexes are forced to conform to cultural expectations about what it is to be male and female in this society. Women's abilities and opportunities are frequently curtailed by such limitations. Women feel great distress from role conflicts, such as when being a good mother conflicts with the role of earning a living. Women may experience distress when their own physical appearances do not meet the dominant culture's standard for female beauty. They are not tall, thin, and blonde. When women are raised to believe that their roles center on being wives and mothers, they feel pain if they fail in those roles, such as by being divorced, infertile, or homosexual. Women who cannot or will not conform to the rigid female role stereotypes, such as large women or lesbian women, are also castigated. Women are taught that their fundamental role is to give to and care for others; if they pay any attention to themselves, they are selfish and therefore fundamentally flawed.

Girls often experience many losses as they give up their dreams in order to conform to parental and societal expectations. Girls often give up feeling good about who they are and instead become obsessed about the size of their thighs or about whether a boy will call. Pipher poignantly stated,

Girls who have recently learned how to bake cookies and swan-dive aren't ready to handle offers for diet pills. Girls who are reading about Pippi Longstocking aren't ready for the sexual harassment they'll encounter in school. Girls who love to practice the piano and visit their grandmothers aren't ready for the shunning by cliques. (p. 53)

Many of these inequities are imposed by educational inequities, religious teachings, cultural imperatives, and media representations. Although some girls, with support, are able to resist such messages, most young girls are like sponges, soaking up the messages, internalizing them, and then acting on them.

The costs are high, and the losses are many, due to such rigid gender socialization processes. Space limitations in this book prevent a thorough discussion of this topic, but perhaps the best instruction is to look at your own life. What were the rules in your family for how a girl or a boy should behave? Were rules different for the boys and the girls? What double standards were imposed? What did you have to give up? What price did you pay? Although individual reflection is valuable, this exercise is even more powerful when discussed in a group.

Internalized Oppression

A further cause of much of women's psychological wounding is a process known as *internalized oppression*. Internalized oppression occurs when the victims of the oppression are led to believe the negative views of their group, as espoused by the oppressor. Pheterson (1986) offered this more comprehensive definition:

Internalized oppression is the incorporation and acceptance by individuals within an oppressed group of the prejudices against them within the dominant society. Internalized oppression is likely to consist of self-hatred, self-concealment, fear of violence, and feelings of inferiority, resignation, isolation, powerlessness, and gratefulness for being allowed to survive. Internalized oppression is the mechanism within an oppressive system for perpetuating domination not only by external controls but also by building subservience into the minds of the oppressed groups. (p. 148)

In a misogynistic society, many women learn to hate themselves. Women are taught, often in subtle ways, to feel inferior to men. Women frequently attribute their success to luck or good fortune, rather than to their own abilities. Women often demonstrate a lack of self-confidence and self-esteem. Women's language is full of qualifiers and apologies. Women may iden-

tify with the oppressor. How often have you heard women say, "I really don't care for women, all my friends are men" or heard therapists say, "I'd much rather work with men

---

Ser Mujer

Haber nacido mujer significa:
poner tu cuerpo al servicio de otros
dar tu tiempo a otros
pensar sólo en función de otros.

Haber nacido mujer significa:
que tu cuerpo no te pertenece
que tu tiempo no te pertenece
que tus pensamientos no te pertenecen.

Nacer mujer es nacer al vacío.
Si no fuera porque tu cuerpo-albergue
asegura la continuidad de los hombres
bien pudieras no haber nacido.

Nacer mujer es venir a la nada.
A la vida deshabitada de ti misma
en la que todos los demás—no tu corazón—
deciden o disponen.

Nacer mujer es estar en el fondo
del pozo, del abismo, del foso
que rodea a la ciudad amurallada
habitada por Ellos, sólo por ellos
a los que tendrás que encantar, que engañar,
servir, venderte, halagarlos, humillarte
rebelarte, nadar contra corriente, pelear,
gritar, gritar, gritar
hasta partir las piedras
atravesar las grietas,
botar el puente levadizo, desmoronar los muros
ascender el foso, saltar sobre el abismo,

lanzarte sin alas a salvar el precipicio
impulsada por tu propio corazón
sostenida por tus propios pensamientos
hasta librarte del horror al vacío
que tendrás que vencer
sólo con tu voz y tu palabra.

To Be a Woman

Having been born a woman
means placing your body at the service of
 others
giving your time to others
thinking only in terms of others.

Having been born a woman
means that your body is not yours
your time is not yours
your thoughts do not belong to you.

Being born a woman
is being born into nothingness.
If it weren't that your body-home
ensures the continuance of the species
you might as well not have been born.

To be born a woman
is to come to nothing,
to a life you do not inhabit
in which everyone else—not your own heart—
determines and decides.

To be born a woman
is to be at the bottom of the well, the moat,
the pit that surrounds the walled city
where They live, They alone: those
you are called to admire, trick, charm,
humiliating and selling yourself.
You must swim against all currents,
rebel, fight, and scream
until you can push the boulders apart
and slip out through the crack,
destroying the drawbridge, tearing down
 the walls,
making it to the moat and crossing the chasm,

leaping without wings from the precipice
impelled only by your heart
sustained only by your mind
until you have liberated yourself
from the nothingness you will only conquer
with your woman's voice, your verb.

Daisy Zamora

than women, they are easier to work with"? Women often become disdainful and critical of other women. These statements hide an underlying misogyny that women have internalized. When women learn the lesson that men are superior and more powerful, who among us doesn't wish to be identified and associated with the more valued and respected group? However, the paradox for women becomes this: If you are female and purport to hold females in low regard, what does that say about you because you are female, too? Nicaraguan soldier and poet, Daisy Zamora (1993), vividly brought to life the pain often involved in being a woman in her poem, "Ser Mujer" (To Be a Woman), yet she ended the poem on a powerful and hopeful note, which acknowledges that women can rebel and fight to find their voice.

The internalized oppression of women varies from woman to woman, often based on her unique experiences in the world. A strong mother or supportive father may have refuted societal expectations of women as second-class citizens. Additionally, lesbian women, women of color, and women of different faiths internalized different messages, based on the specific messages they received in a culture that is homophobic, racist, and anti-Semitic, as well as sexist. As Audre Lorde wrote, "To imply, however, that all women suffer the same oppression simply because we are women is to lose sight of the many varied tools of patriarchy. It is to ignore how those tools are used by women without awareness against each other" (Lorde, 1984, p. 67).

For lesbian women, the internalized oppression of sexism is joined by the internalized aspects of heterosexism and homophobia. The external and internal messages of multiple oppressions takes its toll on the mental and physical health of women. Pharr (1988) commented on the internalized oppression that affects lesbian women, especially their feelings of self-esteem and self-worth:

The messages that society gives lesbians and gay men are that we are sick, immoral, destroyers of the family, abnormal, deviant, immature, etc. It is very, very difficult to grow up in the midst of this constant bombardment and throw off all of these messages without internalizing any of them as true. Yet when we do take them in, we do damage to ourselves and put severe limits on our freedom to achieve everything we can be in the world. (p. 69)

The internalization of homophobia causes serious problems for some lesbian women, yet such difficulties are often misidentified as an indication of the pathology of homosexuality, rather than as a symptom of living in a homophobic culture. Pharr (1988) listed some of the ways internalized homophobia can be expressed, such as isolation, passing as heterosexual, self-hatred, underachievement or overachievement, poor physical health, suicide, abuse of alcohol and other drugs, unrealistic expectations of love relationships, lesbian battering, lack of authentic relationships with heterosexual family and friends, and horizontal hostility toward other lesbians.

Similarly, women of color may experience difficulties due to the internalized messages of racism. Greene (1994) has combined several definitions of internalized racism to describe the experiences of African-American women: "internalized racism is observed in African American women when they internalize both the negative stereotypes about African Americans and their cultural origins and the idealization of White persons and their cultural imperatives, negatively affecting their sense of self" (p. 20). Internalized racism can be felt as self-hatred or directed to other members of the same oppressed group. For instance, Lorde talked about the difficulties sometimes experienced among African-American women in her essay "Eye to Eye." She acknowledged the effects of being "black women born into a society of entrenched loathing and contempt for whatever is Black and female. We are strong and enduring. We are also deeply scarred" (Lorde, 1984, p. 151). As she wrote of some of the conflicts and judgments that are often a part of the relationships among African-American women, Lorde identified their source: "We have not been allowed to experience each other freely as Black women in america; we come to each other coated in myths, stereotypes, and expectations from the outside, definitions not our own" (pp. 169–170).

There is some evidence that African-American girls are more able to resist the dominant culture's messages than European-American or Latina girls are. This resistance may be due to their strong family connections and communities. Yet this resistance does not come without a price. Debold, Wilson, and Malave (1993) noted that while African-American girls often protectively distance themselves from institutions that tell them they are worthless, such strategies may be effective in the short term but in the long run may limit their economic security.

Beyond the internalization of negative messages based on sex, race, and sexual orientation, some women are further stigmatized by religious prejudice and the subsequent internalization of such messages. For instance, issues of anti-Semitism have often been ignored or trivialized in the society as a whole, as well as within the women's movement. Jewish women are often attacked both as Jews and as women. Beck (1990) believes that "most Jews, even the most assimilated, walk around with a subliminal fear of anti-Semitism the way most women walk around with a subliminal fear of rape" (p. 22). The attack on Jewish women both as women and as Jews is dramatically illustrated in the derogatory and stereotypic use of the term "J.A.P." (Jewish American Princess). Beck outlined the ascribed characteristics of this label, which combines misogyny and anti-Semitism to perpetuate a cruel stereotype creating a Jewish female who is manipulative, materialistic, and vulgar. These images are extremely painful to Jewish women, who may internalize such stereotypes into self-hatred or may project them onto other Jewish women.

The socialization of women, especially the internalization of negative messages, is very painful to women. In response, women develop a variety of survival mechanisms. Women learn to dislike themselves and other women; women learn to hate their bodies; women learn to turn anger inward; women commonly experience identity crises; and women struggle with performing to perfection the many roles for which society holds women responsible. Gender-role conflict and gender socialization may also be a critical factor in the development of alcoholism and other kinds of drug addiction among women (Forth-Finegan, 1991).

Male Standards of Mental Health

Another major mechanism for creating the psychological stigmatization of women has been the development of male models of psychological development. The development of such models define maleness and the traits associated with masculinity as the sole standard of psychological health. Women are seen as varying from the standard, and the differences become operationalized as deficiencies.

Although Sigmund Freud was not the first to misdiagnose and pathologize women, he is perhaps the most well known. His ideas were so influential that much of feminist psychological criticism begins with his often misogynist work, leading some to nickname him "Dr. Fraud." Much of the criticism revolves around Freud's concepts of "penis envy" and of women as defective men, and his plaintive question, "What do women want?" Yet it is for his repudiation of the seduction theory that Freud is most often castigated for by feminists. As Judith Herman noted, "The dominant psychological theory (psychoanalysis) was founded in the denial of women's reality" (1992, p. 14).

In 1896 Freud believed he had uncovered the cause of hysteria, a condition affecting a number of his female patients. In presenting his findings to his colleagues, he identified childhood sexual abuse as the etiology calling it the seduction theory. Yet when his colleagues were outraged at his theory, Freud later retracted his argument, only to say that he was mistaken and that the sexual abuse of young girls by their fathers and other male relatives and family friends had been mere fantasies, rather than actual events (Masson, 1984). His change of heart affected the treatment of countless women for many years after, whose experiences with childhood sexual abuse were discounted and disbelieved. On the other hand, Freud has made some important contributions to the mental health field, and his work should not be summarily dismissed. Some feminist therapists find his work helpful and adopt some of his conceptualizations after putting his ideas through a thorough feminist critique.

Sigmund Freud also formulated a model of moral development based on men's experience. He posited that the development of the superego (essentially, the conscience) depends on undergoing castration anxiety. Because women do not experience castration anxiety, Freud concluded that women are morally deficient and immature, compared with men. Other theorists made similar assumptions. Kohlberg (1958) developed a stage model of moral development, based on his study of 84 boys, over a period of 20 years. When he applied this model to women, he, too, found their moral development to be immature.

Another male developmental model is Erikson's (1950) frequently taught "Eight Stages of Man." His model outlines a process of increasing individuation and autonomy. Because women tend to value connections and intimacy, women do not appear as healthy or as normal when they are measured on this scale. This point was made by McGoldrick (1988): "Theories propounded by males have failed to describe the progression of relationships toward a maturity of interdependence. Though most developmental texts recognize the importance of individuation, the reality of continuing connection is lost or relegated to the background" (p. 32). McGoldrick further noted that most of the stages described by Erikson involve individual, rather than relational, issues: "from age one to 20, those characteristics that refer to interpersonal issues—doubt, shame, guilt, inferiority, and role confusion, [all of which are associated with female characteristics]—signify failure" (p. 32).

By combining male models with the Western tendency to polarize ideas, it became easy to operationalize men as healthy, women as unhealthy; men as strong, women as weak; and men as objective and rational, women as emotional and illogical. It wasn't a far step then to place value judgments on the two opposites, deeming those characteristics assigned to men to be superior to those characteristics assigned to women. These gender differences were thought to reflect the innate differences between men and women. Feminist mental health professionals were some of the first to note that such pathologizing of women was political and social, rather than strictly psychological.

Psychiatrist Jean Baker Miller (1976) was just such a pioneer, with her groundbreaking book, *Toward a New Psychology of Women.* Miller reported that this labeling process occurs in the presence of inequality, especially the inequality of power and status, when one group is labeled dominant and the other subordinate. Miller wrote that "once a group is defined as inferior, the superiors tend to label it as defective or substandard in various ways" (p. 6). Dominant groups then tend to label subordinate groups and to assign these groups the tasks and roles the dominant group finds distasteful. The inferior group's "incapacities are ascribed to innate defects or deficiencies of mind or body, therefore immutable and impossible of change or development. . . . It follows that subordinates are described in terms of, and encouraged to develop, personal psychological characteristics that are pleasing to the dominant group. These characteristics form a certain familiar cluster: submissiveness, passivity, docility, dependency, lack of initiative, inability to act, to decide, to think, and the like" (p. 7).

Therefore, much of what was deemed the normal psychological state for women was actually a set of ascribed characteristics, based on power differentials. Men were the powerful group with the ability to define what is normal and what is crazy. It comes as little surprise to note that men found the traditionally valued male characteristics normal and sane and the traditionally ascribed female characteristics as abnormal and crazy.

Psychological Sequelae to Physical Assaults

Although this chapter has emphasized the ways in which growing up female in a patriarchal culture inflicts psychological wounds on females, we must never forget that many of women's psychological symptoms are a direct result of physical violence perpetrated on them. Because violence in the lives of girls and women is so prevalent, practicing social workers should assess every female client they see, to investigate the possibility of a history of sexual, physical, verbal, or emotional abuse. Although many of the mental health problems women present to social workers may result indirectly from women's socialization or from internalized oppression, such problems often arise because of more blatant, external oppressive acts, such as incest, rape, sexual harassment, and battering.

Subsequent chapters of this book detail the dynamics of violence perpetrated against women, such as sexual harassment, sexual assault, and battering. Each of these types of violence has both psychological and physical consequences. Psychological symptoms following such traumas can include depression and anxiety, as well as the symptoms associated with posttraumatic stress disorder (PTSD), such as numbness and hyperarousal. The psychological ramifications of such assaults are detailed in each of the chapters corresponding to each type of abuse. This chapter focuses on the psychological ramifications of being female in a patriarchy, without necessarily also being a victim of violence. Nonetheless, because being female and being a victim of a violent assault are so closely related and so often overlap, the effects of violence must be acknowledged here as well.

For instance, because child sexual abuse is so prevalent but is not discussed in detail else-where in this book (which focuses on the victimization of women), the topic is briefly discussed here. The estimated numbers of women who were sexually abused as children vary widely, depending on the research reviewed and on how the researchers asked respondents about their experiences. The most frequently cited study is Russell's (1983) survey of 930 San Francisco women, which asked 14 separate questions to uncover the various forms of child sexual abuse. The study revealed that before age 14 years, 28% of the women had experienced unwanted sexual touching, and when attempted and completed forcible rapes are added in, the figure for total sexual abuse before age 18 years rose to 38% (Russell, 1983).

Clearly, sexual abuse of girls is prevalent, although often ignored, in our society. Such abuse has lasting psychological consequences that extend from childhood into adulthood. One review of the literature found the following long-term effects for women reporting a history of child sexual abuse: sexual disturbance or dysfunction, anxiety and fear, depression and depressive symptomatology, evidence of revictimization experiences, and suicidal ideas and behavior, particularly when they have been exposed to force, such as violence (Beitchman, Zucker, Hood, DaCosta, Akman, & Cassavia, 1992). Courtois (1988) described more long-term effects of incest in terms of six categories: (1) emotional reactions such as generalized anxiety and fear, depression and feelings of helplessness and powerlessness; (2) negative self-perceptions, including self-blame and shame; (3) physical and somatic effects, including gastrointestinal distress, headaches, and eating disorders; (4) sexual difficulties; (5) difficulties in interpersonal relationships, such as difficulty in trusting other people; and (6) social effects ranging from isolation, rebellion, and antisocial behavior to overfunctioning and compulsive social interaction.

The caution here is that although many of the following mental health problems women report may be consequences of being female in a patriarchal society, such problems may also be the result of having been physically or sexually abused. Every female is at risk, so every woman should be assessed for a history of assault. Two valuable books for working with women who have been sexually assaulted as children are Christine Courtois's *Healing the Incest Wound* (1988), as well as the popular self-help book *The Courage to Heal* (1988) by Ellen Bass and Laura Davis.

The Second Assault: Sexism in the Mental Health Professions

Many times, after a physical assault, women are revictimized by the very professions that are supposed to be helping them. For instance, women who are raped often experience a second assault at the hands of the criminal-justice system when they seek redress from the police and the courts. Similarly, many women who are depressed, anxious, or emotionally wounded experience a second victimization at the hands of the mental health system they turn to for relief and healing, for the mental health institutions have not been free from the sexism prevalent in many other societal institutions.

A now-classic study (conducted by Broverman, Broverman, Clarkson, Rosenkrantz, & Vogel, 1970) demonstrates how culturally defined stereotypes influence the delivery of mental health services, often to the detriment of women. In the study, 70 clinically trained psychologists, psychiatrists, and social workers were administered a sex-role stereotypes questionnaire to determine the traits of a healthy woman, a healthy man, and a healthy adult. As the researchers hypothesized, the clinical judgments of the therapists differed according to the sex of the person, upholding societal sex-role stereotypes. Additionally, the researchers found that the clinicians' description of a healthy adult was nearly identical to their account of an adult male, while the characteristics for healthy women differed from the healthy adult standard. Clinicians were far more likely to suggest

that "healthy women differ from healthy men by being more submissive, less independent, less adventurous, more easily influenced, less aggressive, less competitive, more excitable in minor crises, having their feelings more easily hurt, being more emotional, more conceited about their appearance, less objective, and disliking math and science" (pp. 4–5). Thus, trained clinicians held the same biases as the general public, which often views "healthy adulthood" and "maleness" synonymously.

These stereotypical views of women are ingrained in therapeutic interventions based on male-model theories of psychological health. Most therapies emphasize the intrapsychic functioning of the client or assist clients in learning to adapt to their environments, rather than in learning to change their environments. Although such therapy was believed to be apolitical and value free, such a stance was in and of itself political because it supported the status quo. In addition, the mental health professions reflected the same biases, prejudices, and misogyny that is present throughout society. Instead of women finding relief, they often found blame and judgment. Instead of receiving therapy that values and understands their lives as women, women often found male-biased treatment models and harmful so-called therapeutic strategies. Women who have sought therapy have been labeled hysterics, masochists, fearful of success, codependent, borderline, psychotic or diagnosed as having multiple personalities. Women have been told they love too much, make foolish choices, or enjoy suffering. Not only have the diagnoses been misogynistic, but the therapeutic interventions have been, as well.

Greenspan (1983) identified three myths composing the foundation of many traditional therapies. The first myth is "It's all in your head." That is, a client's problems are determined by unconscious forces within a person's mind, separated from any social, historical, or economic context. The second myth has relied on a medical model of psychopathology, wherein the problem is often deemed an illness that can be cured with proper diagnosis and treatment. Myth number three states that the solution to the illness is *the* expert, who is scientific, objective, and qualified to diagnose and treat the problem. The expert is usually male, a *Father Knows Best* figure.

This male-centered model is detrimental to women when women's problems result from their having internalized the patriarchal culture. Women are taught to defer to a male authority who is assumed to know more about her than she knows about herself. With a male-centered model, women often have ended up diagnosed and either hospitalized, or given tranquilizers. Such therapies have viewed women from a traditional male perspective, with little understanding of the unique difficulties inherent in being female in a patriarchal culture. These traditional therapies have tended to look at problems as being personal, rather than political, the opposite of a feminist stance. For instance, both of us have had numerous experiences with battered women who described their painful attempts to obtain help from therapists who ignored or minimized the violence, tried to get the victims to have more sympathy for the batterers, or even strategized with the victims regarding how to be better wives and mothers so they would not provoke the violence!

Another instance of a sociopolitical problem being personally defined is incest. Louise Armstrong wrote the groundbreaking book on incest, *Kiss Daddy Goodnight* (1978). Her book was the first to break the silence on incest, identifying the problem using a feminist analysis of the underlying dynamics of the rape of children by their fathers. Even after her book was published, however, through the years, the mental health profession, including social workers, have redefined incest as a mental health problem. The rapist father has been transformed into the incest family, and the victimized child or adult survivor has been made a patient requiring treatment. Louise Armstrong (1994) talked about the change:

From a political issue framed by feminists as one of male violence against women and children—a sexual offense on the part of men, for which we demanded accountability, and censure—incest has, in these years, been coopted and reformulated therapeutic ideology, as an illness in women, to be treated. In children, it is a prediction of illness to be treated. (p. 30)

Instead of holding men accountable, society sees the men as victims, too. Mothers are often held just as accountable as the fathers, and civil statutes are written to censure the mother who "knew or should have known" (p. 31). This cautionary tale should lead us to carefully evaluate every so-called treatment strategy for women, which may actually blame women and cease to hold the patriarchy responsible.

Blaming the Mother

Women are blamed not only for their own psychopathology, but for inflicting it on others as well. The psychiatric literature has blamed mothers for causing schizophrenia, homosexuality, and autism in their children. Many mothers feel as though they can't win. If they are caring and involved with their children, they are labeled "overprotective," and if they are not, they are labeled "distant" and "cold." Such terms as "schizophrenogenic mother" and "maternal deprivation" have been attributed to mothers, yet comparable terms do not exist for fathers. Caplan and Hall-McCorquodale (1985) conducted an investigation by reviewing articles in major clinical journals to assess the degree of mother blaming. They found 72 different types of pathology attributed to mothers, ranging from arson and depression to incest and phobias. The child's pathology was attributed, at least in part, to the mother's activity in 82% of the articles and to the mother's inactivity in 43%, contrasted to the father's activity in 43% and the father's inactivity in 39% of the articles.

Sexual Exploitation

Not only do women often receive biased therapeutic interventions from many mental health professionals, but some women are sexually exploited by their therapists, as well. In Catherine Nugent's (1994) review of the literature, she found the prevalence rates of psychotherapist–client sexual exploitation varied, with 7% to 12% of therapists admitting to having sexual contact with their patients. Another study cited by Nugent reported that 65% of psychiatrists and 50% of psychologists surveyed reported having consulted with a patient who had been involved with a sexually exploitive therapist. Nugent's (1994) review of the literature revealed common patterns in the exploitation; for instance, most sexual abuse involved a male therapist exploiting a female client, many of the therapists were involved with more than one client, and the women usually suffered negative consequences.

The Codependency Movement: An Illustration of Pathologizing Women

The diagnosis of codependency is a painful illustration of the pathologizing of women, which serves economic, political, and social needs of society. Krestan and Bepko (1991) remember a time when *codependency* was not even a word, let alone a label adopted by mental health professionals. Before the 1980s, the term literally did not exist. They traced the origins of codependency to the 1930s and 1940s, when the public's perception of alcoholism changed from viewing it as a sign of moral degeneracy to seeing it as a medical problem and then, later, to considering it an addictive problem for which treatment and sympathy were offered. At the time, most of the identified alcoholics were men. With the advent of family therapy and systems theory, clinicians began to look at the wife of the alcoholic man and found her ill as well. In fact, the conventional wisdom in the addiction field often held that she was more ill than he was. Books, articles, and self-help groups proliferated, which promoted the pathologizing of the wife of an alcoholic. Gradually, the definition was generalized and broadened to include almost all women. The symptoms of this newly identified disease were broad and inclusive and included many caregiving behaviors, which women had been taught to consider their responsibility. In fact, feminists argued that codependence was merely another term for a well-socialized woman.

Increasingly, women began to identify themselves as codependents and to attend self-help groups specifically to combat this new "disease". For-profit psychiatric hospitals formed codependency units and insisted that women be hospitalized for 30 days at a time to treat this addiction. This treatment certainly served an economic function, as hospitals, therapists, and publishing companies reaped great profits from books, workshops, therapy, and insurance. Krestan and Bepko (1991) also described the political ramifications of such a diagnosis. By describing the wife and children as sick and in need of treatment, the dominant culture could divert attention and responsibility from the male alcoholic, and codependency became "simply another tool in the oppression of women fostering denial of male accountability" (p. 52).

Unfortunately, traditional therapists rarely adequately addressed the underlying issue involved—that women are often socialized to be caregiving and self-sacrificing, to the detriment of themselves. This disease–addiction model served to stigmatize and pathologize women, rather than to help. Krestan and Bepko redefined the problem. Instead of viewing the problem as one of disease and blaming the woman, they formulated a clinical-intervention model, which identified problematic behaviors to be changed, not a disease that those afflicted were powerless to overcome.

Krestan and Bepko (1991) identified both a pattern of overresponsibility on the part of many women and one of irresponsible behavior on the part of many men. Their framing of the problem in this way allows women to examine and to change problematic behavior while holding men accountable for their behavior, as well. Such a model doesn't blame the victim, and it also acknowledges societal factors, such as gender roles, which teach problematic behavior to men and women. Pathologizing women is almost a national sport.

Tavris (1992) quoted Harriet Lerner: "Our culture dislikes and fears angry women, but is not threatened by sick women meeting together to get well" (p. 203). Tavris further acknowledged that "women get much more sympathy and support when they define their problems in medical terms rather than in political terms" (p. 203).

The codependence movement vividly but painfully illustrates how women are pathologized by the mental health field, often for political and economic reasons. In the 1990s, the term *codependence* is rarely heard. This women's disease has gone out of style, similar to last year's fashions. Krestan and Bepko (1991) summarized the codependency movement, but their words are applicable to many other diagnoses given to women in the past and those sure to arise in the future:

> The codependency movement is probably best viewed as a fascinating and compelling example of the evolution of a social phenomenon. It speaks to the power of our descriptions of reality to invent reality and to invent disease for economic and political gain whereby certain segments of society profit from treating others whose experience is controlled by being defined as sick. It speaks to our tendency to over-identify with negative and pathologizing views of ourselves. And it speaks to our tendency to think in generalized extremes that fail to acknowledge contradiction, complexity, distinction. (p. 64)

Diagnostic and Statistical Manual of Mental Disorders

Some of you might agree that such labeling of women as masochists or codependents was unfortunate, but you might also argue that such pathologizing does not occur today. We would beg to differ with you and cite the current battle that is being conducted today over the *Diagnostic and Statistical Manual of Mental Disorders (DSM)*. The *DSM* is published by the American Psychiatric Association (APA), which describes and categorizes mental illness. The book is extensive and comprehensive, and it appears very scientific, for each disorder is assigned a number, right down to the hundredth of a decimal place. For instance, in the current (fourth) edition, DSM-IV, "Adjustment Disorder with Mixed Anxiety and Depressed Mood" bears the number 309.28 (APA, 1994). This manual has many stated purposes, including the facilitation of reliable diagnoses, a teaching tool for mental health professionals, and a means for gaining reimbursement from insurance companies. For these reasons, the DSM is a powerful book, naming what is, or is not, a mental illness, with serious economic as well as personal ramifications. In fact, Paula Caplan (1995) has called it, somewhat tongue-in-cheek, the "bible of mental health professionals" (p. xviii).

Although the book is claimed to be based on scientific study and objective standards, the manual is riddled with stereotypes and male bias. Many clinicians have been critical of the *DSM* with regard to its treatment of women (e.g., Kaplan, 1983; Landrine, 1989; Walker, 1993), but one of the most effective and vocal critics has been Paula Caplan, a Canadian psychologist. Caplan has written extensively about the male bias, gender stereotyping, and double standards within the mental health profession (Caplan, 1985, 1995; Pantony & Caplan, 1991). As a one-time consultant to a *DSM* task force, she has been in a distinctive position to see what goes into the making of diagnoses of mental illness. She has found that the *DSM* serves economic and political functions, rather than scientific ones. Rather than being based on empirical research, it is more likely to be based on personal bias. Caplan is critical of the *DSM*'s often unquestioned adoption by mental health professionals, including social workers. She wrote,

> *Historically, social workers have been more inclined to take social factors into account in trying to assist unhappy people, but as social worker Ben Carniol has pointed out, even their profession has been turned toward a focus on*

individuals' intrasychic sources of trouble. This has been partly because social work has been influenced by psychiatry and psychology and partly because some social workers who feel powerless to eradicate poverty and other social ills find it less upsetting to act as though the problems come from within the individual. (1995, pp. 62–63)

Although many of the disorders in the *DSM* are problematic, Caplan focused primarily on two. The first is the self-defeating personality disorder (SDPD), originally called "masochistic personality disorder," and the second is the late luteal phase dysphoric disorder (LLPDD), which originally appeared in the *DSM-III-R* (*DSM*, third edition, revised) and was renamed for the *DSM-IV* (fourth edition) as the premenstrual dysphoric disorder (PDD). Caplan's criticism is briefly outlined here. First, neither of these so-called disorders is confirmed by research. In fact, regarding PDD, research on how women are affected by menstruation has been inconclusive and contradictory. Further, although the effects of testosterone on male behavior has been more conclusively related to specific behaviors (Tavris, 1992), there is no mental illness attributed to male hormones. Finally, women who do experience menstrual difficulties should be seeing a gynecologist, not a psychiatrist.

Regarding SDPD, Caplan became involved in the *DSM* work groups in 1985, when *DSM* authors were planning to add a diagnosis of masochistic personality disorder in the next edition. Many other feminist therapists fought the inclusion, arguing that many of the so-called symptoms are merely characteristics of a well-socialized woman or a woman who has survived sexual or physical assaults. For instance, one characteristic listed was "incites angry or rejecting responses from others and then feels hurt, defeated, or humiliated (e.g., makes fun of spouse in public, provoking an angry retort, then feels devastated)" or "chooses people and situations that lead to disappointment, failure, or mistreatment even when better options

are clearly available" (APA, 1987). Additionally, the disorder was not supported by empirical research, which was cited as a precondition for a diagnosis to be included in the *DSM*. Under pressure by feminists in the field, the *DSM* task force compromised by changing the name to self-defeating personality disorder and placing the diagnosis in the appendix. Fortunately, due to its controversial nature, biased underpinnings, and lack of empirical basis, the diagnosis was not included in the *DSM-IV.*

Caplan also made the critical point that diagnoses such as the PDD and SDPD have the potential not only to pathologize, but also to stigmatize women. For instance, in custody cases or employment decisions, the invoking of such diagnoses can seriously harm women. Caplan observed that much of what is labeled "mental illness" is in fact a normal response to common life problems or the result of social injustice.

The double standards and male bias inherent in creating the *DSM* were additionally exposed when Caplan (1995) proposed a new category for the *DSM*, which was meant to be both a consciousness-raising and a thought-provoking tool, but which also had empirical validity, due to a number of supportive research studies. She proposed this new diagnosis, entitled "Delusional Dominating Personality Disorder" (Caplan, 1995, pp. 169–171). The disorder includes such characteristics as inability to establish meaningful interpersonal relationships; inability to identify and express a range of feelings; and tendency to use power, silence, withdrawal, or avoidance, rather than negotiation, in the face of interpersonal conflict or difficulty (p. 169). Although most therapists recognize these descriptions as problems in their male clients, the editors of the *DSM* would not consider it as a diagnosis, despite an abundant empirical base.

We urge social worker colleagues to read more about the problems with the *DSM* before adopting its assumptions wholesale for use in your practice. The labeling of other people is a powerful tool and should not be lightly undertaken. The diagnoses are often more harmful than helpful, often becoming another tool for labeling, pathologizing, and oppressing women. Some *DSM* diagnoses may be helpful for some women in identifying their problems and gaining access to treatment, yet all diagnosis and treatment of women should be made thoughtfully, with the costs and benefits to the client carefully considered.

The Mental Health of Women

In the past, many of women's psychological difficulties in this society were deemed to have resulted from the innate psychological weakness, hormonal imbalances, or intrapsychic processes of women. The advent of feminism has led many mental health professionals to use a new gender lens to reexamine much of traditional thought on the psychology of women. The point here is not to deny that women can become mentally ill or have psychological difficulties, but merely to better understand the etiology of such difficulties. Determining the cause of the problem is critical, for etiology determines the choice of a solution. For instance, if women are understood to be depressed because they are naturally and biologically more emotional than men, then perhaps antidepressants should be prescribed. However, if women are more likely to be depressed because of their inferior status in a patriarchal society, the solutions look very different and suggest major societal and political changes that cannot be accomplished with a pill.

A feminist worldview recognizes that much of what was written and accepted as part of the psychology of women has been based on myths, stereotypes, and sexist theories of human development and psychological schools of thought. Although new feminist theories have been emerging over the past several decades, bias persists even today. Blumenthal (1994) suggested that "the adverse effects of inferior social status, impaired self-esteem, sexual abuse and sexual discrimination, lack of economic equality, and constricted educational and occupational opportunities account, in part, for the higher rates of some mental illnesses in women" (p. 456).

Although the majority of clients seeking mental health services are women, and 70% of all psychotropic medications are prescribed to women, men experience higher rates of mental disorders over their lifetimes than do women (Blumenthal, 1994). In addition, both research and clinical experience demonstrate clear gender differences in the predominance of certain disorders. Disorders more common in women than men include major depressive disorder, dysthymia, seasonal affective disorder, rapid-cycling bipolar disorder, panic disorder, phobias, dissociative disorder, borderline and histrionic personality disorder, and suicide attempts (Blumenthal, 1994).

Some of these diagnoses are problematic, revealing a sexist bias. For instance, psychiatrist Judith Herman reported that the borderline diagnosis is "frequently used within the mental health profession as little more than a sophisticated insult" (1992, p. 123). She recalled that when she was a resident, she had asked her supervisor how to treat borderline patients, only to have him reply, "You refer them" (p. 123). Additionally, the histrionic personality disorder is merely a caricature of the traditional female role (Kaplan, 1983).

Therefore, instead of basing our discussion on the disorders listed previously, the following brief discussions address several difficulties that women describe as problems in their lives: depression, low self-esteem, body-image problems, and eating disorders. We believe that these conditions are symptoms, not of mental illness, but of women's oppression in a patriarchal society. Because each of these topics could easily become a book in itself, we can only present a brief overview of each subject. Each discussion is meant more to challenge the traditional ways of viewing women than to provide a comprehensive discussion of each topic. We encourage you to use the bibliographic references to read more about each of these issues that are painfully prevalent in the lives of women.

Depression

Throughout history, women have been more depressed than men. Today, woman are two to three times more likely to experience depression, and in the United States, one out of every seven women will be hospitalized for depression during her lifetime (Wetzel, 1994). Depression appears to be a multifaceted problem affecting major areas of life, including the affective, cognitive, behavioral, and physical realms. Major symptoms include differing levels of sadness, anxiety, irritability, hopelessness, worthlessness, inappropriate guilt, decision-making difficulties, recurrent thoughts of suicide and death, social withdrawal, lack of interest, headaches, sleeping and eating disturbances, fatigue, and negative rumination about the world, the self, and the future (Wetzel, 1994).

In 1987, the American Psychological Association formed a national task force on women and depression. The task-force members were charged with identifying the risk factors and treatment needs of depressed women by summarizing existing research and synthesizing current theory on women and depression. The task force issued a report entitled "Women and Depression: Risk Factors and Treatment Issues" (McGrath, Keita, Strickland, & Russo, 1990). The study identified these risk factors for women (McGrath et al., 1990, p. xii):

- Women are at greater risk for depression due to a number of social, economic, biological, and emotional factors. The task force determined a need to study women's depression from a biopsychosocial perspective.
- Women's depression is related to certain cognitive and personality styles—that is, avoidant, passive, dependent behavior patterns; pessimistic, negative cognitive styles; and a tendency to focus too much on de-

pressed feelings instead of action and mastery strategies.
- The rate of sexual and physical abuse of females is much higher than previously suspected and is a major factor in women's depression.
- Marriage confers a greater protective advantage on men than on women. Mothers of young children are highly vulnerable to depression; the more children in the house, the more depression is reported.
- Poverty is a "pathway to depression." In the United States, 75% of the people living in poverty (annual income of $5,776 or less) are women and children. Minority women, elderly women, chemically dependent women, lesbian women, and professional women are also high-risk groups for depression and need special attention and support.

Their review of the literature serves to debunk the myths that women are more often diagnosed as depressed because they are more willing to talk about their feelings or more likely to seek help, two commonly offered explanations for the prevalence of depression in women. Women are more depressed, it appears, due to real-life problems facing them, which are often a direct result of being female.

The report stresses the need for careful diagnosis of depression. The recommendation for a diagnostic assessment for women should include "taking a history of sexual and physical violence, and exploration of prescription drug utilization, past and current medical conditions, and a reproductive life history to see how menstruation, birth control, pregnancy, child birth, abortion, and menopause may have contributed to the women's depression" (McGrath et al., 1990, p. xiii). The task force found interpersonal therapy, cognitive–behavioral therapy, and the sociocultural perspective of feminist therapy to be helpful. Antidepressants were found to often be effective in treating some kinds of depression, but many problems were also found with such a treatment plan—such as

QUALITY TIME   Gail Machlis

Gail Machlis humorously addresses the serious problem of women, depression, and the use of antidepressants.

improper diagnosis and monitoring, high discontinuance rates for drug therapy, and the use of drugs that may work differently for women than for men (McGrath et al., 1990).

Self-esteem

Self-esteem is the layperson's term for internalized oppression. The use of the word "self-esteem" is problematic in itself because it suggests that individual women have a problem with their "self" in contrast to the use of the

term "internalized oppression," which has much different implications. Although the following section uses the commonly accepted word "self-esteem," we urge you to change your thinking and begin to substitute the concept of internalized oppression. When this is done, the problem and the solutions look very different.

Women's lack of self-esteem is almost epidemic. In fact, low self-esteem among women is so common it is accepted as an unalterable fact of female life. Women are rarely pleased with who they are. Sanford and Donovan (1984) define *self-concept* or *self-image* as "the set of beliefs and images we all have and hold to be true of ourselves. By contrast, our level of self-esteem (or self-respect, self-love, or self-worth) is the measure of how much we like and approve of our self-concept" (p. 7). Most women, while disliking themselves, look at the problem as a personal one—that is, something is wrong with me. Rarely do women examine—or are they encouraged to examine—how the society affects how women view themselves and each other. In contrast, one feminist therapist said to a female client who reported low self-esteem as a presenting problem, "That is certainly to be expected. How can you value yourself in a society that doesn't value women?" (Diana Storms, personal communication, 1995).

Sanford and Donovan (1984) agree that there is a connection between women's self-esteem and the patriarchal society in which we live. They base their work on four premises that provide a valuable foundation for understanding women and self-esteem (Sanford & Donovan, 1984, pp. xiv–xv):

1. *Low self-esteem among women is largely the result of female oppression in male-dominated culture and society, and constitutes an insidious form of oppression [in] its own right. A woman whose career opportunities, for example, are restricted because of sex discrimination is externally oppressed. But a woman whose career opportunities are restricted because she had been taught to think of herself as lacking in capabilities and not worth much is also internally oppressed.*

2. *Low self-esteem is at the bottom of many of the psychological problems that plague individual women today, and attempts to "cure" these problems without addressing what underlies them can often lead to other problems. For instance, a woman who compulsively overeats or is dependent upon alcohol may be able to change her behavior in that specific regard. But when she does, the low self-esteem behind the original problem will probably manifest itself in other ways.*

3. *Low self-esteem and the psychological problems it gives rise to facilitate the continuation of women's external oppression in a male-dominated world. A woman who is taught from childhood that she is of less value than males, for instance, easily may come to believe it, and her lack of faith in her own value will predispose her to depression and passivity, which, in turn, will make it easier for others to keep her down—down being her proper place.*

4. *The development of self-esteem in individual women is necessary for the advancement of women as a group. Male-dominated culture and society can continue only if women accept and internalize the notion that women naturally are and deserve to be second-class. For a woman to hold herself in high esteem in a world where women are held in low esteem is to tacitly challenge the prevailing social, political, and economic order.*

Because self-esteem is a political problem as well as a personal one, solutions must be political as well as personal. Sanford and Donovan (1984) recognize this fact by presenting "Blueprints for Change," a series of action steps for women to take not only on the personal level, but in the political arena as well. Individual attempts by women to feel better about themselves are often futile when society continues to devalue, objectify, restrict, and blame women.

Body Image and Body Hatred

It seems almost rare for a woman to be happy with her body. The movies, fashion magazines, print advertisements, and television commercials depict a beauty ideal that is not only unrealistic, but unhealthy as well. Women are bombarded with these images of apparently perfect bodies, in spite of the fact that many of the images are either airbrushed or portray preteen and teenage models masquerading as adult women. Such standards of beauty pose special difficulties for women of color, for Western beauty is characterized not only by being tall, thin, and large-breasted, but also by having white skin—and preferably blonde hair. Asian-American women also struggle, like many other women of color, with the concept of European-American beauty. Attempting to conform to such standards may lead to bulimia, breast augmentation, and eyelid alterations (Bradshaw, 1994).

Yet race may also provide some women of color a protective stance in relation to body image. For example, although one study found that African-American women have adopted negative beliefs about body image, eating, and weight, similar to those European-American women display (Pumariega, Gustavson, Gustavson, & Motes, 1994), other studies reveal racial differences, with African-American women and girls reporting more satisfaction and positive feelings toward their bodies than European-American women report (Harris, 1994; Parker, Nichter, Nichter, Vuckovic, Sims, & Ritenbaugh, 1995). In the latter set of studies, when a culturally sensitive survey was designed and administered by African-American researchers, racial differences began to emerge in interviews with African-American girls. For instance, African-American girls focused less on weight as an issue and more on "making what you got work for you" (p. 111). The African-American girls also had a more flexible definition of beauty, which included the importance of style and the concept of older women perceived as being beautiful in their own right (Parker et al., 1995).

In *The Beauty Myth*, Naomi Wolf (1991) theorized that the striving of women to achieve this mythical, limited ideal of beauty is a political weapon used to stall women's advancements in this society. Wolf also illuminated the economic benefits of the beauty myth as she challenged the $33-billion-a-year diet industry, the $20-billion-a-year cosmetics industry, the $300-million-a-year cosmetic-surgery industry, and the $7-billion-a-year pornography industry (Wolf, 1991). Along a similar vein, Rabbi Harold Kushner said in a presentation, "If women across America woke up happy with

their bodies tomorrow, the American economy would collapse" (personal communication, November 10, 1996).

The money many women spend supporting these industries is mind-boggling. Can you image all the good that could be done with this money if used in other ways? How many female candidates would it elect? How many women and children could such money feed and shelter? How many child-care facilities could it operate? Also, the time and energy involved in all these activities are monumental and could be redirected to create a more just society. Yet individual women are often more obsessed with decreasing the size of their thighs than with increasing the number of opportunities for women.

Issues of appearance or beauty ideals are not trivial but often have life-and-death implications for women. Although the research is contradictory, women's experience tells us that breast implants have serious health consequences, often involving autoimmune disorders. Untold numbers of women die from liposuction and other unnecessary cosmetic surgical procedures. In addition, as the following section shows, anorexia and bulimia are life-threatening disorders.

Eating Disorders

Anorexia nervosa is a syndrome in which extreme weight loss occurs due to inadequate food intake, about 90–95% of cases of anorexia occur in young females (Horton, 1995). *Bulimia nervosa* is another eating disorder, typically characterized by self-induced vomiting, which usually begins in the late adolescence of girls and young women. Although both of these disorders produce serious physical consequences, too often, they are treated solely as physical or medical problems without taking gender into account.

Many feminists view eating problems as a result of a culture that values thinness and enforces this prescription for female beauty culturally, socially, and economically. For others, an eating disorder may be an attempt to take back power and control in the one area in which they have some: what they do or do not eat. In *The Obsession: Reflections on the Tyranny of Slenderness* (1981), author Kim Chernin has urged us to look at the underlying meaning for women's obsession with eating and weight. She suggested,

> *The body holds meaning. A woman obsessed with the size of her body, wishing to make her breasts and thighs and hips and belly smaller and less apparent, may be expressing the fact that she feels uncomfortable being female in this culture. A woman obsessed with the size of her appetite, wishing to control her hungers and urges, may be expressing the fact that she has been taught to regard her emotional life, her passions and "appetites" as dangerous, requiring control and careful monitoring. A woman obsessed with the reduction of her flesh may be revealing the fact that she is alienated from a natural source of female power and has not been allowed to develop a reverential feeling for her body. (p. 2)*

Thompson (1992) posed an alternative theory for eating problems. Thompson proposed that eating problems are survival strategies for coping with various traumas, such as sexual abuse, racism, classism, sexism, heterosexism, emotional and physical abuse, acculturation, and poverty. In Thompson's review of the literature, she found a number of incidence studies indicating that between one third and two thirds of women who have eating problems had been sexually abused, and in her own study, 61% of her sample of women were survivors of sexual abuse (Thompson, 1992). Women often binge to anesthetize their feelings, alleviate anxiety, and combat loneliness, and in some cases regain a sense of control. Her theories shift the focus from issues of appearance to the underlying problems of the inaccessibility of economic, cultural, racial, political, social, and sexual justice for women.

Eating disorders are a serious medical problem. In fact, if anorexia nervosa remains untreated, it is estimated that 9% of those affected will die prematurely from suicide, heart ailments, or infections; and only half of the remaining patients are able to recover (Horton, 1995). Clearly, the physical complications should not be ignored when treating this disease, yet neither should its gender implications.

Strategies for Change

PRACTICE ISSUES: EMPOWERING WOMEN

There is no doubt that women are psychologically wounded in this culture. Although the symptoms of these wounds often appear in the personal arena, they are often caused and affected by the political one. The solutions then are many and varied and occur on both the personal and the political levels. It would be both erroneous and futile for the social work profession to attempt to help individual women feel better about themselves without concurrently addressing the political source of the problems that contribute to women's psychological distress. Too often, in many of the helping professions, individual problems are depoliticized and decontextualized. Codependency, incest, depression, and self-esteem are just a few of the many examples that illustrate this point.

To avoid a social work practice that contributes to misogynistic, racist, or homophobic practices, we can use the concept of empowerment to guide our practice. Barbara Solomon was the first in social work to define *empowerment* and to develop this paradigm as a model for social work practice, in her groundbreaking book *Black Empowerment: Social Work in Oppressed Communities* (1976). She defined *empowerment* as "a process whereby the social worker engages in a set of activities with the client or client system that aim to reduce the powerlessness that has been created by negative valuations based on membership in a stigmatized group" (p. 19).

Unfortunately, since the mid-1970s, the term *empowerment* has become overused and even distorted by the political ideologies of various groups. However, the common denominator in empowerment theory remains to increase the control people have over their own lives. Swift and Levin (1987, p. 73) elaborated:

> In order to make it a more precise and useful concept, two central issues should be kept in mind. Empowerment: 1) refers both to the phenomenological development of a certain state of mind (e.g. feeling powerful, competent, worthy of esteem, etc.) and to the modification of structural conditions in order to reallocate power (e.g., modifying the society's opportunity structure)—in other words, empowerment refers both to the subjective experience and the objective reality; and 2) is both a process and a goal.

This definition fits with the perspectives presented in this chapter and in the book as a whole. Addressing the psychological wounding of women in this society means both helping individual women to resist society's socialization process and increasing individual women's feelings of competency, power, and self-esteem. In addition, we must focus on the structural conditions—in a word, *patriarchy*—that cause such conditions to exist. Such a focus is very compatible with social work's emphasis on self-determination, person-in-environment, and social change, as well as the feminist belief that the personal is political.

Barbara Simon (1994, p. 7) offered a definition of empowerment practice, which is both concrete and lyrical:

> The social worker who is intent upon client empowerment attempts to initiate and sustain interactions with clients and client groups that will inspire them to define a promised land for themselves, to believe themselves worthy of it, and to envision intermediate approximations of that destination that they can reach, in a step-by-step fashion, while remaining in reciprocal connection with each other and with a professional guide who offers technical and emotional help.

Although she was not speaking specifically of women, Simon's definition is certainly appropriate to women. Many women have not been allowed the opportunity "to define a promised land" for themselves, as they are instead handed a sex-role stereotype to conform to. Also, even when opportunities and power are accessible, some women continue to feel that they are unworthy or incapable.

The empowerment literature often describes different levels of empowerment. Gutierrez and Ortega (1991) outlined three levels of intervention. First, empowerment on the personal level focuses on ways that individuals can develop feelings of personal power and self-efficacy. Second, empowerment on the interpersonal level stresses the development of specific skills that allow individuals to be more capable of influencing others in a range of settings, including the family, the workplace, and the political arena. Such skills could include everything from assertiveness training to advocacy skills. The third level of intervention is at the level of political empowerment, which emphasizes the goals of social action and social change. In the practice section of this chapter, strategies for personal and interpersonal empowerment are discussed, whereas political empowerment is reserved for the policy discussion, although in reality, each component overlaps.

Personal Empowerment

Gutierrez and Ortega (1991) summarized the psychological process of empowerment as

> changing the perception of the self in society. This includes the development of a sense of group identity, the reduction of feelings of self-blame for problems, an increased sense of responsibility for future events, and enhanced feelings of self-efficacy. This is described as developing a sense of critical consciousness (pp. 25–26).

For women, there are many ways to achieve this level of critical consciousness. There is no single path to either enlightenment or empowerment. For some women, personal experiences with racism and sexism spark the development of critical consciousness that enables them to connect the personal with the political. For some women, consciousness-raising groups or other collective efforts lead to their understanding of their position in the patriarchy and their desire to work for social change. For other women, the process is more academic, via reading and studying about the historical oppression of women and making the connections to present-day conditions. For other women, involvement in grassroots organizing for social justice has developed personal empowerment, while for others, it has been the support, love, and teaching of other women. Although there are many paths on the journey to personal empowerment, therapy has become an increasingly popular path taken by many. Social workers have become interested in psychotherapy, and many are practicing psychotherapists. With this in mind, the major focus here is on feminist therapy, which often constitutes a controversial practice area for social workers. Some criticisms of feminist therapy are also included.

Feminist Therapy

Feminist therapy is based on an empowerment model. Actually, rather than being a complete therapeutic model within itself, feminist therapy is more like a lens for viewing other therapeutic modalities. Feminist therapy is a political and ideological position through which other therapeutic modalities are filtered. For instance, some feminist psychotherapists might describe their theoretical orientation as feminist family therapy or feminist self-psychology.

However, feminist therapy does have its own unique view of women's lives and some of its own particular intervention strategies and techniques. Butler (1985) outlined guidelines for feminist therapy practice, which include awareness of women's oppression based on gender, race, and class; recognition of the sociocultural context; focus on women's empowerment; use of diverse therapeutic modalities through a nonsexist lens and with nonsexist techniques; demystification of power in a therapeutic rela-

tionship; importance of the therapist and other women as role models; benefits of the all-women group approach; the therapist's continuous self-examination and reflection on her values; and encouragement of growth-enhancing experiences in addition to therapy.

Eminent feminist psychologist Laura Brown has found that the most frequent stereotype about feminist therapy is that it is about a woman therapist talking to a woman client about women's issues. Feminist therapy is much more. Laura Brown (1994) made this point most powerfully:

> *Feminist therapy, as one aspect of the feminist revolution, functions to subvert patriarchal dominance at the most subtle and powerful levels, as it is internalized and personified in the lives of therapists and their clients, colleagues, and communities. Unlike other expressions of feminism, which address themselves to external and overt manifestations of patriarchal oppression, feminist therapy also concerns itself with the invisible and sometimes nonconscious ways in which patriarchy has become embedded in everyone's daily life—in our identities, our manners of emotional expression, and our experiences of personal power and powerlessness—to our profound detriment. Unlike other approaches to psychotherapy, feminist therapy concerns itself not simply with individual suffering but with the social and political meaning of both pain and healing. It has as its goals the creation of feminist consciousness and a movement toward feminist action. The first and most important "client" of feminist therapy is the culture in which it takes place; the first and foremost commitment to feminist therapy is to radical social transformation. (p. 17)*

The past two decades have been an exciting time in women's psychology, as countless female mental health professionals have evaluated their own fields from a feminist perspective. The results have been transformative, benefiting not only women, but men as well. For instance, family therapists have breathed new life into traditional family therapy by challenging male concepts such as the importance of rigid boundaries and family hierarchies. Feminist theorists have reframed enmeshment as a desire for connection and have added an analysis of gender and power dynamics within the family (Goodrich, Rampage, Ellman, & Halstead, 1988). Feminist therapy offers critiques of traditional therapies and theories, including the much-esteemed systems theory. For instance, Walters, Carter, Papp, and Silverstein (1988) noted, "Systems therapy discriminates against women by seeking balance and equilibrium for the family system as a unit, without addressing the unequal access of each individual to choice of role" (p. 23). Feminists have analyzed both the power and the gender constructs in the addiction model (Bepko, 1991). Burstow (1992) offered a radical feminist therapy, which is based on radical feminism, radical therapy, and antipsychiatry. (Antipsychiatry, as defined by Burstow, "is a combined movement/perspective that views psychiatry as a fundamentally oppressive institution propped up by hegemony and built on mystification, subordination, and violence.")

However, new theories have not been limited to adapting therapeutic modalities to women's experience; they also include development of new theories of female growth and development, which have profound implications not only for women, but for men as well. These new theories of female growth and development have been postulated based on a woman's experience and perspective, rather than on the traditional practice of developing a model for men and then rating women as being less than or the polar opposite. One such theory has been developed by Carol Gilligan (1982), regarding the moral development of women. Gilligan, who initially worked with Kohlberg (1958), began to notice a dissimilarity in the moral development of women, which she did not label deficient, merely different.

In conducting a study on the moral dilemma confronting women who are considering the option of abortion, Gilligan developed a model for women. The moral imperative for men seems to be rooted in a sense of justice and fairness, as noted by Kohlberg. Gilligan noted

that the moral imperative for women, however, is "an injunction to care" (p. 100). Men seem to view relationships as a hierarchy, with a wish to stay on the top and a fear that others will get too close. In contrast, women view relationships as a web, with a desire to stay in the center and a fear of being too far out on the edge. Using these constructs, the moral development of women does not appear deviant, merely different. The behaviors of both women and men are more understandable when viewed in this context.

Another theory of female development was formulated by Janet Surrey (1985), in conjunction with the Stone Center at Wellesley College. Surrey noted that traditional developmental theories emphasize the importance of disconnecting from early relationships to achieve a separate, autonomous self. Using this model, men appear well-adjusted, and women seem immature. Surrey developed a self-in-relation model, which emphasizes connection over autonomy, and which views relationship as a basic goal of development. Surrey (1985) stated that "the self is organized and developed through practice in relationships where the goal is the increasing development of mutually empathic relationships" (p. 3). Such a theory has important implications for working with women in therapy. Instead of labeling women as being codependent or overprotective, this theory views women's relationships as being central to women's self-concepts. Such a theory also helps describe disruptions in women's mental health status as being primarily caused by disconnections. Feminist therapists have incorporated these theories into their practice, allowing them to view both women and men in a new light.

While successfully addressing issues of gender and power in therapy, feminist therapy has often been criticized for being less successful in confronting issues of religion, class, and race. Public perception has held that therapy is a self-indulgent pursuit of the wealthy. While the traditional focus of therapy has been on middle-

and upper-class, primarily European-American women, feminist therapists are changing the therapeutic culture, adding to their analysis of gender the issues of race, class, and religion.

For instance, Beck (1990) offered several suggestions for therapists working with Jewish clients. Such suggestions include taking the issues of Jewish identity and anti-Semitism seriously; doing the necessary homework, such as learning Jewish history and customs; studying the history of anti-Semitism and its cumulative effects; understanding how Jewish women must deal with two sets of identity issues—that is, those associated with life's developmental tasks and with the development of Jewish identity; realizing how Jewish culture places inordinate pressure on women toward heterosexuality, marriage, and childbearing, intensified in a community where so many millions have been exterminated in recent history; and cautioning against assuming that if a therapist is either Jewish or feminist, she or he will necessarily understand how to work most effectively with Jewish clients (Beck, 1990).

Feminist psychotherapist and social worker Pat Palmer (1996) has found that although the issue of class is often included on a laundry list of dynamics for feminist therapists to be aware of, many therapists don't know what that specifically means in practice. Her article is included in this chapter, to demonstrate to readers some implications of class when seeing working-class women in therapy.

Observations & Commentaries: Pain and Possibilities: What Therapists Need to Know About Working-Class Women's Issues

Patricia Palmer

Publications often list class and classism among the factors therapists need to take into account, but seldom explain what this actually means.[1] I want to tell you some of the things you need to know as therapists about working with working-class women. My understanding comes both from exploring working-class women's writings in the USA and the UK[2] and from my experience as a working-class child and woman, and as a therapist and person in therapy.

First, we need to be aware that when working-class women come into therapy, they may be dealing with another layer of causes that contributes to their symptoms, to their pain and longings, to whatever concerns they present to us. Class experience and classism have created this layer: through the experience of working-class life and through society's treatment of working-class people. These factors have impacted working-class women intrapsychically as they developed from childhood. Class experience and classism are only parts of working-class women's formative experience, but they are integral aspects that therapists must know about and keep in mind as they look for threads running through a woman's life. This is true even when women have become part of the middle class through higher education or a partner who is middle class. Heritage and childhood experience are significant contributers to how people perceive themselves and the world, including what they consider possible for themselves and what they value. Dynamics from the past, internalized messages and unexamined values—whether conscious or unconscious—may be playing out in adult life in ways that do not serve the woman's best interests. Because therapy is so much about increasing possibilities, therapists must be aware of obstacles that impede clients' growth. The issues for working-class women include shame, fear and lowered self-confidence, loss and grief, and feelings of disconnection.

We need to be aware that a working-class woman may have had class-related shaming experiences that have undermined her self-esteem and sense of possibility. These experiences result in disappointment in the self, feelings of not belonging where sufficient possibilities exist, and a sense of not being seen as an individual but as part of a group considered 'less than'. Therapists need to know what these experiences may have involved: clothing, housing and parents' occupations, among others. A working-class woman may fear that her story will not evoke an empathic, attuned response because it is culturally unfamiliar to the therapist. A painful shaming experience I had when growing up occurred at the home of some upper-middle-class people when I stayed with them for a visit. I overheard their conversation about how nothing in my wardrobe was suitable for my appearing in public with them. I felt inadequate, that I didn't belong in the world of greater possibility that they represented to me, and that the clothing defined me and was more important than my personal qualities, such as accomplishment in school and liveliness. Therapists can help clients see that the problem does not come from personal inadequacy but from limitations in other people's perspectives.

Whereas classism results in shaming experiences, growing up in the working-class community often fosters strengths: determination, courage, resourcefulness, empathy, a sense of what is important and commitment to social justice, among others. We need to be aware that these strengths may be present or waiting to be tapped within working-class women we see.

We also need to know that class experience and classism may have contributed to anxiety and lowered self-confidence for working-class women. Problems may come from needing to maintain unwavering determination in the face of immense obstacles, such as poor resources and the absence of a 'life plan', which middle-class people often assume as a given. Many working-class women have lived with a sense of anxious urgency—even desperation—for years, thinking 'if I don't keep going I'll be stuck' (with little money, poor housing, boring job). At the same time, the girl's or woman's family may fear the costs of pursuing goals. The 'safer course' of lowered expectations and saving money as a buffer against hardships, intended to protect her, does not give her the support she desperately needs. Class-related familial responses to pursuing goals vary, including pride in the person's achievement over obstacles, fears that she will be disappointed by classist barriers or that insurmountable expenses may arise, a sense of loss or envy from their own lack of opportunity, a willingness to make great emotional or financial sacri-

fices, discomfort in the world the person has entered, and fear that these new experiences may separate her from them. Conflicting messages may appear simultaneously.

It is important for therapists to know that working-class women usually have a range of class-related losses. Exploring losses helps women to grieve and to identify their longings with a view to getting their needs met in their current lives. Working-class women may especially mourn the loss of opportunity and safety in their lives. They may also grieve for relatives and friends who have suffered poverty, lack of opportunity, illness and even death because of class-related experiences. I grieve for my father who suffered from the effects of influenza and TB most of his life. Some women have so internalized their losses and perhaps their parents' experiences of loss that they do not know what a life of possibility looks like and may need help in creating one. Therapists need a knowledge of community aid/support to help women with few resources.

For working-class women the experience of loss may be intertwined with issues of self-care and connection with other people. As an 11-year-old I was strong but not graceful. In group ice-skating lessons I advanced rapidly because of my strength and balance. I was excited when I advanced to a group which worked on gracefulness and flexibility. Although I couldn't have articulated it then, I longed to develop this side of myself. At that point my father discontinued the ice-skating lessons. He told me that advanced lessons were 'for the children of doctors and dentists and people like that', a message that working-class children often hear. I was deeply disappointed but soon overlaid this with feelings of allegiance to my Dad, whom I saw as wise and courageous in his situation (ill from childhood poverty, hardworking in a poorly paid job) and to 'people like us' who didn't need frivolous things like advanced lessons. In my natural desire to be connected to him I identified with his ideas about expectations and possibilities. It is unfortunate that this connection came at the cost of my longings. Exploring this incident in therapy helped me separate the threads running through it. I can choose now to have a different sense of possibility than my Dad did without feeling disconnected from him and from part of myself. I can experience my childhood longings to feel good about my body and bring them forward into my present life without feeling selfish or frivolous. Having explored this incident I am now better able to discover other longings without the message 'this is not for you'.

The tension between longings and connection can come up particularly when working-class women are going on to new opportunities—in schooling, careers and other areas. They may experience uncomfortable feelings of being disconnected from other working-class people, including fears of losing contact, and being 'better than' or selfish. The resolution in therapy involves helping the woman to reach a decision that feels comfortable to her. In doing clinical work, Ellman has found that opportunity always involves some loss; for oppressed people this loss often includes leaving what feels familiar and what feels good in terms of helping others, and a sense that one is abandoning other oppressed people (B. Ellman, personal communication, 18 April 1995). Ellman recommends asking women if they feel they've achieved enough; if the woman wants to accept the opportunity, she suggests naming the situation as a dilemma and exploring its implications, including losses, challenges and possibilities.

A woman I worked with experienced relief after exploring her dilemma. She felt free to choose the opportunity she deeply wanted without the thoughts that had made her hesitate, 'I'm abandoning . . . I'm better than . . . I'm selfish . . . I'll be lonely'. She went on with her goals knowing that she might lose connection with or not be able to help some people in her current life because her new goals took much of her time, she might grow apart from some people, and some did not support her but for various reasons held her back. Having acknowledged her need to pursue her longings she felt more able to enjoy some current relationships without guilt or fear of being held back. Some people remained an integral part of her life, including some who were unable to take on opportunities themselves at that time but supported her efforts. Her challenges included examining what she could realistically do to help others, exploring who did and did not support

her on this part of her journey, and finding support on her college course. Possibilities included accomplishing what she wants to do, improving the quality of life for herself and her family, supporting and inspiring people in her current life, growing through new connections, and helping oppressed people in her new position.

We must also be aware that connection, both to individuals and to working-class and middle-class people as groups, presents specific challenges for working-class women because they grew up in two worlds: in their families/working-class communities and in the dominant middle-class world. Dealing with two realities will always be necessary—whether they currently live primarily in a working-class or middle-class context—because they carry connections to the working class as part of their feelings and perceptions. Their roots are in the working class, they have bonds with working-class people as parents, siblings, extended family and friends, they know the resiliency and courage of many working-class people, and they have seen other working-class people suffer hardships, which they also know firsthand. Situations like those described above may arise in which they fear or experience disconnection from working-class people.

Working-class women's relationship to the middle-class world is also complex. Working-class women may find themselves attracted to middle-class people because of the sense of safety and possibility they offer and 'because they are not caught up in the same distress' (Trevithick, 1988: 80). This can be healing and stimulating. At the same time, their experience of classism has taught working-class women that they may be shamed, judged and excluded if they don't know or follow the rules of the middle-class world (what to wear, suitable interests, and many other rules). Comments may hurt, 'didn't you ever learn music as a child?—I thought everyone did'. Families of potential partners may let working-class women know that they're unacceptable because they're working-class. These experiences leave them feeling insecure or angry. Working-class women may feel resentful or envious towards middle-class friends because of the ease of their lives. They may also feel uncomfortable with some middle-class possessions and expectations, considering them excessive. They may feel rage at continued injustices. The impact of these feelings is often a sense of disconnection.

Therapists must listen to the full range of working-class women's feelings around their relationships with both worlds, helping them examine how they can use these feelings to foster their best interests, experience connection and express their values. Women can explore how they want to live to pursue both their connections to other working-class people and their own goals. We can validate working-class women's anger and knowledge of injustice and help them examine how they play out in their lives. 'Survivor guilt' and unexamined curtailing of self-development to help oppressed people are counterproductive; considered support, advocacy and social action both on a one-to-one and on a larger scale are empowering.

Therapists can also help working-class women in their relationships with middle-class people and in navigating the middle-class world. Envy and resentment hinder mutual relationships with individual women; we can help women look behind these feelings to their roots: anger and a sense of loss for themselves and other working-class people. Shame limits working-class women's ability to pursue opportunities they want. Women become stronger through learning to recognize oppression and lack of awareness, confronting others on their behaviour or comments, and exploring their internal responses to see when their understandable fear or its exaggerated intensity comes from shaming experiences in the past and not from the present situation. We can also support working-class women and encourage them to look for help from middle-class friends when they decide to explore possibilities—clothing, interests, and other areas—previously unavailable to them. Uncertainty about having opportunities or possessions or about following patterns generally considered middle-class leaves working-class women feeling hesitant and guilty. We can encourage working-class women to use their sense of what is important to decide what feels comfortable or excessive to them while asking questions such as, what is behind this desire? Does this go back to a longing for something that will help me feel comfortable, stimulated, confident, good about myself? Working-class women need the safety and encouragement to ask these questions; having little opportunity for nourishing the self is one of the greatest costs of classism.

The result of this work in therapy around the experience of working-class life and classism is women's ability to see themselves more clearly, what they feel, need, value and will do. Feelings that impede growth, such as shame, inadequacy, anxiety, guilt, hesitancy and insecurity lessen. Working-class women may feel more confident as they pursue goals and more joyful when they arrive where they want to be. They may experience more connection and know more about how they want to live in relation to others. The most significant personal benefits of my research and reflection have been feeling better able to pursue what I need for self-development, more connected to both working-class and middle-class people, and clearer in my values.

ACKNOWLEDGEMENTS

I would like to thank Karen Holmes, Jo Stanley, Pam Trevithick and Valerie Walkerdine for helping me begin this research. I am grateful to Marty Collier, Wendy Nes, Laura Oren, Bob Palmer, Karen Stout and particularly Barbara Ellman, Beverly McPhail and Diana Storms for their support and insights throughout the writing of this paper. Joan Brochstein made helpful comments on an earlier draft.

NOTES

1. Some feminist therapists in the UK and the USA have specifically explored working-class women's issues. Rubin (1978), a family therapist who grew up in the working class, pioneered with a qualitative study of 50 US white blue-collar families. In the UK, Eichenbaum and Orbach (1983) made specific recommendations for bringing discussions of class into training programmes for therapists. Trevithick (1988), a UK social worker and working-class woman, conceived workshops for working-class women, exploring with them many issues central to working-class women's lives. Filming one of Trevithick's workshops, Walkerdine (1990), also a

working-class woman, produced a video for working-class women and therapists. In the USA, Denny (1986), Faunce (1990) and Skodra (1992) have written about working-class women and therapy.

2. Working-class women's writings are rich sources for therapists on the context and internal realities of working-class women. I have not come near to exhausting this resource and more books are appearing. Zandy's (1990) anthology of past and contemporary US working-class women's literary work reflects the diversity of working-class women and offers many suggestions for further reading. Olsen's (1978) essays have inspired other working-class women to voice their experiences. Examining working-class women's writings quickly leads to work by feminist women of colour who have been leaders in exploring the impact of class in women's lives. I suggest the anthologies edited by Moraga and Anzaldua (1983) and by Smith (1983) and the essay collections by Lorde (1984) and hooks (1981, 1984). Taking Liberties Collective (1989), a UK feminist collective composed mainly of working-class women, provides insights into working-class women's lives through an examination of higher education. Ryan and Sacrey's (1984) book of essays by working-class academics contains two essays by women. Recently Tokarczyk and Fay (1993) have edited a collection of essays by working-class women academics.

REFERENCES

Denny, P. A. (1986) "Women and Poverty: A Challenge to the Intellectual and Therapeutic Integrity of Feminist Therapy", *Women & Therapy,* 5(4): 51–63.

Eichenbaum, L. and Orbach, S. (1983) *Understanding Women.* London: Penguin Books.

Faunce, P. S. (1990) "Women in Poverty: Ethical Dimensions in Therapy", in H. Lerman and N. Porter (eds.), *Feminist Ethics in Psychotherapy,* pp. 185–94. New York: Springer.

hooks, b. (1981) *Ain't I a Woman: Black Women and Feminism.* Boston, MA: South End Press.

hooks, b. (1984) *Feminist Theory: From Margin to Center.* Boston, MA: South End Press.

Lorde, A. (1984) *Sister Outsider.* Freedom, CA: The Crossing Press.

Moraga, C. and Anzaldua, G., eds. (1983) *This Bridge Called My Back: Writings by Radical Women of Color.* New York: Kitchen Table: Women of Color Press.

Olsen, T. (1978) *Silences.* New York: Dell.

Rubin, L. B. (1978) *Worlds of Pain: Life in the Working-class Family.* New York: Basic Books.

Ryan, J. and Sacrey C. (1984) *Strangers in Paradise: Academics from the Working-class.* Boston, MA: South End Press.

Skodra, E. E. (1992) "Ethnic/immigrant Women and Psychotherapy: The Issue of Empowerment", *Women and Therapy* 13(4): 81–98.

Smith, B., ed. (1983) *Home Girls: A Black Feminist Anthology.* New York: Kitchen Table: Women of Color Press.

Taking Liberties Collective (1989) *Learning the Hard Way: Women's Oppression in Men's Education.* London: Macmillan.

Tokarczyk, M. M. and Fay, E. A., eds. (1993) *Working-class Women in the Academy: Laborers in the Knowledge Factory.* Amherst: The University of Massachusetts Press.

Trevithick, P. (1988) "Unconsciousness Raising with Working-class Women", in S. Krzowski and P. Land (eds.), *In our Experience: Workshops at the Women's Therapy Centre,* pp. 63–83. London: The Women's Press.

Walkerdine, V. (1990) *Didn't She Do Well.* London: Metro Pictures (0171-434-3357).

Zandy, J., ed. (1990) *Calling Home: Working-class Women's Writings.* New Brunswick, NJ: Rutgers University Press.

The issue of race must be part of the therapeutic hour. Some well-intentioned therapists posit that they are color-blind and treat all clients alike. However, such a stance means that the therapist is not really seeing the client, for race has a profound impact on clients' experiences. In a racist society such as ours, being a person of color has serious implications that cannot be denied or glossed over. Additionally, experiences with racism can also result in a variety of responses and coping strategies, of which the therapist needs to be aware. "Healthy cultural paranoia" and "armoring" were cited by Greene (1994) as adaptive mechanisms employed by African-American women to "decrease their psychological vulnerability in encounters where there is a potential for racism" (p. 23). Therapists may be quick to label such behavior as "oppositional" or "resistant" unless they are knowledgeable about the dynamics of race in therapy. Increasing numbers of books are being written, which address the special needs of women of color in therapy (Boyd-Franklin, 1989; Comas-

Diaz & Greene, 1994; Dufrene & Coleman, 1992). Espin (1994) suggested ethnospecific therapy, where therapists and clients are matched in race, as well as gender. Espin offered advantages of such a match: The therapist can understand the culture, ethnicity, race, and language; the therapist can serve as a better role model; and the power dynamics are more equalized.

Vasquez (1994) reported that recurring racist events lead to depression, anxiety, and posttraumatic stress disorder in Latinas. She reported that each individual "who experiences discriminatory behavior has to struggle to incorporate and deal with the painful experience. It takes extra effort not to feel badly about oneself; it takes extra effort to know what to do with the hurt and anger" (1994, p. 122).

Before and during work with people of different ethnic backgrounds, it is important to undergo ethnicity training, which in reality is a lifelong task. McGoldrick and Giordano (1996) stated that "the most important part of ethnicity training involves the therapist coming to understand his or her own ethnic identity" (p. 22). As previously mentioned, there is a growing body of literature on therapeutic interventions with women and families of many races and ethnicities. For instance, *Women of Color* (1994), edited by Lillian Comas-Diaz and Beverly Greene, includes information on African-American, Native American, Asian, Asian-American, Latina, Jamaican, Indian, and mixed-race women. *Ethnicity and Family Therapy* (1996), edited by Monica McGoldrick, Joe Giordano, and John Pearce, contains a discussion on more than 40 different types of families, based on ethnicity, ranging from Native American to Nigerian, Korean, Amish, Greek, Soviet Jewish, and Slovak families. Clearly, there is much to learn to begin to understand and appreciate the many ethnic and racial groups that are represented in America.

Some practice concepts around ethnicity that McGoldrick and Giordano (1996, pp. 23–24) find useful include the following:

- Assess the importance of ethnicity to patients and families.

- Validate and strengthen ethnic identity.
- Be aware of and use the client's support systems.
- Serve as a "cultural broker."
- Be aware of "cultural camouflage" (using identity as a defense against change).
- Know that there are advantages and disadvantages in being of the same ethnic group as your client.
- Don't feel you have to "know everything" about other ethnic groups.
- Avoid polarization.
- Don't romanticize a culture; not all cultural practices are ethical.

Criticism of Feminist Therapy

Although misogynistic practices continue within the mental health profession today, new generations of mental health professionals are being exposed to literature that refuses to pathologize women, values women's strengths, reframes many of women's responses from pathology to survival mechanisms, and values multicultural diversity. Yet there are drawbacks to the use of therapies as a tool to empower women. For instance, even if therapy is conducted in a feminist, egalitarian manner, for many women, therapy still implies treatment, and women can feel "crazy." This obstacle can be difficult to overcome.

Some feminists question the necessity of therapy for women, particularly certain groups of women. For instance, Chrisler (1989) concluded that feminists therapists should avoid weight-loss counseling because it is not congruent with feminist ideology, with its acceptance of a variety of female sizes and shapes. Lesbian feminists Kitzinger and Perkins (1993) have made a powerful case against therapy, even feminist therapy, with lesbian women. In stating the goal of their book, *Changing Our Minds,* they say, "We want to show how the influence of psychology is to depoliticize, individualize, and privatize our language, and hence to inhibit the development of clear political goals and strategies" (p. 38). Their caution is well taken, for even seasoned feminist therapists can fall into focusing only on the personal, rather than on the political and structural.

Interpersonal Empowerment

There are many ways of facilitating the empowerment of women, which social workers can implement both inside and outside of therapy. Many of the following strategies can be used both in conjunction with therapy and as an alternative to therapy. Some empowerment strategies involve teaching women new skills. Such skills can include assertiveness training or learning how to write a legislator or how to organize a community. Knowledge is often equated with power, and social workers can share what they know with their clients. Additional empowering techniques include bibliotherapy, group work, reframing, resistance, nonsexist child-rearing practices, and research.

Bibliotherapy

Bibliotherapy is a sophisticated word for reading self-help material. Frequently, women are unaware of many aspects of oppression because it was never taught in school. Although educators wouldn't dream of teaching math using only the odd numbers, they teach history, literature, and government portraying only one gender. This sad state of affairs requires us as women to do our own learning and to designate our own "classics." Reading gives women back their history and their role models. Reading enables us to learn from the past, as well as to plan for the future. Such reading can include books on women's history, women's poetry, feminist criticisms of societal institutions, novels by and about women, new psychological research on women, and books written by and about women whose experiences have particularly been marginalized—such as lesbian women, women of color, heavy women, and women with disabilities—as well as more traditional self-help books. The reference books listed at the end of each chapter in this book are a good place to start.

Psychologist Harriet Lerner cautioned women about the wholesale adoption of self-help books aimed at women, however.

> As a journalist once noted, self-help books explain life the way Cliffs Notes explain Tolstoy. Even worse, these books obscure larger contextual issues, detouring readers from challenging class, gender, and racially stratified systems in which we live and our family histories have evolved. For reasons that include both our vulnerability and our strength, women have long been the advice-giving industry's primary consumers. (1993, p. 62)

Lerner gave suggestions for selecting self-help books, including these: Don't buy books telling us that women are sick, do choose books that truly connect the personal and the political, and don't buy books that promote guilt (Lerner, 1993). Some books that Lerner suggests are her own trilogy *The Dance of Anger* (1985), *The Dance of Intimacy* (1989), and *The Dance of Deception* (1993), as well as bell hook's *Sisters of the Yam: Black Women and Self-recovery* (1993) and Wendy Kaminer's critique of the recovery movement *I'm Dysfunctional, You're Dysfunctional* (1992).

Group Work

Isolation is often a hallmark of oppression. Women coming together in dyads or groups can transform this cultural isolation. Women can come together in a variety of groups to offer support, to share resistance strategies, and to confront the root of the problem, rather than focusing on the symptoms. From therapy groups to reading groups, to advocacy groups, the possibilities are endless. Women of the same race and sexual orientation can come together to renew group pride and solidarity, and women from different groups can come together to challenge stereotypes and explore commonalities and differences.

Reframing and Renaming

Reframing and renaming are powerful strategies to empower women. Brown (1987) suggested that therapists can reframe lesbian differences in a positive manner and additionally offered that "fat women can be reconceptualized as having taken power back by taking space, being visible, and violating the rule against feeding oneself" (pp. 302–303). Penis envy can be reframed, for we have rarely met a woman who envied a man's penis but have observed a large number of men who worry about the size of their penis. Perhaps the nonexistent "penis envy" can be replaced by the real-life concerns of "penis insecurity." Gloria Steinem (1983) has urged women to view stretch marks resulting from pregnancy and scars from cesarean births as symbols of experience and courage, to be worn proudly rather than shamefully.

Resistance

Resistance is another strategy to be employed to help women resist the restricting messages of patriarchy. For instance, Debold, Wilson, and Malave (1993) have viewed the mother–daughter relationship as a vital relationship to empower mothers and their daughters. They noted, "Mothers can find themselves unwitting accomplices; they re-create in their daughter's lives the choices they made in their own lives. Women may find themselves subtly encouraging their daughters to accept the same limitations on dreams and power that they had accepted because women know of no other ways to survive in a hostile culture" (p. 84). Debold et al. (1993) have envisioned mothers helping their daughters to resist society's messages that restrict and disempower women, and the authors have detailed various "resistance strategies" for mothers to share with their daughters.

One such resistance strategy is to strive to end sexist child-rearing practices that are detrimental to both girls and boys. Social worker Myriam Miedzian wrote a book entitled *Boys Will Be Boys: Breaking the Link Between Masculinity and Violence* (1991). In it, she theo-rized that "many of the values of the masculine mystique such as toughness, dominance, repression of empathy, extreme competitiveness, play a major role in criminal and domestic violence and underlie the thinking and policy decisions of many of our political leaders" (p. xxiii). She suggested numerous strategies for changing the socialization of boys to decrease the violence in our culture, such as involving boys with child rearing and teaching them conflict resolution.

Research

Research and other forms of knowledge building are invaluable in empowering women. Women must generate new theories of female growth and development, such as those of Gilligan and of Surrey. Women are also reclaiming knowledge that was lost or appropriated, such as midwifery and goddess-centered religions. Social workers can support this knowledge building by conducting research and by building theory. There are many other strategies women can adopt to heal the psychological wounds inflicted by patriarchal practices. Gloria Steinem (1983) has encouraged women to commit "outrageous acts and everyday rebellions" (Steinem, 1983). Table 3.1 lists a few examples related to the myriad topics covered in this chapter.

POLICY FOR CHANGE: POLITICAL EMPOWERMENT

It is not enough for individual people to feel competent and powerful. Political empowerment requires social change, social justice, and a transfer of power among groups in society. Political empowerment can run the gamut from changing policies to running for political office. The levels of empowerment overlap and build on one another, and social workers can weave such strategies into their practice in a variety of ways.

Table 3.1
Empowering Strategies for Women and Girls

- Read Charlotte Perkins Gilmore's (1980) classic semiautobiographical short story, entitled "The Yellow Wallpaper," which is about what happens when a talented woman writer is diagnosed with a nervous condition (neurasthenia), forbidden to write, and forced to rest, presumably in order to recover.

- Be cautious of your use of the *DSM* in your practice. If *DSM* diagnosis is necessary for insurance reimbursement for your client, sit down with your client, and together choose a diagnosis that is the least stigmatizing possible, such as posttraumatic stress disorder (PTSD) or adjustment disorder. If another diagnosis is needed, discuss the potential risks and benefits for the client.

- Start or join an advocacy group that focuses on an issue you are interested in, for which you can reduce the negative impact on how women are portrayed or how women view themselves. For instance, some advocacy groups have reframed being "childless" to being "child-free" and offer support about choosing such a lifestyle, while other groups have advocated the end of discrimination against heavy women through education, support, and advocacy that attempts to change the perceptions and beliefs about body size held by society as a whole, as well as by women in particular.

- Treat yourself to feminist, or feminist ethnospecific, therapy.

- Gather a group of therapists who will meet weekly with you, specifically to address cases presented with a feminist perspective (Goodrich et al., 1988).

- Rent the old movie *Gaslight*. "Watch it over and over until you are confident of the meaning of the verb 'to gaslight,' particularly in this tense: I am being gaslighted. Watch for real-life applications, especially from professors, supervisors, and theorists who are in positions of authority over you" (Goodrich et al., 1988, p. 181).

- Attend trainings on feminist therapy, or provide such training to your colleagues. At multidisciplinary case conferences, present a feminist analysis. Attend ethnicity training, and keep learning about your own and other cultures all of your life.

- As Burstow (1992) recommended demystify psychobabble. Some of her definitions include the following: "diagnosis" is a specific pathologizing label; a "prognosis" is a wild psychiatric guess about what a client will be like in the future; and "acting out" is resisting in ways that upset psychiatric staff (pp. 248–249).

- Explore a range of empowering paths for women, such as support groups, self-help groups that are women-friendly, women's music and spirituality, alternative therapies, and practices such as yoga, dance, and meditation.

- Listen to a variety of women's music, which serves to empower, affirm, and enrich women's lives. A couple of examples are Libby Roderick and Sweet Honey in the Rock.

- Raise your children in a nonsexist manner. Join with other like-minded parents for support. Read the humorous and insightful piece entitled: "X Stories for Free Children:— A Fabulous Child's Story About an Xperiment with Baby," whose parents refused to divulge whether the child is female or male, to the great frustration of friends, family, and the school system (Gould, 1972). Don't give children gifts that stereotype or limit them.

- Mary Pipher has suggested resisting the urge to offer girls advice or too much sympathy. She encourages girls to keep diaries, to write poetry and autobiographies; to search within themselves for their deepest values and beliefs; to observe their own culture with the eyes of an anthropologist in a strange new society; to meditate daily; to learn to separate thinking from feeling; to make conscious choices; to learn to make and enforce physical and emotional boundaries; to learn the skills of defining relationships, managing pain, and modulating their emotional reactions; to look within for validation; and to discover the joys of altruism (Pipher, 1994).

As we have seen throughout this chapter, the power to label and define what mental illness is and who is mentally ill is immense. Social workers must increasingly take an active part in the process to better reflect the reality of women. One place to start would be to become informed about the *DSM* work groups. When new additions are considered, social workers can write letters, organize, and educate the public to protest those policies and actions that are biased against women and that reflect painful sex-role stereotypes.

Many of the psychological wounds discussed in this chapter are the result of policies that punish, restrict, or discriminate against women. Policy efforts involve changing the conditions that produce psychological distress for women. For example, when a woman is sexually harassed at work, she may come to a therapist reporting self-blame, fear, anger, or depression. Although an individual therapist can assist the woman with validating her feelings and outlining her alternatives, the social worker is also challenged with ending the policies and practices that allow such harassment to exist. Another example concerns poor women. As the American Psychological Association task force report on women and depression (McGrath et al., 1990) noted, poverty is a pathway to depression. Social workers can work to change the policies that cause the feminization of poverty. Specific strategies are outlined in Chapter 5, on the economic assault on women.

Additionally, as the task force report on women and depression (McGrath et al., 1990) noted, reproductive issues affect women's depression. As social workers, we should lobby for more research on menopause, menstruation, and pregnancy, and we should support government funding for family planning services and federally funded abortions to allow women choice. Ending the psychological assaults on women also means ending the physical and sexual assaults that often produce these psychological wounds. Later chapters in this book more specifically address these issues.

Although social work therapists in clinical practice might work with their clients around issues related to body image, such as creating new definitions of female beauty and practicing daily self-affirmations, this political issue is also worthy of policy reform. Policy reform may include lobbying for laws that outlaw job discrimination based on body size, joining or starting an advocacy group to end fat oppression, writing advertisers about their depictions of women's bodies in advertisements, or staging protests outside of businesses that exploit and objectify the female body.

Because there is so much work to be done on so many levels, it is important to remember the latter part of the definition of empowerment offered by Swift and Levin (1987): Empowerment is both a process and a goal. Empowering women to overcome their psychological wounding is a never-ending process. However, the ideology of both social work and feminism can guide such a process, helping women not only to survive, but also to thrive.

SUMMARY

The psychological wounding of women is a fundamental assault to consider along a continuum of violence perpetrated against women. Similar to the "problem with no name," identified by feminist author and activist Betty Friedan (1963), such wounding is often unnamed, but pervasive. Gender socialization and internalized oppression can cause many difficulties for women if not recognized and resisted. As discussed, revictimization by the mental health field can be problematic if women's psychological symptoms are taken out of context and not only psychologized, but pathologized as well. Because many social workers are working within the mental health field, it is important to be knowledgeable about identifying these psychological wounds and addressing them in a manner that is both helpful and affirming to women.

REFERENCES

American Psychiatric Association. (1987). *Diagnostic and statistical manual of mental disorders,* (3rd ed.-Revised). Washington, DC. Author.

American Psychiatric Association. (1994). *Diagnostic and statistical manual of mental disorders* (4th ed.). Washington, DC. Author.

Armstrong, L. (1978). *Kiss daddy goodnight.* A speak-out on incest. New York: Hawthorne Books.

Armstrong, L. (1994). Who stole incest? *On the Issues, 3*(4), 30–32.

Bass, E., & Davis, L. (1988). *The courage to heal.* New York: Harper & Row.

Beck, E. T. (1990). Therapy's double dilemma: Anti-Semitism and misogyny. *Women and Therapy, 10*(4), 19–30.

Beitchman, J. H., Zucker, K. J., Hood, J. E., Da-Costa, G. A., Akman, D., & Cassavia, E. (1992). A review of the long-term effects of child sexual abuse. *Child Abuse and Neglect, 16,* 101–118.

Bepko, C. (Ed). (1991). *Feminism and addiction.* New York: Haworth Press.

Blumenthal, S. J. (1994). Issues in women's mental health. *Journal of Women's Health, 3*(6), 453–458.

Boyd-Franklin, N. (1989). *Black families in therapy: A multisystems approach.* New York: Guilford Press.

Bradshaw, C. K. (1994). Asian American women: Historical and political considerations in psychotherapy. In L. Comas-Diaz & B. Greene (Eds.), *Women of color* (pp. 72–113). New York: Guilford Press.

Brown, L. S. (1987). Lesbians, weight, and eating: New analyses and perspectives. In The Boston Lesbian and Psychologies Collective (Ed.), *Lesbian psychologies* (pp. 294–309). Urbana and Chicago: University of Illinois Press.

Brown, L. S. (1994). *Subversive dialogues: Theory in feminist therapy.* New York: Basic Books.

Broverman, I. K., Broverman, D. M., Clarkson, F. E., Rosenkrantz, P. S., & Vogel, S. R. (1970). Sex-role stereotypes and clinical judgments of mental health. *Journal of Consulting and Clinical Psychology, 34,* 1–7.

Burstow, B. (1992). *Radical feminist therapy.* Newbury Park, CA: Sage Publications.

Butler, M. (1985). Guidelines for feminist therapy. In L. B. Rosewater & L. Walker (Eds.), *Handbook of feminist therapy* (pp. 32–38). New York: Springer.

Caplan, P. J. (1985). *The myth of women's masochism,* London: Methuen.

Caplan, P. J. (1995). *They say you're crazy.* Reading, MA: Addison-Wesley.

Caplan, P. J., & Hall-McCorquodale, I. (1985). Mother-blaming in major clinical journals. *American Journal of Orthopsychiatry, 55*(3), 345–353.

Chernin, K. (1981). *The obsession: Reflections on the tyranny of slenderness.* New York: Harper & Row.

Chesler, P. (1972). *Women and madness.* Garden City, NY: Doubleday.

Chrisler, J. C. (1989). Should feminist therapists do weight loss counseling? *Women and Therapy, 8*(3), 31–37.

Comas-Diaz, L., & Greene, B. (Eds.). (1994). *Women of color: Integrating ethnic and gender identities in psychotherapy.* New York: Guilford Press.

Courtois, C. A. (1988). *Healing the incest wound.* New York: W. W. Norton.

Debold, E., Wilson, M., & Malave, I. (1993). *Mother daughter revolution: From betrayal to power.* Reading, MA: Addison-Wesley.

Dufrene, P. M., & Coleman, V. D. (1992). Counseling Native Americans: Guidelines for group process. *The Journal for Specialists in Group Work, 17*(4), 229–234.

Erikson, E. H. (1950). *Childhood and society.* New York: W. W. Norton.

Espin, O. M. (1994). Feminist approaches. In L. Comas-Diaz & B. Greene (Eds.), *Women of color: Integrating ethnic and gender identities in psychotherapy* (pp. 265–286). New York: Guilford Press.

Forth-Finegan, J. L. (1991). Sugar and spice and everything nice: Gender socialization and women's addiction—A literature review. In C. Bepko (Ed.), *Feminism and addiction* (pp. 19–48). New York: Haworth Press.

Friedan, B. (1963). *The feminine mystique.* New York: Dell.

Gilligan, C. (1982). *In a different voice.* Cambridge, MA: Harvard University Press.

Gilmore, C. P. (1980). The yellow wallpaper. In A. J. Lane (Ed.), *The Charlotte Perkins Gilmore reader* (pp. 3–20). New York: Pantheon Books.

Goodrich, T. J., Rampage, C., Ellman, B., & Halstead, K. (1988). *Feminist family therapy.* New York: W. W. Norton.

Gould, L. (1972). X Stories for free children:—A fabulous child's story. *Ms., 1*(6), 74–76, 105.

Greene, B. (1994). African American women. In L. Comas-Diaz & B. Greene (Eds.), *Women of color: Integrating ethnic and gender identities in psychotherapy* (pp. 10–29). New York: Guilford Press.

Greenspan, M. (1983). *A new approach to women and therapy.* New York: McGraw-Hill.

Gutierrez, L. M., & Ortega, R. (1991) Developing methods to empower Latinos: The importance of groups. *Social Work with Groups, 14*(2), 23–43.

Harris, S. M. (1994). Racial differences in predictors of college women's body image attitudes. *Women and Health, 21*(4), 89–104.

Herman, J. (1992). *Trauma and recovery.* New York: Basic Books.

hooks, b. (1993) *Sisters of the yam: Black women and self-recovery.* Boston, MA: South End Press.

Horton, J. A. (1995). *The women's health data book.* (2nd ed.). Washington, DC: Jacobs Institute of Women's Health.

Kaminer, W. (1992). *I'm dysfunctional, you're dysfunctional.* Reading, MA: Addison-Wesley.

Kaplan, M. (1983). A woman's view of the DSM-III. *American Psychologist, 38,* 786–797.

Kitzinger, C., & Perkins, R. (1993). *Changing our minds.* New York: New York University Press.

Kohlberg, L. (1958). *The development of modes of thinking and choices in years 10 to 16.* Ph.D. dissertation, University of Chicago, Department of Psychology.

Krestan, J. A., & Bepko, C. (1991). Codependency: The social reconstruction of female experience. In J. A. Krestan & C. Bepko (Eds.), *Feminism and addiction* (pp. 49–66). New York: Haworth Press.

Landrine, H. (1989). The politics of personality disorder. *Psychology of Women Quarterly, 13,* 325–339.

Lerner, H. (1993, November/December). When bad books happen to good people. *Ms.,* 62–64.

Lerner, H. (1985). *The dance of anger.* New York: HarperCollins.

Lerner, H. (1989). *The dance of intimacy.* New York: HarperCollins.

Lerner, H. (1993). *The dance of deception.* New York: HarperCollins.

Lorde, A. (1984). *Sister outsider.* Freedom, CA: Crossing Press.

Masson, J. M. (1984). *The assault on truth: Freud's suppression of the seduction theory.* New York: Farrar, Straus, & Giroux.

McGoldrick, M. (1988). Women and the family life cycle. In B. Carter & M. McGoldrick (Eds.), *The changing family life cycle* (pp. 29–68). New York: Gardner Press.

McGoldrick, M., & Giordano, J. (1996). Overview: Ethnicity and family therapy. In Monica McGoldrick, Joe Giordano, & John Pearce (Eds.), *Ethnicity and family therapy* (pp. 1–27). New York: Guilford Press.

McGoldrick, M., Giordano, J., & Pearce, J. (Eds.). (1996). *Ethnicity and family therapy.* New York: Guilford Press.

McGrath, E., Kieta, G. P., Strickland, B., & Russo, N. F. (1990). *Women and depression: Risk factors and treatment issues.* Washington, DC: American Psychological Association.

Miedzian, M. (1991). *Boys will be boys: Breaking the link between masculinity and violence.* New York: Doubleday.

Miller, J. B. (1976). *Toward a new psychology of women.* Boston: Beacon.

Nugent, C. D. (1994). Blaming the victim: Silencing women sexually exploited by psychotherapists. *Journal of Mind and Behavior, 15*(1/2), 113–138.

Palmer, P. (1996). *Feminism & psychology, 6*(3), 457–462.

Pantony, K. L., & Caplan, P. J. (1991). Delusional dominating personality disorder. A modest proposal for identifying some consequences of rigid masculine socialization. *Canadian Psychology, 32*(2), 120–133.

Parker, S., Nichter, M., Nichter, M., Vuckovic, N., Sims, C., & Ritenbaugh, C. (1995). Body image and weight concerns among African American and white adolescent females: Differences that make a difference. *Human Organization, 54*(2), 103–114.

Pharr, S. (1988). *Homophobia: A weapon of sexism.* Little Rock, AR: Chardon Press.

Pheterson, G. (1986). Alliances between women: Overcoming internalized oppression and internalized domination. *Signs, 12*(1), 146–160.

Pipher, M. (1994). *Reviving Ophelia.* New York: Ballantine Books.

Pumariega, A. J., Gustavson, C. R., Gustavson, J. C., & Motes, P. S. (1994). Eating attitudes in African American women: The *Essence* eating disorders survey. *Eating Disorders, 2*(1), 5–16.

Russell, D. (1983). Incidence and prevalence of intrafamilial and extrafamilial sexual abuse of female children. *Child Abuse and Neglect, 7,* 133–146.

Sanford, L. T., & Donovan, M. E. (1984). *Women and self-esteem.* New York: Penguin Books.

Simon, B. L. (1994). *The empowerment tradition in American social work: A history.* New York: Columbia University Press.

Solomon, B. B. (1976). *Black empowerment: Social work in oppressed communities.* New York: Columbia University Press.

Steinem, G. (1983). *Outrageous acts and everyday rebellions.* New York: Holt, Rinehart and Winston.

Surrey, J. L. (1985). *Self-in-relation: A theory of women's development* (Work in Progress No. 13).

Wellesley, MA: Stone Center for Developmental Services and Studies.

Swift, C., & Levin, G. (1987). Empowerment: An emerging mental health technology. *Journal of Primary Prevention, 8*(1–2), 71–94.

Tavris, C. (1992). *The mismeasure of woman.* New York: Simon & Schuster.

Thompson, B. W. (1992). "A way outa no way": Eating problems among African-American, Latina, and white women. *Gender & Society, 6*(4), 546–561.

Vasquez, M. J. T. (1994). Latinas. In L. Comas-Diaz & B. Greene (Eds.), *Women of color* (pp. 114–138). New York: Guilford Press.

Walker, L. (1993). Are personality disorders gender-biased? Yes! In S. A. Kirk & S. D. Einbinder (Eds.), *Controversial issues in mental health.* New York: Allyn & Bacon.

Walters, M., Carter, B., Papp, P., & Silverstein, O. (1988). *The invisible web: Gender patterns in family relationships.* New York: Guilford Press.

Wetzel, J. W. (1994). Depression: Women-at-risk. *Social Work in Health Care, 19*(3/4), 85–108.

Wolf, N. (1991). *The beauty myth.* New York: William Morrow.

Zamora, D. (1993). *Clean slate: New and selected poems.* Willimantic, CT: Curbstone Press.

Chapter

4

GENDERED COMMUNICATION

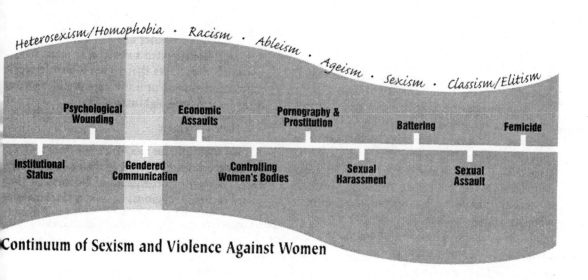

Heterosexism/Homophobia · Racism · Ableism · Ageism · Sexism · Classism/Elitism

| Psychological Wounding | Economic Assaults | Pornography & Prostitution | Battering | Femicide |

| Institutional Status | Gendered Communication | Controlling Women's Bodies | Sexual Harassment | Sexual Assault |

Continuum of Sexism and Violence Against Women

"Sexism" is the name of the sum total of all of the myths, the pain, the deprivation, the destruction that has been perpetrated upon women for centuries and continues today in all parts of the world. It steals our bodies, enslaves our minds, stills our voices. It shackles our children, our own destinies. It works by dividing us along lines of color, language, economics, religion, race, sexual preference. It tells us lies about ourselves and each other. It hides behind the discomfort of using "politically correct" language that sometimes forces us to face harsh reality. Our own voices have to be louder, stronger. We have to speak the words, name the destruction.

Jan Edwards, Women's Issues class member, 1995

*T*his chapter explores the numerous ways in which men and women are treated differently, based on gender, through verbal and nonverbal communication patterns. This type of differential treatment, so common and insidious, is often only *felt*—an emotional and subjective experience—by the victim, who may be unaware of its form but sensitive to its meaning. The study of gendered communication can lead to the identification of practices that contribute to the ongoing oppression of women in society and that negate the leadership of women in social work. To move toward social change, as social workers, we must begin to hold ourselves and others accountable for sexist practices, language, and behavior (Stout & Kelly, 1990).

This chapter addresses the following forms of gendered communication: gender-related language (e.g., modes of address), interruptions, time, space, touch, and cultural misunderstandings. The topics included in this chapter are not separate from those presented in other chapters. Again, components in the continuum are not readily differentiated, as they tend to shade into one another. For example, much of the differential treatment expressed through gendered communication, described in this chapter, may be very relevant when examining sexual harassment in the workplace. Exclusionary language, such as *chairman* and *congressman,* often reflects the reality of the absence of women in key decision-making roles and certainly contributes to women's invisibility once they have taken on those roles. Women who have been battered or sexually assaulted often tell poignant narratives of the power that hateful and negative language has had on their self-esteem and on their feelings of safety. The content of this chapter has direct relevance for social workers in many roles. Administrators need to be aware of the many forms that gendered communication takes, and clinicians need to be aware of the power dynamics that are often reflected in our language, our touch, and our use of space. This chapter examines various forms of gendered communication and then presents strategies for change.

INTRODUCTION TO THE ISSUES

The Power of Language

"Language is our means of classifying and ordering the world: our means of manipulating reality" (Spender, 1980, p. 2). Very simply, language is a means of communicating with others. It's also a powerful form of shaping reality.

As such, it warrants professional attention to examine the many forms language takes and the reality-distorting images it portrays, as well as the contribution that language makes in the reproduction of inequality and hatred. Language has been used to demean women ("dumb blonde," "girl," "jungle bunny"), to show hatred toward women ("bitch," "cunt") and to exclude women ("chairman," "mankind"). Each of these and other forms of communicating about women contribute to the many forms of sexism and violence against women (e.g., the verbal abuse directed toward a woman who is battered, the taunts that create a hostile workplace atmosphere, and the curses still heard in a rape survivor's nightmares).

Hate Language

Barnes and Ephross (1994) define *hate violence* as those crimes "directed against persons, families, groups, or organizations because of their racial, ethnic, religious, or sexual identities or their sexual orientation or condition of disability" (p. 247). In an exploratory study, they used focus groups to determine the types of hate violence people had experienced and their reactions to those experiences. Physical assault, verbal harassment (ethnic slurs, threats, and insults), and mail or telephone threats were the most common crimes reported by participants in the focus groups. Emotional reactions included anger, fear of injury, and sadness. While the violent behavior associated with hate is the form of hate crimes many people most often think about, it is important to highlight that respondents of this study cited hate speech as a key form of violence that affected them.

Kleg (1993) wrote, "Racial and ethnic epithets and offensive jokes penetrate the victim's sinew, striking deep into the heart and mind, vibrating like a thousand drums, and yet, the victim often smiles or nods as if to say, 'It's okay; it does not hurt.' But hurt it does, and even this is an understatement" (p. 179). Kleg reminds us that racial and ethnic hatreds are deeply rooted in U.S. society. We would add that prejudice and hatred toward heterosexual and lesbian women, as well as gay men, is also deeply rooted in this patriarchal society. For example, 92% of lesbian women of color and 85% of European-American lesbians have been the victim of antilesbian verbal harassment, with hateful words directed toward them, such as *dyke, man-hater, queer,* or *pervert* (Comstock, 1991). Savin-Williams (1990) found, "At Yale, Penn and Rutgers 57–73 percent of lesbian and gay youths reported verbal abuse; nearly 90 percent anticipated future victimization" (p. 13). He strongly encouraged parents and teachers not to allow youths to use name-calling such as "faggot" or "dyke"; "otherwise, we may be contributing to suicide, pregnancy, AIDS, sexually transmitted diseases, and drug and alcohol abuse among our adolescent children" (p. 14). Pharr (1988) wrote, "It is not by chance that when children approach puberty and increased sexual awareness they begin to taunt each other by calling these names: 'queer,' 'faggot,' 'pervert.' It is at puberty that the full force of society's pressure to conform to heterosexuality and prepare for marriage is brought to bear" (p. 17).

Kleg lists some of the language of hate: "Nigger, Jungle Bunny, Porch Monkey, Coon, Sambo, Pickaninny, Boy, Wop,. . . , Kike, Sheeny, Christ Killer, JAP, Spic, Beaner,. . . " (p. 178). Additionally, hate language directed toward women includes the words *bitch* and *cunt.* Anecdotal evidence from criminal lawyers and feminist activists suggests that the word *bitch* is frequently invoked before a woman is raped or killed. Some feminist activists encourage women and men to remove this word from their vocabulary for this reason, as it is similar to the word *dyke* being used toward a lesbian while she is being beaten or the word *nigger* in the same context of violence toward an African American. Words of disparagement, such as *bitch, faggot, dyke,* and *nigger* have become words of hate and violence.

MacKinnon (1993) focuses on the inequality inherent in the language (and acts) of hate, with the following vision: "In a society in which equality is a fact, not merely a word, words of racial or sexual assault and humiliation will be nonsense syllables" (p. 109).

Exclusionary ("He/man") Language

Language has been used to exclude women from participation as equals and thus keeps women as invisible outsiders. Spender (1980) wrote that "masculinity is the unmarked form: the assumption is that the world is male unless proven otherwise" (p. 20). Martyna (1980) referred to exclusionary language as "he/man" language. The language of social work has been rife with exclusionary language. A 1987 study by Else and Sanford found that only 10 of 32 social work journals consistently avoided using generic male terms. Social workers routinely say "manpower" when referring to the workforce or to personnel, "manning the hotline" when referring to those who work on or who staff a hotline, "man-in-environment" when referring to person-in-environment, and "mankind" when referring to humans (Stout & Kelly, 1990). This is one area where we believe that a follow-up study may demonstrate progress, in that the use of the generic *man* in professional publications appears to be less frequent than it was during the time period reviewed by Else and Sanford.

Arliss (1991) noted,

> Most of us tend to treat language as a system somehow separate from our lives; as long as we are aware of inconsistencies in the system, they need not cause serious problems. We ought to consider, though, the effects of the exclusion and exception rules on early language users. After all, young children are unlikely to be aware of the subtle difference between the sex-specific he and the generic he. How might they be affected by the famous utterance "One small step for man; one giant leap for mankind"? (p. 31)

Table 4.1 offers a small sampling of nonsexist language as food for thought about the

A Long Beach, California ship welder at the Port of Long Beach. One can only imagine the language she hears on a daily basis as she goes about her work. Photo © 1996 Kim Kulish.

many exclusionary words that creep into language. For more depth regarding the unlearning of sexism in language, several nonsexist dictionaries are available in most feminist and some general bookstores. (For instance, see R. Maggio, 1988, *The nonsexist word finder* [see Table 4.1] and C. Miller & K. Swift, 1980/1988, *The handbook of nonsexist writing*.)

Wood (1994) wrote of Sheldon's experiences with her daughter's use of the generic *he*: "She had noticed that her 6½-year-old daughter used male generic language to describe her stuffed toys. When she asked her daughter why she called a stuffed animal 'he,' her daughter responded that 'there's more he's than she's'". Wood suggests that when women and girls are not made visible through language (and many other sources) then men and boys become perceived as the numerically dominant group—even when they are not.

Many people have been socialized to use exclusionary language, and some have been taught that it is the natural and grammatically correct form. Spender (1980) challenged this notion by explaining the history of the use of exclusionary language. Spender documented

that it was not until 1553 that exclusionary language made its debut. A Mr. Wilson "insisted that it was more *natural* to place the man *before* the woman, as for example in male and female, husband and wife, brother and sister, son and daughter. Implicit in his insistence that males take precedence is the belief that males 'come first' in the natural order" (p. 147, italics in original). His ideas were readily accepted by his audience of upper-class, educated males. Yet it was not until 1746 that a similar discussion reemerged, with grammarian John Kirby formulating 88 grammatical rules. "Rule Number Twenty One stated that the male gender was *more comprehensive* than the female" (Spender, 1980, p. 148; italics in original). Prior to this time, the plural was most often used for the singular; for example, "Anyone can learn nonsexist language if they work hard" instead of "Anyone can learn nonsexist language if he works hard." Even after these grammatical rules were laid down, the use of "they" still dominated, so in 1850, enraged male grammarians who could not tolerate the singular use of the word *they* went to the British Parliament. In 1850, an act of Parliament set into law that *he* would now stand for both *he* and *she* (Bodine, 1975, as cited in Spender, 1980). About 150 years ago, it took an act of Parliament to declare the superiority of *man* in language.

It does not take a historian specializing in English history to know that there were no women in Parliament in 1850. The point here is that what many now perceive as natural and innocent took an act of Parliament to implement. If any social work students doubt that public policy really affects social work practice, we hope they will recall how this example worked, in that male-gendered language is dominate. In any case, exclusionary language was never natural or innocent. Wood (1994) evaluated research on the generic use of *man* and concluded, "Research demonstrates conclusively that masculine generics are perceived as referring predominantly or exclusively to men.

Table 4.1
Nonsexist Language Sampler

Word	Alternatives
Anchorman	Anchor, newscaster, announcer, commentator
Boycott	The authors found that "boycott" is, technically, a nonsexist term. Boycott is named after Charles Boycott who was a wealthy landowner, charged high rents, and was "boycotted."
Busboy	Busser, busperson, dish carrier, dining room attendant
Cowboy hat	Stetson, western-style, rodeo hat
Craftsman	Artisan, craftworker, skilled worker
Chivalrous	Courteous, considerate, protective, valiant, brave
Cover girl	Cover model
Kingdom	Country, land, realm, domain, dominion, territory
Manhandle	Mistreat, maul, batter, force, handle roughly
Manhole	Utility-hole, access hole, sewer hole
Manpower	Workforce, personnel, human resources, labor, workers
Nubile	There is no parallel term for a man. Use is **discouraged.**
Nymphomaniac	There is a parallel term—satyr. In theory, it's a nonsexist word; yet, in reality, we seldom hear the word "satyr." Use is **discouraged.**
Ombudsman	Ombuds, ombud, watchdog, referee, intermediary, monitor, guardian of the public good, regulatory agent
"Politics makes strange bedfellows"	Unless quoting Charles Dudley Warner, use politics makes strange bedmates
Welfare mother	Welfare client/recipient

Source: Maggio, R. (1988). The nonsexist word finder: A dictionary of gender-free usage. Boston: Beacon Press.

When people hear them, they think of men, not women" (p. 126).

A related concern is associated with the issue of "political correctness" (PC) over the past several years. This debate has centered on issues related to naming and the use of exclusionary language. For example, if a colleague is correcting another for saying "Chairman" instead of "Chairperson," other colleagues might chuckle. Someone might note, "Oh, no. The P.C. police are here," which effectively trivializes inclusionary language. Perhaps the words "political correctness" could be renamed "polite conversation" or "plain courtesy." To be inclusionary is to be respectful and can simply be a part of polite conversation. Using inclusion-ary language can also be a political act intended to correct the many years of women's invisibility in written and spoken words.

Negative Language

Negative language is the use of words to demean or lower the status of a person or a group of persons. For example, when adult women of any age are called "girls," their status is lowered. Lakoff (1975), an early scholar on gender differences in language, noted that past the age of adolescence, men are seldom referred to as "boys," except in situations suggesting "an air of adolescent frivolity and irresponsibility," such as in "going out with the boys" (p.25).

(It's critical to acknowledge that African-American men's experiences with the word "boy" have been much different than those of European-American men.) Women professionals, however, are often referred to as "nice girls," "smart girls," or "the Hispanic girl."

Women who successfully control human interactions are often criticized or have doubts cast on their proscribed feminine role. They are often considered "abnormal" and described as "castrating bitches," "domineering," "aggressive," and "witches." Other forms of what can be referred to as negative language are words used to address or describe women in terms associated with foods or animals: *honey, tart, cookie, chick, bunny, dear [deer], fox,* and *filly.* Cose (1993) related the experience of an African-American law professor in this passage: "After addressing the American Association of University Professors on the issue of 'discriminatory harassment on campuses,' she found herself talking to a middle-aged white man who explained that she should not take offense at being called a jungle bunny because 'you are cute and so are bunnies'" (pp. 22–23).

Arliss (1991) described this type of language as "metaphorical language" and noted, "Metaphorical expressions come and go in the form of slang names, but the general trend toward describing females as edible objects and soft, cuddly animals remains a sharp contrast to male metaphors" (p. 40), such as "lucky dog" (as compared to "bitch") or "big cheese" (as compared to "cupcake"). "Certainly, we would be mistaken if we called a man a female dog or a female horse. The metaphors *bitch* and *nag* are reserved for women with irritating behavioral tendencies" (Arliss, 1991, p. 39). Obviously, words such as *cunt* and *whore* are also negative words used to demean women.

The implications of negative language are many. In professional situations (including social work educational settings—both the field and the classroom), none of these words have a place. This does not suggest that words of endearment do not have a place in language. However, in work and academic settings, there are significant power issues operating in the environment, and calling someone a "dear" or a "fox" serves to perpetuate gender inequality.

Modes of Address

The use of modes of address to reinforce differences in perceived status is representative of insidious and subtle factors that lead to the derogation of women. One form of differential use of modes of address is the use of status indicators. Brown (1965) discussed how modes of address are used to indicate status and solidarity. Status is reflected by asymmetry of address, such as when one speaker refers to the other by title and the second speaker counters with a lower-status term in response. An example is a student referring to a school's dean by title and the dean addressing the student by her or his first name. Solidarity is seen when both people use the same familiar or polite form of address, such as two social work managers greeting each other by their first names. Miller and Swift (1980/1988) suggested, "Women are frequently referred to by their first names in circumstances where men are called by their last names" (p. 118).

The following example is a blatant example of the different use of status indicators: "When the Supreme Court handed down its decision that pension plans which pay women less then men are illegal, a wire service dispatch reported, '[Justice Thurgood] Marshall's opinion . . . was joined by Justices Brennan, White, Stevens and Mrs. O'Connor. Dissenting were Chief Justice Warren E. Burger and Justices Powell, Blackmun and Rehnquist'" (Miller & Swift, 1980/1988, pp. 120–121). Mrs. O'Connor!

Stout and Kelly (1990) found, in their exploratory study on differential treatment, that in a midwestern town, female social service managers were addressed by their first names 72% of the time. The male managers were only addressed by their first name 28% of the time. This finding was significant, as the meetings under study were hearings where managers were presenting funding proposals. Although a great deal of care from the commissioners might be expected to ensure that all managers were treated equally during this formal process, women still received unequal treatment.

Time Allocations and Interruptions

Wood (1994) addressed the issue of conversational dominance, citing numerous researchers who have found that in all conversational groupings (heterogeneous and homogeneous gender) (1) boys and men talk more frequently than girls and women do, and (2) boys and men talk for longer time periods. This finding was noted in studies as early in development as preschool (Austin, Salehi, & Leffler, 1987). Similarly, Arliss (1991) stated, "Women have been reported to talk less often and/or for shorter periods of time in laboratory groups, in jury deliberations, and in professional meetings. In each case, researchers concluded that gender did indeed influence who was willing and able to speak in mixed-sex groups" (p. 48).

Stout and Kelly (1990) stated, "Men frequently interrupt women speakers in agency staff meetings, boards of directors meetings, and social work classrooms. Interruptions undermine the verbal input of women managers during decision-making conferences and conversations. They send the message that the women's input is not valuable enough to be heard fully" (p. 62). In this study on the differential treatment of women managers, they found that women managers were interrupted an average of nine times, while men managers were interrupted only two times, on average. After reviewing the literature on interruptions, Arliss (1991) found that in male–male or female–female dyads, interruptions tend to be equally dispersed and are less frequent. Yet with male–female dyads, there are more interruptions, and men do more of the interrupting than do women. Wood (1994), drawing on the work of L. P. Stewart, said that men tend to use

interruptions as a control tactic—to challenge or get the floor, whereas women who interrupt tend to do so to show support, to affirm, or to encourage elaboration. However, after reviewing the literature on male–female interruptions, James and Clark (1993) concluded that no clear conclusions can be drawn regarding whether men are using interruptions to gain control—primarily because of the difficulty in interpreting how an interruption was intended or perceived.

Women's Conversational Style

Tannen (1990), through her popular book *You Just Don't Understand: Men and Women in Conversation*, successfully drew many people's attention to the different conversational styles of men and women. Tannen proposed the following idea for consideration: "If women speak and hear a language of connection and intimacy, while men speak and hear a language of status and independence, then communication between men and women can be like cross-cultural communication, prey to a clash of conversational styles. Instead of different dialects, it has been said they speak different genderlects" (p. 42). Table 4.2 outlines some of the variation which has been observed between men's and women's communication styles.

Tannen's work has been influential for at least two reasons: (1) She introduces to the general public the miscommunication that can occur between men and women, and (2) she does not glorify either style of communication. Many feminists appreciate Tannen's work because she did not encourage women to "talk right"—that is, "like a man." She also analyzed the manner in which men spoke and concluded that their communication style does portray caring and feeling—just differently than how many women tend to communicate. In fact, she helps many women see that many men communicate in the way they do because they care, for example, by giving directives on how to take care of the current issue at hand. Likewise, she

Table 4.2
Typical Female and Male Conversational Style Patterns

Women's Speech	Men's Speech
1. Importance of equality e.g., "I've felt that way, too."	1. Exhibit knowledge, skill, or ability e.g., "You ought to just tell him . . . "
2. Support for others e.g., "I think you've done the right thing.	2. Instrumentality e.g., Problem-solving efforts, focus on information
3. Attention to the relationship e.g., "How did you feel when that occurred?"	3. Conversational dominance e.g., Topic changing, interruptions
4. Maintenance work e.g., "Tell me about your meeting."	4. Absolute, assertive e.g., Direct, forceful, authoritative
5. Inclusivity e.g., "That's interesting."	5. Abstraction e.g., General terms—removed from personal experience
6. Personal, concrete e.g., Personal disclosures	6. Minimal response cues e.g., "yeah," umhmm"
7. Tentativeness e.g., "That was good, wasn't it?"	

Compiled from the following source: Wood, J. (1994). Gendered lives: Communication, gender, and culture. Belmont, CA: Wadsworth, Inc.

helps men learn more about what women are trying to achieve through their interactions with men and with other women; for example, "I don't need information on how to fix it. I know what I need to do. What I need is to talk about how it felt when X happened."

While Tannen (1990) received much popular acclaim for *You Just Don't Understand,* some people have criticized her work. First, although she encourages respect for male and female conversational styles, one reviewer suggested that her examples tell us something different—that the male style appears "frightened, stubborn, hostile, or socially destructive" (Burke, Burroughs-Denhart, & McClish, 1994, p. 484). The same reviewers criticize the book *You Just Don't Understand* for presenting communication as being only gender specific, ignoring class and ethnicity. Kitzinger and Perkins (1993), in their book on lesbian feminism and psychology, spoke about the safety that lesbians

often seek in groups and about the formal rules that they often develop—such as the use of "I statements." They also often use disclaimers (e.g., "this is just my opinion"). They wrote, "This approach is fraught with political danger. Women have always been expected to hedge our speech around with verbal disclaimers—not to speak strongly, to allow plenty of space for changing our minds. This is especially true for white middle-class gentile women, and Caryatic Cardea describes the imposition of this 'ladylike' speech as a form of classism" (p. 147).

Some researchers have concluded that differences in communication styles are not based solely on differences in culture or gender, but also on differences in power. For instance, Tavris (1992) asked for consideration of the following question:

What would happen to your language if you played a subordinate role in society? You would learn to persuade and influence, rather than assert and demand. You would become skilled at anticipating what others wanted or needed (hence "women's intuition"). You would learn how to placate the powerful and soothe ruffled feelings. You would cultivate communication, cooperation, attention to news and feeling about others (what men call gossip). In short, you would learn a "woman's language." But the characteristics of such a language develop primarily from a power imbalance, not from inherent deficiency or superiority in communication skills, emotion, or nurturance. They develop whenever there is a status inequity, as can be seen in the languages of working-class Cockneys conversing with employers, blacks conversing with whites, or prisoners conversing with guards. (p. 298)

It is important to note that the gender-specific differences are not reflected in all men or all women. Many women have learned to conform to the environment. In order to succeed in a patriarchal society, many women have eliminated the "tag questions" (e.g., ya know?) from their sentence structures, have removed personal disclosures from their professional communications, and have taken every assertiveness course offered in their local community. Likewise, many men consider the process aspects of communication and have removed authoritative tones and styles from their professional repertoire. We encourage social workers to become respectful of and to have the ability to read and speak both "genderlects." The development of cross-gender translation skills may become critical for successful social work practice with individuals, couples, families, groups, and supervisees, and for community and political practice.

Cultural Differences in Language Styles

Hurtado (1989) suggested that white women are socialized to be "parlor conversationalists" (p. 848) and that "working-class women of Color come from cultures whose languages have been barred from public discourse, as well as from the written discourse, of society at large" (p. 848). In addition, Henley and Kra-

marae (1991) cautioned that women of color may experience "a lot of interracial 'miscommunication' in talks with both white women and white men" (p. 37) and may experience less sexist male–female miscommunication. Blank and Slipp (1994), in their book *Voices of Diversity*, described many forms of interracial communication. For example, an African-American manager noted, "We're not afraid of verbal conflict. We like to debate openly and to challenge ideas. But if we have an animated argument on an issue, we are seen as hostile or aggressive or as having an 'attitude.' It's as if everyone is comfortable with us only when we are passive. This is a problem, especially for young black workers" (p. 24). Similarly, a Chinese-American worker noted, "We're often blamed for being indecisive. We can make decisions, but we may go about it differently. Usually Asian-Americans will try to reach consensus first, before simply making a decision. We will try to do it without seeming to make the other party lose" (p. 40). As these examples illustrate, gender is not the only variable for consideration when examining communication styles that will emerge in social work practice with women.

In 1973, Haskins and Butts noted, "educators and linguists must first recognize that black English is in fact a language by itself, departing systematically from standard English. Then, these educators and linguists must change the traditional language program from one that treats black English as a deviation to one that concentrates upon teaching standard English as a second language" (p. 53). In their 1993 revision, these same authors observed that African-American English includes Southern (U.S.), Creole, West Indian, and Northern (U.S.) dialects and that many African-Americans oscillate between standard English and African-American English (sometimes called "Ebonics"). They term this code switching "diglossia" (p. 75) and define it as "the use by a society of two different languages, dialects, or language variants to convey two different values or attitudes" (p. 75). Smitherman (1977) passionately noted,

> The speech of blacks, the poor, and other power-less groups is used as a weapon to deny them access to full participation in the society. Teachers harp on the "bad" English of their students; potential employees are denied jobs because they don't talk "right"; future college graduates become force-outs because they write in "nonstandard" English. Yet what is "nonstandard" English is simply the language of "nonstandard" people. Their linguistic usage deviates from the collective dialect of the dominant culture—nothing more, as simple and yet as complex as that. (p. 199)

The use of Ebonics emerged as a controversial issue at the end of 1996, when the Oakland School Board announced its recognition of Ebonics and that it would seek federal dollars for teacher training to increase understanding of the use of Ebonics. Op-ed columnists and government officials began announcing that Ebonics was just bad English and that kids should not be rewarded for speaking that way. We hope that in-depth discussions and debates will occur around this topic, with increased recognition and respect of this linguistic style of speech as an outcome.

Many social work clients and professionals may be using standard English as a second language, by choice or through coercion. Verbal and written communication styles may then reflect differences. Persons from the Deaf community may communicate using American Sign Language, such that a professional interpreter may be required. When language differences and preferences are perceived or judged as deficiencies or as signs of lesser intelligence, inequality is perpetuated.

Nonverbal Communication

Henley (1977) was a pioneer in exposing power issues related to "body politics" (which happens to be the title of her book). She wrote,

> The "trivia" of everyday life—touching others, moving closer or farther away, dropping the eyes, smiling, interrupting—are commonly interpreted as facilitating social intercourse, but not recognized in their position as micropolitical gestures, defenders of the status quo—of the state, of the wealthy, of authority, of all those whose power may be challenged. Nevertheless these minutiae find their place on a continuum of social control which extends from internalized socialization at one end to sheer physical force at the other." (p. 3)

Nonverbal communication can be as powerful a force as verbal communication. The study of proxemics and touch are two more variables for consideration in an examination of gendered communication.

Proxemics

Proxemics is the term used to refer to space and the use of space (Hall, 1968). Wood (1994) reinforced the idea that studying space can reveal the power and status afforded to groups in society. "Space is a primary means by which a culture designates who is important, who has privilege" (p. 160). Wood (1994) and Arliss (1992) have encouraged the use of informal studies to check out how space is used to designate prestige and power. Some of the examples they have used include the following: Who has more space—the secretary or the executive; who in your family has her or his own room, which others do not freely enter; who sits at the head of your dinner table or of the conference-room table at work; what areas in the city have the largest yards or the largest houses?

Proxemics also encourages the examination of the personal space afforded to persons in professional (and personal) situations. Interactional distance tends to reflect gender and power differences. Three feet tends to be the amount of space that seems most comfortable for European Americans (Arliss, 1992, p. 106)—with early studies indicating that people from Latin American countries are comfortable with less social distance (Hall, 1968). Arliss (1991) summarized the research on gender differences related to proxemics: "The fact that women are awarded less space than men, across a variety of situations and relationship types, suggest that a women may be assumed to occupy a position of lesser status" (p. 109).

Touch

Communication scholars refer to communication by touch as *haptics* (Arliss, 1991). Henley (1977, p. 100) wrote of the variations in the use of touch in the United States: "Within a country like the United States, with numerous ethnic minorities, we expect and find also cultural variation: persons of Jewish and Italian descent, or from Spanish-speaking backgrounds such as Puerto Rican and Chicano, are believed to use more tactual expression than those of the dominant Anglo-Saxon-derived culture."

Although the expected cultural variations are supported by evidence, gender-based expectations are not. Henley (1977) challenged the mythology that women are "the touchers," as evidence appears to be to the contrary. Henley wrote, "In this male-dominated society, touching is one more tool used to keep women in their place, another reminder that women's bodies are free property for everyone's use.... One is appalled to consider that something so human, so natural, as touching should be perverted into a symbol of status and power. But a moment's thought reminds us that this is the story of other simple facts of our being, unrelated to status: clothing, shelter, and food have all been turned into status symbols in the competitive struggle" (p. 123). Similarly, Arliss (1991) found that research evidence contradicts the myth that women are the touchers in our society. Wood (1994) suggested that men's socialization to use touch to assert power often leads to actual or perceived sexual harassment. She concluded that women and men need to be attuned to gender patterns of touch, to be cau-

tious, and to "resist those that contribute to sexual harassment" (p. 162). Such behaviors might include putting a hand on a woman's back or elbow to guide her, squeezing her arm, or patting her hand. On a related note, Spain (1992) found that bosses often touch secretaries, whereas secretaries rarely touch bosses.

While much of this chapter has focused on male–female interactions, homophobia also influences communication patterns. Henley and Kramarae (1991) noted that lesbians and gay men have reported that when they touch as an expression of warmth, some straight people misunderstand the touch as a sexual advance. They suggested, "Here, too is the potential for miscommunication based on cultural difference and dominance—that between homosexual and heterosexual cultures" (pp. 38–39). The research on communication and miscommunication between homosexual persons and heterosexual persons is limited and warrants future social work research.

Bringing Differential Treatment into the Classroom

Wood (1994) listed the major findings of a 1982 study by Hall and Sandler, which demonstrate that female and male students are getting different educational experiences. Please note that Wood examined more contemporary literature and concluded that these biases have persisted over time, although the original research was conducted in 1982. Some of the major findings of Hall and Sandler are as follows (Wood, 1994, p. 218):

- *Professors are more likely to know the names of male students than female ones.*
- *Professors maintain more eye contact and more attentive postures when talking to male students than when addressing female students.*
- *Professors ask more challenging questions of male students....*
- *Faculty [members] call on male students more often [than female students].*

- *Female students' contributions are interrupted, ignored, or dismissed more often than those of males.*

Authors' Perspective

We encourage you to compare these findings with your own experiences because some blatant examples of discriminatory practices may be occurring within social work educational environments. African-American, Hispanic, Asian-American, Deaf, gay men and lesbian women have made points illustrating this discussion. Some minority students report that the *only* times when the professor or the students seek their input are when issues of race, ethnicity, disability, or sexual orientation are raised. Many talented minority students have been negatively affected by these overt discriminatory practices. The students we have talked to have also made it clear that the topic is usually about a negative perception of the community they belong to—that is, they aren't asked to talk about the strengths or joys of being part of a particular community or about their own professional interests; they are only being called on as experts on drug abuse, poverty, AIDS, colonias, or gang violence.

The cartoon by Garry Trudeau on the opposite page calls attention to gendered communication in the classroom, as astutely observed by an adolescent girl.

Strategies for Change

*To some, individual practices expressing differential treatment may seem insignificant, considering the vast array of serious problems facing those who are concerned with social justice. . . . The most pressing social justice issue for ac-*tivists may not be to eliminate the word "mankind" or "manning the hot line" from the spoken language. Should we activists choose to participate in a boycott or other form of social action, our first target may not be employers who refuse to shake hands with their women counterparts. However, we must make a strong commitment to examine the cumulative results of the trivialization and exclusion of women through deference behavior, language, and overt power plays through interruptions. It is time to begin holding individuals and organizations accountable for sexist practices. (Stout & Kelly, 1990, pp. 70–71)*

Gendered communication can and does emerge at all levels of social work practice. Exclusionary and negative language, interruptions, and differing allocations of time and space, as well as interracial and gender miscommunications occur in couples and family therapy sessions, group counseling, administrative practice, research development and reports, and community organization and efforts toward activism. Therefore, it is recommended that all social work students and practitioners evaluate their own practices and those of the agencies and groups with whom they are affiliated, with the aim of transforming social work practice.

This type of work has begun. For example, Goodrich, Rampage, Ellman, and Halstead (1988) provided some ideas for reforming the practice of family therapy. They suggested, "However you choose to contribute, make sure that if you were ever accused of being a feminist family therapist, there would be enough evidence to convict you" (p. 181). Some of their suggestions include the following:

- "Since language shapes reality, listen to yourself and your colleagues with a special ear. Usual forms of speech support a sexist outlook, for example, "I'm seeing a man and his wife at 3:30." Suggest alternative phrasing. When the response is "Oh, it doesn't make any difference," note that the impatient reply contradicts itself" (p. 181).

Doonesbury

BY GARRY TRUDEAU

Gender equity remains a critical issue to be encouraged at all levels in the educational process.

- "Monitor family therapy journals for sexist language, sexist assumptions, omission of the feminist perspective, silence on gender issues relevant to the discussion. Write the journal and the authors about your observations" (p. 182).
- "The next time a colleague, student, or client uses the term "girl" to describe a female apparently over the age of sixteen, respond by asking the exact age of the girl in question" (p. 183).

Language can be changed. It is not easy to do so, but it is necessary. Interruptions in social work classrooms and agencies can be stopped. It takes perseverance and risk taking, but it's vital to do so. The next section of this chapter offers suggestions in the areas of personal transformation and group behavior to address differential treatment that occurs in language and nonverbal communications.

PERSONAL TRANSFORMATION

It seems necessary to begin changing behaviors that may be using privilege or that have let the subtleties of differential treatment go unchallenged. The following are some guidelines for change.

Learn to Listen

Three Rivers (1990/1991) offered this analysis:

> People of color and Jewish people have been so all their lives. Further, if we have been raised in a place where white gentiles predominate, then we have been subjected to racism/anti-Semitism all of our lives. We are therefore experts on our own lives and conditions. If you do not understand or believe or agree with what someone is saying about their own oppression, do not automatically assume that they are wrong or paranoid or over-sensitive. (p. 22)

A basic skill in social work practice is listening. Haynes and Holmes (1994) noted, "In order to establish rapport and engage with the client, the social worker needs to develop finely tuned *listening skills*" (p. 275; italics in original). Unfortunately, this very basic skill and practice often goes by the wayside in situations where people are expressing grievances or anger. Baker-Miller (1991) wrote that subordinates often feel anger in response to the way they are treated, yet that anger is not readily accepted by dominant groups. Further, she noted, "It is usually made to appear that subordinates have no *cause* for anger; if they feeling anything like it, there is something *wrong with them.*

They are uncivilized natives, dumb workers, sinful or unloved women,—or in modern parlance, 'sick,' maladjusted, and the like." (p. 184; italics in original).

Authors' Perspective

To illustrate this point, we present a personal experience observed by one of us: Karen Stout. A couple of years ago, I was conducting an 8-hour workshop on the continuum of sexism and violence against women. The women in the group who were vocally and visibly angry about sexism in their environment were continually dismissed by their classmates, both female and male. These women soon became silent and remained so until the end of the workshop. At the end of the workshop, the women asked for the floor and began to present data on the differential treatment that occurred during this workshop: Men interrupted women X number of times, men changed topics X number of times, and the numerical minority of men spoke longer and more often than did the majority of women. Even with this compelling data, these women continued to be dismissed as hysterical, and the topic was changed to challenging the accuracy of their data. It appeared that the people in the workshop group, all graduate social work students, felt extremely uncomfortable hearing anger from women. Because of this discomfort, the information presented was dismissed and negated. Being dismissed and negated, as you recall, was the source of the women's anger. Therefore, a vicious cycle occurred, which served to protect the status quo. If the women who were angry had been listened to and afforded respect, they may have felt validated and supported. Ironically, some of the very dynamics Baker-Miller (1991) described were occurring in the sexism workshop with social work graduate students.

Become Sensitive to the Issues

Wicker (1986), outlined a series of steps for social workers to engage in to confront racism:

- *Form nonhierarchical peer-supervision groups at work, to discuss basic definitions of racism and prejudice; then use a variety of therapeutic techniques, such as role playing, psychodrama, and gestalt tactics, to help one another look at prejudice and racism in clinical work with people of color.*
- *Read literature and nonfiction written by people of color; this step is vital to educating yourself about people who are different and who live in different cultures.*
- *Attend multicultural events. Learn about ethnocentrism and how it alienates the group in power by presuming that only one culture— the dominant culture—exists. Support multicultural events in your community. Feel what it is like to be in the minority. What does this experience teach you about racism?*
- *Attend workshops on "unlearning racism."* (pp. 37–38)

Similar steps can be undertaken in order to combat sexism and heterosexism, as well. Therefore, all helping professionals are encouraged to examine their sexism, heterosexism, and racism and to take steps to become antiracist, antiheterosexist, and antisexist. Recognizing that each person approaches these issues from different racial, class, gender, and cultural backgrounds, some of these actions may be more applicable to some individuals than to others. For example, the first suggestion is to form peer-supervision groups to discuss racism and prejudice. People of color may have had lifelong, daily training with racism and prejudice yet may come from a middle-class background. Therefore, those persons may choose to initiate a peer-supervision group to discuss class and classism issues or to examine heterosexism and homophobia.

Students can make a good start toward reaching these goals of combating sexism, racism, classism, and heterosexism while enrolled in a social work education program.

However, given the strength of the institutional and cultural environment, social workers must really engage in a lifelong struggle against discrimination, such as differential treatment. Some immediate actions to be taken include the following: (1) Buy a nonsexist word-finder dictionary; (2) become a frequent visitor or participant at your university's various cultural centers (African American, Hispanic, Asian American, and Native American, as well as women); (3) read books by African-American, feminist author bell hooks often and thoroughly; (4) ask to have your field placement supervised by someone different than yourself (i.e., feminist supervision for nonfeminists, lesbian supervisor for heterosexual, women of color supervisor for European-Americans—obviously, these are not mutually exclusive or exhaustive categories); (4) enroll in a course on Latina/Latino culture or literary works; (5) become bilingual by learning Spanish, Vietnamese, or Chinese or by becoming an American Sign Language interpreter; (6) interrupt discrimination each time you see or hear it for one 24-hour day, to really grasp the enormity of the problem; (7) address the local school board on the need for true multicultural curriculum development, which includes information on gay and lesbian persons; (8) organize a women's caucus within a social work program; (9) rent *A Handmaid's Tale* from a local video store; and (10) buy a set of nonsexist, nonracist children's books for an agency's waiting room or for your own children's enjoyment. Perhaps a final recommendation could be to learn about and to enjoy women who have made a difference in our world. The song "Rosa" by Libby Roderick speaks to the contributions of a number of notable African-American women.

Rosa

Dedicated to Rosa Parks, the "mother of the civil rights movement," this song is a tribute to African-American women who have inspired me. In 1993, Audre Lorde, one of the world's most honest and courageous voices, succumbed to cancer. You can't kill the spirit.

Rosa call to me, she say,
Don't you take the back of no bus,
Every woman here deserve respect
Ain't nothing too good for us, sweet women,
nothing too good for us.

Nikki Giovanni she tell it like it is,
She say oooooooh, when you're Black like me you
are queen of the world
Ain't nothing too rich for you, sweet women,
nothing too rich for you.

Shirley, she pound her fist, she say no other
voices will do
Women of color got to speak for themselves
Ain't nobody smarter than you, sweet women, no-
body smarter than you.

Rosa . . .

Fannie, Fannie Lou Hamer, say people deserve
enough food
And everybody got the right to vote
Ain't nobody better than you, sweet women, no-
body better than you.

Audre Lorde, surviving cancer, speaking so clear
and so true
She say with women's love and your own bold
vision
Ain't nothing too scary for you, sweet women,
nothing too scary for you.

Rosa . . .

Winnie Mandela, her fist held high, she say my
people are going to be free
Racism trying to make me die but
Ain't nothing too big for me, sweet women,
nothing too big for me.

Alice, Alice Walker, writing us all back home
She say go in search of your mother's garden
And find yourself your own, sweet women, find
yourself your own.

Rosa . . .

Women, if we're gonna be free, it's got to be all
of us or none
While racism lives we all stay in chains
Ain't none of us make it alone, sweet women,
none of us make it alone.

Rosa . . .

Respect Language and the Culture It Represents

Lum (1992) has encouraged social workers to decrease communication barriers when working with people of color. Lum suggested six ways to decrease barriers to communication across cultures: (1) Decrease the language barrier, (2) decrease the nonverbal communication barrier, (3) decrease the preconceptions and stereotypes barrier, (4) decrease the evaluation barrier, (5) decrease the stress barrier, and (6) decrease the organizational constraints barrier. Suggestions for decreasing these barriers include the following: Learn the language; understand your nonverbal behavior, as well as the meanings behind your clients' nonverbal behaviors; get to know both the culture and particular individuals from the culture; and find out about communication channels in your organization (Lum, 1992).

Arroyo and Lopez (1984) wrote of the importance of the Spanish language to Chicanos. They noted, "it must be kept in mind that language reflects an individual's philosophy of life, value system, and (most important) aspects of the personality that one may find difficult to understand or even may not notice without knowledge of the language" (p. 68). Haskins and Butts (1973/1993) reported a finding by Marcos that Spanish-speaking patients "were found to have more pathology when evaluated and interviewed in English as contrasted with the level of pathology when interviewed in Spanish" (p. 79). Reports such as these are reminders of the importance of having bilingual and bicultural social workers and bilingual students in schools of social work.

In an interesting study, Guy (1979) wanted to test a hypothesis about how a patient's use of language may affect a therapist's evaluation of psychopathology in a patient. Guy had a tape made with an actor speaking standard English and a tape made with the same actor using African-American English ("Ebonics"). The findings indicated that African-American therapists thought more highly of the patient (actor) when using Ebonics, whereas the European-American therapists demonstrated a negative bias toward the patient when Ebonics was used. Logan, Freeman, and McRoy (1990) encouraged social workers to include language as a factor when assessing a person's racial identity. They noted that the use of Ebonics may indicate either a traditional or a culturally immersed identity.

Change Language

The American Psychological Association (1994) has set forth three guidelines regarding unbiased language: The first guideline encourages professional writers to be specific. Specificity can allow a fuller description of a client's thoughts, feelings, or behaviors without relying on stereotypical assertions, such as "dependent," "typical female," or "hysterical." The second guideline suggests sensitivity to labels. Nouns used to describe groups tend to change over time, and professional writers need to be respectful of these changes. In addition, this second guideline calls for parallel terms, such as husbands and wives (instead of men and wives), women and men (instead of girls and men or ladies and men). Third, the APA suggests acknowledging participation—that is, referring to survey or research "participants" rather than to "subjects."

The APA (1994) also has suggested eliminating exclusionary (i.e., he/man) language and specifying the sex of a participant only if apropos or required. This sex-specificity guideline is set forth to discourage use of such terms as "lady doctor" or "male nurse." This type of language makes the sex of a person stand out and implies that such person in that position is an exception or an anomaly. Some commonly used verbs also imply gender specificity. For example, a social worker might write, "This child appears to need more mothering." It would be more specific and gender neutral to spell out the particular needs of the child, such as the child needs more active parenting, nurturing, self-esteem building, supervising, or other verbs that would describe what a child may actually need.

The use of inclusive language requires trial and error, as well as vigilance. So very many words and phrases are exclusionary or have developed as pejorative terms. What might be an alternative to cowboy boots? (Western boots.) What about "gentleman's agreement," busboy or busgirl, second baseman, or ombudsman? Again, it is necessary to become more inclusive, yet it takes a great deal of unlearning and sometimes a lot of creativity. What will I tell my daughter the "snowman" is? ("Snow sculpture" might work.)

Authors' Perspective

It helps to have a good support system while trying to change language. Perhaps the members of a social work class could become a laboratory for helping each other if all class members agreed to point out noninclusive language with good humor and were willing to support each other with change. Despite all of the foregoing data and much effort, we have been somewhat frustrated to find that some people insist that (1) language is harmless, and (2) people cannot change what they were socialized to do or say. Speaking personally for a moment, it is our experience that words do hurt and that language can be changed—despite gender socialization or cultural expectations. We know that we have changed our own use of language. We also know that we must keep working on these changes. Most people trying to change their language must work on this transition every single day. Because we have experienced challenges to our change

efforts, we think you may need support, as many people will think you have gone over the feminist edge as you are becoming attuned to your own, and other people's language. Often, this attunement leads parents, friends, lovers, partners, children, and your professors to think you are going too far in your attempt to avoid sexism. When you bring up issues of battering or rape, you may be seen to be aware or to have an agenda, whereas when you bring up issues of gendered communication, you may be perceived as becoming humorless, relentless, demanding, or radical. For this reason, we suggest either using the classroom as a laboratory or searching for a few key people whom you can count on as you begin changing communication styles. We want you to be validated and supported *more than* accused or ridiculed.

In addition, achieving social justice takes time. Your assertion of your rights does not mean that you will be certain to obtain those rights instantaneously; similarly, your assertions in pursuit of gender justice in everyday and professional situations does not mean that you will be sure to receive just or respectful treatment at that instant. For many of us, however, the struggle or the process becomes part of our everyday transformational work. If you accept the definition of *radical* as meaning "root," then we suggest that the changing of gendered communication is radical work at its best.

GROUP BEHAVIOR

Proper monitoring is critical to developing equity in groups. As social workers begin their group practice, the group may profit from being audio- or videotaped. This practice is necessary to carefully evaluate gender equity. It can be informative to monitor the time spent speaking, by gender, in the group. In addition, someone can count and analyze the interruptions. If women or men are interrupting to gain control or as a support measure, this observation can be pointed out to the group. Are some members or groups taking up more space than others? Are titles of address congruent and respectful for all? Are girls and boys, women and men called on with the same frequency, or is one group getting more attention? The American Association of University Women (1991/1994) has pointed out that "in dozens of separate studies, researchers have found that girls receive less attention, less praise, less effective feedback, and less detailed instructions from teachers than do boys" (p. 14). Are social workers also showing this type of inequity in their interactions in groups with girls and boys (or women and men)? Taping (video or audio) can give feedback on this issue. We realize that it is hard enough to feel comfortable when facilitating support, task, community, or therapy groups without *also* having to worry about whether you are being sexist. Yet the effort *will* enhance your effectiveness, as well as communicate respect to *all* of your clients or constituents.

A second broad area for enhancing equity in groups is the recognition of the many task and morale functions that contribute to a successful group. Kokopeli and Lakey (undated) described group task and morale functions and suggested that "understanding these functions can make the difference between a group that flounders and a group that moves" (p. 15). Table 4.3 lists these functions.

A review of Table 4.3 reveals that a stereotypical men's style is reflected in the task functions. As noted earlier in this chapter, "genderlects" are often spoken, and men are more likely to operate in a take-charge mode. The stereotypical women's style is reflected in the morale functions—supporting, nurturing, caring, and helping people to feel comfortable in the group. Kokopeli and Lakey (undated) wrote, "Shared leadership in a feminist vision, then, values the

Table 4.3
Group Task and Morale Functions

Task Functions	Morale Functions
Information and opinion giving	Encouraging participation
Information and opinion seeking	Harmonizing and compromising
Starting initiating	Relieving tension
Direction giving	Helping communication
Summarizing	Evaluating emotional climate
Coordinating	Process observation
Diagnosing	Setting standards
Energizing	Active listening
Reality testing	Building trust
Evaluating	Solving interpersonal problems

Compiled from Kokopeli, B., & Lakey, G. (undated). Leadership for change. Santa Cruz, CA: New Society Publishers.

morale functions highly and sees that the power of the group in the long run is as dependent on the nurturance of its members as on its efficiency in particular tasks" (p. 20).

In addition to placing equal value on task and morale group functions and modeling both kinds of functions, Kokopeli and Lakey (undated, p. 28) also suggested that a period of "silence after proposals are made and before brainstorming begins helps women find more space for speaking up. In Sweden, neighborhood and community groups sometimes use small buzz groups to increase participation and to reduce dependency on the "most articulate" members of the group. Furthermore, a group process observer can be selected and can report on issues related to differential treatment based on gender (e.g., interruptions, time, space, language, and touch) (Kokopeli & Lakey, undated). Finally, caucuses "can help empower people who have been controlled by traditional leaders. Women's and Third World caucuses are well-known; working class, gay and/or lesbian, young people's, and elders' caucuses are also needed in many organizations. By gathering together and comparing notes on what is keeping them quiet in meetings, they can support each other to throw off the old effects of intimidation" (Kokopeli & Lakey, undated, p. 29).

The valuing of both product and process as key variables is necessary to achieve equity in group settings. Tolman, Mowry, Jones, and Brekke (1986), addressing men in social work, pointed out, "Men's groups, however sincere their intentions to end sexism, need to attend consciously to the extent to which competition and hierarchy, rather than cooperation and consensus, characterize their operations. . . . it is all too easy for men to fall into traditional patterns of relating even when they are gathered to work against those patterns and to free themselves from sex-role restrictions" (p. 72). Van Den Bergh and Cooper (1986) find that a focus on process is an enabling and facilitative force. A focus on the group process means that all participants are encouraged to speak and to have an opportunity to place items on the agenda, time is taken to address personal concerns of group members; and feedback and critique loops are built into the process (Van Den Bergh & Cooper, 1986).

POLICY FOR CHANGE

In 1885, the American Association of University Women (AAUW) undertook its first national study to dispel the myth that higher education was harmful to women's health. More than 100 years later, the organization conducted another national study to counter yet another myth—that girls and boys receive an equal education (AAUW, 1992). As a result of this study, the AAUW made a series of recommendations for educational institutions. Next, we present a few of the AAUW recommendations, adapted to be more congruent with social work education and practice.

One important recommendation of the AAUW was to ensure that certification or licensure regulations require coursework on gender issues. Further, it recommended checking for the inclusion of gender-fair and multicultural practice knowledge on licensing tests. There are a number of ways to adapt testing and other licensure requirements for use by social work professionals. For one thing, many schools require a comprehensive examination prior to graduation, these comprehensive exams could be modified to include cases studies that would address gender and multicultural issues. Additionally, licensure requirements could require students to take courses, in-service training, Continuing Education Units, or other comparable training in gender and multicultural issues.

Another area stressed by the AAUW is using work evaluations to assess the degree to which social workers practice in an equitable manner in terms of gender and multicultural values. This practice could be adopted as policy in all types of social work agencies and within academic settings. The University of Houston Graduate School of Social Work now includes as part of its merit-evaluation procedures the information compiled from students' evaluations as to how well individual professors address issues related to socioeconomic class, women, minorities of color, and gay and lesbian persons in the courses they teach. This type of policy can serve to hold a person accountable for "walking the walk" instead of just "talking the talk."

While CSWE requires that all courses include content on women, the organization does not specify what should be taught. The AAUW suggests that issues of power, gender politics, and violence against women are important for educators to address. The AAUW stated, "Better-informed girls [and women] are better equipped to make decisions about their futures. Girls and young women who have a strong sense of themselves are better able to confront violence and abuse in their lives" (AAUW, 1992, p. 85).

Finally, we would propose that social work educational programs consider counting as practice electives various courses on Latino-, African-American, Asian-American cultures or history, as well as similar courses that address gay and lesbian issues. Such courses could help provide the historical and political context so many students often lack regarding issues related to multicultural practice. It might also be useful to engage in dialogue that considers as a practice elective a course on the Spanish language or American Sign Language.

SUMMARY

Gendered communication is an insidious form of sexism and has been used to demean and dismiss women. Power is often reflected in many ways—from the language used, to the offer of an embrace, to the size of a person's office. Becoming aware of the many forms and meanings of communication so often associated with differential treatment can be a source of empowerment. For a woman to be able to name the sexism that once was just a sense that somehow she was not being treated fairly can help to alter women's—and men's—behavior in the group room, the boardroom, and the classroom. Becoming

sensitive to power assertions through gendered communication can be a step toward treating all members of our world fairly and with sensitivity.

Wood (1994) suggested that the United States has always been a rich country through its diversity, yet the language and dominant identity has been misrepresented as homogeneous or as a melting pot. She has encouraged people to explore how to create a new dominant reality—one that celebrates and incorporates all its citizens. A call to action by Wood seems a fitting way to end this chapter:

> *The Reverend Jesse Jackson offered the compelling metaphor of our nation as a family quilt made up of patches having various colors and designs. Another metaphor is that of a collage in which distinct patterns stand out in their individual integrity, while simultaneously contributing to the character and complexity of the whole. If your generation is able to affirm diversity in women and men, as well as in race, class, ethnicity, and affectional preference, then you will have inaugurated a bold new theme in the cultural conversation—one that has the potential to make our society richer and more equitable for all. That is a responsibility and an opportunity that belongs to each of you. (p. 309)*

REFERENCES

American Association of University Women. (1991/1994). Shortchanging girls, shortchanging America. Washington, DC: AAUW.

American Association of University Women. (1992). *How schools shortchange girls.* (Available from the American Association of University Women, AAUW Sales Office, P.O. Box 251, Annapolis Junction, MD 20701-0251.)

American Psychological Association. (1994). *Publication Manual of the American Psychological Association.* Washington, DC: American Psychological Association.

Arliss, L. P. (1991). *Gender communication.* Englewood Cliffs, NJ: Prentice-Hall.

Arroyo, R. & Lopez, S. (1984). Being responsive to the Chicano community. A model for service delivery. In B. while (Ed.), *Colorina White Society.* Silver Springs, MD: NASU Press.

Baker-Miller, J. (1991). The construction of anger in women and men. In J. Jordan, A. Kaplan, J. Baker-Miller, I. Stiver, & J. Surrey (Eds.), *Women's growth in connection: Writings from the Stone Center* (pp. 197–205). New York: Guilford Press.

Barnes, A., & Ephross, P. (1994). The impact of hate violence on victims: Emotional and behavioral responses to attacks. *Social Work, 39, 247–251.*

Blank, R., & Slipp, S. (1994). *Voices of diversity.* New York: American Management Association.

Brown, R. (1965). *Social psychology.* New York: Free Press.

Burke, R., Burroughs-Denhart, N., & McClish, G. (1994). Androgyny & identity in gender communication. *Quarterly Journal of Speech, 80, 482–517.*

Comstock, G. (1991). *Violence against lesbians and gay men.* New York: Columbia University Press.

Cose, E. (1993). *The rage of a privileged class.* New York: HarperCollins.

Else, J. F., & Sanford, M. J. (1987). Nonsexist language in social work journals: Not a trivial pursuit. *Social Work, 32, 52–59.*

Goodrich, T., Rampage, C., Ellman, B., & Halstead, K. (1988). *Feminist family therapy.* New York: W.W. Norton.

Guy, D. (1979). Dialect differences between therapist and patient: It's influence on the clinical evaluations of the therapist. *Dissertation Abstracts International, 39, 2985 B* (University microfilms No. 78-22.048.

Hall, E. T. (1968). Proxemics. *Current Anthropology, 9, 83–108.*

Haskins, J., & Butts, H. (1973/1993). *The psychology of black language.* New York: Hippocrene Books.

Haynes, K., & Holmes, K. (1994). *Invitation to social work.* New York: Longman.

Henley, N. (1977). *Body politics: Power, sex, and nonverbal communication.* New York: Simon & Schuster.

Henley, N., & Kramarae, C. (1991). Gender, power, and miscommunication. In N. Coupland, H. Giles, & J. Wiemann, *"Miscommunication" and problematic talk* (pp. 18–43). Newbury Park, CA: Sage Publications.

Hurtado, A. (1989). Relating to privilege: Seduction and rejection in the subordination of white women and women of color. *Signs: Journal of Women in Culture and Society, 14, 833–855.*

James, D., & Clarke, S. (1993). Women, men and interruptions: A critical review. In D. Tannen (Ed.), *Gender and conversational interaction* (pp. 231–280). New York: Oxford University Press.

Kitzinger, C., & Perkins, R. (1993). *Changing our minds: Lesbian feminism and psychology.* New York: New York University Press.

Kleg, M. (1993). *Hate prejudice and racism.* Albany, NY: State University of New York Press.

Kokopeli, B., & Lakey, G. (undated). *Leadership for change.* Santa Cruz, CA: New Society Publishers.

Lakoff, R. (1975). *Language and woman's place.* New York: Harper & Row Publishers.

Logan, S., Freeman, E., & McRoy, R. (1990). *Social work practice with black families.* New York: Longman.

Lum, D. (1992). *Social work practice and people of color: A process-stage approach.* Pacific Grove, CA: Brooks/Cole Publishing Company.

MacKinnon, C. (1993). *Only words.* Cambridge, MA: Harvard University Press.

Maggio, R. (1988). *The nonsexist word finder: A dictionary of gender-free usage.* Boston: Beacon Press.

Martyna, S. (1980). The psychology of the generic masculine. In S. McConnell-Ginet, R. Burker, N. Furman (Eds.), *Women and Language in Literature and Society* (pp. 69–77). New York: Praeger.

Miller, C., & Swift, K. (1980/1988). *The handbook of nonsexist writing* (2nd ed.). New York: Harper & Row Publishers.

Pharr, S. (1988). *Homophobia: A weapon of sexism.* Little Rock, AR: Chardon Press.

Savin-Williams, R. (1990, Winter). Reactions of gay and lesbian youth to verbal and physical harassment. *Human Ecology Forum,* pp. 12–14.

Smitherman, G. (1977). *Talkin and testifyin: The language of black America.* Detroit: Wayne State University Press.

Spain, D. (1992). *Gendered spaces.* Chapel Hill, NC: University of North Carolina Press.

Spender, D. (1980). *Man made language.* London: Routledge & Kegan Paul.

Spender, D. (1982). *Invisible women: The schooling scandal.* London: Women's Press.

Stout, K. D., & Kelly, M. J. (1990). Differential treatment based on sex. *Affilia, 5, 60–71.*

Tannen, D. (1990). *You just don't understand: Women and men in conversation.* New York: William Morrow.

Tavris, C. (1992). *The mismeasure of woman.* New York: Simon & Schuster.

Three Rivers, A. (1990/1991). *Cultural etiquette.* Indian Valley, VA: Market Wimmin.

Tolman, R. M., Mowry, D. D., Jones, L., & Brekke, J. (1986). Developing a profeminist commitment among men in social work. In N. Van Den Bergh & L. Cooper, *Feminist visions for social work* (pp. 61–79). Silver Spring, MD: NASW Press.

Van Den Bergh, N., & Cooper, L. (1986). *Feminist visions for social work.* Silver Springs, MD: NASW Press.

Wicker, D. (1986). Combating racism in practice and in the classroom. In N. Van Den Bergh & L. Cooper, *Feminist visions for social work* (pp. 29–44). Silver Springs, MD: NASW Press.

Wood, J. (1994). *Gendered lives: Communication, gender, and culture.* Belmont, CA: Wadsworth Publishing.

Chapter 5

ECONOMIC ASSAULT ON WOMEN

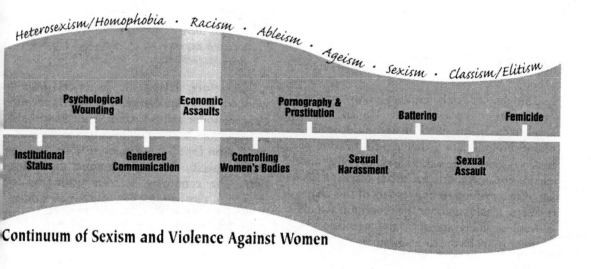

Heterosexism/Homophobia · Racism · Ableism · Ageism · Sexism · Classism/Elitism

| Psychological Wounding | Economic Assaults | Pornography & Prostitution | Battering | Femicide |

| Institutional Status | Gendered Communication | Controlling Women's Bodies | Sexual Harassment | Sexual Assault |

Continuum of Sexism and Violence Against Women

A little girl and little boy are both peering down the front of their respective diapers as the little girl proclaims, "So this explains the differences in our pay!"

> *Classic feminist cartoon on pay inequity*

Men may work from sun to sun,
but women's work is never done.

> *Anonymous saying*

*T*he use of the word *assault* is usually reserved for describing physical or sexual attacks or harm, yet the term seems appropriate in describing the condition of women within the present economic system. Instead of—or in addition to—being attacked by hands or by weapons, women are assaulted with pay inequities, occupational segregation, and glass ceilings. In a capitalist society, money is power and often control. Economics is simply another tool for keeping women one down because a lack of resources translates into a lack of opportunities. Women's labor becomes another resource to be devalued and exploited.

The link between economic and physical assaults is more than metaphorical, however, as it represents reality for women. In fact, homicide is the leading cause of workplace-injury deaths for women (U.S. Department of Labor, 1994a). Additionally, women are sexually harassed and assaulted in the workplace (this issue is detailed in Chapter 8). There is also a connection between economic violence and physical violence because for women, having less money translates into having fewer choices. For instance, the amount of money a woman earns can influence whether she can leave an abusive partner or she can live in a safer neighborhood.

This chapter briefly outlines a range of economic assaults perpetrated on women, but a complete discussion of all the inequities are beyond its bounds. The growing povertization of women is also discussed, as well as policy and practice considerations for social workers. We also offer a caution to our readers of this chapter. When speaking about the economic assault on women, many statistics and numbers are necessary to make the case and prove the point. Although it may be easy to skim over lists of figures, please don't do so. The statistics reflect the lives of women. When reading the numbers, it might be helpful to visualize the faces of the women whose lives are captured in those statistics.

INTRODUCTION TO THE ISSUES

Race, Class, Sex, and Women's Work

The economic assault on women has historical precedents, based on a woman's race, class, and sex. Although this text primarily looks at women's experiences due to their gender, as we have often cautioned, gender cannot be separated from class and race. In looking at economic inequality, the issues are complex and multifaceted. Teresa Amott and Julie Matthaei (1991) have stated,

Race–ethnicity, gender, and class are interconnected, interdetermining historical processes, rather than separate systems. This is true in two senses. . . . First, it is often difficult to determine whether an economic practice constitutes class, race, or gender oppression: for example, slavery in the U.S. South was at the same time a system of class oppression (of slaves by owners) and of racial–ethnic oppression (of Africans by Europeans). Second, a person does not experience these different processes of domination and subordination independently of one another. . . . Hence, there is no generic gender oppression which is experienced by all women regardless of their race–ethnicity or class. (p. 13)

Therefore, laying the historical groundwork for and explanation of women's second-class economic status becomes fraught with difficulties, for there is no common experience of oppression for all women, even when focusing on the specific issue of economic discrimination. The economic discrimination against women in this country has affected all women, but in different ways. We urge our readers to read more specifically about women of different races and classes for a more complete picture of women in America. One such valuable reader is the book by Amott and Matthaei (1991), entitled *Race, Gender, and Work: A Multicultural Economic History of Women in the United States.*

The economic assault on women today is influenced by the historical economic exploitation of women, which varies widely depending on race and class. For instance, Native Americans were oppressed and exploited by forced assimilation and religious conversion, unfair trading practices, violent extermination, racism, and the institution of the reservation system, leading to both their impoverishment and their disempowerment (Amott & Matthaei, 1991). The economic exploitation of women of European ancestry varies widely, from women who lived luxurious upper-class lives in gilded cages, benefiting from their husbands' wealth yet having no access to it, to indentured servants, often treated like chattel, to immigrant women who lived in tenements doing piecework in often-crowded or even hazardous rooms. Historically, Latinas have experienced a wide range of economic statuses, from upper-class women who led pampered and protected, although very restricted, lives to indigenous and *mestiza* women who worked at backbreaking labor (Amott & Matthaei, 1991). Arriving in the United States either by force or by choice, Asian-American women were often exploited as farmworkers, prostitutes, and domestic servants, only to come full circle to be considered the model minority, with some success in educational and professional pursuits (Amott & Matthaei, 1991). This movement has not been without struggle or discrimination, however, as revealed by the racism inherent in the Chinese Exclusion Act of 1882 and the World War II internment camps for Japanese Americans who lost not only their businesses and livelihoods, but their freedom as well. African-American women have suffered due to their sex, race, and often class. Many were

brought to this country in chains and suffered brutal, almost unimaginable treatment at the hands of slave owners. They were exploited not only economically for their labor, but sexually as well. Although educational opportunities after the Civil War enabled some African-American women to become teachers and nurses, the majority were trapped into low-wage work, such as domestic service and sharecropping (Amott & Matthaei, 1991).

Class

It has been widely acknowledged that women have been discriminated against throughout history, on the basis of sex and race. Religious, cultural, and biological theories have often deemed women to be the inferior and weaker sex, while women of color have been doubly hampered by theories of racial inferiority. Class also plays an important role in women's participation in the labor market.

In America, many people tend not to think of class as an important factor in their lives. In

Unionized Latino office workers protest for better wages in downtown Los Angeles. Union membership among women is growing as women organize for increased pay, improved working conditions, and better benefits. Photo © 1996 Kim Kulish.

fact, many think of America as a classless society, especially when compared to the more easily identifiable class systems of the British aristocracy, the czarist system of prerevolutionary Russia, or the caste system of India (Amott & Mathaei, 1991). Yet to fully understand the economic history of women—and its influences on women today—we must have an understanding of class and our economy. The two traditional theories that have led to different schools of thought about our political economy are those of liberalism and Marxism (Abramovitz, 1988). Although many feminists have ignored the class implications in the woman question, socialist feminists have not.

> The socialist-feminist response to the theories of liberalism and Marxism integrates the radical feminist analysis of patriarchal power relations and the Marxist analysis of capitalist class and property relations.... The emerging synthesis locates the oppression of women in the ways that the power relations [of] capitalism (class domination) and patriarchy (male domination) together structure ideology, the social relations of gender and class, and the overall organization of society. The dynamics of racism have also recently begun to be factored into this complex equation. (Abramovitz, 1988, p. 24)

Even though many social workers eagerly understand and embrace the concepts of self-determination and empowerment, others may shudder at the mention of economics, capitalism, and Marxism. Yet these concepts are equally important to social work students, as well as to those in business and economics, for these factors influence the economic status of women. The system of capitalism is structured as a pyramid, with a few wealthy people who own the means of production at the top, and the vast working class below. The move from a bartering and trading society with largely agricultural pursuits to a market economy of an industrialized nation has had profound effects on women.

In most cultures across time, the family was considered an economic unit. Labor within the family was often sexually segregated, with each sex contributing to the well-being of the family. Women's labor was often valued for producing goods and services that allowed the family to survive. The rise of capitalism, the Industrial Revolution, and wage labor had dramatic impact on the economic contributions of women, however. Wage labor was considered a male pursuit and became valued because it earned a salary. Women's labor in the home—cooking, cleaning, rearing children—was unpaid and became devalued over time. However, the labor system was willing to make exceptions for the inclusion of women in the labor force, based on class. Amott and Matthaei (1991) reported that "with the rise of capitalism, women were brought into the same labor system, and polarized according to the capitalist–wage laborer hierarchy" (p. 23). This hierarchy was again based on race, sex, and class, as middle-class women were actively discouraged from entering the labor market, and working-class women were trapped into menial and low-paying work. These trends continue today, with women of color still earning less than European-American women, and women of all colors restricted by the glass ceiling.

Socialist feminists are owed a great debt for bringing class issues into feminist theory. Social workers must continue this emphasis, with a greater understanding of the influence of capitalism and the economy on women who are sometimes forced into the workplace and at other times kept out. For instance, the so-called angry white male often blames women and people of color for his lack of job opportunities when in reality, the job market is dramatically changing, due to new economic trends. The changes brought by the Industrial Revolution are again being revised in this new postindustrial society, which has fewer manufacturing and more service-sector jobs. Poor women are held responsible for a changing economic system while being blamed for the financial assistance they receive, without realizing that the market takes advantage of their status, reaping economic and social benefits by ensuring cheap labor, upholding patriarchal hierarchies, and regulating the lives of women (Abramovitz, 1988). More and more women are speaking up about class issues and how these issues interact with other variables, such as race, gender, sexual orientation, and ableism (Davis, 1981; Penelope, 1994; Zandy, 1990; Zinn & Dill, 1994).

Women Working in the Paid Labor Force

Let's look at a few numbers that begin to paint a picture of employed women in America. The following statistics are from the U.S. Department of Labor Women's Bureau (USDOLWB, 1994a) *1993 Handbook on Women Workers: Trends and Issues.*

- In 1991, there were 99.2 million women over age 16 years in the United States, and 57 million of these women were in the labor force.
- Women held about three fifths of all service jobs, a proportion they maintained during the 1980s.
- Women held nearly two thirds (65%) of the 21.8 million part-time jobs in 1990.
- Of the women working part-time for economic reasons in 1990, 30% were seeking full-time work.
- Women are starting businesses at twice the rate of men.

Women are in the workforce in ever-increasing numbers. Yet, in spite of growing numbers of women in the labor force, wage compensation and job opportunities have not always increased commensurately.

Wage Gap Women have always worked. Whether their labor is paid or unpaid, women's labor is an important, if often unrecognized, contributor to our nation's economy. Women are increasingly moving into the paid work-

force to support their families, gain economic independence, and satisfy personal needs of ambition and or service. European-American women and all people of color are a growing proportion of the workforce, and by the year 2005, they will account for two thirds of all new entrants to the workforce (National Committee on Pay Equity [NCPE], 1994). Nonetheless, women moving into paid employment often find that their work is undervalued and underpaid, affected by pay inequities.

The National Committee on Pay Equity (NCPE, 1994) has defined the *wage gap* as a statistical indicator that is often used as an index of the status of women's earnings, relative to men's. The gap is usually expressed as a percentage, which is derived by dividing median annual earnings for women by median annual earnings for men. In 1963, the wage gap between men and women was 59.6%, and in 1993, the wage gap was calculated at 72%. Although the gap has gradually improved, the rate of improvement is calculated as less than half a penny each year (NCPE, 1994). Additionally, the narrowing of the wage gap is largely credited to a fall in men's real wages, rather than an increase in women's.

Although lists of statistics can be tedious, the following numbers compiled by the National Committee on Pay Equity (NCPE, 1994) are enlightening:

- According to a National Academy of Sciences report, between one third and one half of the wage difference between men and women cannot be explained by differences in experience, education, or other legitimate qualifications.
- College-educated women earn only $2,717 more per year than do white men who have never taken a college course, and they earn $11,667 less than college-educated white men.
- Women earn less, even when they hold the same occupations as men. The U.S. Bureau

FIGURE 5.1   1995 Median Annual Earnings of Year-Round Full-Time Workers

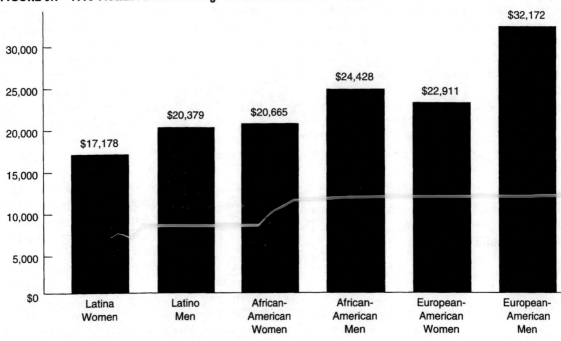

This graph demonstrates earning inequities based on race, and gender.

Source: U.S. Bureau of the Census, Current Population Report, p60–193, Money Income in the United States: 1995 (With Separate Data on Valuation of Noncash Benefits), *U.S. Government Printing Office, Washington, DC, 1996.*

of Labor Statistics data for 1993 indicate that women earn equal pay in only 7 out of 90 occupations identified by the bureau.

- In 1993 alone, the total amount of wages women lost due to pay inequity was near $100 billion.
- The average woman loses approximately $420,000 over a lifetime, due to unequal pay practices.

The updated information in Figure 5.1 shows similar findings.

As we noted earlier, however, economic assaults do not occur solely as a result of a woman's sex, but because of her race as well. It comes as no surprise then to note that the wage gap is even greater for women of color. The National Committee on Pay Equity (1994) reported,

- Women of color experience the most severe pay inequities: African-American women earned only 64 cents, and Hispanic women earned only 54 cents, and European-American women earned 71 cents for each dollar a white man earned.
- A woman of color is four times more likely to be a low-wage worker than a similarly qualified white man.
- Women and people of color are overrepresented in part-time, temporary, and contingent work.
- College-educated Latinas actually earn less than European-American male high-school

graduates. College-educated African-American and Latinas earn $12,873 and $15,984 less, respectively, than their European-American male colleagues.

Pink Ghetto: Occupational Segregation There are many rationales offered for the current wage discrepancies between men's and women's salaries. The reason most frequently cited is the fact that despite some advances into male-dominated fields, women are still segregated into traditionally female-dominated jobs where wages and status are low. According to the National Committee on Pay Equity (1994), in 1993, 61% of all employed women worked in technical/sales, service, and administrative support/clerical occupations. Of the 20 leading occupations for women, 11 are jobs in which women have worked historically (USDOLWB, 1994a). These women-dominated jobs are often referred to as the "pink ghetto" or "pink-collar" jobs, as compared to blue-collar occupations. Although this segregation is not as blatant now as it was in earlier years, when the classified ads were distinctly separated into "help-wanted—male" and "help-wanted—female" columns, occupational segregation continues today on a more subtle level.

The term *women's work* is often used as a pejorative term for any work a male finds distasteful. Women's work is often seen as an extension of women's natural caregiving role, and women cluster into careers of clerical/secretarial work, nursing, teaching, and social work. Because such work is often done by women and is viewed as congruent with a traditionally female role, such labor is undervalued and underpaid. Additionally, occupational segregation, or *crowding* as it sometimes is termed, makes the concept of equal pay for equal work problematic and difficult to assess.

Although male-dominated professions are increasingly being entered by women, Reskin (1993) reported two general patterns that tend to counteract women's entrance into these non-traditional occupations. First, within many of these so-called male occupations, men and women remain highly segregated, with men concentrated in the highest-status and best-paying jobs. For instance, although women are entering the medical profession in ever greater numbers, female physicians tend to be in the more poorly paid and low-status family-practice positions, while male physicians tend to dominate the better-paid, higher-status specialties, such as cardiology and neurosurgery. Reskin also noted a second pattern, demonstrating that women often gain access to male-dominated occupations primarily after changes in work content and declines in autonomy or rewards made the work less attractive to men. This process is sometimes called the "feminization of an occupation" (Reskin, 1993), with pharmacy and veterinary medicine being two such examples.

Glass Ceiling Although the *glass ceiling* is a relatively new term, it is not a new concept. According to the Glass Ceiling Commission of the U.S. Department of Labor (1995), the *glass ceiling* refers to "invisible, artificial barriers that prevent qualified individuals from advancing within their organizations and reaching their full potential" (undated, unpaged fact sheet). In 1991, the Glass Ceiling Commission was created as part of the Civil Rights Act of 1991. The commission was a 21-member body appointed by the President and congressional leaders and chaired by the U.S. Secretary of Labor. The commission was charged with identifying glass-ceiling barriers and expanding policies and practices that would allow women and people of color increased opportunities. The commission released a report in 1995, entitled *Good for Business: Making Full Use of the Nation's Human Capital.* The report reviewed surveys done from the mid-1980s to the mid-1990s, which found that only 3 to 5% of the senior-level jobs in major corporations were held by women, and in 1994, only two women were chief executive officers (CEOs) in Fortune 1000 companies. The report detailed three levels of artificial barriers to the advancement of women (Glass Ceiling Commission [GCC], 1995, pp. 7–8):

1. Social barriers which are often outside the direct control of business and include barriers to educational opportunities and attainment as well as conscious and unconscious stereotyping, prejudice, and bias related to gender, race, and ethnicity.

2. Internal structural barriers within the control of businesses which include outreach and recruitment practices that do not seek or reach or recruit women; initial placement and clustering in staff jobs or in highly technical and professional jobs that are not on the career track to the top; little access to memberships on highly visible task forces and committees; corporate climates that alienate and isolate women; lack of mentoring and management training; biased rating and testing systems; little or no access to informal networks of communication; and counterproductive behavior and harassment by colleagues.

3. Governmental barriers which include lack of vigorous, consistent monitoring and law enforcement; weakness in the formulation and collection of employment related data; and inadequate reporting and dissemination of information relevant to glass ceiling issues.

While an increasing number of women of color are moving into professional roles, the glass ceiling affects women of color more dramatically than their European-American

Ann Telnaes's cartoon depicts male resistance to women's advancement up the corporate ladder.

coworkers. For instance, the same set of data showing that women hold only 3 to 5% of the senior-level jobs in major corporations also reveal that of those women, only 5% are women of color (GCC, 1995). The difficulties for women of color often arise in a complex combination of discrimination due to race, as well as gender. For instance, Sokoloff identified and described some of the issues facing African-American women managers: isolation, lack of mentors, and stereotyping (1992). Sokoloff reported that the "glass ceiling" that often exists for European-American women can be shattered, in contrast to the "Lucite ceiling" described by Henriques (cited in Sokoloff, 1992), which represents a clear obstacle that cannot be broken.

Sokoloff additionally discounted a prevalent myth, dating from the 1970s, about African-American women, which is called the "twofer" myth (1992). This myth came to life in the first years of affirmative action, when employers placed emphasis on hiring women and minorities. According to the myth, African-American women largely benefited from affirmative action because by hiring African-American women, an employer could get "two for the price of one"—that is, an African-American woman could fill the quota for an African American, as well as for a woman. However, this myth has been debunked as untrue, for the largest beneficiaries from affirmative action have generally been European-American women.

It is interesting to note that women in corporate leadership positions see the obstacles to advancement differently than corporate CEOs do. In a survey of Fortune 1000 companies (Catalyst, 1996), female executives cited male stereotyping, preconceptions of women, and exclusion from informal networks of communication as the top obstacles that prevent women from advancing to corporate leadership. In contrast, male CEOs cited women's lack of general management or line experience and their having not been in the pipeline long enough. A notable finding was the fact that women executives were more than twice as likely as CEOs to cite "inhospitable corporate culture" as a barrier to women's advancement. Another demonstration of a gender gap in perceptions of the corporate culture was revealed when only 23% of women agreed that opportunities for women have improved greatly over the preceding 5 years, in contrast to 49% of male CEOs who thought similarly.

Although there is much resistance to the advancement of women and people of color into senior management positions, research shows that such movement is good for business, as well as for achieving diversity goals. A 1993 study of Standard and Poors 500 companies revealed that companies that include women and people of color in management positions produced stock-market records that were nearly two and a half times better than comparable companies without women and people of color in such positions (GCC, 1995).

A growing response to the wage gap, the pink ghetto, sexual harassment, and the glass ceiling is that women are increasingly leaving other people's companies to start their own. For instance, during a 5-year period in the 1980s, businesses owned by women increased from 2.6 million in 1982 to 4.1 million in 1987 (USDOLWB, 1994a). In this same period, receipts from women-owned businesses increased from $98.3 billion in 1982 to $278 billion in 1987, which represents a 183% increase. Additionally, women-owned businesses employed a total of 3.1 million workers in 1987. Although there still remain many obstacles to women owning their own businesses, such as limited access to capital or financing and lack of management and technical expertise (USDOLWB, 1994a), for many women, owning their own businesses can be a solution to many of the economic assaults on women in the traditional workplace.

Working Women Count: A Report to the Nation

In 1994, the Women's Bureau of the U.S. Department of Labor launched an unprecedented survey of American working women. Reaching over a quarter of a million women in 4 months, women responded to what it means to be a working woman today. Women talked about what they liked about their jobs, what they didn't like, and what they would like to change. The Women's Bureau enlisted more than 1,600 partners to help distribute the questionnaire, including businesses, grassroots organizations, unions, daily newspapers, national magazines, and federal agencies. Additionally, a telephone survey was conducted with a scientifically selected, national random sample. When women were asked about their work and their lives, they identified these main concerns (USDOLWB, 1994b, pp. 5–7):

- Improving pay scales and health-care insurance for all were the two top-ranking priorities for workplace change for respondents in both the scientific and the popular samples.
- The number-one issue women wanted to bring to the U.S. President's attention is the difficulty of balancing work and family obligations. Women reported that problems with child care are deep and pervasive, affecting families across the economic spectrum.
- Health and pension benefits were critical concerns. Forty-three percent of women who worked part-time, and 34% of women over 55 years old lacked health-care insurance. These percentages far exceeded the 18% of the general population who lacked health insurance. Fifty-seven percent of respondents gave their pension plans negative ratings, including 23% who had no pension at all.
- Stress ranked as working women's number-one problem. This problem, identified by almost 60% of all respondents, cut across income and occupational groups.
- More than half of the sample, 61%, said they have little or no ability to advance. This pro-

portion increased to 69% for blue-collar workers and 70% for technical workers.
- In the sample, 14% of European-American women, and 26% of women of color reported losing a job or a promotion on the basis of their gender or race. While women of color reported a higher incidence of discrimination, both groups gave high priority to ensuring equal opportunity—50% of European-American women and 61% of women of color.
- Among mothers in the sample, 63% of mothers with children age 5 years and under, and 61% of single mothers gave high priority to getting paid leave to care for children or relatives.
- Of women with children age 5 years and under, 56% said that "finding affordable child care" is a serious problem, and over half of this group (53%) said that "information about and support for dependent care" was a high priority for change.
- In the total sample, 65% said that "improving pay scales" was a high priority for change, and 49% said, "I don't get paid what I think my job is worth."

The survey asked women to tell in their own words both the joys and the frustrations of their jobs, and the survey report shares the stories of many of these women. One such testimony was from a social worker who said, "I have a Master's Degree in this area and I am not paid sufficiently. . . . I worked hard for my education, paid a lot of money and think I am doing a very important job—But not according to my salary!" (p. 23).

This report is an impressive attempt to take the pulse of the nation's working women. The challenge, according to the framers of the report, is "to build high performance workplaces that fully and fairly value women as equal partners in American life" (p. 9).

From Women's Bureau, U.S. Department of Labor (1994b). Working Women Count! A Report to the Nation. Washington, DC: Author.

Mothers in the Paid Labor Force

The term *working mothers* has been used extensively in the 1980s and 1990s, as an increasing number of mothers are moving into the paid workforce. According to Department of Labor statistics (USDOLWB, 1994a), mothers in the labor force numbered 23 million in March 1992, a large increase from the 16 million in March 1980. The same source revealed that 70% of working mothers with preschool children worked full time in March 1992. Mothers working outside of the home face many unique problems and additional stress beyond that of other workers or other parents.

Women who work outside the home remain the primary parent responsible for child-rearing. This responsibility creates a number of difficulties for women, who are often torn between the needs of their families and the needs of their jobs. Women are often in a no-win situation. If they give primary emphasis to their children, they are viewed as not serious about their work, which is reflected in promotions and salary, yet if women give primary attention to their jobs, they are viewed as unfit mothers. Additionally, double standards exist today for working parents: A mother who stays home with sick children is viewed as not serious about her career, while a father who does the same often is congratulated for being such a concerned father.

As a solution, Schwartz (1989) proposed a compromise in her now-infamous article in the *Harvard Business Review,* in which she proposed different tracks for women, the "career primary" and the "career-and-family" women. The quickly dubbed "mommy track" was subject to much scorn and criticism. By relegating women to an alternative track, women once again faced discrimination based on the fact of their motherhood, while fathers suffered no comparable loss for the fact of their parenting.

Due to caregiving responsibilities, women are more likely then men to have gaps in their work histories. A study conducted by Jacobsen and Levin (1995) revealed that mothers who take time off after the birth of a child often return to lower wages, lost seniority, less on-the-

job training, and employers who may believe that the mothers will take another leave at a future date. Upon returning to the workforce, after 3 to 5 years, the intermittent worker's salary is 20% lower than that of women who stayed on the job continuously. Jacobsen and Levin's study found that although wages that drop because of a break from the workplace rise over time, the negative effects are so persistent that they remain discernible even 20 years after the last break ended. Over time, that difference decreases, but women who left never catch up to workers who never left. Mothers who leave also lose contributions into their pensions and profit-sharing funds. Jacobsen and Levin (1995) suggested that the effects of the gap on a woman's lifetime earnings should be taken into account in calculating compensation in divorce proceedings.

One victory for working parents, however, was the passage of the Family Leave Act of 1993. This act mandates unpaid leave for mothers and fathers to care for a sick family member or a new baby. Yet the act is limited, in that the leave is unpaid and doesn't apply to small companies; also, the stigma associated with taking such a leave has kept many parents from taking advantage of its benefits. Much remains to be done to make the workplace more amenable to the needs of working parents. Family-friendly social policies recognize the importance of childrearing by adopting policies for women and men, which allow parents to be responsible both as parents and as employees. Such policies often include paid parental leaves, sick days for children's illnesses, reduced workweeks, flextime, and affordable childcare, often provided on site by the employer.

Women in Social Work

In a profession that teaches the concepts of empowerment, equality, and advocacy, one might expect the social work agencies and workplaces to serve as models of workplace equity. Unfortunately, this is not the case. The social work profession suffers from characteristics similar to those of other female-dominated professions in which the majority of the workers are women, performing tasks that are often perceived as women's work. Gibelman and Schervish (1993) stated that "social work, a profession dominated by women since its inception, shares with nursing, teaching, and library science (also female-dominated fields) lower earnings and status compared with traditionally male-dominated professions, such as law, medicine, and engineering" (p. 445). Sadly, the devaluation of work, pay inequities, and glass ceilings evident in other professions are all too prevalent in our own.

Individual social workers have long felt underpaid and undervalued. Research confirms this perception. According to a study released by the National Committee on Pay Equity in 1987 (cited in Freeman 1991), social work is 1 of the 25 most underpaid occupations. The study "analyzed occupations whose personnel are paid less than would be expected on the basis of the education that is required, the number of hours worked, and the age distribution of its workers" (Freeman, 1991, p. 11) and found that if social workers had been paid according to the same criteria as jobs held primarily by European-American men, they would have earned 50% more than they received.

Not only is the social work profession underpaid in general now, but also Huber and Orlando's (1995) review of the literature documented at least a 30-year history of sexual discrimination within the profession. This sexual discrimination is reflected in income discrepancies between female and male social workers, even when investigators control for other factors, such as age and experience. Gender has been isolated as the major explanation for the wage gap within social work, as male social workers are consistently paid more than female social workers. Huber and Orlando tracked the income disparities, finding that male social workers made $12,359 more in 1974, $6,152 more in 1987, $8,500 more in

1992, and $8,114 more in 1994 (Huber & Orlando, 1995). Huber and Orlando also decry the profession's apparent apathy about correcting the situation. The researchers note that although social workers are willing to advocate for fairness and equity on behalf of their clients, they seem unwilling or unable to do so on behalf of themselves.

Evidence also suggests that the glass-ceiling phenomenon described earlier exists in the social work profession as well. Gibelman and Schervish (1993) analyzed the demographics of the membership of the National Association of Social Workers (NASW). The study found that, compared to female social workers, male social workers disproportionately hold managerial positions, reach these positions earlier in their careers, and earn more money in these positions. The study revealed that a higher percentage of women were more likely to hold direct-service jobs, while a higher percentage of men were more likely to hold jobs described as supervisory or management. This gender pattern only increased with numbers of years of practice.

Because the social work profession is affected by the wage gap and the glass ceiling experienced by other female workers, there are practice issues to be addressed by social workers on behalf of the social work profession. For instance, Huber and Orlando (1995) suggested classes or workshops (either within a degree program or as part of continuing education) on salary negotiations, whereas Gibelman and Schervish (1993) recommended that NASW investigate the glass-ceiling phenomenon within social work and monitor equal access and opportunity for women within the profession. As social workers seek to economically empower women in society, they must address the inequities within the social work profession, as well. Such redress has benefits not only for individual social workers, but for clients as well. If social workers are economically empowered, the profession has more clout and resources to utilize in ending the economic oppression of all women.

Women's Unpaid Labor: Housework, Volunteer Work, and the Second Shift

In our society and most others across the globe, the value of work is often equated with the income it generates. More skilled or prestigious occupations earn higher salaries, along with increased status. In general, money is a reward for a job well done, yet this maxim doesn't extend to women. Women's labor is often invisible. Women often work long hours without compensation, and the value of women's unpaid labor is not calculated in this country's gross national product.

Often, women's work is not even perceived as work. This misperception is true for middle-class women who are full-time homemakers, who call themselves "just a housewife"; for women who work two shifts, one outside the home in the paid labor force and one within the home as unpaid labor; for the women who contribute many volunteer hours that are not valued; for the women receiving government assistance who must work hard to gather available benefits to which she and her children are entitled; and for many women in the Third World whose unpaid or subsistence-wage work gathering fuel, growing crops, or carrying water goes unacknowledged in the economic system.

In the United States, there has been a small movement to recognize the important contributions of women who work inside the home. Popular buttons read "Every mother is a working mother," in response to the newly coined term *working mother*, which customarily refers only to mothers who work outside of the home in paid employment. As consciousness is raised and language changes, more sensitive inquiries include, "Do you work outside of the home as well?" Yet even with a small acknowledgment of women's unpaid labor, we are still a long way from recognizing women's work as the valuable contribution it is.

The Human Development Report (HDR) released by the United Nations Development Programme (UNDP) in 1995 calculated the undervalued, undercompensated labor of women (UNHDR, 1995, p. 6):

- Women work longer hours than men in nearly every country. Of the total burden of work, women carry, on average, 53% in developing countries and 51% in industrial countries.
- Of men's total work time in industrial countries, roughly two thirds is spent in paid activities, one third in unpaid activities. For women, the situation is the reverse. In developing countries, more than three quarters of men's work is in market activities, so men receive the lion's share of income and recognition for their economic contribution—while most of women's work remains unpaid, unrecognized, and undervalued.
- A major index of neglect is that many of women's economic contributions are grossly undervalued or not valued at all—on the order of $11 trillion a year.

Not recognizing women's economic contributions has serious repercussions for women, not only in terms of lack of appreciation and self-esteem, but in lack of economic consideration as well. For instance, the value of women's labor is not calculated into the equation when loans are requested, divorce is considered, or policy decisions are made. As the UNDP HDR (1995) noted, "Men's labor in the marketplace is often the result of 'joint production,' not a solo effort, since much of it might not be possible if women did not stay at home looking after the children and the household" (p. 6).

Phyllis Chesler constructed a "help-wanted ad," which humorously, yet effectively depicted the dilemma of the job of "housewife." She questioned whether many women or men would apply for a job that required intelligence, patience, and energy, at no pay, with long hours, and a trend toward layoffs as the employee approached middle age (Chesler, 1976, p. 97).

Homemakers provide many intangible services that go into the making of a home from cleaning to child and elder care. An estimated salary for the many roles could be as high as $80,000.

Although often viewed as a middle-class European-American woman's issue, this issue affects all women. Women who receive Aid to Families with Dependent Children (AFDC) (now TANF) are often seen as not working by legislators who would force them "back to work" after receiving assistance for 2 years. Women receiving AFDC already work, keeping a home and obtaining benefits for their children. Women who work in the home often depend on their husbands for support, while women receiving AFDC are similarly dependent on the government. This observation lends truth to an old feminist maxim, "Most women are a man away from welfare." Yet a double standard exists, based on class or race, which calls for middle-class women who work outside the home to leave their jobs, to return to the home to care for children, where as poor women are urged to leave their children at home and to find paid employment outside the home.

Women's unpaid labor is an issue not only for full-time homemakers, but also for women who work outside the home. Arlie Hochschild and Anne Machung (1989) gave a name to a problem facing women employed in the paid labor force: "the second shift." Their research documented what employed women already knew—that most women arrive home from work outside of the home only to continue working inside the home in the areas of housework, parenting, and domestic management. Hochschild and Machung (1989) found that 18% of men shared the second shift by doing half (45 to 55% of the work) of the tasks in the aforementioned three categories; 21% did a moderate amount (between 30 and 45%); and 61% did little (between 30% and none of the work).

The volunteer work women have traditionally contributed to their communities is also underrecognized as important work. Histori-cally, men have been financially more able to give monetary contributions to charitable organizations, and such donations are usually tax deductible, whereas women have generously given of their time in volunteer labors that aren't similarly acknowledged or rewarded (Waring, 1988). Independent Sector, a national coalition of more than 800 voluntary organizations, foundations, and corporate-giving programs, documents the trends in volunteering and contributions. Their 1995 report found that in 1993, an estimated 89 million Americans volunteered an average of 4.2 hours a week. Furthermore, among all volunteers in 1993, 44% were male and 56% were female (Independent Sector, 1995). The value of volunteer hours varies over time, but according to the 1994 Economic Report of the President, cited by Independent Sector, volunteer work is calculated at $12.13 per hour.

As more women enter the paid workforce, less time and energy is available for volunteer work. Many nonprofit agencies that rely heavily on volunteers to provide services and to raise funds are hurting from the lack of volunteers. In 1994, the Houston Area Women's Center (HAWC), a nonprofit agency that works with survivors of sexual assault and domestic violence, reported an increase in the number of calls received on their hotline, an increase in number of women and children housed in shelter, and an increase of women attending rape support groups. In fact, the only statistics that decreased over that particular fiscal year were the number of volunteers and the number of volunteer hours served (HAWC, 1995).

The recommendations for changing the valuation of women's unpaid labor are wide-ranging. A longtime recommendation has been for men (including fathers) to become more active participants in housework and childrearing. The benefits would include a renewed appreciation for the value of such work, relieving of women's burdens, and a closer father-and-child bond. While there is some anecdotal evidence that this change is a growing trend, child care and housework remain the primary responsibility of women.

Another recommendation is to demand "wages for housework" (Jones, 1991, p. 218). If society were to pay women for the unpaid labor they now perform, such payment would show the value of women's contribution on behalf of the family and the nation's economy. Another alternative is for women to go on strike to educate others as to the importance of their work. Far too often, work is not appreciated until its absence is noted. This practice has been effective on an individual level, with some mothers going on strike, although such an action is often humorously depicted by the media. Work stoppage was also conducted on a larger scale in 1985, when 22 countries participated in either "time off for women" activities or full-scale strikes to advocate for the calculation of women's unpaid labor, as well as their paid labor, in their countries' gross national products (Waring, 1988).

THE FEMINIZATION OF POVERTY AND THE POVERTIZATION OF WOMEN

In 1978, Diana Pearce coined the phrase the "feminization of poverty" (Pearce, 1978) while documenting the growing trend that the people living in poverty in this nation were increasingly female. Although this phrase is frequently used to highlight the gender issues of poverty, social worker Mimi Abramovitz prefers the term the "povertization of women." Abramovitz feels this term "better captures the long history of female economic impoverishment" (Abramovitz, 1991, p. 380). While the terminology is new, the phenomenon is not.

Far too little attention has been given to poor women and the reasons for their impoverishment. Often, poor women were divided into the *worthy poor,* such as widows, who received support, and *unworthy women,* such as unwed mothers, who received society's castigation and blame. Women's poverty was attributed to

women's lack of work ethic or a personal character defect. Such beliefs have historical roots that continue to influence today's beliefs about poor women, who are often judged to be lazy or promiscuous, having babies to collect government benefits.

One Low-Income Woman's Story

It's easy to lose sight of the economic plight of individual women when statistics are used to portray the economic discrimination of women as a class. To remedy that tendency, presented here is the experience of one Mexican woman named Esmeralda, currently living and working in the United States. Esmeralda's story appeared in the newspaper when the necessity of raising the minimum wage was being debated in Congress and across the country in the fall of 1996.

Esmeralda and her husband José immigrated to the United States in the mid-1980s with their two children, Juán, now 12, and María, now 9. The family did well, as José found work as an asbestos worker while Esmeralda worked part-time in the home, selling home-decorating merchandise. After settling into life in America, they had two more children, Leonel, 5, and Jesus, 3.

Their financial stability began to crumble when José became ill with diabetes and his health deteriorated to the point where he was unable to work. Although he didn't want his wife to work outside the home, her doing so became necessary in order to support the family. With only a sixth-grade education and limited English-speaking skills, Esmeralda's job opportunities were restricted. Esmeralda first found a job cleaning offices at night for $4.35 an hour. She later began working for a discount store at $5.00, then $5.25 an hour, but she is limited to working 4 hours a day, 6 days a week. Because she is a part-time employee, no benefits are accorded her or her family. If she spoke more English, she might qualify for a full-time position with increased pay, yet Esmeralda has had little time to take the English classes she is interested in since she added a second job to support the family.

Esmeralda's second job involve making sandwiches, at $4.25 an hour. After a year, she received a raise, which increased her pay to $4.33. This job also has no benefits and no holidays. The hours are undependable, as she works until enough sandwiches are made or until she has worked 40 hours a week, which ever comes first. Work lasts from midafternoon to 6 or 7 P.M., when she leaves for her job at the discount store. Between jobs, she runs home to see and feed the children. She pays an older neighbor $50 to $60 a week for child care.

José's health has recently improved, so he is working in another state at present. Because his health and job security is unstable, Esmeralda continues to work outside the home. She thinks the increase in the minimum wage will be "a big help." Esmeralda hopes to return to Mexico one day. José mother is seriously ill, and the long-distance phone bills to Mexico mounted up to $200 last month. When looking at her life's hardships and struggles, Esmeralda philosophically states, "But many things pass in a person's life."

Adapted from newspaper article: Perin, Monica (1996, September). Making ends meet with minimum wage jobs. Westside Sun, p. 1. (Names were changed to preserve confidentiality.)

Of course, the reasons for the povertization of women are more complex than such simplistic notions of personal inadequacies. Although it's easy to turn a complex problem into a simple one of personal attributes or faults, poverty is political. Ruth Sidel, in her now classic *Women and Children Last* (1992), listed the many social and economic causes of the povertization of women:

> These include the weakening of the traditional nuclear family; the rapid growth of female-headed families; the continuing existence of a dual-labor market that actively discriminated against female workers; a welfare system that seeks to maintain its recipients below the poverty line; the time-consuming yet unpaid domestic responsibilities of women, particularly

child care; and an administration in power in Washington [the Reagan administration] that is systematically dismantling or reducing funds for programs that serve those most in need. Broader social, political, and economic aspects of life in the United States in the waning days of the twentieth century, such as unemployment; continuing discrimination on the basis of race, class, and age; and the changing nature of the economy also contribute to the impoverishment of women and children. One additional factor that must be mentioned . . . is the continuing notion on the part of women that they will someday be taken care of by a man, that they do not really need to prepare themselves to be fully independent. This lingering remnant of another era is really an example of "culture lag," an idea, a set of beliefs that has lasted long after the conditions that produced them have changed dramatically. This core of dependency is, of course, fostered by almost all the social institutions of our culture, so that breaking out of the traditional role becomes extremely difficult. (p. 15)

Poverty Statistics

The povertization of women is a global phenomenon. According to the United Nations Development Programme's Human Development Report (1995), of 1.3 billion people in poverty across the globe, 70% are women. The report links the increasing poverty of women to "their unequal situation in the labour market, their treatment under social welfare systems, and their status and power in the family" (p. 4). Closer to home, the statistics on the poverty of women in the United States are similarly dismal. According to the U.S. Department of Labor Women's Bureau:

- Women were 51.3% of the U.S. population in 1990, but they made up 57.7% of all persons in poverty.
- There are more than a third as many poor women as there are poor men.
- Poverty among women varies over the life span, with poverty rates being nearly equal for female and male children; women age 18 to 24 experiencing a 60% higher rate of

poverty than men, with the difference declining after age 24; and an increase in the poverty rates as women age, with women's poverty rate about twice that of men among those 65 years and older.

The categories that follow are not all inclusive and are often overlapping, but they begin to outline the categories of women who live in poverty.

Women Receiving Public Assistance

Women who fall, or are pushed, into poverty often turn to the government for support. Entitlement programs have been many and usually have consisted of several programs—namely, AFDC (dissolved under the 1996 so-called welfare reform); Women, Infants, and Children (WIC); and food stamps and housing subsidies (also drastically cut in the mid-1990s). Gener-

ally, such programs are entitled "welfare," and women receiving such assistance are called "welfare recipients."

Far from being touted as honorable women, fallen on hard times and raising our nation's most precious resource, women receiving assistance are caricatured, blamed, and even demonized. Women who receive AFDC have been castigated as "welfare queens" who cheat the system, have additional children to receive more benefits, buy caviar with food stamps, and ride in Cadillacs to the public assistance office. While none of these images comes remotely close to the truth, unfortunately, the formulation of public policy is often based on such caricatures. Additionally, the scapegoating of women who receive AFDC is used as a political tool because being "tough on welfare mothers" has a similar political advantage to

Keefe's cartoon illustrates the attempt to shift economic woes onto the backs of women receiving AFDC benefits rather than other entitlements which benefit corporations.

being "tough on crime" or denouncing new taxes. Such rhetoric often holds sway over the facts.

Entering into this emotional and often volatile debate is the National Association of Social Workers. NASW lobbies Congress on numerous issues, one of which is educating the American people, as well as members of Congress, regarding the realities of welfare. In an attempt to expose the myths and the rhetoric, NASW's government-relations staff compiled the following statistics from congressional and other sources (Landers, 1995, p. 5).

- More than two thirds of the 14 million AFDC recipients are, in fact, children.
- Families receiving AFDC typically have the same number of children as families that do not receive welfare benefits. In 1991, more than 70% of all AFDC families had two or fewer children, more than 40% had only one child, and just 10% had four or more.
- A change in marital status—whether through divorce or through death of a spouse—that results in a female-headed family is the most powerful predictor of whether a person will receive welfare.
- The vast majority (70%) of all people entering the welfare system leave within 2 years, and 50% leave within 1 year.
- Less than 1% of the total federal budget funded AFDC in fiscal year 1991. That percentage has remained basically unchanged since the mid-1980s. In 1991, the average state spent 2% of its revenue on AFDC.
- Families receiving AFDC are about as likely to be European American as African American. In 1991, 38% of families receiving welfare benefits were non-Hispanic European Americans, 39% were African Americans and 17% were Hispanic Americans.
- The average benefit per AFDC family in fiscal year 1992 was $388 monthly or $4,656

annually. Even when payments are combined with food stamps, the benefits are below the poverty level ($11,521 per year for a family of three) in every state and below 75% of the poverty level in almost four fifths of the states.

One of the most comprehensive and important feminist analyses of the impact of social welfare policy on women is the book by Mimi Abramovitz entitled *Regulating the Lives of Women: Social Welfare Policy from Colonial Times to the Present* (1988). Abramovitz moved beyond the myth and exposed the reality of the social welfare policies that have regulated the lives of women across the centuries. Although much of what we hear in the media decries the funding of public-assistance programs, socialist feminists such as Abramovitz have recognized the paradoxical benefits such assistance provides, not only to the individual woman who receives the assistance, but also to the society as a whole.

> *On the one hand, welfare state policies assist capitalism and patriarchy by reproducing the labor force, regulating the competing demands for female labor, enforcing female subordination, maintaining women's place in the home, and sustaining social peace. On the other hand, welfare state benefits threaten patriarchal arrangements. They redistribute needed resources, offer non-working women and single mothers a means of self-support, and provide material conditions for the pursuit of equal opportunity. (Abramovitz, 1988, pp. 35–36)*

Social-welfare policy is a complex issue influenced by the often overlapping dynamics of sexism, racism, and classism. Yet for too long, welfare reform has not been viewed as a woman's issue. When the lives of so many women hang in the balance, however, social workers must be in the front lines when any talk of welfare reform arises. The system is broken and needs to be fixed, but the socially responsible fix means constructive solutions, not punitive measures.

Author's Perspective

About 8 years ago, when I (Stout) was a research assistant for a study at the University of Texas at Austin, I spent a summer driving around Texas, interviewing women who were receiving AFDC. One day, I met a remarkable women, who truly touched my heart and challenged my view on almost everything related to AFDC. I posed to this woman a question that went something like, "Have you ever accepted money for work without reporting it to the Texas Department of Human Services?" She paused and then began her story.

"Do you mean have I ever mowed lawns to get the money for a pair of shoes for my son? Of course I have. What decent mother would not? Have I ever babysat for a neighbor's child and accepted money so I could buy my son's books? Of course I have. Do you want to call that welfare fraud? Then go ahead. Just know that I am a mother. I love my children. And they will have shoes on their feet and books in their hands. And let me tell you something else. . . . these boys' daddy is sitting on death row right now in Texas. I don't believe in the death penalty, I'm a church-going woman. But you need to know that the state of Texas gives me $128.00 a month for taking care of these two boys under AFDC. If the state of Texas kills their daddy, I'll get over $600.00 a month to care for my children. Something is wrong. Something is very wrong. I'm a mother, and no one should be having to think about whether their boys will be 'better off' if their Daddy is executed. Something is wrong."

Women Alone: Divorce, Widowhood, Single Parenting, and Being Old

There does seem to be a common thread running through much of the discussion of the povertization of women. That is, in many cases, as long as a woman is affiliated with a man, her standard of living is enhanced, but when a woman, by choice or by circumstance, is not legally attached to a man, the standard of living declines. This painful fact has long been recognized by those in the women's movement whose goal has been the economic independence of women. Abramovitz (1991) has viewed this situation of women as a class-based double standard, in which there are "strong parallels between middle-class wives' reliance on male wages and poor single mothers' reliance on the welfare state" (p. 381).

Unfortunately, this painful reality for women—that having a man can keep poverty at bay—has been used by some social conservatives to push women into relationships with men. Many so-called welfare reforms offered up since the early 1990s would require teenage mothers either to live at home with their parents or to marry their children's fathers, while other reforms call for making divorces more difficult for all women to obtain. Although such reforms may be well intentioned—that is, seeking to end the impoverishment of women and children—they are implemented in a punitive, controlling manner, which ties women to men. A better proposition would be to help make women more economically independent with more opportunities and choices, not fewer. Let's look at some of the conditions that drive women into poverty: divorce, widowhood, single parenting, and aging.

Divorce   Many Americans' view of divorce was colored by anecdotal stories, such as those told by Johnny Carson, of *The Tonight Show* fame. Johnny bemoaned the cost of alimony payments and painted himself as a poor victim living meagerly while his former wives lived luxurious lifestyles. Although Johnny may have gained the sympathy of some, his story did not reflect reality for millions of divorced women in America. Women are frequently impoverished by divorce. In fact, psychologist Carol Tavris has stated, "If a conservative is a liberal man who has been mugged, a liberal is a conservative woman who's been divorced" (Tavris, 1996).

Whittelsey and Carroll (1995) cited one study reporting that a woman's standard of living drops 30% after a divorce, while a man's rises by 10 to 15%. Another study found that the average income of women dropped 16% following a divorce, while men's rose 23%. Ironically, some of these inequities were caused by divorce law reforms, which were instituted to make divorce more equitable. Yet these so-called reforms often benefit men rather than women and children. As Weitzman (1990) stated,

> Although the divorce law reformers knew that equality between the sexes was not yet a reality when they codified assumptions about equality into the law, they had seen trends in that direction and believed that the new law would accelerate those trends. But the new laws had the opposite effect: it increased economic inequality. It worsened women's condition, improved men's condition, and widened the income gap between the sexes. (p. 333)

Alimony, now called "spousal support," and property settlements were once awarded matter-of-factly to compensate women for their investment in a marriage. However, in 1990, only 15.5% of women who had ever been divorced were awarded alimony payments, and only 32.3% ever received a property settlement (Whittelsey & Carroll, 1995). Frequently, upon divorce, the woman's contributions to the marriage are minimized and devalued. For instance, attorney Frances Leonard stated (cited in Whittelsey & Carroll, 1995), "The greatest loss divorced women suffer is the enhanced earning power the husband gained at his wife's expense while she stayed home or otherwise stunted her earning ability and he proceeded apace with his" (p. 121).

A woman's children are often used as an economic weapon against her. Although the majority of women gain custody of their children after a divorce, in the cases where the fathers fight for custody, fathers win 70% of the time (Whittelsey & Carroll, 1995). Women may give up financial compensation in order to gain custody of their children. When mothers do gain custody, they are often still dependent on the father for child-support payments. By one report, $34 billion in court-ordered child-support payments go unpaid each year (Whittelsey & Carroll, 1995). Due to the high cost of attorney fees, most women cannot afford protracted custody or alimony contests.

There have been many proposed solutions given to reduce the impoverishment of women and children due to divorce. Some are punitive, either forcing women into marriage or taking away women's right to leave marriage. Clearly, this lack of choice and potential for harm is not a satisfactory solution to the decline in women's and children's standard of living after a divorce. Some advocate a return to the fault-based system of divorce. Yet, according to Lenore Weitzman (1990), "We do not have to return to a fault-based system of divorce to alter the economic results of the present system, for the hardships of the present system are not inevitable. What is required to alleviate them is a commitment to fairness, an awareness of the greater burden that the system imposes on women and children, and a willingness to require fathers to shoulder their economic responsibility for their children" (p. 328).

Weitzman would codify these attitudes into law. In fact, many of her recommendations were passed into law in California, and similar legislation is being considered across the nation. Some of her policy recommendations follow: Child-support awards should be designed to equalize the standard of living in the custodial and noncustodial households; child support should be extended to age 21 for college students; sale of the family home should be delayed, in the interests of minor children; "grandmother clauses" should be included, to provide long-married older women who married and lived their lives under the traditional rules; there should be increased judicial education and training about the effects of divorce laws on women and children; and standards for spousal-support awards (based on the standard of living during marriage) should be improved (Weitzman, 1990).

Widowhood   Although studies have generally found that married women are more depressed than their unmarried counterparts (McGrath, Keita, Strickland, & Russo, 1990), marriage does confer an element of economic, if not mental health, advantage. Based on information from the U.S. population census, Holden (1989) was able to offer these insights into widowhood:

- One-third of women in the United States are widowed by the time they reach age 65 years. At age 75, well over half of all women are widowed, and by age 85, over 80% are widowed.
- There is no doubt that married women are (and always have been) more economically secure than unmarried women.
- The economic consequences of being married are most evident when poverty rates of widows and married women are compared. The poverty rate for married women was 7% compared with almost 30% for widows.
- A longitudinal study that followed the same group of women over time revealed a 30% to 50% decline in the average income-to-needs ratio following the death of a husband; this finding led the researchers to conclude that "the transition from wife to widow led to a sharp and permanent decline in economic well-being."

The cause of the economic vulnerability is the accumulation of a lifetime of economic discrimination, such as unpaid labor in the home, sporadic work histories (often in low-paying, part-time jobs), lack of pensions, and the increasing wage gap as women mature. Additionally, although the average age of widowhood for women in the United States is 55 years, social security spousal benefits are not available until age 60, creating a widow's gap (Hatch, 1995).

Single Parenting   Although many families in the United States live in poverty, the likelihood for a family to live in poverty is greatly increased in families headed by females. According to the U.S. Department of Labor Women's Bureau (USDOLWB, 1994a), in 1990, the overall poverty rate for all families was 10.7%. Married-couple families had a poverty rate of 5.7%, while the poverty rate for families with a female head of household was 33.4%. Female-headed households accounted for 3.8 million families out of a total of 7.1 poor families. Most of these female-headed households had children, in fact, out of 3.8 million such families, 3.4 million had children.

These figures represent a substantial increase in the number of women and children living in poverty since the mid-1970s. The Women's Bureau noted that 99% of the increase in the number of families in poverty over a 20-year period was due to an increase in poor families headed by women (USDOLWB, 1994a).

Again, as in so many other circumstances, the figures for women of color are even worse. Of the 5.1 million African-American families with children in the United States in 1990, 2.7 million of them (53.2%) were female-headed households with no husband present. Among these female-headed households, 1.5 million (56.1%) were below the poverty line. The rate of poverty among female-headed Latino families with children was slightly higher (58.2%)

but included only 536,000 families (USDOLWB, 1994a).

Single parents face not only economic hardships, but also social stigmatization. Such families are often called "broken," and the lack of a male in the house is cited as a factor in numerous pathologies. Former Vice President's Dan Quayle's attack on the single-parent television character Murphy Brown is just one example. Such families need support, not condemnation, however. Nichols-Casebolt, Krysik, and Hermann-Curie (1994) cited Sweden and the Netherlands as countries that have social policies benefiting single mothers and keeping their families out of poverty. The package of benefits available in these two countries include "tax-free children's allowances to help cover the costs of raising children; guaranteed child support benefits for all children who do not live with both parents; government-subsidized day care, and a national health care system" (Nichols-Casebolt et al., 1994, p. 24).

One Woman's Story of Single Parenting

My name is Kim. I am a single working mother raising two boys, ages 11 and 10. I have been divorced for 5 years and currently am a secretary at a local utility company. With my limited education and background, I am very limited on good paying jobs. This makes me very dependent on my ex-husband's child support payments. I find finances to be a constant, daily stress. Although I realize I am fortunate to receive child support payments when many women don't, it is still a struggle to make it from paycheck to paycheck.

I always write out my bills prior to payday and once the bills are paid there is little to nothing left. I pay the bills but there is nothing left over for incidentals ... or are they incidentals? Clothing for the boys, haircuts, sending in extra school supplies or goodies for that special school party, and what about clothing for me? I am al-

ways last on the "needs" list. Recently my son asked for some of his money that I keep when he receives it on birthdays and other occasions, but I felt so low when I told him I borrowed his money for groceries but would pay him back on my next paycheck. Now, it looks like it will be two paychecks down the line before I can pay him back.

I grow very anxious and stressed, and it is a continual process of wondering how I can make ends meet. I'm always living on borrowed time. I frequently ask someone to hold a check I have written until payday. I have had to put back items in the grocery store due to going over budget. I have forfeited cable TV and other such items once considered necessities, but now are luxuries I can't afford.

I do have an outstanding credit card bill. I use it for emergencies only, but when I do use it there is no money available to pay it back. I am very fretful as I see this credit card building up, but what can I do when I have a sick child or broken down car? I find myself neglecting my needs for doctor appointments to make sure the children are taken care of. I have a painful foot problem, but I tend to just "live with it" knowing I can't afford to see a doctor.

Daycare is another struggle. My boys still need supervision at certain times but, unfortunately, I have had to choose letting them stay home versus being with a sitter. The money is just not there. I try to supervise my children over the phone after school as I do my daily secretarial work. I guess I am fortunate that I can at least receive phone calls and talk with them. Just yesterday I arrived home to find a broken front porch globe and a broken garage door window (more expenses!!). Summer is just a few months away and I wonder what I will do.

I found myself in a relationship once where I wasn't really serious about the man, but I enjoyed the financial support the relationship brought. It was so nice to see my boys enjoy some of the "little" things in life, like going to the local fair and rodeo and having the boys ride on every ride, eating to our heart's content, and buying souvenirs to boot! I rode an emotional roller coaster for quite a while trying to decide whether the financial ease he brought to my life was worth staying with him. As we struggle day after day, his money brought a relief from some of my struggles as a single working mother.

Older Women Many of our nation's older women are alone, through divorce or widowhood, and some never have married. Although there is some overlap between categories, we consider the plight of older women as a discrete category because, as a group, their poverty is both pervasive and serious. With our culture's focus on youth and beauty, older women have long been the victims of discrimination and prejudice. Ageism is rampant in this youth-worshiping culture, and women are more affected by ageism than men are. While men are considered more distinguished with the onset of gray hair and wrinkled brow, women who are wrinkled and gray are just considered old. Products are relentlessly marketed to older women, and even middle-aged women, purporting to make them look and feel young.

The advent of feminism has led women to look again at the issue of aging and to celebrate the maturity and wisdom old age can bring. Such celebrations must be tempered with reality, however, for although old age can be a time of newfound freedom, many older women find themselves increasingly impoverished as they grow older. Although women are at risk for economic discrimination and poverty throughout their life spans, older women are at higher risk of becoming poor or of continuing to be poorer than their male counterparts. There are many reasons for older women's poverty, most of which are not unique to old age but merely represent the continuation of the wage discrimination women face throughout their lifetimes. That is, the wage gap widens as women age. Among workers age 25–34 years, the wage gap is 83%, yet by age 55–64, women are earning only 64% of men's earnings (NCPE, 1994).

Hatch (1995) described some additional reasons for the inferior economic status of many older women:

> *Although women make up 59 percent of Americans sixty-five and older and 72 percent of those eighty-five and older, old-age economic and health programs are oriented more toward men's needs and life-course experiences than they are to women's. Old age benefit programs are based upon men's work histories and job characteristics. Women are penalized economically for the unpaid family labor they have performed throughout their lives. (p. 182)*

Social security benefits and pension plans are the safety nets that allow many older Americans to live comfortably in their later years. Unfortunately, both kinds of benefit plans are premised on continuous, high earnings. Many women have inconsistent work histories, most often due to their part-time work and their work within the home, due to family commitments. For instance, social security benefits are derived by averaging a worker's lifetime earnings. Women who work inside the home or who take time off from paid employment, therefore, are not accruing benefits. In addition, although women's social security benefits average only 70% of men's benefits, women are more likely than men to rely on social security benefits as their principal source of income (Hatch, 1995). While married or widowed women may receive a portion of their spouses' benefits, women who never married or who divorced before completing 10 years of marriage are not eligible for spousal benefits. Pension benefits are often calculated similarly to social security benefits, and, once again, women's often sporadic work histories or their part-time jobs (which don't include benefits) end up disadvantaging women. Hatch (1995) reported that only 10% of older women receive any private pension income, as compared to 27% of older men, and even among the few women who do receive income from pensions, their average benefits are only one half those of men.

Although the overall economic status of elderly people in this country has gradually improved, there remain segments of the elderly population that are extremely poor, with the poorest elderly people concentrated among African-American and Latina women (Ozawa,

1995). For example, the median income of African-American and Latina nonmarried women age 62 and older is almost half of the income of a European-American women of similar age and marital status (Ozawa, 1995). Ironically, African-American women often have the lowest earning history yet also the highest rate of employment. Elderly European-American women are more likely to have income from private pensions, annuities, and assets, while African-American and Latina women are more likely to receive income from public assistance (Ozawa, 1995).

It is important for social workers to recognize the importance of social security benefits in the lives of older women, especially women of color. Social workers must be involved in any reform of the social security system. Ozawa (1995) recommended that social workers oppose any across-the-board cuts in benefits and advocate instead for revisions in the benefit formulas to lower the benefit levels of high-wage earners and keep intact the benefit levels of low-wage earners.

There have been many successful efforts to organize groups of older women in the past decades. Two wonderful successes are the formation of the Gray Panthers in 1970, by Maggie Kuhn, and the founding of the Older Women's League (OWL) in 1981 by Tish Sommers and Laurie Shields. OWL has become a strong, effective organizing and advocacy group for older women and displaced homemakers. Their goals include education and political change. OWL has a policy agenda that seeks to forestall cuts in programs that benefit women, as well as to develop new programs that help older women to improve the quality of life of their later years.

Discrimination in the Marketplace

This chapter has outlined many aspects of economic discrimination women face. Most Americans are probably aware of pay inequities and glass ceilings, but additional biases are so subtle and pervasive that they are simply taken for granted or appear to be the natural order of things. This category of economic discrimination can be summed up under the rubric "gender-biased pricing practices." These practices are neatly exposed in a little book *Why Women Pay More: How to Avoid Marketplace Perils* (1993), written by Frances Cerra Whittelsey, published by the Center for Study of Responsive Law, and then reissued as *Women Pay More: And How to Put a Stop to It* by Frances Cerra Whittelsey and Marcia Carroll (1995).

These books carefully catalog how women pay more than men for similar services in the marketplace and reveal widespread economic discrimination in all areas of women's lives, including the legal and medical fields, insurance and automotive industries, and even leisure activities such as travel and sports. One of the book's authors revealed her surprise at marketplace abuses as she wrote, "I was, of course, painfully aware that women earn less than men. But I had not realized how devalued our dollars become simply because they are in female hands" (Whittelsey & Carroll, 1995, p. xi). These abuses are widespread, and a few are listed here:

- In Chicago, male and female participants were sent out with a set script to bargain for a used car. European-American women ended up with prices 40% higher than those for European-American men, while African-American women were quoted prices more than three times the markup paid by European-American men.
- A Boston survey found that half the city's dry cleaners charged women customers up to three times more than men to clean a plain oxford-cloth shirt.
- In New York City, women pay an average of $20.00, while men pay only $16 for the same basic shampoo, haircut, and blow-dry in hair salons.

- In California, the Beverly Hills branch of Saks Fifth Avenue was sued for charging women $28 to hem clothing, while men's clothing was hemmed free of charge.

Most of these practices are so long-standing that they are accepted as natural and normal. Yet these practices are merely long-entrenched forms of economic discrimination against women. Many of these practices are based on stereotypes of women as passive and unknowledgeable consumers. Other gender-biased practices prey on women who feel they must conform to the feminine ideal by purchasing cosmetics, undergoing plastic surgery, and spending millions to support the diet industry. For instance, weight-loss programs are big business, with revenues of almost $2 billion in 1993, 90% of their clients being women (Whittelsey & Carroll, 1995).

To overcome such marketplace abuses, women must become more critical and careful consumers. Whittelsey and Carroll list countless ways to address specific abuses, and they offer these general guidelines: "Be assertive, learn about your home and car, be a crafty negotiator, don't let incidents of incompetence or fraud slide, and check with your city's consumer protection office or human rights office to see if there are laws that prohibit businesses from charging women more than men for identical services" (Whittelsey & Carroll, 1995). Whittelsey and Carroll also acknowledge that individual action is not the only remedy and support the adoption of a federal Equal Rights Amendment.

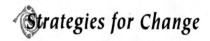 Strategies for Change

---

PRACTICE ISSUES

Economic Empowerment

Social workers can play a vital role in the economic empowerment of women. The specific actions to be taken depend on the particular practice arena in which a social worker is employed. For instance, a social worker working as a psychotherapist can choose to work in a nonprofit counseling agency that provides free or low-cost counseling to women. Similarly, a social worker in private practice can offer a sliding-scale fee, based on a woman's income, or can take on a few cases for little or no cost. Social worker psychotherapists can also acknowledge the economic assault on women by recognizing that many of the mental health problems women exhibit may be related to their life circumstances, rather than to psychopathology. McGrath et al. (1990) reported the link between poverty and depression. Social workers can also be a source for information and referral to clients, regarding a wide variety of both private and public programs that seek to offer economic support to women, such as government-assistance programs, job-training programs, and displaced-homemaker programs.

Social workers practicing within a school setting can focus their efforts on primary prevention of the impoverishment of women. The American Association of University Women (AAUW) has extensively documented how schools shortchange girls, finding even that girls who are highly competent in math and science are much less likely to pursue scientific or technological careers, which often are relatively lucrative (AAUW, 1992). Social workers can provide messages and programs that increase the opportunities available to girls. Whether girls participate in the *Ms.* Foundation's Take Our Daughters to Work Day or other mentoring programs, girls need to know the full range of possible careers available to them. Joline Godfrey has offered many practical suggestions for improving the economic well-being of girls in her creatively entitled book, *No More Frogs to Kiss: 99 Ways to Give Economic Power to Girls* (1995). The suggestions are wide-ranging, from introducing the barter concept to teaching girls about computers to creating scholarships to teaching girls about the stock market.

Economic Organizing

One of the most exciting practice areas for social workers is the economic organizing of women. Social work has a long tradition of community organizing as a mode of practice. In addition, much evidence shows that the collective organizing of women on their own behalf can bring other rewards, in addition to economic gains. For instance, a case study on the grassroots organizing and legislative efforts by a largely female clerical workers union brought about not only pay equity, but also greater appreciation for women's work, increased self-esteem, and attention to other working women's issues (Almeleh, Soifer, Gottlieb, & Gutierrez, 1993). Additionally, experience and research demonstrate that when women become more economically solvent, the entire family benefits as well (Nichols-Casebolt et al., 1994).

Innovative economic organizing on behalf of women has become a global phenomenon involving women of all races and classes (Rowbotham & Mitter, 1994). Such organizing has taken creative and alternative approaches to more traditional economic practices, which often have not met the needs of women. At the United Nations Women's Conference in Beijing, China, in 1995, global efforts were shared, and new concepts, such as microcredit and microenterprise, were explored. Two successful examples are presented here, to illustrate the widely divergent needs and solutions to the empowerment of women through economic organizing.

In most countries, traditional banks see low-income women as poor risks for credit or for loans, yet one well-known success story is now a model for poor women around the globe. The Grameen Bank in Bangladesh began in the late 1970s, mainly as a credit program for low-income women. The bank now reaches nearly 1 million rural clients, more than 90% of whom are women (UNDP, 1995). Loans are much smaller than most banks consider profitable, usually between $25 and $250, yet the recovery rates are phenomenal, about 95% (UNDP, 1995). This dramatic success story illustrates both the innovative practices and the change in beliefs and attitudes about women that are necessary to achieve the financial empowerment of women. Old stereotypes about women's work must be laid to rest, and increased opportunities must be made available to women. The achievement of economic empowerment for women means discarding some traditional banking practices that have favored men and have viewed women as economic liabilities, rather than assets. The UNDP-HDR (1995) noted, "Experience shows that to be responsive to the needs of low-income women, financial services need to provide an informal banking atmosphere; small, short-term loans; nontraditional collateral requirements; simple application procedures with rapid turnaround; flexible loan requirements; ownership and mutual accountability; convenient mechanisms for small savings accounts; participatory lending and savings structures; and participatory management of institutions" (p. 112). Such innovative practices can be adopted in the United States for the benefit of low- to moderate-income women.

Another success story for the economic organization of women was detailed in the bestseller, *The Beardstown Ladies: Common-Sense Investment Guide* (1994). In 1983, 16 European-American women, ranging in age from 41 to 87 years, met monthly at a local church to learn how better to handle their personal assets. Beardstown, Illinois, is a small farming community (population 6,000) on the banks of the Illinois River. Although some members had never invested before, by working and learning together, their investment club has outperformed many other investment clubs and Wall Street experts. The investment of only $25.00

per month has led to a club portfolio of fewer than 20 stocks with an annual return of 23.4%, which is twice that of the Standard & Poors 500 and more than most professional money managers (Beardstown Ladies Investment Club, 1994). The women used the money to expand their businesses, take trips all over the world, and plan for a secure and comfortable old age.

POLICY ISSUES

The economic empowerment of women must concurrently focus on policy and on practice. Amott and Matthaei (1991) remind us that "individual efforts to scale the labor market pyramid will not eliminate economic injustice as long as the hierarchy persists. Instead, collective struggles must begin to challenge the labor market hierarchy itself, as well the other social institutions which reproduce inequality. This will require radical structural changes across the economy, the polity, and the family" (pp. 345–346).

The Congressional Caucus for Women's Issues has introduced the Economic Equity Act (EEA) every year since 1981, in order to seek redress in the area of economic discrimination against women. This omnibus bill comprises many different bills proposing a wide range of provisions to benefit women economically, including the provision of partial benefits to part-time workers; the establishment of a commission to study pay equity; the addressing of pension issues; and—newly added in 1996—the Battered Women's Employment Protection Act, which seeks to help battered women to obtain unemployment insurance and which permits limited unpaid leave for women who are forced to leave their employment to deal with domestic violence or its aftermath. Although the bill includes many policy changes that would benefit women, the focus here is on three topics: pay equity, lesbians in the workforce; and welfare reform.

Pay Equity

Comparable worth (pay equity) is a controversial concept, which has been around since the early days of the second wave of the women's movement. Recognition of the economic discrimination that kept women subordinate and often dependent caused the formation of a pay-equity movement in the 1960s and 1970s. The rallying cry became "equal pay for equal work." In 1963, the Equal Pay Act was passed, which mandated equal pay for equal work. However, the act is viewed as largely a symbolic gesture, which had little impact on women's wages.

The principle of pay equity is based on the theory that "jobs held primarily by women are underpaid in relation to comparable jobs held by men *because the jobs are held by women, not because the jobs are worth less*" (Freeman, 1991, italics in original, p. 13). For instance, although child care and care of the sick and dying are difficult, demanding, and crucial jobs, they have been traditionally undervalued—and underpaid—because women are primarily responsible for performing these jobs.

Although the concept of equal pay for equal work seems simple and fair, the operationalization has proved problematic. The chief obstacle is the issue of occupational segregation. Although it is easy to see that a man and a woman with the same experiences and skills doing the same job should be paid the same, it is more difficult to equate salaries when women and men work at disparate jobs, as is often the case. Therefore, different jobs must be evaluated and their worth compared. Freeman explained (1991):

> *The method of implementing this solution involves the development of a job-evaluation system that would allow the comparison of different jobs in an organization. Under such a system, the relative worth of jobs to the employer is evaluated through the use of an estab-*

lished set of criteria, based on, for example, skill, effort, responsibilities, and working conditions. Jobs are then compensated on the basis of their worth or value to the organization, which presumably results in equal pay for work of comparable worth. (p. 15)

Many feminists see comparable worth as the answer to economic discrimination. Others encourage women to move into traditionally male-dominated occupations to equal out income disparities. However, Barbara Reskin holds that neither of these two solutions are effective because they ignore what she sees as the underlying cause of the income gap. Reskin (1993) stated, "The basic cause of the income gap is not sex segregation but men's desire to preserve their advantaged position and their ability to do so by establishing rules to distribute valued resources in their favor" (p. 199).

Yet there has been some success when pay-equity solutions are applied. One progressive model often cited is the plan for employees of the state of Minnesota. In 1982, Minnesota implemented a pay-equity plan for its state employees. A state study had found that on the average, so-called "women's jobs" were paid 20% less than so-called men's jobs (NCPE, undated). A job-evaluation program was implemented, which rated the value of jobs performed. For instance, a job as delivery-van driver, held mostly by men at the monthly salary of $1,382, was found to be equivalent to a job as clerk-typist, primarily performed by women at a monthly salary of $1,115; the difference between the two positions was $267 per month. Pay-equity adjustments were phased in over 4 years, with the average pay increase approximately $2,200 a year, costing only 3.7% of the state's payroll (NCPE, undated).

Miriam Freeman (1991, pp. 16–17) recommended the following strategies: educating ourselves, our clients, elected officials, agency administrators, and students about the pay-equity issue; finding out how pay equity is being addressed at the state and local levels; holding

NASW unit meetings on pay equity and organizing task forces for action; creating coalitions to achieve pay equity or joining existing ones; advocating for the passage of pay-equity legislation at the national level; advocating for studies of pay equity in our own agencies; joining the National Committee on Pay Equity (NCPE); joining the Women's Equity Action League; working for political candidates who are committed to economic equity between the sexes and the races; and running for political offices ourselves.

The NCPE has offered recommendations for people of color around the issue of pay equity. The NCPE has applauded and supported the growing trend of including pay equity as an issue on the employment and economic agendas of African-American, Hispanic-American, Asian-American, and Native American workers. However, the NCPE also recommended increased educational opportunities, job training, and aggressive affirmative action (NCPE, 1987). Unfortunately, these recommendations fly in the face of political reality as affirmative action programs are being debated and dismantled across the country.

Lesbian Women in the Labor Force

Another group of women who experience unique economic assaults are lesbian women, although specific figures for lesbian women in the workplace are difficult to find. Schneider (1993) attributed this lack of information to the fact that a majority of the literature on lesbian women is concerned with sexual behavior or deviance, so the reality that most lesbian women are employed is often overlooked or minimized. In her study, Schneider found that lesbian women had problems in the workplace that were both similar to and different from those of heterosexual women. For instance, like the majority of women at work, lesbian women were frequently sexually harassed, yet they also faced unique problems, such as whether to identify themselves as lesbians at work.

Lesbian women also face unique economic assaults in the workplace. The economic assault may take the form of job discrimination, as some employers refuse to hire—or they later fire—women who they suspect are lesbian. A major issue for lesbian women is the safety involved in being self-identified as lesbian at work. In one study, 8% of lesbians reported losing a job when their sexual identity became known, and another 2% believed (but did not know for certain) that they lost a job for this reason (Schneider, 1993). Leading a double life is extremely stressful for lesbian women who often must hide their sexual orientation due to fears for their economic security.

Another economic assault is that lesbian workers usually lack health insurance and other benefits for their partners, which heterosexual workers receive for their spouses. This lack of benefits can be costly. In these days of rising health-care costs and insurance premiums, lack of access to a partner's benefits can be a real economic blow. Additionally, paying for the legal costs (e.g., lawyer fees) of filing documents that mimic some of the automatic benefits of state-sanctioned marriage can be an expensive undertaking.

During divorce, lesbian women may have trouble gaining custody of *their* children from a heterosexual spouse. Anecdotal evidence suggests that some lesbian women sacrifice spousal-support or child-support payment in order for the father not to contest custody. This has clear economic impact on divorced lesbian mothers. Where custody is contested, lesbian women are often at the mercy of the particular level of homophobia shown by the judge who is hearing the case or by the state in which the women reside. In addition to their distinctive disadvantages, lesbian women in the workplace also suffer from many of the same policies that affect heterosexual women, such as pay inequities and lack of access to child care. Additionally, however, lesbian women in particular would benefit from specific policy changes, such as the implementation of policies that pro-

hibit discrimination on the basis of sexual orientation and policies that provide benefits for domestic partners. Some cities and businesses have such policies in place, but such efforts must be expanded to ensure that lesbian women in all workplaces are protected. One such policy is the proposed Employment Non-Discrimination Act (ENDA).

ENDA would extend federal employment protections that currently cover most Americans which bars discrimination on the basis of race, religion, sex, national origin, age, and disability to protect Americans of differing sexual orientations. The bill prohibits employers, employment agencies, and labor unions from considering sexual orientation as the basis for employment decisions, such as hiring, firing, promotion, and compensation (Human Rights Campaign, undated). One study found that while 74% of Americans favor preventing job discrimination against gay people, 80% of Americans are not aware that gay people are not covered by current civil rights law (Human Rights Campaign, undated). This proposed law would not give lesbian women and gay men special rights, but would merely provide the same protections that most Americans currently enjoy. Additionally, the law would protect heterosexuals from discrimination based on their sexual orientation. This bill did come to the floor for debate and a vote in the 104th Congress, only to be defeated by a single vote, 49 yeas to 50 nays.

Women and Public Assistance

More has been written about the reform of the welfare system and about "ending welfare as we know it" than about any other social program in recent history. Unfortunately, many of the so-called reforms are subtle and not-so-subtle attempts to scapegoat, blame, and punish women. Mimi Abramovitz, a social worker, believes, "If welfare reform had women's interests in mind, it would promote women's economic independence, instead of self-sufficiency, and provide for systemic labor market reform, individual education, and skill development. More radical proposals would address the underlying cause of poverty among women and of social inequality" (Abramovitz, 1991, p. 382).

Political conservatives blame women's personal inadequacies and the welfare state for the "welfare crisis," as political liberals blame the changing job market. What both groups have in common, note Axinn and Hirsch, is that "both liberals and conservatives call for welfare reform as a way to reform women's behavior" (1993, p. 565). Increasingly, welfare reforms are tied to women's reproductive behavior, their children's immunization records, and school attendance, and a willingness either to marry or to establish the paternity of their children. Axinn and Hirsch noted,

> All of the welfare reform proposals reflect deep-seated beliefs that low-income women are incapable of making good choices for themselves and their children in the absence of coercion. For the most part, the proposals appear to be directed at women's behaviors (particularly single women), rather than men's behavior. And many of these proposals do not reduce welfare costs. Clearly, the driving motivation behind such proposals is to control women in addition to controlling government budgets. (1993, p. 566)

In his first presidential campaign, then-candidate Bill Clinton promised to "end welfare as we know it." Initially, his administration's plan sought to end welfare by helping women to leave the welfare rolls through subsidized child care and increased job training. Yet bowing to political pressure during a campaign year, President Clinton signed the Personal Responsibility and Work Opportunity Reconciliation Act of 1996 into law in August of 1996. This euphemistically worded law amounts to welfare cuts, rather than welfare reform. The new legislation abolishes Aid to Families with Dependent Children (AFDC), as well as other programs, replacing them with block grants to the states. The law also cuts federal funds for a variety of programs that previously provided a safety net for poor women and their children; these cuts total $54 billion over 6 years (Children's Defense Fund, 1996). Under previous law, federal funding in-creased to meet increased need in times of recession, but the new law sets caps on funding, which cannot be increased (Children's Defense Fund, 1996). The law dramatically increases work requirements without a corresponding increase in work opportunities. Although child-care funds have been increased, the funding falls $2.4 billion short of the new need (Children's Defense Fund, 1996). Many new restrictions on aid are included in the new law, including provisions that impose time limits on assistance, as well as requirements that minor parents receive aid only if they are living with their own parents or in another adult-supervised setting. Such restrictions factor in no flexibility for individual hardships or distinctive circumstances.

Social workers have a crucial role to play in monitoring the implementation of this law. The Children's Defense Fund has estimated that the law will push more than 1 million additional children into poverty while deepening the poverty of millions more (Children's Defense Fund, 1996). Advocates for women and children must join together to lessen the harshly punitive impact of this law. The Children's Defense Fund has suggested some specific strategies, such as suggesting that each state create a reserve fund to serve increased caseloads during recessions, to mitigate the overall limits on assistance of 5 years or less per person; and to continue Medicaid, cash assistance, and social service coverage for legal immigrants (Children's Defense Fund, 1996).

Ending welfare as we know it actually calls for ending sexism, racism, and classism as we know it. However, more specific policy changes are advocated by Lynn Phillips, who has offered a seven-step program: (1) Strengthen pay-equity laws; (2) raise the minimum wage; (3) enforce child-support laws; (4) support universal health and child care; (5) strengthen unions; (6) repeal the foreign tax credit; and (7) stump for an international minimum wage (Phillips, 1994). Other welfare reforms involve increased job training for women, greater access to educational opportunities, and greater access to family-planning methods. Ozawa (1994) sug-

A homeless woman prepares dinner in a downtown Los Angeles encampment. Older women are at increased risk of living in poverty. Photo © 1996 Kim Kulish.

gested further policy changes that would establish income security for children and would empower female heads of households, such as these: refundable tax credit for children, child-support assurance, low-interest loans, accumulation of assets through a government-matched savings program, earned-income tax credits (EITC), refundable dependent-care tax credits, continuation of the Job Opportunities and Skills Training (JOST) program, with the addition of health-care coverage and supervised living for teenage AFDC mothers.

If government officials insist on looking at public-assistance programs to reduce the federal and state budgets, then social workers should advocate a major policy and position of looking at so-called corporate welfare or phantom welfare (Huff & Johnson, 1993) or shadow welfare (Abramovitz, 1983) arenas as appropriate avenues for cost cutting. Welfare has typically been perceived as those public-assistance programs that serve the poor, and its very name implies a host of pejorative and stereotypical meanings. Yet corporate America is the recipient of many federal subsidies, including direct expenditures, credit subsidies, tax expenditures, subsidized services, and trade restrictions estimated at more than $170 billion a year (Huff & Johnson, 1993). Although the majority of Americans would agree that the federal budget must be reduced, this reduction should not be accomplished on the backs of poor women and children. Any cuts must include corporate welfare.

SUMMARY

The history of economic exploitation and discrimination against women is a long one. The povertization of women affects all women, from middle-class displaced homemakers to poor women receiving government aid. The common denominator is that women are disadvantaged economically by the institutions in our society that continue to devalue women and their labor. Such discrimination is pervasive and rampant. Lack of economic opportunities keep women subordinate and often financially dependent either on men or on the government. Until this economic oppression is ended, women will remain second-class citizens. This assault is as painful and ugly as the more physical assaults outlined in the following chapters. In a patriarchal, capitalistic society, women and children will continue to be disproportionately poor until the economic discrimination based on gender, race, class, and sexual orientation ends.

REFERENCES

Abramovitz, M. (1983). Everyone is on welfare: "The role of redistribution in social policy" revisited. *Social Work, 28,* 440–447.

Abramovitz, M. (1988). *Regulating the lives of women.* Boston, MA: South End Press.

Abramovitz, M. (1991). Putting an end to double-speak about race, gender, and poverty: An annotated glossary for social workers. *Social Work, 36*(5), 380–384.

Almeleh, N., Soifer, S., Gottlieb, N., & Gutierrez, L. (1993). Women's achievement of empowerment through workplace activism. *Affilia, 8*(1), 26–39.

American Association of University Women. (1992). *How schools shortchange girls: Executive summary.* Washington, DC: American Association of University Women Educational Foundation.

Amott, T. L., & Matthaei, J. A. (1991). *Race, gender, & work.* Boston, MA: South End Press.

Axinn, J. M., & Hirsch, A. E. (1993). Welfare and the "reform" of women. *Journal of Contemporary Human Services, 74*(9), 563–572.

Beardstown Ladies' Investment Club, with Whitaker, L. (1994). *The Beardstown ladies' common-sense investment guide.* New York: Hyperion.

Catalyst (1996). *Women in corporate leadership: Progress and prospects—Executive summary.* New York: Author.

Chesler, P. (1976). *Women, money, and power.* New York: Bantam.

Children's Defense Fund (1996). *Summary of the new welfare legislation and implementing the new welfare law.* Washington, DC: Author.

Davis, A. (1981). *Women, race, and class.* New York: Random House.

Freeman, M. L. (1991). Pay equity and social work. *Affilia, 6*(1), 7–19.

Gibelman, M., & Schervish, P. H. (1993). The glass ceiling in social work: Is it shatterproof? *Social Work, 8*(4), 442–455.

Glass Ceiling Commission. (1995, March). *Good for business: Making full use of the nation's human capital.* Washington, DC: U.S. Department of Labor.

Godfrey, J. (1995). *No more frogs to kiss: 99 ways to give economic power to girls.* New York: HarperCollins.

Hatch, L. R. (1995). Gray clouds and silver linings: Women's resources in later life. In J. Freeman (Ed.), *Women: A feminist perspective* (pp. 182–196, 5th ed.) Mountain View, CA: Mayfield Publishing.

Hochschild, A., & Machung, A. (1989). *The second shift.* New York: Avon Books.

Holden, K. C. (1989). Women's economic status in old age and widowhood. In M. N. Ozawa (Ed.), *Women's life cycle & economic insecurity* (pp. 143–169). New York: Praeger.

Houston Area Women's Center (1995, Spring). *Catalyst: A quarterly newsletter of Houston Area Women's Center.* p. 2 Ostrander, Michellee, Increased awareness of violence against [female] results in higher numbers at HAWC.

Huber, R., & Orlando, B. P. (1995). Persisting gender differences in social workers' incomes: Does the profession really care? *Social Work, 40*(5), 585–591.

Huff, D. D., & Johnson, D. A. (1993). Phantom welfare: Public relief for corporate America. *Social Work, 38*(3), 311–316.

Human Rights Campaign (undated). *This employee is being terminated due to violated company policy. The employee is gay.* Washington, DC: Author.

Independent Sector. (1995). *Giving and volunteering in the United States* (Vol. II). Washington, DC: Author.

Jacobsen, J. P., & Levin, L. M. (1995). Effects of intermittent labor force attachment on women's earnings. *Monthly Labor Review, 118*(9), 14–19.

Jones, K. B. (1991). Marxist feminism. In H. Tierney (Ed.), *Women's studies encyclopedia* (pp. 218–219). New York: Peter Bedrick Books.

Landers, S. (1995, January) Untangling welfare debate's web of myth. *NASW News*, p. 5.

McGrath, E., Keita, G. P., Strickland, B. R., & Russo, N. F. (1990). *Women and depression: Risk factors and treatment issues.* Washington, DC: American Psychological Association.

National Committee on Pay Equity. (1987). *Pay equity: An issue of race, ethnicity, and sex.* Washington, DC: Author.

National Committee on Pay Equity. (1994, Winter). Face the facts about wage discrimination and equal pay. *Newsnotes*, pp. 5–10.

National Committee on Pay Equity. (undated). *Two progressive models on pay equity: Minnesota and Ontario.* Washington, DC: Author.

Nichols-Casebolt, A., Krysik, J., & Hermann-Currie, R. (1994). The povertization of women: A global phenomenon. *Affilia, 9*(1), 9–29.

Ozawa, M. N. (1994). Women, children, and welfare reform. *Affilia, 9*(4), 338–359.

Ozawa, M. N. (1995). The economic status of vulnerable older women. *Social Work, 40*(3), 323–331.

Pearce, D. (1978). The feminization of poverty: Women, work, and welfare. *Urban and Social Change Review, 11*, 28–36.

Penelope, J. (Ed.). (1994). *Out of the class closet: Lesbians speak.* Freedom, CA: Crossing Press.

Perin, M. (1996, September). Making ends meet with minimum wage jobs. *Westside Sun*, pp. 1.

Phillips, L. (1994). Safety net performs vanishing act. *On the Issues*, pp. 37–41.

Reskin, B. F. (1993). Bringing the men back in: Sex differentiation and the devaluation of women's work. In L. Richardson & V. Taylor (Eds.), *Feminist frontiers III* (pp. 198–210). New York: McGraw-Hill.

Rowbotham, S., & Mitter, S. (Eds). (1994). *Dignity and daily bread: New forms of economic organising among poor women in the third world and the first.* London and New York: Routledge.

Schneider, B. (1993). Peril and promise: Lesbians' workplace participation. In L. Richardson & V. Taylor (Eds.), *Feminist frontiers III* (pp. 223–234). New York: McGraw-Hill.

Schwartz, F. (1989, January–February). Management women and the new facts of life. *Harvard Business Review, 67*(1), 65–76.

Sidel, R. (1992). *Women and children last: The plight of poor women in affluent America,* first published in 1986 (1992, 2nd ed.). New York: Penguin Books.

Sokoloff, N. J. (1992). *Black women and white women in the professions.* New York: Routledge.

Tavris, C. (September, 1996). There's a gap, but it has little to do with gender. *Houston Chronicle*, p. 31A.

United Nations Development Programme. (1995). *Human Development Report 1995.* New York: Oxford University Press.

U.S. Department of Labor Women's Bureau. (1994a). *1993 Handbook on women workers: Trends and issues.* Washington, DC: Author.

U.S. Department of Labor Women's Bureau. (1994b). *Working women count! A report to the nation.* Washington, DC: Author.

Waring, M. (1988). *If women counted: A new feminist economics.* London: Macmillan.

Weitzman, L. J. (1990). Women and children last: The social and economic consequences of divorce law reforms. In S. Ruth (Ed.), *Issues in feminism* (pp. 312–335). Mountainview, CA: Mayfield Publishing.

Whittelsey, F. C. (1993). *Why women pay more.* Washington, DC: Center for Study of Responsive Law.

Whittelsey, F. C., & Carroll, M. (1995). *Women pay more.* New York: New Press.

Zandy, J. (Ed.). (1990). *Calling home: Working-class women's writings.* New Brunswick and London: Rutgers University Press.

Zinn, M. B., & Dill, B. T. (Eds.). (1994). *Women of color in U.S. society.* Philadelphia: Temple University Press.

Chapter 6

CONTROLLING WOMEN'S BODIES: HEALTH AND REPRODUCTIVE FREEDOM

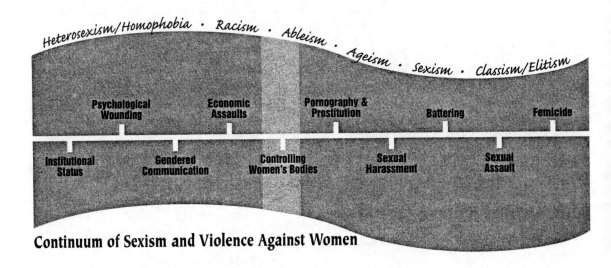

Heterosexism/Homophobia · Racism · Ableism · Ageism · Sexism · Classism/Elitism

Psychological Wounding   Economic Assaults   Pornography & Prostitution   Battering   Femicide

Institutional Status   Gendered Communication   Controlling Women's Bodies   Sexual Harassment   Sexual Assault

Continuum of Sexism and Violence Against Women

I will be the master of what is mine own:
She is my goods, my chattels; she is my house,
My household stuff, my field, my barn,
My horse, my ox, my ass, my anything.

      Petruchio in William Shakespeare, The Taming of the Shrew *(1594)*

$\int$ ince the earliest times of recorded history, men have claimed to own and attempted to control the bodies of women. This control has been codified in laws and in social custom. This chapter focuses on some of the ways in which women's bodies are defined and controlled in a patriarchal society.

Although the claim of ownership of women's bodies is often a factor in the physical violence perpetrated against women, this chapter focuses on the more subtle results of male ownership of female bodies. This ownership results not only in bruises and broken bones, but also in unnecessary surgeries and lack of reproductive choices. The abuse is perpetrated not only by intimate partners but also by doctors and researchers. The major focus here is on how the control of women's bodies has affected both women's health and women's reproductive freedom.

Women's health has been consistently marginalized or just plain ignored. As feminist columnist Katha Pollitt has noted, "The obsession with women's bodies is unfortunately not the same as rational concern for women's health" (Pollitt, 1994, p. 85). It is no coincidence that most of the major health-care scandals of the past decades have been perpetrated on women: Thalidomide, diethylstilbestrol (DES), the Dalkon shield, breast implants, and toxic-shock syndrome are a few of the tragedies that have affected women, leaving them injured, chronically ill or disabled, or, in some cases, dead.

The control over women's bodies extends beyond women's health and into the realm of reproductive rights, as women have fought to regain control over their bodies and their lives. The struggle for women to regain the ability to control their reproductive choices has been a long and difficult fight that continues today. Access to birth control and abortion have marked the struggle over women's ownership of their bodies, as well as the more recent attention given to female genital mutilation.

These issues and their practice and policy implications for social workers are discussed here. Social workers have a prominent role to play in addressing these injustices—from being an advocate in a patient's hospital room, to defending women's access to family planning services, to joining in the efforts to influence policy to make high-quality health care accessible to all Americans.

INTRODUCTION TO THE ISSUES

History of Male Control over Female Bodies

It is believed that long ago, when goddesses were worshipped, women were similarly revered. Part of this past reverence is attributed to the fact that women's bodies brought forth life. This capacity was mysterious and magical.

Additionally, women were society's traditional healers and midwives. Midwives and healers learned their skills from other women, often mothers or aunts, and they passed on their knowledge of healing, of the medicinal uses of herbs, and of ways of handling difficult births (Bogdan, 1990). Women's position in the community was vital and they were well-respected for both their knowledge and their skill. In these pagan times, women were fairly knowledgeable about birth control, often using vaginal sponges or natural abortifacient drugs (Walker, 1996).

With the formation of patriarchy, however, women lost the control they once had over their bodies. Religious, social, and legal institutions gave the power and control over women's lives and their bodies first to their fathers and then to their husbands. This control was codified in laws, as well as sanctified by scriptures. In the Judeo-Christian scriptures, all women were burdened by God's announcement to Eve: "I will greatly multiply thy sorrow and thy conception; in sorrow thou shall bring forth children; and thy desire shall be subjected to thy husband, and he shall rule over thee" (Genesis 3:16).

Throughout history, men thus were granted the power to control women's bodies, as well as their lives. Much of the concern with controlling women's bodies was focused on women's reproductive capacity, and again, law and religion dictated both the information about and the access to birth control and abortion. Women's control of their own bodies was supplanted by control by fathers and husbands, as well as by male judges, legislators, and physicians. Control over women's bodies ran the gamut from guarding and prizing female virginity to deciding how large a rod could be used to beat a wife.

With male control came male definitions and standards. Naturally enough, what was male was claimed as the normative standard, and women's bodies were perceived from a deficit model. Menstruation, once celebrated, was thought shameful and dirty. Women's genitalia—once featured in art, music, and poetry—was found unclean. The natural and normal processes of women's bodies were reviled. Female sexuality and genitalia came to be seen as dangerous, needing to be controlled. Following are just a few examples of male declarations about women, as compiled by Tama Starr in *The "Natural Inferiority" of Women: Outrageous Pronouncements by Misguided Males:*

> The most holy bishop of Mainz was irritated by no annoyance more than the stinking, putrid private parts of women.—Crotus Rubianus (ca. 1520) (Starr, 1991, p. 45)

> I tend to regard the feminine organ as something unclean or as a wound . . . dangerous in itself, like everything bloody, mucous, infected.—Michel Leiris, Age D'Homme (1946) (Starr, 1991, p. 45)

> Dreams, myths, and cults attest to the fact that the vagina has and retains (for both sexes) connotations of a devouring mouth and an eliminating sphincter, in addition to being a bleeding wound.—Erik H. Erikson, "Womankind and the Inner Space" (1968) (Starr, 1991, p. 45).

Sexism and Bias in Medicine

Although control of women's bodies was appropriated by men and their institutions, perhaps nowhere else was the effect more evident than in the medical profession. With the professionalization of medicine, male doctors garnered the power to diagnose, while women healers and midwives were denounced as crones and witches. With the development of the nursing profession, female nurses became doctors' handmaidens. If doctors were analogous to the archetypal father, and nurse to the mother, then female patients played the passive, yet often demanding child. Women were no longer seen as experts on their own lives, and their bodies often remained a mystery even to them.

Regaining control over and knowledge about their bodies was deemed a principal goal of the second wave of the women's movement.

The feminist classic *Our Bodies, Ourselves,* first published in 1971 by the Boston Women's Health Collective, and *The Doctor's Case Against the Pill* (1969), by Barbara Seaman, led the way for women to take charge of their bodies once again. The importance of women reclaiming their own bodies was made by Barbara Ehrenreich and Deidre English (1973) in *Complaints and Disorders: The Sexual Politics of Sickness:*

> The medical system is strategic for women's liberation. It is the guardian of reproductive technology—birth control, abortion, and the means of safe childbirth. It holds the promise of freedom from hundreds of unspoken fears and complaints that have handicapped women throughout history. When we demand control over our own bodies we are making that demand above all to the medical system. It is the keeper of the keys.
>
> But the medical system is also strategic to women's oppression. Medical science has been one of the most powerful sources of sexist ideology in our culture. Justifications for sexual discrimination—in education, in jobs, in public life—must ultimately rest on the one thing that differentiates women from men: their bodies. Theories of male superiority rest on biology. (p. 5)

The control of one's own body is a key to gaining control over one's own life. Yet, as women gain the right to control their own bodies, they must combat political and social institutions, as well as medical and health institutions. Especially around the area of reproductive freedom, women's bodies have become political footballs, where issues are debated not on the merits of women's health, but rather on the degree of control over women. The politics of the gag rule, abortion services, fetal-tissue research, RU-486, and most recently late-term or partial-birth abortions have dominated the debate, rather than the health, safety, and choice of women.

Gender Bias in Medical Practice

The bias within medical practice is confirmed by research. In one study, physicians indicated

Jim Borgman offers a provocative look at how the world would be if men were more likely than women to develop breast cancer.

that female patients were more likely than male patients to make excessive demands, to suffer from psychosomatic illnesses, and to have complaints in which emotional factors were important (Bernstein & Kane, 1981). This gender bias affects not only how physicians perceive women, but also how physicians treat women. Studies have consistently shown that women who are admitted to the hospital with chest pain are less likely to be referred for coronary angioplasty and revascularization than are men (Ayanian & Epstein, 1991; Maynard, Litwin, Martin, & Weaver, 1992). Even when women's cardiac workups were abnormal, women were more than twice as likely as men to have their symptoms attributed to psychosomatic, psychiatric, or other noncardiac causes (Tobin, Wassertheil-Smoller, Wexler, et al., 1987).

Other studies have found that men were more likely than women to receive dialysis or a kidney transplant when suffering from end-stage renal disease (Held, Pauly, Bovbjerg, et al., 1988; Kjellstrand & Logan, 1987).

The biased care that women receive is noted in two tendencies by the medical establishment when treating women: medicalization and genitalization. The *medicalization* of women's health occurs when normal female developmental processes are transformed into diseases, which must then be treated. Examples include how childbirth is transformed from a natural process requiring support and little intervention to a complicated medical procedure, defined as a disability, which requires medical intervention with forceps, medications, fetal monitors, and often surgery. The natural state of menopause—the cessation of a woman's menses—has been medicalized into an estrogen-deficiency disease, requiring hormone-replacement therapy (HRT), despite little knowledge about the long-term effects of estrogen replacement. The menstrual cycle itself was pathologized and a new illness discovered: PMS, or premenstrual syndrome. Tavris (1992) has discussed the "manufacture of PMS" and how the chief beneficiaries of such a syndrome are often the drug companies that market PMS remedies and the shifting labor force, with its periodic changes in the need for women. One of the more blatant attempts to medicalize a woman's body was a publication from the American Society of Plastic and Reconstructive Surgeons, which stated that small breasts were a disease that required medical intervention (cited in Laurence & Weinhouse, 1994).

Another detrimental trend in the traditional practice of women's health is the *genitalization* of women's bodies. For too long, women's health has been equated with maternal health. Women's health traditionally referred to the female reproductive system, and the little research that targeted women was generally focused on this single system. In fact, according to the American College of Obstetrics and Gynecology, about two thirds of women go to a gynecologist for their primary care (cited in Smith, 1992). Through this lens, women are seen as walking uteruses, rather than as physiologically complex human beings.

The medical establishment has controlled women's bodies by asserting that physicians are the sole experts on women's bodies, by hoarding medical knowledge, and by assuming a superior stance. Physician Adriane Fugh-Berman described the pervasive sexism in medical schools, which consists of sexist jokes; inequity in teaching, with male students being given more opportunities than female ones; and misinformation about sexuality and women's health continuing to be taught (Fugh-Berman, 1994). One story she described is especially chilling:

The prevailing attitude toward women was demonstrated on the first day of classes by my anatomy instructor, who remarked that our elderly cadaver "Must have been a Playboy bunny" before instructing us to cut off her large breasts and toss them into the 30-gallon trash can marked "cadaver waste." Barely hours into our training, we were already being taught that there was nothing to be learned from examining breasts. Given the fact that one out of nine American women will develop breast cancer in her lifetime, to treat breasts as extraneous tissue seemed an appalling waste of an educational opportunity, as well as a not-so-subtle message about the relative importance of body parts. How many of my classmates now in practice, I wonder, regularly examine the breasts of their female patients? (pp. 47–48)

The genitalization of women deemphasizes the many other organs that effect women's health, such as heart, lungs, and kidneys. For instance, through much activism and increased public awareness, many women are very conscious of their risk for breast cancer yet remain unaware of their cardiac risk factors. Contrary to conventional wisdom, heart disease is responsible for more deaths in women than are all cancers combined (National Center for Health Statistics, 1994).

Gender Bias in Medical Research

In the not-too-distant past, most research was conducted on men by men, yet each of the various rationales offered to keep women from participating in research simply do not hold up under scientific inquiry. In fact, this attempt to protect women and fetuses actually has had the opposite effect, for little knowledge has been accrued about women's bodies during pregnancy. This lack of information has a serious effect on women, as they and their physicians are forced to make medical decisions based on little or no information. Tavris offered an alternative reason for the lack of funding, citing the old axiom that research is based on what money is available, and male members of Congress have followed the principle that "we fund what we fear" (Tavris, 1992, p. 98). As the following examples illustrate, the common denominator in the current lack of research on women is not science, but sexism.

Because medical research has been conducted almost solely on men, the results are often simply extrapolated to women. An example of this practice is the Physicians' Health Study, in which 22,071 male physicians were recruited for a study to determine the effects of aspirin on mortality from cardiovascular disease (Steering Committee of the Physicians' Health Study Research Group, 1988). The study was terminated early because of the tremendous benefit produced by aspirin in preventing cardiovascular disease in men. The benefits for men are clear, but despite the fact that heart disease is the number-one cause of death for women, not a single woman was included in the study. Hence, the effects of aspirin on heart disease has yet to be determined for women, although some physicians prescribe such a regime for their female patients.

There is no accurate measure to calculate the various assaults on women by the medical establishment. How many women died because their chest pain was deemed to be psychological and they were prescribed a tranquilizer rather than a cardiac intervention? How many women died of uterine cancer because they were given high doses of estrogen to cure menopause before the consequences of HRT were realized? How many women died because the medical establishment abandoned them, and they were forced to seek illegal abortions? Women's bodies have been and continue to be assaulted by the very persons women trust to deliver high-quality health care. Physician John Smith wrote "An unindicated hysterectomy is an assault, but no doctor is ever charged with a crime for doing it" (1992, p. 37).

Although the American Medical Association's Council on Ethical and Judicial Affairs has been slow to respond to the gender bias in medical practice, in 1991, the council issued a somewhat tentatively worded report, entitled "Gender Disparities in Clinical Decision Making." After reviewing the research literature, the council concluded, "Data that suggest that a patient's gender plays an inappropriate role in medical decision making raise the question of possible gender bias in clinical decision making" (Council of Ethical and Judicial Affairs, 1991). The report concluded with a list of recommendations for physicians, such as advising physicians to examine their practice and attitudes for social or cultural bias; to increase research on women's health; to avoid generalizing from research done solely on men and applying the findings to women; and to increase the number of female physicians in leadership roles and other positions of authority in teaching, research, and practice.

Effects of Race and Class on Women's Health

Clearly, women as a class have been marginalized in medical research and practice, which has led to poor health and lack of information about women's health. If the health industry has marginalized women, then women of color have been rendered invisible. For again, not only do women of color battle sexism within the health-care industry, but racism, as well. Class is another important factor in the quality of health care available, for generally more money means better health care. The statistics are clear, convincing, and sobering.

One indication of health is life-expectancy rates, although at first glance, these statistics can be misleading. When comparing the life expectancies of men to women, women's health appears better because women, on the average, live 7 years longer than men. Yet such a measure does not factor in the quality of life and health over the intervening years. Nonetheless, life-expectancy numbers can give us valuable insights, especially when the rates are compared among women of different races. For instance, in 1989, the life expectancy of European-American women was 79.2 years, as compared with 73.5 years for African-American women and 77.1 years for Latina women (NIH, 1992). Some further statistics help complete the picture of the health status of women of color: Death from stroke occurs twice as often in African-American women as in European-American women (NIH, 1992). The rate of death from complications of pregnancy and childbirth are 3.5 times greater for African-American women than for European-American women (NIH, 1992). Although European-American women have a higher incidence of most types of cancers than African-American women, African-American women have higher death rates and lower 5-year survival rates than European-American women for most types of cancer (Horton, 1995). Overall, Latina groups are at a markedly increased risk for diabetes mellitus type II, gallbladder disease, hypertension, stroke, hypercholesterolemia, cardiovascular disease, and obesity (Zambrana & Ellis, 1995). The death rate for Native American women is 6 times higher for alcoholism (10 times higher for women 25–45 years of age), 5 times higher for liver disease and cirrhosis caused by alcohol abuse, 3 times higher for homicide and motor vehicle accidents, and 2 times as high for suicide (Horton, 1995). Also, of the AIDS cases reported among women in 1992–1993, 76% were among women of color (Horton, 1995).

Clearly, the health of women of color is at increased risk in this society. When looking at the differences in the health of women of color, racial rationales may be sought, yet such explanations are simplistic and unsupported. For instance, less than 1% of African-American deaths have been attributed to hereditary conditions related to racial genetic patterns, such as sickle-cell anemia (Jaynes & Williams, 1989, cited in Leigh, 1995).

Two major predictors of poor health are poverty and lack of education (NIH, 1992). These two characteristics occur disproportionately among African-American, Latina, and Native American women. Poverty causes the

A Latina holds her sick child outside a Los Angeles area hospital facing service cutbacks and closing. Cutbacks in healthcare services disproportionately affect poor women and their children. Photo © 1996 Kim Kulish.

conditions that lead to poor health, such as inadequate housing (e.g., risk of injury and illnesses such as lead poisoning), malnutrition, dangerous jobs, little or no preventive health care, lack of health insurance, and lack of access to health care (Leigh, 1995). For instance, many women of color lack private health-care insurance for themselves and their families. Those having only public insurance coverage include 31.5% of African Americans, 18.3% of Latinas, and 6.8% of European Americans (Horton, 1995). Additionally, environmental causes of ill health are increasingly being implicated in some cancers and other diseases because environmental hazards are disproportionately located in poor communities of color.

Racism is also a factor in the lower quality of health and health care that women of color experience. This racism has a long history. One of the founders of modern gynecology, J. Marion Sims, developed a repair for vesicovaginal fistulas (a tear from bladder to vagina, which can cause urinary incontinence and considerable discomfort) by operating on unanesthesized enslaved African-American women (cited by Laurence & Weinhouse, 1994). Racism in medicine also has a more recent history. In 1971 researcher Joseph Goldzieher conducted a study on Latina women in San Antonio, Texas, to study the side effects of the birth-control pill. He devised a study in which a fifth of the sample population received a placebo, and 10 women became pregnant within months. In response to the questioning of his study, Goldzieher is reported to have said, "If you think you can explain a placebo test to women like these, you never met Mrs. Gomez from the West side" (cited in Laurence & Weinhouse, 1994, p. 23).

Racism's effects on health are twofold: (1) Structural racism places barriers of access to high-quality health care, and (2) racism can have direct effects on health by creating physiological changes in the racism victim's body, in response to stress (Leigh, 1995). Clearly, the health of women of color is affected by their race and class, as well as their gender.

Lesbian Women and the Health-Care System

Lesbian women are often an invisible population within the health-care system. The history of their treatment by health-care providers has been abysmal, as their homosexuality was often viewed as a disease to be cured or a criminal act to be punished. The so-called treatment at the hands of the medical and the mental health professions are horrific and have included electroshock treatment, genital mutilation, aversive therapy, and hormonal injections (Stevens, 1992).

Although attitudes have changed over the years, prejudices and stereotypes still abound within the health-care system. Patricia Stevens (1992) examined research about lesbians in the health-care system from 1970 to 1990 and found a mere 28 studies in 20 years. Several of the studies Stevens reviewed focused on the attitudes of health-care professionals toward lesbian women. The studies' findings suggest that lesbianism is still considered an affliction by many health-care providers. Significant numbers of providers were uncomfortable providing services to lesbians and often held stereotypical views of lesbians. In response to a survey, health-care professionals variously described lesbian women as "unnatural," "disgusting," "immoral," "perverted," and "criminal" (Stevens, 1992).

Not surprisingly, lesbian woman's health-care experiences reflect this homophobia and bias. Lesbians often report that the provider's heterosexist assumptions are a problem. According to lesbian clients, such conditions "made them feel invisible and led providers to misdiagnose conditions, provide inadequate treatment, offer irrelevant health teaching, lecture about birth control, ask insensitive and biased questions, make sexist remarks, and alienate lesbians from the entire health care process" (Stevens, 1992, p. 110). Stevens's review of the literature revealed studies demonstrating that lesbians tend to delay seeking health care because of their fears and poor health-care experiences. Financial costs also were a factor in limiting help-seeking behavior. Studies also found that lesbian women expressed an overwhelming preference for female health-care providers, especially if the providers were also lesbians (Stevens, 1992).

Because women have been ignored in health research and lesbian women are an invisible subset of women, there is little information about the specific health-care concerns and risks of lesbian women. Suzanne Haynes of the

National Cancer Institute began to look at the links between cancer and lesbianism in 1992 and found that no studies existed (Whittelsey & Carroll, 1995). By analyzing the risk factors for breast cancer among lesbians, she concluded that lifetime breast-cancer rates may be proportionately higher among lesbians than among all women in general—in fact, it is two to three times higher for older lesbians (Whittelsey & Carroll, 1995). The identified risk factors that were more common among lesbians than among heterosexual women were higher rates of alcohol use and smoking, lower prevalence of childbearing, and inadequate access to health care.

Additionally, lesbian women are less likely to have regular appointments with their gynecologists, often because they have less need of contraceptive information and less chance of acquiring sexually transmitted disease (STD) infections. One study cited by Horton (1995) found that 58% of lesbian women sought gynecological care only when problems occurred, rather than on a regular, preventive basis. This lack of regular preventive checkups also reduces a lesbian's access to screening for breast and cervical cancer. Clearly, much more research must be conducted on the special health-care needs of lesbians. Health-care providers must also examine their institutions and practices to make them more inclusive for women of all sexual orientations.

Profiting from Women's Bodies

Although it is easy to identify misogyny as a cause for controlling women's bodies, another important driving force is the economics that increasingly fuels the direction of health care. Medical intervention on female bodies makes money for doctors, pharmaceutical companies, medical-supply companies, hospitals, and other interests. At one time, the following joke was popular in medical school. Question: What are the symptoms for a hysterectomy? Answer: A Blue Shield card and $250 for the deductible

(Whittelsey & Carroll, 1995). John Smith, an obstetrician and gynecologist (OB-GYN), cited many reasons for the excessive number of hysterectomies, including "hysterectomies are deliberately sold to women by doctors who use the operation as the major source of income" (1992, p. 47).

Naomi Wolf has taken on the $300-million cosmetic surgery industry as profiting from the bodies of women (1991), she also attacked the $33-billion-a-year diet industry, in which the medical profession also takes part. In addition, drugs are relentlessly marketed to women and their doctors (Laurence & Weinhouse, 1994). Although most medications are expensive, the ones sold to women in America seem especially high. For instance, Premarin (estrogen) cost 28 cents a pill in the United States, but only 9 cents in Britain; similarly, Norplant was selling in Sweden and some developing companies for as little as $23, while it was initially sold by Wyeth-Ayerst for $365 in the United States (Laurence & Weinhouse, 1994).

Women's health-care centers often spring up overnight, supposedly to meet the special needs of female patients. However, social workers Marta Lundy and Sally Mason caution that some women's health-care centers "may be more in keeping with the historically exploitative practices of the medical profession where the intent is profit, not comprehensive health care. Women's centers may be primarily a marketing tool" (Lundy & Mason, 1994, p. 118). Some of these misnamed women's centers encourage physicians and other health-care workers to treat, and even hospitalize, women labeled with codependency. Often, the staff members of these facilities have no special knowledge or understanding of women but are interested in profits, rather than women.

Health Concerns of Women

It is beyond the scope of this book to outline the specific health problems women face and how each of these areas have often been ignored, defined, or marginalized by the medical profession. Many good books exist on these topics, and students are urged to read more about each specific health problem (Coney, 1985; Corea, 1985; Laurence & Weinhouse, 1994). Just to highlight some of the issues, several topics are briefly introduced here.

The difference in the number of surgeries performed on women, as compared to men, is startling. Nearly 15 million women have inpatient surgery each year, compared to 8½ million men (Laurence & Weinhouse, 1994). Of the 12 most frequently performed surgical procedures, 7 are unique to women, while only 1 (prostatectomy) is unique to men (Laurence & Weinhouse, 1994). For example, the hysterectomy rate is three times higher in the United States than in any country where comparable statistics are available (Smith, 1992). Smith wrote that "many male gynecologists feel that the uterus is a disposable organ, one that bleeds, cramps, carries babies, and gets cancer" (p. 44).

The course of HIV/AIDS is less understood in women than in men, for early studies focused on the disease in gay men and later in heterosexual men. When the incidence for women increased, little was known about how best to screen, diagnose, and treat women. Women died more quickly after diagnosis, leading some to speculate that the disease had a faster progression in women than in men, although early death was subsequently determined to be more the result of late diagnosis and lack of access to experimental drugs. Another difficulty for women with HIV/AIDS was that the definition of the disease was based on a male model, which created numerous difficulties for women. For instance, to receive disability and other social services, a diagnosis of AIDS is often required. Yet many women who were seriously ill with the disease did not qualify for assistance because they did not have enough of the specified opportunistic infections to be diagnosed as having AIDS. The Centers for Disease Control did expand the definition in 1992 to include invasive cervical cancer, but other conditions that affect only women are excluded, such as vaginal thrush, pelvic inflammatory disease, and vaginal condylomas (Norman & Dumois, 1995).

Women's substance abuse is another area imbued with a male perspective. When women were studied, it was most often in relationship to the effects of her drug use on either her unborn fetus or her ability to parent her children. Numerous articles can be found on fetal alcohol syndrome or on "crack mothers," with only a few articles focusing on women substance abusers in their own right. Additionally, gender differences in substance-abuse progression, assessment, and treatment have been ignored (Forth-Finegan, 1991); National Center on Addiction and Substance Abuse, 1996; Wilke, 1994). Treatment centers that specifically treat women and make provisions for their children are few and far between. For instance, Ferguson and Kaplan's (1994) review of the literature found that of Ohio's 16 treatment facilities for women, only 2 provided child-care services. Another study Ferguson and Kaplan reviewed found that 54% of the treatment facilities in New York City did not treat pregnant women, 67% did not treat pregnant women on Medicaid, and 87% would not treat pregnant, crack-addicted women on Medicaid.

The definition of menopause as an estrogen-deficiency disease, with estrogen as the cure, has raised some serious questions about how disease is defined and treated in women. (As Susan Love, 1997, p. xvii, has asked, "If 'estrogen difficiency' is a disease, are all men sick?"). The rapid prescription of estrogen as a miracle drug was curtailed somewhat with the mid-1970s publication of studies that first linked estrogen to an increase in endometrial cancer (Coney, 1994). Fears of an increase in breast cancer due to estrogen were also reported, along with estrogen's beneficial effects on osteoporosis. With little research to base decisions on, women had little more than the assurances of their doctors, who were aggressively marketed drugs for female patients.

Coney (1994) wrote, "Complicated risk/benefit arguments are put forward, resembling nothing less than an intricate chess game in which bones saved are checked off against malignant tumors in the breasts, and canceled heart attacks are measured against concerns in the uterus" (p. 205).

Increasingly, breast cancer has gained attention, as activists have had to take to the streets and legislatures to get funding for this disease, for which each woman now has a one in eight lifetime risk (Horton, 1995). A strong advocate for the fight against breast cancer is artist and activist Matuschka. Her photograph of herself on the cover of *The New York Times Magazine*, revealing her mastectomy scar, provoked both admiration and condemnation. Her message raises awareness about the possible environmental links to breast cancer, as well as taking on the media for its exclusive portrayal of only "perfect" female bodies. Matuschka's photographs increase awareness, educate the public, promote prevention efforts, and present freedom for women from the tyranny of idealized female bodies.

Reproductive Issues

Reproductive freedom is a women's health issue. Birth control and abortion are intimate matters concerning a woman's control over her own body and her decisions about whether to have children. This simple statement is frequently lost in the political struggles that birth control and abortion have become in this country. Political fervor over abortion has removed the discussion of abortion from the medical arena between a woman and her doctor and has placed it in the political arena, where any interested party can intrude. New drugs and procedures that would terminate a pregnancy are not debated on their merits of safety and effectiveness, but on political clout and number of votes (Lader, 1991). The bodies of women have become battlegrounds on which others fight their ideological wars.

"Beauty Out of Damage." First published by **The New York Times** on The New York Times Magazine *cover, Sunday, August 13, 1993. Copyright 1993 by Matuschka, reprinted by permission of the artist.*

Birth Control and Reproductive Education

One of the early battles fought in these wars was Margaret Sanger's campaign to educate women about their bodies and about birth control, so that women could avoid the unwanted pregnancies and dangerous abortion procedures of the day. Margaret Sanger often told the story of Mrs. Sach, whom she attended as a visiting nurse. Mrs. Sach was very ill with the complications of a septic abortion when Margaret Sanger first met her. When Mrs. Sach begged the doctor for information on how to avoid more pregnancies, the doctor is said to have told her to have her husband Jake sleep on the roof (Chesler, 1992). Three months later, Margaret Sanger was at her bedside again, as Mrs. Sach lay dying of septicemia. In Sanger's attempts to educate women about birth control, she wrote a column for a socialist newspaper, *The Call*, entitled "What Every Girl Should Know" (Chesler, 1992). The column was banned by public censor Anthony Comstock, and the following week, the column was replaced by a blank box, which was titled "What Every Girl Should Know—Nothing: By order of the U.S. Post Office" (Chesler, 1992).

Although birth-control methods and knowledge have come a long way since the days of Margaret Sanger, battles to control women's reproduction continue. For instance, Norplant implants were offered as conditions of probation for poor women, and the French pill mifepristone (RU-486) has fought a long, uphill battle to be tested and accepted in the United States. Although Claude Evin, the French minister of health, called the drug the "moral property of women," the Reagan and Bush administrations, as well as the U.S. Food and Drug Administration (FDA), have led the fight to suppress the drug's use in the United States (Lader, 1991).

The U.S. Supreme Court decision *Roe v. Wade* made abortion legal, based on a woman's constitutional right to privacy. The decision was based on a trimester calculation in which the state's interest in the fetus increased with the viability of the fetus. Although later Supreme Court decisions have allowed restrictions, the basic right of a woman to choose abortion has been upheld. These increased restrictions include parental consent, mandated waiting periods, and denial of public funds for abortion. The rate of abortions has remained relatively constant since the mid-1970s, with the rate being 33.5 per 100 live births in 1992 (National Center for Health Statistics, 1994). This translates into 1.53 million abortions being reported in 1992 (Horton, 1995).

Illegal Abortion: One Woman's Story

Before the *Roe v. Wade* decision, abortion was illegal. Women had few choices regarding how to respond to pregnancy. Since that time, women have begun to break the silence and to share their stories about obtaining illegal abortions. Their stories are as varied as the women who tell them, with some women going to clean medical facilities after office hours, and receiving safe, professional care, whereas other women were forced to go to untrained abortionists in less than ideal conditions. Women often hemorrhaged, developed infections, and even died. This account is given by actor Margot Kidder (1991, p. 98):

> I was told to undress and lie in the bathtub, which I did. John was in the other room. There was no anesthetic, of course. She crammed something through my cervix. It was incredibly painful. I was screaming and crying; I had no idea what was happening to me. Then she used what looked like a douche to shoot some sort of solution up through my cervix. When it was over, I remember lying in the bathtub weeping in pain and overhearing a mumbled conversation in the other room between the woman and John, then she left.
>
> John came in and took me in his arms and put me in bed and explained to me that I was going to go through a lot of pain, but eventually the fetal matter would come out, and I would be fine. I was told to take some pills she'd given us for the pain; we didn't even ask what they were.
>
> I began to go into labor, incredibly horrific pain for I don't know how many hours—ghastly, ghastly pain. I was screaming and clutching John and sobbing and didn't know what was happening. And yet we had made a pact that under no condition would we go to a hospital; we felt we should honor it, for her sake. So I ate the pills she'd given me, which didn't do anything. The pain continued, I was bleeding, I kept passing out.
>
> Finally John said, "I don't care what happens to us; we're going to the hospital." I don't remember how I got there, in an ambulance, a taxi. I barely remember getting into the emergency ward, being rushed on a stretcher somewhere, and then I was out. When I came to—I don't know how many hours later—a doctor and nurse came in, and they looked very scornfully at me, the nurse with a bit of

pity. I was told that I almost died, that the woman had filled me full of Lysol.

Social workers must bear in mind, however, that the legality of abortion and the accessibility of it are two different things. According to Carole Joffe's review of the literature, 84% of all U.S. counties are without abortion facilities, only 12% of OB-GYN residencies require training in first-trimester abortion techniques, and only 6% require training for second-trimester abortions (Joffe, 1995). Increasingly, abortion clinics have been the targets of arson, bombings, vandalism, and disruptive actions, while abortion providers have been harassed, threatened, and even killed.

Abortion activists are generally divided into two groups: prochoice and prolife. Prochoice activists are not necessary proabortion but believe that each woman has the right to control her own body and reproductive options. Prolife groups place primacy on the life of the fetus, usually believing that life begins at conception and often proclaiming that abortion is murder. These two categories cross many religious and political lines, as reflected by the formation of such diverse groups as Republican Women for Choice, Catholics for a Free Choice, and Feminists Against Abortion.

Abortion remains a contentious issue in America, and social workers have not been spared from the fracas. Social workers are on both sides of the issue. NASW has drafted a policy statement concerning abortion, which does not take a position concerning the morality of abortion. The statement refers to the profession's belief in self-determination as the basis for the position that "Every individual (within the context of his or her value system) must be free to participate or not participate in abortion services. Women should have the right to participate in or refrain from abortion counseling" (NASW, 1994, p. 3). The statement lists the services that should be available to all women, including counseling and referral of patients, provided by professionally trained staff members who are knowledgeable of the social and psychological dynamics of unwanted pregnancy and abortion; safe surgical care, as requested; and counseling about and provision of appropriate contraceptive devices (NASW, 1994).

Reproductive freedom involves much more than the issue of abortion. It also includes women's access to contraceptive alternatives. Reproductive freedom means not only access to services, but also freedom from coercion, such as freedom from forced sterilization, forced abortion, and fetal-protection policies that limit women's choices. As new technologies become available, the discussions and debates will continue, for new technologies often bring new ways to control women, such as (a) treating women as incubators rather than human beings and (b) exploiting women as reproductive surrogates (Corea, 1985). Social workers must keep abreast of the many changes and must examine the ramifications of these changes for the self-determination of women.

Fetal-Protection Policies

Fetal-protection policies are protective regulations and laws that attempt to protect each fetus residing in a woman's uterus. Although these policies seem well-intentioned on the surface, many of these policies pit the rights of the mothers against the rights of the fetus. Lesbian stand-up comic Sara Cytron has commented on this state of affairs by saying, "The last time people in this society cared about my rights was when I was a fetus." This humorous account alludes to the priority often given to the fetus over a living, breathing woman. In some discussions, women are treated as walking incubators instead of human beings in their own right. This view of women as animate objects was evident in the initial awareness of the AIDS epidemic, during which initial concern was focused on women as vectors of transmission, with emphasis on how women may transmit the virus to their fetuses or to their male partners, rather than on the effect of the virus on the women themselves.

One type of fetal-protection policy is a set of workplace regulations that target women on the basis of their childbearing capacity (Nuccio & Mama, 1990). Although such policies are often designed to protect women and their fetuses, the policies often have an unintentional (or perhaps intentional) effect of limiting the economic potential of women. The inherent double standard in such policies is rarely addressed, despite the documented danger for male workers and their subsequent children, as well (Nuccio & Mama, 1990). In some cases, women have been encouraged or even economically coerced to be sterilized in order to meet protection policies, only to be transferred or laid off thereafter. Nuccio and Mama (1990) report "the key issue for policymakers and social workers is this: Is the policy based on the *gender* of female workers or the risk to *all* workers?" (p. 47, italics in original). A balance must be achieved, where the rights of females are protected while maintaining the health and safety of all workers.

Another area of fetal-protection policies that seem to favor the fetus over the woman is when punitive policies are aimed at pregnant, chemically dependent women. Women who are both pregnant and chemically dependent often receive little support yet much condemnation. Increasingly, such women are charged with supplying drugs to a minor, child abuse, and even manslaughter (Gustavsson, 1991). Sometimes, they are jailed and even mandated birth control as terms of probation. Gustavsson has noted that "Pregnant women, under certain circumstances, have lost control of their bodies to physicians and the courts" (p. 66). This control is not limited to chemically dependent women. One story that made national headlines is that of the pregnant woman who sued a server and the restaurant for which the server worked for refusing to serve the mother an alcoholic beverage. Again, the double standard is readily observed, for men are not punished or treated in such a manner when the sperm they contribute may also affect a developing fetus. In fact, the latest research demonstrates that a man's sperm is more easily damaged than a woman's egg; biologist Irina Pollard said, "Genetic abnormalities are more often linked with paternal than with maternal DNA damage" (cited in Boyd, 1997, p. 19A). It will be interesting to see whether this new research leads to restrictions, regulations, and punishment of men for the potential damage they contribute to their offspring.

Gustavsson (1991) recommended changing the focus from viewing mothers as the enemy to recognizing that the mother and the child are a couple. She advocated both removing barriers to drug treatment for pregnant chemically addicted women and providing more comprehensive services, which include health care, drug treatment, housing and financial assistance, job training, parenting skills, training in infant care, child care, counseling, and more. The attempt to control women's bodies is not the answer. Too often, such tactics backfire, making women more reluctant to come forward for prenatal care, as well as for drug treatment.

Female Genital Mutilation

Some readers may be surprised to see the topic of female genital mutilation (FGM) discussed in an American textbook in a chapter on women's bodies. Although the practice most often occurs in Africa, the Middle East, and Southeast Asia, immigration has meant that some of these mutilations are being performed in the United States. Also, some older women are coming to U.S. medical centers to seek treatment for complications from mutilating procedures performed on them when they were young girls or to request that the procedure be reversed where possible. Current estimates are that 2 million girls are maimed worldwide each year, with 10,000 girls at risk in the United States each year (Jensen, 1996). When President Clinton signed the Department of Defense appropriations bill, female genital mutilation became illegal in the United States, as of March 29, 1997, due to legislation sponsored by former Representative Patricia Schroeder (D–Colorado) and Senator Harry Reid (D–Nevada). Previously, a handful of states had chosen to make it a felony to perform FGM. In addition to outlawing the procedure, the law also requires data collection on the prevalence of the practice, providing outreach to affected groups, as well as making recommendations to medical schools regarding treatment of its complications (Equality Now, 1996).

Female genital mutilation is usually categorized into three degrees of severity: (1) The *sunna* or *circumcision* is removal of the prepuce or hood of the clitoris, with the body of the clitoris remaining intact. (2) The *excision of the clitoris,* or *clitoridectomy,* is the removal of the clitoris and all or part of the labia minora. (3) *Infibulation,* or *pharaonic excision,* involves removal of the clitoris, the labia minora, and much of the labia majora. The remaining sides of the vulva are then stitched together to close up the vagina, leaving only a small opening for the flow of menstrual blood and urine (Calder, Brown, & Rae, 1993; Ntiri, 1993; Walker & Parmar, 1993).

In Africa, estimates of the number of girls and women who have undergone one of these three procedures is estimated to range from 60 to 70 million (Ntiri, 1993). The procedure is usually performed on a girl anywhere from age 1 week to age 14 years, by a traditional midwife or an older woman, often without the benefit of anesthesia or asepsis. Many complications can result, including hemorrhage, infection, and death. Long-term effects are vaginal disorders, childbirth complications, difficult sexual encounters (often, women must be cut open on their wedding nights for intercourse to take place), scarring, urinary-tract infections, and fistulas (Calder et al., 1993; Ntiri, 1993).

Some feminists have been outspoken about this practice, both here in the United States and in countries where it is traditionally performed. Author–activist Alice Walker and filmmaker Pratibha Parmar have written a book (1993)

and have produced a movie about the practice. In response to those who have branded as cultural imperialists the Western feminists who have spoken out against the practice, Walker has pointed out that FGM is not culture, but torture (Walker & Parmar, 1993).

In 1979, in Khartoum, the World Health Organization (WHO) recommended the abolishment of FGM. Increasingly, the problem is being framed not only as a women's rights issue, but also as a human rights and health issue of global importance. Many African women who have themselves undergone the procedure have organized to end FGM (Jensen, 1996), although many Islamic women argue for the continuation of the practice. Various reasons are given for performing the procedure: to control women's sexuality, to guarantee virginity until marriage, to ensure an economic future for a girl child, to subjugate women, to protect young girls against rape, and to give consideration to hygiene esthetics, and religious ritual (Calder et al., 1993).

Because FGM is occurring in the United States, it behooves social workers to be familiar with the procedure, either when it is requested of providers or when complications arise from having the procedure performed outside of medical facilities. Calder et al. (1993) surveyed Somalian women to see what care they would accept in a Western health-care facility. The women responded that they would first turn to female relatives and then to female nurses, midwives, and physicians. Calder noted that health-care workers have a responsibility to help individuals and families become aware of services available in their communities while also increasing their own knowledge and understanding of other cultures.

The most recent development in the struggle to outlaw the practice involved a decision by the Board of Immigration Appeals, which granted political asylum to a 19-year-old woman from the African nation of Togo, based on her wish to evade FGM. This decision was the first in the United States to recognize the fear of FGM as a legitimate ground for asylum (Dugger, 1996). The board found that the level of harm can constitute persecution, which is the basis for granting asylum. Although detractors of the decision feared the floodgates would be opened for women seeking similar protection, supporters acknowledge that most women do not have the resources or the control over their lives to leave their countries (Superville, 1996). For instance, although Canada recognized FGM as a rationale for asylum in 1993, only half of the roughly 800 claims have been granted in that country (Superville, 1996).

Social Workers and Women's Health

Before we examine the specific practice and policy implications for social workers in this arena, let's look at the position of social workers in health care. Social workers have been active in the women's health movement. Many schools of social work have a separate track or specialty, which specifically trains social work students as medical social workers. In fact, the third largest area of practice in social work is in the medical field, with 13% of social workers employed in medical settings (Hopps & Collins, 1995).

Olson (1994) has noted the similarities between social work and women's health. Both movements share a perspective on health care that addresses the whole person and views that person in the context of her (or his) environment. This shared perspective makes social workers natural allies in the women's health movement. Olson reported the need for organized advocacy and political action. She also added, "it is especially important that social workers turn our congruence with the women's health movement into an active and visible alliance by helping clients to make the personal–political connections, by organizing ourselves, by joining with other like-minded professional groups, and by joining women's health advocacy groups" (Olson, 1994, p. 14).

Social workers have had great impact on practice and policy issues concerning women's health. Two hospital-based social workers who include political activism as part of their jobs are Ellen Parker and Laurie Hackett of the New England Medical Center, who cofounded the Massachusetts Breast Cancer Coalition (Bricker-Jenkins, 1994). Social worker Phyllis Greenberger is executive director of the Society for the Advancement of Women's Health Research, a nonprofit organization established in 1990 to address the lack of research on women's health issues. Clearly, despite many obstacles and in spite of the changing health-care system, social workers are on the forefront in advocating for women's health.

Nonetheless, many obstacles have made it difficult for social workers to act as patient advocates. At times, there seems to have been a lack of interest in women's health by social workers. For instance, one study (Millner & Widerman, 1994) assessed the ways in which social work is addressing issues in women's health care by reviewing the professional journals for articles on women's health. The 11 most prominent social work journals were surveyed over the years 1985–1992, and they were found to include only 36 articles on women's health, 19 articles concerning reproductive subjects, and 17 other articles about issues related to medical diagnoses. The study's authors were disappointed in the small number of articles on women's health, noting that the majority of these articles used the disease perspective of the medical model, and they followed the traditional view of seeing women's health as solely concerning reproductive issues. The authors (Millner & Widerman, 1994) ended with a call to social workers to take a leading role in women's health.

Olson (1994) has outlined some of the structural elements that have affected both women's health care and social workers' efforts to advocate for the health of their patients. Olson cited the enormous economic interests and influences of the pharmaceutical, medical supplies, and insurance industries, as well as the medical profession. Olson also noted the rigidly hierarchical nature of traditional hospital systems, where most doctors are male, and most social workers are female. She also identified the belief in the superiority of medicine, based on so-called hard science, over social work, based on soft-science, as another reason for the devaluation of social workers and their knowledge and perspective (Olson, 1994).

Another difficulty for medical social workers is the dilemma in which they often find themselves, as employees of hospitals and other health-care agencies, which the workers describe as being caught between the proverbial rock and a hard place. That is, social workers are frequently employed by institutions that have a very different agenda than the social worker's agenda of being a patient advocate. This dilemma has become even more difficult, due to the recent pressures to cut expenditures for health care. Some social workers fear that health-care decisions are being made based on cost, rather than patient welfare; this basis for decision making has made the medical social worker's role very difficult. Some social workers have even left the field, citing strains and stresses, as well as ethical dilemmas.

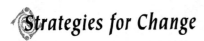

Strategies for Change

PRACTICE FOR CHANGE

The primary practice strategy involves helping clients to regain power and control over their bodies. Empowering clients often involves teaching or sharing information. Social workers can (a) teach clients to obtain a second opinion on major health concerns, (b) inform clients of the growing alternative medicines and therapies, and (c) refer clients to the multitudes of advocacy organizations that exist to inform and educate their members while lobbying for policy changes. An invaluable service that social workers can provide is to teach women to become advocates and informed consumers on their own behalf. Too many women are taught to assume the sick role of a passive, subordinate patient

when active participation in their health care is vital. Social workers should encourage clients to ask questions and to check their physicians' credentials. Social workers can teach clients these skills and can support them in the skill-acquisition process. Social workers can also refer women to the wealth of books currently available on a wide range of women's health issues. Empowerment also involves acknowledging and honoring women's extraordinary strengths in coping with illness in their own lives and in the lives of their families and friends.

Women are leading healthier lives than ever, yet women's health can be further improved by paying increased attention to preventive health care. Social work practice should emphasize preventive care whenever possible. Women, on average, live longer than men, but many women suffer chronic health problems that intrude on their quality of life. Preventive health care—such as exercise, good nutrition, vitamin and mineral (e.g., calcium) supplements, and preventive health services—can help clients and social workers to live healthier lives.

Referrals and Reframing

Support groups are vital to women with acute, chronic, or life-threatening diseases. Too often, women feel isolated and alone. Support groups can provide comfort and validation, as well as a sharing of medical information and experiences. Social workers need either to develop a list of available support groups for client referral or to start such groups if none exist in their area.

John Smith, an OB-GYN and author of *Women and Doctors* (1992), has recommended that women be referred to female gynecologists. He also supports the use of nurse-practitioners and midwives for women's reproductive health care. Social workers should have referral sources of women health-care providers and of male health-care providers who are sensitive to, and trained in, the special health-care needs of women. Again, social workers need to be wary of the so-called women's centers that may give attention to women in pursuit of a profit motive, rather than a sincere desire to meet the special needs of women.

Social workers can also enlarge their referral sources to include alternative treatments. Although alternative therapies were once viewed with some suspicion, they have gained greater acceptance today. Alternative or concurrent therapies may include acupuncture, homeopathy, humor, vitamins, meditation, yoga, special diets, and much more.

An invaluable service that social workers can provide is reframing a woman's body and its functions. For example, menstruation is often viewed as a dirty, shameful process. A study of menstrual-product advertisements (Coutts & Berg, 1993) found that the underlying messages to women are that (a) women's bodies are unclean, (b) women should fear menstrual discovery, (c) menstruation involves tainted femininity, and (d) women require a complex menstrual management system. Women who receive such messages may internalize the messages. Social workers can reframe such thinking while assisting women in celebrating the positive aspects of female bodies.

Similar work can be done regarding menopause and other physiological transitions in a woman's life. Through teaching, sharing, and exploring, social workers can help women to reframe menopause from being an end of womanhood to being reconceptualized as "post-menopausal zest," as described by Margaret Mead. A favorite T-shirt slogan reframes "hot flashes" as "power surges." Women have been taught to criticize, distrust, and be ashamed of their bodies' functions and odors. Women can learn new messages, which celebrate the beauty of female bodies in all their diversity of size, shape, and color. Yet Coney (1994) has cautioned feminists not to overidealize the lives of older women, for each woman's experience must be honored without imposing rosy interpretations on an event that may be disturbing for some women.

The reframing of health issues also means making the personal political. Social worker and breast cancer survivor Mary Bricker-Jenkins (1994) made this point powerfully in writing about her own experience with breast cancer.

> *Social workers must first change the ideological lens through which we view the woman with breast cancer. We must shift from a convex pathological lens—which narrows our focus to the behavior and lifestyle of a victim—to a concave lens through which we can see the strengths of the survivor as well as such impinging ecological contexts as environmental pollution and socioeconomic oppression. These can be scripted into the research questions we ask, the policies and programs we formulate, and every practice encounter we have with women with breast cancer. (p. 25)*

The politicizing of health issues, which may increase women's control over their own bodies, involves a multitude of actions, including demonstrations, lobbying, creating symbols such as pink ribbons for breast-cancer awareness, fundraising, and agency and regulation oversight, to ensure that women are included in research and that women's health issues are funded. Women are increasingly sharing their stories of loss and survival. Joyce Wadler described her experience with breast cancer in her book *My Breast* (1992). Similarly, Lucille Clifton (1996) wrote about her experience with breast cancer in her volume of poetry, *The Terrible Stories*. One of her poems, "lumpectomy eve," is included here.

lumpectomy eve

all night i dream of lips
that nursed and nursed
and the lonely nipple

lost in loss and the need
to feed that turns at last
on itself that will kill

its body for its hunger's sake
all night i hear the whispering
the soft

   love calls you to this knife
   for love for love

all night it is the one breast
comforting the other

Culturally Competent Practice

The pressing health concerns of women of color have implications for all health-care workers in both the policy and the practice arenas. More research is needed to study the racial differences in the incidence, diagnosis, and treatment of disease in women. The current women's health movement has included the special needs of women of color in the call for more participation by women of all races in research—as participants, researchers, and health-care providers. Several landmark reports have been issued by public agencies, including the 1993 report entitled *One Voice, One Vision,* issued by the 1992–1993 Hispanic/Latino Health Initiative, spearheaded by former U.S. Surgeon General Antonia Novello, and the U.S. Department of Health and Human Services reports of the secretary's Task Force on Black and Minority Health, released in 1985 and 1986. Much more research needs to be done, especially in regard to other women of color, including Asian-American and Arab-American women, and other underserved populations of women.

Social workers would do well to become more knowledgeable about the specific health concerns of women of color, as well as about impediments to their receiving high-quality health care. Both practice and research should consider the unique needs and values of women of color. Land (1994) noted that empowerment approaches to health care use cultural values and build on the strengths of the culture. For instance, in reaching African-American women who are at relatively high risk for HIV/AIDS, prevention and early detection practices can be couched in cultural values, such as "linking behavior change to pride in one's culture, noting adverse effects of AIDS in African American communities, and stressing family responsibility to protect the children" (Land, 1994, p. 358). Some other issues to consider when working with African-

American women regarding HIV/AIDS in particular, and regarding other health issues in general, is the need to (a) increase the number of culturally competent health providers, including African-American women; (b) recognize addiction as a problem underlying HIV infection and other issues; (c) treat addiction; (d) include the families of African-American women in treatment; (e) provide child care for women undergoing treatment; and (f) gain access to informal caregivers within the family (Land, 1994).

Cultural sensitivity requires knowledge of the culture, values, and help-seeking behaviors of many different ethnic and racial groups. For instance, Land has noted that many Latinas prefer an informal, familial approach to help giving. Land (1994) stated,

> *Incorporating cultural values in the treatment relationship increases the likelihood of success. These values include establishing trust (confianza) through personalizing the relationship rather than assuming solely a professional posture (personalismo), taking sufficient time to be respectful of the client and family structure (respecto), communicating a personalized sympathetic and empathetic response (simpatía), sharing some personal information with the client, and even acknowledging the value of emulating qualities of the Virgin Mary, such as compassion, patience, endurance, and bravery (Marianisma). (p. 358; emphasis added)*

Religious and folk practices must be also taken into account, as some Latina clients may seek out a *curandero* or a *curandera* (folk healer) or may purchase herbs to treat themselves.

The needs of Native American women are often unique and vary by tribe and region. Tom-Orme (1995) recommended improving the health of Native American women by involving them in their personal health; by increasing their involvement in planning and participation in community-level interventions; by ensuring that health-care services are culturally competent; and by increasing health-profession educational opportunities to enable more Native American women to become health-care providers in tribal communities.

Women of color are leading the way in promoting research and practice that is ethnospecific. For instance, The National Black Women's Health Project was founded in 1989 by grassroots organizer Byllye Avery. The organization sponsors community-based self-help programs, conferences, and educational films and publications. Other women of color are writing books directed at health-care professionals, as well as self-help books for women of color, which highlight their race-specific health concerns (Adams, 1995; Villarosa, 1994; White, 1994). Much more information is available than ever before, and social workers need to be involved in creating and utilizing such resources.

POLICY FOR CHANGE

Social workers must be active in the policy arena, as well as the practice arena, to shape health-care policies that benefit women. Although the education of individual health-care professionals, researchers, and patients is important, reform must also occur at a policy level. This chapter raised many specific problems that are most appropriately addressed in the policy arena, such as ensuring reproductive freedom and prohibiting female genital mutilation. To achieve needed policy changes, social workers can employ a variety of strategies, including letter and editorial writing, lobbying and testifying before Congress, and providing financial support to organizations that are actively engaged in policy formulation and advocacy. Even after policies are adopted, social workers must remain vigilant to oversee the implementation of new policies.

One of the biggest policy issues regarding the control of women's bodies is the reform of the health-care system. Although health-care reform has not always been identified as a woman's issue, this issue has dramatic impact on millions of women. This policy issue has life-and-death implications for the health of women, as many women either have no health insurance or have insurance that does not cover lifesaving procedures or preventive screenings. Health-care reform affects every woman, but especially those at risk, such as poor women, older women, single mothers, and mothers receiving public assistance. Because of the importance of reform, this policy section focuses on health-care reform as it applies to women.

Health-Care Coverage

Lack of universal health-care coverage is a vital issue for social work attention and intervention. The percentage of Americans who have no health insurance is increasing, often because employers are dropping insurance coverage, excluding some employees, or shifting insurance-premium costs to employees who may not be able to afford them (Horton, 1995; National Center for Health Statistics, 1994). Although estimates of the number of Americans without health-care coverage vary, approximately 34 to 37 million people in the United States have no health insurance whatsoever.

Although men are more likely than women to be uninsured, some subgroups of women are uninsured at disproportionate rates. An estimated 19% of women in America are uninsured (Horton, 1995). Lack of insurance is affected by race, age, marital status, and work status. Women of color are less likely to be insured, as are women who are single, divorced, or separated. Women are more likely than men to be in part-time or temporary jobs, or in poorly paid jobs with lower rates of insurance coverage (Horton, 1995). Almost all women over the age of 65 years are insured due to Medicare coverage, although older women are less likely then men to have private coverage to replace or supplement Medicare (Horton, 1995). Additionally, Medicare tends to provide better coverage for the acute and expensive illnesses that are more likely to affect men, whereas it provides less adequate coverage for the chronic illnesses that' are more likely to affect women (Horton, 1995).

Women are affected not only by a lack of health insurance, but also by the inadequacy of insurance coverage. For instance, insurance companies and programs vary in their coverage of many important women's health-care services, such as cancer screening, pregnancy, family planning, and induced abortion (Horton, 1995). The average health-insurance expenditures for preventive health-care services are higher for women than for men (Horton, 1995). Deductible payments or copayments for these services can make these services less affordable for women. For instance, women ages 15 to 44 years had out-of-pocket expenditures for health-care services that were 68% higher than those of men of the same age (Horton, 1995).

Thus, it is clear that health-care reform must continue to be important to social workers. Although some changes are possible at the state level, most of the attention is currently focused at the federal level. During his first term, President Clinton made health-care reform an important part of his administration, appointing First Lady Hillary Rodham Clinton to preside over a special task force on health-care reform. As she combined the roles of First Lady and policymaker, Hillary Rodham Clinton came under harsh personal attack, as well as criticism for the president's Health Security Plan. Although the Clinton plan was not passed, and the issue, as of press time, is on the back burner, health-care reform is nonetheless an issue whose time has come.

Health-Care Reform

Social workers have long been involved in the public debate over health-care reform. Many plans have been proposed in the past and will be proposed in the future. Social workers need to be involved in developing and evaluating various plans; educating other people as to the benefits and costs of each plan; and lobbying Congress and the president for those plans that will best serve social workers and their clients. For instance, social worker Robert Scuka (1994) developed criteria for evaluating competing proposals for health-care reform, including the following: It must (1) guarantee universal access, (2) eliminate the link between employment status and access to health insurance, (3) eliminate cost-sharing impediments to gaining access to health care, (4) eliminate restrictions on preexisting conditions, (5) give priority to guaranteeing primary and preventive care, (6) control the proliferation of expensive medical technology, (7) establish a nationwide system of provider-fee schedules, and (8) establish health-care planning at the national level.

Although these criteria constitute a valuable starting place for evaluating health-care reform, Scuka's evaluation provides no gender analysis. When plans do not specifically address women, women's special concerns are often ignored and marginalized. Health-care reform is a woman's issue, and the unique needs of women must be taken into account when health-care reform is proposed. There are many strategies for achieving health-care reform. The practice strategies discussed here are the formation of study groups and of coalitions. Although each of these topics may more appropriately be included as an aspect of practice, because they are being utilized to promote policy change, they are discussed here in relation to policy.

Study Groups

In their book, *Strategies for Community Empowerment*, Hanna and Robinson (1994) advocated the formation of study groups to empower communities and to work toward transformative social change. They described a group coming together for the dual purpose of developing critical consciousness and of moving people to social change. Before policies can be formulated or advocated, it is crucial to know the issues and to discuss the full range of policy options. Hanna and Robinson's book includes this skill-development exercise:

> *You are a hospital social worker. Large changes are looming regarding health care reform at both the state and federal levels. In your state, the insurance companies and the for-profit medical industries are dominating the reform agenda. You and your coworkers are worried about what might happen in the future, but you feel powerless to have any impact. You decide to initiate a study circle for people to learn more about these issues and the options for reform, and to explore how you might be able to have some influence on the outcomes. How will you go about setting up the study circle? Ask yourself:*
>
> 1. *Who should I invite to participate?*
> 2. *When, where, and how often to meet?*
> 3. *How should we obtain materials to study and discuss?*
> 4. *How will our study group be facilitated?*

This classroom exercise can be used in life outside of the classroom on the very real issue of health-care reform. Some health-care professionals are considering unionization to protect their jobs, as well as to ensure the safety of their patients. A study circle is an ideal format in which to become informed, to debate the issues, and to develop policy initiatives.

Coalition Formation

Building coalitions is an effective practice strategy to utilize to influence public policy. Haynes and Mickelson have noted that "because there is strength in numbers, a lobbyist should include coalition building as a part of his or her total strategy" (1986, p. 70). They provide a definition of *coalition*: "A coalition is a loosely woven, ad hoc association of constituent groups, each of whose primary identification is outside the coalition" (p. 70). Coalitions can increase the clout, media attention, and funding that individual organizations would be unable to muster individually. Haynes and Mickelson noted two contradictory effects of diversity within a coalition: (1) The more diverse the groups are in a coalition, the more powerful the coalition becomes, but (2) the greater the diversity, the more vulnerable the coalition is to being splintered by outside opposing groups.

The Older Women's League (OWL) has spearheaded a coalition of interested women's groups to ensure that women's voices are heard in the health-care debate. The coalition is called the "Campaign for Women's Health" and comprises more than 90 national, state, and grassroots organizations. The coalition has taken an active role in evaluating health-care plans and offering recommendations on what women's health benefits any plan should include. Their mission includes the goal that "all services which are necessary or appropriate for the maintenance and promotion of women's health should be included in a benefits package" (Campaign for Women's Health, 1994). The campaign (Campaign for Women's Health, 1994) established a set of principles that must be incorporated into a national health plan and will only support those plans that assure the following:

- Universal coverage and equal access for all
- Affordable costs
- Mandated comprehensive benefits, including preventive and primary care, the full range of reproductive health-care services, and long-term care
- Access to a full range of providers and settings
- Accountability to include participation of women's health advocates in all commissions and regulatory bodies and to protect against discrimination
- Commitment to protect and advance a women's health-research agenda

The campaign has further detailed the specific provisions required for adherence to these principles. Additionally, Laurence and Weinhouse (1994) believe that woman-friendly health-care reform must include coverage for care by nurse-practitioners and nurse-midwives. The debate about health-care reform is far from over, and social workers must be on the front lines to protect the health of all female clients, who too often have been marginalized, ignored, and discriminated against in the past in health-care practice, policy, and research.

SUMMARY

For too long, women's bodies have been defined, controlled, and regulated by men. This chapter has merely touched the tip of the iceberg in outlining some of the ways in which this control has been legitimized. Happily, one of the biggest successes of the second wave of the women's movement has been the reappropriation of the female body by women. This process continues today, with the struggle for reproductive freedom and the burgeoning interests in development of a women's health specialty. Social workers have been involved in these issues, both as medical social workers and as activists. Empowering women to regain control over their bodies is an appropriate social work task, with much to be accomplished in both the practice and the policy arenas. Although conflicts and ethical dilemmas arise in this often emotionally charged arena, social workers are ideally suited to act as advocates for women, to increase the knowledge, choices, and control women have not only over their bodies, but also over their lives.

REFERENCES

Adams, D. L. (1995). *Health issues for women of color: A cultural diversity perspective.* Thousand Oaks, CA: Sage Publications.

Ayanian, J. Z., & Epstein, A. M. (1991). Differences in the use of procedures between women and men hospitalized for coronary heart disease. *New England Journal of Medicine, 325*(4), 221–225.

Bernstein, B., & Kane, R. (1981). Physicians' attitudes toward female patients. *Medical Care, 19*(6), 600–608.

Bogdan, J. C. (1990). Midwifery. In A. H. Zophy & F. M. Kavenik (Eds.), *Handbook of American women's history* (pp. 370–371; Garland reference library of the humanities; vol. 696). New York: Garland.

Boston Women's Health Collective. (1971). *Our bodies, ourselves: A book by and for women.* New York: Simon & Schuster.

Boyd, R. S. (1997, March 13). Life in womb will be written on your tomb. *Houston Chronicle,* p. 19A.

Bricker-Jenkins, M. (1994). Feminist practice and breast cancer: "The patriarchy has claimed my right breast." *Social Work and Health Care, 19*(3/4), 17–42.

Calder, B. L., Brown, Y. M. R., & Rae, D. I. (1993). Female circumcision/genital mutilation: Culturally sensitive care. *Health Care for Women International, 14,* 227–238.

Campaign for Women's Health. (1994). *A project of the Older Women's League.* Washington, DC: Author.

Chesler, E. (1992). *Margaret Sanger and the birth control movement in America.* New York: Simon & Schuster.

Clifton, L. (1996). *The terrible stories.* Brockport, NY: BOA Editions.

Coney, S. (1994). *The menopause industry: How the medical establishment exploits women.* Alameda, CA: Hunter House.

Corea, G. (1985). *The mother machine: Reproductive technologies from artificial insemination to artificial wombs.* London: Women's Press.

Council on Ethical and Judicial Affairs, American Medical Association. (1991, July 24/31). Gender disparities in clinical decision making. *Journal of* the *American Medical Association, 266*(4), 559–562.

Coutts, L. B., & Berg, D. H. (1993). The portrayal of the menstruating woman in menstrual product advertisements. *Health Care for Women International, 14,* 179–191.

Dugger, C. W. (1996, June 14). Woman wins asylum based on sex rite fear. *Houston Chronicle,* p. 23A.

Ehrenreich, B., & English, D. (1973). *Complaints and disorders: The sexual politics of sickness.* Old Westbury, NY: Feminist Press.

Equality Now. (1996). *Update on female genital mutilation.* New York: Author.

Ferguson, S. K., & Kaplan, M. S. (1994). Women and drug policy: Implications of normalization. *Affilia, 9*(2), 129–144.

Forth-Finegan, J. L. (1991). Sugar and spice and everything nice: Gender socialization and women's addiction—A literature review. In C. Bepko (Ed.), *Feminism and addiction* (pp. 19–48). New York: Haworth Press.

Fugh-Berman, A. (1994). Man to man at Georgetown: Tales out of medical school. In K. M. Hicks (Ed.), *Misdiagnosis: Woman as a disease* (pp. 47–53). Allentown, PA: People's Medical Society.

Gustavsson, N. S. (1991). Pregnant chemically dependent women: The new criminals. *Affilia, 6*(2), 61–73.

Hanna, M. G., & Robinson, B. (1994). *Strategies for community empowerment.* Lewiston, New York: Edwin Mellen Press.

Haynes, K. S., & Mickelson, J. S. (1986). *Affecting change: Social workers in the political arena.* New York: Longman.

Held, P. J., Pauly, M. V., Bovbjerg, R. R., Newmann, J., & Salvateirra, O. (1988). Access to kidney transplantation. *Archives of Internal Medicine, 148,* 2594–2600.

Hopps, J. G., & Collins, P. M. (1995). Social work profession overview. In *Encyclopedia of social work* (19th ed, pp. 2266–2282). Washington, DC: NASW Press.

Horton, J. A. (Ed.). (1995). *The women's health data book: A profile of women's health in the United States.* Washington, DC: Jacobs Institute of Women's Health.

Jaynes, G. D., & Williams, R. M. (1989). Black Americans' health. In G. D. Jayne & R. M. Williams (Eds.), *A common destiny: Blacks and American society* (pp. 391–450). Washington, DC: National Academy Press.

Jensen, R. H. (1996, January/February). Mimi Ramsey: For selflessly striving, despite her own pain, to end the mutilation of young girls. *Ms.,* pp. 51–52.

Joffe, C. (1995). *Doctors of conscience.* Boston: Beacon Press.

Kidder, M. (1991). Margot Kidder. In A. Bonavoglia (Ed.), *The choices we made* (pp. 95–100). New York: Random House.

Kjellstrand, C. M., & Logan, G. M. (1987). Racial, sexual, and age inequalities in chronic dialysis. *Nephron, 45,* 257–263.

Lader, L. (1991). *RU 486.* Reading, MA: Addison-Wesley.

Land, H. (1994). AIDS and women of color. *Families in Society, 75*(6), 355–361.

Laurence, L., & Weinhouse, B. (1994). *Outrageous practices: The alarming truth about how medicine treats women.* New York: Fawcett Columbine.

Leigh, W. A. (1995). The health of African American women. In D. L. Adams (Ed.), *Health issues for women of color: A cultural diversity perspective* (pp. 112–132). Thousand Oaks, CA: Sage Publications.

Love, S. (1997). *Dr. Susan Love's hormone book.* New York: Random House.

Lundy, M., & Mason, S. (1994). Women's health care centers: Multiple definitions. *Social Work in Health Care, 19*(3/4), 109–122.

Maynard, C., Litwin, P. E., Martin, J. S., & Weaver, W. D. (1992). Gender differences in the treatment and outcome of acute myocardial infarction. *Archives of Internal Medicine, 152,* 972–976.

Millner, L., & Widerman, E. (1994). Women's health issues: A review of the current literature in the social work journals, 1985–1992. *Social Work and Health Care, 19*(3/4), 145–172.

National Association of Social Workers. (1994). *Social work speaks: NASW policy statements* (3rd ed.). Washington, DC: NASW Press.

National Center for Health Statistics. (1994). *Health, United States, 1994.* Hyattsville, MD: U.S. Public Health Service.

National Center on Addiction and Substance Abuse. (1996). *Substance abuse and the American woman.* Columbia University.

National Institutes of Health. (1992). *Opportunities for research on women's health* (Summary Report) (NIH Publication No. 92-3457A). Washington, DC: Author.

Norman, E., & Dumois, A. O. (1995). Caring for women with HIV and AIDS. *Affilia, 10*(1), 23–35.

Ntiri, D. W. (1993). Circumcision and health among rural women of southern Somalia as part of a family life survey. *Health Care for Women International, 14,* 215–226.

Nuccio, K. E., & Mama, R. S. (1990). Effects of fetal-protection policies on women workers. *Affilia, 5*(3), 39–49.

Olson, M. M. (1994). Introduction: Reclaiming the "other"—women, health care, and social work. *Social Work in Health Care, 19*(3/4), 1–16.

Pollitt, K. (1994). Hot flash. In K. M. Hicks (Ed.), *Misdiagnosis: Woman as a disease* (pp. 83–86). Allentown, PA: People's Medical Society.

Scuka, R. F. (1994). Health care reform in the 1990s: An analysis of the problems and three proposals. *Social Work, 39*(5), 580–594.

Seaman, B. (1969). *The doctors' case against the pill.* New York: Peter H. Wyden.

Smith, J. M. (1992). *Women and doctors.* New York: Dell.

Starr, T. (1991). *The "natural inferiority" of women: Outrageous pronouncements by misguided males.* New York: Poseidon Press.

Steering Committee of the Physicians' Health Study Research Group (1988). Preliminary report: Findings from the aspirin component of the ongoing physicians' health study. *New England Journal of Medicine, 318*(4), 262–264.

Stevens, P. E. (1992). Lesbian health care research: A review of the literature from 1970 to 1990. *Health Care for Women International, 13,* 91–120.

Superville, D. (1996, June 15). Most can't flee female mutilation. *Houston Chronicle,* p. 25A.

Tavris, C. (1992). *The mismeasure of woman.* New York: Simon & Schuster.

Tobin, J. N., Wassertheil-Smoller, S., Wexler, J. P., Steingart, R. M., Budner, N., Lense, L., & Wachspress, J. (1987). Sex bias in considering coronary bypass surgery. *Annals of Internal Medicine, 107,* 19–25.

Tom-Orme, L. (1995). Native American women's health concerns. In D. L. Adams (Ed.), *Health issues for women of color: A cultural diversity perspective* (pp. 27–41). Thousand Oaks, CA: Sage Publications.

U.S. Department of Health and Human Services. (1991). *Health status of minorities and low-income groups.* Washington, DC: Government Printing Office.

U.S. Office of the Surgeon General. (1993). *One voice, one vision.: Recommendations to the Surgeon General to improve Hispanic/Latino health.* Washington, DC: Author.

Villarosa, L. (Ed.). (1994). *Body and soul: The black women's guide to physical health and emotional well-being.* New York: HarperPerennial.

Wadler, J. (1992). *My breast.* New York: Pocket Books.

Walker, A., & Parmar, P. (1993). *Warrior marks.* New York: Harcourt Brace.

Walker, B. B. (1996). *The women's encyclopedia of myths and secrets.* Edison, NJ: Castle Books.

White, E. C. (Ed.). (1994). *The black women's health book: Speaking for ourselves* (2nd ed.). Seattle, WA: Seal Press.

Whittelsey, F. C., & Carroll, M. (1995). *Women pay more: And how to put a stop to it.* New York: New Press.

Wilke, D. (1994). Women and alcoholism: How a male-as-norm bias affects research, assessment, and treatment. *Health & Social Work, 19*(1), 29–35.

Wolf, N. (1991). *The beauty myth.* New York: William Morrow.

Zambrana, R. E., & Ellis, B. K. (1995). Contemporary research issues in Hispanic/Latino women's health. In D. L. Adams (Ed.), *Health issues for women of color: A cultural diversity perspective* (pp. 27–41). Thousand Oaks, CA: Sage Publications.

Chapter

PORNOGRAPHY
AND PROSTITUTION

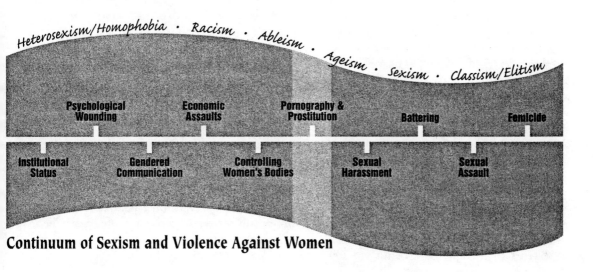

Heterosexism/Homophobia · Racism · Ableism · Ageism · Sexism · Classism/Elitism

| Psychological Wounding | Economic Assaults | Pornography & Prostitution | Battering | Femicide |

| Institutional Status | Gendered Communication | Controlling Women's Bodies | Sexual Harassment | Sexual Assault |

Continuum of Sexism and Violence Against Women

> *The harm is invisible because of the smile, because women are made to smile, women aren't just made to do the sex acts. We are made to smile while we do them. . . . And this smile will be believed, and the injury to her as a human being, to her body and to her heart and to her soul, will not be believed.*
>
> *Dworkin, 1993, p. 283*

*T*his chapter focuses on the sex industry, primarily pornography and prostitution, as forms of violence against women. This chapter purposely directs attention to the harms suffered by women who are used in the sex industry. The focus of the chapter is on the inherent sexism and violence of the sex industry, with less attention focused on (a) the quantitative literature on the correlation between violence toward women and men's use of pornography and (b) the civil-libertarian perspectives that seek to protect the First Amendment rights of pornographers. This approach is not without limitations, and readers are encouraged to further investigate those perspectives that are not highlighted in this chapter (see, for example, the works of E. Donnerstein and of N. Malamuth). However, because pornography and prostitution are rarely included in analyses of violence against women, this chapter focuses more heavily on this underrepresented connection and perspective. Also, material on pornography and prostitution is less often presented in schools of social work; thus, the use of narratives are frequently offered herein, to present the many issues affecting women used in the sex industry. This approach is advocated by Jensen (1995), who has stated, "I argue that instead of privileging the experimental laboratory research that has been so prominent in the debate over pornography during the past three decades, we should look to richly detailed narrative accounts of women and men that can tell us a great deal about how pornography works in the world" (p. 34).

Academic literature has done little to make connections either between pornography and prostitution or among pornography, prostitution, and other forms of violence. Few authors and advocacy groups have framed the issues related to women used in the sex industry as violence. Among those who have applied this analysis are the advocacy group WHISPER (Women Hurt In Systems of Prostitution Engaged in Revolt), Andrea Dworkin, Catherine MacKinnon, and Diana Russell. Their analysis (as is explained in more detail throughout this chapter) does not depict prostitutes or women engaged in pornography as being masochistic or sex addicted or as having unresolved oedipal complexes, self-defeating personality disorders, or other labels, which too often are used to dismiss, justify, or rationalize violence against women. Instead, these activists and scholars encourage the examination of the actual harm done to women used in the sex industry. In other words, the women thus used are identified as subjects, instead of objects. The analysis of pornography and prostitution as a victimless crime cannot continue to occur if the experiences of women who are used in the sex industry are included along the same continuum of sexism and violence that is applied to the experiences of other women: victims of hate language, females socialized to use sexuality to

survive in the patriarchy, and survivors of sexual harassment, battering, sexual assault, as well as the all-too-common victims of femicide (see section in Chapter 11 on the killing of prostituted women). This type of analysis rejects the media and film industry's glamorization of pornography and prostitution. This analysis creates the need to center not only on the harm done by pornography (and other forms of the sex industry) to women outside of the industry (i.e., objectification) but also on the harm done to women who are trapped or used by the industry. This way of thinking has the camera lens zoom in on Linda Lovelace's battered body, instead of on the erect penis penetrating her. In other words, observers see the experiences of women used in the sex industry in context, so that the women's pain and degradation become visible.

The first sections of this chapter address the issues associated with prostitution and pornography—definitions, prevalence, descriptions, and related controversial themes. The final section offers strategies for change on the practice and the policy levels.

INTRODUCTION TO THE ISSUES: PROSTITUTION

Background of the Problem

Jolin (1994, p. 70) wrote that prostitution resulted from the following:

1. *Male sexuality was defined to include promiscuity.*
2. *Female sexuality was defined to dictate chastity.*
3. *Men had the power to enforce both.*

Jolin explained that prostitution exists because of a sexual double standard, where the implementation of the double standard is maintained by the social and economic control of men over women. Among the ancient Greeks, prostituted women often became highly cultured companions of powerful men yet were denied the status of "wife" (Jolin, 1994). In medieval French society, prostitutes were seen as desirable marriage partners, and thus, according to Shrage (1989) "the cultural principles which sustained commercial exchanges of sex in this society were quite different than those which shape our own sex industry" (p. 350). Saints Augustine and Thomas Aquinas tolerated prostitution, asserting that it met basic needs, and the elimination of prostitution would lead to more harmful effects.

In contrast, Martin Luther wanted prostitution abolished and saw prostitutes as "emissaries of the devil who were sent to destroy faith" (Jolin, 1994, p. 72). During the nineteenth century, the feminist movement addressed the issue of prostitution, with notable women such as Elizabeth Cady Stanton and Susan B. Anthony joining in the debate. Stanton and Anthony perceived prostituted women as "victims of licentious men" (Jolin, 1994, p. 73). Other feminists disagreed, and Jolin described them as free-love advocates, who saw marriage laws as more restrictive and harmful than prostitution.

All 19th century feminists agreed, however that inequality was bad for women, that the social and economic forces that permitted setting women aside for prostitution (i.e., inequality) were indeed a problem. What divided them were different conceptions about the role of prostitution in women's struggle for equality.

Social purity feminists like Stanton and Anthony saw prostitution as the embodiment of female inequality, *and free love feminists like Woodhull saw prostitution as the embodiment of female* equality. *For Stanton and Anthony, the prostitute represented the victim of male sexuality and dominance; for Woodhull she represented an empowered woman who had cast aside the shackles of chastity and marriage. (Jolin, 1994, p. 74)*

Just as the nineteenth-century feminists were embroiled in debate over the issue of prostitution, so too are feminists today. The organization Women Hurt in Systems of Prostitution Engaged in Revolt (WHISPER) (undated) suggests that the problem of prostitution has been framed in four ways, and therefore, the ways in which the problem has been addressed has taken different paths. Table 7.1 shows the framework suggested by WHISPER. This range of problem definitions and suggested policy responses indicate that issues related to women used in prostitution are no less controversial than those posed in regard to pornography. Jolin (1994) suggested, "History is replete with challenges to prostitution, followed by decades, even centuries, of relatively quiet tolerance. Yet neither support nor challenges have ever succeeded in freeing prostitution from controversy" (p. 71). The next sections briefly focus on each of the ways in which the problem of prostitution has been framed, giving primary

Table 7.1
Frameworks Used to Address Issues Related to Prostitution

Problem Definition	Policy Response
(1) Prostitution exploits women and children.	(1) Decriminalize [prostitution,] and improve job conditions.
(2) Prostitution is a public health problem, including an AIDS transmitter.	(2) Decriminalize, license, and control [prostitution.]
(3) Prostitution is a "necessary evil" and is inevitable.	(3) Keep it illegal and out of sight.
(4) Prostitution is a form of violence against women and children.	(4) Stop prostitution.

WHISPER, undated. Conference material handouts.

attention to framing the issue of prostitution as a form of violence against women.

Prostitution as an Exploitative System

Groups such as COYOTE (Call Off Your Old Tired Ethics) best exemplify this approach to understanding issues related to prostituted women. COYOTE advocates that prostitution be recognized as a service occupation, that laws against prostitution be repealed, and that prostituted women have their rights as workers protected (Jenness, 1990). COYOTE members suggest that most prostitution is voluntary, and the work is chosen among alternatives (i.e., prostitution is an employment choice). As an employment choice, COYOTE members advocate for employee benefits, from sick leave to workers' compensation insurance (Jenness, 1990). Rather than viewing prostituted women as deviants or victims, COYOTE promotes the idea that their work and their behavior is "sensible and moral" (Jenness, 1990, p. 416). "By invoking and institutionalizing a vocabulary of sex as work, prostitutes as sex workers, and prostitutes' civil rights as workers, COYOTE's claims sever the social problem of prostitution from its historical association with sin, criminality and illicit sex. The social problem of prostitution is firmly placed in the rhetoric of work and civil rights" (Jenness, 1990, p. 417). Similarly, statements by the International Committee for Prostitutes' Rights World Charter and World Whores' Congress advocate for the decriminalization of adult prostitution, abolition of zoning that forces prostituted women to work in certain areas within a city, taxation of earnings, workers' compensation, and voluntary medical care (International Committee for Prostitutes' Rights, 1987).

Many of the supporters of decriminalization perceive prostitution as an economic issue. Jolin (1994) cited Margo St. James as saying, "A blow job is better than no job" (p. 79). Jolin further has encouraged discussion among feminists, because it is women who are dispropor-

tionately being jailed for prostitution. She noted "for the street prostitute, criminalization translates into a very real, very long, and very painful list of daily victimizations and indignities, to which she can add the further burden of becoming the victim of feminist prostitution ideology" (p. 82).

Gamache and Giobbe (1990) address the classism and racism inherent in systems of prostitution. While Gamache and Giobbe see prostitution as inherently violent, not as a choice, they recognize the economic forces that surround issues of prostitution. They suggested, "By maintaining a society in which women are kept economically marginalized, the system of male supremacy ensures that a pool of women will be vulnerable to recruitment and entrapment in prostitution. . . . Lastly, by zoning 'sex shops' into economically depressed neighborhoods, classism makes poor and ethnic women more subject to harassment by pimps and johns" (p. 88).

Prostitution as a Public-Health Problem

This perspective toward prostitution suggests that the activities of prostituted women need to be regulated to protect the public from the spread of sexually transmitted diseases (STDs) and is exemplified by this quote from a newspaper article reporting on prostitution on the South Orange Blossom Trail in Orlando, Florida: "South Trail hookers carry other diseases besides AIDS. They carry contagious skin diseases and parasites, such as lice. Some of their bodies are covered with sores. No victims? How about the wives and children of the men who pay the hookers for sex?" (Quinn, 1995, p. 14A). Note how the responsibility and blame is shifted from the man paying for sex to the woman who is used. The prostitute in this scenario is seen solely as a vector of transmission, rather than as a person in her own right, and the wife and children are solely portrayed as innocent victims.

Although there has been concern for many years about the transmission of STDs between the women used in prostitution and the customers (Johns), Jenness (1990) wrote, "The AIDS epidemic represents the most recent and most dramatic change in the political environment of prostitutes' rights organizations. In addition to posing a health threat to prostitutes, the AIDS epidemic represents a social and legal threat to prostitutes as well" (p. 414). Some communities have struggled with questions about how to address the spread of HIV and AIDS infections. As with other forms of repression, oppressed persons are targeted first. With the AIDS epidemic, the persons targeted first were largely gay men, low-income ethnic-minority drug abusers, and prostitutes.

In the name of public health, many communities considered the option of quarantining people with AIDS. Alexander (1987) wrote,

> The high fear of AIDS underlies the obvious desire for easy "solutions," and could result in such things as mandatory testing, quarantines, employment discrimination, and possibly mandatory sterilization. In 1986, several states considered legislation to require certain groups of criminal offenders—especially prostitutes and sex offenders—to be tested upon conviction and/or as a condition for probation. (p. 257)

Violations of the rights of prostitutes did, in fact, occur; for example, in Seattle, for several months in the mid-1980s, all prostituted women who were arrested were tested for HIV; in 1986, the Food and Drug Administration (FDA) distributed guidelines barring women used in prostitution from giving blood; and in Nevada, women in brothels who tested HIV-positive were fired, and their picture was printed in the newspaper (Alexander, 1987). Alexander urged, "It is up to those of us who are used to reading between the lines and looking for evidence of bias and prejudice to help keep the focus on AIDS and its prevention, not on punishment" (pp. 260–261).

COYOTE members (1987) believe that AIDS prevention and education is critical and suggest that those who wish to help prostituted women should talk to local health officials, mental-health providers, and other medical groups to ask what services and outreach are being offered to prostituted women and to make sure that AIDS-prevention education is being provided both to women used as prostitutes and to their customers.

Another public-health issue associated with prostituted women has been substance abuse. Weiner (1996), in her study of 1,963 streetwalking prostitutes in New York City, found that crack cocaine was the illegal drug they most often used (68.3%), followed by marijuana, powder cocaine, intravenously (IV) injected heroin, and nasally inhaled heroin. Further, her findings indicate that of those who use IV drugs, most did not report using new needles or cleaning needles, and 18.7% reported sharing needles. Weiner's research indicated some differences in drug use among streetwalking prostitutes, which were associated with race or ethnicity. Weiner noted that Latinas had the highest nasal-heroin use rates; African-American women the highest alcohol or crack-cocaine rates; and European-American women had the highest IV-heroin use. In another study of drug use in Manhattan, Graham and Wish (1994) found that of women arrested on prostitution-related charges, 60% tested positive through urinalysis for cocaine use, and 27% tested positive for heroin use. Drug addiction was noted by many of the women arrestees as a reason for their continuing role as prostitutes.

The exchange of sex for crack cocaine has created a body of research literature that certainly relates to prostitution. Forney, Inciardi, and Lockwood (1992) studied the exchange of sex for crack cocaine in rural Georgia communities and in the city of Miami. Although differences emerged on many issues, the authors noted, "For all, the most common means of obtaining crack was in exchange for sex" (p. 82). These authors further noted, "Although these women appeared to understand HIV transmission routes fairly well, few had changed [their own] behaviors to reduce their risk for HIV infection, other than initiating or increasing condom use" (p. 82). Imperato (1992) found that crack-addicted women reported an average of 62.3 different sexual partners within 1 month's time, almost entirely without using condoms or other forms of contraception or disease prevention. Inciardi, Lockwood, and Pottieger (1993) suggested that two types of prostitutes involved with crack have emerged: (1) those who prostitute for money and then buy crack, and (2) those who participate almost exclusively in a sex-for-crack exchange, often in a crack house. Fullilove, Lown, and Fullilove (1992) and Harrison (1995) have described a whole vernacular for women who prostitute for drugs, such as "crack ho" and "skeezer." Even among drug-addicted persons and other prostituted women, women who exchange sex for crack are often viewed as deviant.

Prostitution as a Necessary Evil

Many people believe that prostitution will always exist and that it serves a purpose in society. As noted previously, even Saint Thomas Aquinas expressed the opinion that if prostitution did not exist, sodomy and other crimes would be rampant (Jolin, 1994). However, many of the people who see prostitution as a necessary evil nonetheless regard it as a nuisance and believe that it should be out of sight and NIMBY—not in my back yard—and that criminal sanctions are necessary to keep it marginalized. We can still vividly recall a Texas gubernatorial candidate who boasted of the utility of brothels on the Mexico side of the Texas/Mexico border towns, to "service" young, Anglo Texan men. Picket signs appeared outside of his campaign offices, vehemently protesting women's role of "servicing" young men and the racism implicit in his message for the need for Mexican women to perform this "service."

The idea of prostitution as a necessary evil has a somewhat Victorian quality and serves to perpetuate a virgin/whore image of women: The Madonna, a virginal good woman, is sexually pure until marriage, and during marriage, she does not consent to *certain* sexual practices,

so if her husband desires such sexual acts, then he must discretely seek them elsewhere; in contrast, the whore, a lascivious bad woman, provides sexual services (paid or unpaid) to men but is not a suitable choice for a wife. Pheterson (1987) suggested,

> The prostitute is the prototype of the stigmatized woman. She is both named and dishonored by the word "whore." The word "whore" does not, however, refer only to prostitutes. It is also a label which can be applied to any woman. . . . The whore stigma is specifically a female gender stigma which can be defined as "a mark of shame or disease on an unchaste woman." (p. 215)

Helfand (1987), a former sex-industry worker, wrote about this type of dichotomous thinking, noting,

> People have always been shocked to learn that a nice girl like me could have been a sex industry worker. "I never would have thought. . . ." For years I found a kind of defiant pleasure in their astonishment. Now I want to shout, "Why not? What are your stupid stereotypes that deny my experiences?" But I realize that I shared in the denial, felt as if my work was not the true me but a part I was playing. (p. 103)

Perhaps the work of Greenman (1990) best sums up the view that prostitution is inevitable. Writing about how the so-called straight world helps to keep women in prostitution, she noted,

> The "straight" world implicitly and explicitly helps keep women in prostitution by accepting fallacies: for example, that women "choose" to be prostitutes, that without prostitution more men would sexually abuse "innocent" women and children, that women in prostitution are "sex addicts," and so forth. These misconceptions allow society to blame the victim and keep her in prostitution. People don't want prostitution in their own neighborhood, but can live with it in someone else's. Their attitude seems to be "we don't want our children involved but don't care if someone else's are." (p. 112)

Another concern related to the idea of prostitution as an inevitable piece of life is the history of various national governments in providing women for members of the armed services for their sexual use. In recent years, some attention has been given to the enslavement of women during World War II by the Japanese government, euphemistically termed "comfort women." Most of the women used as comfort women were from Korea, China, Taiwan, and the Philippines, and reports vary, suggesting that from 80,000 to 200,000 women were forced into prostitution (Staff, undated). According to a staff writer of *The East Journal,* Lieutenant General Okamura Yasuji *claims* credit for institutionalizing the use of comfort women. He *claims* that rapes of civilian women stopped once prostituted women were provided for soldiers. He noted, "Today [1938] almost every expeditionary force is accompanied by comfort women, who are thought of as being part of the supply department" (p. 41).

One of these enslaved women recalled the following about a typical week:

> Around eight every morning soldiers would enter. They had condoms. We were not given condoms. Sometimes officers stayed overnight. We had no chance to rest. Each soldier stayed thirty minutes at most. If he was longer the other soldiers began to yell. We each received between ten and thirty men a day. The house was quiet during battles, although gunfire could be heard once in a while. A doctor examined us once a week. If he found even a trace of disease, he immediately gave us an antibiotic. We never received money, but the soldiers brought food such as rice and miso. We had a kitchen and cooked meals ourselves. (Staff, undated, p. 40)

Sturdevant and Stoltzfus (1992) focused their book, *Let the Good Times Roll: Prostitution and the U.S. Military in Asia,* on the complicity of the U.S. government in promoting prostitution for the use of U.S. service men in areas near U.S. bases. For example, they noted, in the Philippines, prostitution is illegal. However, 9,000 of approximately 15,000 "hospitality women" are registered with the Social Hygiene Clinic. The Social Hygiene Clinic is operated by Olongapo Health Department

with the U.S. Navy providing medical supplies and technical assistance (Sturdevant & Stoltzfus, 1992). Around 18,000 so-called club women are registered in bar areas around U.S. bases in Korea, as well. Sturdevant and Stoltzfus (1992) reported that U.S. military police monitor clubs in Korea to make sure that soldiers are not frequenting clubs that have more than the allowable number of women with diseases working—these unregistered clubs are off limits.

These examples are just a few showing how U.S. taxpayers and the government itself may be accepting the inevitability of state-supported prostitution. In reading the accounts of the women prostitutes used by U.S. servicemen, it was difficult to decide whether military involvement fit into this section on prostitution as a necessary evil or it better fit with prostitution as violence against women. The following is one brief excerpt by a 30-year-old woman from Manila, which leads into the next section on prostitution as violence against women:

> He put me in position and suddenly pierced me with his penis in my ass. That's what three hole meant. I thought he was just going to put it in the bottom [vagina]. When he was finished, he gave me P2 [currency exchange]. I really cried then. I thought: "So that's what it is like here if you don't know English. The Americans take advantage of you."
>
> My friend said, "That's right. . . . you have to be wise."
>
> The first time I gave a blow job, I threw up outside. I didn't know that throwing up outside was banned. I carried a small towel with me after that. (Sturdevant and Stoltzfus, 1992, pp. 121–122).

Prostitution as Violence Against Women

The literature from this perspective appears to be fairly scarce in the social work and general academic literature. A group called WHISPER introduced many people in the battered women's shelter movement to this understanding of women used in the sex industry. Wynter

(1987) wrote the following about this perspective in viewing prostitution:

> There has been a deliberate attempt to validate men's perceived need, and self-proclaimed right, to buy and sell women's bodies for sexual use. This has been accomplished, in part, by euphemizing prostitution as an occupation. Men have promoted a cultural myth that women actively seek out prostitution as a pleasurable economic alternative to low-paying, low skilled, monotonous labor, conveniently ignoring the conditions that insure women's inequality and the preconditions which make women vulnerable to prostitution. . . . This myth is so pervasive that when women come forward and expose the conditions they've endured, the injuries they've sustained through systems of prostitution, they are most often disbelieved or considered to be the exception rather than the rule. (p. 266)

From this perspective, prostitution is seen as yet another facet of women's oppression. This perspective acknowledges that there is no free choice to choose prostitution in any country that does not have civil equality. Greenman (1990), writing about the PRIDE (From Prostitution to Independence, Dignity, and Equality) program in Minneapolis, MN, rejected the notion that prostitution is a victimless crime; she suggested,

> Rather, prostitution is a culturally sanctioned system of oppression that uses women, children, and young men as sexual objects. Prostitution, or more correctly, the sex industry, is a multibillion-dollar business that includes pornography, nude dancing, and stripping as well as streetwalking, saunas, out-call services, and brothels. The sex industry uses power and control tactics to supply its customers with human beings who are used as sexual toys. Prostitution is dehumanizing to everyone involved in the industry. (p. 111)

According to WHISPER educational materials (undated):

- 85% of women used in prostitution are substance abusers and addicts
- 85% are adult survivors of childhood sexual molestation or rape
- 83% are victims of assault with a weapon

- 89% are victims of rape 8–10 times a year
- 66% are victims of physical or sexual assault by a pimp
- 57% are victims of kidnapping
- 57% seriously attempt suicide

Greenman (1990) had similar findings to those of WHISPER regarding the violence perpetrated against prostituted women. Noting how difficult it is for women used in prostitution to leave that occupation, she found that most prostituted women are not allowed to keep the money they earn—the pimps have control over the women's money and expenditures. Greenman further noted, "Because most women in prostitution were forced into prostitution as teenagers, they have no marketable job skills and obviously are unable to cite recent work experience to potential employers" (p. 112).

Author's Perspective

I (Stout) worked for one academic year at the Harris County jail, running weekly groups for battered women. The abuse the women had endured was extremely severe. Toward the end of that year, I was surprised to learn that almost all of the women participating in that group were prostituted women whose battering came at the hands of pimps and johns. Women had been thrown from buildings, burned, knifed, and frequently raped. In addition, they had the experience of incarceration, and many had severe scarring from intravenous drug use. Most of the women attending the support groups and educational sessions were African-American or Latina women. Gamache and Giobbe (1990) suggest, "Racist law enforcement policies disproportionately target women of color for harassment, arrest, imprisonment, and fines. These actions create a revolving door through which women are shunted from the street to the courts to the jails and back onto the streets again to raise money to pay these penalties" (p. 88).

The issues related to prostitution are also intricately related to the problems associated with women who are battered. Richie (1996) recorded the story of Doreen, an African-American woman who was arrested for prostitution:

In addition to being battered, he used to rape me. Then he'd say I was such a good slut that I might as well get paid for it, and he'd bring men home and ask them for money to have sex with me. About a year after that started, he took me out to work the street. When I'd get home, the only thing that would stop the abuse was if I brought in lots of money from hooking. . . . My life was hell. I was raped by my husband, then forced to prostitute, raped while waiting for a john, had my money stolen by other girls, with frequent infections, cold, drugged out . . . it was the worst life you can imagine . . . My life was going to be very different from this. I was going to go to college to become a teacher. He's stolen my dreams. . . . I hope I die soon. (p. 115)

In May of 1991, the Minnesota Coalition for Battered Women passed a resolution defining prostitution as violence against women. This action was supported because the board believed that prostitution stems from the same conditions (racism, classism, and sexism within a patriarchal society) as battering. The resolution statement also noted, "Like other battered women, a woman used in prostitution may not be able to escape without abandoning her current home, and often must flee from a pimp/husband/boyfriend who coerces or forces her to turn tricks, or at the very least, benefits financially from exploiting her" (1991, no page number).

The staff of WHISPER developed a handout illustrating the point that women used in prostitution experience tactics of power and control similar to those used on women who are battered (see Figure 7.1 for a visual depiction of the types of power and control used with prostituted women). For example, a woman who is battered by her partner is often isolated (i.e., batterer controls who she sees, where she goes, etc.). A prostituted woman is often isolated by her pimp and by the john

(e.g., moved to different states, controlled in what she can do, isolated in red-light districts or massage parlors, taken to remote areas and left there). A batterer will often use economic abuse against a partner, and so does a pimp or a john. Pimps often take the earnings of a woman used in prostitution or stop her from seeking other employment, whereas johns use economic power to make her comply with their sexual demands and often rob her or refuse to pay her (WHISPER handout, undated). Many similar tactics are used to control battered women and prostituted women. The strategies for change section includes additional information that makes connections between prostitution and battering.

INTRODUCTION TO THE ISSUES: PORNOGRAPHY

As with issues related to prostitution, discussions on pornography are ripe for conflict among feminists, as well as between liberals and conservatives. With the recent increase in the accessibility of sexually explicit and pornographic materials over the Internet, pornography has again become a heated topic of debate. Much of the attention has become focused on children's access to sexually explicit and pornographic materials via the Internet. Education is needed about the danger pornography poses, not only to children, but also to women and men. People need both to understand the many and complex dynamics of issues related to pornography and to confront those issues, rather than shying away because of the conflict so often generated in such discussions.

Defining Pornography

The group Organizing Against Pornography (1986) wrote, "Pornography has existed at least since early Greece. The term is derived from the Latin words 'porne' and 'graphos,' meaning the graphic depiction of female sexual slaves" (p. 1). Andrews (1988, p. 26) noted that feminists often group sexually explicit materials into three categories:

FIGURE 7.1   Sexism and Violence Against Women: Internal and Structural Barriers to Equality with a Focus on Prostitution

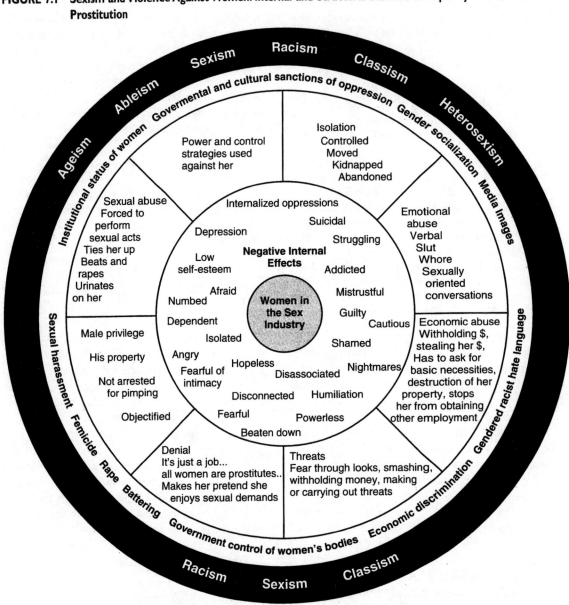

The authors acknowledge the Domestic Abuse Intervention Project in Duluth, MN for the "wheel" concept and WHISPER for the specific forms of violence perpetrated against women used in systems of prostitution.

(1) sex education materials, which are designed by certified professionals and are essential for professional education and for age-appropriate knowledge of human development, (2) erotica, which are nonaggressive sexual stimuli intended to appeal aesthetically and to arouse sexually, and (3) violent or exploitive pornography, which includes aggressive sexuality or dominance/submission. Hardcore pornography graphically represents one party as humiliated or victimized by

force, while softcore *pornography uses more subtle images to portray dominance.*

Jensen (1995) suggested that a feminist approach to pornography "sees pornography as a kind of sexist hate literature, the expression of a male sexuality rooted in the subordination of women, that endorses the sexual objectification of, and can promote sexual violence against, women" (p. 33).

Pulling apart this statement by Jensen, it seems relevant to highlight the following words: *sexist hate literature, subordination, sexual objectification,* and the *promotion of violence against women.* These words suggest that pornography can be seen in the context of sexism, inequality, and violence—the major themes of this text. Dworkin and MacKinnon (1988), pioneers in shaping pornography as a civil-rights issue, offer a very specific definition of pornography, focusing on the harm done to women:

> *Pornography is the graphic sexually explicit subordination of women through pictures and/or words that also includes one or more of the following: (i) women are presented dehumanized as sexual objects, things, or commodities; or (ii) women are presented as sexual objects who enjoy pain or humiliation; or (iii) women are presented as sexual objects who experience sexual pleasure in being raped; or (iv) women are presented as sexual objects tied up or cut up or mutilated or bruised or physically hurt; or (v) women are presented in postures or positions of sexual submission, servility, or display; or (vi) women's body parts—including but not limited to vaginas, breasts, or buttocks—are exhibited such that women are reduced to those parts; or (vii) women are presented as whores by nature; or (viii) women are presented being penetrated by objects or animals; or (ix) women are presented in scenarios of degradation, injury, torture, shown as filthy or inferior, bleeding, bruised, or hurt in a context that makes these conditions sexual.*
>
> *The use of men, children, or transsexuals in the place of women in [the preceding paragraph] is also pornography. (p. 36)*

In reviewing these definitions, the words *dominate, force, objectification,* and *humiliation* are suggested by *pornography.* Recalling that the root meaning of *pornography* is "graphic depic-

tion of female slaves" suggests that the messages of pornography in Western cultures may not have changed greatly since ancient Greek times.

Prevalence

Pornography is everywhere—gas stations, grocery stores, convenience stores, and so-called adult bookstores. Pornography has become a powerful socializing force on sexuality by sheer virtue of its availability and large readership. Baker (1992) noted, "For a young man, acquiring pornography forms a kind of 'rite of passage' into manhood. Older brothers, older men, fathers or other male relatives are likely to be known to have used it. Indeed, these older men often introduce pornography to their juniors" (p. 130). Russell (1993) reported the following information on a "selected" number of issues of pornography sold per year, from data compiled from The National Research Bureau:

Penthouse	4,600,000	*Gallery*	500,000
Playboy	3,600,000	*Oui*	395,000
Hustler	1,200,000	*Chic*	90,000

Add to these figures the average pass-along readership of two to five copies, and as many as 52,000,000 people are being regularly exposed to mainstream pornography—alone (Russell, 1993). These numbers do not include readership data from periodicals such as *Hard Leather, Teenagers in Bondage, Sweet Chocolate, Chair Bondage, Hard Boss, Young Love, Shackled, Black Tit & Body Torture, Swastika Snatch,* or *Oriental Pussy.*

This subscription information illustrates the prevalence of pornography and perhaps, as the titles suggest, some of the content of pornography. To elaborate a bit further, pornography can be purchased almost anywhere, and there is a growing market for homemade pornography (Organizing Against Pornography, 1986). Homemade pornography's growth can be attributed to the access people have to camcorders and the simplicity of recording sexual acts in the privacy of one's home and then finding secondary markets in which to sell one's "homemade" production. The staff of Organizing Against Pornography suggested, "In fact, it's become so pervasive that we're no longer shocked by it. It's time to examine pornography, become aware of its messages and do something about it" (p. 7).

The Problem of Pornography

Matz's (1994) passionate denouncement of pornography complements the definitional points made by Dworkin and MacKinnon (1988) when Matz voiced her own view of the problem with pornography:

> In the production of pornography you take our actual lived pain, violation and destruction and turn it into sexual entertainment: To arouse yourselves, to masturbate, to influence and coerce other women and girls, and to make billions of dollars. You take what we've revealed of the real experience and impact of rape and child sexual abuse: our content, our words, our insights, our dynamics, our feelings, our needs and call it fantasy, fiction, pretend, education or your free speech. You steal it and throw it back at us as trivia! (Common place, insignificant, unimportant.) The fact and experience of our hurt, pain and destruction are "disappeared," vaporized, made invisible, turned into mere representation: not real or actual. (p. 49)

To fully understand the reality of Matz's words, the extent of pornographic messages needs to be addressed. For example, women's real experience with sexual harassment "disappears," is "vaporized," and is "turned into mere representation" by the pornographic magazine *Hard Bosses,* and Native American women's real experiences of rape and torture are "vaporized" by a videogame in which the winner is the player who rapes the most Native American women during the course of the game (staff of Organizing Against Pornography, 1986, slide-show script).

To take women's real experiences with sexism and violence and then sell them as "entertainment magazines" is to sexualize power imbalances. The staff members of Organizing Against Pornography (1986) summarized many

of the ways in which pornography attempts to sexualize power imbalances. The most obvious way in which power is sexualized is through the use of bondage pornography, where women are tied or otherwise immobilized and cannot move. The photographing of disembodied body parts is another common method. Thus, "Women are shown as open mouths, vaginas and anuses inviting penetration. Women also are portrayed as things other than themselves, for example, animals, food, or trash. Presenting women in this way makes it easier for men to mistreat them, and mistreatment is required for arousal" (p. 11).

Pornographic Descriptions

While we are not going to demonstrate common techniques and images of pornography, by printing pornographic pictures in this text, we do suggest that you read *Against Pornography: The Evidence of Harm* by Diana Russell (1993), in which she included hundreds of photos and text excerpts from pornography. In addition we include here five descriptions of pornographic slides put together by the now-defunct group Organizing Against Pornography. Many people, for multiple reasons—such as having survived rape, the sex industry, and other forms of violence against women—have strong, uncomfortable, and unsafe feelings connected to images and descriptions of pornography. For these reasons, we caution readers that the information that follows contains vivid descriptions of pornography, anyone feeling uncomfortable with such passages is encouraged to skip this part of the chapter.

Examples from Organizing Against Pornography

Example Slide One: The cover of *Swastika Snatch* magazine shows Nazi prison guards threatening two nude, vulnerable women. This type of pornography uses the holocaust, an extreme form of racism and hatred, as the means for male sexual entertainment. The text reads, "They became willing sex slaves to the strange fantasies of their captors." Materials like this use weak story lines as an excuse to portray pornography basic theme—that women crave force and pain as part of sexual satisfaction (Russell, 1993, p. 21).

Example Slide Two: In another photo from the *Penthouse* series, a woman [Asian] is bound in an elaborate rope interlacing, especially around her crotch and breasts, to accentuate them. Her arms are tied close to her body, and a mask hides her face, rendering her less-than-human . . . thus, more available for harsh treatment and degradation.

Some of the most brutal, racist pornography in our country uses Asian women. This corresponds with the huge traffic of Asian women into the United States for prostitution and sale as mail-order-brides. . . . (p. 25)

Example Slide Three: This cartoon is from *Gentleman's Companion* magazine. It shows a caveman shoving a club into a woman's vagina and saying, "Don't be silly, nobody hits 'em over the head anymore." This is a take-off on the traditional scenario where the man clubs the woman and drags her back to the cave. The woman is supposedly "turned-on" by the new approach.

Penetration using objects is a form of rape occurring frequently in pornography. Cartoons often portray scenes that would be unacceptable as photographs in magazines such as *Gentleman's Companion, Playboy,* and *Penthouse.* (p. 31)

Example Slide Four: Black women are identified as *Sweet Chocolate* in this magazine. Women of color are referred to as chocolate, brown sugar, coffee or cinnamon, with their skin color sexualized and made the target of violence. The lower caption reads, "It's always their pleasure!" This notion perpetuates the belief that Black women have a voracious sexual appetite, a myth used to justify rape on plantations as well as abuses suffered by Black women today. (p. 39)

Example Slide Five: This *Hustler* cartoon shows a father being sexual with his daughter while she turns down a date with a friend, (quote) "Gee . . . I'd love to go to the drive-in, Tommy, but my dad has some, uh, extra household chores for me tonight." (end quote) The father–child relationship is one of the most frequently abused in our society. One in four female children is sexually abused before she turns 18. By making light of incest, pornography condones this crime. (p. 45)

Coercion and Violence

In addition to being subjected to the negative images of women presented via pornography, women in the sex industry—and especially in the pornography industry—are subjected to coercion and violence. In testimony presented to the U.S. Attorney General's Commission on Pornography, Giobbe (1993) recalled how she was forced into prostitution at age 13 years and that pornographers often exploited her and other young girls. She wrote, "My last pimp was a pornographer and the most brutal of all. . . . He made pornography of all of us. He also made tape recordings of us having sex with him and of our screams and pleas when he beat us, often threatening us with death" (p. 39). Another example is that of Linda Lovelace (the pseudonym of Linda Boreman), who "starred" in *Deep Throat*—a movie that grossed around $600 million (Steinem, 1993). While many of the viewers of this X-rated film focused on the penis shoved down her throat, Boreman and others were more concerned about the visible bruises on her body, which were the result of battering and rape during the making of this film (Steinem, 1993). In addition to being photographed or videoed against their will, women used in pornography are often bound, gagged, and even hung from ropes for the purpose of the specific photograph or video scene. Many people have become so desensitized to the images used in pornography that they cannot see the discomfort or even the pain being experienced by the women used. White (1993), the first African-American council representative in Minneapolis, held hearings on pornography in 1983. He recalled,

> As I listened to these victims of pornography testify, I heard young women describe how they felt about seeing other women in pornography in such degrading positions, how they felt about the way women's genitals and breasts are displayed and women's bodies are shown in compromising postures. And I thought about how during the time of slavery, black women would have their bodies examined, their teeth and limbs examined, their bodies checked out for breeding, checked out as you would check out an animal—and I thought: We've come a long way, haven't we? (p. 291)

In her book *Against Pornography*, Russell (1993) included pictures showing women who are obviously disgusted and in pain, with the purpose of allowing women and men to begin to really see the real women being used in the making of pornography. As was offered in this chapter's opening quote, women used in pornography often have a smile plastered on their face, and that false smile is how they are remembered (Dworkin, 1993). When viewing pornography, it is often consciousness raising to think about how the woman in the photo must have physically or emotionally felt in any particular pose.

The Harm to Men and Therefore to Women

Baker (1992) addressed how pornography harms men, as well as women. He suggested that pornographers' portrayal of women as having voracious sexual appetites arouses men's fear that they will not be able to satisfy their women partners; further, "pornography attempts to assuage this fear by showing that men can satisfy women and graphically explaining to them how to do so. But all of this actually has the effect of making men feel more inadequate, unequal to the challenge, and merely serves to push them further into the apparently safer, unreal world of pornographic

fantasies" (p. 136). Brooks (1995) authored a book titled *The Centerfold Syndrome*. He defined five elements of what he called the "Centerfold Syndrome": voyeurism, objectification, the need for validation, trophyism, and the fear of true intimacy. Each of these elements contributes to a culture that distorts how men, and often women, relate to each other and to women's bodies. Brooks included a list of many ways in which men experience this syndrome. For instance,

> In the middle of a meaningful conversation with an intimate friend he cannot help but break eye contact to stare at an attractive female stranger passing by.
>
> In conversation with a physically attractive woman he cannot avoid looking at her breasts.
>
> A primary sexual outlet is masturbation with pictures of naked women....
>
> When engaging in sex with a loved one, he frequently augments his arousal by imagining an unknown but sexually appealing woman....
>
> He rarely engages in nonsexual touching. (pp. 175–176)

Robert Jensen (1996) allowed readers of the journal *Violence Against Women* into his own life by documenting how pornography helped to shape his own sexuality. In the abstract of this article, Jensen wrote, "From this personal narrative, I show pornography was an important means of sex education in my life; constructed women as objects, which encouraged me to see women in real life that way; created or reinforced the desires for specific acts; shaped and constrained my sexual imagination with its standardized scripts; reinforced racist stereotypes; and eroticized violence for me in a way that not only affected my sex life, but also gave me a sense of control over women" (p. 82). Jensen's openess in describing the many ways in which pornography harmed him and gave him feelings of control over women can be helpful in understanding the many ways in which pornography may have influenced some men. While obviously his narrative does not prove that pornography caused the outcomes he mentioned, it clearly shows that narratives such as his do have an important place in the knowledge base, to aid helping professionals and the public to become sensitive to the range of experiences people have and to build on those narratives through additional research.

The Conflict over Pornography

Although feminists and the general public may agree that pornographic portrayals of women clearly show images of violence, sexism, and control of women, feminists and other people may disagree sharply regarding the attitudes, philosophies, and actions to take in response to those portrayals. Cottle, Searles, Berger, and Pierce (1989) used Q-sort methodology to literally sort out participants' attitudes toward pornography. Their findings indicate that three patterns emerged, which they labeled as "religious-conservative," "liberal," and "antipornography feminist" approaches to the problem of pornography. Religious conservatives tended to focus on the harm to children, family values, and "the moral fabric of society" (p. 313). Antipornography feminists supported the view that pornography harms women and violates their rights. Meanwhile, liberals indicated enjoyment of some forms of pornography, felt that those who wanted to ban such materials were "too moralistic" (p. 317), and were more likely to defend the right to use and produce pornography, based on the First Amendment of the U.S. Constitution.

> Feminists who do not want legislative control of pornography fear that the restriction of pornography will lead to other restrictions and that individual rights and freedom, particularly in areas such as abortion and sexual relationships, will be encroached upon by others who attempt to control what is acceptable or unacceptable for society. . . .
>
> The other side of the controversy is represented by feminists who want to control pornography legally. MacKinnon (1985) has taken the position that pornography infringes on the civil rights of women by silencing them,

> rendering them powerless, and promoting inequality and violence against them. (pp. 14, 97–98)

The debate and conflicts over pornography are not unique or centered within a heterosexual framework. Some lesbian feminist activists have expressed grave concerns over defining pornography as inherently violent and harmful. Other lesbians have taken on central roles in the antipornography movement. In her book *Undressing Lesbian Sex,* Elaine Creith (1996) addressed the conflicts in the debate over pornography. She noted, "The politics of the porn debates are complex and writers on both sides are well informed, passionate, and persuasive" (p. 15). Pornography made by lesbians for a lesbian market introduces both new and age-old questions. Creith posed a few: "Are lesbian pornographers merely continuing to exploit women in their adoption of heteropatriarchal capitalist practice? Or are they responding to a commercial need of a counter culture starved of its own sexual reality?" (p. 14).

Pat Califia (1994) presented many harsh criticisms of the antipornography feminist movement in her collection of essays written between 1979 and 1994. She described fighting the antipornography movement, primarily the leadership of the group Woman Against Pornography (WAP)—based in New York City, in the early days of the movement. She clearly stated her rationale for her struggle against the antipornography movement: "So in the beginning, only leatherwomen were willing and able to take on WAP and its satellite organizations. We did it because we didn't have much choice. We either had to find vehicles for public criticisms of these people or resign ourselves to being drummed out of the women's movement and stand helplessly by while it was turned into a single-issue campaign for moral purity" (p. 12). In an essay titled, "The Obscene, Disgusting, and Vile Meese Commission Report," Califia challenged: "More of us have to start saying that we use porn, like it, and want it to be accessible. Even given the constraints under which it is currently produced, pornography is valuable. It sends out messages of comfort and rebellion. It says: Lust is not evil. The body is not hateful. Physical pleasure is a joyful thing and should not be hidden or denied" (p. 103). Smyth (1994) criticized the group "Lesbians Against Pornography" for not respecting the diversity within the lesbian community. Smyth confronted a fixed notion of the gay and lesbian community, noting, "This is the ground queer politics is constantly contesting, opening up a space for lesbian porn made by lesbians, consensual SM, the use of sex toys, and the right to cruise and fuck without being made to feel less of a feminist" (p. 212).

A critique of the antipornography perspective would not be complete without input from the oft-self-proclaimed cultural feminist critic, Camille Paglia. Paglia (1994) wrote,

Far from poisoning the mind, pornography shows the deepest truth about sexuality, stripped of romantic veneer. No one can claim to be an expert in gender studies who is uncomfortable with pornography, which focuses on our primal identity, our rude and crude animality. Porn dreams of eternal fires of desire, without fatigue, incapacity, aging, or death. What feminists denounce as woman's humiliating total accessibility in porn is actually her elevation to high priestess of a pagan paradise garden, where the body has become a bountiful fruit tree and where growth and harvest are simultaneous. . . . Gay men appreciate pornography as I do because they accept the Hellenic principle that some people are born more beautiful than others. Generic granola feminists are likely to call this "lookism"—an offense against equality. (pp. 66–67)

Finally, Strossen (1995), in her book *Defending Pornography,* also called attention to the diversity among feminists on the issue of pornography. She noted numerous organizations that have been founded with the purpose of opposing the censorship of pornography, such as Feminist Anti-Censorship Taskforce, Feminists for Free Expression, and the National Coalition Against Censorship's Working Group on Women, Censorship, and "Pornography." Strossen suggested that to end violence against women, the focus must be on those who commit the crimes—not directed toward those who create a culture of violence against women (i.e., those who use and create pornography). Further, she has advocated more funding for research and services for victims of abuse and sexual assault—again, with the premise that direct violence is the central issue, not pornography.

Author's Perspective

While most feminists would seek more funding for services for victims and seek accountability for those who directly perpetrate the attacks on women, the conflict over pornography—specifically pornography depicting violence against women—remains. This conflict plays itself out in every forum where pornography is discussed, and in many ways, it has served to immobilize feminists who see it as hurtful to women, regardless of their stand on "free speech." Speaking for myself (Stout), I have largely stayed out of a public debate on controlling pornography since a television appearance shortly after the Minneapolis ordinance was passed (and subsequently vetoed) in the early 1980s. In the television piece, I praised the ordinance and spoke clearly that pornography was harmful to women and depicted inequality. In the same piece, a spokesperson for the American Civil Liberties Union (ACLU) eloquently spoke about the importance of preserving speech in all of its forms and the many oppressions that result when freedoms start being taken away by government. Watching that tape, I felt I had appeared simplistic—"pornography is bad"—and that the ACLU spokesperson had law and tradition behind his words.

In retrospect, I think my emphasis on pornography as harmful to women and as a link in a continuum of violence against women was appropriate and that I allowed myself to be silenced because there are so few voices willing to suggest that pornography is harmful and that we must do something to end the abuse and exploitation of women through this medium. As mentioned previously, pornography is a big business, and there is some real fear for many people about challenging a multi-billion-dollar socially sanctioned business. In the meantime, women in the sex industry continue to be physically and emotionally harmed, and all women become objectified and dehumanized as a result of sexist hate literature. In this vein, the next section discusses more fully the issues relating pornography to the inequality of women, and the practice and policy sections discuss strategies for change to address the use of women in the sex industry.

Pornography and Inequality

Stoltenberg (1990) has clearly documented how he sees pornography as related to male supremacy. He noted,

> *Pornography* institutionalizes *the sexuality that both embodies and enacts male supremacy. Pornography says about that sexuality, "Here's how": Here's how to act out male supremacy in sex. Here's how the action should go. Here are the acts that impose power over and against another body. And pornography says about that sexuality, "Here's who": Here's who you should do it to and here's who she is: your whore, your piece of ass, yours. Your penis is a weapon, her body is your target. And pornography says about that sexuality, "Here's why": Because men are masters, women are slaves; men are superior, women are subordinate; men are real, women are objects; men are sex machines, women are sluts. (p. 64, italics in original)*

Stoltenberg's comments about the institutionalization of male supremacy through pornography are clearly relevant to social workers concerned with the person-in-environment perspective. Once again, it is noted that the many forms of violence against women are inextricably linked to each other. In a similar vein, Baker (1992) has drawn attention to the fact that the misinformation and false representation of women presented in pornographic materials is very similar to the spreading of hate messages about other oppressed people—Jews or African Americans, for example. "It [pornography] tells men that women enjoy many different forms of physical abuse, including bondage, torture, mutilation and even death. The constant repetition of false information is a key part in the maintenance of any oppression: the more it is repeated, the larger the number of people (even in the oppressed group itself) are likely to come to believe that it is true. . . . It is in this way that pornography contributes to the maintenance of discrimination against women in all spheres of life, not merely sexual" (pp. 140–141). Collins (1993) noted how pornography continues to portray African-American women as slaves or bound, as submissive, and frequently with European-American men—all of which serves to perpetuate racism.

When thinking of a continuum of sexism and violence against women, it is important to look at what Baker referred to as hate messages as part of a culture that condones and often even supports violence against women—from the exclusion of women in major policymaking institutions—to male-to-female interruptions and use of time, space, and language—to the sexualizing of violence against women.

After interviews with men who use pornography, Jensen (1995) concluded that

> *For these men, pornography was an important factor in shaping a male-dominant view of sexuality, and in several cases the material contributed to the men's difficulty in separating fan-*

tasy from reality. Pornography was also used by at least one of the men to initiate a victim and break down that young girl's resistance to sexual activity. For several others, it was used as a training manual for abuse, as sexual acts and ideas from pornography were incorporated into their sex lives. (p. 51)

A finding by Senn (1993), however, complements the view that women are objectified by pornography, in that Senn suggested that women are subjects, not objects, who "do not stand idly by as pornography and male consumers act on them" (p. 338). In fact, Senn found that women used psychological coping mechanisms such as denial, reframing, and traumatic forgetting *as well as* "many physical and political steps to exclude pornography from their lives" (p. 338). The many individuals and groups, and the movement work that has occurred since the early 1970s, addressing the issues surrounding pornography and prostitution certainly support Senn's conclusions. From Nikki Craft, an activist leader in the fight against pornography, and civil disobedience acts, to the group Lesbians Against Pornography, to individuals who have examined how the sex industry has affected their lives, women and men are taking steps to confront the sex industry.

Prostitution and pornography remain issues with which women must struggle, within feminist and service-provider communities. The resulting discussions and actions will undoubtedly be fraught with conflict. Perhaps when those working through these issues become more connected with women used in the sex industry, clearer perspectives and voices will emerge.

Strategies for Change

This strategies-for-change section focuses on different approaches to confronting issues related to women used in the sex industry. This first part focuses attention on how two practitioners, Kate Carlson and Claude LaBrosse, who work with men who batter, address issues related to the sex industry in their everyday work. This section is written by those practitioners. The next part ad-

dresses issues related to the organizing of boycotts. The section on boycotts is written in general terms, as issues may emerge related to any of the topics presented in this text, which may require confrontational tactics—such as a boycott. However, the information provided may be helpful should a boycott of some component of the sex industry be needed in your community. Finally, several policy-for-change strategies are discussed in the policy-for-change section.

Confronting the Sex Industry at a Batterers Intervention Project

The PIVOT Project of Aid to Victims of Domestic Abuse is a private nonprofit agency, which provides intervention to perpetrators of domestic violence. The vast majority of the participants in this program are men who have committed assaults against an intimate female partner. Approximately 80% of these men have been arrested and were mandated to undergo treatment through a court order.

The primary mode of intervention offered at PIVOT is group work. After an orientation and individual evaluation, participants are required to participate in a 2-hour group session once per week for a minimum of 18 weeks. Groups are ongoing, with an average of 12–18 participants per group.

The philosophy on which the work at PIVOT is based is the profeminist treatment model of battering intervention, which states that spousal abuse is controlling behavior that serves to give a batterer power over his partner. Abusive behavior is not limited to physical or sexual violence, but rather is viewed as any behavior that has as its purpose the behavioral control of another person. Our primary goal is to promote the safety and self-determination of battered women and children.

The cornerstone of this philosophical foundation is the belief that domestic violence is part of the societal support and acceptance of violence against women, which also includes rape, sexual harassment, femicide, the sex industry, and other forms of oppression, such as inequitable pay. Group work, therefore, includes discussions and exercises that focus on these macrolevel issues, as well as on the participants' individual experiences and beliefs regarding violence and abuse. In addressing the topic of the sex industry in group work at PIVOT, we draw primarily from the messages of WHISPER. Other good sources of information about the sex industry are John Stoltenberg and Andrea Dworkin. As these sources have shown, the sex industry—including prostitution, pornography, and strip clubs—is one of the most clear and undeniable examples of oppression of women. Not only are women and children abused in the making and selling of these products, but they are also blamed and revictimized by a society that refuses to name and confront the abuse.

It has been our experience that both the advantages and the disadvantages of being either a male or a female facilitator seem to be exaggerated when addressing the issue of the sex industry. For that reason, we have explicated the order of the information as presented most often.

As a woman facilitator, the groups see me as a credible representative of a woman's point of view. Therefore, I begin with a discussion of the effects of the sex industry on the women and children used in the industry. The beginning discussion sets some ground rules in the group. Typically, I ask participants to suspend their beliefs about the sex industry, to agree not to make the traditional argument in support of the sex industry, such as "career choice," "freedom of speech," "artistic expression," and so forth, and to attempt to see prostitution, pornography, and strip clubs from the point of view of the person who is being marketed. Participants are then given information about recruitment into the sex industry and asked to talk about the harms of prostitution, pornography, and strip clubs to the women who are used in the industry.

The topic then shifts slightly, and participants are asked to talk about the harms to women in general, and to their own partners in particular. As is true in most discussions regarding abusive behavior, the men generally do not have trouble naming the harms to women. After discussing the effects of the abuse on the victim, the group participants are asked to talk about the messages they have received from using pornography. "How have the messages you

have received from pornographic material affected your attitudes about women?" "How have you compared your partner to images of women that you have seen in pornography?" "What do you think or feel when a woman says 'no' to sexual advances?" "How has the sex industry affected your attitudes about male sexuality?" When addressing the effects of the sex industry on men's attitudes and beliefs, we have found it important to begin from the assumption that the men have used pornography. When this approach is taken, it seems that men are far less resistant to participating in the discussion.

At the conclusion of this section, the group participants are asked to write a plan of how they will confront the sex industry. They are required to focus on personal goals and encouraged to include macrolevel interventions. Typically, participants figure out that they need to stop using prostitution, pornography, and strip clubs in order to contribute to the safety of women.

A male facilitator at PIVOT addresses the issue of the sex industry in a slightly different but equally effective way. Because he is male, he can address how "we" use the sex industry and can establish a commonality of experience. He begins with the concept of "men's unlimited sexual access to women and children" and asks group participants to give examples of this: in the home, at work, on a date, and so on. He has found that there are at least two ways in which it is useful to begin by challenging men to validate the truth of that aspect of male privilege (i.e., "men's unlimited sexual access to women and children"). One way is that men seem readily willing and able to do such validation, naming how that privilege is true at home, at work, on a date, in rape, in pornography, in prostitution, and in the sex clubs; after naming these venues, men seem to be able to explore both the harms to women and children and their personal participation in and usage of these forms of the privilege.

A second way in which this exercise is useful is that men have not seemed to have much need to justify such access, and the standard justifications of "freedom of speech," "career choice," and so on have generally given way to the overwhelming realization of the harms of the oppression that this privilege represents. We theorize that one reason it seems relatively easy for men to take responsibility for the exercise of this privilege is that one component of the privilege itself is the comfort of not having to defend it.

After discussing men's privilege, the focus of the discussion turns to the effect of violence and abuse on the victims. In discussing the effects on the victim, it is sometimes helpful to talk about the "pose" workshops done by Stoltenberg (1994), in which men were asked to replicate pornographic poses, while other men watched and offered suggestions to help the posers to get the pose correct. Another way to frame a discussion regarding how women are victimized in the sex industry, is to ask men whether they would want their daughters to work in the industry. The answer is invariably "no." What follows is usually a productive discussion about what they would fear for her, what her life would be like, and so forth.

As in the first example, the group work is concluded with a discussion regarding what men should do to confront the sex industry in order to work toward safety and self-determination for women.

As in any intervention work that seeks changes in behavior and attitudes, we have obtained mixed results when challenging men who are abusive to work toward confronting the sex industry. Some men have been very resistant to this work, in both subtle and overt ways. We suspect that some of the men who are able to acknowledge both the harms to women and children and the ways in which they have participated in the privilege never move beyond that point in their own work. Although we recognize this lack of progress, it has been our experience that there is still some value in facilitating this work in the groups.

The usefulness of presenting this information to participants is most clear when we ask, "What must responsible men do with this information?" The answer is "we must stop using this privilege; stop using pornography, prostituted women and children, and the strip clubs; and stop presuming our 'right' to be sexual with our partners." The answer is *not* "we have to stop those corrupt women who chose careers in the sex industry." Participants have been willing to take responsibility for their own actions and other men's and have moved away from blaming women in the group

discussions. It has happened that men in our groups have organized to picket a site for a proposed sex club.

There has been usefulness also in demonstrating that men have been willing to maintain the privilege of "unlimited sexual access to women and children" while knowing the harms. When Evelina Giobbe of WHISPER was told that men were able to acknowledge this privilege and how it worked, she exclaimed, "I knew they knew it!"

Kate Carlson and Claude LaBrosse

BOYCOTTS

The use of boycotts is certainly a different, yet complementary, practice strategy from the PIVOT Project group work just described by Kate Carlson and Claude LaBrosse. Shrage (1989) suggested, "prostitution needs no unique remedy, legal or otherwise; it will be remedied as feminists make progress in altering patterns of belief and practice that oppress women in all aspects of their lives. Yet while prostitution requires no special social cure, some important strategic and symbolic feminist goals may be served by selecting the sex industry for criticism at this time. In this respect, a consumer boycott of the industry is especially appropriate" (p. 367). Shrage aptly ties the use of boycotts to the importance of the work being done in programs such as PIVOT, which is altering the beliefs and practices of men who abuse women. Similarly, by asking men to examine the sex industry with a critical eye and with the goal of safety for women, individual boycotts of the industry may be occurring from this group intervention strategy. Large-scale boycotts can also be conducted on a local, national, or international level. This next section suggests some strategies to consider should a community or social work group be evaluating the merits of using a boycott as a change tactic.

Some people are familiar with boycotts because their family has not eaten California grapes for many years due to the growers' exploitation of workers, including the chemical effects on workers. Many young people boycotted products advertised on Howard Stern's radio show after he mocked Tejano music and trivialized the murder of Tejano music star Selena. Persons a few years older may have boycotted Nestles, Libby's, and Stouffer foods, due to those companies' willingness to promote infant formulas instead of breast milk in developing countries, even after it was clear that infants were dying because formula was often diluted to make it stretch a bit farther and because the mothers were unable to obtain fresh, sterile water and were forced to mix formula with water of poor quality. Sometimes entire states have been boycotted. For example, when Coloradans passed legislation denying gay men and lesbian women basic civil rights, many persons chose to schedule meetings and to plan vacations in other states. Boycotts are a familiar tactic in the United States and have often been successful.

Despite the familiarity of the boycott tactic, Kahn (1991) has cautioned that it is difficult for this strategy to be effective, due to the large market base of most retail outlets. He also noted that boycotts demand a great deal of energy and that often a picket in front of the business in question or just a threat of a boycott may be enough to get negotiations started. The multinational connections of business in the global economy are also a deterrent to effective boycotts. A group may believe that the participants are boycotting a local radio station, yet find that the station is connected to a worldwide publishing empire, a sports team, and a favorite clothing manufacturer. Suddenly, a "simple" request for people not to listen to a certain station has become a request to cancel subscriptions to their favorite magazines, to stay home from a sports play-off series, and to refrain from wearing a favorite pair of jeans. Therefore, doing research prior to taking action is critical (Kahn, 1991). Those asked to boycott need to know exactly what commitment they are making.

MacEachern (1994) has reminded boycott organizers that if people are to participate, a significant moral issue must be raised, and people must be angry about the injustice. MacEachern suggested these central points on how to organize a boycott: Carefully choose your target, work with the company first (i.e., try other tactics to resolve the issue before calling a boycott), obtain cosponsors and have cosponsors announce their support of the boycott, and hold a rally and press conference to announce the action. Finally, when the company meets the expectations, end the boycott promptly; or if the boycott has not been successful, do not hesitate to end it and consider using another tactic. Bobo, Kendall, and Max (1991) have cautioned, "The threat of using it [boycott] is more powerful than the weapon itself. But don't make the threat unless you are prepared to go through with it" (p. 39).

POLICY FOR CHANGE

The issues related to the sex industry are many, complex, and intricately woven into the cultural fabric. While evidence of the sex industry enters our space everywhere—from the corner drugstore, to the red-light districts, to billboards advertising "men's clubs," and now even to stock-market pages, with a "men's club" having gone public (a Houston men's club has gone public and now has national stockholders)—it still remains a topic that is seldom discussed. Few therapy groups for women delve into how pornography and other aspects of the sex industry have affected women's lives, and few groups for men have chosen this path, as well. Unfortunately, by reviewing a very short list of services available to prostituted women nationwide (see Table 7.2), we can see that few of our social work agencies are making efforts to provide services for women used in the sex industry. Thus, it appears that policy in this area is ripe for development.

Table 7.2
A Sampling of Organizations Serving Prostituted Women

Covenant House	CA: 213-957-7400
	FL: 305-561-5559
	TX: 713-785-4873
National Runaway Hotline	US: 800-621-4000
Prostitution Anonymous	CA: 619-462-6929
	CA: 510-834-5330
	IL: 312-281-3917
	PA: 215-432-9498
	TX: 713-785-4873
Empowerment Program	CO: 303-863-7817
Sasha Bruce House	DC: 202-546-4900
Genesis House	IL: 312-281-3917
WHISPER	MN: 612-644-6301
PRIDE	MN: 612-729-0340
Bowery Mission	NY: 212-255-3241
New Horizons	WA: 206-328-0115

Information provided by WHISPER; programs shown in bold type are for juveniles; some of the adult programs also serve juveniles.

Agency Policy

Starting at a basic level, social workers need to examine their agencies' policies to determine how prostituted women have been left out of social work services. For example, do local rape-crisis centers, battered women's shelters, youth runaway shelters, and homeless shelters provide outreach services to women used in the sex industry? If not, what are the attitudes of board members, administrators, and paid and volunteer staff members toward prostituted women, topless dancers, strippers, and women used in pornography? Is there fear that serving this population will reduce the agency's current level of community support? Is there concern that staff members do not have the expertise to provide direct or outreach services to this population of women?

More specifically, what training has been provided to agency staff members for working with women used in the sex industry? What academic preparation have social workers had to work with this population?

Another related set of questions to explore has to do with how agencies define violence. Many hotline, counseling, and shelter services define battering as family battering—presumably, with the definition of *family* broad enough to include lesbian women and gay men partnerships. If a prostitute's pimp has abused her, would the prostitute be served under current definitions at job-placement or employment sites? If a pimp (non-live-in partner) or a john had threatened or was stalking a prostitute, would she be defined as a battered woman or as a rape survivor? Gamache and Giobbe (1990) have advocated that prostitutes, by definition, be identified as women who have been battered. They noted, "This approach communicates several important messages to women. It expresses a view that they are victims of an oppressive system who are deserving of assistance. This can be invaluable in freeing women from the self-blame and guilt they may feel due to prevailing social attitudes which hold them accountable for their victimization" (p. 90).

Educational and Professional Policy Development

An incremental change policy is to ensure that schools of social work provide content on what might be termed "stigmatized women." While content on women is required by the Council on Social Work Education (CSWE), specific content on women used in the sex industry, on incarcerated women, and on drug-addicted women is often slight or absent altogether. If content were offered on these topics, social workers might be less wary of joining the debate on issues related to pornography and prostitution. We believe that the voices of social workers could contribute to the current debates over policy, as social workers are less likely to have a single focus on the medicalization or psychologization of the issues and of the persons involved. A person-in-environment approach to policy and practice development is necessary.

As an example of an incremental change effort, students in an advocacy-based social work research course at the University of Houston recently surveyed battered women's shelters in the state of Texas to determine the number of prostituted women being served, the barriers to and fears about serving this population, and the issues that are presenting themselves as the agencies serve this population. One outcome of the survey will be a directory of shelters that are willing to serve this population, which can be used as an outreach tool to encourage prostituted women seeking services to contact a local shelter for battered women. It's a small step, yet a step that may encourage agencies to explore the needs of this population in their communities.

State and local NASW chapters are also potential avenues for influencing local policies that affect women used in the sex industry. A task force to study the needs of prostituted women in communities that have an NASW unit would be a first step toward including this population in social work services.

The Need for Youth Crisis Services

The percentage of youths (young men and women) involved in prostitution who have experienced sexual, physical, and emotional abuse is chilling. Gay and lesbian youths who have retreated to or have been thrown out into the streets by caregivers is also unconscionable. Many of these youths turn to prostitution and drugs for physical and mental survival on the streets. While this nation's leaders often give eloquent speeches expressing their love for children, many youths continue to be deserted by the same leaders and systems that say they care so very much. Caring for youths and funding

youth services needs to become a national priority. Unfortunately, many of the youths who end up on the streets are often not perceived as social work's most desirable consumers. Few philanthropic organizations have been willing to hold galas to raise funds for gay and lesbian youth prostitutes—or for that matter, heterosexual youth prostitutes. Social workers need to make this population a priority as they work to influence policy on services related to children and youths.

SUMMARY

Women used in the sex industry could easily become symbols for the oppression of women worldwide. From being used and abused by military personnel and systems, to taking to the street to provide for the care of young children when the AFDC/TANF check won't cover basic expenses, to batterers who force women into prostitution as part of the exercise of power and control, to the woman working her way through medical school as a topless dancer, women are being used mostly by men for sexual pleasure, to fulfill sadistic fantasies, to avoid intimacy, and to maintain the subordination of women. In a country where an Equal Rights Amendment did not pass, where comparable-worth policies are considered too expensive to implement, and where violence against women is legal—if you pay for it—it appears that the sex industry will continue to thrive. As Shrage (1989) was quoted earlier in this chapter, much of the work to confront the sex industry is already being done by women and men committed to equality for women. We agree with Shrage that the work done in other spheres to enhance the status and quality of life for women will contribute to the beginning of the end of the sex industry. However, as this work is being done, it must include women used in the sex industry in both the analyses of problems and the solutions that are being sought.

REFERENCES

Alexander, P. (1987). Prostitutes are being scapegoated for heterosexual AIDS. In F. Delacoste & P. Alexander (Eds.), *Sex work: Writings by women in the sex industry* (pp. 248–265). Pittsburgh, PA: Cleis Press.

Andrews, A. (1988). A social worker's perspective on pornography. *Affilia, 3*, 23–32.

Baker, P. (1992). Maintaining male power: Why heterosexual men use pornography. In C. Itzine, *Pornography: Women, violence and civil liberties* (pp. 124–144). Oxford, England: Oxford University Press.

Bobo, K., Kendall, J., & Max, S. (1991). Organizing for Social Change. Washington, DC: Seven Lucks Press.

Brooks, G. (1995). *The centerfold syndrome*. San Francisco: Jossey-Bass Publishers.

Califia, P. (1994). *Public sex: The culture of radical sex*. Pittsburgh, PA: Cleis Press.

Collins, P. H. (1993). Pornography and black women's bodies. In D. E. H. Russell (Ed.), *Making violence sexy: Feminist views on pornography* (pp. 97–104). New York: Teachers College Press.

Cottle, C., Searles, P., Berger, R., & Pierce, B. (1989). Conflicting ideologies and the politics of pornography. *Gender and Society, 3*, 303–333.

Cowan, G., Chase, C., & Stahly, G. (1989). Feminist and fundamentalist attitudes toward pornography control. *Psychology of Women Quarterly, 13*, 97–112.

Coyote. (1987). Coyote/National Task Force on Prostitution. In F. Delacoste & P. Alexander (Eds.), *Sex work: Writings by women in the sex industry* (pp. 290–296). Pittsburgh, PA: Cleis Press.

Creith, E. (1996). *Undressing lesbian sex*. New York: Cassell pic.

Dworkin, A. (1993). *Letters from a war zone*. Brooklyn: Lawrence Hill Books.

Dworkin, A., & MacKinnon, C. (1988). *Pornography and civil rights*. Minneapolis: Organizing Against Pornography.

Forney, M. A., Inciardi, J., & Lockwood, D. (1992). Exchanging sex for crack-cocaine: A comparison of women from rural and urban communities. *Journal of Community Health, 17*, 73–85.

Fullilove, M. T., Lown, A., & Fullilove, R. E. (1992). Crack "hos and skeezers": Traumatic experiences of women crack users. *Journal of Sex Research, 29*, 275–287.

Gamache, D., & Giobbe, E. (1990). Prostitution: Oppression disguised as liberation. *National Coalition Against Domestic Violence, 86–90*.

Giobbe, E. (1993). Surviving commercial sexual exploitation. In D. E. H. Russell (Ed.), *Making violence sexy: Feminist views on pornography* (pp. 37–42). New York: Teachers College Press.

Graham, N., & Wish, E. (1994). Drug use among female arrestees: Onset, patterns, and relationships to prostitution. *The Journal of Drug Issues, 24*, 315–329.

Greenman, M. (1990). Survivors of prostitution find PRIDE. *Families in Society, 110–113*.

Harrison, J. (1995). *Gender, power and sexuality: Crack use and abuse among women*. (Unpublished manuscript.)

Helfand, J. (1987). Silence again. In F. Delacoste & P. Alexander (Eds.), *Sex work: Writings by women in the sex industry* (pp. 99–103). Pittsburgh, PA: Cleis Press.

Imperato, P. (1992). Syphillis, AIDS, & Crack. *Journal of Community Health, 17*, 69–71.

Inciardi, J., Lockwood, D., & Pottieger, A. (1993). Women and Crack-cocaine. New York: Macmillan.

International Committee for Prostitutes' Rights. (1987). World Charter and World Whores' Congress statements. In F. Delacoste & P. Alexander (Eds.), *Sex work: Writings by women in the sex industry* (pp. 305–321). Pittsburgh, PA: Cleis Press.

Jenness, V. (1990). From sex as sin to sex as work: COYOTE and the reorganization of prostitution as a social problem. *Social Problems, 37*, 403–420.

Jensen, R. (1995). Pornographic lives. *Violence against women, 1*, 32–54.

Jensen, R. (1996). Knowing pornography. *Violence against women, 2*, 82–102.

Jolin, A. (1994). On the backs of working prostitutes: Feminist theory and prostitution policy. *Crime and Delinquency, 40*, 69–83.

Kahn, S. (1991). *Organizing: A guide for grassroots leaders.* Washington, DC: NASW Press.

MacEachern, D. (1994). *Enough is enough: The hellraiser's guide to community activism.* New York: Avon Books.

Matz, E. (1994). An open memo to men: A brief reflection on pornography leads to a reflective tirade in a statistical mode. *Women and Therapy, 15,* 49–51.

Minnesota Coalition for Battered Women. (1991). Resolution by Board of Directors. (3/15/91) Minneapolis, MN.

Organizing Against Pornography. (1986). *Pornography: A practice of inequality—Facilitators guide.* Minneapoolis, MN: Organizing Against Pornography: A Resource Center for Education and Action.

Paglia, C. (1994). *Vamps and tramps.* New York: Vintage Books.

Pheterson, G. (1987) The social consequences of unchastity. In F. Delacoste & P. Alexander (Eds.), *Sex work: Writings by women in the sex industry* (pp. 215–230). Pittsburgh, PA: Cleis Press.

Quinn, C. (1995, June 29). Victims of a victimless crime. *Houston Chronicle,* p. 14A.

Richie, B. (1996). *Compelled to crime: The gender entrapment of black battered women.* New York: Routledge.

Russell, D. E. H. (1993). *Against pornography: The evidence of harm.* Berkeley, CA: Russell Publications.

Senn, C. (1993). Women's multiple perspectives and experiences with pornography. *Psychology of Women Quarterly, 17,* 319–341.

Shrage, L. (1989). Should feminists oppose prostitution? *Ethics, 99,* 347–361.

Smyth, C. (1994). Beyond queer cinema: It's in her kiss. In L. Gibbs (Ed.), *Daring to dissent* (pp. 194–213). New York: Cassell.

Staff. (undated). The "comfort woman" system: Enslaving women in World War II. *The East, 30,* 38–44.

Steinem, G. (1993). The real Linda Lovelace. In D. E. H. Russell (Ed.), *Making violence sexy: Feminist views on pornography* (pp. 23–31). New York: Teachers College Press.

Stoltenberg, J. (1990). Pornography and freedom. In M. Kimmel (Ed.), *Men confront pornography* (pp. 60–71). New York: Random House.

Stoltenberg, J. (1994). *What makes pornography "sexy"?* Minneapolis, MN: Milkweed Editions.

Strossen, N. (1995). *Defending pornography.* New York: Doubleday/Anchor Book.

Sturdevant, S. P., & Stoltzfus, B. (1992). *Let the good times roll: Prostitution and the U.S. military in Asia.* New York: New Press.

Weiner, A. (1996). Understanding the social needs of streetwalking prostitutes. *Social Work, 41,* 97–105.

White, V. F. (1993). Pornography and pride. In D. E. H. Russell (Ed.), *Making violence sexy: Feminist views on pornography* (pp. 105–106). New York: Teachers College Press.

WHISPER. (undated). Conference material handouts. Distributed October, 1990 in Austin, TX at the Texas Council on Family Violence Annual Conference.

Wynter, S. (1987). WHISPER: Women Hurt in Systems of Prostitution Engaged In Revolt. In F. Delacoste & P. Alexander (Eds.), *Sex work: Writings by women in the sex industry* (pp. 266–270). Pittsburgh, PA: Cleis Press.

SEXUAL HARASSMENT: ASSAULTS ON WOMEN AT WORK AND AT SCHOOL

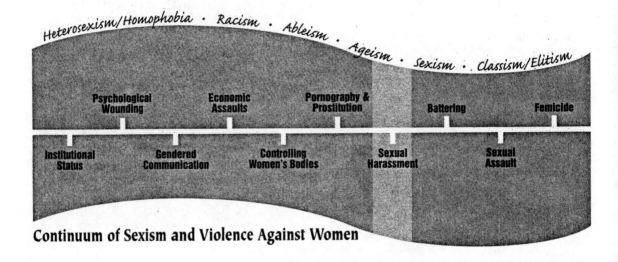

Heterosexism/Homophobia · Racism · Ableism · Ageism · Sexism · Classism/Elitism

Psychological Wounding | Economic Assaults | Pornography & Prostitution | Battering | Femicide

Institutional Status | Gendered Communication | Controlling Women's Bodies | Sexual Harassment | Sexual Assault

Continuum of Sexism and Violence Against Women

My stomach would get sick when I'd hear his chair creak—because I knew he'd be coming back to my desk. I actually even had nightmares involving this man ... I know it made my coworkers (even my male coworkers) uncomfortable ... so it affected all of us

USMSPB [United States Merit Systems Protection Board] Survey respondent

$\int$exual harassment is a serious violation. When compared to other assaults along the continuum of violence, sexual harassment might seem a minor annoyance or inconvenience, but such incidents actually represent serious abuse, which can result in significant physical, emotional, and economic consequences. Although sexual harassment is the newest of the assaults against women to be named and described, Fitzgerald and Shullman (1993) suggested that "sexual harassment is a problem with a long past but a short history" (p. 23).

Three recent events occurring on the national scene have brought the topic of sexual harassment to the attention of the American public, serving as a wake-up call to the dynamics and prevalence of such abuse. These instances include the Clarence Thomas confirmation hearings, where Anita Hill reluctantly brought charges against the Supreme Court nominee in 1991; the revelation of the Tailhook scandal, where Navy pilots harassed and assaulted women at a Las Vegas convention; and the discovery of Senator Robert Packwood's 20-year history of sexually harassing women on his staff, as well as female lobbyists and campaign volunteers. These widely publicized cases brought the subject of sexual harassment to the nation's attention and engendered discussions in the bedrooms and the boardrooms across the country about what constitutes harassment. Yet these cases also demonstrated the underlying difficulties in confronting sexual harassment, as women who brought forth charges found themselves victimized again, with their characters impugned, their motives questioned, and their experiences trivialized. The stereotypes and myths surrounding sexual harassment were often reinforced, rather than challenged.

This chapter confronts the myths by presenting the research on sexual harassment. This body of knowledge has grown in recent years, and much is now known about this insidious problem. Sexual harassment in the workplace and in academia are the focus here, although sexual harassment is prevalent in other public places, such as on the street, in housing, and in social situations. The chapter includes definitions of sexual harassment, the incidence and prevalence of the problem, theories of its causation, its consequences for women, and practice and policy implications of sexual harassment for social workers to consider.

Because this book is devoted to women and their experiences of oppression, this chapter focuses solely on women who are victimized by sexual harassment. The studies and surveys are clear: The majority of the time, men are the harassers and women the targets of harassment. Yet, it must be acknowledged that men are sexually harassed by other men and, less frequently, by women, and women can harass both male and female employees. Nonetheless, these instances are not in the majority and are not the focus of this chapter.

INTRODUCTION TO THE ISSUES

History of Sexual Harassment

Because the phrase "sexual harassment" was not coined until the 1970s, many people erroneously believe that sexual harassment is a modern-day social problem that did not exist in earlier times. However, even though it had no formal name, sexual harassment has been experienced by women for as long as women have walked along public streets or been employed in the workplace. Sexual harassment had no name then; it was merely the way the world was, or business as usual. Yet Catharine MacKinnon, radical feminist attorney and pioneer in the field of sexual harassment, has cautioned that "the unnamed should not be mistaken for the nonexistent" (1979, p. 28).

When historical accounts of women working in the United States are uncovered, women's experiences with sexual harassment on the job surface. A documentary history of women's work in the United States noted, "Women servants suffered uniquely from the indignities of patriarchal control over their personal lives. The sexual double standard often put them literally in a double bind: powerless to resist advances, and even rapes, by their masters and other men, they were nevertheless given the entire blame for being caught in violation of conventional sexual morality" (Baxandall & Gordon, 1995, p. 27).

European indentured female servants, as well as enslaved African women, were at the mercy of men who found them fair game for sexual harassment and sexual assault. As women moved out of the domestic workplaces into factories and offices, the harassment continued at the hands of supervisors and coworkers. With many women forced into factory work to support their families, their responses to sexual harassment were limited due to their economic dependence. As female workers attempted to organize, sexual exploitation was often addressed as an issue, as well as long hours and unsafe working conditions.

The more recent history of sexual harassment began with finally naming the violation in the 1970s. With the second wave of the women's movement and the large influx of women into the paid labor force, women began speaking out in greater numbers than ever before about a troubling phenomenon that interfered with their ability to earn a wage and support their families. The first public outcry on record against sexual harassment took place in Ithaca, New York, in the spring of 1975 (Langelan, 1993). Activists joined with others to start the organization Working Women United Institute, which is often credited for coining the term *sexual harassment* and for conducting one of the first studies on the subject. Early coverage of the issue in *Redbook* and *Ms.* magazines further highlighted the problem. Although the *Redbook* reader survey is frequently discounted because the respondents were self-selected, the informal survey did bring national attention to the subject. In response to the magazine's questionnaire on sexual harassment, more than 9,000 readers responded, with 88% reporting having been personally sexually harassed, while 90% of respondents verified that sexual harassment was a problem in their work environment (Safran, 1976).

The groundbreaking book on the subject of sexual harassment was written by Catharine MacKinnon, entitled *Sexual Harassment of Working Women* (1979). Her book was the first to name sexual harassment as sex discrimination. She wrote, "sexual harassment is argued in this book to be not simply abusive, humiliating, oppressive, and exploitive, but also to be sex discrimination in employment" (pp. 5–6). MacKinnon based her argument on Title VII of the Civil Rights Act of 1964 and the equal-protection clause of the Fourteenth Amendment.

Title VII of the Civil Rights Act of 1964 prohibits discriminatory practices in the workplace. When first introduced, the bill prohibited discrimination based on race, color, religion, or national origin. Discrimination on the basis of sex was not originally included. In an attempt to defeat the measure, such a provision was added at the last moment, proposed by conservative Southern opponents who hoped that such a ludicrous amendment would serve to defeat the entire bill (Petrocelli & Repa, 1992). However, proponents of the bill wanted the other protections so badly that the bill was passed, and prohibition of employment discrimination became law, including discrimination based on sex. At this time the act also established the Equal Employment Opportunities Commission (EEOC) to oversee the law and to issue regulations and guidelines.

Discrimination in educational settings was recognized as a violation of Title IX of the Education Amendments Act of 1972, prohibiting sex discrimination in federally assisted programs. In 1992, the U.S. Supreme Court ruled that sexual-harassment complaints could be filed under Title IX of the federal education laws, and monetary damages could be recovered. Prior to that decision, Title IX applied just to cases of gender inequality in education, such as inequities in funding male and female school sports teams.

Although the Civil Rights Act had been on the books since 1964, it was MacKinnon's treatise that made the act the basis for arguing for protection from sexual harassment. In 1980, the EEOC presented guidelines defining what constitutes sexual harassment in violation of Title VII; stated the manner in which the EEOC would determine whether alleged behavior constituted sexual harassment; held employers responsible for their own acts and for those of their supervisory employees, with respect to sexual harassment; and suggested steps an employer should take to prevent sexual harassment (U.S. Department of Labor Women's Bureau, 1993).

The history of sexual harassment has continued to unfold as court decisions and additional EEOC regulations have been handed down to further refine both the definition of the problem and the subsequent response. For instance, Title VII of the Civil Rights Act was amended by the Civil Rights Act of 1991. Passage of the Civil Rights Act of 1991 allowed compensatory and punitive damages to be awarded for the first time, although a $300,000 cap was put into place. In 1990, the EEOC reissued a lengthy Policy Guidance on Current Issues of Sexual Harassment to help further delineate sexual harassment and employer liability (U.S. Department of Labor Women's Bureau [USDOLWB], 1993).

The nation's court rulings have also had further impact on the issue of sexual harassment. The first decision rendered by the U.S. Supreme Court on sexual harassment under Title VII was *Meritor Savings Bank v. Vinson* (cited in USDOLWB, 1993), which found that a plaintiff may establish a violation of Title VII by proving that discrimination based on sex had created a hostile or abusive work environment; however, such conduct must be "sufficiently severe or pervasive" as to affect a term, condition, or privilege of employment. Another important court decision came in 1991, when the Ninth Court of Appeals ruled in *Ellison v. Brady* that sexual harassment should be viewed from the "perspective of a reasonable woman primarily because we believe that a sex-blind reasonable person standard tends to be male-biased and tends to systematically ignore the experiences of women" (cited in USDOLWB, 1993, p. 211). Although this ruling appears to be beneficial to women—that is, it takes into account a women's perspective—some have criticized the concept as being symbolically helpful, but not practically useful (DeCosse, 1992; Gutek & O'Connor, 1995). The dynamics and definitions of sexual harassment continue to evolve as case law, EEOC regulations, social science research, and public attitudes change in response to new information and greater awareness.

Definitions of Sexual Harassment

As noted, the definitions of sexual harassment continue to unfold. The abusive practice has moved from being perceived as a private trou-

ble experienced by some overly sensitive women in workplaces and educational institutions to being more readily defined as a serious social problem. The most often cited early definition was offered by Catharine MacKinnon (1979) as "unwanted imposition of sexual requirements in the context of a relationship of unequal power" (p. 1). EEOC guidelines issued in 1980 elaborated the definition (cited in USDOLWB, 1993, p. 211):

> *Unwelcome sexual advances, requests for sexual favors, and other verbal or physical conduct of a sexual nature constitute sexual harassment when:*
>
> 1. *submission to such conduct is made either explicitly or implicitly a term or condition of an individual's employment,*
> 2. *submission to or rejection of such conduct by an individual is used as the basis for employment decisions affecting such an individual, or*
> 3. *such conduct has the purpose or effect of unreasonably interfering with an individual's work performance or creating an intimidating, hostile, or offensive working environment.*

These guidelines have been interpreted to outline two broad classes of prohibitive behavior. The first is *quid pro quo harassment,* literally meaning "this for that," which seeks to demand sexual favors by threat of job-related consequences if such favors are refused. Second, a *hostile environment* constitutes sexual harassment, which is pervasive sex-related verbal or physical conduct that is unwelcome or offensive. In 1993, the EEOC amended the original sex-discrimination guidelines to include another category, termed "gender harassment." *Gender harassment* is verbal or physical conduct that denigrates or shows hostility or aversion (Koss, Goodman, Browne, Fitzgerald, Keita, & Russo, 1994, p. 115). Gender harassment, therefore, is harassment that is directed against women as a class, which may not be specifically sexual in nature. Examples of prohibited conduct include epithets, slurs, taunts, and gestures; the display or distribution of obscene or pornographic materials; gender-based hazing; and threatening, intimidating, or hostile acts (Koss et al., 1994).

While the legal definition of sexual harassment is constantly evolving, researchers have concurrently struggled to operationalize the definition in order to determine the prevalence and consequences of sexual harassment across studies with various populations. The trouble with comparing studies across the board is that the definition has been operationalized differently by researchers. Research definitions range from leering glances to actual sexual assaults. A list of behaviors that constitute sexual harassment has been utilized by many researchers, starting with the original list used in the Working Women United Institute study (cited in Koss et al., 1994), which stated, "sexual harassment can be any or all of the following: verbal suggestions or jokes, constant leering or ogling, 'accidentally' brushing against your body, a 'friendly' pat, squeeze, pinch, or arm around you, catching you alone for a quick kiss, the explicit proposition backed by threat of losing your job, and forced sexual relations" (p. 122).

Behavioral lists have advantages, in that they are specific, yet no list can be all inclusive. One of the most widely adapted classification models was proposed by Till (1980, cited by Koss et al., 1994), who surveyed a national sample of college women and then classified their responses into five general categories. Till's categories are

1. *Gender harassment*—generalized sexist remarks and behavior that convey insulting, degrading, and sexist attitudes about women
2. *Seductive behavior*—inappropriate and offensive sexual advances
3. *Sexual bribery*—the solicitation of sexual activity by promise of reward
4. *Sexual coercion*—the coercion of sexual activity by threat of punishment

5. *Sexual crimes and misdemeanors*—gross sexual imposition (attempts to fondle, kiss, or grab) or assault.

Louise Fitzgerald, a prominent researcher in the sexual-harassment field, finds that definitions relying solely on behavioral lists fail to take into account all the components of sexual harassment, including power differentials. After her extensive review of the literature and numerous research studies of her own, Fitzgerald (1990) suggested the following definition:

> *Sexual harassment consists of the sexualization of an instrumental relationship through which the introduction or imposition of sexist or sexual remarks, requests or requirements, in the context of a formal power differential. Harassment can also occur where no such formal differential exists, if the behavior is unwanted by or offensive to the woman. Instances of harassment can be classified into the following general categories: gender harassment, seductive behavior, solicitation of sexual activity by promise of reward or threat of punishment, and sexual imposition or assault. (p. 38)*

Power is an important part of the dynamics of sexual harassment, for sexual harassment is affected by power differentials. In the past, this power differential was frequently operationalized as the power inherent in a hierarchical, vertical organizational structure, such as the power differences present between a supervisor and an employee or a professor and a student. Yet real-life experiences suggest that such power imbalances can occur between two people perceived as equals, such as a male and female coworker, or can even include a male student harassing a female professor.

In defining the power differentials in harassment, Benson (1984) described three possible power relations within sexual-harassment situations: *power sexual harassment*, when the abuser has formal power over the victim; *contrapower sexual harassment*, when the victim has formal power over the abuser; and *peer sexual harassment*, when the sexual harassment occurs between so-called equals. Although studies surveying sexual harassment on college campuses have tended to focus on the harassment of students by professors, several studies have brought to light a problem in which students harass professors, most often male students harassing female professors (Grauerholz, 1989; McKinney, 1990). Although the female professor may have the formal, achieved power of her position, a male student has power ascribed to him by a patriarchal society that values men and deems them superior to women.

The definition of what constitutes sexual harassment seems a torturous process, with complex legal and research definitions. However, not only do various authorities and agencies define sexual harassment differently, so do the two sexes. In a research area full of contradiction and unknowns, the most constant finding is that men and women define sexual harassment differently. Women consistently view a wider range of behaviors as harassing than men do. With few exceptions, this finding has been repeatedly demonstrated. Fitzgerald and Ormerod (1991) found that "the most salient factors in judgments of whether a particular incident constitutes harassment appear to be the severity or explicitness of the incident and the gender of the perceiver" (p. 292). That is, more blatant forms of sexual harassment, such as quid pro quo and more intrusive forms of sexual approach, are seen by both men and women as sexual harassment. Yet there is a large gray area in which women are more likely to define a less explicit behavior as sexual harassment than are men.

The difficulty of operationalizing a definition of sexual harassment is further complicated by the subjectivity of the interpretation of the remark or behavior. The context is all important. For example, Bravo and Cassedy (1992) cited the remark, "Your hair looks terrific" as having various interpretations, depending on the relationship between the parties, how each of them feels, and the tone of voice, as well as body language. For instance,

this remark made by one coworker to another while passing in the hall has a very different meaning when uttered by a male boss while bending over his female secretary and whispering it in her ear.

The definition of sexual harassment is a subjective process, which can produce more questions than answers. What is "unwelcome"? What does a "reasonable woman" view as harassment? Does the intent of the harasser take precedence over the response of the woman who has been harassed? Who decides?

Experiences of Sexual Harassment

Although most kinds of sexism and violence against women have at times been both minimized and joked about, sexual harassment continues to be made light of, while so-called jokes about rape or battering have become generally less acceptable. In a textbook, it is easy to lose sight of the pain of the issue when definitions are laboriously compared and statistics are dryly enumerated. In order to make the issue more real for the reader and to put a face on the problem, the following real-life instances of sexual harassment are related. Remember, these are only a few of the millions of instances that continue to plague women in the offices, classrooms, and streets across America:

- A boss tucked a female employee's paycheck into the fly of his pants, saying "come and get it."
- A male employee slipped a postcard depicting a woman having sex with a goat into the locker of a new female employee.
- A coworker turned up the volume of his tape player and broadcasted the rape scene from a pornographic movie.
- A newly promoted president of the firm said to a female employee, "Either we engage in a sexual relationship, or I no longer need an office manager."
- A supervisor at a factory grabbed a woman employee and forced her face against his crotch.

- The owner of an office building required a female elevator operator to wear a sexually revealing uniform and then fired her for refusing to wear the uniform after being the object of numerous lewd remarks and propositions.
- An undergraduate student at Yale University received a C grade in a course after refusing sexual advances from a professor who promised her an A in the course if she complied.
- A supervisor frequently called female employees "whores," "cunt," "pussy," and "tits."
- Frequent pornographic images of women were displayed, such as a poster depicting a woman lying down with a golf ball on her breasts while straddled by a man holding a golf club, a poster showing a meat spatula pressed against a woman's pubic area, a dart board featuring a woman's breast, with the nipple as the bull's-eye.
- A supervisor fondled a female employee in front of other employees, followed her into the restroom, exposed himself at work, and raped her on more than one occasion.

These are just a few of the instances related in Bravo and Cassedy's book, *The 9to5 Guide to Combating Sexual Harassment* (1992). These instances only begin to touch the surface of the abuse many women face daily as they attempt to go about their lives and earn a living, gain an education, or walk down the street. Be alert to the temptation to minimize the abuse that falls under the rubric of sexual harassment, and understand its relationship to the other abuses along the continuum, from gendered communication to sexual harassment to femicide. Sexual harassment is a serious abuse, often resulting in equally serious financial, emotional, and physical consequences.

INCIDENCE AND PREVALENCE OF SEXUAL HARASSMENT

Workplace

There are many difficulties inherent in measuring the incidence and prevalence of sexual harassment. First, it is difficult to measure what cannot easily be defined. Second, because harassment is legally a civil-rights violation, rather than a crime, its incidence is not reported in national crime statistics that yield other data on crimes against women. The EEOC compiles statistics of complaints filed with the agency, but—like reported rape statistics—these figures are believed to represent only the tip of the iceberg. The Women's Legal Defense Fund (1995) concluded that between 1% and 7% of women who are harassed file a formal complaint or seek legal help, while other studies found that less than 5% of victims ever report the harassment to anyone in authority (Fitzgerald et al., 1988; Livingston, 1982). Studies asking whether a woman has been sexually harassed at work may underrepresent the actual number of incidents because, similar to the dynamics of rape, many women do not identify their experiences as sexual harassment. For many women in the workplace, such treatment is business as usual. Most surveys thus avoid asking employees whether they have been sexually harassed and instead ask about specific behaviors they may have experienced.

With these points in mind, the following review examines the most widely cited studies, which give a picture of the incidence and prevalence of sexual harassment. In 1980, the U.S. Congress commissioned the largest and most highly regarded study on sexual harassment, in which the U.S. Merit Systems Protection Board (USMSPB) surveyed a stratified random sample of 23,964 federal workers. The highlights of the study's findings include the following: 42% of the female respondents reported experiences of sexual harassment; sexual harassment usually occurred over a period of months, rather than being a single, isolated incident; the economic effect of such harassment was nearly $200 million over the 2-year period in which the study was conducted; and 1% of the sample reported actual or attempted rape by coworkers, with this number projecting that 12,000 female federal workers were subjected to rape or attempted rape (USMSPB, 1981). A breakdown of the harassing behaviors into categories found that 10% of the women had been pressured for sexual cooperation, 33% were the target of sexual remarks, 26% the object of unwanted touching, and 15% had been subjected to pressure to date coworkers or supervisors.

The USMSPB updated their findings by repeating the survey in 1980 and again in 1994, with remarkably similar results. In 1987, 42% of women and 14% of men surveyed reported unwanted sexual attention at work during the preceding 2 years, whereas the 1994 survey found that 44% of women and 19% of men reported unwanted sexual attention (USMSPB, 1995). Similar to previous studies, the report found that the most common types of sexual harassment were unwanted teasing, jokes, and remarks; and the most frequent perpetrator was a coworker. Although the figures for sexual harassment in the USMSPB surveys have remained relatively constant, the number of sexual assaults did not. The latest report stated, "the most unsettling statistics coming from the 1994 survey are those involving attempted or actual rape or assault" (USMSPB, 1995, p. 16). The percentage of women who reported having been the victims of rape or attempted rape rose from 0.8% in 1987 to 4% in 1994.

Another important study was conducted by Gutek (1985), which found that 53% of working women reported at least one instance of sexual harassment during their time in the workforce. The sample was representative of the Los Angeles area workforce, based on telephone interviews selected by random-digit dialing. This percentage seems to confirm the high levels of sexual harassment experienced by women in the USMSPB surveys.

Military

The Tailhook scandal by Navy pilots alerted both the public and the military establishment to the pervasive sexual harassment long tolerated within the military culture. The macho image of fighting men who risked their lives for their country and who regarded women—both American and from other countries—as their just reward for their patriotic duty lingered long after women had successfully integrated into all branches of the military service. In 1996, the Pentagon released the report of a massive Pentagon survey, conducted in 1995, which included three survey tools and responses from approximately 47,200 active-duty military personnel. One survey included a list of 25 types of behavior that the Pentagon deems offensive. Of the women who responded, 78% said they had experienced at least one of those behaviors in the preceding year (Department of Defense, 1996).

The most frequently cited perpetrators of harassment were military coworkers, with most of the harassment occurring on military installations, at work, and during day hours. Only 24% of those who experienced an incident of sexual harassment chose to report the incident (Department of Defense [DOD], 1996). Of those who reported the incident, 50% of the women said the person who bothered them was talked to about the behavior, 15% of women indicated that no action was taken, and 23% of the women said that their complaint was discounted or not taken seriously (DOD, 1996). The most common reasons given by women for not reporting the harassment were that they took care of the problem themselves, felt nothing would be done, did not think the problem was important, thought it would make their work situations unpleasant, thought they would be labeled as troublemakers, or did not want to hurt the persons who harassed them (DOD, 1996).

The promising news is that when compared to a survey conducted in 1988, the rate of sexual harassment for female military personnel dropped from 64% to 55%, although it must be noted that these results continue to mean that more than half of all women in the military experience some form of sexual harassment (DOD, 1996). The survey also revealed that over 80% of respondents reported being trained about sexual harassment, almost 90% of respondents knew the process for reporting sexual harassment, and over 60% said that leaders were making honest and reasonable efforts to stop sexual harassment.

As this book goes to press, the latest tragedy of large-scale sexual harassment in the military continues to unfold. Army officials have said that more than 50 women have reported that they were raped, assaulted, or harassed at the Army Ordnance Center and School over a 2-year time frame, with more calls received daily from the toll-free hotline set up for reporting purposes (Houston Chronicle News Services, 1996).

Academic

Studies on sexual harassment have also focused on the academic arena. A 1993 study underwritten by the AAUW entitled "Hostile Hallways" found that 85% of school-age girls and 76% of school-age boys reported experiencing harassing behaviors at school (AAUW, 1993). The gender gap in the response to the harassment is significant, with 70% of the girls reporting having been "very upset" or "somewhat upset," compared with only 24% of the boys (AAUW, 1993). The harassment was so severe that many of the female students reported that they did not want to go to school or talk in class, and many thought about changing schools.

Other research has targeted college populations for study. Benson and Thomson (1982) found that among senior female students at the University of California at Berkeley, 29.7% reported at least one incident of sexual harassment at some point during their college careers. Rubin and Borgers (1990) reviewed the literature on studies conducted in universities during the 1980s and found results that painted a serious picture of sexual harassment on college campuses, including the following: Only 30% of the women on one campus reported *never* being sexually insulted by a man on campus,

whereas 82% of the men reported *never* being sexually insulted by another man; at Michigan State University, among a sample of 478 female juniors, seniors, and graduate students, 25% reported at least one incident of sexual harassment; and at East Carolina University, 33% of the female students reported being harassed by male teachers. The largest study surveyed close to 2,000 female college students at two universities and 642 female faculty members, administrators, and staff members employed at one of the universities. The research found that over 31% of women students and 34% of working women reported some form of gender harassment, and about 15% of the students and 17% of the employed women experienced seductive approaches from their professors or coworkers (Fitzgerald et al., 1988).

In conclusion, it appears that almost one in two women in the workplace and one in three women in academic settings report being sexually harassed. The most frequently reported types of harassment include gender harassment and unwelcome sexual advances. Less often cited were demands for sex in exchange for rewards or threats of punishment and sexual assaults, although the latter do occur with frightening frequency. These data suggest that sexual harassment is one of the most common forms of sexual victimization experienced by women, from elementary school to college and following them into the workplace.

CAUSES OF SEXUAL HARASSMENT

Many theories are offered to explain the occurrence of sexual harassment. Some theories focus on the individual, others the organization, while others implicate society. The most widely cited categorization of theories is the model outlined by Tangri, Burt, and Johnson (1982), which distinguishes among three kinds of theories of causality. The first is the *natural/biological model* of harassment, which interprets sexual harassment as natural sexual attraction between two people. In this model, men are believed to be naturally sexually aggressive, and the behavior that women find offensive is merely viewed as the normal courtship behavior of men.

The second model is the *organizational model,* which holds that harassment is a function of the hierarchical structure of organizations in which supervisors with more institutional power can extort sexual gratification from their subordinates. In this model, while men have traditionally been in positions of power over women, women can harass men if they are in higher positions of power within the organization.

The third model Tangri et al. present is the *sociocultural model,* which suggests that sexual harassment is only one manifestation of the larger patriarchal system in which men are the dominant group. Harassment, therefore, occurs when men assert their power based on the privilege bestowed on men in a male-dominated society. In this model, the sex of the person, rather than the person's organizational position, would be a better indicator of likelihood to harass.

Gutek and Morasch (1982) proposed an alternative theory, named "sex-role spillover," which the authors defined as "the carry over into the workplace of gender-based expectations for behavior that are irrelevant or inappropriate to work" (p. 55). The sex-role spillover is influenced by the sex ratio of men and women at work. Although women working in either male-dominated or female-dominated professions are affected differently, both incur more sexual harassment than women working in sexually integrated workplaces. For instance, in a male-dominated workplace, the male sex role spills over into the work roles, making these work roles incongruent for women. Women are thus seen as female first and work-role occupants second, leading to differential treatment and sexually harassing behaviors. Alternatively, because a traditional female job is dominated by women, the sex role and the work role overlap, and the work role

becomes the female sex role, with all its attendant stereotypes, especially concerning sexuality. Examples include cocktail waitresses and receptionists at engineering or manufacturing firms. In these instances, sexual harassment may be prevalent, although underreported, because it is viewed as part of the job (Gutek & Morasch, 1982).

The on-the-job experiences of management expert Judy Rosener (1995) seem to validate the sex-role spillover theory, and she has illustrated this point in an exercise she conducts in management and leadership seminars. She first asks her audience to list the words associated with the word *leader.* Frequent responses include the words "strong, rational, independent, aggressive, and competitive." Then, she asks female audiences to name the words associated with the word *male,* and they report such characteristics as "strong, controlling, husband/father, brother," as well as "power, macho, and rational." When asking men in the workplace what words they associate with *female,* they reply, "sex, mother/wife, beauty, soft/curves, and sensitive." Rosener (1995) has suggested that "the importance of this word association exercise is that it reveals men's tendency to view women in terms of their sexuality rather than in terms of their leadership potential. Since words structure thought, the lists provide a clue to a source of sexual static for men when they interact with women: they view them initially in a sexual rather than work context" (p. 71).

Another theory of the cause of sexual harassment focuses on the attitudes of men. Pryor (1987) developed a scale called the "Likelihood of Sexually Harassing" (LSH), modeled on scales developed to determine the propensity of men to rape. He found that men who scored high on the scale were more likely to hold adversarial sexual beliefs, find it difficult to assume another person's perspective, endorse traditional male sex-role stereotypes, rate high in authoritarianism, and report a higher likelihood to rape. In a subsequent study, Pryor, LaVite, and Stoller

(1993) expanded on these findings by presenting a social-psychological model, which found that some men harass some of the time. The study demonstrates that both personal (individual) factors and situational factors must be present for sexual harassment to occur. That is, a man must have certain proclivities to harass, as demonstrated on the LSH scale, but also, the work environment must be conducive to such harassment, such as workplace norms that tolerate or encourage sexual harassment.

Another group of theories revolve around misperceptions in communications, largely as a result of gender differences. For instance, Stockdale (1993) examined the role of sexual interpretation of women's friendly behavior as part of an explanation or theory of some forms of sexual harassment. In reviewing the literature, Stockdale reported that "preliminary data suggest that the tendency to sexually misperceive is associated with traditional sex-role attitudes, tolerance for sexually harassing activities, and nonacceptance of feminists' views about sexual harassment" (p. 87). Studies have consistently revealed that some men tend to interpret women's friendly or professional behavior as sexual. Although this explanation does not account for all instances of sexual harassment, it may help to explain some harassing behaviors.

Professor of Linguistics Deborah Tannen, whose books *You Just Don't Understand: Women and Men in Conversation* (1990) and *Talking from 9 to 5: Women and Men in the Workplace: Language, Sex, and Power* (1994) have been best-sellers, has observed various patterns of conversational style influenced by gender. Tannen noted that part of what makes sexual harassment so complex is that the same symbols can have one meaning in one context or to one person and a very different meaning in another context or to another person. She also noted that many rituals associated with men and women grew out of the situation where men and women were most likely to interact in the past—that is, a romantic context. Bringing these old rituals into the relatively new workplace can be problematic (Tannen, 1994).

On the other hand, however, Tannen acknowledges that sexual harassment is not merely about different conversational styles or cultural patterns but is about power, sex, and violence in our culture. Even though not all men are violent and not all men are harassers, Tannen acknowledged the "vague sense of physical threat that many women feel around men, even if there is little or no danger of actual physical violence" (1994, p. 255). It is often this underlying threat that women are aware of and that most men remain totally unaware of that causes some of the misperceptions between women and men.

Tannen has also addressed the fear vocalized by many men in the workplace after Anita Hill aired her charges on national television. Men report fearing that women will falsely accuse them of sexual harassment. This fear seems to shift the power dynamics, as some men believe that a woman's ability to charge them with sexual harassment gives women power over men. This fear is prevalent in the sexual-assault arena as well, as some men report fearing that women will bring false charges. This male fear isn't substantiated in reality, for filing charges of either sexual assault or sexual harassment has proven to be so difficult and damaging for women that most women are reluctant to bring charges. Tannen (1994) wrote,

> The aspect that holds power for most men is the possibility of a false charge, a possibility that many women dismiss as unlikely to happen, since bringing charges is so damaging to the accuser. For their part, many women are insulted by men's concern, which they hear as an accusation that women are manipulative liars. In fact, it is far more common for women to be physically assaulted or sexually harassed than for them to bring false charges, but these reali-

ties do not change the power each fear holds for the individuals who identify with one party or the other. (p. 251)

A feminist view of sexual harassment is multidimensional. From a feminist perspective, sexual harassment is about power and control. It is about men's sexualization and objectification of women in the workplace and academic settings; social control and men's attempt to keep women subordinate; economic exploitation in which women are kept from the traditionally well-paying male jobs; men's feelings of entitlement and superiority; male prerogative over women's lives and women's bodies; the socialization of men, which teaches them that they are superior, dominant, and should be in control; the intersection of sexism, racism, classism, and homophobia in the workplace and school settings; and sexual discrimination.

RESPONSES TO SEXUAL HARASSMENT

In 1991, in front of the Senate Judiciary Committee, law professor Anita Hill charged Clarence Thomas with sexual harassment. She described the harassment, which included graphic descriptions of pornographic films, comments on her personal and sexual appearance, and pressure to accompany Thomas on dates. In her statement to the Senate Judiciary Committee on October 11, 1991, she made the following statements describing her responses to his persistent and unwanted sexual attention:

I declined the invitation to go out with him, and explained to him that I thought it would jeopardize ... what I considered to be a very good working relationship.... I thought by saying no and explaining my reasons, my employer would abandon his social suggestions. However, to my regret, in the following few weeks, he continued to ask me out on several occasions.... Because I was extremely uncomfortable talking about sex with him at all, and particularly in such a graphic way, I told him I did not want to talk

about this subject. I would also try to change the subject to education matters or to nonsexual personal matters, such as his background or beliefs. My efforts to change the subject were rarely successful.... Throughout the period of these conversations, he also from time to time asked me for social engagements. My reaction to these conversations was to avoid them by eliminating opportunities for us to engage in extended conversations.... In January of 1983, I began looking for another job. (Hill, 1995, pp. 337–341)

Hill's responses to Clarence Thomas's harassing behavior were viewed by many as evidence that the harassment did not happen. Full of righteous indignation, some men and women proclaimed that if she had really been harassed, Anita Hill would have aggressively confronted him, filed a complaint, and refused to join him in a move from the Department of Education to, ironically, the EEOC. Yet Hill's testimony of her response is the classic, almost textbook, response of a woman who has been sexually harassed. In the previously cited Pentagon study, 60% of the women who were harassed said that they did not file a formal complaint, usually out of a fear of retaliation. In the 1994 USMSPB study, only about 6% of the respondents who had reported being sexually harassed took formal action (USMSPB, 1995). In the original USMSPB study of federal employees (USMSPB, 1981), almost 10% of the women who were harassed reported changing jobs as a result of the harassment. Even among those women who spoke up when they were harassed, 43% responded that their most assertive response "made no difference."

In the 1994 USMSPB study, the most common response (44% of the respondents) was to ignore the behavior and do nothing (USMSPB, 1995). In contrast, 88% of all survey respondents said that asking or telling a person to stop was the response they believed would be most effective in ending the harassment. Of the respondents who had experienced sexual harassment and who used this tactic, 60% said that it made things better (USMSPB, 1995).

In Benson and Thomson's (1982) study of undergraduate women, students used many indirect tactics to forestall escalation of the sexual harassment, including the following: ignoring sexual innuendoes, bringing a friend to the instructor's office or pointedly leaving the door open, or mentioning that they had a boyfriend or a husband. Students also avoided contact during class time and office hours. Few students directly confronted the professor, citing fear of reprisals such as withdrawing intellectual support and encouragement, criticism of work once praised, and low grades.

Koss et al.'s (1994) review of the literature found a discrepancy between how individuals say they would respond to harassment and how victims actually do respond. Most women predict that they would respond assertively if they were sexually harassed; yet this finding contrasts with research results revealing that the overwhelming number of victims clearly do not respond in this manner. When asked why they don't report harassment, women give many reasons. According to Koss et al.'s (1994) review of the research, these reasons include fear of retaliation, fear of not being believed, feelings of shame and humiliation, a belief that nothing can or will be done, and a reluctance to cause problems for the harasser. In many ways, a woman who reports sexual harassment is viewed as a troublemaker or whistle-blower and is treated accordingly. Some employees leave jobs, are fired, ask to be transferred, while students may drop the class, change majors, or even leave school.

Clearly, the majority of women attempt to avoid confrontation and try indirect tactics to get the behavior to stop. The more blatant the harassment, the more likely women are to confront their harasser and to file charges. Louise Fitzgerald (1993) made a salient point when speaking of women's responses or choices of responses to being sexually harassed, stating, "Women who experience it are frequently faced with choices so aversive as to hardly constitute choices at all: to comply or resist, to report or be silent, to submit or be ostracized, demoted, fired, or worse" (p. 1072).

CONSEQUENCES OF SEXUAL HARASSMENT

Sexual harassment is often viewed by society, and even by social workers, as a mere minor annoyance or petty inconvenience. One professor of political science wrote that "women need to develop a thick skin in order to survive and prosper in the workforce," and she advised women to "lighten up and even dispense a few risqué barbs of their own" (Paul, 1991). This minimization of women's experiences denies the many serious consequences of sexual harassment. The consequences for women can be separated into three general categories, including work-related outcomes, psychological or emotional outcomes, and physical or health-related outcomes. (See Table 8.1 for a complete listing.)

Koss et al. (1994, p. 139) acknowledged,

It is difficult to overestimate the toll that harassment takes on women's lives. Women are disproportionately represented in the most economically vulnerable segments of the labor market. In addition to the millions of single women who support themselves, most married women work from financial necessity, and tens of thousands are the sole support of their families, including a large percentage with small children. Workplace harassment places these women in an intolerable situation. Virtually tens of thousands are forced to tolerate sexual exploitation or run a daily gamut of sexual and emotional abuse as the price of earning a living.

As Table 8.1 makes evident, the outcomes of sexual harassment for women are serious and numerous. Women are affected not only economically, but psychologically and physically as well. When speaking of their experiences of being sexually harassed, many women report feeling violated and compare it to the trauma of rape (Johnson-Gallagher, personal

Table 8.1
Consequences of Sexual Harassment

Work- and School-Related Outcomes

Quit job, fired, transferred, reassigned. Loss of income, seniority, disruption of work histories, problems with references, often a failure to qualify for unemployment benefits. Decreased morale and absenteeism, decreased job satisfaction, damage to interpersonal relationships at work, poor job performance, negative performance evaluations, changes in job plans or career goals, lower productivity. For students, change of academic major or educational program, dropped courses, avoided courses, lowered grades, withdrawal of support and professional opportunities, and derogation of their scholarly work.

Psychological and Emotional Consequences

Fear, lowered self-esteem, lessened confidence, loss of control, disruption of their lives, depression, anger, anxiety, irritability, feelings of humiliation and alienation, sense of helplessness and vulnerability, difficulties with interpersonal relationships with partners, families, friends, shock, emotional numbing, flashbacks, posttraumatic stress disorder (PTSD).

Physical or Health-Related Consequences

Headaches, disordered eating (e.g., binge eating or loss of appetite), gastrointestinal disorders (e.g., nausea), weight loss or gain, crying spells, jaw tightness and teeth grinding, nervousness, sleep disturbances (e.g., inability to sleep or tiredness).

From Koss et al. (1994).

communication, February 27, 1996). Sexual harassment changes women's lives. Women turn to families and friends, therapists, lawyers, doctors, and social workers for help with the consequences of harassment. Social workers have a responsibility to understand the seriousness of the consequences of sexual harassment and to refrain from joining in society's responses to minimize the abuse or to blame the victim.

EXPERIENCES OF SEXUAL HARASSMENT BY SPECIAL POPULATIONS OF WOMEN

Lesbian Women

The sexual harassment of lesbian women at work can take two different forms, depending whether they are or are not hiding their sexual orientation. A closeted lesbian woman is assumed by many in the workplace to be a single,

heterosexual woman. The research literature is generally in agreement that the women most often targeted for harassment are those who are single or divorced. Because a closeted lesbian woman is perceived to be unattached to a man, she may be vulnerable to sexual harassment. In fact, Schneider (1982) found an elevated level of harassment among lesbian women at work, as compared with other women. In a later study, Schneider (1991) reported that 17% of her female sample reported a sexual assault or an attempted sexual assault by someone they knew at work over their employment history. This finding represented 14% of the current self-identified heterosexuals and 20% of the current self-identified lesbians in her study population.

Additionally, lesbian women who are not closeted at work may be subject to sexual harassment based on their sexual orientation, as well as their sex. Although some states and some companies have nondiscrimination policies based on sexual orientation, many lesbian workers have no such protection. Prejudice and homophobia in the workplace create a hostile work environment for lesbian women. Petrocelli and Repa (1992) noted that hostile acts directed at a lesbian are likely to contain elements of animosity toward the woman's gender, as well as her sexual orientation (pp. 2–13). Some people use the terms "lesbian" or "dyke" to refer to any strong and independent woman. If a lesbian woman can show that the harasser treats heterosexual women with similar animosity, she might be able to demonstrate that the harasser is targeting her assertiveness and independence, regardless of her sexual orientation. Petrocelli and Repa (1992) suggested that "A lesbian faced with hostile conduct should stress those elements of her claim that she has in common with other harassed women to fit within the protection of the sexual harassment laws. Her best strategy is to try and show that the hostility toward her is a subspecies of a more general animosity toward all women employees" (pp. 2–13).

Women of Color

Women of color can constitute a vulnerable population to be harassed at work, in school, and in public places, for they are often victims of racial as well as sexual harassment. McClelland and Hunter (1992) modeled a definition of racial harassment on a definition of sexual harassment, stating that racial harassment is "deliberate or repeated unsolicited verbal comments or gestures of a racial nature that [are] unwelcome" (p. 92). The authors distinguished *racial harassment* from *racial prejudice* because racial harassment involves deliberate racist behavior, rather than attitudes, and from *racial violence,* in that the harassment involves unwelcome verbal comments or gestures, rather than physical force.

Therefore, women of color can be harassed due to their race, as well as their gender. As Catharine MacKinnon wrote in her groundbreaking book, *Sexual Harassment of Working Women,* "Apparently, sexual harassment can be both a sexist way to express racism and a racist way to express sexism" (1979, p. 30). The courts have recognized that women of color may face unique patterns of harassment due to their race, as well as their gender. For instance, in *Hicks v. Gates Rubber Company,* the Tenth Circuit Court held that evidence of racially hostile treatment could be combined with that of sexual harassment to establish a hostile work environment toward a female African-American employee (cited in U.S. Department of Labor Women's Bureau, 1993).

Yet sexual harassment has not always been a high-priority issue within the community of women of color. As Marcia Ann Gillespie, current editor-in-chief of *Ms.* magazine wrote in 1992, "No, sexual harassment is not a burning issue for most black women. First you have to get a job" (p. 43). Anita Hill's charges of sexual harassment by Clarence Thomas was especially divisive within the African-American community. African-American feminist Barbara Smith noted that the hearings demonstrated the inextricable links between racism and sexism. She wrote, "It was demoralizing to see how the confrontation reinforced the perception that any woman who raises the issue of sexual oppression in the black community is somehow a traitor to the race, which translates into being a traitor to black men" (p. 38).

Clearly, African-American women and other women of color are victims of sexual and racial harassment. In fact, the U.S. Supreme Court's first ruling on sexual harassment in *Meritor Savings Bank v. Vinson* involved an African-American woman who was severely and repeatedly sexually harassed. Yet whether women of color are harassed more or respond differently than European-American women is not well documented because many researchers do not use race as a variable. There is evidence to suggest that women of color might be more vulnerable to harassment due to economic fac-

Thai women following their release from a clothing manufacturing company where they were held against their will to produce clothing. Asian women have been frequent targets for exploitation, sexually as well as economically, often due to stereotypical beliefs that portray them as passive and subordinate. Also, their immigrant status can make them more vulnerable to abuse. Photo © 1996 Kim Kulish.

tors and stereotypes (DeFour, 1990). DeFour noted that women of color are often financially vulnerable, which may put them at increased risk for being sexually harassed, with fewer alternatives for dealing with harassment. For example, DeFour noted that within the academic arena, women of color are more likely to be dependent on financial aid for their education.

Stereotypes of women of color may also increase their vulnerability to sexual harassment because some of the stereotypes commonly held about women of color relate to their sexual nature. For instance, Latina women are stereotypically viewed as "hot-blooded," Asian-American women are perceived as submissive and exotic sexual partners, Native American women are viewed as devoted to male elders, and African-American women have been perceived as "highly sexed," with "low morals" (DeFour, 1990). Whether these vulnerabilities translate into increased harassment of women of color is uncertain, for the research is limited and often inconclusive.

A few studies focus on the experiences of women of color with regard to sexual harassment. In two studies (Gruber & Bjorn, 1982;

Mansfield et al., 1991), African-American women working in low-status, blue-collar jobs reported a greater frequency and greater severity of harassment, yet in another study (Wyatt & Riederle, 1995), European-American women were more likely to report being sexually harassed than were African-American women. Another study (Yoder & Aniakudo, 1995) consisted of interviews with 22 African-American female firefighters, and every one had been a target of sexual or gender harassment. What was unique about these firefighters was that each one had responded directly to the abuse with responses running the gamut from assertive or verbal aggression to physically aggressive responses, which were generally effective in ending the harassment. Yoder and Aniakudo (1995) speculated that occupational differences, especially the physical nature of their job, as well as racial differences might explain the firefighters' more confrontational responses.

There is a paucity of research on the experiences of Latina women with sexual harassment, and those studies available produce conflicting accounts. For instance, the Navy Equal

Opportunity/Sexual Harassment (NEOSH) Survey included information from 99 Latina female officers and 436 Latina enlisted women. The survey's data suggested that the Latina women did not perceive themselves as uniquely disadvantaged regarding equal opportunity in the Navy (Rosenfeld, 1994). Alternatively, a study of white-collar Chicanas at a public university reported that one third of the respondents described being sexually harassed, and nearly 44% reported encountering discrimination based on gender or race–ethnicity (Segura, 1992).

A study of Chinese students (Tang, Yik, Cheung, Choi, & Au, 1995), designed to determine their perceptions of what constitutes sexual harassment, revealed similar findings to those of American college student populations. That is, the more blatant the acts of harassment, such as quid pro quo and coercive sexual behaviors, the more likely the acts were to be defined as sexual harassment, whereas gender harassment and more covert sexual behavior was not defined as sexual harassment. Also, similar to studies in the United States, Chinese women were more likely than were Chinese men to define particular behaviors as harassing. Clearly, there are some similarities in defining sexual harassment among women of color, but more research needs to be conducted to further illuminate differences and commonalities.

Women in Traditionally Male Blue-Collar Occupations

The sexual harassment research identifies women who are working in traditionally male occupations, often blue-collar positions, as being at increased risk for sexual harassment on the job. In every other assault against women described in this book, the variables of sex, race, and class have important influences on the violence of the assaults. Sexual harassment is no exception. This intersection of variables is most evident when looking at the sexual harassment experiences of women of color in traditionally male-dominated, blue-collar occupations. In a study of women who work on the assembly line in the automobile industry, 36% reported that they had experienced sexual harassment (Gruber & Bjorn, 1982). The study further revealed that African-American women not only receive more harassment than European-American women, but also are harassed more severely. Another study (Mansfield, Koch, Henderson, Vicary, Cohn, & Young, 1991) compared the levels of harassment between women working in traditionally male-dominated jobs, such as tradeswomen and transit workers, and women working in traditionally female jobs, in this case, school secretaries. The study found high rates of sexual harassment and sex discrimination among tradeswomen and transit workers, compared to the rates among women in more traditional women's work, with African-American women also reporting substantial amounts of race discrimination (Mansfield et al., 1991).

Men may feel more threatened when women enter occupations traditionally held by men. Women may also be more subject to having male supervisors in jobs that are traditionally held by men. Also, this subset of women represents the intersection of sex, race, and class oppression, and the multiplicity of factors may be related to the high levels of harassment experienced by these workers. Mansfield et al. (1991) made recommendations to address the increased level of harassment directed at blue-collar, female workers, suggesting career counseling should address the costs and benefits when young women are considering entry into blue-collar, male-dominated work. Although the tradeswomen and transit workers make considerably more money than do school secretaries, they also can expect to encounter more difficult barriers than do secretaries. Mansfield et al. (1991) also called on management, unions, and other work organizations to improve the working conditions for women entering traditionally male work environments.

Social Workers

Although one might hope that agencies that employ social workers are model workplaces devoid of sexual harassment, this is not the case. Instead, social work agencies and educational institutions are merely microcosms of society at large. This condition has been confirmed by several studies that surveyed the level of sexual harassment present in both human services agencies and social work educational institutions (Dhooper, Huff, & Schultz, 1989; Judd, Block, & Calkin, 1985; Maypole, 1986; Singer, 1989). The studies revealed that between 26% and 38% of social workers have experienced unwanted sexual advances, mirroring the results of research on sexual harassment outside of social work workplaces and educational settings. More female social workers than male social workers report being sexually harassed. In Maypole's (1986) study, women were more likely to be harassed by a supervisor or coworker, while male social workers were more likely to be harassed by clients. Verbal harassment was the most commonly reported type of harassment, and like most other victims, social workers tended to ignore, minimize, and indirectly defuse the situation. The most surprising finding came out of the study conducted by Dhooper et al. (1989), which found that three fourths of their social work respondents considered sexual harassment either not serious or only moderately serious. This study also found that a majority of the social workers were not familiar with Title VII of the Civil Rights Act.

These studies inform us that sexual harassment is a problem for the social work profession, as well as for the clients whom social workers serve. Sexual harassment is an issue deserving the attention of social workers and must be focused in two directions. First, as so-

cial workers, we must look inward at our own agencies and educational institutions, as well as looking outward at how sexual harassment affects our clients. These studies indicate the need for interventions within social work, including the education of social work students about the dynamics of sexual harassment, the pursuit of legal remedies, the involvement of social work organizations such as NASW and CSWE, the provision of adequate counseling for victimized social workers, and the practice of lobbying for policy changes. These options and more are discussed in the following section, which addresses the practice and policy implications of sexual harassment.

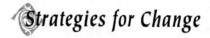

Strategies for Change

PRACTICE IMPLICATIONS

Because sexual harassment is a problem only recently addressed, social workers have the opportunity to help pioneer the field. Because the majority of social work practitioners and clients are female, both client and social worker are at risk of being sexually harassed at work, in school, and in public and social situations. Because the consequences of sexual harassment can be severe—resulting in serious economic, emotional, and physical problems—social workers need to work in both the practice and the policy arenas to address the problem. Within the practice arena, social workers can both assist individuals in dealing with harassment and organize their communities to end sexual harassment.

There is little written work on how to work with victims of sexual harassment. Much of the work draws heavily on the work with women surrounding issues of rape and incest, for there are similarities. For instance, many women who have been sexually harassed feel betrayed because, like victims of incest or acquaintance rape, they often know their perpetrators; both groups of victims are often subjected to blame, which often leads to self-doubt and shame; both kinds of victims are likely to hide the abuse; many feel powerless; as in incest cases, cases of sexual harassment may occur over a long period of time; and both incest and sexual harassment often affect the client in multiple ways, including physical, sexual, and emotional consequences. In dealing with victims of sexual harassment, social workers can use many of the skills they already possess. Individual psychotherapy may be helpful, and group work is recommended (Crull, 1982; Hamilton, Alagna, King, & Lloyd, 1987; Salisbury, Ginorio, Remick, & Stringer, 1986), while still others make a case for family therapy (Woody & Perry, 1993).

Charney and Russell (1994) believe that regardless of the type of intervention, the key therapeutic tasks include empathy, validation, and empowerment. Similarly, Koss (1990) suggested that clinicians may best serve their clients by providing emotional support and a safe forum for expressing feelings, monitoring their clients' physical symptoms and coping behavior, and engaging in specific problem solving. Recommended interventions include (1) validation of feelings that the abuse did happen; (2) a search for meaning, which may include a discussion of gender inequity and current workplace culture and power distribution; (3) expression of anger, which may help clients contain their feelings at the workplace; (4) monitoring of damage to the client's supportive relationships, as well as the impact of stress on the client's coping mechanisms; (5) provision for clients to mourn their losses before rebuilding new beliefs, new lives, and new support systems; (6) offers of hope (Koss, 1990).

Part of support is helping to educate the client about the dynamics of sexual harassment. This education serves to normalize her experiences and feelings, as well as to prepare her to choose from the options she has available. Bibliotherapy can also be helpful, so the client can become knowledgeable about the is-

sues and can make informed choices. One helpful manual comes out of the 9to5 working women's advocacy group, *The 9to5 Guide to Combating Sexual Harassment* (Bravo & Cassedy, 1992).

Crull (1982) and Salisbury et al. (1986) recommended short-term support groups for women who have been similarly victimized. Groups enable women to share their feelings and receive validation by others who have been in the same place. The group may also be a safe place for women to understand why this happened, to discuss legal issues and options, to practice role-playing, and to learn assertive communication. Some groups may evolve into self-directed support groups or activist groups that may assist other women or may speak out to change the system (Salisbury et al., 1986). Group work can be problematic, however, as issues of confidentiality may be threatened, in that group members could potentially be called into court to testify regarding the harassment. At this time, some attorneys are not recommending groups for women who are involved in litigation or other formal complaint processes (Johnson-Gallagher, personal communication, February 27, 1996).

In her work with women who have been sexually harassed, Salisbury et al. (1986) found that women's reactions to sexual harassment seemed to progress in stages. The stages begin with confusion and self-blame, move to fear and anxiety, then shift to depression and anger, before ending with disillusionment. Therapists can assist women through these stages while normalizing their reactions as a natural response to a traumatic situation. Lenore Walker (1994) stated that the most common diagnosis for victims of sexual harassment is PTSD. (This disorder is discussed in Chapter 10, on sexual assault.)

The client who is involved in legal proceedings presents special challenges to the social worker. First, the client must be informed that making a claim of psychological damage will require the client to waive her right to confidentiality, as the therapist may be called to trial to present an assessment of the client (Salisbury et al., 1986). The social worker will need to be cautious in documenting the sessions, as her records could be requested by the courts. Although social workers are not attorneys (usually) and should not advise their clients on legal matters, therapists should encourage clients to research their legal and organizational options. Therapists should also be familiar with the governmental agencies involved in such legal matters, to help facilitate referrals. Salisbury et al. (1986) noted that clients often develop unrealistic expectations about the role of these agencies, whereas the anticipation of concrete, realistic outcomes can positively affect the women's sense of control.

Social workers should have a working knowledge of the ins and outs of taking legal action. For instance, the EEOC only covers workplaces with 15 or more employees. Women who have been harassed in a workplace setting with fewer than 15 employees should file charges with fair-employment agencies on the state or local levels. Clients should also be made aware that there is a time limit on filing a complaint with the EEOC: within 180 days of the incident of harassment, although some state laws extend that limit to 300 days. The EEOC can find that the client has "reasonable cause" or "no reasonable cause," which may shape what steps the client takes next. Additionally, there are many shortcomings of the EEOC system, such as long backlogs, confusing and intimidating forms, unevenness in staff training and knowledge of the issues and options, and the dismissal of many worthy complaints that fail to meet the "reasonable cause" standard (Bravo & Cassedy, 1992). For instance, in 1990, the agency had a backlog of 41,987 discrimination cases nationwide, and fewer than 5% of charges filed with the agency that year were found to have "reasonable cause" (Bravo & Cassedy, 1992).

In acting as an advocate for the client, the social worker can help the client to document

the abuse or to confront the harasser. Numerous books are available to educate the client and the social worker about how to confront harassers (Langelan, 1993; NiCarthy, Gottlieb, & Coffman, 1993; Petrocelli & Repa, 1992). Sometimes the harassment can be stopped by clearly informing the harasser that his (or her) behavior is offensive and unwelcome. This action is not only an effort to get the harassment to end, but also the first step in filing a formal complaint, for the case is stronger if the client can later prove that the harassment continued after the harasser was confronted (Petrocelli & Repa, 1992). Often, a letter is a helpful and less scary way to confront the harasser than is a face-to-face confrontation. Letters should use assertive-communication techniques, including an "I" statement about how the victim feels, the specific behaviors that were found offensive, and what is requested from the harasser. Petrocelli and Repa's book includes sample letters.

This letter can also act as the beginning of a paper trail for documenting the harassment. Petrocelli and Repa (1992) outline a series of steps that can be subsequently taken if this approach does not work. Such steps include collecting evidence, keeping a detailed journal, talking with friends and coworkers, organizing a support group, obtaining a copy of work records, practicing stress-reduction techniques, building support systems, determining whether to file a formal action, and then using formal complaint procedures. Filing a formal complaint can involve various options, such as using the company's sexual-harassment policies, filing a complaint with the EEOC or (under a similar state law) with a state or local fair employment practices (FEP) agency, filing a lawsuit under the Civil Rights Act or FEP laws, or perhaps even hiring an attorney and filing a common-law tort suit (Petrocelli & Repa, 1992).

An alternative to legal proceedings is the issue of mediation. Mediation has been gaining popularity in the past several decades as a reasonable alternative to costly, adversarial litigation. The benefits of mediation include faster resolution, preservation of confidentiality, avoidance of the stress of a hearing, a focus on education rather than punishment, and restoration of working relationships (Gadlin, 1991). Mediation, if done skillfully, can help empower the woman who has been harassed because she is able to confront the harasser in a controlled situation, with support. Other benefits of mediation include the following: developing negotiation skills, facilitating communication, producing mutually satisfying outcomes, healing, and increasing the number of women who are willing to pursue complaints (Gadlin, 1991).

Although confrontation is a scary word for many women who have been socialized to be agreeable and passive, it can be a helpful strategy in ending sexual harassment. Martha Langelan's book *Back Off!* (1993) is full of stories about women, individually and in groups, who successfully confronted their harassers in the workplace, as well as on the street. There is no easy answer or one solution for all women, but assertiveness skills can be taught, practiced, and utilized. Again, the risks and benefits for each woman must be assessed, and support must be given for whatever decision the woman makes.

Secondary Victimization

Numerous reports (Bernstein, 1996; Nancy Johnson-Gallagher, Feb. 27, 1996, personal communication) indicate that since the 1991 court ruling that first allowed women to sue for monetary damages in sexual-harassment cases, the court battles have become increasingly ugly. When suing for emotional damages as a result of sexual harassment, women are subjected to severe scrutiny, as defense attorneys attempt to prove that "alternative stressors," other than the sexual harassment, caused the emotional damages women are alleging. Defense attorneys are suggesting the need to obtain the plaintiff's records from physicians, therapists, personnel records, high school and college transcripts, and court files from divorce and custody cases (cited in Bernstein, 1996). With these aggressive

tactics, once again the victim is revictimized, as personal information such as sexual orientation, history of abortion, and any previous trauma, including childhood incest experiences, are dissected in open court.

In 1994, the U.S. Congress extended the federal rape shield law, which limits the questioning about a victim's sexual history, to civil cases (Bernstein, 1996), but there are many loopholes that still allow such questioning, such as in the discovery process or in bringing such information to the court's attention in the form of medical records. Although some women do prevail, the emotional distress of many women is not attributed to the sexual harassment, and the women leave the court not only empty-handed but also revictimized. As a matter of fact, social worker Nancy Johnson-Gallagher reported that for some women, the secondary victimization at the trial is experienced as worse than the initial victimization (Feb. 27, 1996, personal communication). Additionally, Johnson-Gallagher reported that social workers who testify on behalf of their clients who have been sexually harassed are also victimized, as the defense attorneys are free to ask about the previous history of victimization and mental health treatment of the social worker herself! Clearly, the social worker must weigh the benefits and disadvantages of enduring such an experience, for the social worker as well as for the client, before proceeding.

Working with Men

This practice section has focused on assisting the female victim of sexual harassment, yet social workers may also be called on to answer men's questions and concerns about sexual harassment. Many men question their behavior, worry about false charges, and state that they are unsure how to talk to women in the workplace. These men appear puzzled and confused about the new rules in the workplace and in academia. If the old workplace rules—which accepted the harassment and exploitation of female workers—are no longer "politically correct," some men wonder what behaviors are left. Social workers can respond to some of these concerns by teaching men that talking to women in any setting is merely about common courtesy and respect.

A few guidelines offered at a feminist think-tank session sponsored by Betty Friedan include the following questions to guide men's interactions with women: Would you want your comments published in the company or the community newsletter? Would you like to be seen on television doing this? Would you be doing this if your wife were next to you, or your sister, or your daughter? (Gehry, Hateley, Rose, Stoner, & Friedan, 1994). Panelist B. J. Hateley suggested that women like to be complimented on their work, rather than on their physical appearance. Sometimes, however, this superficial concern and confusion about what is appropriate to say to women in the workplace and other settings is really a smoke screen to disguise male resistance to treating women with respect and dignity. Marian Henley's cartoon offers a wry look at some men's professed

discomfort and confusion surrounding the issue of sexual harassment (see cartoon below).

Community and Research Practice

Langelan (1993) supports community strategies for ending harassment. With social work's emphasis on community organizing, such work is a good fit with social work values and skills. A successful example cited in Langelan's *Back Off!* (1993) was the development of a Hassle-Free Zone in Washington, D.C. In this social action, a coalition of interested organizations joined together to target the harassment of women on city streets. The strategies included educational brochures, public speeches in public parks and subway stops, street-theater skits about harassment, free harassment-confrontation classes, and the photographing and recording of harassers, to aid in reporting harassers to the police. In describing the effects of the campaign, Nkenge Toure (1993) said,

> *Did we succeed in ending street harassment once and for all in Washington, D.C.? No. That may take a few more years. But the Hassle-Free Zone*

Maxine

Marian Henley's cartoon humorously illustrates the difficulty some men experience in understanding sexual harassment.

campaign put the issue of street harassment front and center on the public agenda for our elected officials, the media, and the entire community. We empowered a lot of women, gave a lot of harassers a good reason to think twice, encouraged men to speak up as allies for women, reclaimed some public parks and subway stops, and had a pretty good time doing it. (p. 333)

Such community organizing can inspire us to take on similar projects. Sexual harassment occurs at work, in schools, and on public streets. Our social work practice can creatively address this issue on many levels in many places.

Social work practice also involves continued research on this most pressing issue. The research on sexual harassment is still in its infancy; there is much we do not know. It is difficult to help a woman trying to decide among her options when there is little research to guide us in knowing what actions are particularly effective. Fitzgerald (1993), unarguably the leading researcher in this area, has called for a current, comprehensive, and technically adequate database with which to inform social policy decisions. She has recommended taking the following steps: collection of nationally representative data on prevalence rates in both work-related and educational contexts on an ongoing basis; initiation of basic and applied research through all relevant agencies; specific targeting of research funds for examination of potentially high-risk groups and potentially high-yield topics; and increased emphasis on field research. As social workers, we can respond to this call for research and can build a research base to inform our practice and policy decisions.

POLICY FOR CHANGE

Management

There are several policy initiatives for us to support, as social workers. Yet before we focus our attention on legislative or judicial reform, it would behoove us to focus on our own institutions. We can begin by ensuring that our social work education programs, social service agencies, and other places of employment have a written, posted policy on sexual harassment. The definitions should be clear and expansive. The statement should include an effective resolution procedure. The policy should direct employees to a neutral party, such as an ombudsperson. Too often, sexual harassment policies direct employees to report their grievances to their own supervisors, who may be the very persons harassing them. Policies need to include discussion of consequences, with at least two areas of possible disciplinary consequences. The policy should pledge nonretaliation. Confidentiality should be a part of the process, to protect the anonymity of the complainant, while not being used as an excuse to hinder or subvert the investigation. Fitzgerald (1993) has recommended that employers be required by law to develop a clear policy against harassment, with clear and accessible grievance procedures, while requiring employers to notify employees of the policy, post it prominently, and provide relevant training.

Other ways in which social work managers can prevent harassment in the workplace is by being role models of respectful, appropriate behavior. Studies have shown that organizational tolerance of sexual harassment is often a green light to certain persons with the propensity to harass. Management should send clear signals that sexual, racial, or other harassment will not be tolerated in the workplace. Some of Singer's (1989) respondents, who were deans of graduate schools of social work, agreed that the Council of Social Work Education (CSWE) should take some action in an educational, consultative, or monitoring role.

Additional strategies for ensuring a harassment-free workplace include holding staff in-service meetings and training on the subject, providing exit interviews for employees leaving the agency, having managers walk the floors of the workplace to listen and to observe interactions (Singer, 1989). One brief caution about sexual-harassment prevention training should be noted, though. Too often, training is presented more as a mechanism for organizations to avoid liability rather than as a means to protect victims and ensure a safe and respectful workplace. The tone of training should convey respect for all employees, rather than merely focusing on protecting the agency from legal action.

Legislative and Judicial Reform

Louise Fitzgerald (1993) suggested several legislative initiatives and legal reforms that would benefit women who have been sexually harassed. Fitzgerald recommended that the caps be lifted from the damages allowed by the 1991 Civil Rights amendment, which limits damage awards. Fitzgerald suggested that state unemployment laws be reformed to allow women who leave due to sexual harassment to receive unemployment benefits. Also helpful would be extension of the statute of limitations for filing sexual-harassment charges. Presently, the EEOC mandates that a complaint must be made within 180 days of the incident, and such a short time frame prohibits many women from filing.

Fitzgerald (1993) also recognized the need for judicial reform. As in the cases of rape, cases of sexual harassment that seek justice and accountability in court often end in a second victimization for women. Lawyers representing harassers and their organizations too often seek to win their cases by defaming the victims. Training is needed for judges and attorneys to inform them about the dynamics of sexual harassment. The need for such training is highlighted in two cases cited by Bravo and Cassedy (1992): A woman lost her case of sexual harassment when a photo of the defendant's wife was introduced. The judge ruled that the woman who had been sexually harassed was too unattractive to compete with the wife because "she wore little or no makeup, and her hair was not colored in any way" (p. 37). In another case, a woman claimed that her boss gave her massages, sent her 37 affectionate notes in a 3-week period, and followed her into the bathroom only to have the judge rule that such behavior did not constitute harassment. The judge found that the boss was acting like a "faithful dog, . . . protective . . . , constantly expressing his affection" (p. 37).

Special populations of women who are vulnerable to sexual harassment could benefit from policy changes that directly affect their double, or triple vulnerability. For instance lesbian employees could benefit from specific workplace policies that prohibit discrimination on the basis of their sexual orientation, as well as creation of a safe work environment that is free of heterosexism and homophobia (McNaught, 1993). Further discussion of this issue is found in Chapter 5, on the economic assault on women. Women of color can benefit from policies and practices that directly relate to their race, as well as their gender, such as diversity training of managers and employees. Title VII also protects employees from discrimination based on race.

Fitzgerald (1993) has reminded us that ultimately, primary prevention is the only true solution. She reported that social policy initiatives must be formulated to elevate women's inferior status in the workplace. Fitzgerald recommended two programs that unfortunately have come under fire in recent years: affirmative action and aggressive recruiting practices of women, especially women of color. Other recommendations supported by Fitzgerald (see also Chapter 5, on the economic assault on women) include helping women move into jobs traditionally held by men; eliminating discrimination based on sex, race, and sexual orientation in hiring and training; moving women into top management; and adopting prowoman and profamily policies, such as paid family leave and child-care assistance.

SUMMARY

Clearly, sexual harassment is a serious and pervasive problem women face when obtaining an education, working outside of the home, and—sometimes—even walking down the street. The problem has serious consequences for women emotionally and physically, as well as economically. Social workers have much to learn about this issue in order to end such assaults, including within social work institutions and human service agencies. By becoming better informed, social workers can support their clients in weighing the clients' options, as well as working to change attitudes and policies that allow such harassment to continue.

Until women's status in society in general is elevated onto an equal plane, sexual harassment will probably continue in our nation's offices, streets, and schools. Sexual harassment is merely one symptom of a society that privileges men while subordinating and devaluing women. The social work role is to assist women to empower themselves while working to end the oppression of women.

REFERENCES

American Association for University Women. (1993). *Hostile hallways: AAUW survey on sexual harassment in American schools*. American Association of University Women Educational Foundation.

Baxandall, R., & Gordon, L. (Eds.). (1995). *America's working women: A documentary history*. New York: W. W. Norton.

Benson, D. J., & Thomson, G. E. (1982). Sexual harassment on a university campus: The confluence of authority relations, sexual interest, and gender stratification. *Social Problems, 29*(3), 236–251.

Benson, K. A. (1984). Comment on Crocker's "An analysis of university definitions of sexual harassment." *Signs, 9*(3), 516–519.

Bernstein, A. (1996, July/August). Sexual harassment suits: The fight for damages gets uglier. *Ms.,* pp. 7, 18–20.

Bravo, E., & Cassedy, E. (1992). *The 9to5 guide to combating sexual harassment*. New York: John Wiley & Sons.

Charney, D. A., & Russell, R. C. (1994). An overview of sexual harassment. *American Journal of Psychiatry, 151*(1), 10–17.

Crull, P. (1982). Stress effects of sexual harassment on the job: Implications for counseling. *American Journal of Orthopsychiatry, 52*(3), 539–544.

DeCosse, S. A. (1992). Simply unbelievable: Reasonable women and hostile environment sexual harassment. *Law and Inequality, 10,* 285–309.

DeFour, D. C. (1990). The interface of racism and sexism on college campuses. In M. Paludi (Ed.), *Ivory power: Sexual harassment on campus* (pp. 45–52). Albany, NY: State University of New York Press.

Department of Defense, United States. (1996). *1995 Sexual Harassment Survey*. (No. 410–96). Washington, DC: Author.

Dhooper, S. S., Huff, M. B., & Schultz, C. M. (1989). Social work and sexual harassment. *Journal of Sociology & Social Welfare, 16*(3), 125–139.

Fitzgerald, L. F. (1990). Sexual harassment: The definition and measurement of a construct. In M. Paludi (Ed.), *Ivory power: Sexual harassment on campus* (pp. 21–44). Albany, NY: State University of New York Press.

Fitzgerald, L. F. (1993). Sexual harassment: Violence against women in the workplace. *American Psychologist, 48*(10), 1070–1076.

Fitzgerald, L. F., & Ormerod, A. J. (1991). Perceptions of sexual harassment: The influence of gender and academic context. *Psychology of Women Quarterly, 15,* 281–294.

Fitzgerald, L. F., & Shullman, S. L. (1993). Sexual harassment: A research analysis and agenda for the 1990s. *Journal of Vocational Behavior, 42,* 5–27.

Fitzgerald, L. F., Shullman, S., Bailey, N., Richards, M., Swecker, J., Gold, Y., Ormerod, A. J., & Weitzman, L. (1988). The incidence and dimensions of sexual harassment in academia and the workplace. *Journal of Vocational Behavior, 32,* 152–175.

Gadlin, H. (1991). Mediation principles in dealing with complaints of sexual harassment. In M. A. Paludi & R. B. Barickman (Eds.), *Academic and workplace sexual harassment* (pp. 58–61). Albany, NY: State University of New York Press.

Gehry, F., Hateley, B. J., Rose, S., Stoner, M., & Friedan, B. (1994). The politics of empowerment: A paradigm shift in thought and action for feminists (New questions beyond the feminist focus on sexual harassment: It is helping us move from victimhood to empowerment, or is it a diversion?) *American Behavioral Scientist, 37*(8), 1122–1137.

Gillespie, M. A. (1992, January/February). We speak in tongues. *Ms.,* pp. 41–43.

Grauerholtz, E. (1989). Sexual harassment of women professors by students: Exploring the dynamics of power, authority, and gender in a university setting. *Sex Roles, 21*(11/12), 789–801.

Gruber, J. E., & Bjorn, L. (1982). Blue-collar blues: The sexual harassment of women autoworkers. *Work and Occupations, 9*(3), 271–298.

Gutek, B. A. (1985). *Sex and the workplace.* San Francisco, CA: Jossey-Bass.

Gutek, B. A., & Morasch, B. (1982). Sex-ratios, sex-role spillover, and sexual harassment of women at work. *Journal of Social Issues, 38*(4), 55–74.

Gutek, B. A., & O'Connor, M. (1995). The empirical basis for the reasonable woman standard. *Journal of Social Issues, 51*(1), 151–166.

Hamilton, J. A., Alagna, S. W., King, L. S., & Lloyd, C. (1987). The emotional consequences of gender-based abuse in the workplace: New counseling programs for sex discrimination. *Women & Therapy, 6,* 155–182.

Hicks v. Gates Rubber Co., 833 F. 2d 1406 (10th Cir. 1987).

Hill, A. F. (1995). Statement of Professor Anita F. Hill to the Senate Judiciary Committee, October 11, 1991. In R. Baxandall & L. Gordon (Eds.), *American working women: A documentary history* (pp. 337–341). New York: W. W. Norton.

Houston Chronicle News Service. (1996, December 12). More harassment claims, *Houston Chronicle,* p. 21A.

Judd, P., Block, S. R., & Calkin, C. L. (1985). Sexual harassment among social workers in human service agencies. *Arete, 10*(1), 12–21.

Koss, M. P. (1990). Changed lives: The psychological impact of sexual harassment. In M. Paludi (Ed.), *Ivory power: Sexual harassment on campus* (pp. 73–92). Albany, NY: State University of New York Press.

Koss, M. P., Goodman, L. A., Browne, A., Fittzgerald, L. F., Keita, G. P., & Russo, N. F. (1994). *No safe haven: Male violence against women at home, at work, and in the community.* Washington, DC: American Psychological Association.

Langelan, M. J. (Ed.). (1993). *Back off! How to confront and stop sexual harassment and harassers.* New York: Simon & Schuster.

Livingston, J. A. (1982). Responses to sexual harassment on the job: Legal, organizational, and individual actions. *Journal of Social Issues, 38*(4), 5–22.

MacKinnon, C. A. (1979). *Sexual harassment of working women.* New Haven, CT: Yale University Press.

Mansfield, P. K., Koch, P. B., Henderson, J., Vicary, J. R., Cohn, M., & Young, E. W. (1991). The job climate for women in traditionally male blue-collar occupations. *Sex Roles, 25*(1/2), 63–79.

Maypole, D. E. (1986). Sexual harassment of social workers at work: Injustice within? *Social Work, 30*(1), 29–34.

McClelland, K., & Hunter, C. (1992). The perceived seriousness of racial harassment. *Social Problems, 39*(1), 92–106.

McKinney, K. (1990). Sexual harassment of university faculty by colleagues and students. *Sex Roles, 23,* 421–438.

McNaught, B. (1993). *Gay issues in the workplace.* New York: St. Martin's Press.

Meritor Savings Bank v. Vinson 477 US 57 (1986).

NiCarthy, G., Gottlieb, N., & Coffman, S. (1993). *You don't have to take it!* Seattle, WA: Seal Press.

Paul, E. F. (1991). Bared buttocks and federal cases. *Society, 28*(4), 4–7.

Petrocelli, W., & Repa, B. K. (1992). *Sexual harassment on the job.* Berkeley, CA: Nolo Press.

Pryor, J. B. (1987). Sexual harassment proclivities in men. *Sex Roles, 17*(5/6), 269–290.

Pryor, J. B., LaVite, C. M., & Stoller, L. M. (1993). A social psychological analysis of sexual harassment: The person/situation interaction. *Journal of Vocational Behavior, 42,* 63–83.

Rosener, J. B. (1995). *America's competitive secret: Utilizing women as a management strategy.* New York: Oxford University Press.

Rosenfeld, P. (1994). Effects of gender and ethnicity on Hispanic women in the U.S. Navy. *Journal of Social Psychology, 134*(3), 349–354.

Rubin, L. J., & Borgers, S. B. (1990). Sexual harassment in universities during the 1980s. *Sex Roles, 23*(7/8) 397–411.

Safran, C. (1976, November). What men do to women on the job: A shocking look at sexual harassment. *Redbook,* pp. 149, 217–224.

Salisbury, J., Ginorio, A. B., Remick, H., & Stringer, D. M. (1986). Counseling victims of sexual harassment. *Psychotherapy, 23*(2), 316–324.

Schneider, B. (1982). Consciousness about sexual harassment among heterosexual and lesbian women workers. *Journal of Social Issues, 38,* 75–97.

Schneider, B. E. (1991). Put up and shut up: Workplace sexual assaults. *Gender and Society, 5*(4), 533–548.

Segura, D. A. (1992). Chicanas in white-collar jobs: "You have to prove yourself more." *Sociological Perspectives, 35*(1), 163–182.

Singer, T. L. (1989). Sexual harassment in graduate schools of social work: Provocative dilimmas. *Journal of Social Work Education, 25*(1), 68–76.

Smith, B. (1992, January/February). "Ain't gonna let nobody turn me around." *Ms.,* 37–39.

Stockdale, M. S. (1993). The role of sexual misperceptions of women's friendliness in an emerging theory of sexual harassment. *Journal of Vocational Behavior, 42,* 84–101.

Tang, C. S., Yik, M. S. M., Cheung, F. M. C., Choi, P., & Au, K. (1995). How do Chinese college students define sexual harassment? *Journal of Interpersonal Violence, 10*(3), 503–515.

Tangri, S. S., Burt, M. R., & Johnson, L. B. (1982). Sexual harassment at work: Three explanatory models. *Journal of Social Issues, 38,* 33–54.

Tannen, D. (1990). *You just don't understand: Women and men in conversation.* New York: William Morrow, Ballantine.

Tannen, D. (1994). *Talking from 9to5: Women and men in the workplace: Language, sex, and power.* New York: Avon Books.

Toure, N. (1993). The hassle-free zone campaign. In M. J. Langelan (Ed.), *Back off! How to confront and stop sexual harassment and harassers* (pp. 331–333). New York: Simon & Schuster.

U.S. Department of Labor Women's Bureau. (1993). *Women workers: Trends and issues.* Washington, DC: Author.

U.S. Merit Systems Protection Board. (1981). *Sexual harassment of federal workers: Is it a problem?* Washington, DC: United States Government Printing Office.

U.S. Merit Systems Protection Board. (1995). *Sexual harassment in the federal workplace: Trends, progress, continuing challenges.* Washington, DC: United States Government Printing Office.

Walker, L. E. A. (1994). *Abused women and survivor therapy.* Washington, DC: American Psychological Association.

Women's Legal Defense Fund. (1995). *Sexual harassment: Legal and policy issues.* Washington, DC: Author.

Woody, R. H., & Perry, N. W. (1993). Sexual harassment victims: Psychological and family therapy considerations. *American Journal of Family Therapy, 21*(2), 136–144.

Wyatt, G. E., & Riederle, M. (1995). The prevalence and context of sexual harassment among African American and white American women. *Journal of Interpersonal Violence, 10*(3), 309–321.

Yoder, J. D., & Aniakudo, P. (1995). The responses of African American women firefighters to gender harassment at work. *Sex Roles, 32*(3/4), 125–137.

Chapter 9

WOMEN WHO ARE BATTERED

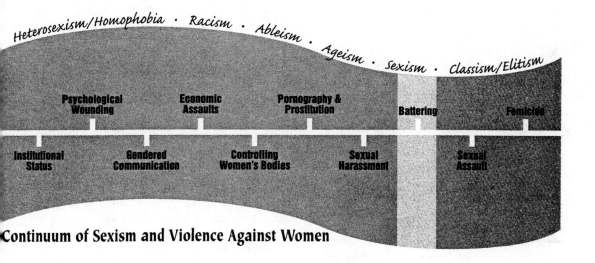

Heterosexism/Homophobia · Racism · Ableism · Ageism · Sexism · Classism/Elitism

| Psychological Wounding | Economic Assaults | Pornography & Prostitution | Battering | Femicide |

| Institutional Status | Gendered Communication | Controlling Women's Bodies | Sexual Harassment | Sexual Assault |

Continuum of Sexism and Violence Against Women

In her heart, she [each woman who has been battered] is a mourner for those who have not survived.

In her soul she is a warrior for those who are now as she was then.

In her life she is both celebrant and proof of women's capacity and will to survive, to become, to act, to change self and society. And each year she is stronger and there are more of her.

Andrea Dworkin

This chapter focuses on the many issues related to women who have been battered by intimate partners. It begins with a broad orientation to problems such as the prevalence and severity of violence in intimate relationships, the use of marital rape and psychological abuse, cultural barriers, and reinforcements to violence. This discussion of issues is followed by an introduction to some theoretical debates currently being voiced within the battered women's shelter movement. Finally, strategies for change are addressed, looking specifically at using social work skills on behalf of women who have been battered and then focusing on practice with African-American, Latina, Asian-American, and lesbian women.

Strategies for change also include policy issues that are currently being debated in different spheres (agency, community, state, and federal).

INTRODUCTION TO THE ISSUES

Violence against women in families takes place in the context of close relationships. It seems unbelievable to many people—including the victims of the violent acts—that violence occurs between people who know each other well, who have a bond of love between them, and who may even share children. Moltz (1992), addressing family therapists, stated, "as we look at violence and abuse in the family, our idea of the *family* changes, from a place of safety to a place of danger, from a context of nurturance to a context of nightmare" (p. 223). Dworkin (1993), a formerly battered woman, has alerted us to the contradictions inherent in discussing battering,

> The husband's violence against her contradicts everything she has ever been taught about life, marriage, love and the sanctity of the family. Regardless of the circumstances in which she grew up, she has been taught to believe in romantic love and the essential perfection of married life. Failure is personal. . . . Marriage is a woman's proper goal. Wife-beating is not on a woman's map of the world when she marries. It is, quite literally, beyond her imagination. (p. 102)

Despite many people's illusions that the home is a place of safety, comfort, and warm feelings, it is within the context of families that women are being threatened, pushed, slapped, yanked, slammed into walls, grabbed, slugged, burned, knifed, raped, kicked, and any other imaginable (or unimaginable) form of violence. With these types of violence occurring within close relationships, partnerships, and marriages, the literature is very mixed on what to even name this issue: "problem" or "reality." As noted in Chapter 4 on gendered communication, language is a very important part of

constructing reality. Criticism has been leveled against professionals for the type of naming that has been attached to the issue of battering. Jones (1991) spoke strongly about the language choices of social scientists:

> 'Domestic violence.' 'Spouse abuse.' 'Partner abuse.' 'Marital strife.' 'Relationship discordance.' 'Familial dysfunction.' 'Nonverbal miscommunication.' Social scientists study these things. You'll notice, however, that these terms conjure no images. Like Orwellian Newspeak, they aim to keep us from seeing what's what. No mention of warfare here. Rather, these terms whisper of insubstantial numbers and vague 'social problems,' affecting (we must assume) not real individual women but 'relationships' and 'families,' mostly in other people's neighborhoods, in a more or less egalitarian manner. (p. 13)

In this textbook, we tend to use the words "battered women" instead of *domestic violence, spouse abuse, couples violence,* or the currently popular *domestic dispute* to address this issue, and we note, throughout this text, that the focus is on violence against women. However, even this language is problematic, as described by hooks (1989),

> This label 'battered woman' places primary emphasis on physical assaults that are continuous, repeated, and unrelenting . . .
>
> Most importantly, the term 'battered woman' is used as though it constitutes a separate and unique category of womanness, as though it is an identity, a mark that sets one apart rather than being simply a descriptive term. It is as though the experience of being repeatedly violently hit is the sole defining characteristic of a woman's identity and all other aspects of who she is and what her experience has been are submerged. (pp. 87–88)

The point made by hooks is critical to understanding the dynamics of battering. For this reason, we often use a few more words to describe the violence (e.g., "a woman who is battered," as well as "a battered woman") to guard against having any reader walk away with the idea that being battered is a woman's sole identity. As may be recalled from the introduction of this text, we noted that one lack associated with this text is that we cannot address all of the wonderful aspects and joy related to being a woman. Here we want to join with hooks by noting that women who are battered are poets, writers, professors, students, social workers, mothers, daughters, artists, engineers, mathematicians, sisters, and colleagues. Women who have been hit are funny, silly, gorgeous, tall, thin, differently abled, serious, older, sad, joyous, victorious, and confident. There is no profile, feeling state, or profession that is a battered woman. She is you, me, your sister, and your friend, with all of our respective strengths and vulnerabilities. This is probably best understood by reviewing the prevalence data for battering.

Prevalence Data

Acts of violence against women by intimate partners occur with shocking frequency. The prevalence data can be confusing because of the differing numbers that appear in professional and lay publications to describe this social problem. When reviewing statistics on prevalence, it is important to bring into that analysis basic research knowledge. Different samples and different operational definitions of abuse will yield different data. In addition, as Bachman and Saltzman (1995) have brought to our attention, there is an added difficulty involved in estimating rates of violence against women: "Many factors inhibit women from reporting these victimizations both to the police and to interviewers, including the private nature of the event, the perceived stigma associated with one's victimization, and the belief that no purpose will be served in reporting it" (p. 1).

In considering the variety of samples, the National Crime Victimization Survey (Bachman & Saltzman, 1995) found different rates of violence by age group, with women between ages 19 and 29 years experiencing a rate of 21.3 per 1,000 women, as compared to rates of 9.6 for women ages 12–18 years and of 10.8

for women ages 30–45 years. Using an alternative means of categorizing abuse victims, Stets and Straus (1989) have focused on the fact that different types of relationships (dating, cohabiting, and marriage) have different prevalence rates of battering. These authors found this pattern for rates of battering: cohabiting (35 of 100 couples), dating (20 of 100 couples), and married (15 of 100 couples). Women separated from their intimate partners had the highest rates of victimization (compared to divorced, married, or never-married women), with an alarming 82.2 rate per 1,000. Browne (1993) analyzed prevalence studies and found that between 21% and 34% of women in the United States will be battered by a male partner. U.S. Bureau of Justice statistics showed that women were six times more likely than men to be victimized by a spouse, ex-spouse, boyfriend, or girlfriend (Harlow, 1991). Despite differences among reported data, most reports agree that battering is a serious social problem and an important issue for social workers to address.

Severity

It is as critical to understand the frequency with which battering occurs as it is to recognize the severity of the violence women are experiencing. Dworkin (1993) has recounted some of the violence she experienced as a battered wife,

> *I remember, of course, that I was hit, that I was kicked. I do not remember when or how often. It blurs. I remember him banging my head against the floor until I passed out. I remember being kicked in the stomach. I remember being hit over and over, the blows hitting different parts of my body as I tried to get away from him. I remember a terrible leg injury from a series of kicks. I remember crying and I remember screaming and I remember begging. I remember him punching me in the breasts. (p. 103)*

Gondolf and Fisher (1988) found that among Texas women who sought shelter services, 9% had been burned, 81% slapped, 57%

choked, 75% punched, and 43% had a weapon used against them. Further, 70% of Texas women who sought shelter had been threatened that they were going to be killed; 42% had their children threatened; 53% had been abused while pregnant; and 27% had been sexually abused. Severe injuries requiring hospitalization, such as head injuries and broken bones, occurred with 10% of the sample. Of the Texas women who sought shelter, 14% had attempted to commit suicide. Gondolf and Fisher noted that by comparing these data to other studies, it appears that these women were more severely abused than were those in other samples (such as Dallas women in Stacey and Shupe's study [1983]; Rocky Mountain battered women in Walker's [1984] study). Nonetheless, a great deal can be learned about the *severity* of violence by looking at these Texas data, while refraining from generalizing these data to other states and other service (i.e., outpatient, nonshelter residential, or general public) populations.

What meaning can be attached to these data on the scope and the severity of battering? How can social workers not grow numb while reading this type of description of the frequency and severity of violence? We have a nagging fear that readers are highlighting all of the facts and figures, yet attaching no meaning to the injury of women. A social work graduate student told us a couple of years ago that a slap wasn't really that awful, and that we shouldn't make that big of a deal over a slap. At this time, we'd like to address you personally to ask you to think carefully about such a statement. What does it physically feel like to have an adult partner slap you? Punch you in the stomach? What does it psychologically feel like to have a lover, a partner, tell you that he or she is going to kill you? Can you picture what the perpetrator's demeanor might be at that moment? Can you imagine what your demeanor is at that moment? Over half of the sheltered battered women in Texas have been choked. Can you imagine what the experience of being choked

must mean? What kind of terror must these women have felt? What kind of pain must they have incurred?

Jeff Basen-Engquist (personal communication, January 1995), who has done extensive work with men who batter, cautions those who might minimize "just a push" or "just a slap" by suggesting that "just a slap" might cause a woman to fall. When she falls, she might hit her head on a coffee table, such that "just a slap" may cause a woman's death. Basen-Engquist's caution is an important one. Minimization will not save lives or help individual women. All violence has the potential to cause serious or even lethal harm.

Formerly battered women have often been willing to poignantly recall their experience of being battered to help social workers gain a fuller picture of the meaning of violence as they experienced it. Andrea Dworkin's (1993) words about being battered can provide more context for us to consider:

> *If one survives without permanent injury, the physical pain dims, recedes, ends. It lets go.*
>
> *The fear does not let go. The fear is the eternal legacy. At first, the fear infuses every minute of every day. One does not sleep. One cannot bear to be alone. The fear is in the cavity of one's chest. It crawls like lice on one's skin. It makes the legs buckle, the heart race. It locks one's jaw. One's hands tremble. One's throat closes up.... Inside, one is always in upheaval, clinging to anyone who shows any kindness, cowering in the presence of any threat. As years pass, the fear recedes, but it does not let go. It never lets go. (p. 103)*

Similarly, an 18-year-old anonymous contributor to *Teen Voices* wrote of her fear, noting,

> *I still feel threatened, even after a year of having the restraining order. If I see him on campus, I'm afraid he is going to hurt me. For awhile I was very afraid of going out, for fear of seeing him. It gets easier, but the fear will always be there. I wrote this for those of you who are entering, or are already in, college. I want you to know that this can happen to you.... The pain*

*does go away, but the memories will stay for-
ever. I have gone through counseling, and I now
know that what happened was not my fault and
that I was not alone and even if I was, I am
strong enough to make it in this world. I want
all of you to know this—you are not alone. No
one deserves to be beaten up. (Anonymous,
1995, p. 20)*

Verbal, Psychological, and Power Abuse

By adding to the pain of physical abuse the fear
reported by many women who are battered,
any discussion of battering gains increased
depth. Other dimensions for consideration include psychological and verbal abuse, plus the
misuse of power that women experience in conjunction with fear and physical violence. Shasta
County Women's Refuge in Redding, California, in the early 1980s developed a test for battered women. Some of the test questions (and
answers) follow:

1. Are you dumb?
   (Yes, he's told you that quite often.)
2. Are you ugly?
   (Yes, he's told you so, remember you haven't
   fixed yourself up since he married you.)
3. Are you a bad mother?
   (Yes, he's told you you never take care of
   the children.)
4. Do you have good kids?
   (No, he's told you they're always screaming
   and fighting when he's around.)
5. Are you sexy?
   (No, he's told you if he doesn't want to go
   to bed with you no one else would want to.)

Shepard (1991) noted that emotional abuse
is more common than physical abuse and that
emotional abuse attacks a woman's self-worth.
Further, emotional abuse "can increase the batterer's control by making the victim feel that
she deserves to be abused and that she has no
other options" (p. 89). Follingstad, Rutledge,
Berg, Hause, and Polek (1990) surveyed 234
women who had been physically abused. A full
98% of these women reported emotional

abuse, with 72% of this same sample believing
that emotional abuse had had a stronger impact
on them than had the physical abuse. Ridicule
was reported by the participants as the most
negative form of psychological abuse. Walker
(1984) found that 34% of those she studied
had no access to a checking account, and 27%
had no access to cash. These numbers include
women who worked outside of the home. In
1989, Tolman published an instrument being
developed to measure the psychological maltreatment of women by male partners. It included 58 items, such as these: put down her
physical appearance, called her names, acted
like she was a servant, acted insensitive to her
feelings, acted jealous or suspicious of her
friends, and blamed her when he was upset.
Scales measuring psychological abuse and control are a very useful complement to assessment
inventories that measure physical abuse and
control to gain a more complete understanding
of the abuse women are experiencing.

These studies are a reminder that physical
violence is only one aspect of the abuse women
experience in the home. Many of their lives become very restricted and isolated—by force,
not by choice. It is also important to stress that
a woman does not have to be hit, slapped,
beaten, or raped daily to be controlled. Shepard (1991) suggested that intimidation is an
important factor to keep in the forefront when
working with women who are battered. "Intimidation includes behaviors that are meant
to frighten the victim. Angry stares, slamming
doors, punching or smashing objects, pound-
ing fists on the table, yelling and physically
crowding her space are examples of intimidating behaviors. When physical abuse has occurred in the past, these behaviors threaten the
victim with the possibility of more violence
and reinforce the batterer's control" (Shepard,
1991, p. 89).

The Domestic Abuse Project in Duluth,
Minnesota, developed a "Power and Control
Wheel" (see Figure 9.1) to sensitize people to
the many forms that power and control take

FIGURE 9.1   The Power and Control Wheel

The Power and Control Wheel provides information to aid in the assessment, as well as the intervention, process.

within an abusive relationship. The wheel directs attention to tactics of intimidation, emotional abuse, isolation, minimizing, blaming, using children, male privilege, economic abuse, coercion, and threats—all of which are tactics frequently used to disempower and to control. Lesbians who are battered have the additional issues of power and control related to heterosexism and homophobia to tackle, as well as the dynamics of intimidation, isolation, and so on. This misused power, portrayed in the power and control wheel, in many ways mirrors the societal systems also used to disempower women (economic inequality, sexism in the language, hate language, blaming the victim and pathologizing women, sexual harassment in the workplace, and other forms of sexism and violence). Contrast the power and control dynamics with the dynamics required for equality (see Figure 9.2) in relationships: fairness, nonthreatening behavior, respect, trust and support, responsible parenting, shared responsibility, and an economic partnership. The concept of equality is quite a contrast from the dynamics that most women who are battered (emotionally and/or physically) experience in their homes and in society.

Marital Rape

Another reality confronting battered women is marital rape. Frieze and Browne (1987) reported that 33–46% of battered women have been sexually assaulted by their batterer. Finkelhor and Yllo (1985), in their important early work on marital rape, suggested that many people choose to think of marital rape as an argument over sex and the husband (male partner) wins. Yegidis (1988) suggested that marital rape is part of a syndrome of abuse. Further, she suggested, "Practitioners should be sensitive to the possibility that their clients are being sexually assaulted as well as physically or emotionally abused by their partners and should be prepared to intervene actively" (p. 68).

Marital rape, despite the benign manner in which the public tends to perceive it, involves humiliation, degradation, anger, and violence. Read carefully about Burleson's (1989) torturous experience with marital rape,

> He started by throwing around the kitchen table and chairs. Next, he threw me down and kicked me. He sat on my chest to keep me from getting up. He ordered me to take off all my clothes and he whipped me with a belt. He choked me. He held a pillow over my face and attempted to suffocate me. He dragged me down the hallway by my hair. He held a butcher knife to my throat. He shoved a loaded shotgun into my vagina. He made me sit in the bathtub while he urinated on me. Then he raped me. Finally, with the Easter

> sunrise, his anger subsided. But, once he took a good look at my battered and bruised body, he refused to let me leave. So, for 2 days, he held me and our six year old son hostage in that trailer. (p. 9)

Anna Belle Burleson is now a formerly battered woman and founder of the Formerly Battered Women's Task Force of Central Texas. In 1996, Burleson was honored as NASW's Citizen of the Year and is the Program Director of the National Domestic Violence Hotline (1-800-799-SAFE).

Cultural Oppression

The central thesis of this text is that violence against women must not be separated or compartmentalized from other forms of oppression women face. Therefore, one can never separate the social, legal, economic, and political realities that further constrain or control the battered woman. Shepard (1991) suggested, "Human service professionals, including social workers, have tended to de-emphasize social–cultural factors by focusing on internal psychological processes and interactional dynamics" (p. 88). Richie (1996) has spoken to this contextual issue by describing her work with imprisoned African-American women:

> The more I learned about the lives of the African-American battered women in jail, the more I came to understand just how profoundly set up (or entrapped) they were. In the private sphere of their lives they were deeply misunderstood by the people closest to them, betrayed by their loyalty to their families and communities, and abused and degraded in their most intimate relationships. At the same time, they were trying desperately to exist in a social world that was determined to condemn them, only to be exiled from the broader society that failed to deliver promised opportunity and rewards. To this, add the social context of an unresponsive social service system, a meanspirited and repressive public welfare agenda, increasingly aggressive law enforcement policies, and growing intolerance for women who cannot or do not "fit in" to dominant society ... and their gender entrapment becomes clearer. (p. 5)

FIGURE 9.2   The Equality Wheel

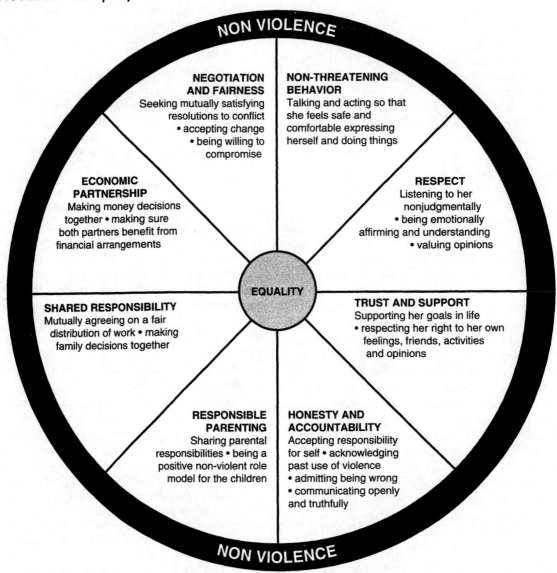

The Equality Wheel suggests ways in which nonviolence can be demonstrated in relationships.

In an important study that looked at consequences of battering beyond the intra- or interpersonal realm, Shepard and Pence (1988) found that being battered had a profound effect on a woman's job performance. For example, 55% of this sample had missed work as a result of abuse; 62% had been late or had to leave work early, as a result of battering; 24% had lost a job, in part because of being battered; and 56% had been harassed by the abuser at work, either in person or by phone. Others in the sample did not attend school or seek employment, either because the batterer forbade it or because their self-esteem and confidence was weakened as a result of being battered. These authors suggested, "In assessment and service planning, social workers must examine the extent to which abuse contributes to employment difficulties. Programs geared to assist women with job placement and training must look beyond women's educational and employment histories to determine what factors may have contributed to their erratic performances" (p. 59).

Davis and Srinivasan (1995) held focus groups with battered women to assess "what helps battered women get out of abusive relationships and survive and grow once they are outside of these relationships" (p. 51). Some of these data are presented later in this chapter, to help focus the discussion on practice strategies with battered women. However, during the course of the focus groups, Davis and Srinivasan obtained descriptions of cultural values and institutions that did not support or validate the battered woman's experiences. For example, many members of the clergy supported so-called traditional family values and encouraged women to return to the batterer. The Center for Prevention of Sexual and Domestic Violence, led by Marie Fortune, has worked for more than a decade to change the culture of religious institutions to ensure that women are no longer victimized within these institutions. Fortune and Wood (1988) wrote, "whether or not our religious institutions can be changed remains to be seen. But in the meantime, many women turn to their faith traditions when they face the crisis of sexual or domestic violence. They deserve to find a faithful response so that they need not abandon their faith in order to stop their victimization" (p. 120).

In October of 1996, a formerly battered woman spoke to the crowd at a candlelight vigil in remembrance of battered women who had been killed. She told the crowd that she had done all of the "right things"—protective order, press charges, divorce; yet now no one will hire her, neighbors don't believe the abuse really happened, and her husband still has all of the power and control in life. Another woman

spoke to the issue that her former partner was being released from a 2-year jail sentence at any time, and what was she to do now? These issues speak to the complexities of issues that face women who have been battered, which force advocates to broaden the scope of relief and safety beyond reliance on the criminal-justice system. Figure 9.3 is a Coordinated Community Action Model, which suggests the many ways in which all segments of our society (media, clergy, education, justice, employers, government, and social service providers) must work together and within their own spheres to make batterers accountable for violence. Wood and Middleman (1992) wrote, "There is not an end to the problem of woman assault. Not as long as gender-based inequality is built into the fabric of society. . . . In the meantime, enlightened women and men have to help women who are trapped in the current social arrangements to get out from under" (pp. 93–94).

Using the Children, and the Effects of Battering on Children

Children are often used as weapons against the woman who is battered. In countless situations, women have been told by batterers, "You can leave, but I'll keep the kids. No court in the country will give you these kids after I get done with you." Children have been kidnapped from schools after women fled multiple state lines to become free of abuse. Children are also often hurt in the cross fire of violence (Roy, 1988). Bowker, Arbitell, and McFerron (1988) found, "The worse the wife beating, the worse the child abuse" (p. 164). Davidson (1994) concisely spells out the harm to children in homes where their mother is being battered:

> There is no doubt that children are harmed in more than one way—cognitively, psychologically, and in their social development—merely by observing or hearing the domestic terrorism of brutality against a parent at home. Experts report that the immediate impact of children's exposure to domestic violence "can be traumatic—fear for self, fear for their mother's safety, and self-blame." (p. 1)

FIGURE 9.3   The Coordinated Community Action Model

DESIRE TO MAKE

SOCIAL SERVICE PROVIDERS
• Design and deliver services which are responsive to battered women and children's needs • Require staff to receive training on the etiology and dynamics of DV • Oppose the "pathologizing" of DV and exclusive control of the "field" by "degreed professionals" • Shift the focus

HEALTH CARE SYSTEM
• Develop and utilize safe and effective methods for identification of DV • Provide referral, education, and support services to battered women and their children • Refrain from overly prescribing sedative drugs to battered women • Utilize accountable documentation and reporting protocols for DV • Devote a percentage of training equitable to DV cases handled

GOVERNMENT
• Enact laws which define battering as criminal behavior • Enact laws which provide courts with progressive consequences in sentencing • Adequately fund battered women's service agencies and violence prevention education • Commute sentences of battered women who kill in self defense • Heavily tax the sale of weapons and pornography to subsidize sexual and physical violence prevention and intervention efforts

JUSTICE SYSTEM
• Regularly disclose relevant statistics on DV case disposition • Utilize methods of intervention which do not rely on the victim's involvement • Devote a percentage of training equitable to DV cases handled • Vigorously enforce batterer's compliance, and protect women and children's safety, with custody, visitation, and injunctive orders • Adopt a "pro-arrest policy" • Provide easily accessible and enforceable protection orders

YOU

EMPLOYERS
• Condition batterers continuing employment on remaining nonviolent • Intervene against stalkers in the workplace • Safeguard battered employee's employment and careers by providing flexible schedules, leaves of absence, and establishing enlightened personnel policies • Provide employment security to battered employees • Provide available resources to support and advocate for battered employees

MEDIA
• Prioritize subject matter which celebrates peace and nonviolence • Spotlight efforts which promote nonviolence • Devote an equitable proportion of their media "product" to battered women and children's needs • Educate about the dynamics and consequences of violence, not glorify it • Cease labeling DV as "love gone sour," "lover's quarrel," "family spat," etc. •Stop portraying the batterer's excuses and lies as if they were the truth

CLERGY
• Speak out against DV from the pulpit • Routinely assess for DV in premarital and pastoral counseling • Seek out and maintain a learning and referral relationship with the DV coordinated community response system • Oppose the use of biblical or theological justification for DV • Reject patriarchal dominance as a preferred social pattern

EDUCATION SYSTEM
• Support and educate teachers to recognize and, respond to symptoms of DV in students lives • Teach violence prevention, peace-honoring conflict resolution and communication skills • Acknowledge gender bias in teaching materials and develop alternatives • Require education about relationships at all levels • Teach that it is the civic duty of all citizens to oppose oppression and to support those who are oppressed

A DIFFERENCE

Violence, power, and control over women is much more than an interpersonal problem. The Coordinated Community Action Model suggests ways in which communities can respond positively to address the needs of women who have been battered.

Jaffe, Wolfe, and Wilson (1990) noted the diversity of children's responses to witnessing and being caught in the cross fire of domestic violence. Reviewing the research findings on children's developmental differences in response to battering, the authors report that these trauma-

tized infants tend to have poorer health, have more sleep problems, and scream more than infants who do not experience family violence in the home. Traumatized preschoolers are likely to exhibit signs of terror: yelling, irritability, shaking, hiding, or stuttering. Developmental regression may also occur. Older children of battered mothers are reported to be more secretive about what is occurring in their homes. They may show aggression outwardly and often show anxiety through nail biting, hair pulling, or even running away. Males are more likely to show aggression and disruptive behavior, while females tend to have more somatic complaints and to be withdrawn, passive, or clinging. Arroyo and Eth (1995) suggested that moral development may also be affected by witnessing family violence. Children may learn that hurting another person often goes unpunished, that it may not be viewed as wrong, and that negative consequences of violence are nonexistent.

Data on children who witness violence and who are often victimized, along with their mother, cast suspicion on the notion that the children are experiencing a good home life. There is tremendous pressure for women to keep their marriages intact, and there is tremendous internal and external pressure for women to protect their children from harm. This conflict is important to address in working with the woman who is being battered, with safety of the woman and child as the central focus of therapy.

Miedzian (1995) encouraged prevention of violence, suggesting,

> If we want, we can decrease violence. Instead of just giving lip service to family values, we need laws and programs that will help families raise decent children. American boys need to be protected from a culture of violence that exploits their worst tendencies by reinforcing and amplifying the atavistic values of the masculine mystique. Women's lives and freedom are threatened constantly by men raised in this culture. We all deserve better. (p. 23)

Gender Socialization for Fixing Abusive Relationships

White (1985/1994) warned that a woman's pastor might read to her a Bible passage from Ephesians 5:21: "'Wives, submit yourselves unto your own husbands,' and urge you to make the sacrifice for your family" (p. 72). With strong religious prescriptions and cultural expectations that women are responsible for getting the family through hard times through nurturance, sacrifice, and putting others' needs ahead of her own, some women have a great deal of emotional conflict over ending a relationship. A woman may be hopeful that the violence will end. She also sees, from time to time, during the respite and contrition stage of the cycle of violence (Walker, 1979), the loving man she married. She may be experiencing a great deal of conflict about what she can do to make things better. Often, a woman will appear in treatment to find out what she can do to help her batterer. Even when women seek our services with a focus on helping themselves, periodically, the discussion will revert to the batterer or to how she can change her partner to prevent the emotional or physical abuse.

Given this context, we briefly present information on the batterer, with the hope that those working either with battered women or with batterers will seek out additional information to aid in clinical or community practice. Further, the information presented has been obtained primarily from samples of men who are battering women. Therefore, it cannot be assumed that this information can be generalized to lesbian batterers.

Characteristics of Men Who Batter

In 1976, David and Brannon presented four factors to describe contemporary masculine roles: No Sissy Stuff, The Big Wheel, The Sturdy Oak, and Give 'Em Hell. Long (1987) believes that these characterizations give us a clear portrait of men who batter.

> No "real man" acts, thinks, feels like a woman. Interwoven with this is a behavioral pattern of egotism and self-centeredness, expectations of control and success, alienation from personal weakness, and the need to maintain separateness (independence) as more powerful than the desire to sustain unity (dependence) . . . the individual batterer uses violence at the level he deems necessary to make up for his sense of inadequacy,

his perceived sense of loss of power or control, or as an outlet for his sense of rage at an unfair world in which he can never live up to the expectations of being masculine. In line with his fear of, sometimes hatred for, and envy of the feminine, he carries out his violence against the woman in his life, fulfilling social prescriptions found in institutional sexism. (p. 306)

Lindsey, McBride, and Platt (1993) list 14 characteristics of abusive and violent men: controlling, lacking in assertiveness skills, repressed, undependable or overresponsible, overstimulated and chaotic, fearful of abandonment, unable to handle criticism, socially isolated, masked by façade, misogynistic, holding irrational beliefs, alienated, obsessive, and having low self-esteem (p. 21). Further, these authors (Lindsey et al., 1993, p. 21) list a belief system held by many men who batter:

- The world is a dangerous place
- I will survive
- I can trust only myself
- I will get what I want when I want it
- I'm doing nothing wrong
- I won't get caught
- If I get caught, I can talk myself out of the situation
- If I can't get out of it, the consequences will be light

Such a belief system ends up with the man feeling entitled. This is why many people who work with men who batter and with women who have been battered answer the question, "Why do men batter?" with, "Because he can." He believes he can, that he won't get caught, and that even if he is caught, the consequences will be light. His belief system is supported by our patriarchal culture and all of its institutions: the helping professionals who don't address the violence, the police who don't arrest the batterer, the religious leader who excuses the violence, the courts that look the other way, and the families, neighbors, and friends who minimize the violence.

Holtzworth-Munroe and Stuart (1994), in an excellent review of the literature on typologies of male batterers, suggested three descriptive dimensions that are most commonly used to distinguish among batterers. *Family-only batterers* are generally reported to engage in the least severe marital violence, to exhibit little psychopathology, and to be less likely to have violence-related legal problems. *Dysphoric/ borderline batterers* are often found to perpetrate moderate to extreme battering, including sexual abuse. "These men are the most dysphoric, psychologically distressed, and emotionally volatile. They may evidence borderline and schizoidal personality characteristics and may have problems with alcohol and [other] drug abuse" (p. 482). The third cluster of batterers, according to the hypothesis of Holtzworth-Munroe and Stuart, named *generally violent/antisocial batterer,* not only engage in moderate to severe woman battering but also have the most extensive history of criminal behavior and are more likely to have substance-abuse problems and to have an antisocial personality disorder. Batterer typologies are being developed and researched with the hope of being able to distinguish factors associated with different types of batterers in order to better understand and implement suitable treatment and prevention strategies. Batterer typologies are not without controversy. The "Trial of the Century," the *State of California versus OJ Simpson,* had experts arguing with experts over whether OJ Simpson fit the pattern of a severe (i.e., femicide perpetrator) batterer.

What then might be a response to a battered woman who asks, "What can I do to help him?" Gondolf (1989) suggested, "Men are more likely to change when they perceive a real crisis that threatens their future, set in motion by the victim" (p. 81). He also suggested that her demands for the violence to stop have to be nonnegotiable and to employ multiple consequences and interventions (i.e., tell neighbors, family, friends, and encourage them to call the police if they suspect violence; call the police when abused or threatened; contact a shelter for support; and alert other agencies to the violence). Finally, Gondolf noted, "A woman facing violence needs as much reinforcement as she can muster. She should feel that she has the right to support and intervention. And hopefully her community is ready and willing to offer them to her. Stopping violent men is something we all have to do" (p. 88).

Fear × Physical Violence × Psychological Abuse × Misuse of Power × Marital Rape × Cultural Oppression × Child-Custody Issues × Gender Socialization × Men's Feeling of Entitlement = the beginning of understanding the dynamics of battering on a woman's life. It's not a complete picture but contains critical factors to keep in mind when (a) assessing the violence used against women, (b) assigning meaning to battering, and (c) intervening with battered women.

Critiquing Mental Health Models— The Psychologization of Battering

Ellen Pence (1988) offered a wonderful analogy to assist helping professionals in understanding how the *sole* application of a mental health model fails to give an adequate understanding of battered women. She suggested that you imagine that in half of your classroom, 100-pound sandbags hang over each person's head. Your instructor, at the push of a button, can release those heavy bags to fall on you at will. Half of you sit under those bags, with the threat of them being released on you day after day. The other half of the class sits, discusses, and moves around without fear. After a few weeks, those who sit under the bags will participate much less in class discussion, be more timid, and become extremely compliant. Six months later, clinical social workers come in to test the class, using psychological variables. The students on the side of the room with the bags are assessed as dependent, as pathological liars, and as nonassertive. The students on other side of the room are assessed as being psychologically healthy.

This experience is similar to what happens to women who have been battered. They are tested in their postvictimized state and then compared to women who have not been victimized. Based on this assessment, they become labeled not as survivors of violence but instead with mental health jargon or diagnoses. Rosewater (1988) noted, "Repeatedly I have seen professionals fail to distinguish the symptoms of victims of violence from the symptoms of the sufferers of mental illness or to understand their interplay" (p. 200). Continuing, Rosewater noted two common errors: "the extreme fearfulness (paranoia) and confusion created by repeatedly experiencing violence are misdiagnosed as psychiatric symptoms, and/or the woman is diagnosed as having a character disorder, which is seen as a *predisposition* for the violence that occurs.... Either way, she is clearly a loser in the mental health care delivery system" (p. 200, italics in original).

As a result of testing after victimization, battered women have been portrayed as women who have low self-esteem and who are helpless, codependent, unhealed survivors of childhood sexual abuse or who lack assertiveness skills. Much of the existing research focused on factors that are correlated with battered women, who are then offered treatment strategies focused on individual characteristics of battered women, such as offering assertiveness training to counter the deficit of nonassertive behavior. Unfortunately, such research was conducted *after* a woman was battered. As a result of the many research reports on the personal and interpersonal deficits of battered women, it becomes easier for professionals to personally distance themselves from the problems of battering. It allows professionals to assume that the low self-esteem and nonassertiveness of a woman who gets battered thereby *allows* battering to continue because of the same supposed character traits. We cannot even begin to count the number of people who have emphatically stated to us that they would never be battered. This statement assumes that battering is somehow a woman's choice or her responsibility or that she can always control her partner. This type of attitude taints social work practice, despite social work training and values related to examining the person-in-environment, understanding ecological levels, and practicing in a nonjudgmental manner. Tifft (1993) wrote, "Even though women are now less likely to be overtly blamed, battering continues to be interpreted in ways that tacitly reinforce notions of women's complicity in the violence" (p. 5).

Similarly, the treatment models for men who batter, which are based on traditional mental health models, are fraught with contradictions and may even place women in danger. The models used for working with men who batter are remarkably similar to treatment strategies that minimize violence, which are too often used with women who have been battered. Adams (1988) discussed several traditional mental health models and offered a pro-feminist criticism of these models. First, the *insight model* assumes impaired ego functioning and as a result, "Insight therapy seeks to help the abusive man become more aware of how he has been affected by past experiences so that he can learn to respond more appropriately to present relationships" (p. 179). Adams cited one survey finding that a shocking 90% of the programs saw "increasing self-esteem" as a top treatment goal, with only 14% of the programs listing "having the abuser take responsibility for his violence" (p. 180) as a top treatment goal. Insight models also assume that treatment interventions should be nonthreatening. Adams has worried that when the danger of violence is ongoing, "therapists cannot afford to get stuck on other issues or to wait for the client to develop insight. Taking the time to create a safe environment for the batterer can sometimes mean perpetrating an unsafe environment for his partner" (p. 181).

Second, with *ventilation models*, Adams (1988) suggested, "Openly expressing anger and resentments was thought to ensure against storing up hostile aggression until its potentially explosive discharge, or against its conversion to other symptoms such as physical complaints, depression, and 'passive–aggressive' behavior" (p. 182). Adams firmly suggested that men who batter do not need "permission from experts to continue to vent their anger with little regard for its consequences to others" (p. 183).

Third, Adams (1988) reviewed *cognitive-behavioral* and *psychoeducational models*. Many of these models bring us closer to treating the dynamic of the use of violence in a relationship. Underlying the cognitive-behavioral model is the belief that because violence is a learned behavior; it can be unlearned. Techniques such as assertiveness and relaxation training are used to teach men alternative behaviors. Psychoeducational models often rely heavily on self-observation with anger logs. Those using a cognitive-behavioral or psychoeducational model (or some combination thereof) vary in how or whether they include an analysis of battering as an abuse of power and sexist behavior. Adams noted, "This approach is weakest when its practitioners fail to adequately integrate a political understanding of battering that identifies and confronts its sexist underpinnings" (p. 191).

Failure to develop the problem of battering as a form of power and sexist control leaves treatment models for men and for women focused on individual and interpersonal dynamics. Adams (1988) concluded by asserting, "Therapists who try to trade insights, fair fighting, or reasons for men's nonviolence are missing what one ex-batterer describes as the whole point of his violence—that *might makes right*. Persistently challenging that right is the most fundamental responsibility for therapists and others" (p. 196, italics in original). Challenging that right is the contribution of pro-feminist treatment models. Within feminist writings, at least two clear perspectives are being debated. One perspective notes that women who are battered develop, because of the battering, psychological symptoms—such as learned helplessness (Walker, 1979) or battered women's syndrome (Walker, 1984). This perspective has been useful to help professionals, laypersons, and women who are being battered to understand, in part, how women get "stuck" (i.e., the age-old question of "Why do women stay?"). Another perspective insists that there is nothing helpless about a survivor of battering. In fact, quite the contrary, the woman shows amazing resourcefulness aimed at trying to end the violence (Bowker, 1993; Gondolf & Fisher, 1988). This perspective is useful for the purposes of focusing on a woman's strengths and toward acknowledging all of the system failures she has confronted: the minister who told her to try harder, the police officer who told her to calm down or she'd be arrested, or the social worker who insisted that assertive communication would help her. Both perspectives include a structural analysis recognizing the sexism, control, and violence that oppress women. Both of these perspectives are briefly summarized here.

Learned Helplessness

Lenore Walker, in her pioneering 1979 book *The Battered Woman,* wrote about learned helplessness. Learned helplessness affects problem-solving capacities. "Repeated battering, like electrical shocks, diminish the woman's motivation to respond. . . . Secondly, her cognitive ability to perceive success is changed. She does not believe her response will result in a favorable outcome, whether or not it might. . . . Finally, her sense of emotional well-being becomes precarious" (pp. 49–50). The way we have commonly explained this phenomenon goes like this: A partner says he (or she) hits a woman because she is dressed too seductively. The woman never again dresses this way. The next time, she is kicked because she did not take out the trash. She always takes out the trash in the future. Eventually, the violence becomes more frequent and more severe, and the

woman turns to her family for help. Her mother and father sit her down and give her advice on how to be a better wife and how she must not divorce; think of the children. The violence continues. The woman continues to try different strategies (leaving, begging, praying, yelling, therapy, etc.), yet the violence continues. She has learned that nothing she does can stop the violence.

There were probably other choices, other options she might have employed. However, the woman did not see those choices, and her partner certainly did not present her with options or choices. The batterer is in control of the violence used. So when questions are posed such as, "Why didn't you leave?" (Well, she did but she was brought back—by force) or "Why didn't she ask her parents for help?" (She did, but they didn't), she is not so subtly being blamed for not making choices that may not have existed for her or for not seeing a full range of choices in the middle of violence and abuse. Walker (1993) summarized, "In the case of battered women with learned helplessness, they do not respond with total helplessness or passivity; rather, they narrow their choice of responses, opting for those that have the highest predictability of creating successful outcomes" (p. 135).

Cycle of Violence

In the same early work, Walker (1979) described a three-stage cycle of violence, the first stage of which is tension building. This stage is typified by "minor" battering—throwing things, increased emotional abuse, and increased feelings of fear. The second stage, the acute battering incident, is what most people think of as "battering." This is the physical violence part of the cycle—often the briefest part of the cycle. "According to reports from battered women, only the batterers can end the second phase. The woman's only option is to find a safe place to hide" (p. 61). This time period is when women often seek the services of social workers (and other helping professionals). The third phase is called "kindness and contrite loving behavior" (p. 65). Apologies, tears, begging for forgiveness, and lots of promises are characteristic of this phase. If the woman sought outside assistance after the acute battering stage, then early in social work practice with her, this "kinder and gentler" stage may be occurring. The abuser says it won't happen again. Beautiful love letters are written. Flowers arrive on the hour. The children are treated to fun times, and so is the woman who was battered. This is a very confusing and powerful stage. In this era of emphasis on "family values," the personal and societal pulls to make the marriage work are incredibly strong. With these pulls on the abused woman (and so many more, such as love and basic economic survival), many women decide to give their partner one more try. Often, the cycle is set back in motion to be repeated and repeated. (It's important to note that not all women experience this cycle in this manner. Some women never receive an apology, or flowers, or experience any contrite behavior. Also, the contrite stage often gets shorter as time passes.)

Battered Women's Syndrome

Battered women's syndrome is a category of posttraumatic stress disorder (PTSD). There are many symptoms of PTSD, which Herman (1992) sorts into three classes: hyperarousal, intrusion, and constriction. *Hyperarousal* includes an exaggerated startle response and hypervigilance on the part of the survivor. These symptoms can result in difficulty sleeping and easy irritability. *Intrusion* causes the event to be continually replayed in the survivor's head. These recollections are recurrent, terrifying, and very stressful for the person reexperiencing the trauma. To prevent these troubling symptoms, many survivors attempt to avoid stimuli that would invoke recollections (Herman, 1992). *Constriction* refers to the generalized numbing state many survivors enter. The survivors may

complain of a loss of interest in normal activities and a decreased ability to feel emotions. Symptoms of depression and anxiety are common. These symptoms can begin immediately after the trauma or may develop after a latency period of months or years following the trauma.

Woman as Survivor

Gondolf and Fisher (1988) proposed that battered women are not passive victims suffering from learned helplessness (Walker, 1979). Instead, they noted, battered women are survivors who have consistently demonstrated active help-seeking behaviors. Bowker (1983) found that as the prevalence and severity of battering increased, more help-seeking behaviors were exhibited. Ten years later, Bowker continued to echo this theme. Bowker (1993) noted, "The student or professional reading about learned helplessness might conclude that all battered women are helpless. Nothing could be further from the truth. The data ... show that many battered women work very hard to free themselves from violence.... Otherwise, how could we explain the fact that so many previously battered women are now living free of violence?" (p. 157).

These types of studies are important for beginning the process of renormalizing battered women after years of psychic assault, misdiagnosis, and treatment that often blamed them or stigmatized them for the violence. Increasingly, research is supporting the notion that while women are frequently victims of horrid acts of violence, their behavior is that of a survivor— not a helpless victim. However, Gondolf and Fisher (1988) rightfully acknowledge that helping professionals will see violence-related symptoms when coming in contact with battered women. Women who have been battered often present with traumatic shock symptoms, introspective thoughts regarding their role in the demise of the marriage (feelings of failure), and separation anxiety, including fear of reprisal, fears about custody issues, financial insecurity, and the fear of the unknown in a world not all that friendly to women such as female single parents (Gondolf & Fisher, 1988).

The theories related to the battered women's syndrome and learned helplessness are falling under increasing criticism for class, race and ethnic, and heterosexist bias. Clearly, the idealized model of the battered woman, in a racist, sexist, classist society, is that of a European-American, heterosexual, and middle-class woman. Richie (1996) noted, "Diane Lewis and other African American feminist criminologists suggest that understanding the experiences of women of color in the criminal justice system requires an examination of how stereotypes about Black women (e.g., they are more violent, less controllable, and less feminine) contradict the dominant ideology about women's roles (passive, family-based)" (p. 154). Moore (1995) related this concept specifically back to the battered women's syndrome in her compelling article entitled, "Battered Woman Syndrome: Selling the Shadow to Support the Substance." Moore described the work done on battered women's syndrome as an example of the inherent flaws in "gender essentialism," which is defined in Moore's work as "the notion that a unitary essential woman's experience can be isolated and described independent of race and other experiences" (p. 13). Moore strongly criticized the use of battered women's syndrome, describing it as oppressive for all women, and in different ways. Implicitly the syndrome points to a sameness in women and implies that the woman who has been battered suffers from a psychological disability. Further criticism of battered women's syndrome is included in Chapter 11.

Interaction Models and Couples Therapy: A Case Against

Another set of debates, centered around theoretical orientations, surrounds the use of couples treatment when a woman is being battered. Adams (1988) discussed the *interaction model* at length and found it flawed on a number of issues. He noted, "Proponents of the interaction

model philosophically justify their use of couples counseling as the treatment of choice by drawing on the family systems literature" (p. 184). Adams continued, "Since the violence itself is seen as but one aspect of an ongoing dysfunctional pattern that has rather arbitrary beginning, middle, and end points, it is presumed to have a nonlinear circular causality" (p. 185). The goal then becomes for each partner to come to see how she and he contribute to the circular problem. Couples counseling ends up placing the woman in a difficult position:

> Though she is expected to be open about her feelings, air her grievances, and report her husband's violence, to do any of these things places her in grave danger of continued violence. Many battered women report that past family therapy sessions were followed by violent episodes. The threat of continued violence leads battered women to communicate their feelings and concerns in an indirect manner, which is often misinterpreted by couples counselors as noncompliance. (p. 187)

Golden and Frank (1994) have strongly suggested, "Women who are being beaten, intimidated, or controlled by their partners are not free to engage in the kind of open dialogue that counseling promotes" (p. 636). These authors continued,

> What social workers do not know about domestic violence can kill our clients. Social workers have been trained in a variety of approaches (for example, behavior modification, family systems, psychoanalysis) that seem generally useful with other kinds of clients and issues. Imposing these models on our work with violent couples, however, not only may prove ineffective but also may actually exacerbate the danger of assault. (p. 637)

Bograd (1984) questioned the assumption that the real issues in families where men use violence are issues such as poor communication or dependency. She wondered whether perhaps it is not the violence that perpetuates the poor communication and dependency symptoms. Some conjoint therapists have set up guidelines suggesting that couples work is not recommended with severe violence. Bograd suggested that this stand implies that mild violence may be acceptable.

Authors' Perspective

In a talk at the 1993 Futures Conference, I (Stout) made the following comments about the use of couples work with women who are battered:

> I believe that services to battered women and batterers will change in the next 10 years. My fear is that services will not change from the traditional couples/family therapy models because as professionals we recognize the damage these "services" can do. The social work profession has a long way to go before we can say that we adequately address the special needs of women, including battered women, in treatment. It seems almost everyone receives training on the DSM-III-R (an increasingly misogynist publication) and almost everyone receives training in family therapy—however, only a few social workers each year receive training on working with women, or on empowerment strategies. Police departments have changed their practices tremendously in the past 15 years. They changed, not because their practices were killing women, but because of multimillion-dollar civil law suits—which they lost. I fear that social workers are going to be included in the next group of lawsuits if we do not begin to value the lives of women, end the minimization regarding violence against women, and work to ensure the safety of battered women throughout every step of the treatment process. Helping professionals should not require such a wakeup call.

This statement was intentionally strong, to encourage social workers to pay attention to safety issues. Both of us (Stout and McPhail) know of feminist therapists who, reluctantly, have agreed to take on a couple only because the couple was going to see someone who would see them *together*—period. The therapists (and mediators who are in similar situations) felt that the only hope for the safety of the woman was for someone who knew about the dynamics of domestic violence to take on the case. Goldner (1992) described such a situation, "I no longer automatically send people away with a politically correct referral to women's support groups and male batterer's groups, because most won't go. As one woman with a broken nose angrily told me when I made such a suggestion, 'I am not a battered woman'" (p. 58). We have also heard of some successful outcomes from feminist therapists and mediators. Therefore, the old adage of "never say never" may be appropriate here. Bograd (1992) addressed the issue of couple treatment and the controversy surrounding its use. While she "largely supports the stance" of not using couples therapy, she pointed out that the debate has been too limited over a narrow treatment choice. She noted,

> Debates about treatment unit alone also distract us from careful analysis of what should be the focus of treatment with batterers. In other words, seeing a couple together or apart is not a sufficient criterion of an ethical or feminist-informed practice. Rather, that is to be determined by what issues are addressed in couples or individual work, how the man is approached, how the reasons for his violence are construed, and whether one is dedicated—not only to ending his violence—but also to helping construct a marriage without coercion or control of any kind on his part. (p. 253)

Avis (1992) also passionately called our attention to some of the critical variables needed in family treatment by suggesting that therapists must stop colluding with the misuse of power and name the abuse and the abuser. Otherwise, she contended, family systems will continue to violate those with less power.

Our experience tells us that avoiding the use of couples treatment is the safest course of action, with professional exceptions made after carefully weighing all of the lethality factors, control dynamics, and other relevant factors related to the two individuals who insist on couples treatment.

"I Do Couples Work. How Will I Know Whether the Woman Is Being Battered?"

Suman and Edwards (undated, no page number) developed a "Family Violence Training Curriculum" for use by Child Protective Services, Region IV, in Texas. They listed seven indicators of men who may be battering a woman:

1. He constantly speaks for his partner during an interview and strongly resists having her interviewed separately.
2. The woman is described by her partner as being clumsy, incompetent, crazy, or stupid, or in other derogatory terms.
3. He is overly solicitous and condescending to his partner.
4. He admits to the existence of violence but minimizes its frequency or severity.
5. When confronted with his abusive behavior, he blames his partner and refuses to accept responsibility.
6. He appears to have excessive control over her life or acts jealous.
7. He appears excessively rigid in his expectations of traditional sex roles.

In addition, the following factors are worth watching for: Does he constantly criticize her? Does he accuse her of coming on to other men? Does he complain about her having friends?

Does he seem like the perfect man, and the woman appears angry and crazy? A classic example of this nice-guy image is a May, 1995, homicide in Houston, Texas, where a man shot and killed his former womanfriend. The paper reported,

> The justice of the peace who released Patrick Walker from jail four months ago said Thursday that he was convinced the defendant was a nice kid with no criminal record who seemed genuinely remorseful for trying to shoot his ex-girlfriend in the head.... "He was a real smart kid. He was valedictorian of his class. He had no criminal history at all." (Reinert, 1995, p. 33)

These points will give some red flags to work with. They do *not* identify a batterer, however. In the case of the police allowing a batterer to be released from jail, it's easy to say, "I wouldn't make this mistake." However, it is worth noting that most police officers have much more training on criminal behavior and often have more training on domestic violence than do most social workers—as domestic-violence training for police officers is mandated in many states. Most social workers have not been under legislative or professional mandates to learn about criminal behavior or domestic violence. Therefore, it seems imperative that social-service and health-care providers conduct one or more violence assessments with all clients or patients. If violence is uncovered during the course of treatment, working closely with a supervisor and local resources to address the needs of all family members is warranted.

Strategies for Change

This section highlights practice strategies that are important when working with women who have been battered; it includes issues related to safety; demonstrating respect; building connections; group work; practice concerns specific to Latina, African-American, Asian-American, and lesbian women; and community practice. Finally, policy-change strategies are introduced.

As mentioned previously, we believe that change is necessary on all levels before violence against women will cease to exist in this world.

SAFETY, SAFETY, SAFETY

It cannot be emphasized enough how much of the treatment literature ignores this critical issue, which is relevant at every single phase of practice with women who have been or who are being battered (or when working with men who batter). It is important to say *boldly* and clearly: The number-one practice issue must always be to ensure the safety of the woman. This is true for women seeking shelter services, group treatment, outpatient counseling, or inpatient medical or mental health services. It is also true for administrative practice, research practice, or community practice. It is true for women who are just now leaving the relationship, for those who are still working within the relationship, and for those who are separated or divorced. Walker (1994), in her book *Abused Women and Survivor Therapy,* suggested, "The two most important goals in survivor therapy are to ensure the woman's safety and to restore her sense of control over her life. . . . Without genuine safety, the victim cannot give up coping strategies that protect her from further psychological harm" (p. 303). Safety is a key issue.

A key to being attuned to safety issues is conducting a thorough assessment, which includes numerous questions on violence within and outside of the home. It is infrequent (although not rare) for a woman to respond affirmatively to the question, "Are you a battered woman?" Has this label been associated with a deficit model and, as such, sometimes feels negative to women. It is often necessary to ask about specific behaviors, such as, Have you ever been pushed, shoved, slapped, threatened, forced to have sex against your will, raped by your partner, frightened by your partner, or restricted from leaving the home? (See Sonkin,

Martin, & Walker, 1985, for a sample violence-assessment instrument, and see Campbell, 1995, for a lethality-assessment inventory.)

Once a woman has been identified as being in danger from battering, it is suggested that she develop a safety plan or an escape plan. (When working with men who use violence, it is also suggested that the men develop a safety plan [Adams, 1988].) *Safety plans* vary widely and must be made individually with women, as class, sexual preference, and race–ethnicity make resources and needs different. For example, safety planning usually involves working with the woman to see whether she can put aside (hide) some money to help her in the event of the need to escape quickly. For some women, accumulating enough money for a phone call and bus fare to a shelter may be all that can realistically be expected. Other women may be able to plan for gathering money for a deposit and the first few months of rental housing. To blanketly encourage all women to save for 3-months rent would blatantly be harmful for many. Common elements of safety planning include having the phone number of a shelter; knowing where and how to get an order of protection; obtaining extra keys for the house and car; gaining access to money and documents such as birth certificates, social security cards, and vehicle registration (Kilgore, 1992); hiding some clothes; and possessing current or prior court orders. When possible, it's helpful for women to plan to bring a favorite toy for each child and to bring a few family treasures (photo albums or jewelry her grandmother gave her). Safety planning is important, and it is just as important that the responsibility for predicting the violence and doing something about it is not placed solely on the woman who has been battered. Unfortunately, some social workers (and other helping professionals) have used safety planning as another way to suggest that male violence is a woman's responsibility. Professionals and laypersons have also not been sensitive to the increased danger a woman is in as she is psychologically or physically preparing to leave. Therefore, safety planning must be handled as a life-and-death matter—not as a routine checklist of things she *must* do. Some situations will clearly warrant that the woman should not have the shelter number available and she should not be sneaking or hiding cash, for example.

Edleson and Tolman (1992) broaden this discussion of safety planning by suggesting that social workers maintain an ecological perspective at all times when addressing the issues related to women who are battered. They noted,

> For a woman's safety to be enhanced, she must have resources to protect herself, including shelter and other supportive programs. The police and court system must be willing to follow through on protective actions, including arrest, issuing and enforcing orders for protection, and proper sentencing. The better the linkages between the various actors, the more effectively her safety can be protected. (p. 50)

Concern for the safety of women was the primary strategy-for-change recommendation. Although safety is often neglected, perhaps the single most important thing professionals (as well as friends, family, and community institutions) can do for women who have been battered is to value and respect her right to freedom from violence. The next few sections address social work practice with women who have been battered: general practice principles, practice with groups, practice with institutions and communities, practice with lesbians, and practice with women of color. In addition, some of the strategies offered elsewhere in this book apply to practice with battered women—for example, information presented on gendered communication, substance abuse, using the media to effect change, and expert testimony.

There is no one profile for a battered women. Follingstad, Laughlin, Polek, Rutledge, and Hause (1991) found that women who had been battered fell into five statistical clusters. They noted, "Because beliefs, reasons for staying in the relationship, abuse history as a child,

willingness to use resources, ability to predict violence, presence of high levels of emotional abuse, and assertiveness differ between these groups, one major intervention with battered women would not suffice unless it was excessively comprehensive" (p. 200). Therefore, we do not offer a singular prescription to use with each abused woman who presents in your practice.

GENERAL PRACTICE-FOR-CHANGE PRINCIPLES

What Helps Battered Women?

1. Draw on women's knowledge of what is right and what is wrong with their lives.
2. Give the women information about resources that can enable them to leave and eventually live without their abusers.
3. Mobilize the resources of family and friends. . . . Contrary to the message that is given in many substance abuse programs, family members do not need to (and should not) use confrontational tactics with their loved one. What they should communicate is their belief in the woman's experience, their concern for the woman's welfare, and their willingness and ability to support her when she is ready to make a change in her life.
4. Listen without judging. . . . We need to move away from this need to understand, which often leads to blaming and labeling, and instead just validate the women's stories.
5. Provide suggestions while supporting the women's right to make their own choices.
6. Groups with other women who have had similar experiences are essential for battered women to move beyond their sense of self-blame and to nurture the hope that change is possible.

From the work of Davis, L., & Srinivasan, M. (1995). Listening to the voices of battered women: What helps them to escape violence? Affilia, 10, 49–69.

Demonstrating Respect and Listening

Demonstration of respect is important for effective social work practice with battered women. Too often, professionals use their knowledge to inform clients what is right or wrong with their lives. Like all other clients, battered women need the opportunity to convey their reality and to have that reality acknowledged. An early publication on battered women by Ball and Wyman (1977–1978) noted several rights of battered women. A few of those rights include:

- She has the right to be treated as an adult.
- She has a right to express her own thoughts and feelings.
- She has a right to develop her individual talents and abilities.
- She has a right not to be perfect.

Those basic rights will be violated if social workers leap to rescue the woman without listening to her narrative and feelings. Further, it is critical to allow women to draw their own conclusions about their relationships, their lives. For example, often professionals who have read something about domestic violence want to use their newly found knowledge or political perspective to inform women of what is wrong about their thinking. For example, a woman who was slapped repeatedly because dinner was not on time might state, "I knew I was wrong to be late with dinner, but the baby was crying and so I got behind on my dinner preparations." At this time, many might rush to exclaim, "You didn't do anything wrong!" While we may recognize that women do not provoke violence, that she did no wrong, it is important to allow the survivor to come to this conclusion on her own. Probing into her feelings, her gender ideology, and her experiences with her partner's violence, she can reach the conclusion that her actions did not make her partner hit her and that helping her baby was not wrong. If she reaches this conclusion, she will own that feeling, that consciousness, instead of merely saying, "My social worker says

it's not wrong to be late with dinner. My social worker says that a woman taking sole responsibility for meals is just another example of patriarchal oppression."

Ellman and Basen-Engquist (1994) suggested that a woman who presents her issues at the personal level needs to be engaged at the personal level. In the preceding example, the woman is feeling responsible for the violence. She is speaking about this responsibility on a personal level, not as part of a political analysis. Ellman and Basen-Engquist suggested that professionals have to initially stay inside the battered woman's subjective experience in order to hear her distinct, personal experience. Sometimes persons working with survivors of violence skip the listening part—they've heard it before and may even be protecting themselves from further trauma by not listening. If we do not hear, are we not believing her? Are we minimizing her pain? Are we discounting her analysis? If so, are we mimicking the behavior of the abuser? To launch into a political analysis may in fact be objectifying her (Ellman & Basen-Engquist, 1994)—that is, "She's just another battered woman, and we're experts on battered women, and we know what to do and she doesn't." A time will come (and it may come quickly) that we can move *with* her toward a politicized analysis. Again, education is critical to help her see that the violence is not her fault or responsibility; such education is part of the process of good social work with women who have experienced violence, yet the basic rules of listening, empathizing, and starting where the client is should not be thrown away as part of the transformational process. Goodrich, Rampage, Ellman, and Hallstead (1988) noted some common mistakes made by feminist therapists when working with women who have been abused. One common mistake is outlined here:

Saving her against her will. *The greatest mistake that a therapist can make with a client like Angie is to try to pry her out of a bad relationship "for her own good." Such a strategy indicates to the client that she is neither being heard nor accepted by the therapist. It places the therapist in the untenable position of validating the societal bias which tells Angie that she is not competent to make her own decisions or form her own judgments. (p. 178; emphasis in original)*

The goals of practice become to validate the woman's pain; to help the woman see her options, mobilizing resources that might assist her; to help her see herself in a new light; to address her fears; to let her know that you do not believe she deserved or caused the violence; and to help her understand the dynamics of violence so that she has new information to make decisions with. If social workers rush in with "getting her to leave" or "making sure she does not go back" as the only goal, her goal of trying to stop the violence but keep the relationship may be trivialized or disrespected. Leaving or not returning is often a way of "fixing things," but the battered woman often does not know that harsh reality initially.

Resource Sharing

According to Davis and Srinivasan's (1995) research, battered women reported that shelter services provided validation, sources of emotional support, and information. Battered women (current and former) need validation that they did not deserve the abuse, that they can take care of themselves (and their children), and that they can make the right decisions for themselves. The women expressed the need for emotional support, comfort, and a social network. Finally, the women in the focus groups noted that they needed information that shelter staff were often able to provide about resources, alcoholism, and the cycle of violence.

For helpful practice with battered women, providing several shelter contact numbers, publicizing those contact numbers, and sharing resource information with battered women or frightened women is essential (Davis & Srinivasan, 1995). This observation suggests that social workers and advocates for battered women know resources and processes for obtaining protection orders, gaining access to low- or no-cost legal services, applying for Temporary Assistance for Needy Families (TANF) and food stamps, applying for low-income housing, contacting the victim's assistance department at the county district attorney's office, and referring to programs that work with men who batter.

Making Connections and Building Community

A control strategy often used by men who batter is to isolate the woman. Drawing on self-in-relation theory developed through the Stone Center Colloquia, Surrey (1991) wrote, "Our conception of the self-in-relation involves the recognition that, for women, the primary experience of self is relational, that is the self is organized and developed in the context of important relationships" (p. 52). Too often, the focus with each battered woman has been on separating (physically, emotionally, and financially) from the abusive man and encouraging her to be independent. Women's developmental theory has offered a great deal in recent years about the need for relationships, mutuality, and empathy in women's lives. Reconnecting with family and friends and getting validation from those significant persons can give a formerly isolated woman a tremendous head start toward a life free from abuse.

Families and friends often need help to understand the impact that violence has had on their significant other and on their relationship with her. They may believe or say, "Well, maybe the violence was not her fault, but it's her fault for not leaving" or "We wanted to help but *she* shut us out," and they may have a great deal of anger toward her. Just as professionals and victims need education about battering, so do victims' families. The physical, emotional, financial, and social control the perpetrator has exercised made it very difficult for connections to stay intact and—certainly—to stay unblemished. The survivor's behavior toward family and friends often needs to be reframed as survival skills requiring courage and strength to counter the perception that she didn't care or listen, or that she placed them in danger. (Many men who batter will threaten those who help the battered woman. When she turns to her family for help, he may strike out against her *and* them. Some family and friends will blame the woman for the abuse and violence the man inflicted on them.)

Groups for survivors can also provide connection and community. Groups are great places to laugh, share stories, mourn losses, and receive validation, support, and information. Other battered women can often give the real information about how to get the police to pay attention, who to avoid in the benefits office, and how to get children to behave appropriately without resorting to violence.

Empowerment and Building Success

Again, many battered women are seeking information, support, and education. Women will look for resource information and for shared power. Part of the power to be shared is knowledge. It's important to share knowledge, including knowledge of community resources. One of the things that can happen to survivors is that they have been deprived of the freedom to make choices from a full realm of possibilities. Survivors need to be able to gain control through making choices; yet, for some, the full array of choices may be overwhelming, and that's where guidance and suggestions can help her to clarify *her* priorities, rediscover self-efficacy, create connections with others, and set goals for herself. It is important to ensure successes for women who have been battered. For each battered woman, it can be helpful to suggest things that she has done and can do to regain some control in her life. Social workers must also address the issues that confront women who have very few choices in their lives, due to economic or educational disadvantages, racist communities, immigration laws, or language barriers. Opportunities must be created, which allow choice, true self-determination (based on choice), and the use of our advocacy skills to confront the systems that limit women's opportunities. Working with multicul-

tural alliances is a step in the right direction to ensure that *all* women's needs are addressed.

Chapter 1 of this text offered Tifft's (1993) description of empowerment. Tifft suggested, "Empowerment can be fostered by *contact* to counter feelings of isolation, *awareness* to contravene mystification, and *action* to negate domination and oppression" (p. 145). At this point in practice with a woman who has been battered, she has you and her family (one would hope) to counter her feelings of isolation, *awareness* is rushing into her consciousness, you are helping her demystify what has been happening in her life, and she is taking action. She has reached out to you. That is action. She has found safety for herself and her children. That is action. Walker (1994) concurred that empowerment is not just about independence. She wrote,

> Empowerment does not only suggest independence, but also the movement past personal independence to interdependence—the state of being independent and sometimes dependent—with other people again. Thus, the woman's interpersonal relationships, including family and friendships, become an important part of therapy. (pp. 303–304)

Ten Reasons Why Women Do Not Leave a Batterer

1. The batterer promised to kill her if she leaves.
2. The batterer promised to kill her family and their children if she leaves.
3. The batterer has a gun and says he (or she) will use it.
4. The last three times she called a shelter, it was full.
5. The last time she went to her parents for refuge, the abusive partner dragged her out with a knife to her throat.
6. She heard on the news that kids without fathers in the home join gangs.
7. She was told that the batterer would never hurt her again and, this time, the batterer sounded like he (or she) meant it.
8. Her minister told her she would be sinning if she left her partner.

9. The batterer says that he (or she) has changed, maybe he (or she) has this time. . . .
10. Reality: no job, no access to cash, no car, no place to go. . . .

The reality is that millions of women have and millions more will leave partners who use violence against them. Shelters are full from the day that they open. Let's replace the old question, "Why do women stay?" with a new question: "What can we do to help?"

PRACTICE WITH GROUPS

The basic principles underlying groups for battered women include the fundamental recognition that battered women are the experts on their experiences, and all-women groups are helpful for building trust and intimacy.

Authors' Perspective

In 1984, NiCarthy, Merriam, and Coffman published a book titled, *Talking It Out: A Guide to Groups for Abused Women.* For persons new to groups, this book (even though it is a bit dated) offers a tremendous amount of concrete, practical information on work with women who have been battered. This book is a useful starting point for those who are developing ideas for groups and issues related to women who have been battered. For example, NiCarthy, Merriam and Coffman suggested that within a 2-hour group format, facilitators should include time for introductions, brags, an activity, a break, a safety check, and the dreaded paperwork. We (Stout & McPhail) have had successful experiences using the group ideas offered by NiCarthy, Merriam, and Coffman (1984), such as "Creating a Pamphlet for Abused Women" (p. 90) and "Valued Traits and Vulnerabilities" (p. 105).

Wood and Middleman (1992) offer a "three-task sequence" for working with battered women in groups. These sequential tasks are (1) mutual support, (2) consciousness raising, and (3) taking action.

Mutual Support

This phase invites women to talk about the battering they have experienced. The social worker's responsibility is to help the women to express their feelings and to use those feelings to connect the women. This process is described by Wood and Middleman as a time of catharsis and rushing this process is not advised. "Because the women talk about feeling humiliated, degraded, and powerless, it is important for them to participate in their own way: some by listening, some by talking about what they are up against, some by trying to help others" (p. 90). Through this process, the women become close and demonstrate caring for each other, which sets the stage for the second task of consciousness raising.

Consciousness Raising

This critical task requires that the group worker place the problem of the battering of women in a context of "a larger pattern of harsh treatment to which women are subjected in a society controlled by men" (Wood & Middleman, 1992, p. 90). This perspective allows the context to emerge more fully, so that they realize that they are not responsible or to blame for the violence they have endured. The social worker has the important responsibility to "challenge their rationalizations and validate their anger as they come to see the ways in which they have been systematically limited by their partners and by the social institutions from which they have sought help" (p. 91). This can be a very difficult process and further requires that the social worker focus on each woman's strengths as she struggles with the complex individual and structural challenges that have and will confront her. Wood and Middleman (1992) cautioned that this is a time when some women will begin to think of leaving the group and suggest that the social worker bring up the issue of leaving, with encouragement to stick with this group of women who care and understand.

Taking Action

Finally, and importantly, Wood and Middleman (1992) suggested taking action as a sequential task. This phase may be a time for specialists (e.g., someone from the district attorney's office, a Women for Sobriety representative, or a local activist) to meet with the group, for resources to be shared by those within and from outside of the group, and for emergency plans to be developed. Psychodrama is suggested, as well as role-play, writing letters, and practicing what they want to say to significant others. Action work can often include networking with other groups, voting, and lobbying.

We like the model presented by Wood and Middleman (1992) and add that many women are able to engage in action with positive results without having to participate in a support or consciousness-raising component of a group. Projects such as The Clothesline Project may be a way for women to become involved in expressive, healing actions regardless of prior or current group participation. The Clothesline Project is a visual display of shirts, designed by survivors or her loved ones, to bear witness to violence against women and to help the healing process through creating personal tributes.

Ten Things Anyone Can Do to Help

1. The next time you see or hear a woman being battered, call the police.
2. Volunteer for a battered women's shelter.
3. Start a clothesline project in your community.
4. Ask your religious leader to obtain training in battering.
5. End violence, including spanking, in your own home.
6. Every time a candidate for public office sponsors a forum, ask what the candidate is proposing to help battered women.
7. Listen to and support women who are being battered.
8. Give a talk on homophobia to your local shelter staff.
9. Donate antiracist and antisexist books to your local shelter.
10. Ask a battered woman how you can help!

PRACTICE IN THE COMMUNITY

Domestic violence is a worldwide problem. This section highlights some of the many community efforts occurring around the world with the purpose of ending violence against women. In 1993, a United Nations report was issued, detailing the international problem of violence experienced by women in the home. This report gives numerous examples of institutional and grassroots efforts around the world. A few of these efforts are listed here.

- In Bangladesh and India, women use street theater, puppet shows, and songs to raise public awareness.
- In Indonesia, Argentina, and the Dominican Republic, comic books have been produced.
- The University of Buenos Aires offers a postgraduate training program in family violence. Similar programs are offered in Costa Rica and at the University of El Salvador.
- Volunteer networks in Canada are assisting with transportation for women living in rural communities.
- In China, the government displays information for victims on city bulletin boards.
- In Papua New Guinea, a reggae song "Noken Paitim Meri" ("Do Not Hit Your Wife") has become popular.

Most U.S. states have a council or network on family violence, which is often actively working on community education and legislative strategies. For example, the Texas Council on Family Violence has an annual conference, which provides excellent educational programs for persons interested in learning more about batterers, women who are battered, working with children who are battered, grant writing, and legislative initiatives. They have also produced a film about domestic violence and the workplace, which shows how domestic violence affects battered women when they are at work and which suggests steps that can be taken to safeguard employees who are being battered or stalked. Such initiatives on state and local levels can enhance social workers formal education. Also, many organizations serving battered women are seeking volunteers, trainers, and paid employees.

In addition to efforts launched to educate and intervene with adult women who have been battered, many communities have begun programs aimed at preventing violence through working with children to encourage future generations to develop skills and values to resolve conflict nonviolently. Gamache and Snapp (1995) have highlighted six common strategies used to address the prevention of violence with children:

1. *Peacemakers*—These programs highlight famous peacemakers as role models (Dr. Martin Luther King, Mohandas Gandhi, Mother Teresa) and encourage compassion and responsibility for people globally.
2. *Affective education*—These programs focus on self-esteem, labeling feelings, and empathizing with others.
3. *Skills education*—Often, the skills taught in such programs include assertiveness, self-control, conflict resolution, and problem solving.
4. *Values education*—The promotion of caring, trust, respect, positive family interactions, and responsibility are often core themes promoted in values-education programs.
5. *Family life education*—Preparing students for parenting and partnership responsibili-

ties are often the focus of these groups or classes, with experiential learning opportunities often built in.

6. *Violence education*—Violence-education programs often have the goal of counteracting the numbing that comes from living in a violent culture. Participants are often helped to see the images and actual violent acts that surround them—in movies, on MTV, in videogames, and on the playground.

Worldwide, efforts are being undertaken to end violence in the home. Outreach efforts to adult women and men, as well as to children, are important ingredients to making the family place of respect, safety, and stability.

PRACTICE WITH WOMEN OF COLOR AND LESBIAN WOMEN

As noted in the issues section, theories on battering have come under criticism for what Moore (1995) described as "gender essentialism." This concept suggests that some feminists believe that gender should be the unifying thread when looking at women's experiences of partner violence. This color-blind approach has hindered the knowledge and skill base for working with women of color and lesbian women. The following sections address issues for consideration with Latina, African-American, Asian-American, and lesbian women.

Latinas

Zambrano (1985, p. 8) posed the following questions and statements for Latinas to consider:

- ¿Estás tú en una relación donde hay abuso?
- ¿Tiene miedo al hombre con quien vive?
- Cuando no más me pegaba a mí, no estaba tan mal, pero ahora le pega a los niños.

- Estoy cansada de ser humillada en frente de la gente.
- La única manera de parar la violencia es matarlo.
- No puedo soportar otra golpiza, la próxima vez, me voy a morir.
- Nunca me había forzado a tener relaciones sexuales, ahora me amenaza y me asalta brutalmente.
- Quiero sentirme segura en mi propia casa.

Zambrano (1985, p. 225) has reminded us that the Latina suffers double discrimination and that we *must* have bilingual and bicultural staff members available for "Puertorriqueña, Domincana, Mexicana, Guatemalteca, Salvadoreña, Cubana, and Chicana" women. She noted that divorce is not acceptable in many Latino communities and that it may take time for a Latina who is being battered to make a decision to leave her partner. She also wrote, "Latinos are not accustomed to revealing their feelings to outsiders. . . . The battered Latina may find it difficult to express herself at first or may not confide one hundred percent of what is going on. Be patient. It is best that you gain her confidence before you start questioning her" (p. 227).

Although whole groups of people are often lumped together under the rhetoric of "Hispanic," differences between groups are often wide and have important implications. Castillo makes this point:

> Among Latino/as in the United States today there is a universe of difference. There is a universe of difference, for example, between the experience of the Cuban man who arrived in the United States as a child with his parents after feeling Castro's revolution and the Puerto Rican woman who is a third generation single mother on the Lower East Side. There is a universe of difference between the young Mexican American aspiring to be an actor in Hollywood in the nineties and the community organizer working for rent control for the last ten years in San Francisco, although both may be

> sons of farmworkers. . . . There is a universe of differences among all of these individuals, yet Anglo society says they all belong to the same ethnic group: Hispanic. (Castillo, 1994, p. 29)

This universe of difference is essential to remember, especially during discussions on specific practice approaches to take with any population, in this case with Latinas who have been battered. While it would be stereotypical and incorrect to assume that Latinas presenting themselves for battered women services may not fully disclose their situation or may be undocumented Zambrano cautioned not to immediately ask questions about the woman's citizenship status, as this line of questioning may frighten the woman who *is* undocumented. This issue is critical in the current environment, given the hostility being shown toward documented and undocumented immigrants alike in the United States. Zambrano suggested that when presenting legal and other options to battered women, social workers should explain the options for all women, including the specific options available for undocumented women. An undocumented woman has often been threatened with deportation by her abuser, such a threat is a control mechanism to keep the battered woman trapped (Davidson, 1994). Further, using the legal system for remedy may be an unfamiliar concept for a woman has come from a country with a judiciary that was "an arm of a repressive government [in which] persons who prevail in court are persons with the most money and the strongest connection with the government" (Davidson, 1994, p. 19), or even for a woman who has grown up in the United States, who has seen injustice in law enforcement and judicial systems based on race, ethnicity, and social class.

Flores-Ortiz (1993) clearly noted that the goal of treatment for Latino families is "to seek in the culture of the family resources and solutions to end the violence, the exploitation, and the pain" (p. 176). She has felt that to provide a culturally integrated model of treatment, an agency must make a commitment to addressing the individual and collective needs of the whole family. The first critical step toward this goal is to conduct a lethality assessment. If fatal risk is present, then separation is encouraged and is presented as an effort to protect everyone and as a way to save the family. Next, an evaluation is necessary, which includes a psychological evaluation of all family members and an assessment of cultural needs (national origin and history of and reasons for migration).

Flores-Ortiz (1993) suggested these therapeutic goals: "(1) to stop the violence and victimization, (2) [to] learn new ways of problem solving, and (3) to examine critically the cultural, social, and political roots of their violence" (p. 178); such goals can be reached through gender-specific group therapy, which is primarily psychoeducational, followed by group or individual therapy focusing on connecting the prior learning to a feeling level. These phases of treatment (often lasting 7–10 months) can then, Flores-Ortiz suggested, be followed by brief (10 sessions) family or couple therapy. Intergenerational family therapy, modified by Bernal and Flores-Ortiz, for Latinos, "is resource based and attempts to foster a dialogue in the family where issues of trust, loyalty, respect and justice can be addressed" (p. 181). While we do not advocate couples therapy, Flores-Ortiz's plan for a 7- to 10-month separation, with all family members participating in individual therapy may be sound. Obviously, if the abuser has not participated in counseling or has not made substantial progress toward ending violence and abuse, then couples therapy would not be recommended. However, after this length of separation and treatment, with careful attention to safety and individual check-in safety points built in for the woman, couples therapy may be useful.

Gutierrez and Ortega (1991) expressed the view that intragroup interaction can be an important empowerment process and that groups are a great environment in which to explore new attitudes, as well as possibilities for social change. Gutierrez and Ortega continued, noting that "contact with other Latinos, from different subgroups, can provide a means for perceiving common cultural and political interests. . . . As these beliefs become more important to the individual, they will have a greater impact on subsequent attitudes, behaviors, and the empowerment process" (p. 27). (See Figure 9.4 for a Power and Control Wheel in Spanish.)

African-American Women

Villarosa (1994) began a discussion on battering in the AA community by noting,

> *Battering is serious business, but all too often in our community it's a laughing matter. We spent years cracking up at Redd Foxx on Sanford and Son as he chased Aunt Esther around the room threatening her with a fat lip. We snap our fingers to old blues songs where singers boast of using guns to dispose of unfaithful women. And we think nothing of dancing to rappers who brag about offing bitches and hos. . . .*
>
> *Many others swallowed Shahrazad Ali's advice in her book* The Blackman's Guide to Understanding the Blackwoman, *in which she recommends the use of an open-handed slap to the mouth as a disciplinary tool to tame wayward women. (p. 504)*

Collins (1991) framed the issue of the battering of women in African-American families to include race, gender, and class oppression. Collins suggested, "An Afrocentric feminist analysis of abuse generally, and domestic violence in particular, must avoid excusing abuse as an inevitable consequence of the racism Black men experience (p. 188)." First, however, Collins reminded readers of "the great love Black women feel for Black men" (Collins, 1990, p. 183). She illustrated this message by asking us to examine slave narratives, love poems, and African-American women's music so that we can more fully understand the relationship between African-American men and

FIGURE 9.4 Power and Control Wheel and Equality Wheel

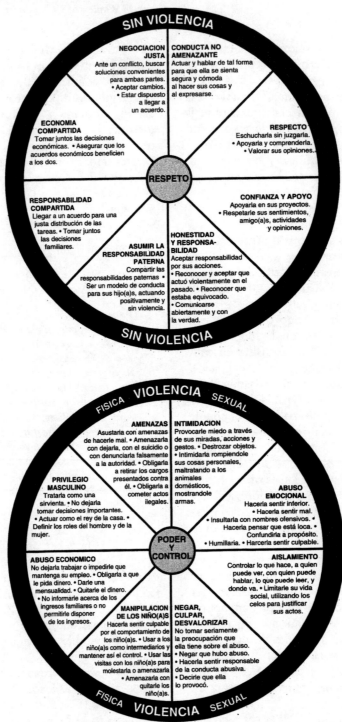

For Spanish-speaking women, this Power and Control Wheel and Equality Wheel was developed for the Boston Healthy Start Initiative by the Domestic Abuse Intervention project.

women. White (1985/1994) noted that because African-American women live in the same racist environment as African-American men do that women "cannot help but be sympathetic to what they suffer. . . . Though we have surely been divided as African-American men and women, our mutual suffering has prevented us from completely turning our backs on each other" (p. 22).

Collins (1991) has acknowledged that African-American women, such as Alice Walker and Ntozake Shange, who break the conspiracy of silence (p. 187) have, at times, been censured.

White (1985/1994) cautioned African-American women to leave counseling if the counselor suggests any of the following:

> *Under no circumstance should you continue to see a counselor who tells you violence is a natural part of Black life; who says you provoked your partner; who does not believe you are in serious danger when you say you are; who uses any kind of racial slur; who forces you to try counseling techniques that make you uncomfortable; or who suggests you relieve the stress in your life with alcohol, drugs or increased sexual activity. (p. 62)*

White (1985/1994) has encouraged the use of support groups—preferably a support group comprising only African-American women. She suggested that support groups can help a woman regain her self-esteem, humor, and strength. "Likewise, seeing other Black women cry and express their vulnerabilities can free you to let down your defenses and stop being the 'strong black woman'" (p. 65). White also addressed the role that the African-American church has had in the lives of many African-American women. White has cautioned that many African-American (as well as European-American) clerics have not yet received adequate training on issues related to battered women. White reported one woman's experience with her pastor, who said to her, "Jesus dropped the charges, so why

can't you?" (p. 72). Given that many religious institutions have not yet adequately addressed issues related to violence in families, White suggested, "it is perhaps best for you to remember that scriptures can be interpreted in many ways and that a family in which there is constant upheaval, violence and abuse is not the 'holy family' your pastor may urge you to 'save'" (p. 73).

Soraya Coley and Joyce Beckett (1988) examined practice issues that working with African-American battered women may present. They suggested that African-American women may be less likely to seek shelter services; therefore, more outreach services are needed within the African-American community—such as with black churches, beauty shops, organizations, and community centers. Further, organizational structures need to reflect the diversity of the community being served. Coley and Beckett wrote, "From boards and committees to staff positions, multiethnic perspectives are needed to develop policies, procedures, and programs that encompass cultural differences" (p. 485). The physical environment of a shelter is also critical to examine. Coley and Beckett have stressed the importance of having toys, dolls, books, adult reading materials, posters, and pictures that reflect the diversity of the shelter residents and suggest that black churches and organizations might help donate materials directed to an African-American constituent group. Lockhart and White (1989) have reminded us to examine social-class issues when addressing issues related to women who are battered. Their research, from a southeastern city, found that African-American middle-class women experienced more violence than did lower-income or upper-income African-American women. Stereotypes abound that low-income women are those most abused, and this research reminds us to commit outreach resources to all social-class communities.

Richie (1996) did intensive interviewing with African-American battered women who were imprisoned. Her analysis of gender entrapment is acutely sensitive to issues of class and race, and it includes perspectives from women who may not normally be included in discussions on battered women (i.e., women who have been arrested on drug, prostitution, and other charges related to illegal activities). She framed her analysis to offer a much-needed perspective, which suggests that the means for survival of battering takes many forms, including illegal activity, and that these women deserve our concern and assistance, and they must be included in theory building. At a 1996 keynote address at the Texas Council on Family Violence, Richie told of African-American women who asked friends, family members, or attorneys to bring them cash, in quarters, to court hearings in order to purchase Lifesaver candy. These battered women then proceeded to eat rolls and rolls of lifesavers until tears filled their eyes. Why? So they could appear sad on the witness stand as they spoke of the abuse they had survived instead of appearing as furious as they felt. This example, told by Richie, speaks to the necessity of creating theory that is inclusive of the experiences of all women—not just the women whose behavior current theories are able to explain or predict.

Asian-American Women

Huisman (1996) interviewed 18 service providers whose clientele included battered Asian-American women and found several needs specific to Asian-American women which must be addressed. A major constraint Huisman reported was language. Because of the number of different languages represented by the term *Asian,* many programs do not have staff members or translators available to address the diversity of Asian-American communities. Often, when translators were used by program personnel, as reported in Huisman's article, women felt some mistrust of the translators, who did not understand the dy-

namics of batterers. In addition, language barriers limit the Asian-American woman's access to information, which often exacerbates her fear.

Another barrier facing many Asian-American women is fear of deportation and of the U.S. legal system. With the passage of the Violence Against Women Act in 1994, many advocates hope that immigrant Asian-American women's fear of deportation can be assuaged, yet the provisions of the act are so complex that an attorney or immigration expert may be needed to determine individual women's status. Finally, cultural constraints also emerge, which can affect battered Asian-American women, such as fear of ostracism or of losing face and religious beliefs ("paying dues for past lives, belief in fate and destiny, belief that suffering is virtuous" (Huisman, 1996, p. 278).

Dasgupta and Warrier (1996) conducted intensive interviews with 12 college educated, professional Indian-American women who had been battered. These research participants exemplified many of the issues outlined by Huisman (1996). Dasgupta and Warrier wrote, "irrespective of age, religion, restrictiveness of parents, and location of childhood development, each woman in this sample stated that [she] had unconsciously internalized the belief that a wife is secondary to her husband" (p. 246). One of the study participants spoke of her romanticized idea of marriage, "For me, India and its traditions were completely glorified. I wanted to marry an Indian man, because then the marriage would last for ever and ever" (p. 248). These women reported economic control and limitations placed on their mobility, as well as physical abuse. Physical abuse was noted to escalate when a woman would challenge her husband's authority or would assert her own autonomy. Fear of being ostracized was a theme that prevented these women from talking of abuse to members of the Indian-American community and also a factor keeping women in their marriages. Uncertainty about legal affairs was also noted, including fear that the husband would automatically gain custody of children. Class issues also emerged, as many of the women felt pressure to maintain their economic status, even in the face of gender subordination.

Dasgupta and Warrier (1996) have suggested,

> Although Asian Indian immigrants have been celebrated in this country as a "model minority," our experiences of working within the community contradict this simplistic perception of the group. It is our contention that the community maintains its façade of tranquility and success by disowning problems that emerge within it. . . . A case in point is the denial of wife abuse in our community. This refusal to acknowledge the existence of woman abuse, along with our socialization into a restrictive women's role and status as immigrants, complicates the Asian Indian women's experience of abuse within the family. (pp. 253–254)

Lesbian Women

Over the years, Suzanne Pharr (1986), a former chairperson of the National Coalition Against Domestic Violence (NCADV) Lesbian Task Force, has been frequently asked questions about battering in lesbian communities. The following are three frequent questions she is asked and her responses (pp. 203–204):

Question 1. Don't you think that with women the violence is more often mutual?

Answer 1: There are those who believe in mutual battering, both among lesbians and non-lesbians. I am not among them. When one works with the complexity of relationships and the layers of truth in a life, one sees the surfacing of an imbalance of power in violent relationships, a greater need or will or ability to

dominate and control on the part of one partner. To deny this difference is to trivialize the battering or to risk adding to the disempowerment of the abused.

Question 2: Should we work with the battered lesbian and her abuser together?

Answer 2: Those people working with battered women who believe in putting the battered woman and the abuser (and often the sexually abused child) in the same room together for therapy somehow believe that there is equal power in the world, and these same people, when working with battered lesbians, will want the abused and the abuser to sit down together. This arrangement always has seemed to me to place the relationship above the importance of the individual and the empowerment of the abused woman.

Question 3: Should we assume the violence is the same as heterosexual violence with the same dynamics?

Answer 3: There is an important difference between the battered lesbian and the battered non-lesbian: the battered non-lesbian experiences the violence within the context of a misogynist world; the lesbian experiences violence within the context of a world that is not only woman-hating but is also homophobic. And that is a great difference.

The isolation of lesbians who are battered is a treatment issue that needs serious attention. Lobel (1986) noted that lesbians are less likely than heterosexual women to turn to their families for support. Two reasons were suggested: (1) It would be difficult for a closeted lesbian to confide in her parents that her partner (female) is physically harming her; and (2) some women who are *out* (open about their sexual orientation) to family members may fear that disclosure of abuse will reinforce their family members' negative stereotypes about the relationship and the lifestyle the woman may have been defending and educating their families about (Hammond, 1986). Similarly, Benowitz (1986) suggested, "We fear fueling society's hatred and myths by speaking openly about lesbian battering. We fear hostile responses from police, courts, shelters, or therapists" (p. 200). Hammond (1986) has drawn our attention to the support that many lesbian women draw from the lesbian community, noting that the partners often share close friends. The victim may fear that disclosure will isolate her, should mutual friends express disbelief or minimize the abuse. Other lesbian women (for example, rural women and some closeted women) are isolated from a lesbian community and fear that by confronting the violence, they will be left entirely alone (Hammond, 1986).

Many lesbian feminists "take pride in our strength and fortitude as individuals, and in our ability to survive and grow even stronger. It is hard for our friends to see us, strong and tough-minded women that we are, as victims of abuse from partners. . . . It is hard for us to acknowledge that a woman we love is capable of being cruel, violent, and brutal" (Hammond, 1986, p. 195). Morrow and Hawxhurst (1989) noted that a common myth is that feminist lesbians do not batter. Renzetti (1992) found that counselors of lesbians were interested in changing the victim, such as by finding out how she provoked the violence, by focusing blame on the victim's substance use or abuse, or by examining codependency issues. The women who had sought counseling in Renzetti's study were dissatisfied with the "counselor's denial that battering was a serious problem in the relationship" (p. 99).

Screening for group membership is important for the population of battered lesbians. NiCarthy, Merriam, and Coffman (1984) addressed this issue by noting that minimally, the group facilitator should inquire whether any couples are present and that facilitators may need screening procedures to ensure that abusers do not also attend the group sessions. An abuser may feel she is *the* victim and may come to the group, seeking services. Obviously, the lesbian who

is being battered will have her safety jeopardized in such a situation.

Social workers have a responsibility to ensure that outreach and community education efforts include strategies to reach out to lesbian women and to make resources available and comfortable for lesbian victims. As Morrow and Hawxhurst (1989) suggested, "the therapist may need to perform advocacy functions, such as in-service training to shelter staffs, identification of 'safe houses' within the lesbian community, or other innovative activities" (p. 61). In addition, staff members often need to be retrained to use gender-neutral terms for identifying the partner of the victim. To assume that the partner is a "he" would be heterosexist bias and may make it harder for a lesbian who has been battered to disclose the true nature of her situation with the social worker.

POLICY FOR CHANGE

Despite social work's historical commitment to confronting injustice on all ecological levels, too often, change efforts designed to assist women who are battered have been limited to the intra- and interpersonal realm. The following discussion highlights policy arenas that are relevant to creating change for battered women and for their children.

On September 13, 1994, the *Violence Against Women Act* was signed into law (Public Law 103-322). The Violence Against Women Act mandates interstate enforcement of protective orders; establishes a national hotline; and provides training for state and federal judges. It also makes gender-motivated violence a civil rights violation (National Coalition Against Domestic Violence, January/February, 1995). This act required 4 years of intense lobbying to pass. Social workers need to monitor the implementation process to ensure that the act lives up to its promise.

According to the National Coalition Against Domestic Violence (April, 1995), a congressional survey found that many insurance companies discriminate against women who have been battered; that is, many companies consider domestic violence a preexisting health-related condition and therefore deny women *health coverage.* In 1995, legislation sponsored by Representative Schumer and Senator Wellstone was proposed, which would prohibit this type of practice by insurance companies. Social workers need to be vigilant to ensure that discriminatory practices such as this one are stopped and must advocate for women who have been harmed by this practice.

Provisions in state or national policies that limit the number of times a woman can receive *AFDC* or *TANF* over a lifetime are of grave concern for those committed to helping women who have been abused. Women often leave the abusive partner numerous times before they are able to finally leave or escape. AFDC and TANF offer critical life-support systems for some mothers and their children fleeing from violence. Further, requirements that force recipients to reveal paternity for child-support enforcement reasons can endanger a women who is attempting to escape violence. As the National Coalition Against Domestic Violence (1995, March) suggested, "Urge your representatives to support reforms to the welfare system that offer real opportunities and provide the support families need to achieve self-sufficiency (p. 2).

Many states and localities now have *preferred-arrest policies.* These policies suggest to police that making an arrest is the preferred response to a report from a battered person (Yegidis & Renzy, 1994). Yegidis and Renzy found that of 51 situations in which Floridian women in their study had been battered and had had police intervention, only 12 arrests were made. Of the 51 battered Floridian women, only 8 knew of the police policy of preferred arrest. Social workers need to educate their clients about preferred-arrest policies, as "a better-informed constituency will make demands on the police for a higher quality of intervention than is currently available" (p. 69). Yegidis and Renzy (1994) and Hirschel and Hutchison (1991) suggested that training is a critical element of ensuring the implementation of preferred-arrest policies. Police officers' work, in many ways like the work of social workers, involves a great deal of discretion in decision making. Training designed to sensitize officers to victim issues, as well as to the preferred-arrest policy itself, can move officers to more carefully consider the arrest option (Hirschel & Hutchison, 1991). As more states are adopting preferred-arrest or mandatory-arrest policies, social workers must be ever so vigilant to simultaneously provide officers with training on homophobia, classism, and racism. We must guard against having these policies becoming mandatory for low-income men of color, while men of race or class privilege continue to be served by the current system (i.e., no arrest). Further, laws need to include cohabitation and same-sex partners as eligible households for the arrest policy. (See Berk & Newton, 1985, Sherman & Berk, 1984; Stark, 1990 for more discussion and research findings on deterrent effects of arrest.)

Similarly, *alternatives to incarceration* may be preferred by some women who have been battered. While there are many good reasons for incarceration, the reality is that the courts are not consistently sending clear messages about assaults on intimate partners (Other forms of sentencing . . . , 1996). Tolman, a social work professor at the University of Michigan, was quoted as noting that many women who have been battered rely on the income of the batterer. While some people may see alternatives to incarceration as being easy on offenders, for some battered women, it would be a preferred alternative.

Saunders (1994) succinctly stated, "Joint custody should rarely be recommended in domestic violence cases. Conditions for visitation should be determined by the types of risk factors in the men who batter and their willingness to complete specialized treatment for physical abuse" (p. 56). A critical factor for a woman who has been battered is her safety and the safety of her child (or children). Most *child-custody decisions,* but especially joint-custody decisions, require that the battered woman continue to have contact with the person who has abused her. As social workers, we must critically assess safety issues for the children and for the woman. Supervised visitation should be considered as one possible alternative. Saunders noted, "Supervised visitation may provide important father–child contact that prevents idealization of the absent father" (p. 56).

Agencies have policies and practices that can either support or harm women clients who have been or are being battered. Agency staff members must assess each component of their program to ensure that the needs of women and children are being addressed. For example, do agency billing practices jeopardize the safety of a woman who is being battered? If the woman is seeing a social worker without the knowledge of her partner, a bill sent to her home may risk her safety. Do agency staff members routinely call to remind people of their appointments? Again, this practice involves a safety issue. Is the waiting room child friendly? Do social history and assessment forms include coverage of emotional, sexual, and physical violence, as well as economic controls? Have agency staff members had training on PTSD? Are the phone numbers of local shelters posted in visible places? Does the agency have a Teletype Device for the Deaf (TDD) so that deaf women can contact a social worker? Does the agency staff and its board of directors reflect the diversity of the community and include formerly battered women?

Resources

National Domestic Violence Hotline
(800) 799-SAFE (7233)
(800) 787-3224 (TDD)

Asian Women's Shelter
San Francisco
(415) 731-7100

New York Asian Women's Center
(212) 732-5200

National Coalition Against Domestic Violence
(303) 839-1852

Family Violence Prevention Fund
(415) 821-4553

National Clearinghouse for the Defense of Battered Women
(215) 351-0010

The Clothesline Project
(508) 385-7004

SUMMARY

The problems associated with battering cut across all practice spheres and, therefore, require a commitment from all levels of practice (including policy practice)—from the individual worker in her or his office contracting with a client to a community group to international policy set forth by the United Nations. Although the literature on battering has proliferated in recent years, there is still tremendous work to be done. This work includes more careful analysis of battering in lesbian relationships and violence directed toward migrant workers, women used in systems of prostitution, immigrant women, and women of color. There is no one solution for ending violence against intimate partners, yet there are important roles social workers can play at all system levels, and we encourage social workers to make a commitment to visualize the world without domestic violence and then to take the steps needed to end violence in our individual and collective lives.

REFERENCES

Adams, D. (1988). Treatment models of men who batter: A profeminist analysis. In K. Yllo & M. Bograd (Eds.), *Feminist perspectives on wife abuse* (pp. 176–199). Newbury Park, CA: Sage Publications.

Anonymous. (1995). Violence against women on college campuses. *Teen Voices, 3,* 18–20.

Arroyo, W., & Eth, S. (1995). Assessment following violence-witnessing trauma. In E. Peled, P. Jaffe, & J. Edelson (Eds.), *Ending the cycle of violence: Community responses to children of battered women* (pp. 27–42). Thousand Oaks, CA: Sage.

Avis, J. (1992). Where are all the family therapists? Abuse and violence within families and family therapy's response. *Journal of Marital and Family Therapy, 18,* 225–232.

Bachman, R., & Saltzman, L. (1995, August). Violence against women: Estimates from the redesigned survey. *Bureau of Justice Statistics: Special Report.* Washington DC: U.S. Department of Justice.

Ball, P., & Wyman, E. (1977–1978). Battered wives and powerlessness: What can counselors do? *Victimology, 2,* 545–552.

Benowitz, M. (1986). How homophobia affects lesbians' response to violence in lesbian relationships. In K. Lobel (Ed.) *Naming the violence* (pp. 198–201). Seattle, WA: Seal Press.

Benson, C. (1992). Judiciary committee report documents domestic violence. *The Feminist Majority Report, 4,* p. 4.

Berk, R. & Newton, P. (1985). Does arrest really deter wife battery. *American Sociological Review, 50,* 253–262.

Bhattaharjee. (1992). Cited in Dasgupta & Warrier.

Bograd, M. (1984). Family systems approaches to wife battering: A feminist critique. *American Journal of Orthopsychiatry, 54,* 558–568.

Bograd, M. (1992). Values in conflict: Challenges to family therapists' thinking. *Journal of Marital and Family Therapy, 18,* 245–256.

Bowker, L. (1983). Beating wife-beating. Lexington, MA: Health.

Bowker, L. H. (1993). A battered woman's problems are social, not psychological. In R. Gelles & Donileen Loseke (Eds.), *Current controversies on family violence* (pp. 154–165). Newbury Park, CA: Sage Publications.

Bowker, L., Arbitell, M., & McFerron, J. R. (1988). On the relationship between wife beating and child abuse. In R. Gelles & Donileen Loseke (Eds.), *Current controversies on family violence* (pp. 133–153). Newbury Park, CA: Sage Publications.

Browne, A. (1993). Violence against women by male partners: Prevalence, outcomes, and policy implications. *American Psychologist, 48,* 1077–1087.

Burleson, A. B. (1989). Speech at crime victim's memorial. FBW Task Force Newsletter, July. (Available from FBWTF, Box 530104, Austin, TX 78753.)

Campbell, J. (Ed.). (1995). *Assessing dangerousness.* Newbury Park, CA: Sage Publications.

Coley, S., & Beckett, J. (1988, October). Black battered women: Practice issues. *Social Casework,* pp. 483–490.

Castillo, A. (1994). Massacre of the dreamers. New York: Plume.

Collins, P. (1991). *Black feminist thought.* New York: Routledge.

Dasgupta, S., & Warrier, S. (1996). In the footsteps of "Arundhati." *Violence Against Women, 2,* 238–259.

David, D., & Brannon, R. (Eds.). (1976). *The forty-nine percent majority: The male sex role.* Reading, MA: Addison-Wesley.

Davidson, H. (1994). *The impact of domestic violence on children: A report to the president of the American Bar Association.* (Available from the American Bar Association Center on Children and the Laws, Washington D.C., 1-202-331-4086).

Davis, L. V., & Srinivasan, M. (1995). Listening to the voices of battered women: What helps them escape violence. *Affilia, 10,* 49–69.

Dworkin, A. (1993). *Letters from a war zone.* Brooklyn, NY: Lawrence Hill Books.

Edleson, J., & Tolman, R. (1992). *Intervention for men who batter: An ecological approach.* Newbury Park, CA: Sage.

Ellman, B., & Basen-Engquist, J. (October, 1994). Battered women as the focus. Presented at the 13th Annual Family Violence Conference, October 5–7, 1994, Austin, TX. (Audio tape available from Gem Tapes, 4801 24th St., Lubbock, TX 79407. 1-800-383-5567).

Finkelhor, D., & Yllo, K. (1985). *License to rape: Sexual abuse of wives.* New York: Holt, Rinehart and Winston.

Flores-Ortiz, Y. (1993). La mujer y la violencia: A culturally based model for the understanding and treatment of domestic violence in Chicano/Latina communities. In N. Alarcon, R. Castro, E. Perez, B. Pesquera, A. Riddell, & P. Zavella (Eds.), *Chicana critical issues* (pp. 169–182). Berkeley, CA: Third Woman Press.

Follingstad, D., Laughlin, J., Polek, D., Rutledge, L., & Hause, E. (1991). Identification of patterns of wife abuse. *Journal of Interpersonal Violence, 6,* 187–204.

Follingstad, D., Rutledge, L., Berg, B., Hause, E., & Polek, D. (1991). The role of emotional abuse in physically abusive relationships. *Journal of Family Violence, 2,* 107–120.

Fortune, M., & Wood, F. (1988). The Center for the Prevention of Sexual and Domestic Violence: A study in applied feminist theology and ethics. *Journal of Feminist Studies in Religion, 4,* 115–122.

Frieze, I., & Browne, A. (1989). Violence in marriage. In L. Ohlin & M. Tony (Eds.), *Family violence* (p. x). Chicago: University of Chicago Press.

Gamache, D., & Snapp, S. (1995). Teach your children well: Elementary schools and violence prevention. In E. Peled, P. Jaffe, and J. Edelson (Eds.) *Ending the cycle of violence* (pp. 209–231). Thousand Oaks, CA: Sage.

Golden, G., & Frank, P. (1994). When 50-50 isn't fair: The case against couple counseling in domestic abuse. *Social Work, 39,* 636–638.

Goldner, V. (1992, March/April). Making room for both/and. *Networker,* pp. 55–61.

Gondolf, E. (1989). *Man against woman: What every woman should know about violent men.* Bradenton, FL: Human Services Institute.

Gondolf, E., & Fisher, E. (1988). *Battered women as survivors.* New York: Lexington Books.

Goodrich, T., Rampage, C., Ellman, B., & Halstead, K. (1988). *Feminist family therapy.* New York: W.W. Norton.

Gutierrez, L., & Ortega, R. (1991). Developing methods to empower Latinos: The importance of groups. *Social Work with Groups, 14,* 23–43.

Hammond, N. (1986). Lesbian victims and the reluctance to identify abuse. In K. Lobel (Ed.), *Naming the violence: Speaking out about lesbian battering* (pp. 190–197). Seattle: Seal Press.

Harlow, C. (1991). Female victims of violent crime. *Bureau of Justice Statistics.* Washington, DC: U.S. Department of Justice.

Herman, J. L. (1992). *Trauma and recovery.* New York: Basic Books.

Hirschel, J. D., & Hutchison, I. (1991). Police preferred-arrest policies. In M. Steinman (Ed.), *Woman battering: Policy responses* (pp. 49–72). Cincinnati, OH: Anderson Publishing.

Holtzworth-Munroe, A., & Stuart, G. (1994). Typologies of male batterers: Three subtypes and the differences among them. *Psychological Bulletin, 116,* 476–497.

hooks, b. (1989). *Talking back.* Boston: South End Press.

Huisman, K. (1996). Wife battering in Asian American communities. *Violence Against Women, 2,* 260–283.

Jaffe, P., Wolfe, D., & Wilson, S. K. (1990). *Children of battered women.* Newbury Park, CA: Sage.

Jones, A. (1991). Introduction. In D. Ferrato, *Living with the enemy* (pp. 12–15). New York: Aperture Foundation.

Kilgore, N. (1992). *Sourcebook for working with battered women.* Volcano, CA: Volcano Press.

Lindsey, M., McBride, R., & Platt, C. (1993). *Amend: Philosophy and curriculum for treating batterers.* Littleton, CO: Gylantic Publishing.

Lobel, K. (1986). (Ed.) *Naming the violence: Speaking out about lesbian battering.* Seattle, WA: Seal Press.

Lockhart, L., & White, B. (1989). Understanding marital violence in the black community. *Journal of Interpersonal Violence, 4,* 421–436.

Long, D. (1987). Working with men who batter. In M. Sher, M. Stevens, G. Good, & G. Eichenfeld (Eds.), *Handbook of counseling and psychotherapy with men* (pp. 305–320). Beverly Hills: Sage.

Miedzian, M. (1995). Learning to be violent. In E. Peled, P. Jaffe, & J. Edelson (Eds.), *Ending the cycle of violence: Community responses to children of battered women* (pp. 10–26). Thousand Oaks, CA: Sage.

Moltz, D. (1992). Abuse and violence: The dark side of the family. *Journal of Marital and Family Therapy, 18,* 223.

Moore, S. (1995). Battered Woman Syndrome. Selling the shadow to support the substance. *Quarterly,* summer 10–13.

Morrow, S., & Hawxhurst, D. (1989). Lesbian partner abuse: Implications for therapists. *Journal of Counseling and Development, 68,* 58–62.

National Coalition Against Domestic Violence. (1995, January/February.) Update. (Available from NCADV, P.O. Box 18749, Denver, CO 80218. 1-303-839-1852.)

National Coalition Against Domestic Violence (1995, March). *Welfare reform will put battered women at greater risk.* (Available from NCADV, P.O. Box 34103, Washington, D.C. 20043-4103.)

National Coalition Against Domestic Violence (1995, April). *H.R. 1191 and S. 524 victims of abuse access to health insurance act.* (Available from NCADV, P.O. Box 34103, Washington, D.C. 20043-4103.)

NiCarthy, G., Merriam, K., & Coffman, S. (1984). *Talking it out: A guide to groups for abused women.* Seattle: Seal Press.

Other forms of sentencing are suggested for batterers. (1996, October). *Houston Chronicle,* p. 12F (WN/Chicago Tribune).

Pence, E. (1988). Working with battered women: From personal crisis to social change. Presentation at the Battered Women and Justice Conference, St. Louis, Missouri. Conference sponsored by the Women's Self-Help Center, St. Louis, MO.

Pharr, S. (1986). Two workshops on homophobia. In K. Lobel, *Naming the violence: Speaking out about lesbian battering* (pp. 202–222). Seattle: Seal Press.

Reinert, P. (1995). JP regrets his release of suspect. *Houston Chronicle,* p. 33A.

Renzetti, C. (1992). *Violent betrayals: Partner abuse in lesbian relationships.* Newbury Park, CA: Sage.

Richie, B. (1996). *Compelled to crime: The gender entrapment of battered black women.* New York: Routledge.

Rosewater, L. (1988). Battered or schizophrenic? Psychological test can't tell. In K. Yllo & M. Bograd (Eds.), *Feminist perspectives on wife abuse* (pp. 200–217). Newbury Park, CA: Sage.

Roy, M. (1988). *Children in the crossfire: Violence in the home—How does it affect our children?* Deerfield Beach, FL: Health Communication.

Saunders, D. (1994). Child custody decisions in families experiencing woman abuse. *Social Work, 39,* 51–59.

Shepard, M. (1991). Feminist practice principles for social work intervention in wife abuse. *Affilia, 6,* 87–93.

Shepard, M., & Pence, E. (1988). The effects of battering on the employment status of women. *Affilia, 3,* 55–61.

Sherman, L. & Berk, R. (1984). The Minneapolis domestic violence experiment. *Police Foundation Reports,* pp. 1–7. (Available from Police Foundation, 1909 K St. NW, Suite 400, Washington, D.C. 20006).

Sonkin, D., Martin, D., & Walker, L. (1985). *The male batterer.* New York: Springer Publishing.

Stacey, W., & Shupe, A. (1983). *The family secret: Domestic violence in America.* Boston: Beacon.

Stark, E. (1993). Rethinking homicide: Violence, race, and the politics of gender. *International Journal of Health Services, 20,* 21.

Stets, J., & Straus, M. (1989). The marriage license as a hitting license: A comparison of assaults in dating, cohabiting, and married couples. *Journal of Family Violence, 4,* 161–180.

Suman, B., & Edwards, K. (undated). *Family violence training curriculum.* Travis County Child Protective Services, Region Six, Austin, State of Texas.

Surrey, J. (1991). The "Self-in-Relation": A theory of women's development. In J. Jordan, A. Kaplan, J. Miller, I. Stiver, & J. Surrey, *Women's growth in connection* (pp. 51-66). New York: Guilford Press.

Tifft, L. (1993). *Battering of women: The failure of intervention and the case for prevention.* Boulder, CO: Westview Press.

Tolman, R. M. (1989). The development of a measure of psychological maltreatment of women by their male partners. *Violence and Victims, 4,* 159–177.

United Nations. (1993). *Strategies for confronting domestic violence.* New York: Author.

Villarosa, L. (Ed.). (1994). *Body and soul: The black women's guide to physical health and emotional well-being.* New York: HarperCollins.

Walker, L. (1979). *The battered woman.* New York: Harper & Row.

Walker, L. (1984). *The battered woman syndrome.* New York: Springer.

Walker, L. E. A. (1993). The battered woman syndrome is a psychological consequence of abuse. In R. Gelles & Donileen Loseke (Eds.), *Current controversies on family violence* (pp. 133–153). Newbury Park, CA: Sage Publications.

Walker, L. E. A. (1994). *Abused women and survivor therapy.* Washington, DC: American Psychological Association.

White, E. C. (1985/1994). *Chain, chain, change.* Seattle, WA: Seal Press.

Wood, G. G., & Middleman, R. R. (1992). Groups to empower battered women. *Affilia, 7,* 82–95.

Yegidis, B. (1988). Wife abuse and marital rape among women who seek help. *Affilia, 3,* 62–68.

Yegidis, B., & Renzy, R. (1994). Battered women's experiences with a preferred arrest policy. *Affilia, 9,* 60–70.

Zambrano, M. (1985). *Mejor sola que mal acompañada.* Seattle, WA: Seal Press

Chapter

10

SEXUAL ASSAULT

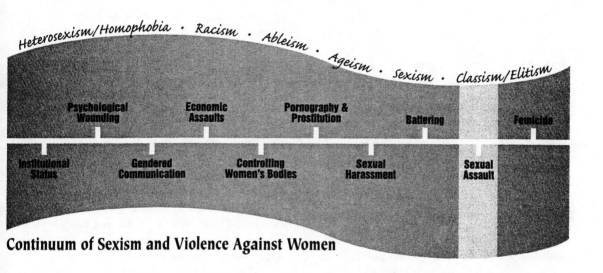

Heterosexism/Homophobia · Racism · Ableism · Ageism · Sexism · Classism/Elitism

| Psychological Wounding | Economic Assaults | Pornography & Prostitution | Battering | Femicide |

| Institutional Status | Gendered Communication | Controlling Women's Bodies | Sexual Harassment | Sexual Assault |

Continuum of Sexism and Violence Against Women

Rape is like bad weather. If it's inevitable, relax and enjoy it.

Oft-quoted rape "joke"

*R*ape. The word itself can evoke fear while the crime evokes nightmares. Sexual assault is a devastating trauma that forever changes the life of a woman who is victimized. The study of rape is a study in contrasts, however: The crime is often marginalized, yet frequently sensationalized. Women alter their lives daily in order to avoid rape; in contrast, men rarely change their behavior for this reason. Many Americans hold firm beliefs about rape, yet many of their attitudes are based on myth and misinformation. Although rape has a long, horrific history spanning centuries, only within the past several decades has the subject been brought into the public arena for debate and action.

In this chapter, we discuss some of these complexities and inconsistencies. Much controversy surrounds the subject of sexual violence, including even the recognized definitions and prevalence of rape. The discussion here ranges from the history of rape to its present-day manifestations. A feminist analysis of rape is presented.

Acquaintance rape and marital rape receive special attention, as does the way in which sexual assault affects African-American women, Latinas, lesbian women, imprisoned women, and women with disabilities. The chapter ends with practice and policy implications that work to "deny rape a future" (Brownmiller, 1975, p. 404).

A note of caution must be sounded at this point. Rape is not a curious phenomenon that occurs on a planet in a distant galaxy. It is impossible to remain a dispassionate and impartial observer when talking about an issue that affects us all, for rape survivors and perpetrators are not only your clients, but also your friends, your neighbors, and, perhaps, you. Keep in touch with your own feelings, biases, and beliefs. As the chapter explains, most women are taught to fear rape. Reading the chapter may bring up fear and anxiety that many of us tend to ignore and deny as we go about our lives. If you are a rape survivor, the chapter may bring up long-buried memories and feelings. The authors urge each student to seek support in order to learn, heal, and grow.

Although child sexual abuse is a serious and pervasive problem, this chapter focuses on the sexual assault of adult women. Incest and other forms of child sexual abuse constitute a serious violation that must be addressed by society at large, as well as by social workers. Too often, this topic has been ignored; leading feminist incest pioneer Louise Armstrong noted that the incest taboo is not a prohibition of the actual sexual violation, but rather the open discussion of the subject (Armstrong, 1978). Many important books and articles have been written on this most horrific form of abuse, and we urge readers both to become knowledgeable about the dynamics of the abuse and to work to end such assaults.

INTRODUCTION TO THE ISSUES

Feminist Analysis of Sexual Assault

Early in the study of sexual assault, rape was believed to be a sexual act committed by men with a diagnosable mental illness, who were unable to control their sexual impulses. Research was conducted on prison populations of convicted rapists and focused on identifying and treating their psychopathology. Some researchers proposed alternative models of causation, including biology, citing abnormal brain functions and hormonal levels, while others looked for social causes in the family, identifying dominant mothers and weak fathers as the culprits. When it became impossible to differentiate the rapists from so-called normal men, rape victims were studied to determine how they precipitated the attacks on themselves. To counter this misogynistic research, a feminist analysis of rape emerged.

Feminist theory has revolutionized the way our society views rape. Feminists have reconstructed rape to look beyond individuals and into the social—political—historical realm to account for the occurrence of rape in this society (Brownmiller, 1975; Griffin, 1971). Feminist theory holds that men do not rape due to biological urges or to individual psychopathology; rather, as the dominant sex in a patriarchal society, some males feel entitled to take what they want from the subordinate sex. Within this theory is the belief that rape serves a purpose for patriarchy. It keeps women subservient to men.

In fact, some radical feminists hold that rape is not merely the by-product of a patriarchal culture, but the foundation of the patriarchy itself. In the feminist classic on rape, *Against Our Will: Men, Women, and Rape,* Brownmiller (1975) theorized,

> *Man's discovery that his genitalia could serve as a weapon to generate fear must rank as one of the most important discoveries of prehistoric times, along with the use of fire and the first crude stone axe. From prehistoric times to the present, I believe, rape has played a critical function. It is nothing more or less than a conscious process of intimidation by which* all men *keep* all women *in a state of fear (pp. 14–15; emphasis in original)*

Brownmiller theorized that this female fear is responsible for society's organization into heterosexual couples and the resulting nuclear families. Although other theories have speculated that love, motherhood, or biology cause the majority of women to align themselves with men, Brownmiller cited fear of rape as the motivating factor that forces women into monogamous, heterosexual relationships with one man in order to seek protection from all other men. This control of women—and of the children produced from their bodies—is believed by some feminist theorists to be the beginning of the concept of ownership and private property.

Rape is a tool of dominance, power, and control. Sexual assault is committed not by a few men who are mentally ill, but by many men who possess a sense of entitlement with regard to women. Rape is, therefore, a political statement, as well as a crime against an individual woman. Rape becomes a tool that some men use to demonstrate their dominance and women's subordination. Rape is additionally used by some men to send a message to other men, especially during times of war, using women's bodies as the intermediary. Robin Morgan made this point by citing Claude Levi-Strauss's theory that men use women as verbs to communicate with other men, for example, communicating total defeat or revenge (Morgan, 1992).

Although most researchers and clinicians working in the arena of sexual assault acknowledge, at least in part, the feminist analysis of rape, there are some who look beyond patriarchy for answers to why men rape, for although most rapists are men, not all men rape. Many researchers espouse a theory of sexual aggression that integrates a multiplicity of factors. Many of these factors consider individual proclivities toward rape in men, including such risk factors as lifestyle impulsivity, antisocial personality, social competence, sexual fantasies, sadism, irrational attitudes, cognitive distortions, issues of control and dominance, disinhibitors, and sexual abuse in childhood (Prentky & Knight, 1991). Other factors examine influences of a hostile home environment, involvement in juvenile delinquency, hostile attitudes and personality characteristics, and a high level of sexual promiscuity (Malamuth, Sockloskie, Koss, & Tanaka, 1991). Feminists even disagree among themselves, with feminist Naomi Wolf (1993) finding that feminist theories constructed on the premise of women as sexual victims can backfire, creating "victim feminism," rather than "power feminism."

Effects of Racism

A further criticism of a feminist analysis of rape is that it identifies sexism as the central premise of rape, without including a detailed analysis of racism as an organizing principle (Burrell, 1993; Davis, 1981; Edmonds, 1992; hooks, 1981). Theorists posing this criticism believe that racism is so closely bound to sexism and classism (Davis, 1981) that the two (or three) cannot be considered separately. They charge that the stereotypic myths of the animalistic African-American male rapist, the immoral African-American woman, and the pure European-American woman not only fueled the lynching of thousands of African-American men, but also allowed European-American men to continue to dominate the social order. Davis (1981) stated, "An effective strategy against rape must aim for more than the eradication of rape—or even sexism—alone. The struggle against racism must be an ongoing theme of the anti-rape movement, which must not only defend women of color, but the many victims of the racist manipulation of the rape charge as well" (p. 201).

We fundamentally agree with the feminist analysis for the basis of explaining not only rape, but also patriarchy. We additionally believe that the most comprehensive explanation of rape is a multidimensional theory with racial–social–biological–cultural–historical constructs. The racist and classist implications of rape are vital to understanding sexual assault, in addition Sanday (1981) reports that rape is also a cultural phenomenon.

Cultural Effects

Sanday (1981) was able to distinguish between societies she described as "rape prone" versus "rape free" in a review of 186 sample societies, ranging from the Babylonians in 1750 B.C. to North America in the late 1960s. A rape-prone society was defined as one in which "the incidence of rape is high, rape is a ceremonial act, or rape is an act by which men punish or threaten women" (Sanday, 1981, p. 9). Rape-prone societies were further characterized by acceptance of interpersonal violence, male dominance, and sexual separation. In these societies, rape was either largely overlooked or allowed by the culture. Sanday (1981) wrote, "Sexual violence is one of the ways [in] which men remind themselves that they are superior" (p. 25).

Yet Sanday also found cultures that were rape free. The similarities of these cultures is "the ceremonial importance of women and the respect accorded the contribution women make to social continuity, a respect which places men and women in relatively balanced power spheres" (p. 17). Sanday's findings suggest that rape is not a normal or a natural phenomenon of all societies, as a result of male biological imperatives or innate aggression, but rather represents a by-product of male-dominated societies. In such societies, rape is supported by society's many institutions, including the criminal-justice system.

Response of the Criminal-Justice System

When men rape and men also write the laws, the practice of rape and the protection of rapists becomes codified into law. Lord Chief Justice Matthew Hale, the famous seventeenth-century English jurist, wrote, "Rape is an accusation easily to be made and hard to be proved, and harder to be defended by the party accused, tho never so innocent" (cited in Brownmiller, 1975, p. 369). His view found its way into American law through the adoption of English common law by the new colonies. Even into the twentieth century, Hale's words were often used as instruction for the jury in cases of rape. "Hale's Dictum," as it was known, prejudiced countless juries as it sought to portray men as innocent and women as vindictive. Ironically, instead of the mythical vindictive women frequently charging rape, rape is the most under-reported crime in the nation, and the documented charges of false allegations are comparable to the numbers of false allegations for other felonies.

With such skepticism pervading the legal system, it should come as little surprise to learn that the rates of conviction in rape cases are abysmally low. In fact, a report entitled *The Response to Rape: Detours on the Road to Equal Justice* (1993), prepared by the majority staff of the Senate Judiciary Committee found the following:

- Of all the victims of rape, 98% never see their attacker caught, tried, and imprisoned.
- Over half of all rape prosecutions either are dismissed before trial or result in an acquittal.
- Almost one quarter of convicted rapists never go to jail or to prison.
- Another quarter receive sentences in local jails, where the average sentence is 11 months.
- A robber is 30% more likely to be convicted than is a rapist.
- A rape prosecution is more than twice as likely as a murder prosecution to be dismissed, and it is 30% more likely to be dismissed than is a robbery prosecution.
- A convicted rapist is 50% more likely to receive probation than is a convicted robber.

Such statistics are appalling and lead some to suggest that rape survivors obtain little justice.

DEFINITIONS OF SEXUAL ASSAULT

The definition of *rape,* as defined by most states, is "a sexual assault in which a man uses his penis to commit vaginal penetration of a victim against her will, by force or threats of force or when she is physically or mentally unable to give her consent" (Warshaw, 1988, p. 12). Early legal definitions often added the phrase "a woman, not his wife," to exempt married men from being prosecuted for raping their wives. It was not legally possible for a husband to rape his wife, although many wives knew it was physically possible.

Most states have not only removed the marital exemption, but also broadened their statutes to include other types of bodily penetration with objects other than the penis, in orifices other than the vagina. Other states have included gender-neutral terms for the victim, to acknowledge the sexual victimization of men. Additionally, some states incorporate different levels of sexual assault, to include a continuum of sexually coercive behaviors, which range from criminal sexual exposure, unwanted kissing, fondling, sexual contact, and attempted rape, to rape.

Although the definitions of rape and sexual assault appear simple and straightforward, they are not. Many myths and stereotypes about rape distort the definition of rape held by the public, as well as by judges, prosecutors, and juries. A common presumption is that rape occurs when a stranger jumps out of the bushes and violently physically and sexually assaults a woman while holding a weapon. Therefore, when a wife is raped by her husband or a woman by her date, she receives little or no support in labeling it rape, even when it meets the legal definition of rape. This disallows women from defining their experience as rape, for the majority of rapes are committed by someone the victims knows, with no weapon used, and little physical force

applied, although it is sexual activity without her consent (Koss, 1987).

Studies have found that the three factors that correlate most to how the rape is perceived by the criminal-justice system are these: a prior relationship between the victim and the offender, lack of force and resistance, and evidence corroborating the victim's account (Estrich, 1987). Additionally, these factors are all assessed from a distinctively male point of view. For instance, resistance for a man may be fighting, kicking, and punching, while resistance for a woman may be saying no, crying, stiffening the body, dissociating, or finally acquiescing to the assault in order to survive. What seems passive to men can be active resistance from a woman's perspective. Additionally, rape charges are taken most seriously when a weapon is involved. To a man, a weapon often means a knife or a gun, yet from a woman's perspective, a weapon can be a man's hands, his penis, his larger physical size, or his threats of violence.

The question of consent is also a complex matter subject to interpretation. Almost all definitions of sexual assault include a statement of the victim's nonconsent, yet how this consent is operationalized varies widely. When a woman in this society says "no," her refusal is often taken as a sexually coy "maybe" or "try harder." In some definitions, nonconsent is viewed as behavior—that is, struggling or fighting. Yet women are frequently advised not to struggle, for such behavior may enrage the rapist and increase the severity of the injuries. If the woman did not struggle, police and prosecutors often do not define the assault as rape. Women, therefore, are caught in a classic Catch-22 situation: damned if they do, damned if they don't. Furthermore, there are nonviolent ways in which women are sexually coerced by a combination of cultural factors, including economic coercion, assumptions about the nature of sex and marriage, and gender roles (Muehlenhard, Powch, Phelps, & Giusti, 1992).

Rape Poem

Marge Piercy

There is no difference between being raped
and being pushed down a flight of cement steps
except that the wounds also bleed inside.

There is no difference between being raped
and being run over by a truck
except that afterward men ask if you enjoyed it.

There is no difference between being raped
and being bit on the ankle by a rattlesnake
except that people ask if your skirt was short
and why you were out alone anyhow.

There is no difference between being raped
and going head first through a windshield
except that afterward you are afraid
not of cars
but half the human race.

The rapist is your boyfriend's brother.
He sits beside you in the movies eating pop-
    corn.
Rape fattens on the fantasies of the normal
    male
like a maggot in garbage.

Fear of rape is a cold wind blowing
all of the time on a woman's hunched back.
Never to stroll alone on a sand road through
    pine woods,
never to climb a trail across a bald
without that aluminum in the mouth
when I see a man climbing toward me.

Never to open the door to a knock
without that razor just grazing the throat.
The fear of the dark side of hedges,
the back seat of the car, the empty house
rattling keys like a snake's warning.
The fear of the smiling man
in whose pocket is a knife.
The fear of the serious man
in whose fist is locked hatred.

All it takes to cast a rapist is seeing your body
as jackhammer, as blowtorch, as adding-
    machine-gun.
All it takes is hating that body
your own, your self, your muscle that softens
    to flab.

All it takes is to push what you hate,
what you fear onto the soft alien flesh.
To bucket out invincible as a tank
armored with treads without senses
to possess and punish in one act,
to rip up pleasure, to murder those who dare
live in the leafy flesh open to love.

One case in Austin, Texas, outraged the state
and the nation, with regard to what constitutes
consent. A woman was raped at knifepoint by
a man she did not know, who broke into her
apartment uninvited, through a window, at 3
A.M. (Phillips, 1993). Finding herself with little
choice, the woman asked the rapist to wear a
condom to protect herself from sexually transmitted diseases and pregnancy. The original
grand jury did not charge the assailant with
rape because they believed that by requesting
the man to wear a condom, the victim had in
fact consented. After protest from an outraged
community, the case was resubmitted to a second grand jury, and the assailant was charged
with, and later found guilty of, aggravated sexual assault and burglary.

The limited legal definition—combined
with the skeptical interpretation of the law by
police, prosecutors, judges, and juries—has led
feminists to note that rape is not illegal in this
country, merely regulated. In no other crime is
the victim scrutinized, judged, and blamed
more than the defendant. Women who are
raped often find themselves alone, without support from the criminal-justice system or family
and friends.

Victims, Survivors, Thrivers

In the past, a woman who was raped was frequently described as the "victim." However, this
term denotes powerlessness and often stigmatizes
women who have been raped. The more favored
term is "survivor," which is more representative of
the courage and determination of women who
physically survived an assault, for 6.5% of all female

homicide victims were also raped (cited in Sorenson & White, 1992).

Lifton (1980, p. 117) defines a *survivor* as "one who has encountered, been exposed to, or witnessed death, and has himself or herself remained alive." Because most women who have been sexually assaulted fear death at the hands of the perpetrator (Gordon & Riger, 1989), this definition certainly describes their experience. Some clinicians use the term *survivor* more specifically to denote a woman who has not only physically survived the attack, but psychologically recovered as well.

It is easy to see why many women would want to distance themselves from the word *victim*, but it is not possible to distance themselves from the reality that they were sexually victimized. For the truth is, the term *victim* does describe the state of helplessness of many women at the moment of their attack. There is a concern that if the term *survivor* is used exclusively, more focus will be placed on celebrating the woman's survival and less focus on ending the victimization of all women at the hands of men.

Artist and activist Matuschka decries the use of the word *survivor* in her own struggle with breast cancer. She finds the term limiting and restrictive because merely surviving the cancer is only a small part of the experience. She wants the focus to be on living but realizes the obvious problems in referring to women as "livers"! Matuschka asked women for input on a new name and several suggested the word "thriver," which she has adapted as most representative of the goals of recovery (Matuschka, personal communication, March 28, 1996).

A feminist perspective values having women name and define their own experience. The term *survivor* was appropriated by women within the rape-crisis movement, to further empower and validate the woman who has been raped. In this chapter, the terms *victim* and *survivor* are both used, sometimes interchangeably, but usually, the term *victim* is used to describe the sexually coerced person close to the time of the victimization, and the term *survivor* is used to refer to the woman after the assault, and perhaps *thriver* can be used to recognize the strength of women to not only survive, but also flourish,

change, and grow after catastrophic events in their lives. Although the discussion of semantics here may seem tedious to some, feminists recognize the power of language and naming, as noted in Chapter 4, on gendered communication.

PREVALENCE

Trying to establish the prevalence of rape is frustrating and difficult. Although many numbers have been quoted throughout the years, there is still much controversy surrounding the issue of how many women are sexually assaulted each year. The main difficulty in determining the prevalence of rape in this society is due to the inadequacies of the measures used by the two federal sources of crime victimization: the Uniform Crime Reports (UCR), which are published by the Federal Bureau of Investigation (FBI), and the National Crime Survey (NCS), compiled under the auspices of the Bureau of Justice Statistics.

The figures from the UCR offer very little value because the report defines rape in the very narrowest manner—that is, penile–vaginal penetration. The numbers also represent only the rapes reported to police. Rape has long been recognized as the most underreported crime; therefore, the UCR does not adequately reflect the incidence of rape in this country (Koss, 1992).

The NCS is a nationwide, household-based survey of crime victimization. Although its intent is to develop a more accurate portrait of crime victimization in the nation, it too has many limitations, thereby preventing its numbers from providing an accurate portrayal of sexual assault in the United States. Although the questions asked by the NCS have been revised to be more sensitive to the incidence of sexual assault, Koss (1992) suggested that independent data sources reveal that rape incidence may be 6–10 times higher than that shown in current NCS estimates.

With this in mind, the best statistics come from several respected studies by researchers well versed with their subject. Russell (1984) conducted interviews with a probability sample of 930 women in the San Francisco area, and 44% reported having at least one experience that met the legal definition of rape or attempted rape. Another important study was conducted by Koss, Gidycz, and Wisniewski (1987), who surveyed a national sample of college students, which found that 53.7% of women respondents revealed some form of sexual victimization—that is, 14.4% reported forced sexual contact, 11.9% reported sexual coercion, 12.1% reported attempted rape, and 15.4% reported rape.

The National Victim Center and the Crime Victims Research and Treatment Center (NVC & CVRTC) jointly commissioned the study reported in *Rape in America: Report to the Nation* (1992), directed by noted sexual-assault researcher Dean Kilpatrick. The study was a 3-year longitudinal study of a national probability sample of 4,008 adult women. The results are sobering.

- Every single minute in America, there are 1.3 forcible rapes of adult women; 78 women are forcibly raped each hour.
- Of adult American women, 13% have been victims of at least one forcible rape in their lifetimes. One out of every eight adult women—or at least 12.1 million American women—has been the victim of forcible rape.
- More than 6 out of 10 rape cases (61%) occurred before the victims reached the age of 18 years.
- Only 16% of rapes are ever reported to police.

Although the numbers may vary from study to study, the conclusions do not. Rape is a serious crime, which affects millions of women across the nation. When rape can be counted in minutes, a serious, pervasive problem exists.

The Voices of Rape Survivors

When reading statistics in a textbook, it is both a habit and a defense mechanism to be busily highlighting the numbers with a colored marker,

without acknowledging that these numbers describe the lives of real women, each with her own story to tell and nightmare to relive. It is important for social workers to hear the voices of women, so social workers can't easily distance themselves from the pain and fear that such stories bring to the surface. Legal anthropologist Patricia Easteal collected the stories of sexual-assault survivors in Australia, resulting in the book, *Voices of the Survivors* (1994). Following are brief accounts of a few of the stories, as related by the survivors.

> In the marriage I was raped forcibly or else I would submit for fear of what might happen. Handcuffs, guns, knives were used for intimidation. The worst incidents occurred while I was pregnant the last time. I was seven months pregnant. I was handcuffed and violently raped—he threatened to cut the baby from me. I went into premature labour and had the baby. It has taken me years to remember all the details. No one even asked if I was OK.

> I initially thought it was not rape as it was oral—severe beating. Happened in 1984. Still feel unclean and have worn away the enamel on my teeth with continual brushing, Had AIDS test and tests for other STDs. Have not dealt with the issue and feel as though I should have worked through the feelings. Not sure now whether it has been resolved or not. Police took me to the hospital and photographed the bruising. Also had to take my (young) son with me. At court his lawyer said it could not have been traumatic because he had previously been my lover.

> I was raped by two guys. I had a couple of drinks and someone put something in one. They dragged me to an oval and raped me. I felt it was my fault for having a drink and couldn't do anything because I was out of it. I felt till this year I was nothing and this incident really made me a fragile, insecure woman, scared of men. I am thankful to a woman counsellor who has helped me to trust this year. (Female, raped when she was 23 [years old])

> About six months after the rape I told my mother about it. She slapped by face and told me I was a slut. It is little wonder that I never went to the police when my own mother was conditioned to think/react this way. It compounds the victimisation of women. I believe my sex life has

been affected by the rape and indeed my very loving marriage ended because of sex related problems. (Raped by a date when she was 15 [years old])

All throughout the rape, he kept on calling me a prostitute and saying, over and over again, 'You love it don't you!' When I said, 'No I don't' he seemed not to hear me and just kept saying it again.

These women's voices are compelling and remind us never to minimize sexual assault. Although these women are Australian, their experiences could just as well have occurred in the United States or any other nation in the world. Although women of the world speak in many languages, rape experiences cause women to speak in one voice, in a common language of hurt and pain.

DYNAMICS OF RAPE

The Female Fear

Although not all women are raped, almost all women fear rape. The only crime women fear more than rape is murder (Gordon & Riger, 1989), and cultural beliefs have long held that sometimes it is better to be killed than to be raped. On a daily basis, women rearrange their lives and their activities to avoid the danger of rape. Not only are women affected physically about what space they choose to occupy and when, but women also bear the brunt of the psychological burden of living in fear.

Griffin (1979) acknowledged this fear:

I have never been free of the fear of rape. From a very early age I, like most women, have thought of rape as part of my natural environment—something to be feared and prayed against like fire or lightening. I never asked why men raped; I simply thought it one of the many mysteries of human nature. (p. 272)

Although men may experience a generalized fear of crime, the fear of rape in everyday life remains uniquely female.

An interesting exercise to demonstrate this point is to ask men what they have done today to avoid rape. Most will look puzzled or laugh, as though the question was an amusing joke. For the most part, however, women will have a different reaction: Women can list specific protective steps they have taken, such as carrying their keys in their hands, walking with determination, traveling in groups of women, purchasing mace or guns, and avoiding going out at night.

Gordon and Riger (1989) undertook a study of women in Chicago, Philadelphia, and San Francisco, and their research reveals that the amount of fear a woman experiences varies according to many factors, such as her childhood experiences and her acceptance of rape myths. Their conclusions suggest that "fear of rape is central to the day-to-day concerns of about a third of women, a sporadic concern for another third, and of little concern of another third, although these women take precautions to prevent it" (p. 21). This pervasive female fear may limit the mobility and opportunities of women and is often exploited for social, political, and even economic gain, as women are exhorted to buy guns, mace, and other personal-safety devices. All women are taught to fear the possibility of rape, but women who have been raped report feeling great fear during the attack and even years later. Most rape victims report having feared for their lives during the assault (Gordon & Riger, 1989), whereas many continue to express fears, such as being left alone and being out at night (Wyatt, 1992), long after the rape occurred.

Rape Myths

Rape myths are so common in our society that these myths distort every facet of rape, including prevalence rates, prevention efforts, conviction rates, survivor treatment, and legal policy. Burt (1980) first defined, discussed, and developed a measure of rape myth acceptance (RMA). Lonsway and Fitzgerald (1994) provided a review and a critique of the literature of RMA and offered their own, expanded definition of rape myths. Rape myths are "attitudes and beliefs that are generally false but are widely and persistently held, and that serve to deny and justify male sexual aggression against women" (1994, p. 134).

The purpose of rape myths is to enforce a system of sexist and racist oppression. See Table 10.1 for a list of myths and their refutations. Myths that blame women for the rape shift the blame from the perpetrator to the victim and allow men to justify their sexual aggression. Accepting rape myths also serves to minimize the seriousness and prevalence of rape. Additionally, RMA may act as a defensive or denial mechanism for unraped women, for if these women can blame the rape victim's appearance or behavior for her rape, then women who haven't been assaulted can retain the illusion that rape only happens to other women, who somehow deserved or provoked the attack.

Many demographic and background variables have been studied in relation to RMA, from sex, race, education, and occupation variables; to knowing a rape survivor and knowing about rape. According to Lonsway and Fitzgerald's (1994) review of the literature, the only variable that consistently is confirmed is gender—that is, women are less likely to believe and to accept rape myths than are men. In reviewing beliefs, behaviors, and attitudes about rape in relationship to RMA, they found the following fairly consistent relationships, in addition to gender: (1) individuals with higher levels of RMA tend to hold more traditional sex-role attitudes, (2) individuals with higher levels of RMA tend to hold more negative attitudes toward women, and (3) men who report greater likelihood of raping women also report higher levels of RMA.

In looking at RMA, it is important to analyze the degree of acceptance not only by so-

ciety, our clients, and their families, but also by us. The degree of RMA can affect how we view, support, and treat our clients who are rape survivors. Dye and Roth (1990) studied how therapists' attitudes toward sexual assault affects their treatment of clients. They found that therapists holding more negatively prejudiced attitudes toward sexual-assault victims tended to employ more treatment strategies that blamed the victim for the assault. The study also found that younger therapists, female therapists, and psychologists and social workers were more likely to have positive and understanding attitudes toward victims than were other therapists (Dye & Roth, 1990).

Acquaintance Rape

Acquaintance rape is often referred to as "hidden rape" (Warshaw, 1988) or "unacknowledged rape" (Koss, 1987). One of the biggest misconceptions about sexual assault is that the assailant is a stranger, and this scenario is assumed to be the only true form of rape. In fact, however, the majority of rapists are someone known to the victim. A survey by Koss et al. (1987), conducted on a nationwide sample of college students, revealed that 84% of the completed rapes involved an offender known to the victim, and in 57% of the rapes, the perpetrator was a date. In Russell's landmark study, 88% of the rape victims knew their attackers (cited in Warshaw, 1988). The risk of being raped by an acquaintance is four times greater than the risk of being raped by a stranger (Warshaw, 1988).

Because society is taught rape myths, and one of the most common myths is that rapes are committed by strangers, acquaintance rape is often not acknowledged as rape. However, rape is rape—that is, unwanted sexual assault is rape, whether the victim knows the assailant or not. Acquaintance rape involves forced sexual activity, where the perpetrator is known to the

Table 10.1
Common Rape Myths

Rape Myths	Rape Realities
1. Women routinely lie about rape for their purposes.	Although false charges of rape are often widely publicized, FBI statistics suggest that only 2% of rape charges are false; this rate is lower than or comparable to the rate for other felonies (cited in Lonsway & Fitzgerald, 1994). One source of mistake in cataloging false charges is combining them with unfounded charges. *Unfounded charges* mean that there is not enough evidence to pursue the case. Critics suggest that the rate of unfounded rape charges is a greater reflection of police skepticism than of women's deceit.
2. Only bad women are raped.	All women are potential victims of rape. Rape crosses all divisions of race, class, sexual orientation, age, and ability. Belief in this myth helps men justify rape while enabling women to believe it can't happen to them because it only happens to other women.
3. You can't rape an unwilling woman (often uses the analogy, "you can't thread a moving needle").	Women can be overcome by force, threat of force, and fear for their lives. A man's physical strength, use of weapon, or psychological intimidation makes rape possible. This myth denies the existence of any legitimate victims of forcible rape (Koss, 1987).
4. Women who are raped must have provoked the rape by leading men on or dressing provocatively.	This myth serves to blame the victim for her rape while excusing male responsibility. Rape is about men's behavior, not women's.
5. Most rape is committed by African-American men against European-American women.	This myth combines elements of racial and sexual oppression, which serves a number of functions, not the least of which is that it serves to keep racial and sexual hierarchies in place, with white males firmly ensconced at the top. The fact is that the majority of rapes are intraracial, not interracial.
6. Most women secretly desire rape and enjoy rape.	Some women may fantasize about a forceful sexual encounter, but fantasy and real life are two different things. As Koss (1987) stated, "there is a big difference between dreaming about a commanding, handsome, and powerful man whose degree of forcefulness is at the control of the dreamer and facing a real life rape" (p. 16). This myth once again blames women for their own victimization.
7. Men rape because they are oversexed and do not have an available partner.	Rape is not about sexual impulses and sexual availability. Rape is about power and control. Men who rape are often married or have a willing sexual partner.

Continued

Table 10.1
Continued

Rape Myths	Rape Realities
8. It can only be called rape if the assailant is a stranger who has a weapon and causes great physical injury.	This myth causes rape to be narrowly defined, which lets men abdicate responsibility for their sexually coercive behavior. The majority of rapes are committed by men known to the woman, only a fraction involve weapons, and the physical force involved is usually mild to moderate (Koss and Harvey, 1987). This myth makes it difficult for women to label their experiences as rape and to hold men accountable for the sexual victimization of women.
9. Rape is perpetrated by a few men who are mentally ill.	Although numerous studies have attempted to identify the rapist as suffering from a specific mental illness, research has not upheld this belief. Most rapists cannot be diagnosed with a psychopathology that causes them to rape. Rapists seem to be little different from normal men, except perhaps that they are often very traditional men with beliefs about the proscribed sex roles of men and women and a belief in male dominance and control.
10. Our society abhors rape and gives rapists long and harsh sentences.	Although society seems to abhor rape, actually, rape is not only tolerated, but even condoned and regulated. According to one study, 98% of all victims of rape never see their attacker caught, tried, and imprisoned; almost one quarter of convicted rapists never go to prison or to jail; and another quarter receive sentences in local jails, where the average sentence is 11 months (Senate Judiciary Committee, 1993).

victim, either casually, having met through a common activity or a mutual friend, or in a closer relationship, as steady dates or former sexual partners (Warshaw, 1988). The hallmark of acquaintance rape is that there is usually some basis for a relationship that creates an element of trust in the victim.

Campus rape is a subset of date rape that occurs on campus or between college students who are dating or have met at a campus event. College students are a high-risk group for rape. The sexual victimization of women peaks first in the 16- to 19-year-old age group and second in the 20- to 24-year-old age group, with 45% of all alleged rapists who are arrested being under the age of 25 years (Koss, 1987).

Survivors of acquaintance rape are more likely to blame themselves for the assault than are survivors of stranger rape. Police, family,

and friends are more likely to blame her, too, often questioning her behavior and judgment. Although some might attempt to minimize acquaintance rape and its impact, studies have shown aftereffects in acquaintance and date rape similar to—or more severe than—those in stranger rape. For instance, one study revealed that acquaintance-rape victims rate themselves less recovered than do stranger-rape victims for up to 3 years following their rape experiences (Warshaw, 1988). Some reasons may be due to the acquaintance-rape survivors' reluctance to tell people of the experience; either the perceived or the real lack of support from family, friends, and police; and the increased feelings of self-doubt, guilt, blame, and betrayal. A *Ms.* study (Warshaw, 1988) found that in a comparison of survivors of acquaintance rape and stranger rape, in both groups, the psychological aftereffects of rape were profound and included feelings of diminished self-worth and increased fear and anxiety.

Marital Rape

At one time, the term *marital rape* was an oxymoron, for it was believed to be impossible for a wife to be raped by her husband. This belief has a long legal history, going back to the seventeenth century, when influential legal scholar Matthew Hale wrote, "The husband cannot be guilty of rape committed by himself upon his lawful wife, for by their mutual matrimonial consent and contract, the wife hath given up herself in this kind unto her husband, which she cannot retract" (cited in Finkelhor & Yllo, 1985, p. 2) This judicial decree has influenced American law for centuries.

Traditionally, most state statutes included a "marital rape exemption"—that is, criminal codes specifically excluded the husband from prosecution for raping his wife. By giving a man such immunity, Finkelhor and Yllo (1985) termed the marriage license a "license to rape." Due to successful feminist advocacy over the past three decades, "as of July 5, 1993 marital rape is a crime in 50 states. Thirty-one still have some exemptions from prosecution if 'only' simple force is used, or if the woman is legally unable to consent due to the severity of a disability (temporarily or permanently, physically or mentally)" (National Clearinghouse on Marital & Date Rape, undated).

Marital rape has often been romanticized, such as in the depiction of marital rape in the movie "Gone with the Wind," when Rhett carries a kicking and screaming Scarlett up the stairs, only to portray her with a self-satisfied smile in the morning. Such Hollywood versions of marital rape is pure mythology. Instead of smiling the next morning, women who are raped by their husbands tend to describe their feelings as betrayal, anger, humiliation, and guilt, with long-term effects reported as the inability to trust men, an aversion to intimacy

and sex, and a lingering fear of being assaulted again (Finkelhor & Yllo, 1985).

The prevalence of marital rape is well documented. Russell (1982) reported that 14% of the women who had married once or more than once reported having been raped by their husbands. This percentage translates into the figure that in one in seven marriages, marital rape has occurred. Finkelhor and Yllo (1985) reported from their survey that 10% of the married or previously married women said their husbands had "used physical force or threat to try to have sex with them" (pp. 6–7). Forced sexual activity included, but was not limited to, forced vaginal and anal intercourse, forced oral sex, forced sexual activity with his friends or with animals, bondage and beating, insertion of a variety of items into her vagina and anus, and taking pictures of these activities without her consent.

A prevalent myth about marital rape is that it represents a minor squabble over differences in sexual desire or frequency. To the contrary, Finkelhor and Yllo (1985) concluded that marital rapes were often frightening and brutal events occurring in the context of an exploitative and destructive relationship. One study (Riggs, Kilpatrick, & Resnick, 1992) compared physical and sexual assaults committed by either strangers or spouses and found that 64% of the women who had been sexually assaulted by their husbands reported the attack was one of a series of such assaults, and 36% reported thinking they would die during the assault. Finkelhor and Yllo (1985) were able to identify three types of marital rape, which closely align with Groth's (1979) typology of men who rape (see Table 10.2). According to this classification, men who rape their wives do so for different reasons and with different degrees of force.

Revictimization of Rape

One disturbing research finding is that women who are sexually abused as children seem to be

Table 10.2
Types of Marital Rapes and Rapists

Types of Marital Rape (Finkelhor & Yllo, 1985)	Characteristics of Marital Rape	Types of Rapists (Groth, 1979)	Characteristics of Rapists
1. Force-only rape	Husbands use only as much force as necessary to coerce their wives into sex	Power rapist	Power is the dominant motivating factor. "Sexuality becomes a means for underlying feelings of inadequacy and serves to express issues of mastery, strength, control, authority, identity, and capability" (Groth, 1979, pp. 310–331).
2. Battering rape	Forced sex, combined with beatings	Anger rapist	Physical brutality is a hallmark. His aim is to hurt and debase his victim, which may include forcing her to perform sexual acts he regards as degrading.
3. Obsessive rape	May or may not use force; husbands' sexual interests are often strange and perverse	Sadistic rapist	"There is a sexual transformation of anger and power so that aggression itself becomes eroticized" (Groth, 1979, p. 44). He takes pleasure in her pain and suffering. Assault may include bondage and torture, with bizarre or ritualistic qualities.

at increased risk for sexual revictimization as adults (Mayall & Gold, 1995; Russell, 1986). Although initially such research may be viewed with some concern for the potential to blame the victim, this research can have important practice implications for those working with both survivors of childhood sexual abuse and survivors of adult sexual assault.

Finkelhor and Browne (1985) outlined four dynamics resulting from child sexual abuse, which may place survivors at increased risk of revictimization: (1) traumatic sexualization in which a child's sexuality is shaped in a developmentally inappropriate and interpersonally dysfunctional fashion as a result of the abuse; (2) betrayal, where the child discovers that someone on whom they depended caused them

harm; (3) stigmatization involving negative connotations, including shame and guilt, that are not only communicated to the child but also incorporated into the child's self-image; and (4) powerlessness in which the child's will, desires, and sense of efficacy are continually denied.

Mayall and Gold (1995) listed many explanations that do not blame the victim for her revictimization while connecting the previous abuse to the present abuse. For instance, traumatic sexualization may lead women to have more sexual partners, which may place them at increased risk. Explanations offered for the increased sexual activity include "earlier disinhibition of adult sexual activity, reinforcement received for being sexual, attempting to gain control over a past traumatic event, learned helplessness in the face of sexual advances, and feeling valued only for their sexuality" (Mayall & Gold, 1995, p. 39). Additionally, Mayall and Gold sounded a cautionary note: "any study of revictimization that studies characteristics of female victims is working with only a small piece of the overall picture since most any of the variance in sexual aggression is accounted for by the male perpetrator. Any woman is at risk of becoming a victim of a sexual assault if she is in contact with a sexually aggressive male" (p. 40).

Aftermath of Rape

With the high prevalence of sexual assault occurring across the country, a social work practitioner is certain to encounter women who have been raped. The practice arena where the survivor is encountered will determine many of the practice issues. For instance, a medical social worker employed in an emergency room will focus on crisis management with a recently raped woman. A social worker at a rape-crisis center may be organizing groups of survivors who want to share their experiences. A social worker in private practice may see a woman who comes in with a variety of vague complaints, which may represent an unresolved sexual assault that occurred a number of years beforehand.

Following is a discussion of the aftereffects of sexual assault. Some of the effects tend to occur immediately after the assault and some years later. Although several areas surrounding sexual assault are subject to some disagreement, such as prevalence and definitions, all researchers and clinicians agree that rape is a serious trauma, with both short-term and long-term effects for survivors.

Numerous studies have been conducted on the aftereffects of sexual assault. The studies reveal similar patterns of response for many women, whether they were raped by an acquaintance or by a stranger. To further assist with our understanding, the reactions are separated into three categories: emotional, physical, and behavioral (see Table 10.3).

Although rape survivors exhibit many similar reactions following an assault, it would be a mistake to generalize these feelings to all women and expect a singular reaction. For instance, a stereotypical female response to a trauma portrays women as hysterical and very emotional, yet many rape survivors are numb or in shock and present a very calm, collected demeanor. This should not be interpreted to mean that the assault was not upsetting to the victim or lead us to question whether the assault occurred at all. Burgess and Holmstrom (1974) have named these two response styles as *expressed style* and *controlled style,* respectively. An *expressed style* involves an open expression of feelings of fear and anxiety, through such behaviors as crying, sobbing, and restlessness. A *controlled style* is characterized by a calm, subdued affect, in which the survivor may appear relatively emotionless.

Rape in America: Report to the Nation (NVC & CVRTC, 1992) studied the differences in mental health between a population of women who had been sexually assaulted and women who had never been victims of assault. Almost one third (31%) of rape survivors had developed symptoms diagnosed as posttraumatic stress disorder (PTSD). Rape survivors were 6.2 times more likely to develop PTSD than were women who had never been victims of assault. Although depression is a problem facing many women in today's society, rape survivors were 3 times more likely than nonvictims of assault to have ever had a major depressive episode. Rape victims were 4.1 times more likely to have contemplated suicide and 13 more times more likely to have attempted suicide than their nonassaulted counterparts. Last, the study found that rape victims had higher rates of drug-related problems (e.g., alcoholism) than did nonassaulted women. Other studies (Burgess & Holmstrom, 1974; George, Winfield, & Blazer, 1992) have similarly found an increased incidence of drug (e.g., alcohol) use.

Table 10.3
Impact of the Assault

Emotional

Fear, humiliation, embarrassment, anger, revenge, worry, terror, confusion, self-blame (especially prevalent in acquaintance rape), anxiety, depression, experiencing intrusive memories of the attack, numbness, mistrust of men, chronic depression, lowered self-esteem, betrayal (especially prevalent in marital rape), lingering acute fear of being assaulted again, shock, sadness, hatred, and development of PTSD.

Physical

Soreness, bruising, shaking, trembling, racing heart, rapid breathing, irritation and trauma to the throat (especially for women forced to have oral sex), tension headaches, fatigue, sleep and appetite disturbances, nightmares, startle reflex, nausea, gastrointestinal irritability, cystitis, rectal bleeding and pain (especially by women forced to have anal sex), vaginal irritation, burning, discharge, physical injuries of varying severity, sexually transmitted diseases, and pregnancy.

Behavioral

Avoidance of sex, decreased frequency of sexual activity, development of specific sexual problems, avoidance of men and situations that remind the survivor of the assault, nightmares, changing residences and phone numbers, suicidal actions, and drug (e.g., alcohol) addiction.

This table was compiled from the following sources: Burgess & Holmstrom, 1974; George, Winfield, & Blazer, 1992; Kilpatrick, Resnick, & Veronen, 1981; NVC & CVRTC, 1992; Wyatt, 1992.

SPECIAL POPULATIONS OF RAPE SURVIVORS

African-American Women

There is perhaps no more tragic chapter in the history of sexual assault than the rape perpetrated on African-American women who were enslaved by European-American slaveholders. Enslaved African-American women were viewed as property, and therefore laws prohibiting rape were not applied to them. Although racist beliefs held that African-American men were frequently raping European-American women, the reverse was actually true—that is, European-American slaveholders frequently raped African-American women.

Angela Davis wrote of the stereotypes of African-American women and men, which she described as political inventions:

> The portrayal of Black men as rapists reinforced racism's open invitation to white men to avail themselves of sexually of Black women's bodies. The fictional image of the Black man as rapist has always strengthened its inseparable companion: the image of the Black woman as chronically promiscuous. For once the notion is accepted that Black men harbor irresistible and animal-like sexual urges, the entire race is invested with bestiality. If Black men have their eyes on white women as sexual objects, then Black women must certainly welcome the sexual attention of white men. Viewed as "loose women" and whores, Black women's cries of rape would necessarily lack legitimacy. (Davis, 1981, p. 182)

Acceptance of this stereotype as truth led to the belief that pure European-American southern women needed protection from African-American rapists. These stereotypes fueled the lynching of African-American men in the American South. These myths remain influential today, despite the fact that the majority of rapes occur intraracially. When African-American men are convicted of rape, they are more likely than their European-American male counterparts to receive harsh prison sentences, and when African-American women are raped, they are less likely to be believed than are European-American women (Edmonds, 1993).

The prevalence rates for the rape of African-American women are often troublesome, for studies reveal that African-American women are less likely to disclose incidents of rape than are European-American women (Wyatt, 1992). Williams and Holmes (1981) reported that in their study, African-American females, in comparison with European-American and Mexican-American women, are disproportionately victims of rape. Yet in another study, although African-American women reported a higher proportion of attempted rape than did European-American women, there was not a significant difference in the amount of completed rape (Wyatt, 1992). Wyatt (1992) also demonstrated many commonalities between the African-American and European-American rape survivors; for instance, both groups report similar short- and long-term effects of the rape, including fear, anger, anxiety, depression, and preoccupation with the rape incident.

African-American women may be at greater risk for sexual assault. African-American women are also significantly more likely than European-American women to give explanations for their victimization due to circumstances involving their living situations (Wyatt, 1992). This finding corroborates Williams and Holmes's (1981) report that African-American women are more likely to use public transportation, to have jobs with long working hours, and to live in high-crime areas. Each of these elements may be risk factors for sexual assault.

African-American women are more reluctant to report rape for many reasons. Due to numerous oppressive actions by the police toward people of color, the police are often perceived as racist. African-American women may not feel comfortable or confident that they will be be-

lieved because the credibility of African-American women as rape victims has never been as firmly established as it has been for European-American women (Wyatt, 1992). Additionally, because most rape is intraracial, some African-American women fear the consequences of reporting rape by African-American men. "For African American women, the rape conviction of an African American man is never simply a question of guilt or innocence. We bear the burden of reconciling our desire to see the guilty punished with our fear of racism and injustice" (Burrell, 1993, p. 88). Burrell observed that the rape of an African-American beauty pageant contestant by boxer Mike Tyson was a case that divided the African-American community, with many African Americans supporting the survivor yet some African-American organizations working for Tyson's release.

Latinas

Before citing the few studies available that report on Latinas' experiences with rape, a word is needed about Latinas in general. The use of the word "Latina" is more accepted today to describe women than is the word "Hispanic," although the descriptor "Chicana" is preferred in some areas of the country. It is difficult to generalize about Latinas because they constitute such a diverse group. Part of the diversity is due to the different national origins of Latino men and women living in the mainland United States, with 60% of Latino men and women coming from Mexico, 22% from South or Central America, 12% from Puerto Rico, and 5% from Cuba (Vasquez, 1994). These different origins can result in variations of language, cultural considerations, and beliefs. Other important factors include class and degree of acculturation or assimilation. The differences are monumental between a middle class, bilingual third-generation Chicana and a Latina who recently arrived in the United States from El Salvador, who does not speak English. Vasquez (1994) has cautioned about generalizing about

Latinas in her writings, stating "we must remember that the descriptions that follow in this section are applicable to some Latinas, some of the time, for a period of time" (p. 117). Her point is well taken and is applicable to the following discussion.

In examining the history of women in Mexico, Williams and Holmes (1981) identified the Spanish colonization, the *encomienda* grant system, and the colonial Catholic church as influencing the present-day sexism and racism experienced by Mexican-American women. Both the family and the church place a special burden on Latinas, for to be raped is "to dishonor or disgrace not only her, but her family and husband as well" (Williams & Holmes, 1981). Saint María Goretti is so honored because she died resisting the attack of a rapist. This historical perspective may explain the research finding of Williams and Holmes (1981) in their study in San Antonio, Texas, which revealed that Mexican-American women seem to be the most adversely affected by the rape experience, as compared to African-American and European-American women. This finding was confirmed in a more recent study, conducted in Florida (Lefley, Scott, Llabre, & Hicks, 1993), where Latinas (chiefly Cuban-American women) who were raped reported higher psychological distress than did African-American and European-American women victims. Additionally, the researchers reported that the Latinas presented with significantly more obsessive–compulsive thinking and use of denial and avoidance as coping responses. The study also revealed that Latinas, both those who had been sexually assaulted and a control group who had not been assaulted, were more punitive and blaming of victims than were European-American respondents (Lefley et al., 1993). For the purpose of this study, Latina participants were "restricted to those with parents born in a Spanish-speaking, Latin American or Caribbean country who (if married) were married to Hispanics" (p. 625).

Rape prevalence rates appear to be lowest for Latinas, as compared with other women.

Sorenson and Siegal (1992) found that a lifetime prevalence of sexual assault among European American was 2.5 times that of Latinas. Although the lower incidence of rape among Latinas (95% of the Latinas in the sample were of Mexican heritage, 56.8% were born in Mexico) may be attributed to reluctance to report or difficulties due to language barriers, another rationale is offered by the researchers: "While traditional Mexican culture includes patriarchal notions rejected by feminists, it may also include factors that serve to protect its members from sexual aggression" (Sorenson & Siegal, 1992, p. 100). For example, traditionally Latino culture forbids young girls to date, and older girls must be accompanied by a chaperone. Findings also revealed that Latinas were less likely to report the assault than were European-American women, and they were less likely to use health services or to consult a psychotherapist about the assault.

Many other research studies have similarly found an underutilization of mental health and support services among Latina women. Two factors that are frequently cited are the lack of geographic accessibility to these resources and the lack of culturally and linguistically appropriate services (Sandra Lopez, personal communication, April 23, 1997).

Social worker Sandra Lopez (personal communication, April 23, 1997) stated "the manner in which a Latina female would perceive sexual assault has a lot to do with her level of acculturation, that is, how connected is she to her traditional values, and how much does she identify with the dominant culture. In addition, level of acculturation would influence how a Latina would perceive help-seeking behaviors and helping resources." In her own practice, clinical social worker Sandra Lopez finds that traditional Latinas are less likely to use services such as a rape support or incest survivor group, preferring instead family support systems. Agencies have noted this preference and seem to be more creatively reaching out to the Latina community by doing more outreach, working with recognized Latina community resources such as churches and schools, and hiring more bilingual staff.

One area concerning Latinas, which has received little attention, is the experiences of immigrant and refugee women. Arguelles and Rivero (1993) found that traditional theories of transnational migration focusing on economic and political rationales offer only partial explanations of the experiences of Latinas who come to the United States. In their interviews with more than 100 Latinas who had migrated transnationally (including from Mexico, Guatemala, and El Salvador), repeated instances of rape, incest, battering, and homophobia led often to their migration to the United States. Unfortunately, abuse often recurred here in the United States, at the hands of family members, strangers, and in one recorded instance, "an officer from 'la migra'" (Immigration and Naturalization Service [INS]) (p. 265). The women were often reluctant to report the abuse that occurred in the United States, for fear of being deported or raped by police officers. These Latinas also reported having few resources to cope with the trauma of such assaults and adopted such coping strategies as dressing like men, intimidating others with behavior, buying guns, living anonymously so that family members and friends couldn't find them, or turning to religious or spiritual resources (Arguelles & Rivero, 1993).

Lesbian Women

There are no separate statistics kept on lesbian women who have been sexually assaulted, yet there is anecdotal evidence that lesbian women may be targeted because of their lifestyle. "Some women are raped specifically because they are lesbian and the violence is a means of demonstrating the abhorrence felt towards a lifestyle that contradicts the assumption 'all women need men'" (Orzek, 1989, p. 114). Lesbian women may face a less sympathetic response from institutions because they are con-

fronted not only with sexism, but also with homophobia and heterosexism.

Just as heterosexual women are raped by spouses, as well as by strangers, so, too, does it appear that similar dynamics exist for lesbian women. Waterman, Dawson, and Bologna (1989) surveyed a small sample of gay men and lesbian women to determine whether sexually coercive behaviors existed within same-sex relationships. Participants were asked, "Have you ever forced a partner to have sex against his/her will?" and "Has your partner ever forced you to have sex against your will?" (Waterman et al., 1989, p. 120). Of the 36 self-identified lesbians who participated in the study, 8.3% reported being perpetrators of "forced sex," and 30.6% reported being victims of forced sex by their same-sex partners. Although the small sample size makes it difficult to generalize, social workers need to pay attention to sexual assaults of lesbians from both inside and outside of their relationships.

As social workers, we must also examine our own biases and heterosexist beliefs in working with lesbian women. Many questions routinely asked of sexual-assault survivors reveal underlying heterosexist assumptions. For instance, rape survivors are frequently asked when was the last time they had intercourse, what method of birth control they use, or whether they had a prior sexual relationship with their assailant. These questions may pose special difficulty for lesbian women who may or may not choose to disclose their sexual orientation in order to fully answer the questions. Orzek (1989) suggests that such questions be asked with sensitivity to the possibility of alternative lifestyles of women who have been assaulted.

More research must be conducted regarding the effects of sexual assault on lesbian women and their partners because many dynamics remain unknown. Wertheimer (1990) described a gay and lesbian grassroots organization founded in response to incidents of antilesbian and antigay violence in New York City. The New York City Gay and Lesbian

Anti-Violence Project provides a number of services, such as short-term crisis intervention, police advocacy, court monitoring, referrals, and individual and group counseling. Wertheimer noted that not all communities can or will create special services for lesbian and gay victims of violence. He suggested that such work can be done by other community agencies that do the following: become trained in special issues of lesbian and gay clients, including how to create nonprejudicial agency environments; engage in outreach, using agency publications that explicitly refer to services available for lesbian women and gay men; and issue nondiscriminatory policies that explicitly include sexual orientation (Wertheimer, 1990).

Women with Disabilities

The Disabled Women's Network in Toronto reported that disabled women are sexually assaulted three times as often as able-bodied women or TABs (temporarily able-bodied persons) (Burstow, 1992). This number calls our attention to another often invisible group of rape survivors: women with disabilities. The term "women with disabilities" is used here instead of "disabled women," to suggest that such women are women first and disabled second (Sue Carver, personal communication, 1995).

Before working with sexually assaulted women with disabilities, it is important to look at our own stereotypes and biases. Too often, mental health professionals pathologize, infantilize, or marginalize women with disabilities. Our stereotypes lead us to believe that "women with disabilities" means women in wheelchairs, rather than women who have a wide variety of disabilities, such as hearing or vision impairment, developmental delays, or chronic mental illness, as well as physical disabilities. The Americans with Disabilities Act defines *disability* as "a physical or mental impairment that substantially limits one or more of the major life activities" (Americans with Disabilities Act, 42 United States Code, Sec. 12102).

Although the statistics vary, research suggests that sexual victimization of women with disabilities is greater than that of the general population, for these women are often more vulnerable to sexual exploitation and assault. Andrews and Veronen's (1993) review of the literature identified eight factors that increase the vulnerability to victimization among persons with disabilities: (1) People with severe disabilities may depend on others for care, leading them to be compliant and trusting of caregivers; (2) people with disabilities are still denied basic human rights and may feel more powerless than other people; (3) offenders may target people with disabilities because they believe the offenders are at less risk of discovery; (4) many survivors who have a disability encounter difficulty being believed; (5) people with intellectual impairments are less likely to have been educated about sexuality, so they may be less able to recognize, understand, and resist sexually abusive or exploitive situations; (6) people with disabilities may be relatively socially isolated and lonely, and more vulnerable to exploitation through manipulative relationships that initially appear to be affectionate and indicative of social acceptance; (7) people with disabilities may be more challenged in attempts to take risk-reducing precautions or to resist actual assaults; and (8) mainstreaming that is implemented without considerations for each person's capacity for self-protection may place disabled women at high risk for victimization.

Sexual assault may have unique ramifications for women with disabilities. In some illnesses, such as multiple sclerosis or lupus, stress can aggravate the illness. Even though no overt physical injuries occur as a result of a sexual assault, the assault may cause serious physical complications (Sue Carver, personal communication, June 5, 1995). Another complication for women with disabilities is their more limited choices after an assault. For instance, some women choose to move after a sexual assault occurs in their home. This option may not be available to a woman with a disability whose housing is determined by wheelchair accessibility, subsidized rent for specific independent-living housing, or proximity to caregivers. Additionally, women with communication disabilities may find it difficult to disclose the abuse, and women with chronic mental illness may disclose the abuse but not be believed.

It helps to hire a social worker or other service provider with special skills and training in working with women with disabilities. The Houston Area Women's Center in Houston, Texas, offers such a program for women with disabilities and is able to offer specialized care, training, public education, and therapy groups for women with disabilities. This model program has received statewide recognition for its pioneering work. Although it's desirable to hire a person with special understanding of women with disabilities, the entire staff needs to be trained in the unique issues that may confront women with disabilities who are sexually assaulted.

Andrews and Veronen (1993) suggest these examples to eliminate barriers for people with disabilities: (a) public-awareness activities that target people with disabilities; (b) information and referral services that screen for callers with disabilities and provide access to those with speech and hearing impairments; (c) 24-hour availability of appropriate transportation, interpreters, and other communication assistance; (d) physical accessibility of all facilities; (e) designated personnel who are trained to respond to victims with disabilities at survivor-services agencies; (f) designated personnel trained to monitor risk reduction and to respond to victims at agencies that serve people with disabilities; (g) adaptive services by medical practitioners, psychotherapists, and others, so that special needs are met; (h) promotion of an inclusive atmosphere, where survivors with disabilities feel welcomed by other clients and caregivers. Clearly, women with disabilities are too often a neglected yet vulnerable population of sexual-assault survivors. Increasingly, the social work profession is acknowledging that

ableism may constitute another way to oppress and discriminate against a class of people. Addressing the needs of women with disabilities is an issue whose time has come.

Incarcerated Women

Women who are incarcerated are also often a forgotten or invisible group of women. These stigmatized women often receive little attention and few services. From April 1994 to November 1996, the Women's Rights Project for the Human Rights Watch conducted research into the sexual abuse of female prisoners in a report entitled *All Too Familiar: Sexual Abuse of Women in U.S. State Prisons* (Human Rights Watch Women's Rights Project, 1996). Little is known about sexual assault behind prison walls, for there has been no systematic survey of the problem, and much of the evidence tends to be anecdotal. The Human Rights Report is based on a 2½-year research project that examined women in five states: California, Georgia, Michigan, New York, and Illinois, as well as the District of Columbia. Based on interviews with 60 current and former inmates, the report described serious sexual abuse from male correctional employees, who vaginally, orally, and anally raped their female prisoners. Mandatory pat-frisks are used as an excuse to grope women's breasts, buttocks, and vaginal areas. The report noted that not only is actual or threatened force used, but also male correctional employees "exploit their ability to provide or deny goods and privileges to female prisoners to compel them to have sex or, in other cases, to reward them for having done so" (p. 1).

Incarcerated women are especially vulnerable to such abuse, as grievance or investigatory procedures are either nonexistent or ineffective. Some female prisoners have taken legal action themselves in class action suits, winning settlements while the U.S. Justice Department Civil Rights Division has won convictions in seven cases since 1990, involving male correctional employees who were abusing female inmates (Holmes, 1996). Such legal remedies and the reported abuse itself seem to be only the tip of the iceberg. The problem has been brought to the forefront, in part by the dramatic increase in the number of female prisoners from 25,000 in 1980 to almost 116,000 in 1995 (Holmes, 1996).

Strategies for Change

PRACTICE IMPLICATIONS

With the high incidence of sexual assault, social work practice may frequently involve providing services to sexual-assault survivors. Depending on the survivors' help-seeking behavior, the social work practice strategies will range from crisis intervention to more long-term psychotherapy interventions. Social work practice may include individual work with survivors, group work, and community organization and education. Inclusive in this model are techniques borrowed from various other therapies, which may be helpful to the sexual-assault survivors, including crisis intervention, supportive counseling, prolonged exposure, and anxiety management. As demonstrated throughout this book, the preferred practice models combine feminist principles with social work values and strategies. These ideologies are both comprehensive and complementary.

In the 1970s, Ann Burgess, a psychiatric nurse, and Lynda Holmstrom, a sociologist, pioneered the work that led to our present-day understanding of rape survivors. By studying women and children survivors of rape who sought treatment at Boston City Hospital, Burgess and Holmstrom (1974) identified a pattern of women's responses to sexual assault, which these researchers termed "rape trauma syndrome." Their model includes two distinct stages: (1) the acute phase, and (2) the long-term reorganization process. These stages identify the victim's response to rape, providing a road map for rape-crisis counselors, social

workers, and therapists. Other clinicians have elaborated on the model (see Table 10.4 for an outline of several stage models). Most recently, rape-practice models have focused on the role of PTSD for survivors of sexual assault.

Posttraumatic Stress Disorder (PTSD)

In the 1980s, mental health professionals began to make the connection between rape survivors and war veterans, between battered women and prisoners of war. Although, on the surface, these traumas appear very different, the underlying experiences are very similar, leading to common symptoms and diagnoses of PTSD. Although it might seem a far-fetched comparison to some people, the terrifying experiences of war veterans and political prisoners in foreign countries produced the same intense terror and helplessness that rape survivors and battered women experience here at home.

Although the diagnosis of PTSD is relatively new, first appearing in 1980 in the third edition of the *Diagnostic and Statistical Manual of Mental Disorders* (DSM-III), the actual disorder is not. Psychiatrist Judith Herman has recounted the "forgotten history" of PTSD, which first was labeled hysteria in the late nineteenth century, as it primarily affected women; the second surfacing of the disorder was in its resurrection as shell shock or combat neurosis in both World Wars I and II and later in Vietnam; and the disorder once again surfaced with the sexual and domestic violence named by feminists (Herman, 1992). The hallmark of the diagnosis is undergoing a trauma. In the DSM-III-R, the trauma was described as "a psychologically distressing event that is outside the range of usual human experience" (American Psychiatric Association [APA], 1987, p. 247). Unfortunately, with the frequency of rape and domestic violence, this description was not accurate, for such violence was too often well within the range of normal female experience. In the *DSM-IV* (fourth edition of *DSM*), the criterion changed to exposure to a traumatic event if "the person experienced, witnessed, or

Table 10.4
Four Stage Models of Sexual Assault

Model Name	Stages	Characteristics
Rape Trauma Syndrome (Burgess & Holmstrom, 1974) A syndrome of behavior, somatic, and psychological reactions, which is an acute stress reaction to a life-threatening situation.	1. Acute phase disorganization	Disorganization, shock, disbelief, fear, somatic manifestations, self-blame.
	2. Long-term reorganization	Coping behaviors; changing residences and phone numbers; finding support; continuing experiences of nightmares, fears, and sexual problems.
Phases of Victim's Reaction to Rape (Sutherland & Scherl, 1970) A specific predictable sequence of response to rape.	1. Acute reaction (few days to few weeks)	Shock, dismay, anxiety anger, fear.
	2. Outward adjustment	Pseudo-adjustment, with elements of denial and suppression, resumption of activities, assertions of feeling well and needing no further assistance.
	3. Integration and resolution	May be triggered by specific incident, such as a glimpse of a man who looks like the assailant; depression and obsessive memories of the rape; must integrate new view of herself.
Empowerment Model for Counseling Rape Survivors (Worell & Remer, 1992)	1. Prerape	The sum total of what a woman knows about rape, including her life experiences, sex-role socialization, rape-myth acceptance, fear of rape, and societal attitudes, beliefs, and responses to rape.
	2. Rape event	All events immediately preceding, during, and following the rape; victim's needs are to escape, then to survive.
	3. Crisis and disorganization (few hours to a year)	Feeling shocked, helpless, out of control, and vulnerable to negative, blaming reactions by others; undergoing various reactions, from hysterical to numb; needing to regain a sense of control, to make decisions about reporting and about medical care; needing to be accepted and understood.

Continued

Table 10.4
(Continued)

Model Name	Stages	Characteristics
Empowerment Model for Counseling Rape Survivors (Worell & Remer, 1992)	4. Outward satisfactory adjustment and denial	Attempt to get their life back to normal; deny and minimize importance of rape; often a useful resting place, but may exhibit depression and nightmares.
	5. Reliving and working through	Denial lifts, and nightmares and flashbacks may occur; symptoms similar to crisis stage, although rape may have occurred years before; feels like she is going crazy.
	6. Resolution and integration	Integrates the rape into her life; makes meaning for herself about the rape; enhances her existing coping skills, appreciates her strengths, moves from "victim" to "survivor."
Trauma and Recovery (Herman, 1992) Treatment of trauma	1. Safety	Empowerment is key: establishing sobriety, building social support, using techniques to manage stress, making environment safe, regaining control of her life and body, managing symptoms.
	2. Remembrance and mourning	Review of life before trauma, recounting of trauma with affect, review of the meaning of the event, grieving of the losses.
	3. Reconnection	Creating a future, developing new relationships, no longer feeling possessed by the trauma, repossessing the self, possibly finding a survivor mission.

was confronted with an event or events that involved actual or threatened death or serious injury to the physical integrity of self or others" and the person's response involved "intense fear, helplessness, or horror" (APA, 1994, pp. 427–428). It is easy to imagine, and research confirms, that a rape survivor meets these criteria. The symptoms of PTSD fall into three categories, including (1) intrusive reexperiencing of the trauma, (2) persistent avoidance of stimuli associated with the trauma and numbing of general responsiveness, and (3) persistent symptoms of increased arousal (APA, 1994).

In one study of 95 female rape survivors, 94% of the women met symptomatic criteria for PTSD at an average of 12 days after the assault, this decreased to 65% an average of 35 days postassault, and decreased further to 47%

an average of 94 days after the assault (Roth-baum, Roa, Riggs, Murdock, & Walsh, 1991). The study's findings led to several conclusions. First, although PTSD is a prominent reaction following rape, it is not universal, and second, not all rape survivors require treatment because half of them seem to recover spontaneously. According to a review of the literature, how a woman reacts after a rape relies on many factors, including the particular characteristics of the crime, present and past psychological resources, developmental level, life stress, and social support (Koss & Burkhart, 1989).

There remains considerable controversy over the PTSD diagnosis, with debate over whether it should continue to be included as an anxiety disorder or would be better classified as a dissociative or depressive disorder (Davidson & Foa, 1991, 1993). Another alternative is to form a new set of diagnostic criteria based on the etiology of the disorder, rather than the symptoms, perhaps called "disorders of psychological trauma" (Davidson & Foa, 1991). Herman (1992) advocates for a new diagnosis that will better define and describe the syndrome that follows prolonged, repeated trauma, such as spousal abuse and repeated marital rapes, called "complex post-traumatic disorder." Much clinical work and research remain to refine the diagnosis to better explain and understand the process of trauma, especially in relation to women who have been victims of violence.

Crisis Intervention

Selecting the appropriate intervention depends on which stage the survivor is in when the social worker comes into contact with her. If it is within hours or days after the assault, crisis intervention is the treatment of choice (Holmstrom & Burgess, 1974; Koss, 1987; Williams & Holmes, 1981). Slaikeu (1984) stated, "a crisis is a temporary state of upset and disorganization, characterized chiefly by an individual's inability to cope with a particular situation using customary methods of problem solving, and

by the potential for a radically positive or negative outcome" (p. 13). This representation describes the experience of a sexual-assault survivor. A medical social worker employed in an emergency room may have this contact, a social worker at a rape-crisis center may be called into the hospital to act as the survivor's advocate, or the person who has been assaulted and who needs your guidance may be your best friend, your neighbor, or your family member.

Earlier in the chapter, we described the range of emotions and behavior a survivor may be experiencing. In response, the social worker can begin to administer "psychological first aid." Slaikeu (1984) described the five components of psychological first aid: (1) Make psychological contact, (2) explore dimensions of the problem, (3) examine possible solutions, (4) assist in taking concrete action, and (5) follow up. This process includes many skills inherent in social work practice, including listening, making empathic statements, communicating concern, and inviting the survivor to talk. The social worker should offer support and non-blaming acceptance. The survivor's primary needs are safety and privacy.

The social work role is to support and guide the client through the process. This process is a little more difficult with a sexual-assault survivor, analogous to walking a tightrope. For instance, in comparison to practicing psychotherapy, a hallmark of crisis intervention is that the social worker is more directive. However, the client has undergone a situation in which complete control was taken away from her. This contradiction—to be directive without being controlling—makes a social worker's task difficult. The immediate needs fall under the following categories: social support, medical assistance, and law-enforcement involvement.

First, the rape survivor needs to make decisions about whom to call. These decisions should be hers; she should also decide whether she makes the calls or the calls are made by others on her behalf. Offer choices and support. A social worker can help her brainstorm who will be most supportive to her in the present situation. This discussion should also include who will come to get her and where she will go. If the attack occurred at her home, many survivors will naturally be reluctant to return home. The home of family or friends may be preferable. Many survivors will return home after changing their locks and their phone numbers. Many survivors who were raped at home move to a new residence.

Also, medical assistance is frequently an immediate need. Depending on the severity of the injuries, such assistance may receive first priority. Medical attention will involve treatment of serious injuries received during a violent rape, preventive treatment for birth control and sexually transmitted diseases, and collection of forensic evidence (Koss and Harvey, 1987). After receiving treatment for injuries, the survivors can make some choices about receiving antibiotics for sexually transmitted diseases and the "morning-after" pill to prevent pregnancy that might occur as a result of the rape. Preferably, the collection of forensic evidence will be done by a sexual-assault nurse examiner (SANE) using a prepared standard rape kit. Although such an examination can be felt by the rape survivor to constitute a second assault, such information is necessary to apprehend the assailant. The social worker, with the client's permission, is encouraged to stay with the survivor and support her during the exam.

With the increased awareness today about the heterosexual transmission of HIV/AIDS, contracting the virus as a result of the assault is a growing concern among rape survivors. Recent rape survivors were four times more likely to be concerned about contracting HIV/AIDS as a result of the rape, when compared to all rape victims surveyed in the *Rape in America: Report to the Nation* (NVC & CVRTC, 1992). Therefore, crisis intervention must include a discussion of HIV/AIDS transmission and phone numbers for confidential testing at a later date. Safer sex practices should be instituted by the survivor and her partner until follow-up testing reveal no transmission of the virus.

Finally, the client must make a decision as to whether to report the attack to the police. The survivor has several options to consider about making a report (Texas Dept. of Health Sexual Assault Prevention-Crisis Services and Texas Association Against Sexual Assault [TDH & TAASA], undated). A formal complaint can be filed, in which the survivor cooperates throughout the criminal justice process as a victim–witness. The formal process of reporting can include an initial statement to police, being photographed to show injuries, (in some states) being polygraphed, giving a formal statement at a later date, identifying the suspect, and testifying at the trial. The survivor also has the choice to end her participation at any point. The survivor could also choose to make an informational report to the police, without further contact. Last, the survivor or a designated person could choose to make an anonymous "third-party" report. It's helpful to weigh with the client the risks and benefits of reporting. The client should be supported if she does report, but not criticized if, for whatever reason, she is unable or unwilling to inform the police. One benefit to reporting the crime is to be eligible for crime-victim compensation, which may be available to cover medical and other expenses (Holzman, 1993).

The local rape-crisis center is usually a good referral source, with the approval of the survivor, so a trained volunteer may come to provide additional support and act as an advocate for the survivor. The number and location of the nearest rape-crisis center should be given as a referral for follow-up questions, counseling, and rape-survivor groups.

Treatment

Due to the many psychological consequences of rape, many rape survivors can benefit from therapeutic intervention. However, few victims seek mental health treatment immediately after a rape, so victims are more likely to see physicians than mental health professionals (Koss et al., 1994). Women may eventually seek psychotherapy, however, as many of the effects of rape are long-term. For instance, one study concluded that for many women, the psychological aftereffects of physical and sexual assaults may last for years, with the survivors in the study averaging more than 13 years postassault (Riggs, Kilpatrick, & Resnick, 1992). These long-term effects may bring survivors in for counseling weeks, months, and even years after the assault.

Assessment

Because many women may be reluctant to disclose a history of sexual assault, the social worker must ask specifically for a woman to divulge such information. It should be a routine part of history taking to ask a client about any experiences with sexual victimization. Just asking the woman whether she has been raped is not enough. As stated many times previously, many women do not define their experiences as having been rape. A more general question might be asked: "At any time in your life, have you received unwanted sexual attention or forced sexual activity from either someone you knew or a stranger?" Even if the therapeutic relationship has not progressed far enough for the client to feel safe to reveal such a traumatic incident, the client knows that this is a subject the social worker is willing to acknowledge and discuss. The door has been opened.

If the client reports an incident of sexual assault, the social worker should not assume that the assault is still an issue for the client. Koss & Harvey (1987) have recommended assessing the degree of rape resolution using a model by Forman (1983), which evaluates several areas: First, assess the client's ability to discuss the rape; if the client is reluctant to discuss the rape or she continues to blame herself, the rape may yet be unresolved. Second, listen for signs of her present postrape responses, which may indicate an incomplete resolution, such as a continuing startle reflex, hyperarousal, intrusive memories, guilt, shame, and avoidance of sexual relationships. Third, try to gain an understanding of the meaning the client ascribes to the rape; if the client is able to verbalize that even though the experience was traumatic, she was able to survive, learn, and grow, this may be a more adaptive response than the client who still feels guilt and self-blame. Fourth, evaluate the social support the client received at the time of the assault and that she receives currently, as an indicator of rape resolution. If her family and friends were critical of her and her relationships with others remain strained, this may signal unresolved feelings about the rape. Fifth, if there has been an extreme reaction to a recent, seemingly minor event, the present reaction can be a reactivation of the past assault. The amount of time that has passed since the assault is generally a poor indicator of the client's level of rape resolution. Sexual assault that occurred years ago can remain problematic for a woman who never had the support or opportunity to integrate the rape experience into her life.

Individual Psychotherapies

The debate over the best treatment for women who fit the PTSD diagnosis continues. As reported earlier, half of rape survivors will resolve the trauma with a decrease in symptoms, without intervention. For the remaining women, clinical treatment may be appropriate. One study compared the efficacy of three treatment modalities with rape survivors, including stress inoculation training, prolonged exposure, and supportive counseling (Foa, Rothbaum, Riggs, & Murdock, 1991). *Prolonged exposure* (PE) involves the survivor reliving the rape scene by imagining it as vividly as possible, with homework including exposure to the feared and avoided stimuli. *Stress inoculation training* (SIT) involves teaching the client many coping skills centered around anxiety management, such as deep muscle relaxation, controlled breathing, stopping of unwanted thought, cognitive restructuring, guided self-dialogue, and role playing. *Supportive counseling* (SC) methods, adapted from rape-crisis center protocols, involve general problem solving, with the therapist taking an indirect and unconditionally supportive role. The study found that PE seemed to be the best treatment in the long term, with SIT being most helpful in the short term (Foa et al., 1991). Additionally, a new intervention currently being used is called "eye movement desensitization and reprocessing" (EMDR) therapy, in which the client tracks the rapid movement of the therapist's fingers, based on a relationship between saccadic eye movements and memory desensitization (Koss et al., 1994). Research is being conducted on its effectiveness, although early reports are promising.

Groups

Women coming together in groups to share their experiences has a long history in feminist practice. From formal women's organizations to informal talks around the kitchen table, women have been sharing their experiences and seeking support from other women. The consciousness-raising groups in the second wave of the women's movement were credited for transforming personal concerns into political agendas. Sexual-assault survivors coming together as a group to discuss their experiences can be a vital part of recovery.

Yassen and Glass (1984) have developed a model for sexual-assault survivors groups, which is time limited and focused on themes and topics specifically related to the sexual assault. Each group's goal is to resolve the emotional turmoil resulting from the sexual assault. Yassen and Glass (1984) suggested that the group members be interviewed beforehand to select group members in a similar stage in resolving the trauma, with a minimum guideline of at least 6 months having passed since the time of the assault. Their groups are a mixture of open-ended and topic-oriented discussions, which include such topics as self-esteem, trust, power and control, guilt, mourning and loss, and anger.

Many rape-crisis centers sponsor survivor groups, and such a center may be an appropriate referral for your client. If such groups are not available, or if assistance is sought in addition to individual and group work, it sometimes helps to read books relating accounts of other women's stories. Feminist psychologist Laura Brown recommended Scherer (1992) "for a first-person account of a heterosexual white middle class woman rape survivor who had strong support and contrast it with Fine's (1992) account of the experience of a poor heterosexual African-American woman whose social network was fragile even before she was raped" (Brown, 1994, p. 172). For rape victims, sharing their own stories and learning the stories of other women can be very validating, affirming, and comforting. It can also lead to political action and advocacy. The Internet provides unique opportunities for women to "chat" together about their experiences and to share successful strategies and resources. Some rape-crisis centers have sites on the world wide web (www). Through their website, the Rape Crisis Center of San Antonio, Texas, was able to link an isolated, hearing-impaired rape survivor in Scotland to a rape survivor in Los Angeles, and the two women began a supportive e-mail conversation (Shannon, 1996).

Treatment Issues

Cultural Analysis of Rape

In line with both the social work emphasis on person-in-environment and the feminist perspective that the personal is political, it is important to relate the client's experience with sexual assault to the rape-prone culture in which we live. The discussion may include talking about rape myths that the client believes and the myths people have told the client since the assault. Refuting the myths can help the client stop blaming herself for the rape and can enable her to define her experience as rape. Naming one's own experience is an essential feature of feminist therapy. Koss and Burkhart (1989) hypothesize that "until victims can be affirmed in the reality of victimization—that is, that they are not to blame for their injury—they cannot complete the emotional process of transforming guilt into anger and depression to grief" (p. 32).

Multicultural Issues

The effect of the rape on the survivor is influenced not only by cultural considerations but also by issues of race, ethnicity, and religion. Research supports the notion that race may affect the beliefs held by the survivor and her family about the rape, as well as her willingness to gain access to resources and her coping responses. For instance, in some cultures, rape is considered such a shameful event that the survivor may not feel able to turn to family and friends for support (Holzman, 1994). A Eurocentric model of therapy centers on openness in communication and avoidance of keeping secrets, and this approach may be inadvisable for some women who face more serious consequences in disclosing the assault, rather than keeping quiet (Holzman, 1994). Another Eurocentric belief is the value of expressing anger or sadness, while in some cultures, public displays of either of these emotions would be unacceptable. Merely talking about the assault is unacceptable in many cultures. Using indirect references to the assault, such as metaphors and third-party references may be appropriate when working with Southeast Asian women (Kanuha, 1987). Referring women to resources in their own communities, where available, is helpful.

Additionally, the survivor's religious beliefs can play an important role in her recovery. For some women, their religion and their spiritual leaders are a comfort, but for others, these can increase the women's shame. Again, the woman knows what is best for her. Culturally appropriate care can be difficult and can create dilemmas for the client when values conflict between what is best for the client and what is required of her by her culture. Holzman (1994) reminded us that an important guide is to always remember that the client has to live with herself in her community. Further, Holzman stated,

> We are not serving her if we try to choose for her, either in the direction of defying cultural values or deferring to them. We can be most helpful by helping her to identify the conflicting pulls she is experiencing, to explore the costs and the benefits of her various options, and to find solutions that work best for her. (p. 93)

Rape is a crime that affects not only the victim, but also her family and her community. Work with the rape survivor must always keep this fact in mind, while supporting the survivor in ways that make her feel safe and heard.

Remembrance and Mourning

Koss and Harvey (1987) reported that discussing the details of the rape can foster catharsis and desensitization. Herman (1992) also noted the importance of the survivor telling her story, or testifying, and then beginning to mourn the many invisible or unrecognized losses. The goal is not merely to dwell on the details of the act, but to more fully understand how the client perceived the event. The client's behaviors during the rape may be a cause of her blaming herself. For instance, women who did not physically resist during the assault often feel guilt and shame, and they question their own behavior. Knowing this, the therapist can begin to reframe the behavior to help the client begin to appreciate what she did to survive.

Sharing the experience will almost certainly bring up a multitude of feelings for each client. She may be sad or angry. Such responses are normal and need to be validated. Some specific strategies for dealing with the anger may include using imagery to confront the assailant, using a punching bag, or engaging in strenuous physical activity. The client should be warned that talking about the assault will frequently bring up all the old feelings she thought she had successfully contained. It may get worse before it gets better. The client will need to rally social support from family and friends.

Rebuilding Shattered Assumptions

One of the most devastating realities about sexual assault is that it represents not only a physical attack, but also a psychological one. The victim's beliefs and assumptions about herself and her world are shattered by rape. Janoff-Bulman (1992) has done extensive work in this area and has identified three fundamental assumptions many people hold about the world: (1) The world is benevolent, (2) the world is meaningful, and (3) the self is worthy. A trauma, such as rape, causes each of these assumptions to be called into question. The world is suddenly seen as a dangerous, unpredictable, meaningless place inhabited by evil. The survivor's sense of self is often shaken, and she may see herself as ruined, dirty, or blameworthy. However, Wyatt (1992) has challenged Janoff-Bulman's theory, as applied to African-American women. Wyatt believes that under the dual oppressions of sexism and racism, many women of color do not have assumptive worlds allowing that the world is a good place populated with good people.

Janoff-Bulman (1992) posited that for the trauma to be resolved, these assumptions must be reassessed, and new assumptions must be adopted. One strategy that survivors often employ is comparing themselves to others, whether real or imagined, and considering themselves fortunate. A survivor may say, "At least I wasn't killed." In Janoff-Bulman's views, some survivors may use self-blame as an alternative strategy for regaining control over their lives. However, although self-blame may be helpful to the survivor in the short term in understanding her assault (e.g., "I shouldn't have gone to his room"), it has long-term effects that often delay the resolution of the rape. A third strategy, described by Janoff-Bulman and others in the trauma recovery field, is the survivor's attempt to "make meaning" of her assault. Survivors may look at the experience for lessons to be learned or benefits to be gained. Survivors of tragedy often verbalize how the experience caused them to reprioritize their lives and enjoy life's simple pleasures, which they had previously taken for granted. Some survivors develop a "survivor's mission" (Herman, 1992), which causes them to adopt a cause and help other survivors. Such rape survivors work at rape-crisis centers, testify before legislative committees to lobby for rape law reform, and others start sur-

vivor-support groups. Social workers can help facilitate this process by supporting clients in rebuilding their worlds and making meaning of how the rape experience fits into their lives.

Cognitive Restructuring

Part of the process of refuting rape myths and reevaluating worldviews and assumptions is to restructure not only what the survivor feels about the rape, but also how she thinks about it. The social worker can assist the survivor to adopt new beliefs about the sexual assault. Worell and Remer (1992) illustrated such a reappraisal. A self-blame cognition may initially be presented as "I should have been able to see that he was dangerous" and then transformed into "He deliberately portrayed himself as trustworthy" and then, "Society misled me to believe that only strangers commit rape" (p. 212). Additionally, a self-blame cognition may include a statement such as "I should have fought harder and longer" to a restructured cognition such as "He was larger and stronger than I. If I had fought more, I might have been more physically hurt and I probably still wouldn't have been able to avoid being raped" (p. 212).

Other Issues

Many other issues will arise for the survivor, which are beyond the scope of this chapter to fully discuss. As reported earlier, there is a marked increase in the use of alcohol and other drugs among survivors, who may abuse substances to dull their pain. Assessments or referrals to appropriate support groups or treatment centers for addictions are helpful. A major part of rape recovery involves mourning the losses resulting from the rape and honoring and supporting the grief process. Assisting the survivor in developing new coping mechanisms may be necessary. Persistent symptoms may need to be treated in a targeted fashion—such as by using specialized techniques for anxiety management, depression, or sexual dysfunction—yet such targeting must be accomplished within the context of the entire rape, for picking out one symptom to work on in isolation is like missing the forest for the trees. Koss (1993) recommends treatment innovations especially of multicultural approaches, programs for adolescent victims, and treatments for victims with multiple diagnoses.

Recovery

Most survivors would agree that the memory of the rape never totally subsides but will always be a part of the victim's life. For each victim, there is no going back to the person she (or he) was before the assault. Yet many survivors resolve the rape and are able to resume a full life. In a study by Zollicoffer and Remer (1989), cited by Worell and Remer (1992), survivors identified the following concepts as illustrating their recovery and resolution:

1. Working through feelings so that they are no longer overwhelmed by rape-related emotions
2. Integrating the rape into their lives so that the rape no longer controls their lives
3. Accepting the reality of the rape, including acknowledgment that the rape occurred and that it was traumatic
4. Helping others by counseling and supporting other survivors who have been raped
5. Perceiving support from others, as the survivors shared their feelings and thoughts about the rape—if they could share without being blamed or judged, and if they were listened to emphatically, then survivors felt validated and less isolated and stigmatized
6. Loving, appreciating, and forgiving themselves—that is, learning to trust themselves to perceive accurately and to make good decisions and judgments (p. 218).

With these indicators as a guide and a support for social work, practitioners can help the victim to move to survivor, and to thriver. The feminist perspective of "the personal is political" and the social work concept of "person-in-environment" uniquely qualify feminist social workers to assist rape survivors with trauma resolution. These same ideologies lead social workers,

sometimes accompanied by their clients, on a further path of policy and advocacy.

POLICY IMPLICATIONS

The present environment allows and even encourages rape to exist, but to change this environment demands a revolution. Such a revolution means the end of a patriarchal society in which men are viewed as dominant and superior, and women are defined as subordinate and inferior; the end of the power imbalances between men and women; the end of the sexual objectification of women; and the confrontation of racism, sexism, classism, homophobia, sex-role stereotypes, and other forms of oppression and discrimination. The revolutionary social-change approach must be multidimensional, working on many levels on a variety of interrelated issues.

Legal Reforms

Many legal reforms at both the state and the national level have been instituted in the area of rape law reform. For instance, definitions of rape have been broadened to include a wider array of acts and perpetrators, including the victim's spouse. Independent corroboration of rape is no longer required in most states, and rape-shield laws are in place to protect the privacy and sexual history of the survivor. Although the benefits of such reform are still being debated (Goldberg-Ambrose, 1992), there has been significant progress.

One strategy in a feminist social work model focuses on legal reforms to advocate for incremental legislative change. A list of reforms vary from state to state, but might include the following:

- Broadening the definitions of rape to include a variety of assaults
- Prohibiting the polygraphing of rape survivors as a requirement before proceeding with their cases
- Forming judicial-review task forces to document differential treatment for women of

color who have been raped and differential sentencing for men of color who have raped

- Gaining increased funding for rape-crisis centers and telephone hotlines
- Advocating for "women-centered" laws and interpretations—for instance, Edmonds (1992) has advocated for a change in how consent is viewed, "That is, 'real rape' would be defined by the presence or absence of an explicit yes, not by how much violence there was or how little the victim knew her assailant" (p. 97)
- Making admissible the expert testimony on rape trauma syndrome and rape myth acceptance
- Ensuring longer sentences for convicted rapists
- Passing of legislation providing sexual assault survivors with effective privacy protections that will prevent media disclosure of their names and addresses (NVC & CVRTC, 1992)
- Removing marital exemptions for rape from the state statutes that still include it

Even these reforms, however, are subject to challenge. Edmonds (1992) has decried harsher penalties and longer sentences for convicted rapists, for she argues that such changes disproportionately affect African-American men, who are more likely than European-American men to be convicted of rape. Edmonds (1992) recommended new jury instructions to replace Hale's Dictum. She suggested, "explicit instructions to the judge, the prosecutors, and the jury that it is a crime of law to allow any negative preconceptions they have based upon the race of the victim or the defendant to enter into their judgment" (p. 98).

As social workers, you may wish to research the sexual-assault statutes in your state. Although legal reforms would go a long way in treating rape survivors more fairly and perpetrators more severely, however, such work is like closing the barn door after the cow is already out. Additional reforms must focus on prevention and social change.

Political Change

The political change required to change this rape-prone culture encompasses much more than legislative change; it means transforming our entire culture to respect and value women. Social workers must work to make rape a political issue in this country. Stoltenberg (1993) described rape as a national-security issue and suggested making rape an election issue. When was the last time you heard candidates talk about their views on rape in their campaign or party platforms? Party platforms often decry political terrorism without addressing the domestic terrorism or sexual terrorism that exists within our borders. By writing editorials, asking tough questions of legislators, or organizing "Take Back the Night" marches, social workers must make rape a political issue.

Stoltenberg further proposed speaking out against the pornography industry as a purveyor of prorape propaganda. Stoltenberg is not the first to associate the issues of rape and pornography. In fact, Robin Morgan's observation is frequently cited, "Pornography is the theory and rape the practice" (Morgan, 1992, p. 88). Although studies do not conclusively link pornography as a causative factor in rape, it does seem to play a role. Studies undertaken on college campuses reveal that after repeated viewing of movies depicting sexual violence against women, men are less likely to empathize with the victim and more likely to blame her for her own victimization (Donnerstein, Linz, & Penrod, 1987). Executed serial murderer Ted Bundy pointed to his use of pornography as related to his attacks on women.

Educational Change

Feminists and other social-change activists are realizing that attitudes cannot be legislated. No matter how good the laws are, it is people who enforce and interpret them. Changes in laws have made it somewhat easier for rapists to be prosecuted and for rape victims to be protected, yet if the jury still believes in rape acceptance myths, all is lost. There must be a comprehensive educational effort to teach the nation about sexual assault.

Most police officers and prosecutors receive special training about sexual assault, but judges and juries are not trained. Koss (1993), acknowledging that victims are more likely to visit a physician than mental health professional, advocates for inclusion of material on rape in the health-care curriculum as well as provision of rape victim sensitive care in all health-care settings. Additionally, we need nationwide, systematic training programs for adolescents about the realities of violence, sex, and power. Many creative and exciting programs are now available to teach adolescents about sexual assault, especially date rape. With an increasing number of social workers practicing in school settings, discussion of these issues is an important practice consideration.

However, much educational work remains to be done before the adolescent years. Gender inequalities in the realms of power, sexuality, and aggression start much earlier than the teenage years. As soon as one infant is wrapped in a pink blanket and the other in blue, the socialization begins whereby boys learn to feel entitled and girls learn to assume caregiving roles. Although sex-role stereotypes are slowly changing, many still exist and are strictly enforced by parents and other family members, friends, and many social, religious, and political institutions. In the book *Transforming a Rape Culture* (Buchwald, Fletcher, & Roth, 1993), many authors took a critical look at ending our rape-prone culture by proposing multifaceted solutions. Many suggested solutions involved the socialization process. Myriam Miedzian (1993), a social worker, wrote, "If we are serious about *significantly* decreasing our rape rates, we must move men, and especially young boys, away from a definition of masculinity that centers on toughness, power, dominance, eagerness to fight, lack of empathy, and a cal-

lous attitude towards women. For as long as these values (which I refer to as the 'masculine mystique') prevail among many men, rape will continue to be viewed by them as proof that they are 'one of the boys,' that they are 'real men'" (p. 155).

Changes in socialization are needed for young girls, as well. Buchwald (1993) has a long laundry list of strategies to teach girls to enable them to be strong enough to resist and change the rape-prone culture. Her list includes telling our daughters what helped us to survive growing up; giving girls our attention and approval; enlisting fathers as active allies to remake the culture; telling girls the truth by replacing ignorance with knowledge and shame with insight; enlisting women mentors and role models; finding ways for girls to play and work together; forming action groups to convince media leaders to reform the presentation of women; choosing toys and stories that don't reinforce gender stereotypes; being part of the solution ourselves; and encouraging girls to be ecstatic. Her strategies could result in revolutionary new ways to raise girls and transform the society in which they learn and live.

Profeminist men are actively working on this issue to change the way men think about women, rape, and male privilege. Men Stopping Rape is an organization of men who actively engage other men in men-only groups to discuss the issues and to challenge their beliefs. The process is twofold, both inward and outward directed. Biernbaum and Weinberg (1991) have described the process: "The process we initiate is and support is *inward*-directed: confronting the rapist within, understanding his complicity in the rape culture, and learning how to be a man without rape. We defer until later the outward-directed process of learning how to confront rape–supportive behaviors in others and to safely intervene to stop the violence of others" (p. 23). Another outspoken man on the topic of rape is author and activist Rus Funk, who wrote *Stopping Rape: A Challenge for Men* (1993).

SUMMARY

This chapter has detailed the trauma of rape. This violent assault causes women to experience disruptions both physically and psychologically. Working with rape survivors means attending not only to their physical needs but also to their psychological needs, remembering to honor their ethnic and cultural values while providing safety and respect. In looking at rape, however, it is clear that social workers cannot limit their practice to treating individuals, whether they are survivors or perpetrators. Rape is not an isolated symptom to be plucked out of society. It is an act that is often supported, condoned, tolerated, encouraged, and regulated by a patriarchal society that gives men a sense of entitlement and privilege. The conditions in society that allow rape to flourish must be confronted. For rape to end, racism, sexism, classism, and homophobia must also end. Stopping rape is a call to action and a challenge for social workers.

REFERENCES

American Psychiatric Association (1987). *Diagnostic and statistical manual of mental disorders, Third Edition-Revised*. Washington, DC: American Psychiatric Association.

American Psychiatric Association (1994). *Diagnostic and statistical manual of mental disorders, 4th edition*. Washington, DC: American Psychiatric Association.

Andrews, A. B., & Veronen, L. J. (1993). Sexual assault and people with disabilities. *Journal of Social Work and Human Sexuality, 8*(2), 137–159.

Arguelles, L., & Rivero, A. M. (1993). Gender/sexual orientation violence and transnational migration: Conversations with some Latinas we think we know. *Urban Anthropology and Studies of Cultural Systems and World Economic Development, 22*, 259–75.

Armstrong, L. (1978). *Kiss daddy good-night: A speak-out on incest*. New York: Hawthorne Books.

Biernbaum, M., & Weinberg, J. (1991). Men unlearning rape. *Changing Men, 22*, 22–24.

Brown, L. S. (1994). *Subversive dialogues: Theory in feminist therapy*. New York: Basic Books.

Brownmiller, S. (1975). *Against our will: Men, women, and rape*. New York: Simon & Schuster.

Buchwald, E. (1993). Raising girls for the 21st century. In E. Buchwald, P. Fletcher, & M. Roth (Eds.), *Transforming a rape culture* (pp. 179–200). Minneapolis, MN: Milkweed Editions.

Buchwald, E., Fletcher, P., & Roth, M. (Eds.). (1993). *Transforming a rape culture*. Minneapolis, MN: Milkweed Editions.

Burgess, A. W., & Holmstrom, L. L. (1974). Rape trauma syndrome. *American Journal of Psychiatry, 131*(9), 981–986.

Burrell, D. E. (1993). Myth, stereotype, and the rape of black women. *UCLA Women's Law Journal, 4*(87), 87–99.

Burstow, B. (1992). *Radical feminist therapy: Working in the context of violence*. Newbury Park, CA: Sage Publications.

Burt, M. R. (1980). Cultural myths and supports for rape. *Journal of Personality and Social Psychology, 38*(2), 217–230.

Davidson, J. R. T., & Foa, E. B. (1991). Diagnostic issues in posttraumatic stress disorder: Considerations for the DSM-IV. *Journal of Abnormal Psychology, 100*(3), 346–355.

Davidson, J. R. T., & Foa, E. B. (Eds.). (1993). *Posttraumatic stress disorder: DSM-IV and beyond*. Washington, DC: American Psychiatric Press.

Davis, A. (1981). *Women, race & class*. New York: Random House.

Donnerstein, E., Linz, D., & Penrod, S. (1987). *The question of pornography: Research findings and policy implications*. New York: Free Press.

Dye, E., & Roth, S. (1990). Psychotherapists' knowledge about and attitudes toward sexual assault victim clients. *Psychology of Women Quarterly, 14,* 191–212.

Easteal, R. (1994). *Voices of the survivors.* North Melbourne, Victoria, Australia: Spinifex Press.

Edmonds, E. (1992). Mapping the terrain of our resistance: A white feminist perspective on the enforcement of rape law. *Harvard BlackLetter Journal, 9,* 43–100.

Estrich, S. (1987). *Real rape.* Cambridge, MA: Harvard University Press.

Fine, M. (1992). *Disruptive voices: The possibilities of feminist research.* Ann Arbor: University of Michigan Press.

Finkelhor, D., & Brown, A. (1985). The traumatic impact of child sexual abuse: A conceptualization. *American Journal of Orthopsychiatry, 55,* 530–541.

Finkelhor, D., & Yllo, K. (1985). *License to rape: Sexual abuse of wives.* New York: Free Press.

Foa, E. B., Rothbaum, B. O., Riggs, D. S., & Murdock, T. B. (1991). Treatment of posttraumatic stress disorder in rape victims: A comparison between cognitive-behavioral procedures and counseling. *Journal of Consulting and Clinical Psychology, 59*(5), 715–723.

Forman, B. (1983). Treating victims of rape. *Psychotherapy: Theory, Research, and Practice, 20,* 515–519.

Funk, R. E. (1993). *Stopping rape: A challenge for men.* Philadelphia: New Society Publishers.

George, L. K., Winfield, I., & Blazer, D. G. (1992). Sociocultural factors in sexual assault: Comparison of two representative samples of women. *Journal of Social Issues, 48*(1), 105–125.

Goldberg-Ambrose, C. (1992). Unfinished business in rape law reform. *Journal of Social Issues, 48*(1), 173–185.

Gordon, M. T., & Riger, S. (1989). *The female fear.* New York: Free Press.

Griffin, S. (1979). *Rape: The Power of Consciousness.* New York: Harper & Row.

Griffin, S. (1990). Rape: The power of consciousness. In S. Ruth (Ed.), *Issues in feminism: An introduction to women's studies* (pp. 272–282). Mountainview, CA: Mayfield Publishing.

Groth, N. (1979). *Men who rape.* New York: Plenum.

Herman, J. L. (1992). *Trauma and recovery.* New York: Basic Books.

Holmes, S. (1996, December 28). How pervasive is sexual assault on female inmates by guards? *Houston Chronicle,* p. 5A.

Holmstrom, A. and Burgess, L. (1974). Rape trauma syndrome. *American Journal of Psychiatry, 131*(9), 981–986.

Holzman, C. G. (1994). Multicultural perspectives on counseling survivors of rape. *Journal of Social Distress and the Homeless, 3*(1), 81–97.

hooks, b. (1981). *Ain't I a woman: Black women and feminism.* Boston: South End Press.

Human Rights Watch, Women's Rights Project. (1996). *All too familiar: Sexual abuse of women in U.S. state prisons.* New York: Author.

Janoff-Bulman, R. (1992). *Shattered assumptions: Towards a new psychology of trauma.* New York: Free Press.

Kanuha, V. (1987). Sexual assault in Southeast Asian communities: Issues in intervention. *Response, 10,* 4–6.

Kilpatrick, D. G., Resnick, P. A., & Veronen, L. J. (1981). Effects of a rape experience: A longitudinal study. *Journal of Social Issues, 37*(4), 105–122.

Koss, M. P. (1992). The underdetection of rape: Methodological choices influence incidence estimates. *Journal of Social Issues, 48*(1), 61–76.

Koss, M. (1993). Rape: Scope, impact, interventions, and public policy responses. *American Psychologist, 48*(10), 1062–1069.

Koss, M. P., & Burkhart, B. R. (1989). A conceptual analysis of rape victimization: Long-term effects and implications for treatment. *Psychology of Women Quarterly, 13,* 27–40.

Koss, M. P., Gidycz, C. A., & Wisniewski, N. (1987). The scope of rape: Incidence and prevalence of sexual aggression and victimization in a national sample of higher education students. *Journal of Consulting and Clinical Psychology 55*(2), 162–170.

Koss, M., Goodman, L., Browne, A., Fitzgerald, L., Keita, G., and Russo, N. (1994). *No safe haven: Male violence against women at home, at work, and in the community.* Washington, DC: American Psychological Association.

Koss, M. P., & Harvey, M. (1987). *The rape victim: Clinical and community approaches to treatment.* Lexington, MA: Stephen Greene Press.

Lefley, H. P., Scott, C. S., Llabre, M., & Hickes, D. (1993). Cultural beliefs about rape and victim's response in three ethnic groups. *American Journal of Orthopsychiatry, 63*(4), 623–632.

Lifton, R. J. (1980). The concept of the survivor. In J. E. Dimsdale (Ed.), *Survivors, victims, and perpetrators: Essays on the Nazi Holocaust.* Washington, DC: Hemisphere.

Lonsway, K. A., & Fitzgerald, L. F. (1994). Rape myths: In review. *Psychology of Women Quarterly, 18,* 133–164.

Majority staff of the Senate Judiciary Committee. (1993). *The response to rape: Detours on the road to equal justice.* Washington, DC: Senate Judiciary Committee.

Malamuth, N. M., & Sockloskie, R. J., Koss, M. P., & Tanaka, J. S. (1991). Characteristics of aggressors against women: Testing a model using a national sample of college students. *Journal of Consulting and Clinical Psychology, 59*(5), 670–681.

Mayall, A., & Gold, S. R. (1995). Definitional issues and mediating variables in the sexual revictimization of women sexually abused as children. *Journal of Interpersonal Violence, 10*(1), 26–42.

Miedzian, M. (1993). How rape is encouraged in American boys and what we can do to stop it. In E. Buchwald, P. Fletcher, & M. Roth (Eds.), *Transforming a rape culture* (pp. 153–163). Minneapolis, MN: Milkweed Editions.

Morgan, R. (1992). Theory and practice: Pornography and rape (1974). In R. Morgan (Ed.), *The word of a woman* (pp. 78–89). New York: W.W. Norton.

Muehlenhard, C. L., Powch, I. G., Phelps, J. L., & Giusti, L. M. (1992). Definitions of rape: Scientific and political implications. *Journal of Social Issues, 48*(1), 23–44.

National Clearinghouse on Marital & Date Rape. (undated). *State Law Chart.* Berkeley, CA: Author.

National Victim Center & Crime Victims Research and Treatment Center. (1992). *Rape in America: Report to the nation:* Arlington, VA: National Victim Center; and Charleston, SC: Crime Victims Research and Treatment Center.

Orzek, A. M. (1989). The lesbian victim of sexual assault: Special considerations for the mental health professional. *Women and Therapy, 8*(1/2) 107–117.

Phillips, J. (1993, May 14). Man convicted in condom rape; sentencing today. *Austin American-Statesman,* pp. A1, A19.

Prentky, R. A., & Knight, R. A. (1991). Identifying critical dimensions for discriminating among rapists. *Journal of Consulting and Clinical Psychology, 59*(5), 643–661.

Riggs, D. S., Kilpatrick, D. G., & Resnick, H. S. (1992). Long-term psychological distress associated with marital rape and aggravated assault: A comparison to other crime victims. *Journal of Family Violence, 7*(4), 283–296.

Rothbaum, B., Foa, E. Riggs, D., Murdock, T., and Walsh, W. (1992). A prospective examination of post-traumatic stress disorder in rape victims. *Journal of Traumatic Stress, 5*(3), 455–475.

Russell, D. E. H. (1982). *Rape in marriage.* New York: Collier Books.

Russell, D. E. H. (1984). *Sexual exploitation: Rape, child sexual abuse, and workplace harassment.* Beverly Hills, CA: Sage Publications.

Russell, D. E. H. (1986). *The secret trauma: Incest in the lives of girls and women.* New York: Basic Books.

Sanday, P. R. (1981). The socio-cultural context of rape: A cross-cultural study. *Journal of Social Issues 37*(4), 5–27.

Scherer, M. (1992). *Still loved by the sun: A rape survivor's journal.* New York: Penguin Books.

Senate Judiciary Committee (May 1993). *The response to rape: Detours on the road to equal justice.* Prepared by the majority staff of the Senate Judiciary Committee. Washington, DC.

Shannon, K. (1996, April 21). Internet gives rape victims sympathetic ear. *Houston Chronicle,* p. 8A.

Slaikeu, K. A. (1984). *Crisis intervention: A handbook for practice and research.* Boston, MA: Allyn & Bacon.

Sorenson, S. B., & Siegel, J. M. (1992). Gender, ethnicity, and sexual assault: Findings from a Los Angeles study. *Journal of Social Issues, 48*(1), 93–104.

Sorenson, S. B., & White, J. W. (1992). Adult sexual assault: Overview of research. *Journal of Social Issues, 48*(1), 187–195.

Stoltenberg, J. (1993). Making rape an election issue. In E. Buchwald, P. Fletcher, & M. Roth (Eds.), *Transforming a rape culture* (pp. 213–224). Minneapolis, MN: Milkweed Editions.

Sutherland, S., & Scherl, D. J. (1970). Patterns of response among victims of rape. *American Journal of Orthopsychiatry, 40*(3), 503–511.

Texas Department of Health Sexual Assault Prevention/Crisis Services and Texas Association Against Sexual Assault (undated). *Advocate Training Manual*. Austin, TX: Author.

Vasquez, M. J. T. (1994). Latinas. In L. Comas-Diaz & B. Greene (Eds). *Women of color: Integrating ethnic and gender identities in psychotherapy* (pp. 114–138). New York: Guilford Press.

Warshaw, R. (1988). *I never called it rape*. New York: Harper & Row.

Waterman, C. K., Dawson, L. J., & Bologna, M. J. (1989). Sexual coercion in gay male and lesbian relationships: Predictors and implications for support services. *Journal of Sex Research, 26*(1), 118–124.

Wertheimer, D. M. (1990). Treatment and service interventions for lesbian and gay male crime victims. *Journal of Interpersonal Violence, 5*(3), 384–400.

Williams, J. E., & Holmes, K. A. (1981). *The second assault: Rape and public attitudes*. Westport, CT: Greenwood Press.

Wolf, N. (1993). *Fire with fire*. New York: Ballantine Books.

Worell, J., & Remer, P. (1992). *Feminist perspectives in therapy: An empowerment model for women*. Chichester, England: John Wiley & Sons.

Wyatt, G. E. (1992). The sociocultural context of African American and white American women's rape. *Journal of Social Issues 48*(1), 77–91.

Yassen, J., & Glass, L. (1984). Sexual assault survivors groups: A feminist practice perspective. *Social Work, 252–257.

Zollicoffer, A. M., & Remer, P. (1989). Untitled manuscript. As cited in Worell & Remer, *Feminist Perspective in Therapy*, 1992. Chichester, England: John Wiley & Sons.

Chapter 11

BATTERED WOMEN WHO KILL AND FEMICIDE: THE FINAL ACTS OF VIOLENCE AGAINST WOMEN

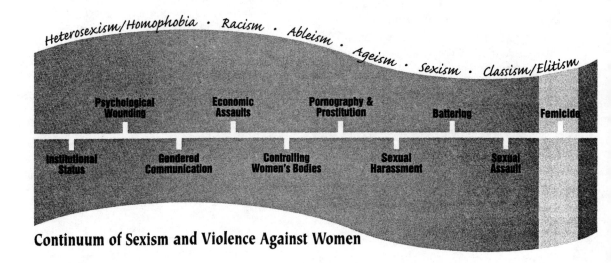

Heterosexism/Homophobia • Racism • Ableism • Ageism • Sexism • Classism/Elitism

| Psychological Wounding | | Economic Assaults | | Pornography & Prostitution | | Battering | | Femicide |

| Institutional Status | | Gendered Communication | | Controlling Women's Bodies | | Sexual Harassment | | Sexual Assault | |

Continuum of Sexism and Violence Against Women

We dedicate this Libby Roderick song to Rebecca Wight, murdered on the Appalachian Trail, and to all lesbian women.

How Could Anyone?

How could anyone ever tell you
You were anything less than beautiful?
How could anyone ever tell you
You were less than whole?
How could anyone fail to notice
That your loving is a miracle?
How deeply you're connected to my soul.

Word and music by Libby Roderick © Libby Roderick Music 1988.

*T*his chapter introduces the many issues associated with the last item on the continuum—femicide. It is related to other chapters in this text in a multitude of ways, as no one aspect of the continuum is distinct from other aspects. For example, the link to pornography and prostitution is clear and is illustrated through the content on snuff films and on the killing of women used in prostitution. Women have been killed as the end result of sexual harassment, and it is not unusual to hear of a woman being killed by an estranged partner on the job site. As noted in previous chapters, women who are sexually assaulted or battered are sometimes killed. Even the language of hate is linked to femicide, as it often is expressed during the physical acts of killing. The common elements of violence against women all too often terminate with the lethal ending of femicide.

This chapter is divided into two major issue sections. First, issues related to battered women who kill are presented. Second, the emerging literature addressing the killing of women—which has been named *femicide*—is reviewed. Following these problem descriptions, strategies for change are addressed. For some readers, parts of this chapter may be shocking (e.g., the material on snuff films and on the media's lack of attention to the killings of women of color) and difficult to come to terms with, due to the finality of the violence. The victims are dead or, in the case of battered women who kill, incarcerated. Therefore, it may be harder to think of ways in which professionals and individuals can intervene. For this reason, the first part of the strategies-for-change section addresses activism skills, and the second part discusses issues related to providing expert testimony in cases of battered women who kill. These change strategies are presented to encourage the channeling of anger and outrage into positive action to end both the imprisonment of battered women who kill in self-defense and the tragic loss of life through femicide.

INTRODUCTION TO THE ISSUES: BATTERED WOMEN WHO KILL

Murder is a difficult topic area for many professional social workers and laypersons to address. Despite the accumulation of literature on

battered women who kill, little research has emerged from social work literature on this topic. Social workers are in important positions to offer assistance before a situation turns lethal, as well as after a death has occurred. As service providers, social work professionals have become increasingly involved with adult victims and perpetrators of violence in four direct-service areas. First, as shelters for battered women increasingly have become staffed by professionally trained personnel, greater numbers of social workers have been employed in shelters to work with victims of physical, psychological, and sexual abuse inflicted by intimate partners. Second, many localities are developing programs for batterers, and social workers are among those who are initiating and facilitating such programs. Third, social workers routinely provide marital and couples counseling. Fourth, social workers are employed as probation and parole officers as well as employees within correctional institutions. As such, social workers need to be informed and educated on the issues related to battered women who kill.

Male violence is responsible for most of the homicides in the United States. When men kill, they most often kill other men. When men kill women, they most often kill their former or current female partners. When women kill men, they most often kill their current male partners. Reynolds (1987) estimated that 800 U.S. women were incarcerated in 1987 for murdering an intimate partner, and Kabat (1991) estimated that there are 2,000 women in the United States serving prison time for an offense related to defending themselves against a man who battered them. O'Shea (1993) found that of 45 women on death row, around 49% had been abused and were on death row for the murder of an abusive partner.

It is reported that when women kill men, they most often do so in self-defense (Browne, 1987; Rashche, 1993; Walker, 1989). Totman (1978) found that of 30 women incarcerated for murder in a California prison, 29 had been battered, and 20 indicated that they had been trying to protect their children or themselves when the homicide occurred. Walker (1989) documented that of those women she studied who killed with a gun, 76% used the gun the male partner had threatened to use against her. This literature suggests that (a) the majority of women imprisoned for homicide were battered by the person they killed; and (b) violence against the woman who killed had escalated in severity and prevalence over time. While many people predict that such killings could be prevented if battered women would just leave the relationship, the literature suggests that the victims of battering felt that the violence against them would escalate if they tried to leave the batterer. For example, Browne (1987) found that almost all the battered women she studied were afraid the batterer would kill them and did not believe that leaving the batterer would protect them from being killed. (See the section on heterosexual intimate femicide in this chapter, for a review of the literature on separation and lethality risk.) According to the literature, despite the fear and the escalating violence, battered women do not want to kill their abusers; they just want the battering to stop. For instance, Jones (1980) concluded that battered women who kill want to end the battering but do not want their batterers to die.

Age-Old Assumptions About Self-defense

Battered women who kill are in a unique legal position. While most of the women and most of their advocates see the homicide as an act of self-defense, the laws of self-defense have been premised on many assumptions that work best in situations of men fighting men. Gillespie (1989) suggested that men and women are treated very differently under the rules of self-defense, even though the law itself would not appear to discriminate. This differential treatment develops from assumptions underlying self-defense laws. One assumption is that it is not "manly" to kill an unarmed person. The premise underlying this assumption is based on

the notion that the two adversaries will be about the same size, strength, and fighting ability. Hands and feet are not generally considered serious threats. In the case of battered women who kill, they are most often beaten repeatedly with "cumulative physical and emotional damage being inflicted. . . . Yet despite all of this indisputable suffering, the case law in many states continues to assume that the harm inflicted by an unarmed assailant's hands or fists is not sufficiently 'grievous' to give rise to a right of self-defense" (p. 43). Gillespie also has described the notion that if a woman has been beaten repeatedly, yet has not been killed by these beatings, then there is the assumption that the outcome would not have been different on the day she killed her batterer. Battered women often report feeling or seeing something different on that day, but it may be as subtle, yet serious, as a look in the eye or a tone of the voice.

Another obstacle is the imminence requirement. One cannot kill a person too presumptuously or too belatedly and still justify self-defense. Gillespie advocated, "When a man who has beaten her up before says to his wife, 'This time I really am going to put you in your grave,' it is hardly reasonable (or just) to expect that woman to wait, for the sake of the imminence requirement, until his hands are around her throat and she is losing consciousness before she acts to save herself" (p. 69).

Further, the issue of excessive force haunts many battered women who kill. When laws were developed in this country, there was an assumption that men knew how to use a gun. With such an assumption, it is expected that a person will try to *not* kill the attacker.

A woman who, terrified, unfamiliar with firearms, having no confidence in her ability to hit the broad side of a barn, starts firing and doesn't stop until the gun is empty, can find herself facing a homicide conviction although her actions met all of the other requirements of self-defense law. The difference between a serious crime and no crime at all can be the panicked firing of just one bullet too many. (Gillespie, 1989, p. 92)

With these types of assumptions embedded in case law and in the hearts and minds of the general public who serve as jurors, the legal situation for battered women who kill has been called "battered justice." Those who oppose clemency efforts for battered women who kill often argue that persons advocating clemency for imprisoned battered women are providing women with a "license to kill." The staff of the National Clearinghouse for the Defense of Battered Women (1991) explained instead that such advocates are merely suggesting that juries have the right to hear all relevant evidence (i.e., jurors need to hear of the prior violence in the relationship).

A Study of Imprisoned Battered Women

Stout and Brown (1995; Stout, 1991) reported findings related to imprisoned battered women in the state of Missouri. Stout and Brown found that 17 of 18 imprisoned women, included in the Missouri prison sample, had committed no prior violent crime. In fact, most did not even have traffic violations prior to their conviction for murder. Sixteen of the 18 reported being beaten by the hands of a man who professed to love her, 14 reported having unwanted sex with the batterer, and 7 reported being raped within 2 hours of a battering incident. Several women reported that their abusers had battered or had sexually assaulted their children. Most of these women saw the homicide as an act of self-defense. They had a high level of fear toward their abusers. Many had called the police at least one time prior to the final incident. Most were not permitted to present evidence of the abuse they suffered during the relationship to the judge or the jury. Despite these findings, half of these women were sentenced to life in prison, without the possibility of parole.

Life, without the possibility of parole, sentences these women to a life with little hope. No one will be reviewing their case to look for good behavior. Clemency is often seen as their only real hope. Advocacy by social workers, attorneys, and battered women's advocates is the route to clemency for these women and those in similar positions throughout the country. (See the policy section of this chapter for more on clemency; see also the accompanying boxed information.)

The vision of Sue Osthoff, director of the National Clearinghouse for the Defense of Battered Women, seems an appropriate way to close this section on battered women who kill:

> *We dream about a world where there is no violence against women and children. A world where women won't have to choose between killing someone or getting killed. A world where kids and women are safe in their own homes. A world where people who love each other don't hurt each other. A world where life doesn't hurt so much that we want to drink or do drugs to survive. A world where we have the right to control our bodies and our destinies. A world where we have economic independence. A world where difference is celebrated, not hated. We dream of a world very different than our own; we dream about a world where there is truly justice for all. (Osthoff, 1992, p. 2)*

Author's Perspective

In the early 1990's, I (Karen Stout) began working with an 18-year-old woman who had killed her husband in self-defense. I found this young woman's narrative and the decisions she was going to have to make absolutely compelling and frightening. At the same time, I was writing scholarly articles on battered women who kill. One night, after an exhausting few days writing an "objective piece," I wrote this story to satisfy my own need to really tell about a battered woman who killed, in contrast to the "scholarly" work I was engaged in.

The Woman-Child. Jo was 12 years old, a child, when she began hanging out with her future husband's sister—her best friend. Her best friend's brother thought she was cute, and I would wager that she also thought she was cute. At age 14, a woman-child, she began getting serious about this man, her best friend's brother, four years her elder. My best guess is that "getting serious" can be translated into "began sleeping with"—yet she blushes when I probe into her woman-child vocabulary. At age 15, on her birthday, she conceived her first child with this man. Shortly thereafter, the abuse began. While being slapped, grabbed, punched, choked, yanked, pulled, and threatened, she developed into womanhood.

By tenth grade, she was a battered woman, a high school dropout, a mother, and a wife. She had no friends outside of her husband's family. The hair yanked from her head, broken clavicle, broken bone under her eye, and broken fingers marked her as his woman-child. Leaving him, begging him, and loving him were her survival strategies. "But Jo, I love you. I can't live without you. I won't do it again. Come back to me." Such was the language of seduction; no, the language of power and control that he used to entice her back.

He battered a child. He battered a woman-child. What gave him the right? Isolated, unskilled, uneducated, and battered she was. I bet she was a gorgeous child. Tall, thin, careful about her appearance, with a youthful taste in clothes. At age 18, when I met her, she was gorgeous and quite the adolescent. Willful. Determined no one could say she did wrong. Seeking independence yet not having anywhere to go. Just a delightful adolescent.

Not quite. She's been charged with first-degree murder. A murderer. A murderess. A criminal. An offender. Yet she's none of those things. I already said she's delightful, willful, a battered woman-child,

a mother, a daughter, and an adolescent. I don't find her the least bit offensive.

He slapped her over and over and over. Slapped with the front of his hand and then slapped with the back of his hand. Over and over and over. He ripped her gown off. She won't say she was afraid of being raped. What myth, what barrier, keeps a woman-child who's being slapped over and over and over and her nightgown ripped off of her from saying that she was afraid of being raped? So those are my words. I think he was going to rape her. She's afraid. She's terrified. She wants him to stop. "Just stop." "Quit hitting me." "Why are you doing this to me?" "Why?" "Why?" "Stop."

She picks up the knife on the counter. Then she remembers being on the floor with him. She's trying to stop the bleeding. She tries so hard to stop the bleeding. She has to call for help. He's bleeding. Run, Jo, run. She's at the neighbors phoning the ambulance. The sirens scream. The ambulance arrives. The police arrive. They take him away.

The police took her away, too. They told her they were putting her in protective custody so his family could not kill her. She trusted them. She told them of her fear, her pain, her anguish, her act of self-defense. They lied. The next day, they booked her on first-degree murder charges. The woman-child is now 18 years old. An adult. She'll be tried in adult court for an adult crime. Can't they see she's just a battered woman-child?

She struggles with whether to plead guilty or no contest or not guilty. She believes a jury will know she did not mean to kill him. She just wanted him to stop. He was beating her. He ripped her gown. She defended herself. It's a risk. It's self-defense, but a risk.

How can I advise her? She wants me to tell her what to do. I cannot. I won't be sitting in prison for life for bad advice. I can't read the minds of potential jurors. I think she's a child, a delightful woman-child. What if they think she's a murderer? Oh, I forgot to tell you. She's also six months pregnant with her third child. Please don't gasp. Don't make it sound like, "Oh, that changes everything." It changes nothing. The child is not his. I'm glad it's not his child. Another man offered comfort or maybe he offered passion. I don't know. I just know she's pregnant, and she's afraid the jury will think she's a "slut." What an awful word. She was embarrassed to even tell me she is pregnant. What kind of stigma do we place on people who wish to have a child? People want to place stigmas on women who have abortions, and then they want to place stigmas on women who have their children. Craziness. The child is going to be a boy. She's pretty excited.

She pleaded no contest to manslaughter. A plea bargain. Now we wait for the sentencing hearing. No word yet. She's invited me to the hearing. I'll go but I'm afraid. I'm afraid she'll be sentenced and I'm afraid my rage will burst if this woman-child is sent to prison. How selfish I am. She may go to prison and I'm worried about myself. She says his family has threatened that if the judge does not send her to prison they will kill her right there in the courtroom. That scares me, too.

The punching, beating, yanking, grabbing, and slapping has ceased; her hair is growing back; her bones are mended—but what will happen to her? Can she mature into a woman, or will her development always be stunted as a battered woman-child? Will her child be born in prison or in her home? I don't

know. With a B.S.W., M.S.W., and Ph.D. in Social Work, I just do not know. I just know I want her to someday be free.

As for me, I don't know what will happen to me either. I guess I'll keep sitting in committee meetings. I guess I'll keep teaching research methodology, research practicum, macro social theory, and women's issues. I guess I'll continue to write dispassionate, objective, and scholarly research articles. But my heart is with Jo. My heart is with her peers sitting in prisons across the country. Maybe I can tell their stories. Maybe someday they can all be free. Maybe someday we can all be free. What gives men the right? What gave him the right? What will happen to Jo? What will happen to me? I just do not know. . . . I really do not know, but I do care. Jo, I do care. Be free wherever you are, wherever you go, whatever you become. Just be free.

"Jo" was incarcerated for 4 years. She was given the maximum sentence (20 years) by the judge. I can, to this day, still hear her screams when the sentence was pronounced. Her case has been reviewed for clemency, and she received a unanimous decision by the clemency review committee to have her sentence commuted to time served and was forwarded to the Governor. As the result of a clemency review, Jo was released from prison.

INTRODUCTION TO THE ISSUES: FEMICIDE

Since the mid-1970s, social scientists have participated in the development of new concepts, theories, and research on violence against women. Social scientists and practitioners have written of women who have been harassed, battered, raped, and incestuously assaulted. In comparison, the killing of women (femicide) has received negligible attention as a form of violence against women.

The term *femicide* was first introduced at the 1976 International Tribunal on Crimes Against Women (Russell & Van de Ven, 1976). According to Russell and Van de Ven, the word *femicide* was introduced because "we must realize that a lot of homicide is in fact femicide. We must recognize the sexual politics of murder" (p. 144). Russell (1982) noted the appropriateness of the word *femicide*: "This word cannot be found in dictionaries yet, but it is important because it focuses attention to the fact that when women are killed it is not accidental that they are women" (p. 286).

There are, of course, other words that can be used to describe the killing of women. *Homicide* is a word that may be used to describe the killing of one person by another, without respect to gender. *Domestic violence* is a word choice that has been used to describe a range of violence, from beatings to homicide, by members of the same household. The word *uxoricide* is available to describe the killing of wives by husbands, and Dworkin (1974) introduced the word *gynocide* with the definition of "the systematic crippling and/or killing of women by men" (p. 16). *Femicide* is the word choice for the next sections of this chapter. It was chosen because the word *femicide* clearly identifies a subgroup, women, under the broader topic of homicide. While the word *femicide* focuses on gender, Radford and Russell (1992a, 1992b) have reminded us that "femicide has no respect for race, culture, age, class, or sexuality" (p. 143).

The Killing of Lesbian Women

Robson (1992) documents a long and tragic worldwide history of the institutionalization of the killing of lesbian women. Some of her findings include the following:

- In 1477, in Germany, a girl was drowned for "lesbian love" (p. 41).
- "A small town near Venice, Italy, adopted a statute in 1574 that forbade sexual relations of 'a woman with a woman if they are twelve [years old] or more,' ordering as punishment that 'she shall be fastened naked to a stake in the street of Locusts and shall remain there all day and night under reliable guard and the following day shall be burned outside the city'" (citing Crompton, 1981, p. 16) (p. 41).
- In 1602, the Portuguese government broadened the list of crimes that could be punishable by death to include lesbian acts.

Unfortunately, prejudice, discrimination, and violence against lesbian women did not end in the sixteenth, seventeenth, or even twentieth century. A 1988 murder captured the nation's attention when, on May 13, 1988, Rebecca Wight was murdered while camping with her partner, Claudia Brenner, on the Appalachian Trial in Pennsylvania. Claudia Brenner was shot five times—once each in the arm, face, and top of the head, and twice in the neck. Claudia Brenner described her terror and recovery from antigay violence in the book *Eight Bullets* (Brenner & Ashley, 1995; see the following account).

Eight Bullets

The First Bullet: When the first bullet hit me my arm exploded. My brain could not make the connections fast enough to realize I had been shot. I saw a lot of blood on the green tarp on which we lay and thought for a split second about earthquakes and volcanoes. But they don't make you bleed. Rebecca knew. She asked me where I had been shot. We had encountered a stranger earlier that day who had a gun. We both knew who was shooting us. Perhaps a second passed.

The Second Bullet: When the second bullet hit my neck next I started to scream with all my strength. Somehow the second bullet was even more unbelievable than the first.

The Third Bullet: The third bullet came and I now know hit the other side of my neck. By then I had lost track of what was happening or where we were except that I was in great danger and it was not stopping.

The Fourth Bullet: I now know a fourth bullet hit me in the face. Rebecca told me to get down, close to the ground.

The Fifth Bullet: The fifth bullet hit the top of my head. I believe Rebecca saw that even laying flat I was vulnerable, and she told me to run behind a tree.

The Sixth Bullet: The sixth bullet hit Rebecca in the back of her head as she rose to run for the tree.

The Seventh Bullet: The seventh bullet hit Rebecca's back as she ran. It exploded her liver and caused her to die.

The Eighth Bullet: The eighth bullet missed.

It is not surprising that Stephen Roy Carr believed us both dead. He shot to kill. The Neck. The Head. The Back. A single-bolt action rifle that he loaded, shot, and unloaded eight times. Surely he believed us both dead or he would have used more of the twenty-five rounds of ammunition he left in his haste to get away.

He shot from where he was hidden in the woods eighty-five feet away, after he stalked us, hunted us, spied on us. Later his lawyer tried to assert that our sexuality provoked him.

He shot us because he identified us as lesbians. He was a stranger with whom we had no connection.

I am the statistic we speak of when we talk of hate violence. Rebecca is the statistic who is not with us. She is one of the murdered. Murder is a horrible word to incorporate into your day-to-day vocabulary. But it is unfortunately part of the vocabulary of our community. When accidents happen that take a

life of a loved one, we find ways of incorporating that loss into our moral fabric, though we suffer. When death comes through the intentional actions of another, it is harder to bear. The horror of intentional unprovoked murder threatens to extinguish the warmth of the human soul.

Statistics, those impersonal numbers we are struggling so hard to collect, are about those murders. They are about real people. They are about me. And Rebecca Wight. And Charlie Howard. And Anthony Milano. And James Zaplolarti. And Rod Johnson. And so many other victims on the continuum of antigay violence. Statistics about murder, death, and tragedy are personal to me. Each one has a face and a story, a family, a lover, a life damaged, a grieving process, the pain of loss, and fear, nightmares, images, anger, and the incredible frustration of absolute injustice.

Before May 13, 1988, I believed that we, as lesbians and gay men, could be harassed. With words most likely. I had accepted the potential harassment gay people are accustomed to, the kind of harassment that comprises two-thirds of reported statistics to the National Gay and Lesbian Task Force Anti-Violence Project. The kind we must stop accepting.

I did not consider brutal murder born of hatred and ignorance. Nobody should have to worry about brutal murder. I didn't. I lived my life, chose my love respectfully and honorably as I believe all people should. I thought I was playing by the unwritten rules that would keep me safe. The rules that keep us more hidden than we need to be. The rules that didn't keep me safe. Because brutal attempted murder happened to me. And killed Rebecca. We need to stop following rules that limit us, and act to make the world the place we want it to be. The fact that violence and crimes are targeted against a particular group, in this case gay and lesbian people, requires a societal response. This state government needs to lead that response by passage of the legislation we lobby for today.

Stephen Roy Carr did not succeed in killing me. I survived that day and the months that followed when my life was consumed with pain and loss. I commit myself to not relinquishing any part of my life. For if I let fear take any part of my freedom, Stephen Roy Carr will have succeeded in his goal. We cannot give up any more lives, or parts of our lives, our freedom, or our civil rights, to the forces of violence, whether organized in Far Right hate groups like those that attacked Rod Johnson, or unorganized actions like the one which killed Rebecca and nearly killed me.

As I'm speaking now, I can feel the lump on the side of my tongue caused by the bullet that shredded my tongue. It is a continual reminder of the shooting, which I feel dozens of times every day. I'm asking you to also be reminded, of your commitment to action, education, and change.

Thank you.

This tragic murder, thankfully, was not sanctioned, dismissed, or trivialized by the justice system. The murderer was sentenced to life without the possibility of parole for the murder of Rebecca Wight. Claudia Brenner has fulfilled her dream to become an architect and a mother. She is also an activist who uses her grief and her physical and emotional suffering to challenge people to change their attitudes and behaviors that allow violence against lesbians and gay men to persist.

Racist Femicide

Grant (1992) documented the murders of 12 African-American and 1 European-American woman, all within a 2-mile radius, in Boston, over a 4-month period in 1979. Russell and Ellis (1992) brought to our attention that while the "Atlanta Child Murders" of 1978–1980 focused on the murder of 26 African-American male children, there were also 38 murdered girls and women found during that time period. These crimes remain unsolved. Russell and El-

lis (1992) suggested "Indifference by the police and the media to this slaughter of women reveals the extent to which racist sexism, or sexist racism, continues to flourish in the United States" (p. 162). In California, the Black Coalition Fighting Back Serial Murders (BCFBSM) was founded in 1986 because of concern about the serial murder of African-American women in Los Angeles. In 1991, BCFBSM noted, "We felt at the time and still feel that the serial murders, the problems with the investigation, and the low-profile media coverage of these murders were all examples of women's lives not counting, and Black women's lives counting least of all, and that they exposed a double standard in policing in our city and country" (p. 1).

In 1990, most of the country was chilled as serial murders of women students at the University of Florida—Gainesville were reported, yet no such attention was focused on the murders of low-income African-American women in the same area over a longer time span (*Memory & Rage*, December, 1990, p. 3). Singer (1992) noted that the killing of Native American women also goes unnoticed by mainstream media. She wrote,

> *When women of color are killed, little attention is paid to these crimes in the news media and we hardly hear about them in comparison with the femicidal murders of white middle-class women. A woman in Albuquerque, New Mexico, who worked in the coroner's office noted that during 1985–86 at least five American Indian women (mostly Navajo) had been raped and killed and their bodies dumped in the Jemez Mountains about 60 miles northwest of the city. These stories received virtually no news coverage. I had not heard about these murders despite the fact that I was attending the University of New Mexico in Albuquerque at that time. (p. 171)*

Femicide by Male Intimate Partners

Canadian novelist Margaret Atwood once asked a male friend why men feel threatened by women. He replied, "They are afraid women will laugh at them." She then asked a group of women why they felt threatened by men. They answered, "We're afraid of being killed" (Caputi & Russell, 1992, p. 13).

The evidence of women killed by husbands and male intimates is not new information discovered in the 1980–1990s by feminists, behavioral scientists, or the public at large. As early as 1911, MacDonald noted, "There are thousands of innocent persons murdered in the United States each year. Most of these are helpless women" (p. 91). MacDonald, in a study examining the efficacy of the death penalty as a deterrent to crime, examined data from England and Wales from the years 1886–1905. During this time span, 487 murders were committed, with 124 wives murdered by husbands, 76 mistresses murdered by male partners, and 39 female sweethearts murdered, indicating that nearly half of these murders were the killing of females by their male intimate partners.

In 1948, von Hentig cautioned, "when a man is found murdered we should first look for his acquaintances; when a woman is killed, for her relatives, mainly the husband and after that her paramour, present or past" (p. 393). A decade later, in a study of Philadelphia, Wolfgang (1958) found that 41% of female homicide victims were killed by their husbands. Okun (1986) noted, "since the founding of America's first battered women's shelter in 1974 through the end of 1983, well over 19,000 Americans have died in incidents of woman abuse or other forms of conjugal violence" (p. xiv). As a result of femicide, a national organization, Parents of Murdered Children, was founded in 1978 by a Cleveland, Ohio, couple whose daughter was murdered by her ex-boyfriend. In more recent times, advocacy groups have developed across the country to address femicide (see the accompanying box).

Organizations Combating Femicide

Black Coalition Fighting Back Serial Murders
P.O. Box 86681
Los Angeles, CA 90086-0681

Body Counts
P.O. Box 5931
Portland, OR 97228

Clearinghouse on Femicide
P.O. Box 12342
Berkeley, CA 94701-3342

Coalition to Stop the Green River Murders
2536 Alki Ave., SW, Box 129
Seattle, WA 98116

Family Violence Network
P.O. Box 854
Lake Elmo, MN 55042

Vigil Project
P.O. Box 21105
Santa Barbara, CA 03121

Women's Project
2224 Main St.
Little Rock, AR 77206

Women We Honour Action Committee
22 Parfield Dr.
Toronto, Ontario M2J 1B9, Canada

National Coalition Against Domestic Violence
Remember My Name Project
P.O. Box 18749
Denver, CO 80218

From Radford, J., & Russell, D. E. H. (Eds.). (1992b). Femicide: The politics of woman killing. New York: Twayne Publishers, and from A Newsletter of the National Coalition Against Domestic Violence Update (1995, January/February), P.O. Box 18749, Denver, CO 80218.

Demographics of Heterosexual Intimate Femicide

An average of four women die each day in this country, as a result of intimate femicide (Stout, 1987, 1989). Browne (1987) suggested that the estimates of how many people die as a result of battering (either the victim or the perpetrator—i.e., battered women who kill their batterers) would increase if better information was available related to whether a woman who commits suicide did so as a result of battering. In Browne's comparison study of women who are battered and battered women who do kill, 31% of nonhomicidal battered women had threatened to commit suicide, and 48% of the battered women who killed had made such threats.

According to Dawson and Langan (1994), 62% of European-American family murder victims were wives, and 53% of African-American family murder victims were wives. Firearms were used in 42% of family murder cases, as compared to 62% of nonfamily murders. Wilson, Daly, and Wright (1993) found that separated wives were at greatest risk and that having a husband 10 years or more older than the wife also increased the risk of femicide. Wilson et al. also found that married women have a nine times greater chance of being killed by a husband than by a stranger. Stout's (1990) national review of intimate femicide for the years 1980–1982 found that victim ages ranged from 16 to 91 years (16 was the youngest age included in the analysis), with the modal age group being 25–29 years. In Stout's (1993) study of intimate femicide perpetrators imprisoned in Missouri, 52% had killed women who had divorced, had separated from, or had broken up with their murderers. The highest rates of intimate femicide occur in the southwestern and southeastern regions of the country (Stout, 1991).

Demographics of Femicide Followed by Suicide

Marzuk, Tardiff, and Hirsch (1992) reviewed the murder–suicide literature and noted that over 90% of murder–suicides were committed by men, with studies showing that 50–86% of the male perpetrators were Caucasian. In reviewing the literature, these authors found that estrangement increases risk and that there was evidence of spousal abuse reflected in many of the studies. Rosenbaum (1990) reviewed police records in Albuquerque, along with trial reports and some interviews with the family and friends of the deceased. In 11 of the 12 murder–suicide cases in Rosenbaum's sample, European-American or Latino middle-class males were the perpetrators. The men were older than their victims; the men showed jealousy; and the women partners had often separated from the men or were undergoing

personal growth. Hanzlick and Koponen (1994) reviewed 12 cases of male perpetrators of murder–suicide from a 4-year period (1988–1991). With these cases, 92% of murder–suicides were committed with a firearm, and there tended to be one murder victim in each case, most often a female victim. In a Kentucky study, the female victim of a murder–suicide had separated from her partner in 15 of 37 murder–suicide cases, and in 7 of those 15 cases, she had obtained a protective or restraining order against the partner who eventually murdered her (*Journal of the American Medical Association [JAMA]*, 1991).

Factors Associated with Heterosexual Intimate Femicide

Numerous factors have been associated with lethality in the literature. A strength of the research to date is that it incorporates feedback from battered women on their perceptions of dangers; it reflects the realities of those who work with the battered women's shelter movement; most of the factors do not blame the victim; and the research gives good risk-assessment guidelines for working with battered women. Unfortunately, there continue to be problems in developing a lethality assessment, due to the obvious problems associated with lethality—the victim is not able to present her experiences, and with femicide–suicide, both the offender and the victim are dead. Therefore, the data accumulated most often tell how many or what percentage of cases have certain factors present. Occasionally, correlational data are presented. There are no true predictors, nor are there causal data to examine. Despite limitations in establishing causality due to obvious ethical prohibitions, assessment for lethality risk continues to be seen as a critical function of responsible social work practice. The following is a list of factors that appear in most studies on lethality: threats or attempts of homicide or suicide, presence of a weapon in the home, marital rape or sexual assault, substance abuse, violent jealousy, child abuse, control of daily activities, violence outside of the home, high

verity and frequency of abuse, isolation,
ause during pregnancy, and poor general men-
al functioning (Browne, 1987; Campbell,
995; Hart, 1988; Sonkin, Martin, & Walker,
985; Stuart & Campbell, 1989). In addition to
nese factors, the demographic information
oted in the previous sections can give addi-
ional assessment information.

In addition to these factors associated with
he batterer and with the woman who is bat-
ered, Stout (1987, 1989, 1992) published fac-
ors associated with intimate femicide from her
national study, which included state factors, as
well as individual ones. She found the following
factors to be correlated (at a statistically significant level) with lower rates of intimate femicide in a state: higher numbers of shelters,
higher numbers of rape-crisis centers, greater
percentages of women (compared to men) in
the state house, and larger percentages of
women in the combined state house and senate.
Women's unemployment rate was positively
correlated with intimate femicide. Further,
states that had statutory protection for victims
of battering had fewer women killed than did
states without such statutory protection. For
example, states that had civil injunctive relief,
had temporary injunctive relief, defined physical abuse as a criminal offense, provided for arrest without a warrant, and provided funds for
shelters or set standards for shelters all had
lower mean rates of intimate femicide.

Social workers have a responsibility to be attuned to the environment in which violence is allowed to persist, as well as to provide care for
those affected by the violence. Tremendous challenges still lay ahead for social workers to protect women's lives. Social workers must continue
to struggle with the many factors that may be associated with this tragic loss of life (Stout, 1989).

Snuff Films, Killing of Women and Men Used in Prostitution, and Other Misogynistic Acts

Snuff films refer to the actual or simulated
killing of women in the production of pornographic films. Generally, the man achieves an
orgasmic climax in the film just as the woman
is killed. "In so-called snuff movies, the production of pornography results in the actual
killing of women, usually black or Third
World women deceived or coerced into participation" (Radford & Russell, 1992b, p. 5).
Snuff is also the name of a movie, which
promised to show the murder and dismember-
ment of a woman. The advertisement of this
movie drew on racism and misogyny to entice
viewers to pay money to watch the killing of
women. LaBelle (1992) described the U.S. history of this movie:

> The film first surfaced in 1975 shortly after
> the New York City Police Department an-
> nounced that they had confiscated several
> "underground" South American pornographic
> films containing actual murder footage. These
> films were given the name "snuff" films be-
> cause the actresses were murdered (snuffed
> out) in front of the cameras in order to excite
> the jaded sexual palates of a select pornogra-
> phy audience that requires death rather than
> mere sex as an aphrodisiac. The curiosity of
> the regular pornography market was whetted
> by this police discovery, and the idea of a
> commercialized "snuff" film was born. (p.
> 189)

Pickets were mobilized throughout the country.
While New York City theater owners continued
to show the movie, pickets and legal actions
were successful in preventing its showing in San
Diego, Denver, Buffalo, Los Angeles, Monti-
cello, and San Jose (LaBelle, 1992).

In 1991, the book *American Psycho* was
scheduled to be released by Simon & Schuster. The
prepublication manuscripts described the sexual
torture of women, with the torturers using power
drills and acid. The contract for this book was
canceled by Simon & Schuster—despite the
$300,000 advance given to the author. Vintage
and Knopf books then paid the author $75,000
for the manuscript. Extensive protests and boycotts were directed at Vintage and Knopf publishers. While the book made some best-seller lists
upon its release, it quickly dropped out of sight

(though it may still be on the shelves of some book-stores) (*Memory & Rage,* July–September, 1991).

Killing of Women and Men Used in Systems of Prostitution

Thorson (1996) wrote about the killing of 19 women and four men in Minneapolis since 1986–seven of the murders since May of 1996. All of these murder victims were women or men used in systems of prostitution. Thorson cited quotes from Evelina Giobbe, director of education of Women Hurt in Systems of Prostitution Engaged in Revolt (WHISPER) to analyze the public apathy toward these killings. Giobbe described in her comments her perception of the public's attitude by noting, "Oh well, that's not me, I have nothing to worry about. Nothing could be further from the truth. . . . The fact that this individual kills women he believes are prostitutes for whatever reason he believes prostituted women don't deserve to live, doesn't mean that he isn't killing women, that he isn't killing human beings" (Thorson, 1996, p. 9). Similarly, PRIDE (From Prostitution to Independence, Dignity, and Equality) spokesperson Kristin Berg was quoted as saying, "Why should it surprise us when they are murdered? There's not a lot of people to stand up for them. Their tricks . . . are not standing up [and speaking] for the women" (cited in Thorson, 1996, p. 9).

As a "bridge between this tragedy and hope for the future" (Thorson, 1996, attributed to Giobbe), a memorial garden was dedicated, with memorial tiles for each of the victims. Giobbe summarized the importance of the memorial:

> It was an important visual statement . . . an important social lesson for all of us: The woman next to you digging the roses and laughing with you right now, hands in the dirt with you right now, could be dead in the alley tomorrow. These are real people, these are real women . . . and we need to do something serious about that. If we don't, we'll just keep making tiles, I guess, and to tell you the truth, I don't want to do that. (cited in Thorson, 1996, p. 9)

Fantasies of Murder on the Internet

The information superhighway, with its computer bulletin boards, was hailed as an exciting new wave of the future, which would bring new opportunities to learn and engage in dialogue with people around the world. Although the medium is new, the messages are not. The dehumanization, sexually objectification, and threatening of women has merely taken on a new technological twist. Pornography and images of violence against women have proliferated. The information highway may have become just another dead end for women. Take this June, 1995, example: A judge dismissed charges against a University of Michigan male student who wrote on the Internet about his fantasy of raping and killing a female classmate. In addition to posting his rape and murder fantasy, this student sent messages to another person about wanting to "do it" to a young girl first, as they are more innocent and easier to control. His correspondent agreed and further added that young girls' bodies would be more fun to hurt. The correspondent preferred 13- to 14-year-olds instead of college-age women (Houston Chronicle News Service, 1995, p. 18A).

The prosecution felt that the University of Michigan male student had gone beyond protected speech (i.e., the rape/murder fantasy had developed into a plan of action). A woman student was named. The method of her rape and murder was outlined. The male writer corresponded with another man about doing it. The judge ruled that the male student's actions were protected by free speech, however. The ruling was hailed by the American Civil Liberties Union (ACLU) and mourned by many persons who work with the victims of male violence. Susan McGee, executive director of the Domestic Violence Project in Washenaw County, Michigan, stated that the ruling "shows the judicial system in the United States is more interested in men's rights to torture, beat and harass women than it is in women's right to live their lives in peace and safety" (Houston Chronicle News Services, 1995, p. 18A).

While courts can make rulings calling such fantasies "musings" or "protected speech," for many women, such musings are the equivalent of yelling "FIRE!" in a crowded theater (unprotected speech), as most women tend to take the subject of femicide quite seriously. No one knows whether this college man is another Mark Lépine—who in 1989 killed 14 women college students in Montreal and who during the slaughter, kept referring to them as "fucking feminists" (Radford & Russell, 1992b, p. 6).

Strategies for Change

The finality of violence discussed in this chapter has the potential to immobilize social workers and other people, due to the enormity of the problems that must be resolved to end the imprisonment of women who kill in self-defense and to end the slaughter of women. Again, it needs to be emphasized that the strategies for change included in this chapter are not intended as ends in and of themselves; all of the change strategies discussed in this book and all of the issues put forth need to be addressed to begin to confront sexism and violence against women. Elsewhere in this text, we discussed the tactics of using the media and lobbying to effect social change (Chapter 2, on institutional status); empowerment strategies (Chapter 3, on psychological wounds), and facilitation of non-sexist groups (Chapter 4, on gendered communication). These strategies would also be useful to challenge femicide and to advocate on behalf of battered women who kill. In a continuum model, all of the issues are interconnected and become indistinguishable from one another. The following strategies-for-change subsections focus on more visible and confrontational community-organizing tactics: community activism and expert-witness testimony. While these tactics are seldom highlighted in traditional social work education programs, there are times when messages need to get to the public in a powerful manner, such as by staging a demonstration or by working as an expert witness for battered women who kill. In addition, this section presents specific practice issues related to battered women who kill.

COMMUNITY ACTIVISM

However carefully community organizing may be publicly described—whether as a search for acceptability and respectability or for simple safety and security—it is intrinsically radical. It is a demand for fundamental change, for reapportioning, for restructuring. (Kahn, 1995, p. 569)

The social work profession has a long and proud history of activism and organizing. Kahn (1995) has reminded social workers of the work of Jane Addams. "Jane Addams herself, one of the founders of social work as a profession, was a radical, a feminist, a trade unionist, a pacifist, a socialist, an agitator, and an organizer" (citing Evans, 1989, in Kahn, 1995, p. 571). Keep in mind the words used to describe Jane Addams on her route to justice: *A radical*—while being a radical has become a pejorative word, it simply means getting to the root; we may hope that being radical is the goal of most social work practice. *A feminist*—this word, too, has noble meanings regarding the work for equality for women but has been turned into a word of accusation. Jane Addams won a Nobel Peace Prize for her work. The labels attached to her memory are offered as encouragement to you as you work for justice. To end the murder of women and to find justice for battered women who kill in self-defense, it may be helpful to look at the past efforts of oppressed groups as a guide to the future.

Weil and Gamble (1995) emphasized that racism in the United States made it absolutely essential for ethnic and racial groups to organize for their survival: Native Americans have reestablished indigenous governance systems and have invested in their own economic and social development activities; African Americans have founded their own organizations and mutual-aid societies, from the Underground Railroad to the civil rights movement, and they have engaged in political-change strategies; Latino populations have participated in countless community-development and change activities, from political organizing to Alinski-style tactics; and Asian-American communities have developed service systems, fought for internment reparations, and initiated development work within refugee populations (Weil & Gamble, 1995). Women of all ages, class backgrounds, races, ethnicities, and sexual orientations have also organized to challenge injustice. Weil (1986) reminded us of women activists such as Emma Goldman and Frances Perkins with the union movement; Alice Paul, a champion for equal rights; Fannie Lou Hammer and Angela Davis, leaders in the civil and welfare rights movements; Delores Huerta, Wilma Martinez, and Antonia Hernandez, with La Raza, the United Farm Workers (UFW) movement, and the Mexican American Legal Defense and Education Fund (MALDEF); and Maggie Kuhn, with the Gray Panthers.

Middle-class European-American women have a great deal to learn from the activism and risk taking by women of color. Hurtado (1989) suggested that women of color often acquire survival skills as early as age 5 years. As a consequence, many have developed survival groups, such as informal networks and alternative health-care provisions and have begun early in life to organize for political and social change. This early development is in contrast to that of many European-American middle-class feminists, who did not recognize oppression based on gender until adulthood. "Lacking experience in challenging authorities and white men in particular, white feminists often seem surprised at the harshness with which the power structure responds to threat, and they do not have well-developed defenses to fend off the attacks. They often turn their anger inward rather than seeing it as a valid response" (Hurtado, 1989, p. 852). While middle-class European-American feminists may be engaging in feminist therapy, Hurtado suggested, "feminists of Color train to be urban guerrillas by doing battle every day with the apparatus of the state. Their tactics are not recorded or published for others to study and are often misunderstood by white middle-class feminists. One basic tactic is using anger effectively" (p. 853).

Authors' Perspective

Using anger effectively is at the root of why we chose the practice strategies of community organizing for the chapter on battered women who kill and on femicide. Speaking for ourselves, it makes us angry that women who defended themselves are sitting in prison with sentences of life without parole. It makes us angry that books are published and sold, which describe the systematic mutilation and killing of women. Farenthold wrote in the introduction to Garland's (1988) work on women activists, "In moments of high emotion, as well as in moments of stark rationality, these women activists point to anger as a principal motivator underlying their thinking and their behavior. Anger is often at the center of their transformations from private actors in restricted universes to public leaders in universes encompassing all the important issues of the day" (p. xvii).

Organizing Demonstrations

Si Kahn (1991) suggested, "Tactics provide a living education. They can sharpen the skills that our members have: public speaking, thinking on their feet, learning to work together, thinking strategically. Tactics can build a sense of solidarity within the organization" (p. 165). Demonstrations can provide such opportunities for building solidarity and for exposing an issue to the public. Marches and demonstrations have been used as successful lobbying tactics and for gaining public support for a cause or issue. According to Fairness and Accuracy in Reporting (FAIR) (undated), demonstrations can be effective means to effect change. FAIR offered a series of suggestions to think about for organizing demonstrations. Their first suggestions relate to preparing—doing homework (e.g., Have all other avenues of protest been exhausted? What times are most convenient for community members to attend? FAIR suggested considering lunch times, late afternoons, or early mornings.)

Second, FAIR has reminded organizers to put thought and effort into publicity, noting that groups generally need at least a week to get out adequate publicity. Publicity often includes contacting the primary and secondary media outlets in your area and providing them with a brief summary of your grievance. A third point relates to those signs and placards that are so often seen at public demonstrations. These are used to catch people's attention and, thus, the reason why slogans and catchy phrases are so often used. Once people are intrigued, they are more likely to pick up the fact sheets or position papers put together by the organizing committee. Conversely, belligerent signs or chants can dissuade people from involvement with your cause. Finally, it is often helpful to have one or two spokespersons to address the crowd or to work with the media. For large crowds, public-address systems, podiums and lecterns, musicians, and featured speakers are often planned (FAIR, undated).

Demonstrations can be valuable for attracting attention to the atrocities associated with the killing of women and the injustices associated with battered women who kill in self-defense. They can also be cathartic for those who work with such issues day in and day out, as well as for victims and survivors to be able to speak and act out in relative anonymity. We have witnessed many rape survivors and recent victims borrow protest signs during a daily protest, which occurred for at least 1 month, in front of a gubernatorial candidate's office who made what he considered jokes about rape. Action, in and of itself, can often be a healing and

an invigorating activity. One type of demonstration is a symbolic demonstration. This type of demonstration is discussed in the next section.

Symbolic Demonstrations

Symbolic demonstrations are probably familiar to most social workers. Each time people see a red ribbon on someone's lapel, people remember those who are living with or who have died from HIV/AIDS. At prochoice rallies, women often carry clothes hangers as reminders of the lives of women lost prior to legal, safe abortions. A pink ribbon worn on the lapel is a reminder of women who are living with or who have died from breast cancer. The Clothesline Project uses T-shirts as symbols of women who have been victims of violence, just as the Quilt Project uses quilt patches to tell the stories of people with HIV/AIDS. To conduct a symbolic demonstration, one needs only an issue and a symbol or a symbolic gesture (e.g., candles or silence) to represent the issue. The remainder of this section is devoted to describing symbolic demonstrations on behalf of femicide victims—with the hope that these ideas will be replicated across the country or that new creative energies will enliven a new effort initiated on behalf of murdered women.

- In 1991, life-size figures of women who have been killed by current or former partners were carried by protesters in front of the Minnesota Capitol. In addition, one figure was named the "Uncounted Woman" to reflect all of the women whose calls for help were unheeded (*Memory & Rage*, June, 1991). On October 18, 1997, "The Silent Witness Project" will have culminated in a march on Pennsylvania Avenue in Washington, D.C. Organizers expect that each state will have participated in this project, with life-size wooden figures painted red and bearing the name and story of each intimate femicide victim who died in 1994 (National Coalition Against Domestic Violence, 1995b).

- Capilano College in North Vancouver, Canada, is raising funds for a wall bearing the names of women murdered in that area (*Memory & Rage,* January–March, 1992).
- On December 6 of each year, many organizations around the world gather for the International Day of Remembrance for Women in memory of the 14 women killed in Montreal for being feminists. Fourteen minutes of silence (1 minute for each victim) is generally observed (*Memory & Rage,* October–November, 1990).

EXPERT-WITNESS TESTIMONY

Working as an expert witness can involve several different roles, from working with the defendant and her attorney during initial interviewing, case building, and setting up bail packages, to serving as a witness in court (Maguigan, 1995).

Case Building and Bail Packages

Maguigan (1995, p. 13) wrote,

> *Many lawyers are ill-equipped for the first interview of a defendant who has just killed her intimate partner. The displays of horror, guilt, anger, and grief which greet the interviewer are daunting. The first thing to bear in mind is that a lawyer cannot hope to deal with all of the client's problems. The second is that a lawyer can and must consult with an expert in order to locate resources to assist the defendant personally and to assist the defense team in preparing for trial.*

In this situation, an expert is someone who understands the realm of experiences of a woman who has been battered, who can provide or can locate resources to assist the defendant and who can help the attorney sort through any misperceptions the attorney may have about battered women (Maguigan, 1995). Social

workers are often uniquely qualified to assist in this work, as they may provide information not only about battering, but also about issues related to class, race, gender, and age, both of which are important to an attorney to help her or him prepare a case in the best interest of the defendant. The issue of battering, in particular, is central throughout the case, for as Maguigan has pointed out, many lawyers, juries, and judges get caught up with the question of whether the woman fits the stereotypical notions of who is a battered woman and lose focus on the real question: "whether a particular defendant acted reasonably on the occasion which led to her prosecution" (p. 16). When attention gets diverted to whether the woman charged was a "good" or "real" battered woman, the "inquiry works to the enormous disadvantage of women who fall outside the dominant stereotype, which is usually white-identified, and assumes 'passive' and 'helpless' behavior patterns" (p. 16).

Social work experts, in collaboration with attorneys, can help set up bail packages that might connect the defendant to shelters, support groups, or counseling or other services as a condition of release. Experts can encourage fact-finding through photographs, 911 calls, witnesses to past abuse, earlier police reports or orders of protection, as well as mental health treatment or past assistance from a shelter. The role of the expert here is to alert attorneys to the possibility of such evidence and to work with the attorney in obtaining and interpreting the evidence.

Court Testimony

Two types of court testimony are often asked of experts. The first type of testimony relates to providing information on battering to the court. The second type generally provides the educational component, as well as providing a specific evaluation of the woman charged with a homicide offense.

Educational Testimony

Blackman (1992), a frequent expert witness in cases of battered women who have killed or injured the men who battered them, suggested that expert testimony is often needed on (1) the psychology of battered women (which often leads to the question of "why does she stay"), and (2) the prevalence of battering in society. Issues outlined by Blackman, which can aid the judge or jury on the societal implications of battering include the following: "The limited availability of shelter space, the real difficulties associated with finding child care, good paying jobs and a safe place to live contribute in a very real way to the problems faced by women whose men injure and terrorize them" (p. 13). Similarly, Galliano and Nichols (1988) suggested that one of the roles of the expert witness is to educate the judge or the jury about the nature of battering and to describe how it is that some women may not be able to leave the dangerous partner. Experts should be prepared to address the dynamics present in the power-and-control wheel (see Chapter 9, on battering), which affect the context of battering in many relationships.

Evaluation

There is no one evaluation model used by expert witnesses in cases of battered women who kill. Some witnesses base most of their evaluation on the battered women's syndrome, as presented by Walker (1979, 1984). Others find that the battered women's syndrome, as traditionally applied, does not fit well in many cases (Stark, 1995)—for example with gay men and lesbian women who kill their partners in self-defense (Bricker, 1993) or with persons of color (Volpp, 1994). Experts are often called on to evaluate a woman accused of killing her intimate partner, to determine whether the woman "acted reasonably on the occasion which led to her prosecution" (Maguigan, 1995, p. 16). Just as there is no typical woman

who is battered, there is no typical battered-woman-who-killed case. However, Coha (1992) described some aspects of evaluation and testimony:

> General expert testimony can be combined with an assessment of the battered woman. This means that an expert who is also qualified to do a diagnostic interview (i.e., psychiatrist, psychologist, social worker) can assess the defendant, present information regarding her state of mind, and address her perception of imminent danger. The expert would review the history of violence from testimony of the survivor, witnesses, work record, medical records, police reports, etc. The expert could discuss the range of strategies that the survivor used to protect herself. The results of the assessment interview can be discussed in relation to knowledge about battered women including battered spouse syndrome. (unnumbered page 4)

Qualifying as an Expert Witness

Social workers (at all degree levels) can often qualify as expert witnesses. To be prepared to be admitted to the court as an expert, Coha (1992) suggested that the social worker build a résumé reflecting experience in the field of domestic violence. Some of the areas to build include

- Trainings attended and presented on the related topic areas (including lectures)
- Specific job titles and responsibilities working in domestic-violence programs
- Number of survivors worked with
- A résumé addendum, which lists the books and articles read on the subject

Any publications the social worker authored would be included in the main part of the résumé. Persons seeking to do expert-witness work might consider studying the literature on the topic, seeking consultation from expert staff at the National Clearinghouse for the Defense of Battered Women, apprenticing with a local expert, and working closely with an attorney for preparation. Understanding the adversarial court system is also crucial.

Author's Perspective

Speaking personally for a moment, I (Stout) have found expert witnessing to be excruciating work. It takes a great deal of preparation prior to meeting a defendant, working with her attorney can also be very time-consuming, and the actual testimony is difficult. I enjoy the teaching aspect of talking to jurors about women who are battered. I do not enjoy cross-examination, where the sole purpose is to discredit me personally or professionally. Like all aspects of social work practice, expert-witness practice requires knowledge and skill development, as well as an in-depth analysis of personal and professional values on the issues that may emerge during testimony. Fortunately, the National Clearinghouse for the Defense of Battered Women has invaluable resource (reading) material, as well as staff consultation available for experts. In addition, many schools of social work have joint programs with law schools. It may be possible to gain experience in settings such as moot courts while still in school.

FOCUS ON PRACTICE STRATEGIES FOR BATTERED WOMEN WHO KILL

Social workers are in a unique situation to address the needs of battered women before trial and after. Several issues could be addressed by *the profession,* to ensure that social workers have the knowledge and skills to provide direct and advocacy services to battered women who kill. An important step toward providing direct and advocacy services is to understand the dynamics of victimization and survival specific to women who have been battered. This step includes challenging the myths that so often cloud the issues related to battering, such as "It would never happen to me," or "She'd be out of this situation if she had just left the batterer." Understanding of the woman who has been battered can often place advocates in conflict with their agencies' goals and policies. For example, social workers who work in agencies with goals that include the preservation of the family may find that services are limited for women who are seeking to unify their family—without the abuser. This situation requires that agencies recognize and value the single parent and provide the full range of services to this family form.

Interdisciplinary work is also often critical to fully addressing the needs of battered women who kill. Advocates who do not have formal academic credentials can often be important allies and sources of information for professionals and for the accused or convicted woman. Attorneys, particularly defense attorneys who are often seen as the adversary when working with battered women, often become the most needed resource for a battered woman who has killed. It has been said that in confronting oppression, the development of unlikely allies is critical. In this case, good working relationships with defense attorneys can mean the difference between freedom and lifelong incarceration or even death for battered-women-who-kill defendants. Other allies accustomed to working with interdisciplinary teams are the staff members at the National Clearinghouse for the Defense of Battered Women (125 S. Ninth Street, Suite 302, Philadelphia, PA 19107). This agency has compiled a tremendous resource library on the social science and legal literature related to women who have been battered and to battered women who have killed. They also sponsor a National Advocate Network and publish a newsletter dedicated to informing advocates of the important work that is occurring around the country.

Social workers can *advocate* for more shelter services and more programs for men who batter, to address the needs of battered women in their community before violence escalates and one of the partners is killed (Stout, 1991). This suggestion also relates to the problem of femicide. In my (Stout's) dissertation research (Stout, 1987), I found that there was a negative association between the murder rate of women in a state and the proportion of shelter services offered in a state, in relation to its population; that is, where there was a higher number of shelters for the population of battered women, there were fewer women killed in those states.

POLICY FOR CHANGE

Clemency Review

Beyond social workers' roles as direct-service providers, social workers have been involved as advocates for legislative and judicial reform. Across the country, advocates have been encouraging legislatures and governors' offices to address the issue of battered women who kill. According to the National Clearinghouse for the Defense of Battered Women (1991), several states have initiated case reviews and clemency efforts on behalf of imprisoned battered women. For example, in December of 1990, Governor Richard Celeste granted executive clemency to 25 battered women who were incarcerated in Ohio prisons (National Clearinghouse for the Defense of Battered Women, 1991). In December of 1990, the King County Coalition Against Domestic Violence in Seattle, Washington, encouraged the governor of Washington to review 65 cases in that state. Twenty-five states had clemency organizing projects underway by 1992 (National Clearinghouse for the Defense of Battered Women, 1992).

Battered women who kill present unique issues for exploration from the legal and social work community. In recent years, due to a "get-tough-on-crime" attitude, many people have begun advocating for harsher penalties for those who commit violent crimes. Caught in the middle of this get-tough attitude are battered women who have killed their abusers. With more than 800 battered women in prison at this time for killing an abusive partner, their plight warrants investigation and advocacy from the social work community. Social workers can encourage PACE (Political Action for Candidate Elections) and the national staff and state units of NASW to work actively to support or initiate clemency and case-review hearings in their state.

Gun Control

Despite the best efforts of the firearms industry and its supporters to portray gun ownership as a guarantor of personal safety, the reality presents quite a different picture. Like their male counterparts, women rarely use guns to kill criminals or stop crimes. In fact, in 1992 for every time a woman used a handgun to kill a stranger in self-defense, 239 women were murdered with handguns. (Glick, 1994, p. 2)

The firearm industry and the National Rifle Association have developed an extensive marketing campaign to sell guns to women and to increase women's support for curbing gun-control legislation. Glick (1994) suggested that the marketing techniques employed are based on myths regarding violence against women. These myths include the following (Glick, 1994, p. 33):

1. *Stranger rape is the most common violent crime against women.*
2. *Most homicides stem from criminal attacks by strangers.*

3. *People who want to kill themselves will find a way no matter what; if a firearm is not available, they will merely use other means.*
4. *Guns, especially handguns, are effective self-defense tools.*

As pointed out in previous chapters and in this chapter, (1) acquaintance rape and marital rape is more prevalent than is stranger rape, and (2) a woman is more likely to be killed by someone she knows—her husband, ex-husband, or manfriend—than by a stranger. Women are killed by strangers in less than 10% of femicide cases.

Advocates for women who have been battered have long been concerned about the availability of firearms and the frequency with which those firearms are used to threaten, frighten, hurt, and kill battered women. In 1994, the Violence Crime Control and Law Enforcement Act addressed gun ownership by men who batter: "The new law states that [people are] prohibited from possessing a firearm if they are currently subject to a restraining order prohibiting them from 'harassing, stalking, or threatening an intimate partner or child of such intimate partner, or engaging in other conduct that would place an intimate partner in fear of bodily injury to the partner or child'" (NCADV, 1995a, p. 7). For further information about gun-control measures, the following section provides contact information for several national groups.

Organizations Concerned About Gun Violence

Women Against Gun Violence
6505 Wilshire Boulevard,
Suite 417
Los Angeles, CA 90048
(213) 651-4601

Violence Policy Center
2000 P Street, NW,
Suite 200
Washington, DC 20036
(202) 822-8200

Handgun Control, Inc.
1225 I Street, NW
Washington, DC 20005
(202) 898-0792

Coalition to Stop Gun Violence
100 Maryland Ave.,
NE, Suite 402
Washington, DC 20002
(202) 544-7190

Compiled from information from Glick, S. (1994). Female persuasion: A study of how the firearms industry markets to women and the reality of women and guns. (Available from Violence Policy Center, 2000 P Street, NW, Suite 200, Washington, DC 20036.)

SUMMARY

Femicide is the final act of violence against women. In the struggle to stay alive, some battered women have defended themselves with lethal force, and many are currently serving long sentences for this defensive action. Snuff films tell women that their lives are cheap, as does the killing of wives, women partners, lesbians, women of color, and women used in the sex industry. Projects such as the "Silent Witness Project" and the creation of a memorial in a park in Minneapolis are attempting to put faces on femicide. To end the slaughter of women, it will take courageous women and men to put an end to all the components included on a continuum of sexism and violence against women. With equality, perhaps the word *femicide* will never have to be added to a dictionary, and all of the other forms of sexism and violence against women will be faded memories. Perhaps our president will declare that her grandchildren will never know a time when political, economic, and social equality for women did not exist, and the Catholic pope will use her influence to ensure that women have full control over their bodies, their lives, and their hopes and dreams. Women will be free, not only to reach for the stars, but also to walk alone at night under them. Finally, the tragic loss of life will end because of what each of us did to change ourselves and our world.

REFERENCES

Black Coalition Fighting Back Serial Murders (1991, March 10). Statement to grassroots organizing meeting on police abuse. In *Memory & Rage* (insert), January–March 1992. (Available from Clearinghouse on Femicide, P.O. Box 12342, Berkeley, CA 94701.)

Blackman, J. (1992, Winter). Two kinds of experts on battered women: Can you be one? *NJ Coalition for Battered Women Newsletter,* p. 13

Brenner, C., & Ashley, H. (1995). *Eight bullets: One woman's story of surviving antigay violence.* Ithaca, NY: Firebrand Books.

Bricker, D. (1993). Fatal defense: An analysis of battered woman's syndrome expert testimony for gay men and lesbians who kill abusive partners. *Brooklyn Law Review, 58,* 1379–1437.

Browne, A. (1987). *Battered women who kill.* New York: Free Press.

Campbell, J. (1995). Prediction of homicide of and by battered women. In J. Campbell (Ed.), *Assessing dangerousness: Violence by sexual offenders, batterers and child abusers.* Thousand Oaks, CA: Sage.

Caputi, J., & Russell, D. (1992). Femicide: Sexist terrorism against women. In J. Radford & D. E. H. Russell (Eds.), *Femicide: The politics of woman killing* (pp. 13–21). New York: Twayne Publishers.

Coha, A. (1992). *Defending battered women: The role of the expert witness.* (Available from NCDBW, National Clearinghouse for the Defense of Battered Women. 125 South 9th St., Suite 302, Philadelphia, PA 215-351-0010.)

Dawson, J., & Langan, P. (1994). *Murder in families: Bureau of Justice Statistics, U.S. Department of Justice.* Annapolis, MD: U.S. Government Printing Office.

Dworkin, A. (1974). *Woman hating.* New York: E.P. Dutton.

FAIR: We Interupt this Message, Media Activist Toolkit, Challenging Myths & Stereotypes in the News. FAIR: New York.

Galliano, G., & Nichols, M. (1988). Mental health professional as expert witness: Psychosocial evaluation of battered women accused of homicide or assault. *Journal of Interpersonal Violence, 3,* 29–41.

Garland, A. W. (1988). *Women activists.* New York: Feminist Press.

Gillespie, C. (1989). *Justifiable homicide.* Columbus: Ohio State University Press.

Glick, S. (1994). Female persuasion: A study of how the firearms industry markets to women and the reality of women and guns. (Available from Violence Policy Center, 2000 P. Street N.W., Washington, DC 20036.)

Grant, J. (1992). Who's killing us? In J. Radford & D. E. H. Russell (Eds.), *Femicide: The politics of woman killing* (pp. 189–194). New York: Twayne Publishers.

Hanzlick, R., & Koponen, M. (1994). Murder–suicide in Fulton County, Georgia, 1988–1991. *American Journal of Forensic Medicine and Pathology, 15*(2), 168–173.

Hart, B. (1988). Beyond the "duty to warn": A therapist's "duty to protect" battered women and children. In K. Yllo & M. Bograd (Eds.), *Feminist perspectives on wife abuse* (pp. 234–248). Newbury Park, CA: Sage.

Houston Chronicle News Service (1995, June 22). Death tale by e-mail not a crime: Student acquitted in murder fantasy. *Houston Chronicle,* p. 18A.

Hurtado, A. (1989). Relating to privilege: Seduction and rejection in the subordination of white women and women of color. *Signs,* pp. 833–855.

Jones, A. (1980). *Women who kill.* New York: Fawcett Crest.

Journal of the American Medical Association. (1991, October 6). Homicide followed by suicide—Kentucky, 1985–1990. *JAMA, 266*(15), 2062.

Kabat, S. (1991, June). Remarks from presentation at Harvard School of Public Health, Center for Health Communication.

Kahn, S. (1991). *Organizing: A guide for grassroots leaders.* Washington, DC: NASW Press.

Kahn, S. (1995). Community organization. *Encyclopedia of social work* (pp. 563–568). Washington, DC: NASW Press.

LaBelle, B. (1992). Snuff—The ultimate in woman hating. In J. Radford & D. E. H. Russell (Eds.), *Femicide: The politics of woman killing* (pp. 13–21). New York: Twayne Publishers.

MacDonald, A. (1911). Death penalty and homicide. *American Journal of Sociology, 16,* 88–115.

Maguigan, H. (1995). *A defense perspective on battered women charged with homicide: The expert's role during preparation for and conduct of trials.* (Working paper prepared for Women's Judges' Fund for Justice, April 1995 Roundtable. Available from Women's Judges' Fund for Justice, 815 15th Street, NW, Suite 601, Washington, DC 20005.)

Marzuk, P., Tardiff, K., & Hirsch, C. (1992). The epidemiology of murder–suicide. *JAMA, 267,* 3179–3183.

Memory & Rage (1990, October–November). *Newsletter of the Clearinghouse on Femicide.* (Available from Clearinghouse on Femicide, P.O. Box 12342, Berkeley, CA 94701.)

Memory & Rage (1990, December). *Newsletter of the Clearinghouse on Femicide.* (Available from Clearinghouse on Femicide, P.O. Box 12342, Berkeley, CA 94701.)

Memory & Rage (1991, June). *Newsletter of the Clearinghouse on Femicide.* (Available from Clearinghouse on Femicide, P.O. Box 12342, Berkeley, CA 94701.)

Memory & Rage (1991, July–September). *Newsletter of the Clearinghouse on Femicide.* (Available from Clearinghouse on Femicide, P.O. Box 12342, Berkeley, CA 94701.)

Memory & Rage (1992, January–March). *Newsletter of the Clearinghouse on Femicide.* (Available from Clearinghouse on Femicide, P.O. Box 12342, Berkeley, CA 94701.)

National Clearinghouse for the Defense of Battered Women. (1991, January). Twenty-five battered women granted clemency in Ohio. *Network Update: Newsletter of the National Clearinghouse for the Defense of Battered Women.* (Available from NCDBW, 125 South 9th St., Suite 302, Philadelphia, PA 19107; 215-351-0010.)

National Clearinghouse for the Defense of Battered Women. (1992). Daring to believe in justice. *Double-Time: Newsletter of the National Clearinghouse for the Defense of Battered Women.* (Available from NCDBW, 125 South 9th St., Suite 302, Philadelphia, PA 19107; 215-351-0010.)

National Coalition Against Domestic Violence. (1995a, January/February). Firearms and Domestic Violence. *NCADV Update.* (Available from the NCADV, P.O. Box 34103, Washington, DC 20034-4103.)

National Coalition Against Domestic Violence. (1995b, January/February). Remember my name. *NCADV Update.* (Available from the NCADV, P.O. Box 34103, Washington, DC 20034-4103.)

Okun, L. E. (1986). *Woman abuse: Facts replacing myths.* Albany: State University of New York Press.

O'Shea, K. (1993). Women on death row. In B. Fletcher, L. Shaver, & D. Moon (Eds.), *Women prisoners: A forgotten population.* Westport, CT: Praeger.

Osthoff, S. (1992, November). Changing the world. *Double-time, A Newsletter of the National Clearinghouse for the Defense of Battered Women, 1*(3 & 4), 1–2.

Radford, J., & Russell, D. E. H. (1992a). Femicide and racism: Introduction. In J. Radford & D. E. H. Russell (Eds.), *Femicide: The politics of woman killing* (pp. 143–144). New York: Twayne Publishers.

Radford, J., & Russell, D. E. H. (1992b). *Femicide: The politics of woman killing.* New York: Twayne Publishers.

Rasche, C. (1993). "Given" reasons for violence in intimate relationships. In A. Wilson (Ed.), *Homicide: The victim/offender connection,* Cincinnati, OH: Anderson.

Reynolds, L. (1987, April). *Executive summary of the second national workshop on female offenders.* Raleigh, NC. (Available from NCDBW, 125 South 9th St., Suite 302, Philadelphia, PA 19107; 215-351-0010.)

Robson, R. (1992). Legal lesbicide. In J. Radford & D. E. H. Russell (Eds.), *Femicide: The politics of woman killing* (pp. 40–45). New York: Twayne Publishers.

Rosenbaum, M. (1990). The role of depression in couples involved in murder–suicide and homicide. *American Journal of Psychiatry, 147,* 1036–1039.

Russell, D. E. (1982). *Rape in marriage.* New York: Macmillan Publishing.

Russell, D. E. H., & Ellis, C. (1992). Annihilation by murder and the media: The other Atlanta femicides. In J. Radford & D. E. H. Russell (Eds.), *Femicide: The politics of woman killing* (pp. 161–162). New York: Twayne Publishers.

Russell, D. E., & Van de Ven, N. (Eds.). (1976). *The proceedings of the International Tribunal on Crimes Against Women.* East Palo Alto, CA: Frog in the Well.

Singer, B. (1992). American Indian women killing: A Tewa Native woman's perspective. In J. Radford & D. E. H. Russell (Eds.), *Femicide: The politics of woman killing* (pp. 170–173). New York: Twayne Publishers.

Sonkin, D., Martin, D., & Walker, L. E. A. (1985). *The male batterer.* New York: Springer.

Stark, E. (1995). Re-presenting woman battering from battered woman syndrome to coercive control. *Albany Law Review, 58,* 973–1026.

Stout, K. D. (1987). *Intimate femicide: Individual and state factors associated with the killing of women by men.* Austin: University of Texas at Austin.

Stout, K. D. (1989). "Intimate femicide": Effect of legislation and social services. *Affilia: Journal of Women and Social Work, 4,* 21–30.

Stout, K. D. (1991). Women who kill: Offenders or defenders. *Affilia, 6,* 8–22.

Stout, K. D. (1992). Intimate femicide: An ecological analysis. *Journal of Sociology and Social Welfare, 19,* 29–50.

Stout, K. D. (1993). Intimate femicide: A study of men who killed their mates. *Journal of Offender Rehabilitation, 19,* 81–94.

Stout, K. D., & Brown, P. (1995). Legal and social differences between men and women who kill intimate partners. *Affilia, 10,* 194–205.

Stuart, E. P., & Campbell, J. C. (1989). Assessment of dangerousness with battered women. *Issues in Mental Health Nursing, 10,* 245–260.

Thorson, J. (1996, September 18–October 1). Women in prostitution confront apathy in wake of murders (p. 9). Minnesota Women's Press.

Totman, J. (1978). *The murderess: A psychological study of criminal homicide.* San Francisco: R & E Research Associates.

Volpp, L. (1994). (Mis)identifying culture: Asian women and the "cultural defense." *Harvard Women's Law Journal, 17,* 57–101.

von Hentig, H. (1948). *The criminal and his victim.* New Haven, CT: Yale University Press.

Walker, L. E. (1979). *The battered woman.* New York: Harper & Row.

Walker, L. E. (1984). *The battered woman syndrome.* New York: Springer.

Walker, L. E. (1989). *Terrifying love.* New York: Harper & Row.

Weil, M. (1986). Women, community, and organizing. In N. Van Den Bergh & L. Cooper (Eds.), *Feminist visions for social work* (pp. 187–210). Silver Springs, MD: NASW Press.

Weil, M., & Gamble, D. (1995). Community practice models. *Encyclopedia of social work* (pp. 577–594). Washington, DC: NASW Press.

Wilson, M., Daly, M., & Wright, C. (1993, July). Uxoricide in Canada: Demographic risk patterns. *Canadian Journal of Criminology,* 263–291.

Wolfgang, M. (1958). *Patterns of criminal homicide.* New York: Wiley.

Chapter

12

PERSONAL AND PROFESSIONAL IMPLICATIONS: A CONVERSATION WITH SOCIAL WORKERS

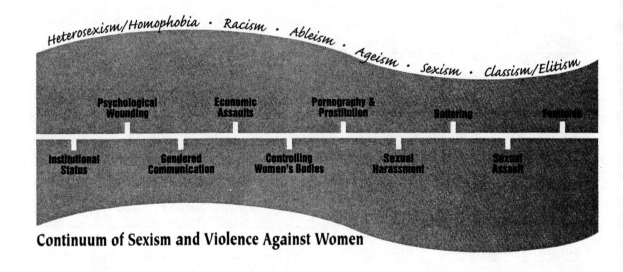

Heterosexism/Homophobia · Racism · Ableism · Ageism · Sexism · Classism/Elitism

Psychological Wounding   Economic Assaults   Pornography & Prostitution   Battering   Femicide

Institutional Status   Gendered Communication   Controlling Women's Bodies   Sexual Harassment   Sexual Assault

Continuum of Sexism and Violence Against Women

> *You may forget but*
>
> *Let me tell you this: someone in some future time will think of us*
>
> Sappho (born ca. 612 B.C.)

Sexism and violence against women present themselves in a multitude of forms and are manifested in one or more forms in the lives of women and men throughout the life cycle. Understanding the multidimensional levels of sexism and violence against women is an important step toward effective social work practice, as well as self-awareness as a professional social worker.

312

COMMON THEMES

This book has presented a continuum of sexism and violence against women, with each chapter delving into the specific dynamics of the various assaults against women. Throughout the chapters, common themes emerged. These commonalities help to make our point that the many aspects and expressions of violence are interrelated—that is, one cannot merely look at rape as an isolated event but must take into account the range of violence perpetrated against women and the culture that supports, condones, and even regulates such violence.

Both women's experience and empirical research confirm that violence against women is pervasive in this society. When incidents of violence against women are counted as occurring in minutes and seconds, it is epidemic. Even women not personally touched by violence live in fear of violence. The violence is pervasive also because it takes so many forms. Physical violence is especially traumatic and tragic, yet women are assaulted daily by institutional sexism and patriarchal systems of economics and medicine. The violence affects women on all levels, not only physically, but psychologically and economically as well.

Another common theme presented in this book and in the continuum model is that it is not possible to separate the violence perpetrated against women based on their gender from issues of race, class, and sexual orientation. In almost every instance, the effects and prevalence of assaults against women are deepened if the woman is a woman of color, a low-income woman, or a lesbian, or some combination thereof. Although gender as a variable is important, it does not arise in a vacuum but is intertwined with race, class, and sexual orientation, as well as ableism and appearance-based oppression, such as fat oppression and lookism. These interactions make both the problems and the solutions more complex and multifaceted, yet, for real change to occur, all of these factors must be addressed.

The various chapters in the book also illustrate that women are most likely to be assaulted by someone they know, rather than by a stranger. Frequent responses often blame the victim for her own victimization. Another common theme is that the institutions that are supposed to assist women after the assault often deliver a second assault. As we saw in Chapter 2, on women's institutional status, the institutions in our society are formed to protect and benefit the patriarchy. Women's experiences with such institutions are often unjust, and the social work profession is not immune from charges of injustice. The sociocultural fabric of our society often supports, minimizes, or ignores sexism and violence against women. The boys-will-be-boys mentality survives even when women don't. Marital rape is not illegal but is merely regulated; for instance, in many states, a man can legally rape his wife as long as he doesn't beat her, as well. Changes are being made, but they are coming slowly, against great resistance.

Another common theme that arises is the horrific consequences of the violence in the lives of women. Being a victim of violence changes a woman's life, and she is never quite the same again. The violence tends to affect women physically and emotionally, leaving both physical and psychic scars. Femicide is the ultimate violence against women, and this book presented the many ways in which women are killed, from being battered by husbands to being ignored by medical researchers.

In rape, sexual harassment, battering, femicide, the perpetrator is predominantly male and the victim female. Overwhelmingly this differentiation by sex is the case. The male quest for dominance and control underlies many of these crimes. The feminist analysis of the violence against women has identified the role of male dominance and has incorporated it into the pursuit of solutions. In looking for solutions, each chapter reiterated the importance of working on all levels concurrently—that is practice and policy, micro and macro, personal and political. Empowerment on all levels—personal, interpersonal, and political—is key, remembering that empowerment is both a process and a goal.

STRENGTHS OF WOMEN

By working on all levels, we remember that the ultimate goal is not the provision of better services to women who have been harassed, raped, or battered, but the elimination of such abuses. Policy changes should not be a Band-Aid temporarily helping in healing, but should work toward eradicating oppressive forces from our society. In addressing policy changes, prevention of violence is key, and much of our efforts must focus on changing attitudes, as well as laws.

Feminists frequently cite an anecdote of a woman who sits on a riverbank enjoying the sun and the water when another woman is pushed down river by currents and cannot swim. The first woman on the bank jumps in and pulls the second woman to the shore. Several more times, this incident is repeated with other women needing to be saved from drowning, until the woman on the shore is so tired herself that she almost drowns trying to save each successive woman. Finally, she must ignore the cries of another drowning woman as she heads upstream. When the drowning woman demands to know where the swimmer is going, the swimmer replies, "to find out who is pushing women in." This story urges us to go to the head of the river, to look for root causes of sexism and violence against women. We must contextualize and politicize sexism and violence if we are to keep women from drowning.

We hope that although this book focused on the victimization of women, you could see the strengths of women on every page, as well. For women often not only survive the violence, but also manage to thrive. Women help each other heal. Women organize, protest, and change policies. Women write groundbreaking books to uncover injustices and conduct eye-opening research to guide the policy and practice debates. Women continue to give birth and

raise their children in spite of an unjust world, while continuing to make the world a safer, saner place for their children to inherit. Women have led or played an invaluable role in every major social-change movement in this country, despite the often overwhelming odds and obstacles. Therefore, although this book has focused on the oppression of women, we hope you never forget for a moment the coexisting strength, courage, and determination of women.

Alexis de Tocquevilles, French observer and political analyst, critiqued life in America in the early 1800s. His commentaries on life in America are often quoted, for as an outsider, he had a unique perspective to offer. One of his least quoted commentaries, however, which rarely appears in history texts, is his view of American women. He wrote, "if I were asked, now that I am drawing to the close of this work, in which I have spoken of so many important things done by the Americans, to what the singular prosperity and growing strength of that people ought mainly to be attributed, I should reply, To the superiority of their women" (Tocqueville, 1956, p. 247).

We must agree with de Tocqueville's observation: Our country is what it is today due to the strength and courage of women. To view women from an empowered perspective, we need a strength-based assessment. Women are not merely victims, but survivors. To see only how women are oppressed is to miss the beauty, strength, and hope of women, who have survived centuries of oppression to grow stronger, wiser, and more determined.

PROFESSIONAL IMPLICATIONS OF WORKING WITH SURVIVORS OF VIOLENCE

Vicarious Victimization

If social workers are to make the connections among aspects of violence and address the complexities of violence against women, they must risk having to pay the costs—professional and personal. This section reviews two studies that address the costs of working with survivors and presents strategies for social workers to maintain their own mental health, as well as safety. As a way of beginning a discussion on the impact some professionals feel when confronting violence against women, we explore some findings from a study by Karen Stout and Sharon Thomas (1991) and an article by Ferol Mennen (1990). The Stout and Thomas study examined issues related to safety, self-protection, perceptions of job-related fear, and actual assaults on staff members in battered women's shelters; the Mennen article addressed the dilemmas and demands of working with adult survivors of sexual abuse.

Stout and Thomas (1991) sought to explore the impact of fear and dangerousness in the lives of shelter staff members, with the following research questions directing the development of a survey instrument: What is the cost to caregivers who interact hourly, day after day, within the confines of shelter walls with women residents who are emotionally, sexually, and physically beaten and beaten down? Are the workers afraid that violence will be directed toward them? Have they been threatened or assaulted? Have their lives changed since beginning their work to end violence against women? What suggestions do shelter workers have for professionals regarding how to deal with fear and danger in practice?

A survey questionnaire was developed and distributed nationwide, in order to obtain preliminary information from shelter workers. A simple random sample of shelters in the United States was drawn from a directory of nationwide shelter services. Seventy-five shelters were randomly drawn from the population data provided by the directory. Survey responses were obtained from 44 different shelters from 19 different states, with both rural and urban shelters represented.

The exploratory study's findings on fear and dangerousness related to shelter work provided some very basic information on the feelings of shelter workers regarding fear and danger in their practice setting. The data indicated that within 82% of the shelters nationwide, workers were at times (albeit "seldom") fearful of physical harm to themselves. Only workers within 18% of shelters never felt fearful of physical harm because of their work in a shelter. This information speaks to the awareness workers had of the potential violence they faced from the perpetrator of violence against the victim and even from shelter residents. It tells us that workers, on occasion, have been afraid of physical harm. Workers also reported being threatened as a result of their professional role at the shelter. These threats were from partners of victims, from adult and child residents, and from unknown men. Threats ranged from the use of a weapon to verbal intimidation. The potential of violence following threats are reflected by the shelters across the country where a worker was actually physically assaulted and by shelters that have had a break-in. All but one of the shelter break-ins were by male partners of residents. Although most shelter break-ins did not involve any injury to a staff member, 22% of shelters nationwide have had break-ins during which a worker was injured. Further, the majority of shelter staff respondents reported that their concern for their own safety has increased since working at the shelter. The majority of respondents also reported that they had more concern for other people's personal safety from violence, as well. It appears that working with victims of male violence may affect people's feeling of vulnerability or may increase their awareness of the prevalence and severity of violence against women. Another finding supports this conclusion, as workers overwhelmingly reported being more aware of violence on television, in advertisements, in child interactions, in movies, and in other aspects of life since working at the shelter—which reflects awareness of a continuum of violence against women (and children).

Most shelter workers who participated in the study reported having more difficulty in interpersonal relationships since beginning their work at the shelter. In examining the possible reasons for more stressful interpersonal relationships, shelter workers reported increased stress, diffuse anger, and more difficulty feeling trust.

Women who work with battered women had numerous suggestions on how to deal with fear and danger. Some of their recommendations (Stout & Thomas, 1991), can be categorized into four major themes, such as the following:

- *Stress management*—Take mental health weekends. Have hobbies outside of work. Exercise. Take regular vacations. Work for better salaries. Be involved in community activities. Learn stress-management techniques.
- *Safety planning*—Learn self-defense. Implement safety precautions and procedures in and out of your home. Have emergency plans of action in the work setting, and conduct drills. Trust gut feelings as warning signals. Befriend the police.
- *Staff support*—Schedule regular staff-support meetings. Have supervision groups just to address issues of stress and fear. Schedule a staff retreat. Address fears regularly with a supervisor.
- *Reality*—Never minimize the danger of your environment. Face fear, and talk about it. Always be cautious, and never think, "It will never happen to me."

These results cannot be generalized to all social workers or to all professionals working with women. These findings are introduced with the hope that you will be alerted to some of the issues you may confront as you become more aware of the prevalence and severity of sexism and violence against women. NiCarthy, Merriam, and Coffman (1984) presented similar issues for persons facilitating groups for women who have been battered. They noted

that group leaders often feel disruption in their lives during the first few weeks of working with this population. They warn that nightmares, sleeplessness, and anxiety are not uncommon. In fact, they noted the following reactions, which are similar to the reactions found by Stout and Thomas (1991) (NiCarthy, Merriam, & Coffman, 1984, p. 150):

1. A heightened awareness of the physical and emotional dangers inherent to women in this society (such as rape, incest, and physical and emotional abuse)
2. Anger toward men in general and toward offenders of all kinds in particular
3. Suspicion of, or distance from, any man with whom you are currently involved
4. Increased feeling of helplessness about your own ability to end or decrease battering
5. Generalized fear

Mennen (1990) reviewed the "dilemmas and demands" (p. 72) of working with adult survivors of sexual abuse. She noted that managing the emotional content of client narratives is often difficult. She stated, "The intensity of the work and the skills necessary to manage therapy with these clients may leave a worker feeling drained, confused, incompetent, frightened, and overwhelmed.... Furthermore, the texts seldom acknowledge that feelings of compassion and sisterhood with those who have been victimized are part of the therapy process" (p. 77). Other demands and dilemmas include economic and time constraints. Long-term needs of survivors may not be met, due to agency or funding-source limitations on how many and how long counseling sessions can be. Survivors may need reassurance and assistance during off hours, and social workers have to make difficult decisions on how to address both the clients' needs and their own. Working with this population of survivors may also present ethical dilemmas, including the rage that social workers may feel because confidentiality may keep them from exposing another professional who sexually abuses clients or a professional who was not helpful—or even was hurtful—to the client (Mennen, 1990).

Mennen offered suggestions for those working with adult survivors of sexual abuse. The first strategy or suggestion is to consider forming a *consultation group* with other professionals working with this population. She suggested, "Through cooperative efforts, it is possible to learn how to deal with some of the more complex problems, including constraints imposed by agencies, late-night calls from clients, anger, and the emotional demands of treatment" (p. 82). The second strategy offered is *self-management*. This strategy calls for alertness to signs of burnout and for consideration of limits on the number of cases in each worker's caseload. Third, Mennen believes that *team therapy* can be a useful strategy. This treatment strategy encourages the use of two therapists to work with the most traumatized clients; for example, one way of offering this treatment is for the client to be seen in individual therapy with one social worker and in a group with another. Finally, Mennen calls for *social action and professional education* to address the issue. Mennen aptly closed her article with the following "call to action": "Ultimately each social worker must make a commitment to social change and understand that treating the sequelae of sexual victimization is not the answer. A society that continues to devalue women and children will be plagued by sexual abuse and the dilemmas faced by the survivors and their helpers" (p. 84).

Working directly with survivors of sexism and violence requires not only knowledge of the issues and therapeutic processes, but also professional support and consultation. As Stout and Thomas's (1991) and Mennen's (1990) articles suggest, the work is not easy and requires us to be attuned to safety and personal issues, burnout, and the necessity for agency policies to adequately address women's concerns; in addition, social workers often need to work on multiple fronts: with consumers, agency administration, and the public, as well as community

and national policymakers. The noting of such implications is not intended to scare social workers away from such work, as our knowledge, skills, and values are desperately needed. The work, on each front, can be enormously satisfying and empowering if social workers take care of themselves and their clients on all levels. It is our hope that by suggesting red-flag areas to watch out for, social workers might be better prepared for the struggles, challenges, and joys of working with female victims and survivors of male violence.

Social Workers' Own Issues

Because the majority of social workers are women, we are confronted with the same sexism and violence faced by our clients. There are no comfortable "us" versus "them" distinctions. As this text has illustrated, female social workers face sexual harassment, sexual assault, and pay inequities. In fact, some social workers enter the profession due to a traumatizing event that has served to politicize them and lead them to assist other survivors, as well as to make changes at a political/community level.

In the past, such experiences would have been perceived negatively by social work professionals and by many consumers, alike. Yet due to changes in perception, many of them achieved through the self-help movement, such experiences are viewed more positively, with the increased understanding that those who have been thrown in the river can often help another drowning survivor through the process of recovering, healing, and even organizing. Many valuable self-help books have been written by survivors, and many successful advocacy groups are fueled by women who have overcome oppressive circumstances.

Therefore, social workers who have been affected by sexism and violence (and who hasn't?) are the ideal allies, counselors, and collaborators for victims of sexism and violence. One caution is that the client's wounding may reopen some old wounds of the social worker.

It is helpful for the social worker to have dealt with issues herself and to be continually open to reexamining the issues, whether in therapy, self-help, political consciousness-raising groups, or clinical supervision. For instance, Courtois (1988) noted that a former victim may have a fuller understanding of survivor experiences, reactions, and difficulties in overcoming a history of incest, yet she needs to be able to separate her own past issues from the client's present issues. A social worker who has been victimized herself may be seen as more of a liability in social work settings that tend to psychologize the problem and less of an obstacle in those settings that tend to politicize the problem.

A feminist approach to sexism and violence does not exclude a social worker from working with a client who faces similar issues, nor does it mandate that the social worker must have experienced that issue in order to understand it. A feminist stance values appropriate self-disclosure, being aware of all the implications, and connecting with other social workers in therapy, supervision, consultation, discussion groups or organizing.

Connecting the "Isms"

It would be regrettable if—while becoming increasingly attuned to gender issues—social workers did not also develop a commitment to addressing oppression from perspectives other than gender. It is only to the benefit of the patriarchal culture to focus only on gender oppression, without making the connections and commitments necessary to confront oppression wherever it manifests. Smith (1986) called to our attention, "A black feminist perspective has no use for ranking oppressions, but instead demonstrates the simultaneity of oppressions as they affect Third World women's lives" (p. 49). She continued, noting, "Until black feminism, few people besides black women actually cared about or took seriously the demoralization of being female *and* colored *and* poor *and* hated"

(p. 55). Very similarly, we need to look inward and work outward to understand and confront ageism, classism, heterosexism, and ableism. The consciousness that you raise and the work that you do to challenge these oppressions will serve to strengthen and heighten your analysis of gender oppression.

It was shocking and disturbing to hear some feminists declare that racism had nothing to do with the O.J. Simpson trial, dubbed the "Trial of the Century." This case brought into public debate the sexism and violence inherent in femicide, the racism of many legal and law-enforcement systems, and anti-Semitism, as well as multiple issues related to class and class privilege. This case reminds us of the "Stages in the Development of Cross-Cultural Awareness," developed by Christensen in 1984 and presented in the 1995 book *Racism in the Lives of Women: Testimony, Theory, and Guides to Antiracist Practice.* Many persons who denied issues other than gender in the O.J. trial appeared to have no awareness (Stage 1 of Christensen's model) or only a beginning awareness of racial oppression. Similarly, those who denied gender oppression as a factor in the trial also appeared to have little awareness of gender issues.

Christensen (1995) suggested a model of five stages of cross-cultural awareness for persons from a majority cultural, ethnic, or racial background and from persons from a minority cultural, ethnic, or racial background:

Stage 1: Unawareness The person at this stage is often unaware of or denying all but the most glaring acts of racism. It often takes a specific event, which has personal meaning and importance, to move past this stage. An example is a student who had thought little about homophobia until the assassination of Harvey Milk, the first openly gay elected city official, in San Francisco. At that time, she was moved to attend the candlelight march in San Francisco. Even though her parents grounded her for a month after she attended this symbolic demonstration, she was still moved to tears 10 years later as a result of this experience and felt that it changed her life as far as her commitment to ending discrimination against gay men and lesbian women.

Stage 2: Beginning Awareness In this stage, people begin to question assumptions or their own status as members of cultural, ethnic, or racial groups. Majority members may want to "dissociate self from sharing responsibility for suffering and harm of disadvantaged and oppressed minority groups" (p. 215), and minority members may begin to feel a sense of shared experience with members of their own group or other oppressed minorities, but "with ambivalence" (p. 215). This stage is reminiscent of all the debates about affirmative action, in which many European Americans acknowledge that racism exists, *but* insist that they should not be penalized for something they did not create or support. The transition from this stage often includes a relationship that provides "intimate and intense" opportunities to learn.

Stage 3: Conscious Awareness This stage represents an awareness of cultural, ethnic, and racial differences, but the person is struggling with how to integrate this knowledge. A person with conscious awareness may be passionate, angry, curious, and quite knowledgeable about racial oppression but may be unsure how to use this knowledge in providing family services, for example. To work through this stage involves "the working-through of feelings and responses related to powerful and prolonged soul-searching and learning experiences" (p. 216).

Stage 4: Consolidated Awareness People working in this stage have an involved commitment for social change and for intergroup understanding. Differences are seen as positive. For racial, ethnic, or cultural minority-group members, this stage brings with it a pos-

itive acceptance of their own groups and a desire to help others of their own group to reach this understanding. An example of how social work practice may be affected by this stage would be the social worker who uses her or his awareness of racism to initiate program changes that confront institutional racism. Christensen (1995) described the transition from this stage as "an affair with the heart" (p. 216), with a shifting of allegiance from a group to humankind.

Stage 5: Transcendent Awareness Persons experiencing transcendent awareness have incorporated their cross-cultural awareness as a way of life and are comfortable in all environments. Christensen (1995) described a feminist therapist operating at this stage:

> *T. is a psychiatrist of Hispanic descent who has comfortably integrated feminist and anti-racist approaches. She is perfectly bilingual and uses the surname of her African-American husband. She finds herself equally able to establish rapport with patients of African-American, immigrant Hispanic, and European backgrounds. As a dark-skinned Cuban, she is rather amused by the surprise on the faces of those meeting her for the first time who appear to think that dark skin and psychiatry are antithetical. (p. 225)*

Appreciating, respecting, and understanding diversity is a critical component of a feminist analysis. Haynes and Holmes (1994) presented this classroom exercise for your consideration:

> *Look around the classroom where you are now sitting and note the differences represented by the individuals in a single room. Multiply that number of differences by 250 million, the approximate U.S. population in the 1990 census. Consider the possible combinations of gender, ethnicity, age, sexual orientation, physical capabilities, religious preference, abilities, interests, and life experiences represented by 250 million lives.*

For persons with racial, class, gender, age, and sexual-orientation privilege, becoming aware of one's privilege, as well as of oppression, is critical. McIntosh (1989) explained European-American privilege in this manner:

> I have come to see white privilege as an invisible package of unearned assets which I can count on cashing in each day, but about which I was "meant" to remain oblivious. White privilege is like an invisible weightless knapsack of special provisions, maps, passports, codebooks, visas, clothes, tools and blank checks. (p. 10)

She made a list of 26 ways in which she can assume white privilege on an everyday basis. Her examples range from "Whether I use checks, credit cards, or cash, I can count on my skin color not to work against the appearance of financial reliability" (p. 11) to "I can criticize our government and talk about how much I fear its policies and behavior without being seen as a cultural outsider" (p. 11). McIntosh noted that it is easy to avoid examining privilege or domination, "for in facing it [my own privilege] I must give up the myth of meritocracy. If these things are true, this is not such a free country" (p. 11). By recognizing and confronting our own uses of race, class, gender, and sexual orientation as a way to dominate or to escape uncomfortable situations, we can begin to directly confront oppression. In contrast, the ignoring of oppression does not promote social work values related to social justice. A newspaper columnist, Juán Palomo (1991) addressed the issue of silence after 10 young men murdered a gay man (Paul Broussard) in Houston, Texas, as he was leaving a gay bar. His words, important reminders of our responsibility to confront oppression, conclude this section:

> The gay rights activists are right: Silence does equal death.
>   When we fail to speak up, we are sanctioning the hatred or ignorance of people like my co-worker and correspondents. And it is such hatred and ignorance that tells stupid kids it's OK to go around beating up the Paul Broussards of the world.

> I didn't know Paul Broussard, but I am not going to let Houston forget him, or how he died—or why.

MESSAGE TO MALE SOCIAL WORKERS

When confronted with the evidence of the systematic oppression of women by this patriarchal society, many men grow defensive. Individual men often say, "Well, I am a nice guy and I would never hit or rape a woman," just as many European-American people say, "I am not racist; I don't burn crosses in the yards of people of color." This denial of overt sexist or racist acts prevents men from examining the ways in which they do oppress women and the benefits of male privilege. These defense and denial mechanisms prevent men from working with women to end the oppression of women. Until men begin to work with women, we will achieve only incremental changes, for the battering, raping, and killing will not end until men stop battering, raping, and killing women.

Some men go on the offensive when women begin to describe how they have been oppressed by this patriarchal society. Some men charge "male-bashing" or "reverse discrimination," or some say that women choose to have breast implants or women provoke rape. Admittedly, it is difficult to be a man when faced with the horrors that men, as a class, have perpetrated against women, as a class. These defensive strategies—denial of personal responsibility, taking the offensive, blaming women for their own victimization—are understandable, if not acceptable. By speaking of the oppression of women, we intend to open men's eyes, rather than to bash men, and we hope to provide a level playing field, rather than to assert special privileges.

Many men have embraced feminism and the vision it provides, for feminist ideology offers benefits for men, as well as for women. Without power hierarchies and rigid gender-role stereotypes, men are freed, as well. Some men have incorporated feminist concepts into their lives, although in different ways. Tolman, Mowry, Jones, and Brekke (1986) have identified two philosophically distinct groups of men: the male-liberation model and profeminist men. The male-liberation position has realized the drawbacks of the male sex role, such as competitiveness, emotional restrictions, and alienation from children and family life. These men decry these restrictions and seek personal solutions. They may say that they are as oppressed as women, call themselves victims, and organize around father's rights. Unfortunately, such a stance does not look at how men oppress women or how men benefit from male privilege.

The profeminist men take a different tack. In this analysis, "Profeminist men are seen as oppressors benefiting from the domination of women. The negative aspect of male roles are addressed but are not equated with the systemic, pervasive oppression of women" (Tolman et al., 1986, p. 64). The solutions sought by profeminist groups, therefore, are not merely focused on the men themselves but also seek to end the oppression of women. Tolman et al. (1986) listed principles for a profeminist commitment: developing a historical, contextual understanding of women's experiences; being responsible for themselves and for other men; redefining masculinity; accepting women's scrutiny without making women responsible; supporting the efforts of women without interfering; struggling against racism and classism, as well; overcoming homophobia and heterosexism; working against male violence in all its forms; refusing to set up a false dichotomy by taking responsibility for sexism; acting at the individual, interpersonal, and organizational levels; and attending to both process and product.

We urge male social workers to join the vital work of other profeminist men. An increasing number of men are active in confronting male privilege and in working to end the oppression of women, and their work is must-read material for men in social work (Brooks,

1995; Funk, 1993; Stoltenberg, 1989). Men's organizations that work on these issues can help end the isolation some men feel when trying to break out of traditional masculinity.

It is a long, hard process to begin to acknowledge male privilege, for men are often taught not to see or to acknowledge it. Nonetheless, men are not alone in dealing with their history as oppressors. European-American women and men must work to deal with their learned racism and with how they benefit from European-American privilege. Heterosexual men and women must address their heterosexual privilege and must actively work to end the oppression of lesbians and gay men. Women must work to overcome their internalized sexism. It's difficult work for us all. It's time to move past feeling defensive and to begin the work that will ultimately benefit all people.

The social work profession needs men— not to improve the credibility of the profession or to monopolize the managerial or academic positions, but to work beside and with women, to end the discrimination, sexism, and violence against women, as well as to address all the other power-based hierarchies. It will take all our energy and talents to prevail. Profeminist men are welcome to join us.

PERSONAL CHALLENGES

Awakening to the many sources of sexism and violence against women, is often a transformational process. Often, before social workers can completely see the implications of sexism and violence for their clients' lives, they are confronted with the realities of their own lives—with all their joys, complexities, contradictions, and challenges. We (Stout and McPhail), too, continue to have awakenings on the implications of this material for our everyday private and public lives. Did we disproportionately call on more male than female students today? If my daughter saves her own money, can I stomach it if she buys that

Barbie she desires? Some days, we feel our own anger emerge toward ourselves and other people, for the daily injustices we confront. Other days, our own laughter erupts at seeing what a well-socialized gender-role follower someone is. Because of the personal implications of this material, we have each written a personal note regarding some of our own experiences with confronting sexism and violence against women. Our hope is that our notes may encourage you to explore your own process of becoming more conscious of these issues and to validate the contradictions inherent in the multifaceted lives of you and those you know as we work together to end sexism and violence against women.

A Personal Note from Beverly

In this last chapter, Karen and I wanted to add a personal note about doing work in the field of violence against women. It is difficult and demanding work, and we wanted to offer you the benefit of our learning and experience. Being a feminist social work practitioner is both a curse and a blessing because in order to assume more than a theoretical orientation when working with clients, a feminist perspective must become a way of life that colors all of your thinking. It involves looking at the world through a gender lens, and they are not rose-colored glasses.

The most difficult part is that I am often angry. I am amazed that other people can read the newspaper and or watch the news and then continue nonchalantly throughout the day. Far from feeling nonchalant, I am enraged by the stories, one after another, that tell of the violence against women and the pervasive discrimination against women that is ongoing in this society. I write editorials and letters to my congressional representatives and senators; I join the protest marches; I call reporters, my legislators, and others; I volunteer on campaigns; and I seek to educate others on the issues. It can be exhausting, never-ending work. Some of my friends and neighbors are amazed that I see the world this way and react in such a fashion, yet I am amazed that they do not! Some feminist friends say that they felt

anger in only one stage of gaining a feminist consciousness, and they have developmentally moved through that stage, yet my anger continually mobilizes and motivates me.

Although anger can be mobilizing, it can also be draining. It is important to be centered in my chosen priorities and connected to the people in my environment. This dynamic is different for different people but may involve a spiritual or religious dimension. Intertwined with this search for meaning is also a search for self. This process is complex and lifelong. Many techniques can be employed in the journey, including meditation, prayer, tai chi, yoga, reading, and ritual.

I have learned over time, however, that I cannot do it all. I have learned to say no to many of the requests for my time and money and have had to pick a few major issues to target. It's helpful to have other interests and a fun, relaxing hobby. However, this solution is often problematic, for sexism so imbues every facet of our lives that escape is nearly impossible. For instance, I am a member of a herpetological association and, upon discovering the sexism in that organization, wrote an article for the association newsletter, entitled, "The Gender Politics of Snakes." Going to the movies is chancy too, for some of my friends have come to dread my feminist analysis.

Feminist sensitivity can be hard on the family, as well. It's a fine line I walk to hold my husband accountable for his own sexist behavior without holding him accountable for the behavior of all men. He has learned and grown as I have, but it can make for a complex and conflictual relationship. I have two sons, as well, and raising feminist sons in this culture is a challenge. Do you give them guns as toys? Do you let them play football? If you force your feminist agenda on them, are you merely re-creating the power imbalances feminists decry? Feminist child-rearing practices are new, often untried and unproved. I feel that I am making it up as I go along. Some days, I am gratified and others horrified. The same son who said, "Mommies don't do homework, they do housework!" also questioned why there are no women on the SWAT (special weapons and tactics) team when a class field trip took him to the police academy. I talk to other feminist mothers, and we search for answers together.

There are benefits to being a feminist social worker, as well. I have met wonderful feminist social work role models who are an inspiration to me. My relationships, although at times more conflictual, are also more intimate and gratifying. I am part of a social-change movement that I firmly believe is changing the world, and I feel honored and privileged to participate in it. Such work is personally challenging, and I continue to learn and grow every day around issues of sex, race, class, ableism, and sexual orientation. It's a lifelong process, and I am a lifelong student. This process is energizing.

I am learning about the history of women, and their lives inspire and motivate me. I meet all kinds of women who have survived and thrived in this often misogynistic culture, and their strength and beauty are incredible. I have intimate relationships with women and view them as allies, rather than competitors. I have learned more about myself and the forces that shaped my life, and I have learned to like and respect my body and myself. These are the gifts of feminism.

A Personal Note from Karen

I still take pride in saying the "F" word—feminist. I am a feminist, an educator, a scholar, a mother, and a wife. I grew up on a farm in the Midwest, and at times, I am confused about the origins of my ideology. Is it my feminism or my rural roots that have instilled in me the belief that all persons have important roles to play in our communities, in our world? Perhaps, instead, is it my generalist social work training that fits best with my belief that social workers have an obligation to work on multiple fronts to confront oppression? I'd like to think that rural values, social work values, and feminist values all fit together to provide a road map for transformational change. I've chosen a journey toward transformational change and have never looked back or regretted the path I have chosen.

Feminism has given me a tremendous power—a language and a context in which to describe the wrongs in our world, as well as a vision for what that world might be. It has offered me connections to persons of color, the poor, sexual minorities, and older adults. As I see the oppression I have experienced as a European-American woman, I can begin to see the oppression I share with other oppressed groups, as well as the differences in our experiences. Examining European-American privilege and heterosexual privilege offers me challenges and conflicts that are important experiences to work with and through. Those challenges and conflicts only enhance the power I can feel—a shared power and connection that lessens the feeling that I have to do it all. I have partners, coconspirators, and revolutionaries to share in the work that must be done!

With that power comes pain. I cried after my daughter's first preschool holiday party when every single 3-year-old girl received a soft, cuddly animal or a Barbie, and every little boy received an action figure or a motor vehicle—except the little boy for whom we purchased a toy, who was unhappily looking at the book and the woman police officer action figure he received. I was furious when, at a demonstration following the slaughter of a gay man by 10 teenagers, I saw very few women present and could identify only a couple of social workers in attendance. Has our work been in vain? Doesn't anyone care? Why wasn't the demonstration called by heterosexual activists to say, "No more!" instead of the endangered group always being the people who have the responsibility to call for change? With awareness, everyday life can bring with it a sadness, a recognition of a loss, a flash of rage. . . .

Like Beverly, I am a mother. As I write this, I have an 8-month-old daughter and a 4-year-old daughter. Although my husband and I have formed a "Parents of Daughters" action group, to work toward changing educational systems that have traditionally been harmful to girls and women, it still seems like an impossible task to raise a child in nonsexist, nonviolent manner, despite a unified commitment within the home.

The hard work we do at home is constantly undermined by the media, the preschool environment, friends, and other cultural influences. Also, the work we do at home, as Beverly described, is often uncharted. We have been shocked by the lack of support we've found for not spanking our oldest child and for trying not to humiliate or verbally abuse her in any way. Most observers seem to find it humorous or ridiculous. Some seem to fear she will become a wild child. While I have not read of accounts of mass murderers who were raised with love, respect, empathy, and nonviolence, it seems that some people fear that children who are not physically punished will be the next generation of social deviants. Other observers are concerned that our children have access to books on gay parents and that we only have women or African-American Santa Clauses in our home; these observers feel that our daughters may be deprived of knowing their own ethnicity while we want her to see all of the possibilities and the goodness of all members of our society. In general, parenting is hard work. Nonsexist, nonviolent, multicultural parenting demands taking risks and just hoping that what you are trying to do will do some good and certainly will do no harm.

The contradictions in my life sometimes silence me. How can I write on sexism when I can still find so many examples in my own life, especially in my face during this time when I'm nursing an infant? How did the power shift, and how will I find satisfactory arrangements that allow for caring for my youngest child in the way I choose in a world where I am still expected to perform all of my other professional and personal responsibilities? Yet this process I am undergoing does enhance my learning, and the silent times can give me the opportunity for the reflection, values clarification, and analysis that I hope will make me a better role model for my daughters, a more human professor in the classroom, and a more challenging participant in the academic world, which has little regard for babies in the ivory tower. (I must note here how absolutely supportive my own school has been about my baby's presence.)

Feminism has brought me power, pain, and tremendous joy. Working on this textbook, with all of its challenges and limitations, has also brought me joy. The opportunity to read so much on so many topics and to work with Beverly has been exciting. Listening to my daughter repeat the words of a book Beverly gave her on being a girl is joyous—words that are hard for her to pronounce, such as *courageous, independent, capable,* and *strong* are powerful coming from such a little one. Returning from a speakout against battering, my little Brenna began imitating a speech made by one of the organizers. She pretended to have a microphone in her hand and forcefully said, "I'm angry. Boys stop hitting girls. Men stop hitting women. Girls stop hitting boys [my daughter is always fair]. I'm so angry." Such moments are precious and inspire me to keep up the work that must be done to keep women from drowning in that deep, wide river. Being able to teach courses on women's issues, feminist practice, and confrontation of oppression is a truly wondrous experience, allowing me to learn and grow from the women and men I have the opportunity to work with. For giving all of this joy to me, I thank those women who came before, who paved the path for my generation to reach for the stars. My hope for each of you is that some of the work of my generation will provide support for you as you carry on the important work that must be done to confront sexism and violence against women.

RESOURCES

Finally, we want to leave with you an abbreviated resource list. We hope that you have found the material presented in the text helpful and that you will desire to seek out additional information. The materials listed in Table 12.1 are some of the key sources we found to be valuable as we learned more about and wrote about the different elements of the continuum.

Table 12.1
Resource List

Author	Title	Element
Adleman & Enguidanos (Eds.) (1995)	*Racism in the lives of women*	Gendered communication
Harbeck (Ed.) (1992)	*Coming out of the classroom closet*	Gendered communication
hooks (1995)	*Killing rage*	Gendered communication
Maggio (1988)	*The nonsexist word finder*	Gendered communication
Miller & Swift (1988)	*The Handbook of nonsexist writing*	Gendered communication
Spender (1980)	*Man made language*	Gendered communication
Stout & Kelly (1990)	"Differential treatment based on sex"	Gendered communication
Wood (1994)	*Gendered communication*	Gendered communication
Amott & Matthaei (1991)	*Race, gender, and work: A multicultural economic history of women in the United States*	Economic assault
Ozawa (1989)	*Women's life cycle and economic insecurity*	Economic assault
Sidel (1986)	*Women and children last*	Economic assault
Waring (1988)	*A new feminist economic history of women in the United States*	Economic assault
Brown (1994)	*Subversive dialogues: Theory in feminist therapy*	Psychological wounding
Caplan (1995)	*They say you're crazy*	Psychological wounding
Tavris (1992)	*The mismeasure of woman*	Psychological wounding
Adams (1995)	*Health issues for women of color: A cultural diversity perspective*	Women's health
Boston Women's Health Collective (1992)	*The new our bodies, ourselves*	Women's health
Laurence & Weinhouse (1994)	*Outrageous practices: The alarming truth about how medicine mistreats women*	Women's health
Jenson (1996)	"Knowing pornography"	Pornography
Russell (1993)	*Against pornography: The evidence of harm*	Pornography
Greenman (1990)	"Survivors of prostitution find PRIDE"	Prostitution
Delacoste & Alexander (1987)	*Sex works: Writings by women in the sex industry*	Sex industry
Bravo & Cassedy (1992)	*The 9to5 guide to combating sexual harassment*	Sexual harassment
Koss, Goodman, Browne, Fitzgerald, Keita, & Russo (1994)	*No safe haven: Male violence against women at home, at work, and in the community*	Sexual harassment, Sexual assault, battering

Continued

Table 12.1
Continued

Author	Title	Element
Paludi (Ed.) (1990)	*Ivory power: Sexual harassment on campus*	Sexual harassment
Browne (1987)	*Battered women who kill*	Battering and homicide
Davis & Srinivasan (1995)	"Listening to the voices of battered women"	Battering
Dworkin (1993)	*Letters for a war zone*	Battering and violence against women
Ferrato (1991)	*Living with the enemy*	Battering
Buchwald, Fletcher, & Roth (Eds.) (1993)	*Transforming a rape culture*	Sexual assault
Finkelhor & Yllo (1985)	*License to rape: Sexual abuse of wives*	Wife rape
Riger & Gordon (1981)	"The fear of rape: A study in social control"	Rape (fear of)
Russell (1984)	*Sexual exploitation*	Rape, incest, sexual harassment
Russell (1990)	*Rape in marriage*	Wife rape
Brenner (1995)	*Eight bullets*	Femicide
Radford & Russell (Ed.) (1992)	*Femicide: The politics of women killing*	Femicide
Stout (1989)	"Intimate femicide': Effect of legislation and social services"	Intimate femicide

REFERENCES

Adams, D. L. (1995). *Health issues for women of color: A cultural diversity perspective.* Thousand Oaks, CA: Sage Publications.

Adleman, J. & Enguidanos, G. (Eds.). (1995). *Racism in the lives of women: Testimony, theory, and guides for antiracist practice.* New York: Harrington Park Press.

Amott, T., & Matthaei, J. (1991). *Race, gender, and work: A multicultural economic history of women in the United States.* Boston, MA: South End Press.

Boston Women's Health Collective. (1992). *The new our bodies, ourselves.* New York: Simon & Schuster.

Bravo, E., & Cassedy, E. (1992). *The 9to5 guide to combating sexual harassment.* New York: John Wiley & Sons.

Brenner, C. (1995). *Eight bullets.* Ithaca, NY: Firebrand Books.

Brooks, G. (1995). *The centerfold syndrome.* San Francisco: Jossey-Bass Publishers.

Brown, L. (1994). *Subversive dialogues: Theory in feminist therapy.* New York: Basic Books.

Browne, A. (1987). *When battered women kill.* New York: Free Press.

Buchwald, E., Fletcher, P., & Roth, M. (Eds.). (1993). *Transforming a rape culture.* Minneapolis, MN: Milkweed Editions.

Caplan, P. (1995). *They say you're crazy*. Reading, MA: Addison-Wesley Publishing.

Christensen, C. P. (1995). *Racism in the lives of women: Testimony, theory, and guides for antiracist practice*. New York: Harrington Park Press.

Courtois, C. (1988). *Healing the incest wound: Adult survivors in therapy*. New York: W. W. Norton.

Davis, L., & Srinivasan, M. (1995). Listening to the voices of battered women: What helps them escape violence. *Affilia, 10*, 49–69.

Delacoste, F., & Alexander, P. (1987). *Sex work: Writings by women in the sex industry*. Pittsburgh, PA: Cleis Press.

Dworkin, A. (1993). *Letters from a war zone*. Brooklyn, NY: Lawrence Hill Books.

Ferrato, D. (1991). *Living with the enemy*. New York: Aperture.

Finkelhor, D., & Yllo, K. (1985). *License to rape: Sexual abuse of wives*. New York: Free Press.

Funk, R. E. (1993) *Stopping rape: A challenge for men*. Philadelphia: New Society Publishers.

Greenman, M. (1990). Survivors of prostitution find PRIDE. *Families in Society*, pp. 110–113.

Harbeck, K. (Ed.). (1992). *Coming out of the classroom closet*. Binghamton, NY: Harrington Park Press.

Haynes, K. S., & Holmes, K. A. (1994). *Invitation to social work*. New York: Longman.

hooks, b. (1995). *Killing rage*. New York: Henry Holt.

Jenson, R. (1996). Knowing pornography. *Violence Against Women, 2*, 82–102.

Koss, M., Goodman, L., Browne, A., Fitzgerald, L., Keita, G., & Russo, N. (1994). *No safe haven: Male violence against women at home, at work, and in the community*. Washington, DC: American Psychological Association.

Laurence, L., & Weinhouse, B. (1994). *Outrageous practices: The alarming truth about how medicine mistreats women*. New York: Fawcett Columbine.

Maggio, R. (1988). *The nonsexist word finder: A dictionary of gender-free usage*. Boston: Beacon Press.

McIntosh, P. (1989, July/August). White privilege: Unpacking the invisible knapsack. *Peace and Freedom*, pp. 10–12.

Mennen, F. E. (1990). Dilemmas and demands: Working with adult survivors of sexual abuse. *Affilia, 5*, 72–86

Miller, C., & Swift, K. (1988). *The handbook of nonsexist writing* (2nd ed.). New York: Harper & Row.

NiCarthy, G., Merriam, K., & Coffman, S. (1984). *Talking it out: A guide for groups for abused women*. Seattle: Seal Press.

Ozawa, M. (Ed.). (1989). *Women's life cycle & economic insecurity: Problems and proposals*. New York: Praeger.

Palomo, J. (1991, July 9). Paying the cost for being silent. *Houston Post*.

Paludi, M. (Ed.). (1990). *Ivory power: Sexual harassment on campus*. Albany: State University of New York Press.

Radford, J., & Russell, D. E. (1992). *Femicide: The politics of the killing of women*. Boston: Twayne Publishers.

Riger, S., & Gordon, M. (1981). The fear of rape: A study in social control. *Journal of Social Issues, 37*, 71–92.

Russell, D. E. (1984). *Sexual exploitation*. Beverly Hills, CA: Sage Publications.

Russell, D. E. H. (1990). *Rape in marriage* (2nd ed.). Bloomington and Indianapolis: Indiana University Press.

Russell, D. E. H. (1993). *Against pornography: The evidence of harm*. Berkeley, CA: Russell Publications.

Russell, D. E., & Van de Ven, N. (Eds.). (1984). *The proceedings of the International Tribunal on Crimes Against Women*. East Palo Alto, CA: Frog in the Well.

Sidel, R. (1986). *Women and children last*. New York: Penguin Books.

Smith, B. (1986). Some home truths on the contemporary black feminist movement. In N. Van Den Bergh & L. Cooper (Eds.), *Feminist visions for social work*. Silver Spring, MD: NASW Press.

Spender, D. (1980). *Man made language*. London: Routledge & Kegan Paul.

Stoltenberg, J. (1989). *Refusing to be a man: Essays on sex and justice*. New York: Meridian.

Stout, K. D. (1989). "Intimate femicide": Effect of legislation and social services. *Affilia, 4*, 21–30.

Stout, K., & Kelly, M. J. (1990). Differential treatment based on sex. *Affilia, 5,* 60–71.

Stout, K. D., & Thomas, S. (1991). Fear and dangerousness in shelter work with battered women. *Affilia, 6,* 74–86.

Tavris, C. (1992). *The mismeasure of woman.* New York: Simon & Schuster.

Tocqueville, A. de. (Edited and Abridged by Richard D. Heffner, 1956, renewed 1984). *Democracy in America.* New York: NAL Penguin, Inc.

Tolman, R., Mowry, D., Jones, L., & Brekke, J. (1986). Developing a profeminist commitment among men in social work. In N. Van Den Bergh & L. Cooper (Eds.), *Feminist visions for social work* (pp. 61–79). Silver Springs, MD: NASW Press.

Waring, M. (1988). *If women counted: A new feminist economics.* New York and San Francisco: Harper.

Wood, J. (1994). *Gendered lives: Communication, gender and culture.* Belmont, CA: Wadsworth Publishing.

CREDITS

Chap. 1, p. 10: © 1996 Photo by Kim Kulish. Reprinted with the permission of the artist.

Chap. 2, p. 14: Reprinted with permission of Turtle Island Records. Words and Music by Libby Roderick © 1987 Libby Roderick Music.

Chap. 2, p. 19: © 1996 Photo by Kim Kulish. Reprinted with the permission of the artist.

Chap. 2, p. 20: Printed with the permission of Barbara Mikulski.

Chap. 2, p. 30: *Nancy* reprinted by permission of United Feature Syndicate, Inc. © 1989.

Chap. 2, p. 38: © 1996 Photo by Kim Kulish. Reprinted with the permission of the artist.

Chap. 2, p. 40: From THE MOON IS ALWAYS FEMALE, by Marge Piercy. Copyright © 1980 by Marge Piercy. Reprinted by permission of Alfred A. Knopf, Inc.

Chap. 3, p. 47: "To Be a Woman" from *Clean Slate* by Daisy Zamora (Curbstone Press, 1993). Reprinted with permission of Curbstone Press. Distributed by Consortium.

Chap. 3, p. 59: "QUALITY TIME" cartoon by Gail Machlis is reprinted by permission of Chronicle Features, San Francisco, California. © 1994.

Chap. 3, p. 66–70: Reprinted by permission of Sage Publications Ltd. from Pat Palmer, "Pain and Possibilities: What Therapists Need to Know About Working Class Women's Issues" in *Feminism and Psychology*, Vol. 6, No. 3, copyright 1996.

Chap. 4, p. 82: © 1996 Photo by Kim Kulish. Reprinted with the permission of the artist.

Chap. 4, p. 91: DOONESBURY COPYRIGHT 1993 G. B. Trudeau. Reprinted with permission of UNIVERSAL PRESS SYNDICATE. All rights reserved.

Chap. 4, pp. 93–94: Reprinted with permission of Turtle Island Records. Words and Music by Libby Roderick © 1988 Libby Roderick Music.

Chap. 5, p. 103: © 1996 Photo by Kim Kulish. Reprinted with the permission of the artist.

Chap. 5, p. 108: Reprinted with the permission of Ann Telnaes. © 1992.

Chap. 5, p. 117: Reprinted with the permission of Mike Keefe. Copyright 1992.

Chap. 5, p. 131: © 1996 Photo by Kim Kulish. Reprinted with the permission of the artist.

Chap. 6, p. 137: Jim Borgman cartoon reprinted with special permission of King Features Syndicate. Copyright © 1997.

Chap. 6, p. 140: © 1996 Photo by Kim Kulish. Reprinted with the permission of the artist.

Chap. 6, p. 144: "Beauty Out of Damage." First published by *The New York Times* on *The New York Times Magazine* cover, Sunday, August 13, 1993. Copyright 1993 by Matuschka, reprinted by permission of the artist.

Chap. 6, p. 151–152: LUCILLE CLIFTON: "lumpectomy eve", copyright 1996 by Lucille Clifton, with the permission of BOA Editions, Ltd., 260 East Ave., Rochester, NY 14604.

Chap. 8, p. 199: © 1996 Photo by Kim Kulish. Reprinted with the permission of the artist.

Chap. 8, p. 205: MAXINE! COMIX © Marian Henley. Reprinted by permission of the artist. © 1993.

Chap. 9, p. 216: Reprinted with the permission of The Domestic Abuse Intervention Project. 206 West Fourth Street, Duluth, MN 55806.

INDEX